HANDBOOK OF
APPLIED SOCIOLOGY

HANDBOOK OF
APPLIED SOCIOLOGY

Frontiers of Contemporary Research

Edited by

Marvin E. Olsen
Michael Micklin

PRAEGER

PRAEGER SPECIAL STUDIES • PRAEGER SCIENTIFIC

Library of Congress Cataloging in Publication Data
Main entry under title:

Handbook of applied sociology.

Includes index.
1. Sociology—Addresses, essays, lectures.
2. Social problems—Addresses, essays, lectures.
3. Social institutions—Addresses, essays, lectures.
4. Social services—Addresses, essays, lectures.
I. Olsen, Marvin Elliott. II. Micklin, Michael.
HM51.H248   301   81-5891
ISBN 0-03-052076-2   AACR2

Published in 1981 by Praeger Publishers
CBS Educational and Professional Publishing
A Division of CBS, Inc.
521 Fifth Avenue, New York, New York 10175 U.S.A.

23456789 052 98765432

Printed in the United States of America

Dedicated to the memory of David P. Street, a cherished colleague and dear friend who sought to apply sociology throughout his short career.

PREFACE

Beyond the frontier lies the wilderness, waiting to be explored. The frontiers of applied sociology are vast and raw, and the wilderness beyond is virtually unknown. The purpose of this book is to identify and describe the current frontiers of knowledge and action in selected areas of applied sociology, so that we can penetrate them and expand the scope and contributions of this field.

Several kinds of readers should find this book useful. Undergraduate sociology and other social science students who are considering a career in applied sociology can utilize the book as an introduction to the field and a guide in identifying their specific interests. Graduate students in sociology and related fields who are preparing to do applied sociology can draw on the book as a reference to recent work in their areas of specialization. Academic sociologists and other social scientists who are concerned about the relevance of the discipline to the real world can read the book for an overview of the present state of the art in applied sociology. Social workers and other practitioners can investigate the book to discover sociological concepts, theories, and research findings that are applicable to their work. Finally, nonsocial scientists who are interested in particular social issues or problems can use the book to explore current sociological efforts to deal with those situations.

Each chapter examines a broad area of contemporary applied sociology. All of the authors are currently working on the frontier of their specialty and hence are personally familiar with the state of the art in that area. The book is divided into five parts. Part A, "Developing Applied Techniques," covers several research and programmatic techniques that are particularly important in applied sociology. Part B, "Improving Social Institutions," looks at five forms of social organization that are crucial components of modern societies. Part C, Reducing Social Inequities, examines efforts to eradicate different forms of social inequality. Part D, "Providing Social Services," asks how adequately several vital services are being

vii

rendered in modern society. Part E, "Ensuring Human Survival," deals with four imperatives that are crucial for the survival of human life on this planet.

To give some coherence to this wide-ranging tour of the frontiers of applied sociology, all of the chapters follow one of two standard formats. The first five technique chapters are divided into these five sections: What Is _____ ? How Is _____ Implemented? How Has _____ Been Used? What Has _____ Accomplished? Where Is _____ Going? The remaining 19 substantive chapters then follow this common format: What Are The Problems? What Do We Know? What Are We Doing? What Have We Accomplished? Where Are We Going? Within these major section headings, however, each author handles the material in his or her own way. All of the chapters contain one additional feature. Included in the list of references at the end of each chapter are five suggested items for further reading in that area. Each of these is marked with an asterisk before the author's name and is followed by a brief annotation.

The idea for this book was originally suggested to us by Professor Richard Hill of the University of Oregon, who is deeply concerned about the future of applied sociology. We greatly appreciate his strong encouragement in launching this endeavor. Our primary debt of gratitude is to the 30 other people who contributed to writing this volume. All of them put great effort into surveying the frontiers of their respective areas. In addition, organizing and coordinating the work of this number of people would have been impossible without their considerate and pleasant cooperation. Finally, behind every book is a secretary who contributes countless hours of typing and other assistance, and in this case our sincere thanks go to Adeline Dinger.

Marvin E. Olsen
Michael Micklin

Seattle, Washington
March 1981

CONTENTS

ix

LIST OF TABLES

LIST OF FIGURES

PROLOGUE: PROBLEMS AND PROSPECTS OF APPLIED SOCIOLOGY *

David P. Street and Eugene A. Weinstein

The winds of political and intellectual upheaval have now moderated sufficiently that dispassionate analysis of the question of the problems and prospects of applied sociology is again feasible. One can ask whether sociology can contribute sufficiently to our understanding of how social institutions come into being, operate, change, and affect the people who deal with them to be of use to any set of consumers besides sociologists themselves. Are we far enough along to design the Utopia if those in power would only listen to us or, even better, cede that power to us—or would the result be an Orwellian travesty? (Remember, in *1984*, Big Brother was a sociologist.) Should we even aspire to designing and creating Utopia, or is the role of the sociologist only that of the dispassionate dissector, who for his own edification and that of his students and colleagues, slices beneath the surface of everyday social life to visualize the forces that shape it.

These are complex questions that require complex answers. Despite the existence of a great array of sociological products that indicate substantial promise for applications in the "real world," sociologists' products tend to be spotty and do not cumulate to provide a coherent and convincing basis for action in our major institutional settings. Take the case of U.S. race relations: On the one hand, one of social science's greatest achievements is that it has played the leading intellectual role in change in this nation in substituting a social-structural and cultural view for a biological one as the dominant interpretation of differences between blacks and whites. The field's efforts have resulted in a plethora of worthwhile research studies as well as in numerous policy proposals. On the other hand, it is correct to say that major policy debates

*Reprinted by permission from *The American Sociologist* 10 (May 1975): 65–72.

and decisions dealing with race over the last two decades have proceeded in the absence of really adequate evidence.

Technical and methodological deficiencies, and the lack of sufficient research, disable sociology in achieving legitimacy as a guide to public policy. Further, the resistances of established social institutions and political pressures generated on significant issues can also undermine this legitimacy. Our awareness of the scope of this problem is enlarged by the writing of Gouldner (1970), who argues that in the absence of a strong and aware commitment to the creation of a social science explicitly directed to positive social change, the sociologist will often be unguided and insensitive to the uses to which his findings may be put. Lacking such a perspective, the sociologist has made the totality of his findings available for mishandling by established groups in a relatively mindless way. Nor has research yielded a comprehensive and compelling demonstration of sociological conclusions relevant to public policy.

Thus, the potentials for an applied sociology are substantial, but the difficulties are great, the issues very complex, and the potential as yet unrealized. The remainder of this discussion will seek to clarify these issues with the aim of better understanding the conditions under which applied sociology might be most fruitfully pursued.

THE DEMAND FOR SOCIOLOGY

No doubt the demand that sociology have immediate relevance to the solution of society's problems, or at least that it provide definitions of society that can help individuals solve their own problems, is now very high. Witness: The growth in universities of sociology faculties and enrollment over the past decades; efforts to extend sociology to the high school; the readiness of federal officials to use a sociological approach, such as "opportunity theory," as a basis for designing antipoverty programs; substantial interest in incorporating sociology into training management personnel and professionals in many fields; the great reliance placed on scientific sampling and polling in public life; the increasing numbers of sociologists appointed to federal commissions and advisory boards; and the leading role played by sociologists in the environmental protection and population control movements. Another index of the demand for sociology is its increasing incorporation into everyday life: The interest in sociology of the mass media (a "Behavior" section in *Time Magazine* and "Behavior Editors" for *Newsday* and other newspapers), or the inclusion of much of the argot of the professional sociologist ("power structure," "social class," "roles," and "norms") into common parlance.

Presumably the demand for sociology will continue and probably it will grow. Modern industrial society is so complex, it changes so rapidly, it features so much mobility, and it produces so much disagreement and protest that the need for sociology to help to comprehend the scene is omnipresent. The mass media are hungry for interpretations of the great number of social and political events that they present every day, and thus they thirst for social predictions and interpretations. The creation of truly nationwide media in a country that is quite heterogeneous in terms of regions, ethnicity, and other attributes implicitly demands interpretations from a comparative perspective, one which is thereby highly congruent with sociological styles of thought.

It is precisely the high demand for sociology, given that the field has not adequately arrived at a clear definition of what either sociology or applied sociology is to be, that creates severe problems for the field. We can think of sociology as having developed in three principal ways: First, it has developed as a scientifically oriented aspect of scholarly endeavor; second, while sociology has developed as an independent contribution to the general enlightenment, it also has grown as a reflection or offshoot of this enlightenment. Its analysis expresses as well as reflects the "demystification of the world" found in modern, secular society, and its content depends upon an acceptance of the plausibility of an Enlightenment that made man and society the legitimate objects of secular public analysis. Third, increasingly sociology has developed as an aspect of modern mass culture. As sociological terminology and perspectives move undiminishedly into the popular parlance, sociology is progressively sought after as a definer of the present and a seer of the future. These three aspects of development—scientific and scholarly, reflector and participator in the general enlightenment, and creature or captor of mass culture—are linked together within the same pool of consumers by virtue of the growth of a great system of mass higher education—and therein lies a great deal of ambiguity about the role of sociology.

As a result, the discipline finds itself, on the one side, committed to the relatively slow and careful development of its knowledge as an academic discipline and teaching field and, on the other, to the attractions of the potentials for receiving attention in mass society. The attractions include the opportunity to do large-scale action research, produce reams of impressive findings, and make publicized pronouncements about the problems, future, and solutions of the society. One consequence could be to further what Levine (1970) discusses as the premature institutionalization of sociology. The result of this process, Levine says, has been to freeze in or conventionalize sociological theories, perspectives, and conclusions before their worth, and the character of the sociological enterprise itself, could be well established.

Widespread institutionalization of applied sociology could present a similar problem. The sociologist runs a great risk of overselling his capacities, especially because in America there is such a great demand for immediate results. Oversell and failure to produce immediate results could ultimately be interpreted by the potential users as an indication that sociology really cannot deliver. The potentialities of sociology then may come to be discredited. Witness Saul Alinsky's pronouncement (1972): "Asking a sociologist to solve a problem is like pre-scribing an enema for diarrhea." Or, most likely, sociologists could assume the stance of educated pundits, persons to be consulted (but whose counsel need not be paid much heed). And because the pundit-sociologist's energies and perspec-tives would become captive to the demands of mass culture, the mission of developing a really adequate applied sociology would remain unfulfilled.

The upshot is not, however, to seek to return sociology to the ivory tower. With all its impurities, sociological knowledge is too important to be monopo-lized by professors. We have a true dilemma, one that cannot be solved either on the side of scientific purity and long-range development of knowledge or on the other side of immediate and therefore superficial relevance. The solution is not to seek to reduce the demand for sociology, either in the classroom or in the world of practical affairs, but instead to seek to clarify to potential users how sociological results can be interpreted. If sociology is related to the world with-out being oversold, it will not end up simply being an aspect of mass culture, but instead can be an important component of scholarly work relevant at many points to the choices of men.

PROBLEMS OF PRODUCT AND USER

All or almost all policy-oriented researchers are in some way flawed or limited by their own methodology, or their implications are debated on these grounds (cf. Williams and Evans, 1969). Many of these difficulties are matters of technique and resources and in principle are soluble. There are limitations inevitable in the sociologist's product, however. First, sociological knowledge is restricted by the fact that the practitioners of necessity are limited in the extent to which they can experiment on human subjects. In this, sociology appropriately encounters the same difficulty as does medical research properly practiced, in that there is the injunction in the first instance to do no harm. Second, sociological knowledge is limited by the fact that ordinarily—and especially in American society—the basic structural variables cannot be directly manipulated; thus some hypotheses must go untested. For example, we know about institutional racism, and we can document its effects, but we cannot manipulate the basic structural variables that we might hypothesize give rise to it. Third, it must be recognized that while sociology is crucial in understanding the world, it cannot yield precise (or even reliable) predictions or timeless theories. In *The Poverty of Historicism* (1957) Popper correctly argues that the search for overall historical forecasts is hopeless, precisely because man is capable of influencing his future and because the accumulation of science means that he may have unforeseen tools for doing so in that future. Thus, Popper counsels doing "short-run social forecasting" for "piecemeal planning." This makes sense, and it is one way in which social scientists can be especially useful in the more mundane decisions of the real world.

At the more general level, what sociologists ordinarily do is provide basic perspectives or metaphors for thinking about the world, ones that only rarely yield relatively precise predictions. It is important to recognize that the ultimate utility and limits of these perspectives can be gauged only after they have a history of being useful or not—useful not only in formal replications regarding the predictions, but more importantly useful in recurrent applications of the general perspective. This last point can lead us to understand why it is that sociologists can so often be wrong about a particular diagnosis or forecast. (The "end of ideology," recurrent revisions of population projections, and the 1950's optimism about race relations are but a few cases in point.) All of this is deflating to the image of an omnipotent applied sociology. It is also comforting, because sociology indeed *cannot* create *1984*. Essentially, what it means, once again, is that sociologists will not do good applied work until they recognize and communicate the limits as well as the potentials of what they are doing.

The problem of use is not, of course, that of the producer alone. The reaction to a variety of large-scale and important studies has been frivolous or even scornful. Thus, President Nixon and Congress reacted to the findings of the pornography commission, which failed to discover evil effects flowing from reading of pornography, by condemning and voting "untrue" the results before they were even announced. Similarly, the Nixon administration declared unacceptable the principal findings of its commission on drug usage on legalization of marijuana use before these results were made public.

More generally, audiences to whom the research can be addressed are selective in where and when they allow research, what they consider to be sociological research, and how they use the research. Researchers are often kept away from the data central to the study they are doing because it is considered to be too "sensitive." Decision makers often show a fundamental misunderstanding of the nature of sociological inquiry, or are very selective in what they take from the research findings. Results that do not please them are frequently said to be the result of inadequate methodology or insufficient concern with the "realities."

Thus it is that applied sociology is disabled both by deficiencies in the producers, product, and potential users and by lack of effective conceptualization and communication by both producers and users of its role, potentialities, and limits. It is now incumbent on us to seek to specify an improved model of the relationship between producer and user. Before doing so, we must consider the question of whether or not a "genuine" sociology is possible.

THE FUNDAMENTAL PROBLEM OF BIAS

Numerous doubters and critics have raised the question of whether or not sociology truly can address itself to the improvement of the human condition, rather than be consciously or unconsciously self-serving or self-confirming. This is a "sociology of knowledge" question—an issue in which the creation of sociological knowledge about social and political predispositions to hold certain kinds of matters to be true has resulted ultimately in an attack upon the sociological position. Thus it is asked: Are not sociologists encapsulated by their own "conventional wisdom?" Does not "knowledge" often serve the purposes of a ruling class or political regime? And are its producers so well rewarded for their role that they are unaware of their function?

The recent history of sociology in the United States provides some spectacular affirmative instances, some touched on briefly already. Sociologists have long been aware of the revolutionizing impact of rising expectations, but the racial tensions of the 1960s took the discipline (or at least most of its practitioners) completely by surprise. Ideology, one leading scholar claimed in the 1950s, had come to the end in the rise of affluence and the forging of mass consensus (Bell, 1950). The only dark cloud was hyperconformity. How well did this imagery serve a consensus-oriented political system? How well does it describe the society only a decade later? Or how well do today's trade unions fulfill the early Marxian prediction of their critical role in revolutionary change?

Despite these and many more instances, we believe that a sociology that genuinely serves the human condition is possible. Our reaction is in two parts:

1. We make an analogy to Karl Mannheim's solution (1936) of the "free-floating intellectual." Such persons have a great leeway in what they do or say. They are in a sense "classless," and from this position can take an "objective" and "enlightened" view of the social structure. It is useless to debate whether or not on the present American scene any one ever becomes totally "classless"; no one ever does. One can, however, suggest that in relative terms, U.S. sociologists can, to a considerable degree, transcend pure class interests. Indeed those who complain most vociferously about sociologists having "sold out" are sociologists themselves (sometimes quite wealthy through inheritance or marriage). Further, the institutionalized mechanisms of academic freedom, such as tenure (leaving aside whatever extent they may serve classroom teaching effectiveness), provide a degree of protection little known elsewhere in the society. The vast majority of sociologists operate outside the presumed norms of conformity induced by federal or "establishment" grant getting. Clearly, academics are influenced by their easy reception of "revealed truth" and their over preoccupation with such opinions as are promulgated in *Newsweek* or *The New York Review of Books*. However, a model of external pressure is not required to account for this fact; indeed, we might point to their laziness as a better explanation.

2. We have the notion that, over the long run, regime-oriented sociology is undone by the essential perspectives and findings of the discipline. Marx, Durkheim, and Freud were fundamentally skeptical of the functioning of their society, as were Veblen, Weber, and Simmel. Much of their perspectives remains alive. Further, whatever the regime-serving or self-serving biases of the sociologists, there is an empirical quality to scientific work that tends to undermine these biases. As Swanson notes (1971), the events we observe do "...'bite back'—to

confirm or disconfirm our hypotheses." What this means in practice is that inadequate theoretical approaches become not so often overtly rejected as diminished in heuristic appeal, becoming forgotten or seen as irrelevant. A good example is the writings of Sumner, in his *Folkways* (1906) and *What Social Classes Owe Each Other* (1883). His work fell by the wayside not principally because it was politically conservative (you cannot change anything until the folkways change, he said repeatedly), but because it became clear that Sumner's conceptions just could not carry one very far analytically or empirically.

Our hypothesis, then, is that over time sociology will have a relatively independent existence, not principally justifying either the regime or revolution. This does not deny that from time to time the discipline will show emphases embodying particular political biases—sometimes to the right, sometimes to the left, and sometimes internally divided. Our presumption is that the sociological enterprise as presently constituted is ultimately self-correcting on this matter, continually seeking some equilibrium between theories emphasizing social consensus (which may move it to the political right) and theories stressing social conflict (which may move it to the left). As Dahrendorf (1958), Coser (1956), and various other observers have indicated, there is no genuine sociology that lacks either of these emphases.

MODELS OF APPLIED SOCIOLOGY

What model of applied sociology would we suggest? The answer is largely apparent in what we have said so far. Obviously, we reject the model of the social scientist as *philosopher-king*, the model held by the nineteenth century founder of the discipline, Auguste Comte (1877), and apparently held presently by psychologist B.F. Skinner (1971). Clearly we find irrelevant the *scientistic* model, in which the practitioner proceeds as if he were utterly "value neutral" and were able to direct his work solely on "purely scientific" grounds. As our discussion of bias has implied, this is not to negate the views of Weber (1949) and others that sociology can proceed to draw empirical conclusions as (and if) distinguished from the sociologist's personal preferences. Among the many alternative models we could discuss, three merit rather detailed attention: *social engineering, radical sociology*, and *enlightenment* (on the first and third, Janowitz, 1970).

Social Engineering
This is the traditional model of applied work, and, of course, derives from the model of professional engineering. Scott and Shore (1974) are eloquent about the limits and possibilities of this approach. Under this model, the client has a specific problem he wishes to have solved, and he engages specialists to aid him in solving it. The specialists are presumed to have technical and/or conceptual skills that enable them to produce the data needed to specify the solution. Thus,

client groups may engage survey research institutes to use their technical skills in designing interview schedules, drawing samples, and conducting survey interviews; or specialists in group dynamics may be engaged to use their skills in conducting T groups; or researchers may be brought in to evaluate the effectiveness of a given experimental effort in a public agency.

A great deal of useful applied sociology has been generated under this model, and no doubt this will continue to be the case. However, there are major problems of a social engineering model if one looks to it as the basic approach to applied sociology. It tends to be mindless, adapted too greatly to the problem definitions of the client. Thus, the sociologist may have very little control over the kinds of data he will analyze, the questions he will ask of the information that is available, *or the uses to which his analysis will be put*. This may sharply reduce the effectiveness of the research, for the sociologist thereby is led not to look into the totality of the social institution or into fundamentally important phenomena contained within it.

Radical Sociology

This is where much of the action has been in recent years. Gouldner (1970) contends that "reflexive sociology" would have to be at the same time a radical sociology. From this perspective one would always be hypercritical of the regime and established institutions; one would come fundamentally to emphasize a conflict model of society. Certainly Gouldner is correct that to adopt a radical perspective is to enhance one's praxis. Clearly, very useful research could be done from this perspective. However, the radical sociology model has several deficiencies. First, it leaves out the other required emphasis of sociology, that of looking at social stability and consensus. Second, it implies that a great many of the phenomena of the social life are not worth studying, for they are only seen as epiphenomena of the underlying exploitative and class relations. By such exclusions, the self-corrective function of research is aborted and radical theory becomes revealed truth. Third, by becoming so politicized, the sociologist is likely to find himself unable to achieve access to settings in which useful applied work could be done, and to find his findings and judgments discredited due to the accusations of political bias.

Enlightenment

The social engineering model sharply distinguishes between the client and the sociologist, while the radical sociology model perhaps removes the client entirely while substituting a group of intended beneficiaries. Under the enlightenment model, the assumption that sociologists provide the answers to the clients' questions in a straightforward way is abandoned. Instead, it is assumed that whatever sociological research is done will be placed in context by sociologists, whose task it is to enlighten the decision makers in as broad a way as possible. A sociologist may be hired by the user, but he is not beholden to that user. The sociologist attempts to use his sociological knowledge to communicate the broad range of problematics of theory and data, enlightening the user to the sociological perspective. Simultaneously, in Janowitz's words (1970:250), the model would "reject the view that sociological knowledge produces definitive answers on which policy and professional practice may be based." Further, we would assume that the communications to the elites are not the sole product; they would be coupled with enlightening communications to relevant publics and to the society at large.

In many ways, the enlightenment model seems to be the most appropriate model for much of applied sociology—assuming, of course, that no single model will predominate and that applied sociologists may use a mix of models in any given instance. The principal advantages are that the model avoids both oversell and unconditional acceptance of the user's definition of the problem. Nor does it make an overly sharp distinction between pure and applied sociology, a distinction which is more apparent than real. The knowledge gained in either kind of effort can be transmitted to the other, and the theories used in doing both should be identical or compatible. The most difficult problem with the enlightenment model would seem to be that the applied sociologist might become overly committed to the status quo, for the model requires that he be in relatively intimate contact with elite groupings. Thus, the use of the enlightenment model must recognize the need for a reflexive sociology, that is, a need to have a self-critical awareness of the integrity of his work and the uses to which it can be put. Then it can be a significant guide to applied sociology without requiring that one couple to it a commitment to radical sociology or to the immediate and total improvement of mankind.

Mixed Models

Clearly, these models are ideal types. An applied sociology cannot be exclusively any one because the range and variety of questions to which it is legitimately directed cannot all be handled within a single model. For example, even operating generally under the enlightenment model, the sociologist might try to find appropriate places to focus on manipulable variables and bring these to the attention of decision makers who would then require knowledge best developed through an engineering model approach.

The true test of an applied sociology is whether it can lead to more humane and effective decisions. Different models seem more effective for different levels of decisions. Applied sociology should be able to help ordinary people, not only policy makers, in their interchange with social institutions. The radical model gives generalized guidance for this purpose but it is limited in its implications to those who are already committed to revolutionary praxis. Implications from work done under the engineering model could give similar guidance, but there is a problem in bringing together the consumer's problems and available knowledge. Such a function could be served at the grassroots level by a social work profession in partnership with both enlightenment and engineering-oriented applied sociology.

A second test is whether applied sociology can assess the effect of existing institutional practices on the clients served and, as a corollary, the effects of changes in those practices. These seem to be straightforward engineering questions. But the engineering model is particularly vulnerable to the tunnel vision of the client's definition of the problem, a handicap that reverberates throughout the research process. Some aspects of the radical model may be invaluable as a corrective to the consequences of the engineer's frequent insensitivity to his own assumptions regarding the institutions he is studying.

Finally, a third test of applied sociology is whether it can be used as a basis for designing better social institutions. This is hallowed ground for radical sociology. We are concerned, however, about the reluctance of the users of the radical model to question their own assumptions. The enlightenment model, predicated on humane values but open to correction regarding its perspectives on implementing those values, seems to us to be especially well suited for addressing applied problems of this level. But, again, we must note the dangers of unwitting cooptation of enlightenment sociologists. A radical model may be necessary to spur reflexivity, even if not at the core of applied sociology.

SOCIOLOGY AND SOCIETY

The central conditions making possible a truly useful applied sociology are not those internal to the discipline or the minds of the practitioners, however. The central conditions are those of the society at large. In all societies, sociology could help in the *efficient* making of some decisions, whether humane or otherwise, with the social engineering model. However, the positive impact of such a science for man would be extremely limited in societies that are highly ideologized. Neither totalitarian right societies nor totalitarian left ones have regimes that can permit an enlightened and thus critical sociology. For example, Nazi Germany made use of a bastardized anthropology of race in the effort to justify anti-Semitism, while in the Soviet Union sociology has principally been either Marxist ideological exegesis or the accumulation of masses of statistics on "nonsensitive" matters.

We propose that sociology is likely to have its greatest utility in societies that are committed to humane and rational planning and that are "governable." These conditions suggest the likelihood that large-scale social experimentation can be made but without an insistence on immediate results and totalistic planning, such that enlightenment and improvement in social practices can be brought about through changes in policies of public agencies and relevant professional groups. This does not imply a commitment to excessive incrementalism, but it does recognize that social science cannot help forge new social policies and practices overnight.

The approximation of contemporary American society to these conditions is very much in doubt. Under a high commitment to *laissez faire*, humane and rational planning is extremely difficult and governability is dubious. American society shows a mix, with the heavy *laissez faire* commitment persisting despite the growth of statism and ambivalent aspirations to the welfare state; what we seem to have is collectivism without social planning. Indeed, plans come to be seen only as political documents or slogans. For the generations coming to political age in the 1960s and 1970s, their experience with assassinations and of an apparently interminable Indo-Chinese war, coupled with the problems in the economy that would seem to indicate that the Keynesian solutions were insufficient, have been given little reason to have faith in the possibility of enlightened social planning. U.S. society is becoming so complex, the proposals for reform are so many, and the protests on all sides mount so high, that it becomes difficult for any set of proposals, no matter how well based in sociology or other knowledge, to seem like anything but another set of slogans or demands. Under these conditions, it becomes increasingly legitimate for decisions to be reached through compromise (and "logrolling") among all parties to the issue. In the process, all parties come to be seen, and legitimately so in this system, as pressure groups (Lowi, 1969)—or, in more recent times, all become discredited. The role of sociological knowledge becomes that of the role of the "sociologists' pressure group"—and a weak one at that!

Thus, the prospect for applied sociology approaching its promise is by no means assured. In a society ridden with conflict and protest and lacking a commitment to rational planning or the means to implement effectively such plans as it has, sociology would be in the public spotlight. But, the danger is that it would become an aspect principally of mass culture. Indeed, sociology might even contribute to the immobilization of society by promulgating conceptions confirming that the attributes of the citizens and/or the society make genuine change impossible. It is our conclusion that such a development is far from inevitable. Sociologists communicating both the potentialities and limits of their work can at least help in the effort to see that it is not.

REFERENCES

Alinsky, Saul. 1972. "Interview with Saul Alinsky." *Playboy*, March 1972, p. 64.

Beil, Daniel. 1955. *The End of Ideology: On the Exhaustion of Political Ideas in the 50's*. New York: The Free Press.

Comte, Auguste. 1877. *Cours de Philosophie Positive*. Paris: Bailliere.

Coser, Lewis A. 1956. *The Functions of Social Conflict*. Glencoe, Ill.: Free Press.

Dahrendorf, R. 1958. "Out of utopia: toward a reorientation of sociological analysis." *American Journal of Sociology* 64 (Sept):115–127.

Gouldner, Alvin W. 1970. *The Coming Crisis of Western Sociology*. New York: Basic Books.

Janowitz, M. 1970. "Sociological models and social policy." In *Political Conflict: Essays in Political Sociology*, edited by Morris Janowitz, pp. 243–59. Chicago: Quadrangle Books.

Levine, D. 1970. "Sociology confronts student protest." *School Review* 78 (Aug):529–541.

Lowi, Theodore J. 1969. *The End of Liberalism*. New York: W.W. Norton.

Mannheim, Karl. 1936. *Ideology and Utopia*. London: Routledge and Kegan Paul.

Popper, Karl. 1957. *The Poverty of Historicism*. Boston: Beacon Press.

Scott, R. and A. Shore. 1974. "Sociology and policy analysis." *American Sociologist* 9 (May):51–59.

Skinner, B.F. 1971. *Beyond Freedom and Dignity*. New York: Alfred A. Knopf.

Sumner, William G. 1883. *What Social Classes Owe Each Other*. New York: Harper and Brothers.

_____. 1906. *Folkways*. Boston: Ginn.

Swanson, Guy E. 1971. "Review symposium on *The Coming Crisis of Western Sociology*." *American Sociological Review* 36 (Apr):320.

Weber, Max. 1949. *Max Weber on the Methodology of the Social Sciences*. Edward Shils and H.A. Finch, trans. and ed. Glencoe, Ill.: Free Press.

Williams, W. and J.W. Evans. 1969. "The politics of evaluation: the case of head start." *Annals of the American Academy of Political and Social Science* 385 (Sept):118–32.

Part
A

DEVELOPING
APPLIED
TECHNIQUES

Writing over four decades ago, Robert Lynd contended that "However great a part 'pure curiosity' and 'the *disinterested* desire to know' may have played in the acquisition of scholarly knowledge and natural science, it has been the *interested* desire to know in order to do something about problems that has predominately motivated social science, from the *Wealth of Nations* down to the present."* Nevertheless, the history of sociology suggests that this claim is not totally accurate. Until very recently sociologists have viewed colleagues who apply sociological knowledge to the solution of problems as second class citizens of the discipline. Perhaps because of this pervasive invidious distinction, as well as their differing objectives, applied sociologists have developed a set of techniques that are not commonly taught in standard courses on sociological methods.

If the aim of applied sociology is "to know in order to do something about problems," then several kinds of knowledge are required. First, the dimensions of the problem must be identified. This may involve one or both of two techniques. On the one hand, empirical indicators of the nature and extent of the problem must be developed. For example, to indicate poverty we might measure the proportion of all families below the government's official poverty line. On the other hand, the applied researcher may want to assess in advance the likely social consequences (both intended and unintended) of a proposed action. For instance, what impacts might an affirmative action program have on both employees and employers?

A second kind of knowledge needed by the applied sociologist concerns alternative strategies for handling, reducing, or eliminating problems. Again, two different techniques fall in this category. One involves the organization of material and human resources into programs designed to combat specific problems. Development of programs to deliver needed services to the elderly, the poor, and unwed mothers illustrate this technique. The second technique is intervention into ongoing organizations or programs to reduce conflicts that may be hindering their effectiveness. For example, sociologists may apply their expertise to labor-management negotiations or to resolving interracial conflicts.

The third kind of knowledge used by applied sociologists stems from the need to determine whether efforts to do something about a problem are achieving the desired results. This technique of evaluation research involves measuring the effects of a program, apart from the effects of other factors influencing the problem, as well as formulating guidelines to improve program performance. In recent years, large-scale evaluation studies of school bussing, family planning, and income maintenance programs have been conducted by sociologists.

---

*Robert S. Lynd. *Knowledge for What? The Place of Social Science in American Culture.* (Princeton, N.J.: Princeton University Press, 1939), pp. 114–15.

3

The chapters in this section review the current state of development of each of these five applied techniques: social indicators, impact assessment, program development, conflict intervention, and program evaluation. The authors discuss the varied uses to which these techniques have been put as well as the difficulties associated with their implementation. They are also concerned with how these procedures can be improved.

Sociologists have always had an intellectual interest in the problems of society. But only recently have they begun to develop specialized techniques for doing something about these problems, through the application of sociological knowledge. Achievement of the ultimate goal of applied sociology—improving the quality of life in society—will depend heavily on the imagination and skill we exercise in developing the tools of our trade.

1 SOCIAL INDICATORS

Judith Innes de Neufville

Numbers can play powerful roles in both political and intellectual realms. They are potent media for communication and provide unambiguous standards for which public agencies can be held accountable. They shape definitions of public programs and the means for their solution. Public action is far more likely with problems that are measured, since any disparity between what exists and what is desired is then readily apparent. Quantitative data are accepted as factual far more readily than other kinds of information. They make abstract ideas concrete and provide a link to the empirical world that allows us to test the ideas. The simplicity and power of quantification force clarity of thought. Numbers permit us to apply formal models to empirical reality and to manipulate and analyze a large amount of information in a sophisticated way.

WHAT ARE SOCIAL INDICATORS?

A Link Between Meaning and Data

For numbers to work so powerfully they must be more than merely statistics; they must be indicators, that is, measures of something. The difference between indicators and data is not obvious from a superficial inspection. The difference depends on the statistic and whether it has meaning in the context of an application. To say that there are 250 families on welfare in Berkeley is merely to recite a piece of data that is of little intrinsic interest. However, to say that 25 percent more families are on welfare this year than last year is more meaningful because it makes a comparison. After further investigation of the factors influencing the figure, one may be able to use it as a social indicator, reflecting poverty, unemployment, or perhaps simply the behavior of welfare agencies.

The literature contains many different ideas about what social indicators are or should be, but this chapter uses a broad and inclusive definition. Social indi-

5

cators are measures of significant social phenomena. The notion of "social" implies that the phenomena have to do with relationships, interactions, and the well-being of social groups. Such phenomena may be significant because they are valued concerns in a society or because they help us to understand how the society works. Some critics have argued that indicators must be regular trend data or have unambiguous normative implications. Nevertheless, the most fundamental aspect of social indicators is the self-conscious attempt to measure social phenomena. To determine the best forms and most productive uses for such measures will require more exploration.

Social indicators, like all measures, have the paradoxical quality of being simultaneously abstractions from reality and concrete data. They are constructions, the design of which may be based on theoretical notions, yet they allow us to make sense of raw data. The reading on a thermometer tells us the temperature because we know the relationship between heat and the expansion of mercury. Similarly, the number of violent crimes per capita may be understood as an indicator of the level of alienation in a population if one can demonstrate a link between social violence and alienation.

More precisely, a social indicator is a set of rules specifying who or what should be counted and how the resulting data are to be structured. A crime indicator, for example, would include rules on which crimes to count, over which time periods, and within which jurisidictions, as well as rules about whether each crime is to be given equal weight and whether the figures should be reported as a proportion of population or in some other way. Each of these decisions has significance for what we will then "see" concerning violent crime and its changing patterns. An indicator is a lens which permits us to look at data from a particular perspective.

The critical position of indicators, standing between meanings and data, between the subjective and the objective, makes them philosophically and pragmatically important as a subject of study. While the design of an indicator can radically affect what we see and understand, there can be no definitive guide as to how the indicator ought to be designed. The appropriate design is contingent on the theories and the values that we choose to apply to a particular situation. A well-chosen indicator can be central to a political dispute; one that does not correspond to the user's view of the issue is likely to be ignored. Moreover, the meaning of an indicator is not uniformly attached to a set of numbers, but can vary depending on where and how it is applied. Therefore, the study of social indicators cannot confine itself to methods for manipulating statistics. It must also address the processes and purposes of their use and the theoretical contexts for their interpretation.

A further complication of social indicators is that they acquire meanings that go beyond what they are explicitly designed to cover. They become symbols, as do many aspects of policy language (Edelman, 1977). The crime rate may be viewed as an indicator of moral deterioration or economic breakdown of society, although the demonstrable linkage may be slight. Much of the writing on social indicators overlooks this symbolic dimension, although inappropriately ascribed meanings affect public policies in perverse ways. Policies may be proposed that will change an indicator, but really are intended to change what the indicator represents in the public mind. For example, efforts to lower the crime rate through stricter deterrents are apt to have little effect on public morality. Alternatively, some policies are wrongly judged to have failed on the basis of indicators that, on closer examination, are not good representations of the policy's goals.

Social Indicators in Public Policy

Social indicators are to public policy like prose to Molière's Bourgeois Gentilhomme. Policy has depended on them for generations without their being labeled as "social indicators." The idea of applying quantitative data systematically to policy making dates back at least to seventeenth century Britain, when censuses were taken to aid in the planning of national mercantile policy. The social survey had its origins in nineteenth century social reform, when concern with the living and working conditions of labor led to massive, path-breaking studies. The most potent early examples of quantitative information in policy making, however, were the measures of employment, prices, construction, and wholesale trade that were used to help predict the course of the business cycle in the early twentieth century. Other economic measures, such as national product, income, and inflation, were critical in designing economic policies after World War II.

Meanwhile, a presidential committee reported on social trends in the early 1930s (President's Research Committee, 1933), and governments regularly collected data on housing, employment, family income, and consumption. These social indicators have played a less visible, but still significant, role in decision making. Dramatic improvements in the methods of survey research, including the development of stratified sampling in the 1930s, made feasible far more extensive use of social data. With the advent of the computer and advanced techniques of data manipulation in the 1960s, the technological capability existed for a systematic effort to gather and use social indicators.

Economic indicators provided a double-edged inspiration for the social indicators movement, which is reflected in ambivalent expectations. On the one hand, the success of economic indicators in influencing policy seemed to confirm the power of quantitative information, and it encouraged a faith in our ability to diagnose and solve social problems. It meshed nicely with a policy emphasis on large-scale, quantitative modelling. On the other hand, the proponents of social indicators argued that these measures would provide an alternative to economic indicators, diverting public attention from economic to social concerns. They would rescue us from the "new Philistinism" of economic materialism and encourage us to focus on the quality of life, on satisfactions and well-being, rather than on product and income. While some analysts contended that social indicators were merely extensions of economic indicators, broadened to include satisfaction, the majority saw them as different in style and application. The very idea of rational calculation—reducing social problems to simple, quantifiable dimensions so that tradeoffs and predictions could be made—is foreign to the characteristic approach of sociologists and social theorists, who are apt to place more emphasis on process and hard-to-quantify phenomena such as values and attitudes. Accordingly, social indicators are evolving in new ways that diverge sharply from the economic indicator model.

HOW ARE SOCIAL INDICATORS IMPLEMENTED?

Social Indicator Design

The task of indicator design is to transform a concept into something that can be counted and to provide a form in which the numbers will be meaningfully combined and presented. One begins, for example, with a concept of community health and then selects something measurable—such as local mortality or morbidity, self or physicians' assessment of health status, days lost from work, or length of life. These data must be transformed and presented as a rate or special index that has the desired meaning, like the life expectancy measure. This task may involve taking a special survey or locating and manipulating existing data. Compromises are inevitably required, since the ideal concept can never be perfectly embodied.

Even the simplest concepts for which we seek indicators are what Kaplan (1964) calls "open concepts." They have fuzzy, undefined elements and, when applied in different contexts, may have different meanings. For example, to a toddler a book would be anything with hard covers and pages, including an empty notebook, but to a librarian it would have to have a certain content and publication format to be classified as a book. Librarians classify many bound and published volumes as journals. A faculty tenure review committee might count an unpublished manuscript as a book, however, while a republished collection of articles would very likely not qualify for consideration.

As another example, there is no hope of measuring health without a clear set of ideas about what constitutes a healthy person and how we can recognize such a person. Moreover, the values we hold about the kinds of ailments that are worthy of public concern and the ideas we have about appropriate actions to deal with health problems will influence the sort of health indicator that is chosen. The professional or intellectual perspective within which an indicator is designed will contain many of these determinants. Ramsøy (van Dusen, 1974: 41) describes the implications of applying four different frames of reference to the design of health indicators. The therapeutic approach, for example, envisions treatment as the solution to health problems, defines health as absence of clinically diagnosed illness, and measures individual health status. The epidemiological view, on the other hand, is concerned mainly with prevention. It focuses on the health risks of populations "at-risk" and produces indicators related to the causes of ill health, particularly in the environment. While the therapeutic framework results in indicators of the prevalence of clinical disease in the population, the epidemiological approach is likely to result in indicators of the health risks of different groups or of environmental health hazards. The first set of measures will suggest a need for medical treatment and the second for preventive policies. Each profession defines indicators in terms of the solutions it can apply to the health problem.

The circularity of theories, professional capabilities, indicators, and policy solutions is inevitable (Rittel and Webber, 1973), but it runs counter to a popular view that indicators can be value-free. Indicator design, even in its details, is guided by prior models, values, and purposes. For example, a common conception of poverty is the level of income below which a family cannot participate fully as citizens. Theories of political participation will emphasize the importance of being able to afford newspapers and a television set, while a concern with economic opportunity will stress being able to purchase adequate clothing for school or work. Nutritionists' theories will tell us what foods people need to function at full capacity. Even the decision to depend on a survey for the data, instead of using some less reactive form of data gathering such as looking at housing and consumption patterns, implies a set of assumptions about how accurately people will report their incomes and expenditures.

Once one steps beyond the selection of a perspective to define the concept, the next design choice is about the type of connection the indicator and concept will have. The measure might correlate with the phenomenon; it might represent some part of it; it might be causally linked; it might be in several parts, representing different dimensions; or it might attempt to represent all elements of the concept in an aggregated or composite index. As an indicator of recreational activity, for example, one could use recreation expenditures (a correlated measure); use of national parks (a partial measure); satisfaction with use of leisure time (a causally linked indicator); time, money, and satisfaction attributable to recreation (a multidimensional indicator); or a summation of all recreation activities, weighted by average per capita use of each in hours (an aggregated index). The choice among these is largely a practical matter, dictated by what one has the time and money to do and by the purposes for the measure. It will also require some substantive connection to the type of policy issue under consideration. In the presentation and use of an indicator it is critical to make explicit its link to the basic concept. For example, increased use of national parks should not be assumed to indicate increases in other recreational activities, particularly ones that are dissimilar or which provide alternatives to parks (such as travel abroad).

Indicators all involve comparisons, and establishing what comparisons to make is a third important design decision. A bald fact, such as the number of poor people in a city, indicates nothing, except when it is compared with something else, such as the number of poor in the city last year, the number of poor in another city, or the nonpoor population of the same city. The basis of comparison is critical, for it helps to shape the way those who use the indicator will view the problem. There are misleading comparisons. A comparison ought to be made only with a population that could potentially be affected by the phenomenon. It is deceptive, for example, to give unemployment rates based on the total population. The number of unemployed should be compared to the total employable population, or the rate will continually fluctuate with births or other factors relevant to employment. Many comparisons are clearly dictated by the purpose of the indicator. Many have policy implications. For example, one can compare IQ levels by race, by race and location, or by location alone. One measure might suggest different policies for the races, while another might argue for programs targeted at school systems.

A fourth design issue is aggregation. Any indicator depends on counting and adding items that are somewhat different from one another. This is done by translating the amounts of the different items into a common metric. To add apples and oranges, they can all be translated into pieces of fruit, pounds of weight, or dollars of price. Even a simple indicator, such as years of education, involves a decision to count each year of schooling as equivalent, although the amount of learning acquired may differ greatly, and some schools produce significantly more learning than others.

For most indicators, the aggregation problem is far more substantial and explicit than in these examples, and can involve complex theoretical issues. The Gross National Product, for example, involves a common valuation of all products and services in dollars to reach a single index of national productivity. Market prices are the weighting factor for many goods, but government services have to be valued at their cost. No weight is given to volunteer services, regardless of their contribution to welfare, nor is housework included. To avoid double counting, the concept of final value to consumer is used, so raw materials and intermediate goods are not valued. Each of the decisions involved in this aggregated index is a theoretical and value-based choice. Many future indicators will face parallel problems as they focus on measuring overall quality of services or environments. When there is no logical or comprehensible way to combine components using a meaningful metric such as price or satisfaction, the option of preserving separate indicators in a disaggregated, multidimensional form should not be forgotten. Several separate indicators can provide a profile on the phenomenon that might be lost in an aggregate measure.

Other design considerations are also important and should not be arbitrarily determined. For example, the frequency of collecting and producing an indicator can be related to the speed of change of the phenomenon and the capacity of the system to respond to change. The U.S. government measures price changes monthly because monetary and fiscal policy can be activated on short notice, but purchasing patterns of the average family are only determined every ten years because they change slowly. The cost of producing an indicator should be related to its likely impact on policy and to the costs that might be affected by its use. Additionally, a measure should not be more precise than our capacities to analyze it. If theories give us only crude guidance concerning the implications of changes in an indicator, it is wasteful to develop precisely high figures. Generating such figures may mislead others into treating the results as more accurate than they really are (Alonso, 1968:248).

Validating Social Indicators

There are no routine, mechanical tests to determine whether an indicator is valid; that is, whether it means what it is used to mean. The problem is difficult because of the peculiar nature of indicators at the intersection of data and ideas. An indicator's validity depends on both and yet is not totally determined by either.

Of the various validation techniques, intuitive or experiential validation is the simplest. One can tell by one's experience, or members of a group can tell by their shared experience, how much money it takes to live on, or whether years of education indicates achievement. But such subjective validation can be misleading when used alone. There is no intuitive reason to think the movement of a needle on a speedometer would indicate car speed, or the length of the mercury in a thermometer would indicate temperature. One recognizes the validity of these measures because of previously known relationships.

A different validation strategy is to see if the indicator's movements follow the same pattern as those of another indicator of the same phenomenon. The unemployment rate from the Current Population Survey should move up and down along with unemployment insurance figures or with an index of help-wanted ads. Survey responses about the favorite tourist attractions in the United States should coincide with visitor figures to those attractions. For this validation procedure to work, however, the indicator must represent a defined concept and cannot be simply a measure with no external meaning.

An indicator can also be validated by observing whether its movements in relation to indicators of other variables correspond to established predictions. This approach takes advantage of prior theory about the phenomenon. Unemployment indicators can be validated by looking at their relationship to employment and the composition of the population and labor force. This type of validation is most effective when an indicator is originally derived from a causal model of the problem. It also requires that the indicator represent a meaningful phenomenon.

These validation approaches all depend on the acceptance of a particular frame of reference and set of theories, which may also require validation. An indicator measuring health as diagnosed disease will decrease along with the number of doctors, as predicted, but still might not be a good indicator if one is interested in physical and mental well-being. The only way to determine what the indicator should be measuring is ultimately through a social and political process. Policy makers, data users, and the public can play a role in the design of an indicator, provide feedback, and suggest changes when it does not reflect the phenomenon as they experience it. Users often know best what an indicator means in application and whether it is working. Moreover, the theories applicable in one society or period may not be equally relevant in another. A valid indicator in one context is not necessarily valid in another. The divorce rate, for example, can be a valid indicator of family instability in a period or society where divorce is an accepted practice, but not elsewhere. This contextual problem raises questions about the validity of many long-term, continuous statistical series, and of cross-cultural, comparative social indicators. (For further discussion of validation, see de Neufville, 1978–79).

Agencies to Produce Social Indicators

The kind of agency that produces an indicator influences that indicator's character and credibility. Any agency is most responsive to its own constituencies and puts its own mission first. It will, accordingly, produce indicators reflecting this priority (President's Commission on Federal Statistics, 1971). The major types of agencies that produce social indicators are 1) statistical agencies with no other responsibility, like the Census Bureau, 2) central management agencies, like the Office of Management and Budget, 3) quasiindependent statistical bureaus in agencies with policy responsibility, like the Bureau of Labor Statistics, 4) statistical offices of operating agencies, like the statistics branch of the Social Security Administration, 5) operating agencies themselves, like a police department or the FBI, 6) private profit-making organizations, such as the Gallup Poll, and 7) university-based or nonprofit research groups, such as the University of Michigan Survey Research Center.

Differences abound among these agencies. A central statistical agency has to please many masters and tends to provide data that are both technically sound and credible, but it is often too broad in its mission to choose statistics that have immediate pertinence to policy and too cautious in its activities to be responsive to new demands. An agency with responsibility for programs will typically place program needs first and is likely to have more understanding of policy but less technical expertise in data collection and management. Its main reason for collecting data is for internal administration rather than for public information, and such an agency may avoid indicators that reveal information that could be used against it. Operating agencies tend to collect data in inconsistent and self-serving ways because data collection is not their main mission. They often have little credibility with either the public or social science users, particularly with controversial data. The FBI crime indicators, for example, are seldom used in social science research and have little impact on public policy because of their biases and technical limitations (de Neufville, 1975:101ff).

The private firm or university-based group plays a role in developing experimental indicators, measuring attitudes, and dealing with sensitive subjects. Quality control can be best assured for such groups through openness about their methodology, competitiveness, and concern for their reputation. Several such groups play important roles in social indicator production.

The most successful source of social policy indicators, however, has been the quasiindependent statistical agency. Such an agency can develop technical expertise and commitment to methodological excellence. It is also close enough to ongoing policy issues to maintain some relevance, and its staff deals with a sufficiently limited set of subjects to become substantive experts. The Bureau of Labor Statistics, often in conjunction with the Census Bureau, has produced some of the most important and widely used social indicators thus far, such as the unemployment rate, the Standard Family Budgets, and the Consumer Price Index.

HOW HAVE SOCIAL INDICATORS BEEN USED?

Frameworks for Applying Social Indicators

No single organizing scheme is best for applying social indicators. If one is interested in indicators for specific research tasks, then the purposes of the research and the theories on which it depends provide the framework. However, if one needs time-series social indicators as part of a general system for analytical and policy use, an organizing scheme is essential. Several major alternatives have been proposed that are not mutually exclusive, but that do represent different emphases.

The approach taken by governments to formal social reporting (see, for example, U.S. Department of Commerce, 1977, and United Kingdom Central Statistical Office, 1970ff) has been to develop indicators corresponding to a set of social concerns that match, more or less, public understandings of how social life is organized. In practice, these correspond closely to the missions of the service-providing institutions. The most typical topics are housing, health, employment, public safety, income, education, and a few others. The indicators all have some link to well-being, as illustrated by crime rates and years of education (Ferris, 1975:81). The Organization for Economic Cooperation and Development (OECD) has created such a framework by achieving agreement among nations on social objectives such as minimal standards of living, and through successive iterations it has developed ways of measuring those concepts (Christian, 1974:69). The objective is to compare social well-being among member nations. This approach is connected with policy questions and has an intuitive popular appeal. However, it constrains our understanding of the dynamics of society and the experiences of people, which are not compartmentalized into housing or educational systems.

A second framework is a social change perspective. It draws its categories and concepts from social theory and purports to deal with fundamental social forces. While no one has developed a full set of indicators based on this view, some work is based on it. Concepts might include, for example, alienation, mobility, or family structure. Social processes and structures are the principal foci, not well-being. Data such as years of education, which are outputs of the service sector, are less important than population surveys, particularly cohort or longitudinal studies. Some governmental reports do reflect these concerns, but it remains to be seen whether this framework can be linked to policy objectives and whether governments will be willing to make the significant expenditures required for such measurement. An even more difficult obstacle will be the development of concepts and theories to the point where it is clear what should be measured and how to interpret the indicators.

A third approach, not necessarily distinct from the first two, is to develop social indicators explicitly on the basis of causal models. One would start with a theoretical or policy question and develop a causal analysis, out of which indicators would be chosen. To understand occupational changes in society, for example, Land and Pampel (1977) designed an indicator of occupational prestige that grew out of a model linking changes in the production system with bureaucratization. This approach is the most likely to produce meaningful and useful measures. The most effective public policy indicators have been based on such causal models (de Neufville, 1975). However, they require many years to develop and depend on a systematic body of theory, which exists for only a few important social issues.

A fourth strategy is to develop indicators as part of a system of social accounts, analogous to financial balance sheets. The social system can be thought of as using inputs in the form of resources and producing outputs in the form of human welfare. An input to one part of the system is an output from another part. Given this matrix of linkages, it is possible, at least in principle, to measure the overall welfare of the whole society and to estimate the costs and benefits of particular policies in terms of the inputs they require and the outputs they contribute to that welfare. Some of the earliest schemes for social indicators envisioned a large matrix, identifying all the interrelationships between inputs and outputs of social processes and institutions. For example, labor can be seen as an input to education and achievement as an output, which, in turn, is an input to work. This scheme is attractive because it has been worked out in detail for economic development planning, among many other purposes, and could be adapted to social concerns. Moreover, its effort to summarize diverse values is an appealing simplification for policy making.

Major problems have arisen with this accounting model, however, and it loses its appeal as the full implications of its application become apparent. The data demands are tremendous. Accounting must be done for everything, including much that is difficult to measure, like the costs of pollution or the social benefits of a park. To identify the interrelationships among all the components of the matrix is even more problematic. For example, how much is health education worth in terms of health care costs or labor productivity? Most significantly, to make an accounting system work, all goods or activities must be transformed into a common metric. Unlike prices in economic accounting, we have no common measure that is applicable to a social accounting framework.

The fifth and currently most discussed application for social indicators is measuring the quality of life. Here the central idea is that indicators should reflect the experience of living in a community or nation. These indicators are based on individual perceptions and satisfactions and involve the impacts of social and economic activities and environments on people's lives. A lot of creative activity now focuses on this much-neglected dimension of social policy. Considerable attention is being given, for instance, to measuring and interpreting attitude data (Campbell, et al., 1975; Andrews and Withey, 1976) and to methods for combining information to indices of life quality. The effort to develop composite indexes has the same pitfalls as accounting schemes, however. They require vast amounts of data and a common metric. And little has been done to determine the relationships between attitudes and objective situations, which will be essential if quality of life indicators are to have policy implications. Moreover, if these indicators can be linked to models of societal behavior, they will provide more powerful tools for both research and policy formation.

Some people argue that social indicators should be performance measures with clear implications, so we can interpret a move up or down as good or bad. Some argue that input measures are not useful, while others insist that they are an essential part of any policy indicator system. It is becoming clear that each of the perspectives has merit and that they can be mutually supportive. An ultimate scheme for usable social indicators will incorporate many system levels and will include indicators of environments, production processes, distributional systems, and levels of well-being for nations, groups, institutions, and individuals. (For an outline of such a framework, see McIntosh, et al., 1977.)

Each of these concepts represents an objective for the application of social indicators. But while these frameworks and indicators are being developed, public decisions are made and analysis and research go on. Imperfect measures can be better than none. The task of social indicators research is not only to work toward long-term goals, but also to learn ways of using imperfect indicators while recognizing their limitations.

Current Applications of Social Indicators

Social indicators have been applied in a wide variety of contexts and are becoming increasingly pervasive in public decision making and social science research. The most familiar application is in social reporting. Most of the developed nations, including the United States, have produced social reports, ostensibly to provide an assessment of social trends and problems. While these assessments depend heavily on existing data, they have set a precedent in bringing together a set of social indicators into a single report. Many U.S. states and localities have also begun some form of social reporting. While few of these efforts are highly sophisticated or institutionalized, they reflect the popular appeal of the idea. (For a bibliography of many of these, see California Office of Planning and Research, 1977.)

Social indicators have often been applied in policy making at the visible, public level. Perhaps most importantly, they have been used to focus public attention on problems and to define them. For example, the rising crime rate keeps the issue of crime in the public eye, but crime is defined in terms of the activities included in the index, which does not take into account white-collar crime. Such indicators can subdue arguments about whether a problem is getting better or worse, and they provide a sense of the scale of the problem. They influence the shape, direction, and scope of policy, which is frequently designed with the intent of influencing the indicator. The goals for a new program, like constructing six million units of standard housing, often grow from the use of an indicator, such as the number of families in substandard housing. The policy of constructing standard housing (as opposed to some other housing or other welfare policy) is advanced by the public attention given to a housing indicator that focuses on this aspect of housing quality. The indicators that are most often used in policy contexts tend to be simple and comprehensible, and they tend to cover areas in which there is considerable agreement on definitions and on the need for action. These indicators with critical policy consequences must be designed with particular care.

Social indicators lend themselves well to making comparisons among areas. Researchers have used indicators to compare the quality of life in various U.S. cities, and the Bureau of Labor Statistics' annual comparisons of living costs in different cities always attract much public attention. Social indicators are used by cities and counties in the United States to identify needy neighborhoods and other areas as targets for federal funds. These rankings of neighborhoods also receive considerable attention in the local press and may arouse the concern of local residents (de Neufville, 1979).

Social indicators can play a role in social needs assessment and social planning at the local level. While this is not widely and systematically done at the present time, the practice is growing, partially as a result of federal requirements for documenting needs. Indicators have also been used as program triggers. For example, when unemployment in an area goes above a certain level, it can set in operation a program of extended unemployment benefits. A particular level of an indicator can become a normative standard and be incorporated into the administration of programs. Thus, the official poverty line may become the cut-off income for welfare assistance or for college scholarships.

Social indicators have also been incorporated into formulas for allocating funds from state and federal governments to communities and from international agencies, such as the United Nations or World Bank, to member nations. The funding level may depend on such indicators as the number of people in poverty, the number illiterate, the percentage living in urbanized areas, or the percentage of housing stock that is substandard. For example, such formulas are widely used in the United States as a basis for federal block grant funding to communities. While many people argue that they are simply convenient ways of circumventing political disputes, they ostensibly provide objective social criteria for dispersing of funds.

Social indicators also play a part in the design and evaluation of programs. These applications are as numerous as the types of programs, so it is difficult to classify them. In general, it is necessary to know the characteristics of the population and the size and location of the social problems a program is addressing. For example, U.S. regulations demanding affirmative action hiring and evaluation of the impacts of programs on minorities have increased the importance of indicators for all minority groups. Although standard social indicators can often be used in designing and evaluating programs, it is sometimes necessary to develop new indicators and collect new data to coincide with the intent of the program.

WHAT HAVE SOCIAL INDICATORS ACCOMPLISHED?

The notable accomplishments of social indicators are, in some respects, unexpected and subtle, while some of the expected achievements have not materialized. Social indicators, as conceived of in the 1960s, have not yet radically changed policy making or social science. Such changes require decades to define measures, gather data, produce indicators, discover what they show, and reorient theory or policy processes to incorporate these new kinds of analysis. Expectations that indicators could be promptly incorporated into decision making were quite unrealistic and were based, in part, on an oversell of social indicators as a panacea for policy problems. However, specific social indicators have continued to influence public discussion of major social policy issues. Moreover, the impact of the social indicators movement has been pervasive and significant, though hard to pinpoint. It has contributed to raising the level of understanding of social measurement and to improving the quality of effort applied to measurement in both policy making and social science research.

Social reporting, through publication of compilations of national or local social indicators, has not had the impact on public policy that had been hoped for (Caplan and Barton, 1978). Decision makers simply do not use these books, although some of them use the data on which the books are based. Nonetheless, the publications are much in demand, and it has been suggested that their important function is to make the general population conversant with data about social phenomena, rather than to enlighten those who are already familiar with the problems. A substantial market for these reports, for instance, was found in Canada among college and high school teachers (Brusegard, 1978).

A few selected social indicators have had key roles in national social and economic policy since the turn of the century. These indicators were the outgrowth of considerable thought and effort and were specifically designed to influence policy. They have been linked to some of the most controversial policies of the period and have themselves received much public attention. Their influence has been largely mediated through legislators, high-level officials, interest groups, the media, and public opinion.

Many social scientists initially believed that social indicators could become tools, or even weapons, for technicians and bureaucrats in disputes over policies, and that indicators would be important for program design, prediction, and evaluation. Instead, indicators have turned out to be tools for laymen and legislators more than for bureaucrats. And while the measurement concepts and methods developed for social indicators have aided program design and evaluation, more finely tuned and specifically designed information is frequently required for these purposes. The use of social indicators as predictors of change (as opposed to merely projecting trends), or as early warning systems to alert us to impending crises, will not be possible even in the foreseeable future. Those activities will require a substantive understanding of social forces that we are still far from achieving.

The role of social indicators in public policy discussion should not be belittled, however. Measures of poverty, the cost of living, unemployment, housing quality, family composition, racial mix, and health status of soldiers have all had profound influence on national policy in the United States. Measures of the number of people in poverty, first developed in England in the nineteenth century, called public attention to a major social problem, showing that it was far more extensive than had been thought. The particular measure used—the income level at which basic subsistence was not possible—helped to encourage the development of policies directed toward people below that level, such as minimum wage laws and supplemental food and housing. A more generous definition of poverty, in contrast, would permit policies to aid the poor in other ways, such as family counseling or job training. Measures of poverty were particularly important in formulating and publicizing governmental antipoverty programs in the 1960s.

Cost of living measures and the Standard Budget developed by the United States Bureau of Labor Statistics during World War I have been used to set government pay scales, to help adjudicate wage disputes under wartime wage controls, and to set benefit levels for income support programs. They have also been central to discussions of antiinflation policies. Measures of housing quality have been important in establishing and funding many types of housing programs. Racial mix measures have been critical in establishing programs for compensatory education and bussing to achieve racial balance in schools.

A report on the Negro family, published by the Department of Labor in 1965 and known as the "Moynihan Report," popularized the idea that the difficulties blacks were having in reaching economic parity with whites were largely due to the higher proportion of black families headed by females. In subsequent years, the percentage of female-headed families was increasingly used as an indicator of social disorganization. This indicator was also used in the experiments with guaranteed family incomes that were conducted during the early 1970s.

Probably the most influential social indicator has been the unemployment rate. This figure, now collected monthly through a large national survey, gives the percentage of the labor force that is actively looking for work. It is a technically sound and sensitive indicator and represents a definition of unemployment, which, at least at the outset, commanded considerable public agreement. After it was established, labor and business stopped collecting their own data and arguing over the number of unemployed persons, and Congress was able to proceed to a more substantive discussion of what actions to take. When the Employment Act was passed after World War II, it contained the implicit requirement that the president annually acknowledge this figure and establish policy to deal with unemployment if the figure was high. A presidential advisory council of economists, plus a joint congressional committee with a subcommittee on statistics, guaranteed that policy makers would use and understand the unemployment indicator. It had the added advantage of fitting nicely with theoretical models of the economy based on Keynesian thought, which then dominated economic policy. Consequently, the indicator could be readily interpreted and policies could be proposed that would affect it.

All the indicators mentioned in the preceding paragraphs are collected and produced by well-respected government agencies that are not typically seen as biased. All of these indicators are funded and produced regardless of current policy disputes, and they cannot be readily changed. If one doubts whether these indicators are influential, consider the political disputes that have taken place over them (de Neufville, 1975, Ch. XII). Unions attacked the cost of living index during World War II when it was used to regulate wage increases. They did studies to demonstrate that it was an inaccurate measure of living cost. Congress and a federal court used the standard budget to override a Nixon Administration policy to permit wage increases to only a small proportion of the working force during a period of wage and price controls. When unemployment figures were high, the ensuing publicity led the administration to remove some Bureau of Labor Statistics officials and attempt to change the way the data were collected and presented. U.S. social reports were all several years in the making because of the fears of public officials that figures they considered inappropriate would be published. Regularly published, institutionalized social indicators erode the ability of public agencies to design and conduct policies independently of public opinion. Most of the important social policy indicators have been produced at the instigation of legislatures wanting greater oversight and not voluntarily by agencies.

Social indicators have also been valuable for administrative purposes. Their use in allocating funding and setting benefit levels in many public and private programs has made the whole process more objective and accountable. This is no minor concern, as billions of dollars and the well-being of millions of individuals are at stake. Social indicators have played a decisive role in the identification of needy communities within metropolitan areas and have called the attention of local officials to problem neighborhoods that otherwise might have passed unnoticed.

The foregoing are all instances in which social indicators have influenced public decisions. Whether or not that influence has been in a desirable direction is another matter. Even the comparatively well-thought-out indicators used in national policy formation are not ideal. Many analysts have taken issue with the female-headed family indicator of social disorganization, noting that its validity depends on a particular view of the role and structure of the family. There are major questions today about the validity of the unemployment measure because it does not include the underemployed, who many analysts believe constitute a large part of the problem. There is no definitive way to assess whether the use of these indicators has been, on balance, beneficial. In each case, we can only say that an indicator that corresponds to social scientists' and public conceptions of a social phenomenon—in other words, an indicator that has been validated—has helped to inform the decision process. Most of the indicators cited meet this criterion to some degree. As conceptions change, however, the indicators may also have to change. If one recalls that indicators are lenses we design to see something in a particular light, it becomes obvious that we must change them along with our understandings of society and the policies in which we are interested. Policy indicators must often be designed along with policy, rather than before it, if they are to be successful.

Finally, social indicators have helped to widen and deepen the understanding of social measurement among many groups, from social scientists to journalists and the general public. They are contributing to making us more "numerate" as a society, helping to raise the standards used in social measurement, and increasing our awareness of the pitfalls of quantitative analysis. The social indicator movement has helped change the character of public discussion over social policy, imbuing it with more objective information.

WHERE ARE SOCIAL INDICATORS GOING?

Social indicators are here to stay. They have become part of the vocabulary of both public policy and social science. Within the disciplines that concern themselves with social policy, many individuals have made long-term commitments to working on problems of social measurement and indicator design.

Sessions on social indicators are now dependably a part of annual meetings in many professional fields. The topic is highly interdisciplinary, drawing the interest not only of sociologists, but also of statisticians, philosophers, economists, and policy analysts. As such, it is a rich and rapidly evolving subject of study. A journal devoted solely to social indicators (*Social Indicators Research*) has appeared regularly for some years and shows no signs of running out of material for publication. Two newsletters (*Social Science Research Council*, 1973 ff; *Special Interest Group on Social Indicators*, 1977 ff) provide a forum for communication among indicator practitioners.

Many trends in the development and application of social indicators seem likely to continue, although some are less desirable than others. Other developmental needs exist which, without deliberate effort, may never be met. Presumably, the urge to accumulate and bank large quantities of social data and to invent all-encompassing schemes for indicator construction and application will continue. These notions are invariably attractive to many researchers. However, such efforts contribute little to policy formation or social understandings (de Neufville, 1978). More important is work on the theoretical foundations of social indicators, so they can be linked to causal models of social and political change. The selection and design of new indicators to mesh with specific policy concepts will also be important. An incremental approach to the development of social indicators is not only more likely to receive support than a massive scheme, but it is also more likely to produce useful results.

Quality of life measurement will continue to develop, one hopes with a greater link to basic causal understandings and possible policy interventions. Interest in social indicators of attitudes and perceptions will lead to methodological advances in techniques for gathering such information and to methods for relating it to objective situations.

Needs for data at the local government level will grow, along with an improving technology for data production and use. Social indicators for local areas are likely to become more important, but will have to be available on a neighborhood or other small-area basis to correspond to local policy decisions.

One hopes that the two most important trends will continue. First, the social indicators ideal will continue to influence researchers and analysts to set higher standards for social measurement, both in methods and in policy relevance. Second, social indicators will become widely understood by many publics. As working measures linking the messy world of data with the tidier world of theory, social indicators of the future cannot be designed in isolation from either of those worlds.

REFERENCES AND SUGGESTED READINGS

Alonso, W. 1968. "Predicting Best with Imperfect Data." *Journal of the American Institute of Planners* 34:248–55.

Andrews, F.M. and S.B. Withey. 1976. *Social Indicators of Well-Being: Americans' Perceptions of Life Quality*. New York: Plenum.

Brusegard, D. 1978. "Rethinking Nation Report." *Social Indicators Research* 6:261-72.

California, State of, Office of Planning and Research. 1977. *Putting Social Indicators to Work: An Annotated Bibliography*. Sacramento: Office of Planning and Research.

*Campbell, A., P. Converse, and W.L. Rodgers. 1976. *The Quality of American Life: Perceptions, Evaluations and Satisfactions*. New York: Russell Sage Foundation.

This is the most thorough and thoughtful analysis of satisfaction data currently available. It is a report on a massive U.S. survey and contains the results of a cross-sectional study of satisfactions with such things as residence, work, and family life, along with a careful analysis of the social factors influencing these perceptions. It is an important work for those interested in making use of subjective data as part of social indicators.

Caplan, N. and E. Barton. 1978. "The Potential of Social Indicators." *Social Indicators Research* 5:427-56.

Christian, D. 1974. "International Social Indicators: The OECD Experience." *Social Indicators* 1:69-86.

*de Neufville, J.I. 1975. *Social Indicators and Public Policy: Interactive Processes of Design and Use*. Amsterdam, Holland: Elsevier.

A number of the ideas in this chapter are further developed in this book, which is a study of the actual design and use of social indicators in public policy. It includes case studies of the development and use of three indicators—unemployment, standard budgets and poverty lines, and crime rates—exploring how and why they were or were not used. It also outlines in more or less text fashion important design considerations for social indicators, such as date collection methods, design strategies, and institutional arrangements for production and use.

——. 1978-79. "Validating Policy Indicators." *Policy Sciences*. 10:171-88.

——. 1978. "Statistics and Knowledge. *Society*, (Nov/Dec):10-12.

——. 1979. Social Indicators in Local Government. *American Statistical Association Proceedings*. Social Statistics Section.

Edelman, M. 1977. *Political Language: Words That Succeed and Policies That Fail*. New York: Academic Press.

Ferris, A.L. 1975. "National Approaches to Developing Social Indicators." *Social Indicators Research* 2:81.

*Gilmartin, K., R.J. Rossi, L.S. Lutowski, and D.F.B. Reed. 1979. *Social Indicators: An Annotated Bibliography of Current Literature*. New York: Garland.

This is the most current bibliography and a useful starting point for those interested in social indicators.

Kaplan, A. 1964. *The Conduct of Inquiry*. San Francisco: Chandler.

Land, K.C. and F. Pampel. 1977. "Indicators and Models of Changes in the American Occupational System." *Social Indicators Research* 4:1-23.

McIntosh, W.A., G.E. Klongland, and L.D. Wilcox. 1977. "Theoretical Issues and Social Indicators: A Societal Process Approach." *Policy Sciences* 8: 245–67.

President's Commission on Federal Statistics. 1971. *Federal Statistics*, vol. I, ch. 2, Washington, D.C.: U.S. Government Printing Office.

President's Research Committee on Social Trends. 1933. *Recent Social Trends, I.* New York: McGraw-Hill.

Rittel, H. and M. Webber. 1973. "Dilemmas in a General Theory of Planning." *Policy Sciences* 4: 155–69.

*Rossi, R.J. and K.J. Gilmartin. 1979. *Handbook of Social Indicators*. New York: Garland STPM Press.

This is the only textbook thus far available describing social indicators and systematically dealing with the problems and methods of design. It is easy to read and accessible to the nontechnician. It provides an excellent introduction to the field.

*Social Indicators Research. Dordrecht, Holland: Reidel.

This journal is where the majority of methodological work on social indicators now appears. It covers a full range of social indicator topics and includes useful book reviews.

Social Science Research Council. 1973 ff. *Social Indicators Newsletter*. Washington, D.C.

Special Interest Group on Social Indicators Research. 1977 ff. *Social Indicators*. R. Rossi and K. Gilmartin, ed. Palo Alto, Calif.: American Institutes for Research.

United Kingdom Central Statistical Office. 1970 ff. *Social Trends*. London: Her Majesty's Stationery Office.

U.S. Department of Commerce. 1977. *Social Indicators, 1976*. Washington, D.C.: U.S. Government Printing Office.

van Dusen, R.A., ed. 1974. *Social Indicators 1973: A Review Symposium*. Washington, D.C.: Social Science Research Council.

2 IMPACT ASSESSMENT

Kurt Finsterbusch

Social impact assessment (SIA) is a relatively new but increasingly important technique used by applied social scientists to assist public officials and other policy makers in formulating, selecting, and implementing programs and projects. For the purposes of this chapter, programs provide services and projects involve the construction of facilities.

WHAT IS SOCIAL IMPACT ASSESSMENT?

Purpose and Practitioners of SIA

The purpose of a SIA is to estimate the likely consequences of proposed programs and projects on individuals, groups, neighborhoods, communities, regions, institutions, and other social units. This knowledge will, one hopes, give decision makers a fuller understanding of the potential consequences of their actions. Together with assessments of environmental and other types of impacts, SIAs help determine whether or not a proposed activity should be undertaken and whether actions are necessary to prepare for its impact.

Associated with the process of SIA is a network of scholars, applied social scientists, and agency personnel. C.P. Wolf has been instrumental in linking SIA professionals through meetings and the newsletter *Social Impact Assessment*. SIA professionals are also active in the environmental and applied sections of the American Psychological Association and the American Sociological Association.

The SIA community is growing rapidly and gaining in stature. Its literature is proliferating but is still chaotic and difficult to review, since much of it is in government reports with limited distributions. As a sociological specialty, SIA is still in its pioneer period and is filled with the excitement of exploring new territory.

NEPA and SIA

To some degree, policy makers have always considered the social conse-quences of policies in their decisions. Until the National Environmental Policy Act (NEPA) of 1969, however, social impacts seldom received systematic study and due consideration. NEPA requires that environmental impact statements (EIS) must be prepared for all federal actions that significantly affect the envir-onment. As the concept of environment has been broadened to include social conditions, NEPA has become the major stimulus to the development of SIA as a social science specialty and a growing concern with the social impacts of agency decisions. NEPA also tends to open agency decision making more to the public by enabling people to learn how they will be affected by a proposed project. Furthermore, the EIS process gives citizens an opportunity to complain at hearings and in writing. These inputs from interested parties often lead to projects or program modifications.

The courts are partially responsible for making the EIS process effective and more available to the public. Liroff (1978a:5) has reviewed the history of NEPA in the courts and concludes that the courts have generally "... insisted on rigorous compliance ..." to the procedural requirements of NEPA and " ... gen-erally have had little patience with pro forma compliance...." At the same time, the courts have assiduously avoided judging the substantive merits of agency decisions, which limits the extent to which they can improve the EIS process. The courts have, however, opened up the EIS process. They treat NEPA as a full disclosure law whose purpose is to alert government agencies and the public to the consequences of the proposed action (Liroff, 1978a:7).

The latest chapter in the history of NEPA is the new regulations for NEPA that were promulgated by the Council on Environmental Quality (CEQ) in the *Federal Register* on November 19, 1978. These regulations seek to reduce paper-work, eliminate delays, and improve the decision process. They set limits to the number of pages and length of time for EISs and recommend that only real or competitive alternatives be evaluated and only on the important dimensions. Which issues are important and "deserving of study in the EIS" are determined by the agency "in consultation with affect parties." One purpose of this provision is to "reduce the possibility that matters of importance will be overlooked in the early stages of a NEPA review" (CEQ, 1978: 55982).

Another provision of the 1978 NEPA regulations requires

> agencies to produce a concise public record, indicating how the EIS was used in arriving at the decision. This record of decision must indicate which alternative (or alternatives) considered in the EIS is preferable on environmental grounds. Agencies may also discuss preferences among alternatives based on relevant factors including economic and technical considerations and agency statutory missions. (CEQ, 1978:55980)

This provision will not insure that due consideration be given to environmental and social effects, but it will make it more difficult to ignore them, especially since interested parties read EISs carefully with slings and arrows poised.

One additional regulation is the requirement for "accurate documents as the basis for sound decisions." This means drawing

> upon all the appropriate disciplines from the natural and social sciences. ... A list of people who help prepare documents, and their professional qualifications, shall be included in the EIS to encourage professional responsibility and ensure that an interdisciplinary approach was followed. (CEQ, 1978:55980)

The goal of these provisions is to increase the efficiency and effectiveness of the EIS process. Efficiency is to be enhanced by eliminating the study of non-essential issues, reducing time and page lengths, studying only promising alternatives, and focussing on critical issues. Effectiveness is to be enhanced by allowing inputs from affected parties earlier in the process, strengthening the link of the EIS to the agency decision, and revealing who is responsible for each part of the EIS.

HOW IS SIA IMPLEMENTED?

This discussion of the methodology of SIA is complicated by the fact that there are actually three different methodologies: 1) the methodology required by NEPA and CEQ, 2) the way SIA is actually done, and 3) the way SIA should be done. Each of these methodologies is described below.

NEPA and CEQ Requirements
Section 102 (2) (c) of NEPA reads:

> (A)ll agencies of the Federal Government shall...(c) include in every recommendation or report on proposals for legislation and other major Federal actions significantly altering the quality of the human environment, a detailed statement by the responsible official on—
> - (i)   the environmental impact of the proposed action,
> - (ii)   any adverse environmental effects which cannot be avoided should the proposal be implemented,
> - (iii)   alternatives to the proposed action,
> - (iv)   the relationship between local short-term uses of man's environment and the maintenance and enhancement of long-term productivity, and
> - (v)   any irreversible and irretrievable commitments of resources which would be involved in the proposed action should it be implemented.

The recent CEQ regulations elaborate NEPA's requirements by specifying that the EIS not only discuss direct and indirect effects and their significance for each alternative—including the alternative of no action—but also indicate their 1) "energy requirements and conservation potential," 2) "natural or depletable resource requirements," and 3) "urban quality, historic and cultural resources, and the design of the built environment" (CEQ, 1978:55996). These regulations also call for the inclusion of appropriate mitigation measures. In contrast to the NEPA statement, CEQ's requirements demand that some action alternatives be thoroughly assessed for comparison with the proposed action.

The NEPA and CEQ regulations give little concrete guidance on how to conduct an environmental impact assessment. The following six step methodology is implicitly suggested, although other methodologies are not prohibited:

1. Design the project or program.
2. Select a few promising alternatives and include the alternative of no action.
3. Select the critical impacts or issues to be studied using inputs from affected parties.
4. Estimate the critical direct and indirect impacts and their significance.
5. Design mitigation measures for the negative impacts.
6. Answer several special questions such as:
    (a) What are the adverse environmental effects that cannot be avoided should the proposal be implemented?
    (b) What is the relationship between local short-term uses of man's environment and the maintenance and enhancement of long-term productivity?
    (c) What are the energy requirements?
    (d) What are the natural resource requirements?
    (e) How does it affect the quality of the urban environment?

This methodology fails to specify: how the project, its alternatives, and its mitigation measures are designed; how impacts are estimated; how the special questions are to be answered; and how the assessment of impacts is to be used in the selection of one alternative for implementation. It specifies that a comparative framework be used but fails to specify how choices are to be made on the basis of the comparisons. It recommends the use of affected parties for selecting critical impacts for study but not for drafting alternatives. It further implies that the impact assessment is to be used in the design of mitigation measures, and that the impacts of these modifications should in turn be assessed.

Actual SIA Techniques

The methodology of the SIA as actually practiced in the production of EISs is often less sophisticated than the minimal methodology described above. Generally, few impacts are assessed, the study is not designed to help select the best alternative, and little attention (if any) is devoted to developing mitigation measures. A study of 1975 and 1976 highway EISs that considered at least two construction alternatives revealed that few impacts of any kind were even mentioned in the average EIS and very few were studied in any depth (Finsterbusch, 1977). For example, only 41 percent of these EISs mentioned impacts on neighborhoods.

The numerous ways of conducting an SIA can be grouped into six general approaches, with considerable variety within each approach.

Armchair Analysis. Much legislation is drafted and many agency policies, programs, and projects are designed on the basis of someone's personal and subjective judgment. A rationale is then developed to support that decision. This rationale is a kind of armchair SIA, which points out the vices of the alternatives and the virtues of the selected policy. The analysis tends to be unsystematic, based on personal judgments, and obviously biased. It is this kind of uninformed decision making that the professional SIA movement is trying to replace.

Historical Narrative. Some policy studies use a historical narrative approach that describes the evolution of the original project design and then identifies how inputs from interested parties and considerations of project consequences have brought about modifications in its design. The resulting story of the decision process demonstrates how open, reasonable, and rational the decision makers have been. Though the historical narrative is inadequate as a SIA, it does recognize that decision making is a process that intertwines design and analysis in a series of assessment cycles.

Impact List. Most EISs use the impact list approach. Regulations often require that certain impacts be studied, and many EISs dutifully report on only those impacts. In such cases, the EIS is based on the minimum amount of research acceptable to the reviewing agencies. For example, in many EISs the total discussion of the proposed project's impact on wildlife was that "the project will have no significant affect on wildlife." No evidence was advanced to support this claim. EISs of this kind can hardly contribute to the design of alternatives or the choice between them.

Rational Linear Study. The rational linear approach is currently being used in most of the better EISs. This methodology begins with goals that are carefully thought out for the program or project. The program or project and its alternatives are then designed to achieve those goals. Next, criteria for goal attainment are specified according to which the alternatives are to be evaluated. These criteria encompass many project impacts. Measurements or estimates are made for each alternative on each criterion and displayed for comparative review by decision makers and the public. This approach allows for an informed decision. It is rational because it evaluates projects in terms of the goals for which they are designed. It is linear because it marches through a set of logical steps from goals to project design to information collection and analysis. Its shortcoming is its failure to see goals, design, evaluation, and decision making as an interactive cyclical process. Goals and criteria cannot be fixed at the beginning of the study because they change as the study progresses, influenced by both the information collected and by the reactions of affected parties.

Cost-Benefit Analysis. When the rational linear approach tries to quantify all of its measures and translates them into monetary values it becomes a cost-benefit analysis. The transformation of social impact measures into monetary values is usually impossible to do in a way that is comprehensible to most people. What is the monetary value of the strain placed on household members when they are forced to move to a new neighborhood because a highway project has bulldozed their former home? There is evidence that such moves contribute to the death of elderly people. How can a price be put on such impacts? These difficulties have kept cost-benefit analysis out of most SIAs, even though some economists have strongly advocated this practice.

Filtering Cycles. This approach is currently being recommended by many SIA practitioners. It uses several study cycles. In the first cycle the need for a project or program is reexamined and general goals and specific objectives are specified. The second cycle explores and assesses a wide range of alternatives on important but easily ascertained criteria. Many alternatives can be quickly eliminated as too expensive, too risky, too interfering, too ugly, etc. The third cycle seriously studies the more likely candidates and tries to eliminate all but a few finalists. These are modified to eliminate their worst features and to enhance their best. The final cycle estimates the impacts of the finalists in depth and provides an information base for choosing between them. Possibly, one alternative will stand out as superior to the others on most of the important dimensions. It is more likely, however, that no alternative is clearly best, so that a choice must be made that somewhat arbitrarily weighs some criteria more heavily than others.

Ideal SIA Steps

The process of conducting a SIA can be divided into three broad steps: impact estimation, response determination, and policy improvement. The first step is to identify and estimate the probable impacts of a policy, program, or project on individuals, groups, organizations, communities, social institutions, and other social units. The second step is to determine the likely responses of impacted parties to the proposed activity. These responses may include both actions and attitudes. This step may not be required by CEQ regulations, but it is necessary for informed decision making. These responses must be determined in order to estimate some of the indirect impacts of the action and to warn decision makers of some of its political consequences. The third step is to revise the proposed activity to minimize negative impacts and maximize positive ones. These steps are described in the following paragraphs (for a further treatment, see Finsterbusch and Motz, 1980).

Impact Estimation. SIA cannot be reduced to a simple formula. It will always involve judgments that cannot be routinized. Over time, however, research traditions evolve for specific types of SIAs. They develop rapidly for relatively standard projects such as highways and slowly for relatively unique projects such as an offshore deepwater port. These research traditions reduce the number of ad hoc research design judgments and give continuity to successive studies. At the present time, however, most types of SIAs lack research traditions worthy of emulation, and hence require continual initiative, innovation, and intelligence. The following comments are therefore not prescriptions, but rather general guidance for SIA researchers who must depend heavily on their own judgment.

Social impact estimation involves a cyclical process, as described above. Normally, a SIA begins with a description of the program or project and information on the environmental and economic impacts of the project that are supplied by other members of the interdisciplinary research team. (When social programs are assessed the interdisciplinary information flow would probably go in the opposite direction.) Then the social impact assessor develops a relatively exhaustive list of potential social impacts. This list should include impacts that are direct and indirect, likely and unlikely, short-term and long-term, significant and insignificant. It should be as inclusive as possible, because its major purpose is to see that no significant potential impact is overlooked. Indirect impacts are identified by considering each major impact and developing an impact list for it.

To generate this inclusive impact list, several heads are better than one and different perspectives, disciplines, and interests are better than homogeneous ones. All interested parties and appropriate experts should be invited to contribute to the list. Differences among contributors protect against oversights.

The next task is to select the impacts that should be studied from the inclusive list. Again, sensible judgment rather than rigid rules should be used, although the following criteria can serve as guides: 1) probability of impact, 2) intensity of impact, or the value of both benefits and costs, 3) extent of impact, or the number of people impacted, 4) selection by affected parties and 5) probability of causing important higher-order impacts.

The assessor must then estimate—for each alternative—the extent, intensity, and probability of its impacts. Procedures for making these estimates cannot be prescribed in detail, since numerous factors such as budget, time, required accuracy levels, degree of public cooperation will affect one's choice of methods. In all cases, however, three types of information are pooled when estimating social impacts: the results of current research on the situation, lessons from past case studies, and judgments of experts. The full range of research procedures in the social sciences—from preset questionnaires and unstructured interviews to government statistics and direct observations—can be used in SIAs to describe the present situation and how individuals and organizations expect to be impacted. Past cases of the same or similar events, programs, or projects can be reviewed for guidance on the consequences of the proposed event, program, or project. Experts can also be consulted for their judgments about probable social impacts. This last process is usually rather unstructured, but sometimes it is highly structured, involving criticism from other experts and successive revisions. The final assessment of possible impacts must be a judicious combination of these three types of data.

Response Determination. The line between impact estimation and response determination is vague. Responses include both attitudes and actions. Impacts on individuals are tied in with their attitudes, and the actions that affected parties take in response to a public action may cause further impacts. Nevertheless, we can consider response determination as the second major step in a SIA.

The SIA researcher provides policy makers with the current attitudes of the public toward the project or program and estimates of how those attitudes will change over time. Current attitudes are measured through hearings and private communications and in a more systematic and representative fashion through surveys. Expected future attitudes are estimated from knowledge of public opinion in similar previous cases. For example, a common finding from past cases is that people learn to live with projects that change their residential environments far better than they expected in advance. In general, negative attitudes tend to attenuate over time.

Even more difficult than predicting attitudes is the task of predicting future actions of individuals and organizations if the proposed innovation is implemented. Of particular interest to decision makers is the possibility that affected parties will attempt to block or alter the proposed program or project. The existence of such a desire can be ascertained by a survey, but the will to act on that desire is more difficult to discern. The key factor here may be a leader who can mobilize people to act. Another possible action by affected parties is to adapt to the new conditions. Decision makers, however, need to know *how* people will adapt. Different adaptations lead to different indirect consequences, and often a certain kind of adaptive response is essential to the success of the program or project. For example, increasing the tax on gasoline as a strategy for reducing gas consumption may have little effect on drivers or it may stimulate a move to smaller cars, increase car pooling, crowd public transportation, and/or reduce traveling.

Techniques for predicting responses of affected parties are still experimental and largely untested. For example, one technique that has been developed for this purpose is a cumulative interactive interviewing procedure. Spokespersons for the various affected parties are interviewed in the order that they are likely to respond to the proposed activity. In this way the spokespersons indicate how their group will respond not only to the innovation, but also to the actions of other affected parties. Spokespersons are also asked to comment on the responses from other parties. When opposing parties agree about the actions that each party will likely take, the assessment probably contains little bias. This procedure is interactive because reactions, suspicions, and comments of other parties are fed back to spokespersons as questions when they are reinterviewed.

Improving Proposed Activities. The last step in the SIA process is to improve proposed policies, programs, or projects by modifying or supplementing them. The study of impacts and responses often identifies problems in the design of the proposal and elicits suggestions for altering it. In addition, the SIA researcher should have detailed knowledge of its potential negative social impacts and thus will be in a position to design impact mitigation measures that will not significantly interfere with program goals. These modifications, however, should be subjected to another regular assessment cycle, since they might have unintended negative consequences that could cancel out their benefits.

Special SIA Techniques

This is not the place for a detailed description of special SIA techniques (see Finsterbusch and Wolf, 1981, for descriptions of numerous techniques). Instead, let us briefly examine a few special techniques that represent efforts to address particularly vexing research problems. The major problem in SIA is how to predict future impacts of current activities. Usually these future impacts are predicted on the basis of present trends, common sense assumptions, and guidance from the impacts of previous cases. Sometimes a special technique called scenario analysis is employed to predict future impacts in a more organized manner. Several scenarios are constructed on the basis of either 1) carefully worked out relationships between variables and clearly stated assumptions, or 2) speculation and intuition. *The Limits to Growth* (Meadows, et al., 1972) scenarios used mathematical relationships, many recorded assumptions, and computer generated projections. Scenarios based largely on natural or economic factors are also commonly generated mathematically. Such scenarios are often arranged into high, medium, and low projections based on optimistic, normal, and pessimistic assumptions concerning the predicted range of consequences for each causal relationship. These projections usually appear quite reliable, because they are based on countless reasonable numbers. In fact, however, they normally contain countless guesses, some of which have low probabilities of occurrence.

Most scenarios constructed for SIA are based largely on guesswork, however, and contain few numbers except for population projections. These scenarios are qualitative and highly intuitive. Several plausible storylike scenarios are often created to give decision makers an idea of the range of possible outcomes. Most likely the scenarios will be arranged along an optimism/pessimism continuum, but they may contain very different story lines and involve very different assumptions.

Another problem in SIA that requires special techniques is the identification of subtle second- and third-order impacts (i.e., impacts of impacts, and impacts of those impacts). This process relies heavily on the use of informed judgment, although knowledge of past cases can inform these judgments. The primary procedures here are cross impact matrices and the delphi technique. Both are designed to improve subjective judgments. A cross impact matrix places predicted impacts along both the rows and the columns of a matrix, with one side representing causes and the other representing effects. The SIA analyst indicates in each of the cells of the matrix whether these two impacts are likely to effect each other and how this will occur. Sometimes a matrix is also used to cross impacts with objectives or evaluation criteria, so that the research can indicate how various impacts affect these factors. In general, the cross impact matrix helps to organize one's thoughts, but it does not really generate new knowledge.

The delphi technique is used to both identify potential impacts and to estimate the extent of those impacts. It is a purely subjective technique, designed to improve the reliability of subjective estimates of impacts made by experts. It involves several rounds of interviews with those experts. In the first round, the experts privately express their judgments concerning potential impacts. Means and standard deviations are then computed for the entire group of experts and fed back to them before their second round of judgments. Persons whose judgments are quite divergent from the mean can then reconsider their extreme views. The experts may also be given the opportunity to react to detailed criticisms of their views in the second round of interviews. Unless a third round is necessary to achieve closure, the group mean judgment and the degree of consensus are reported, along with deviant positions. This report gives decision makers a "best" estimate by a group of experts, as well as an indication of the amount of agreement or disagreement among them.

Another problem area in SIA is the need to obtain information from people in a relatively inexpensive manner. Telephone surveys and mailed questionnaires are cost-cutting techniques that can be used when the biases introduced by unlisted telephones and high nonresponse rates are not critical. An alternative technique that can be used to obtain data inexpensively is the mini survey (see Finsterbusch, 1976a and Finsterbusch, 1976b for an extended discussion of this technique). This is simply a survey of a randomly-selected, small sample of respondents—often about 40. It does not produce precise estimates of the characteristics of the population in question, but it can provide very useful information. The crude reading of public attitudes toward a potential activity that a mini survey can provide is far better than no knowledge. Moreover, a sample of size 40 or 50 has far greater statistical reliability (i.e., a smaller potential error range) than many people realize, so that increasing the sample size to 400 or 500 is often not cost effective in terms of measured accuracy.

HOW HAS SIA BEEN USED?

The main application of SIA is in environmental impact statements, (EISs), as mandated by the National Environmental Policy Act. Another notable use of SIA is in technology assessment (TA), although few contain detailed assessments of many social impacts. Other uses of SIAs are wide ranging. They are required for projects conducted by the Agency for International Development and for major domestic urban projects with federal support. Some states and counties are also conducting SIAs. The use of SIAs is slowly expanding as public decision makers increasingly accept this procedure as a legitimate part of public policy formation.

SIA in Environment Impact Studies

The National Environmental Policy Act requires EISs for all federal actions that significantly affect the environment. Two types of actions are subjected to the EIS process—single projects and continuing programs. The vast majority of EISs are written for single projects such as a highway, a dam, a power plant, an airport, or a housing project. EISs are also written for ongoing agency programs in such areas as flood protection, water quality standards, community development, timber management, coal leasing, and coastal zone management.

EISs vary tremendously in quality. Some consider few alternatives, identify few impacts, report little evidence for their statements, and provide almost no assessment of social impacts. The majority are rather sketchy but give enough information on the available alternatives to provide some guidance in choosing among them. A few are massive research efforts that produce a great deal of information about the estimated impacts of the proposed project and its alternatives. Sometimes too much information is produced. The EIS on the proposed Kaiparowits power plant and transmission line system in southern Utah is over 2,500 pages in length, and in the judgment of Bardach and Pugliaresi (1977: 25): "Most of this material is not worth reading," because it is not germane to the Department of Interior's decision on the project.

An illustration of a major EIS with an extensive SIA component is the one proposed in 1974 for the West Side Highway Project in New York City (U.S. Department of Transportation, 1974). The study considered five alternatives. Under the Maintenance alternative, the existing West Side Highway would be repaired (an elevated portion collapsed in 1973), reopened, and serviced with periodic maintenance. Under the Reconstruction alternative, major structural deficiencies would be corrected through partial reconstruction and general rehabilitation. The Arterial proposal was to replace the existing West Side Highway with an at-grade arterial roadway with a transitway underneath it. The Inboard alternative would remove the existing West Side Highway and replace it with a six-lane interstate highway, a new transitway, and a rebuilt West Street. The Outboard alternative would also remove the present West Side Highway and provide instead a six-lane interstate highway, a new transitway, and a rebuilt West Street, but would locate the new facilities just offshore and remove existing waterfront facilities. The report's summary of the major socioeconomic impacts of these alternatives reads as follows:

> The Maintenance and Reconstruction alternatives would stimulate no highway related redevelopment, and would initiate few positive effects on adjacent communities. By reinforcing existing land uses on the West Side and precluding positive land-use changes far into the future, these

alternatives would likely produce counter-productive effects for both adjacent communities and the City alike.

The Arterial alternative offers rapid implementation of the new roadway, followed by a more lengthy period for rail transit construction. It would enhance the marketability of the Battery Park City project and would stimulate early speculation and redevelopment along the West Village waterfront. Pressures for substantial change both off-shore and upland would be intensified by the rail transit development, especially at station locations and in the meat market area. Development initiatives from the private sector would mandate significant public involvement within the next ten years, in order to moderate the timing and intensity of change affecting predominantly privately owned areas.

The Inboard proposal anticipates the development of a project over a ten-year period. Preservation of existing land uses and facilities would be the primary guideline, with redevelopment focused on the narrow strip of land adjacent to the existing facility. Rapid speculative change would be less intensive than in the Arterial alternative, allowing for both City and community involvement in the development process. Development of new land resources would be limited to recreation space utilizing a covered section of the new facility along the West Village.

The Outboard alternative would have the effect of spreading future changes over a longer period of time, beyond the ten year construction period, and focusing redevelopment energies on newly created off-shore land rather than adjacent upland areas. Both public and private commitments to such an extensive redevelopment proposal would be large, but the longer lead time provided would allow for the formulation of community oriented control mechanisms and an orderly development program. The potential for new housing in off-shore areas could be used to moderate demand in adjacent communities and relieve pressures for residential expansion into those industrial areas that the City is attempting to stabilize. Extensive open space is another resource which could be developed for the benefit of local communities. Although long-term in nature, the Outboard alternative would create conditions that stimulate extensive, deliberate changes as distinct from the less controlled and largely deteriorating changes of the Maintenance and Reconstruction alternatives, the speculative conditions of the Arterial alternative, and the limited changes of the Inboard alternative. (U.S. Department of Transportation, 1974:172)

In addition to the above comparisons the study assessed the direct impacts of the highway alternatives in each of the following areas: construction employment, highway user cost savings, parks and waterfront access, visual effects, changes in travel and traffic patterns, parking, public transit, impacts on energy consumption, air quality impacts, noise levels, water quality impacts, impacts on public facilities, impacts on public utilities, displacement of housing and commerical properties, relocation of households, impacts during construction, and costs. However, the EIS did not examine the possible impacts of any of the alternatives on the probable lines of development of the highway corridor.

Let us also briefly review four other EISs with prominent SIAs to indicate how they affected the final policy decisions. The first of these shows how an EIS can affect the choice between action and no action. It studied the effect of the proposed extension to Kennedy Airport in New York on Jamaica Bay and surrounding neighborhoods. The Port of New York Authority requested the National Academy of Sciences to conduct the assessment. An interdisciplinary research team of 25 experts recommended against the airport extension because air traffic noises already had very detrimental effects on area residents, so that additional air traffic would be highly undesirable. Furthermore, it concluded that "any runway construction will damage the natural environment of the Bay and reduce its potential use for conservation, recreation and housing" (Jamaica Bay Environmental Study Group, 1971:1). Partly as a result of this study and partly as a result of public outcry against the project, the Port Authority decided against the airport extension.

An example of the use of SIA in choosing between competing alternatives is provided by the Chicago Crosstown Expressway Study (Pikarsky, 1967). This study used the filtering approach involving several assessment cycles. In the first cycle the need for the highway was established, largely on the basis of travel studies. The second cycle used a highway spacing technique to determine the most promising corridors for the highway. The third, fourth, and fifth assessment cycles selected, through successive eliminations, the Belt Railroad alignment alternative. In each cycle equal weight was given to three parallel studies: social impacts, engineering aspects, and land use. The Belt Railroad alignment was chosen over the Cicero Avenue alignment because it had a better SIA score, even though it had a lower score on engineering aspects and a nearly equal score on land use.

The move of the Navy Oceanographic Center from Suitland, Maryland to Bay St. Louis, Mississippi illustrates how a policy decision can shape the SIA rather than the SIA affecting the decision. The move was made despite the severe negative social impacts it would cause. The Navy Department tried to minimize the negative social impacts in the EIS and to demonstrate significant economic savings to justify the move. Both the economic and social analyses were highly questionable, however. For example, the EIS argued that black employees who relocated to Bay St. Louis would not suffer discrimination in housing. The evidence was letters from top officials in major real estate agencies and housing developments, who reported that their firms did not have discriminatory practices. In reality, black employees who visited Bay St. Louis to appraise the situation for themselves claimed they found considerable discrimination.

The EIS for the proposal to extend I-66 from the Beltway into Washington D.C. involved a highly politicized decision. Neighborhood groups in the proposed highway corridor fought long and hard against the highway on the grounds that it would adversely affect their neighborhoods. Secretary Coleman of the Department of Transportation finally rejected the I-66 extension. Shortly thereafter, the Council on Environmental Quality (1976) assessed six years of experience with the EIS process and cited the I-66 study as an example of an EIS that identified serious negative impacts of a project and led to its cancellation. Later the decision was reversed and construction on I-66 was quickly begun, providing a forceful reminder that decisions on such projects are a part of politics.

SIA in Technology Assessments

Most technology assessments thoroughly discuss the technology involved and its expected economic and environmental impacts but give relatively little attention to social impacts. For example, the TA conducted by the Office of Technology Assessment on offshore ports, offshore drilling for oil and gas, and floating nuclear power plants, discusses numerous political aspects but no social impacts. In some cases—such as blast furnace innovations—the social impacts do not warrant extensive analysis. In other cases, however, the social impacts are not analyzed simply because the task is too difficult.

The wide range of TAs is illustrated by the following selected list of studies funded by the Office of Exploratory Research and Problem Assessment Research Applications in the National Science Foundation: remote sensing of the environment, earthquake prediction, biological substitutes for chemical pesticides, controlled environment agriculture technology, life-extending technologies, human rehabilitation techniques, orographic snowpack augmentation in the Colorado River Basin, cashless-checkless society, integrated hog farming, alternative work schedules, hail suppression, and large air transport.

An important component of TAs is their policy recommendations. TAs are policy studies, commissioned to recommend courses of action. Good recommendations, however, cannot be formulated without a proper assessment of their full impacts, and they will not be heeded unless those assessments are convincing. Melzer's study of the "Social Uses of India's Television Satellite," reported by Coates, illustrates that TAs sometimes produce strong recommendations against the use of technology under existing circumstances. Melzer made the following points:

> The TV-satellite provides an unduly high capacity for mobilizing its audiences in an undifferentiated manner. It combines this characteristic with a very poor performance in the distribution of information which to a minimal degree is adapted to the developmental needs of the audience.

Detailed information for adults can only be distributed under the high risk of conflicts amongst states on questions of informational policy.

In the sector of teacher training and school programs, INSAT reaches sufficient or reasonable results only in arrangements which must be ruled out for political reasons at the present time. (Coates, 1975:55–56)

He concluded that "INSAT's technical structure is too poor and too inflexible to meet the exigencies of development in India." He therefore recommended either further development of INSAT's technical structure or replacing it with a decentralized communication system.

Sometimes strong recommendations on important issues cannot be made because the SIA is inconclusive. The Nuclear Regulatory Commission (1975) did a TA on nuclear power energy centers locating from ten to 40 power plants at one site. An important consideration was whether to locate nuclear energy centers near "old" towns or to create new towns along with the centers. Most of the experts consulted in the study supported expanding or revising "old" towns rather than starting new towns. Some of their reasons for this were that new towns would probably be underfinanced, would be too homogeneous to provide quality communities, would require too much federal involvement, and would take too long to develop a stable social structure. On the other hand, the study also noted that new towns compare favorably with control communities in Burley and Weiss' study (1976). The TA could not recommend the new town option, however, because all but one of the communities studied by Burley and Weiss were located near metropolitan areas and may not have been relevant for predicting impacts of energy centers in rural settings.

Other SIAs

The potential applications of SIA are nearly infinite. Appropriate subjects for SIAs include not only public projects or programs, but also many anticipated events or developments. Some of these other applications of SIA are illustrated in the following paragraphs.

In addition to EISs and TAs the federal government has also sponsored many other policy studies that have included SIAs. One example is the study of the "Effects of Socioeconomic Impacts on Inter-Regional Allocations of Potential Increase in Coal Production" by Gilmore and Moore (1977). Their major conclusions were that labor-management conflicts in central Appalachia will cause serious production shortfalls, and that boom town problems must be alleviated in central Appalachia and the West to enhance production.

State and local governments and private organizations have also commissioned SIAs and will likely do this more frequently in the future. For example, the Sacramento County Community Development and Environmental Protection Agency is committed to the policy that "... decisions concerning growth management cannot reasonably and equitably be addressed without a full information document which encompasses a credible and comprehensive consideration of three basic elements: environmental, economic, and social" (Wolf, 1978:15). This agency now produces such assessment documents.

Another example of an SIA being directed at the impacts of social change and economic development is the study of "current and expected changes in the social environment" of Mornington Peninsula, Australia. An important part of the study was a survey of 387 peninsula residents. In general, they preferred a quiet life style and opposed rapid growth and development, although controlled growth was viewed favorably.

Sometimes a federal, state, or local government agency conducts or funds an SIA at the request of private interests. For example, the United Farmworkers of America (UFW) have demanded impact assessments on research pertaining to labor-displacing farm machinery. When the University of California refused to assess the labor impacts of its mechanization research, the UFW had a bill introduced into the California State Assembly requiring social and employment impact statements before public funds could be used for such research. The bill was withdrawn only when the governor promised to appoint a special committee to study the issue.

An impact assessment with nongovernmental sponsorship is the Rand study of the "Urban Impacts of Federal Policies," funded by the Charles F. Kettering Foundation. The study analyzed many diverse federal policies and drew three major conclusions:

> First, little is known about both the probable and the actual consequences of federal policies....
>
> The second conclusion of the study is that different regions and different metropolitan areas respond quite differently to market trends....
>
> The third conclusion ... is that although they are not the primary cause, federal policies have tended to support urban decentralization. (*Rand Research Review*, 1978:7–8)

The first conclusion acknowledges that federal policies have unexpected effects. For example, the interstate regulation of natural gas has the unintended effect of restricting supplies in the Northeast and relocating gas-consuming industries to gas-producing states. The significance of the second conclusion is that an urban problem can originate in different sources and require different solutions in various contexts. The decentralization effects of federal policies identified in the third conclusion refer to suburbanization and regional shifts. The major policies contributing to these changes include the interstate highway program, the regulation of the transportation industry, federal mortgage policies, income tax allowances for home ownership, and industry investment tax credits. These policies have made it more economical for many industries and people to move to the perimeters of cities.

WHAT HAS SIA ACCOMPLISHED?

It is difficult to assess the accomplishment of SIAs. They have only recently been used for public actions, and their effects have not been systematically studied. There have been many discussions of the deficiencies of the EIS process and the impacts of NEPA, but little analysis dealing specifically with SIAs. Nevertheless, several observations can be made with some assurance.

Both the Jamaica Bay/Kennedy Airport and the Chicago Crosstown Expressway studies demonstrate that SIAs in EISs can affect public decisions. Most commentators, however, are skeptical about the amount of influence that SIAs actually exert. The SIAs in many EISs are so weak or biased that they should not influence the decision. In other cases, the SIA may be reasonably well-done but is given short shift in the decision. Often in such cases, cost-benefit analysis is the principal evaluation criterion for the engineers and economists who currently occupy many positions of authority in government agencies. SIA faces an uphill climb to respectability and influence. That climb will be arduous, partly because of prejudice and partly because of the primitiveness of SIA methodology. The role of subjective judgment in both SIA information generation and analysis is often excessive, and much of the quantitative data is extraneous padding. Except for population projections, many SIAs tend to have low credibility or little relevancy. Nevertheless, SIAs are gaining influence because they are improving and because social impacts are being given greater weight in public decisions.

New Dimensions in Public Decisions

In the past decade, public officials have become much more sophisticated in evaluating the actions taken by industry or government, and have become more aware of the full range of impacts of projects or programs. In particular, they are becoming more cognizant of those impacts called externalities, which are not counted as either income or expenditures of the project. If a new highway lowers the value of adjacent properties and increases the value of other properties, these losses and gains are not borne by the state that builds the highway and are not included in the state's costing of the project (though a sophisticated cost-benefit analysis would estimate the tax losses and gains to the state). Social impacts such as property value losses and gains are experienced by individual property owners and hence are externalities to the direct costs and benefits of the project. The main thrust behind the growing consideration of externalities in public decisions has been an increasing awareness of the need to take environmental consequences into account, but SIA is also benefiting from this development.

Social impacts have also increased in importance in public decisions for three other reasons. First, the public has become much more active during the past 15 years in influencing, challenging, and blocking decisions, often on the basis of the social impacts of those decisions. Bureaucrats who prefer to be left alone to make their decisions in peace have found that they will have little peace unless they take social impacts into account and design their projects to minimize negative social impacts. The second factor increasing the role of social impacts in public decisions is the SIA movement. SIA is an ideological cause for some and a professional self interest for many others. In addition, SIA is a banner behind which many officials, affected parties, and public commentators rally. Finally, another factor affecting the role of SIA in public decisions is the legal system. NEPA and CEQ regulations are now being interpreted by the courts to require SIAs in EISs.

Changes in Agency/Public Relations

An unanticipated effect of SIAs has been to stimulate citizen involvement in public decision making. SIAs provide vehicles for injecting the attitudes and interests of individuals and groups into the decision-making process. The surveys and interviews conducted for SIAs become communications by citizens to decision makers. SIAs also focus the attention of officials on impacts that deeply concern the public. As a general rule, the more aware public officials are of negative social impacts the more interested they are in ameliorating them. Furthermore, the identification of negative social impacts makes affected parties more aware of their plight and better enables them to protect their interests. In this manner, SIAs have permanently changed the relationship between government agencies and the public.

Increasing the Policy Research Effort

Since there is no indication that SIAs have led to a commensurate reduction in other types of research on policies, projects, and programs, we can conclude that SIAs have increased the total research effort. This consequence has caused a minor backlash that is usually directed implicitly rather than explicitly at SIAs. The recent CEQ requirements to reduce paperwork by limiting the length of EISs and to avoid "accumulating masses of background data" partly reflects this backlash. These regulations can be interpreted, however, as objecting to incompetent SIAs (dealing with peripheral matters) but as supporting competent SIAs.

A persuasive attack on the excessive costs of EISs has been made by Bardach and Pugliaresi (1977). They cite a court decision that required the Bureau of Land Management to prepare 212 EISs at an estimated cost of $100 million for investments like fencing and water holes on 150 million acres of public rangeland. The EIS cost will be a large fraction of the total costs of the investments. They also give examples of excessively lengthy reports, arguing that "much of an EIS consists of trivia or pure formalities" (Bardach and Pugliaresi, 1977:26). Their critique includes trivial SIAs, but it should be pointed out that most of their examples are of trivial environmental impacts such as birds colliding with offshore, oil drilling platforms at night. They complain that both trivia and length blur the proper focus on EISs and therefore their effectiveness.

Evaluations of NEPA

The results of NEPA have been disappointing to those who expected it to promote basic reform in agency decision making. Other commentators, with more realistic expectations, have been pleased with its results. In this section we review the ongoing debate over the achievements of NEPA.

There is considerable agreement that the scientific quality of the environmental and social impact assessments of most EISs is low. The knowledge base for EIS work is underdeveloped, the research is of low caliber, and the review process is not very demanding. Friesema and Culhane (1976) have carefully evaluated the quality of several hundred SIAs in EISs and judge them to be generally very inadequate. They fault most SIAs as too narrow, unspecific, methodologically deficient, and lacking in analysis. "The primary deficiency of social impact assessment in EIS is that the statements usually consider only one social consequence—the economic impact of the project" (Friesema and Culhane, 1976:343). EISs are careful to describe the economic benefits of a project and often use these benefits to justify its implementation. Changes in social variables are "rarely considered," and when noted:

> It is common for EIS's not to assert the directionality of the effects, much less the magnitude. Possible social impacts, if noted at all, are merely listed. Nor are the implications of change in some social variable likely to be discussed. (Friesema and Culhane, 1976:343)

Another failure of omission concerns mitigation. "The authors are aware of no EIS which proposes a mitigation strategy for a social impact...." They also claim that EIS methodologies "are often crude or blatantly inappropriate" and provide many illustrations of that claim. Finally, they point out that much of the social impact data presented in EISs are not analyzed and that the implications of social impacts for specific groups are not explored. In sum, Friesema and Culhane find that the majority of EISs do not contain what might be considered even a minimal SIA.

The consensus among commentators is that most EISs are unsatisfactory. But are they efficacious? Do they affect decisions, and, if so, do they beneficially affect decisions? Opinions are divided on this question. CEQ (1977) evaluated six years of the EIS process and reported many cases in which the process did have significant effects on agency decisions in terms of either introducing project design changes or stopping projects altogether. CEQ builds a positive case for the EIS process, but it should be noted that their appropriations from Congress depend on such evidence. Friesema and Culhane (1976) provide a less biased case for the positive effects of the EIS process. They criticize the quality of EISs but praise their effects. They do not assume that decisions are improved because the EIS process is more rational than traditional decision making. Most "bad" decisions are not due to bad information. Rather, EISs change the politics of decision making in two ways. They give environmentalists and negatively affected parties formal entry into the decision-making process (normally by responding to draft EISs), and they provide a basis for subsequent court action. Since such groups have not been well represented in public decisions in the past, the EIS process has redressed that imbalance. The effects of this influence have been modifications in project designs and killed projects. "The authors estimate that agency decisions have been altered to some degree in approximately half the decisions in which they have participated" (Friesema and Culhane, 1976). Their case for the positive effects of the EIS process rests mainly on killed projects, however. They assume that most project cancellations are net benefits to society, although it must be remembered that many groups lose benefits when projects are stopped.

Andrews (1976) also judges the EIS process to have positive effects for three reasons. He argues that the process forces decision makers to consider new issues, that it makes agency decisions open for inputs by other agencies, and that it invites public comments and gives affected parties a voice in the process. Andrews admits that processual improvements improve public actions only as long as environmentalists and affected parties are politically active. On the other side of the issue, Schnaiberg and Meidinger (1978) are critical of the effects of the EIS process because they believe it inherently favors development and economic interests over environmental and social interests. The EIS is inevitably biased because adverse ecological consequences cannot be empirically demonstrated and must be understated, while economic and user benefits are adequately reported. Bardach and Pugliaresi (1977) argue, however, that uncertainty in assessing environmental impacts leads to the opposite result, since adverse environmental effects are exaggerated.

The most devastating attack on the effects of the EIS process is by Fairfax who argues that:

> NEPA has been a disaster for the environmental movement and for the quest for environmental quality.... Litigation under NEPA and preoccupation with the NEPA process truncated pre-existing and potentially significant developments in the definition of agency responsibility for environmental protection and in citizen involvement in agency deliberative processes. (Fairfax, 1978a)

Her arguments about the legal standing of challenges to development projects before the passage of NEPA and the ineffectiveness of the EIS process in providing tools for affected parties to influence the public decisions have been challenged by Liroff (1978b) and Culhane (1978). But Fairfax (1978b) has tried to answer her critics, and the debate goes on.

To summarize, the quality of EISs is generally low, and the effectiveness of this process in improving public decisions is in doubt in most cases. In other words, it is not clear that the EIS process has produced many benefits. A final question is whether it costs too much. Bardach and Pugliaresi (1977) argue, using examples, that EISs often waste considerable money. CEQ takes an opposite stance. Though 20 federal agencies spent $150 million in 1975 alone on EISs, a study of 29 major EISs found that preparing a typical EIS cost only about .1 percent of the total project costs. CEQ also presents evidence that challenges the view that the EIS process has been legally costly. Though nearly 7,000 draft EISs were filed in the period of its review, only 60 led to temporary injunctions and only four produced permanent injunctions. Perhaps the verdict of the future on the EIS process will be that it has been modestly beneficial because the modest benefits it produces for society are at even more modest costs.

WHERE IS SIA GOING?

SIA has a bright but troublesome future. Bell (1973) writes about the United States becoming a postindustrial society in which the knowledge industry expands considerably and assumes a more central role in society. In other words, more knowledge will be used in making decisions in both private enterprise and government. We expect the growth and development of SIA to be a part of this process. The extent to which SIA becomes institutionalized as an important component of policy decisions depends mainly on three developments: the political battles over SIA, the expansion of the knowledge base for SIA, and the technical improvement of SIA.

The Politics of SIA

SIA is a battleground for groups with conflicting interests over program or project impacts. It is also a battleground for researchers and bureaucrats whose work opportunities are affected by the importance given to SIA. Environmentals, homeowners, and many other groups may suffer negative social impacts from potential programs and projects. They have an interest in the study of social impacts and the increased consideration of social impacts in decision making. Businesses, facility users, and many other groups may have opposing interests and hence view SIA as impeding useful projects. The decision maker is caught in the middle. Since the traditional ties of decision makers have generally been with businesses and facility users, they tend to share a bias against SIA. However, the definition of their roles as public servants means that they must be concerned about the interests of opposing groups and at least pay lip service to the importance of SIAs. Furthermore, the orientations of the many decision makers are shifting away from business to a more academic, environmentalist, or social service concern. That shift is painfully slow, however, and SIA is presently more tolerated than appreciated.

The battles over SIA are often small ones. They include many hiring or promotion decisions, such as whether a sociologist or an engineer is hired for a position, or whether an environmentalist or an official with years in the lumber business is promoted to the position of project director. They also include such issues as the portion of an agency's research budget that will be spent on SIAs. These decisions seem to go against SIA much of the time, but, nevertheless, the SIA community is growing rapidly.

The Expansion of the Knowledge Base

If SIA is to have a greater role in the future it should be earned. The knowledge base for SIAs is currently embarrassingly small. For example, relocation of residents is a major social impact of many construction projects, but there is no first-rate scientific study of the effects of forced relocation. Unemployment is a major social consequence of government actions, but basic research on the social and psychological effects of unemployment is embryonic. There has been some research on the social and psychological effects of noise on people, but much more needs to be known in order to assess the impacts of the noise produced by many public facilities.

The knowledge base for SIA must be expanded considerably. It is time for the generous funding of basic research on the social and psychological aspects of events that are commonly produced by public actions. It is also time for increased funding of two kinds of applied research. First, the impacts of past projects should be more often studied to provide a better basis for predicting impacts of future projects. Second, the accumulation of knowledge in SIA should be fostered by sponsoring quality efforts to draw together and synthesize available knowledge. The efforts to date are generally quick, superficial, and uncritical.

The Development of SIA Methods

Methodological development is a great requirement of SIA. Subjective estimates play too great a role in SIAs, and more objective methods are needed to replace them. Some aspects of SIAs must be quick and dirty. Methods that retain the quickness while removing the dirt are needed. The use of experiments in assessing social impacts has regrettably been almost completely ignored. The list of needs for methodological improvements in SIA is long, which is a major reason why it is imperative that many capable social scientists enter the field of SIA.

REFERENCES AND SUGGESTED READINGS

Andrews, R.N.L. 1976. "Agency Responses to NEPA: A Comparison and Implications." *Natural Resources Journal,* 16 (Apr):301.

Bardach, E., and L. Pugliaresi. 1977. "The Environmental-Impact Statement vs. the Real World." *The Public Interest,* 49 (Fall):22–38.

Bell, D. 1973. *The Coming of Post-Industrial Society.* New York: Basic Books.

Burley, R.J. III, and S.F. Weiss. 1976. *New Communities U.S.A.* Lexington, Mass.: Lexington Books.

Coates, J.F. 1975. "A Technology Assessment of India's Television Satellite INSAT." *Journal of the International Society for Technology Assessment,* 1 (Sep):55–56.

*Cottrell, W.G. 1951. "Death by Dieselization: A Case Study in the Reaction to Technological Change." *American Sociological Review,* 16:358–65.

This article tells the story of the unanticipated consequences for a small town of the conversion from steam to diesel engines on a western railroad line. The town became obsolete with the conversion to diesel. The railroad wrote off its investments in the town as a loss against profits, but it never calculated the economic, social, and psychological losses suffered by the townspeople.

Council on Environmental Quality. 1976. *Analysis of Six Years Experience by Seventy Federal Agencies.* U.S. Government Printing Office.

_____. 1978. "National Environmental Policy Act Regulations." *Federal Register,* 43,230 (Nov 29).

Culhane, Paul J. 1978. "Letters to the Editor." *Science,* 202:1034–36.

*Dixon, M. 1978. *What Happened to Fairbanks?* Boulder, Colo.: Westview Press.

Fairbanks expected the Trans-Alaska Oil Pipeline to bring many benefits. It did not anticipate the many headaches. Dixon describes the social impacts of the pipeline on Fairbanks and how the community responded to the changes.

Fairfax, S.K. 1978a. "A Disaster in the Environmental Movement." *Science,* 199 (Feb 17):743–48.

_____. 1978b. "Letters to the Editor." *Science,* 202:1038–40.

Finsterbusch, K. 1976a. "The Mini Survey: An Underemployed Research Tool." *Social Science Research,* 5 (Mar):81–93.

_____. 1976b. "Demonstrating the Value of Mini Surveys in Social Research." *Sociological Methods and Research,* 5 (Aug):117–36.

_____. 1977. "An Analysis of Environmental Impact Statements for Federal Highways," Mimeo. University of Maryland (Apr).

*Finsterbusch, K. and C.P. Wolf, eds. 1981. *Methodology of Social Impact Assessment,* Second Edition. Stroudsburg, Pa.: Hutchison & Ross.

This is the major work on SIA methodology. It presents the state of the art from conceptual frameworks and general approaches to specific research techniques.

Finsterbusch, K. and A.B. Motz. 1980. *Social Research for Policy Decisions.* Belmont, Calif.: Wadsworth.

Friesema, H.P., and P.J. Culhane. 1976. "Social Impacts, Politics, and the Environmental Impact Statement Process." *Natural Resources Journal,* 16:339–56.

*Gilmore, J.S. 1976. "Boom Towns May Hinder Energy Resource Development." *Science* 191 (Feb 13):535–40.

The boom town is a case of extreme social impacts resulting from a project. This article sketches the social changes commonly experienced by boom towns and how they in turn reduce productivity at the project causing the boom.

Gilmore, J.S. and K.D. Moore. 1977. "Effects of Socioeconomic Impacts on Inter-Regional Allocating of Potential Increase in Coal Production." Denver: Denver Research Institute.

Jamaica Bay Environmental Study Group, National Academy of Science. 1971. *Jamaica Bay and Kennedy Airport: A Multidisciplinary Environmental Study.* Washington, D.C.

Liroff, R. 1978a. *Judicial Review Under NEPA—Lessons for Users of the Water Resources Assessment Methodology (WRAM).* Vicksburg, Miss.: Environmental Effects Laboratory, Waterways Experimental Station, U.S. Army Corps of Engineers.

_____. 1978b. Letters to the Editor," *Science* 202:1036–38.

Meadows, D.H., J. Randers, and W.W. Behrens, III. 1972. *The Limits to Growth.* New York: Universe Books.

Pikarsky, M. 1967. "Comprehensive Planning for the Chicago-Crosstown Expressway." *Highway Research Record* 180:35–51.

Rand Research Review 2(Spring 1978).:7–8.

Schnaiberg, A. and E. Meidinger. 1978. "Social Reality Versus Analytic Mythology: Social Impact Assessment of Natural Resource Utilization." Paper presented at the annual meeting of the American Sociological Association. San Francisco.

U.S. Department of Transportation and New York State Department of Transportation. 1974. *Draft Environmental Impact Statement for West Side Highway Interstate Route 478.* Washington, D.C.: U.S. Government Printing Office.

U.S. Nuclear Regulatory Commission. 1976. *Nuclear Energy Center Site Survey— 1975.* Springfield, Virginia: National Technical Information Service.

*Wolf, C.P., ed. 1974. *Social Impact Assessment.* Milwaukee: Environmental Design Research Association.

This is the first commercially published effort to describe SIA and to provide substantive articles on social impacts.

_____. 1978. "Sacramento County Social Impact Study." Social Impact Assessment 25 (Jan):15.

3 PROGRAM DEVELOPMENT

Arthur B. Shostak

From its very outset abroad as guided in the 1800s by social engineers like Comte and Saint-Simon, and from its distinctly applied origins in the United States as guided in the early 1900s by socially-concerned practitioners like Small and Giddings (Haskell, 1977), sociology has been inextricably involved with a social invention known as program development (PD). Broadly composed of three distinct components—identification of the goals of a program, implementation of the program, and evaluation and consolidation of the entire effort— PD can claim the distinction of being the major representative of sociology to the world at large. This is, of course, something of a mixed blessing for all parties.

While strong on good intentions, PD remains disappointing to date in execution and self-advancement. This track record, however, does little to dent the ardor of practitioners, many of whom regard PD as *the* critical test of the ultimate worth of armchair, blackboard, and counting types of sociological effort. Until our conceptual, theoretical, and methodological activities result in new and significant gains, however, and the communication loop has all sociologists really learning from PD feedback, our discipline will remain far from the "complete" science its activist founders envisioned over 150 years ago.

WHAT IS PROGRAM DEVELOPMENT?

Underlying Assumptions
No effort at introducing PD would be complete without mention of at least five of its critical axioms.

First, applied sociologists drawn to PD campaigns take as an article of faith the notion that change programs can actually be designed, and that there are very few imperatives or inviolable relationships capable of prohibiting systematic intervention. Second, many sociologists believe that PD demands that synthesis of otherwise disparate lines of academic work. So long as the division of labor in the behavioral sciences does violence to the real-world realities of organizational programs, PD practitioners must innovate in bold interdisciplinary ways. Third, many insist there is no universally preferred form of PD. While on some dimensions all PD programs are similar (each involves personnel, resources, goals, and internal contradictions), the programs also have enough unique characteristics (such as their history or leadership) to ensure a need to custom tailor at least some aspects of any PD process to the specific problem at hand.

This, in turn, helps explain the last two of the five axioms. PD is necessarily a collaborative, rather than an autocratic enterprise. As such, it is grounded in both scientific generalizations *and* in unique material best known to actual program participants. The PD user, as an outsider, must therefore earn the trust and cooperation of key program members to function effectively. Finally, program participants must sense the PD sociologist's confidence in their ability to continue improving the program long after the sociologist-consultant has departed. This confidence in the client's desire to grow and develop promotes the democratic potential of PD methodology and helps prevent it from being distorted to serve manipulative and authoritarian ends.

Objectives of PD

Sociologists serve as PD consultants in every major institutional area (business, legislation, education, health care, and so on), and the variety and complexity of problems to which PD is applied seemingly increases all the time. Generally, organizations call for PD help for two major clusters of problems: 1) matters of conflict, disruption, ineffective methods, unclear assignments or expectations, and leadership failures, and 2) matters of outmoded routines and inadequate risk taking; lack of imagination and creativity; absence of challenge, zest, and stimulation; excessive complacency; and false certitude. Consultants typically respond by trying to help the organization gather data and diagnose the situation. They help set goals and objectives for a PD exercise, implement the new program, and evaluate its initial product. Thereafter, consultants generally help guide revisions to strengthen both the reform impetus and the cadre that originally sponsored the entire undertaking.

Given this remarkable range of tasks, sociologists who serve as PD specialists confront a wide and dizzying array of organizational questions. Some of these are obvious, but many more are veiled and vexing. For example:

- Who really wants the PD effort to succeed, and why? To fail, and why? To be altered, and how and why?
- What objectives of the proposed program stir the most and the least opposition or support? Why, and with what intractability?

- What is the relevant history of recent PD efforts in this organization, and why? In the organization's competition, and why?
- Which of the various tools available to a PD specialist (such as surveys, interviews, simulations, and team exercises) engender the most and the least opposition or rewards? Why, and with what intractability?
- How likely is a post-PD capacity for managing change to be more effective and efficient than was true before the PD exercise? How can this possibility be strengthened?

Coursing through all such concerns is the obligation of the PD professional to honor the ancient and sage obstetrical adage: *Primum non nocere* (First, do no harm).

HOW IS PROGRAM DEVELOPMENT IMPLEMENTED?

Any guide to the classic steps in the PD process should keep in mind a biting caution raised recently by the British book reviewer, Tony Gould. Concluding his critique of still another new methodology text, a sociology "rule book for those who need to be taught to be perceptive," Gould (1979:595) suggests that "reading it in a library may be as much help as consulting a manual in order to learn to kiss." PD is also best understood by the doing of it, though a few pointers in the following areas can be shared apart from such involvement. The following paragraphs identify seven major steps in the PD process.

Diagnosis

Securing valid information about existing conditions as they relate to goal achievement is the first and, in many ways, possibly the most decisive PD task (French and Bell, 1973). Based on a more-or-less explicit framework of ideas, the diagnostic research for a PD project commonly examines attitudes, openness, climate, norms, patterns of decision making, and so on (Levinson, 1972). Naturally concerned with the "structure" or "grammar" of an organization, PD diagnosis goes further to explore organizational "rhetoric" as well. Attention is paid "not just to the rules of the game, but the many, often conflicting purposes people hope to realize by playing the game, and the strategies and tactics (including cheating) by which they try to realize them" (Goodenough, 1974:435–36).

These sorts of hidden organizational agreements can undo PD efforts almost before they ever get underway. Uncovering them can be exceedingly difficult because of three dilemmas mentioned by Argyris and Schon (1974): 1) individuals are reluctant to publicly "own up" to a minority position they privately hold, 2) individuals harbor negative fantasies of the terrible consequences of being unmasked, and 3) "going public" is a difficult skill to learn even when one is willing to accept the risks. Accordingly, the initial diagnosis stage in the PD process frequently entails far more sleuthing and "crap-detecting" (Postman and Weingarten, 1969), as well as far more building of courage into fearful respondents than is commonly suggested in our formal and pristine texts on the subject.

Earning and maintaining intimacy of an unexpurgated kind is indispensable if PD practitioners are to learn how program members (and relevant outsiders) really define and act in their particular world. Wherever possible, they should participate directly with program members, or (as a poor substitute) spend generous allotments of time in both structured and unstructured conversations with them. PD, in short, requires a quality of "grounding" that can only be attained with considerable time and effort. Among its many other rewards, such familiarity, as Mangham (1977:18) drolly points out, "breeds concepts."

Especially strategic here is uncovering the "dominant coalition" in an organization. Kotter (1978:20) describes this as "the objectives and strategies (for the organization), the personal characteristics, and the internal relationships of that minimum group of cooperating employees who oversee the organization as a whole and control its basic policy making." While the dominant coalition sometimes overlaps with the highest formal leadership, it may exclude particular officers and/or include others. Because this coalition occupies the top positions of power it often has tremendous influence on all programs—a piece of local reality no PD specialist ever minimizes.

Overall, however, PD projects frequently enter this initial diagnostic stage on a weak footing. "There are few activities in applied social change that are more important than the definition of the social problem. Sadly, the mechanical task of defining social problems is one of the most neglected areas of applied social research" (Zaltman and Duncan, 1976:32-33). To facilitate this process, Zaltman and Duncan (1977:34-40) suggest two cogent prescriptions for identifying variables in approaching a problem situation, which they call the "metatheory" and "open systems" designs. Since acceptance of a particular definition of the problem profoundly influences both the approach and the prospects of PD project success, much additional care must be paid to this task.

Data Collection

For an organization to obtain "a valid image of itself in the present, develop a clear picture of its problems, and construct realistic maps to guide it toward improvement," PD practitioners must seek data through questionnaires, interviews, observation of behavior, analysis of organizational records, and other such methods (Nadler, 1977:5). Considerable skill is required in choosing the type of data desired and deciding how to collect it. Related methodological craft is needed to determine how to aggregate, disaggregate, and analyze this data. In addition, since information is power (Pettigrew, 1972), data collection methods involve sensitive political considerations vital to the success of any PD effort.

More specifically, program members are commonly uneasy about sharing the full story with an inquiring PD outsider, especially if data collection stirs questions about the discretion, loyalty, maturity, or professionalism of either the respondents or this outsider. As data collected under a cloud of suspicion are often not trusted and can be readily challenged by the PD opposition, winning and holding the confidence of respondents is critical. Information that is viewed as valid, accurate, and unbiased is the goal, and such information can be a powerful motivating aid in a soundly-grounded PD process.

Nadler (1977:185) helps here with a unique discussion of a whole range of questions and issues concerning the various uses of data as an organizational-change tool. His cautions are especially relevant, as in the advice that "knowing what questions to ask of the data that has been collected is as important as (and perhaps more important than) the specific techniques of asking those questions."

Feedback

Sound data collection rests on an analytic plan with direction and purpose, including some clear idea of what to do with the data once they are collected. This information must be understandable, descriptive, and verifiable. It should also be limited (to prevent overload), relevant (about areas of activity that can be influenced), comparative (to provide relevant bench marks), and open-ended (presenting the data as a starting point for further exploration rather than as an end point).

Critical in this matter is the feedback meeting, for it is "at the center of the question of whether feedback will produce change" (Nadler, 1977:152). PD specialists use this occasion to promote dialogue about the data's long-term meaning and applicable solutions, as well as to explore how this information bears on problems immediately at hand. Because many people often feel uneasy, defensive, or frightened about what to expect—even while some few are excited and hopeful—feedback meetings can be remarkably challenging and complex.

Typical of attendant problems is the resort at such sessions to name calling, personal griping, or the verbal punishing of others:

> The format of such a meeting should always be problem focused and centered on actions. If the matter of racism were raised, it would hardly be productive to spend time in making changes and counter charges as to who is or is not racist. The problem-solving stance should be: What actions do we need to take to eliminate any feelings that racism occurs in our team? Then the focus of the group's attention is on planning and action-taking—not on name-calling or derisive confrontation. (Dyer, 1977:130)

Pivotal in such a PD strategy is the assumption that people actually prefer to act in "neighborly ways" if only given half a chance to do so (Bennis, 1969: 37).

Above all, the feedback meeting is a strategic opportunity to raise questions about commonly unexamined assumptions: "The interventionist must be able to offer (or at least have the skills to work with the client to develop) an alternative interpretation, an alternative script, and series of parts....Without this, feedback is not worth a candle and may even be an irresponsible activity" (Mangham, 1978:138). Only as program members come to question the previously unquestioned, and to believe that departures from the status quo are plausible and profitable, does the PD process really begin to move. Accordingly, PD specialists attack the paralyzing notion that a situation unchanged for a long time is somehow thereby unchangeable. A climate is sought in which program participants no longer embrace the status quo, but rather construct, perceive, or at the very least become open to new PD alternatives for their own situation.

Goal Setting

PD outcomes can be heavily influenced, and sometimes even doomed to failure, by weaknesses in the basic definition of project goals. If goals are left poorly defined, much unnecessary ambiguity, anxiety, and uncertainty are also highly likely (Kold, et al., 1974). Lack of clarity here will confound later evaluation efforts and heighten the project's vulnerability to negative rumors about its real worth and probable lasting effects.

In addition to clarifying goals, PD practitioners confront the task of helping program members add to their lofty goals others that are more realistic, specific, and proximate (short-run and tangible). Participants can then gain new confidence in what is being attempted through the project's incremental stages: "Both rational strategy and meaningful evaluation grow out of this" (Rothman, et al., 1976:4).

Undoubtedly, the most novel issue here is the orientation of project goals around unrecognized rewards that can actually result from errors. Pressures traditionally exist, of course, in favor of not making errors. "Then, if there is no such payoff, if errors occur in prediction or control, the chances are they will be suppressed or ignored rather than learned from—except the lesson: do not hire the same PD agent again" (Mirvis and Berg, 1977:318). In contrast with this old formula, certain PD reformers are campaigning now for goals that are more compatible with experiments, risk taking, and learning from mistakes. Such goals would help free PD practitioners and clients from the unreasonable notion that knowledge and skill every time guarantee successful change results. Errors could therefore be seen not so much as demoralizing "failures" as special guides to learning: "As errors show the change participants the limits of their knowledge, they will also make them more aware of themselves, what they do, and what they might do to change themselves and their organizations" (Mirvis and Berg, 1977:326).

Supporters of this novel perspective help clients lower unreasonable expectations of PD ventures. They can view so-called errors with far less anxiety and can respond to them much more effectively. "Just as practitioners have sought to create the open problem solving necessary for change in the past, so they will seek to create the open error-embracing norms necessary for learning in the future" (Mirvis and Berg, 1977:329).

Implementation

PD intervention, guided by the project's progress in diagnosis, data collection, feedback, and goal setting, is responsive to specific pointers derived from decades of experience:

- Ideas should be weighed largely independent of the people who suggested them, though with some sensitivity to the significance of their parentage.
- A series of short-term plans of reaching desired objectives should be very specific with regard to exactly what activities will be undertaken, by whom, drawing on what resources, and by what target date.
- Every meeting in the PD scenario should build an agenda for the next meeting (unfinished business, progress reports, "trouble" reports, etc.).
- Every meeting should include some mention of the program's present strengths as well as the weaknesses that spur the PD effort; exclusive concentration on problems can discourage all in a counter-productive way.

These guidelines, and numerous others (Hausser, et al., 1977:66–82), can carry a PD project a considerable distance, especially when linked to a powerful theory of organizational dynamics (Kotter, 1978).

Options for program implementation are numerous, perhaps limited only by the creativity of the PD collaborators. For example:

Employ various forms of slack resources. These resources, which may be in the form of financing, knowledge, ideas, personnel, or physical facilities, can be increased or decreased just like any other policy variable. They can be used to reduce complexity so as to reshape problems into more soluble forms (March and Simon, 1958).

Create new self-contained units. The design problem here is to decide which roles are to be combined into a self-contained unit, and to what level of the organization it will report.

Promote new lateral relations. The challenge in this case is to employ and formalize decision processes that cross lines of authority, so as to move priority decisions down to lower levels of the program or organization. The design problems here revolve around "who should be represented, what the mechanism should be, and to what organization level the mechanism should operate" (Galbraith, 1973:80,110).

• *Sponsor a "fair trial."* The program members are asked to specify a temporary period during which they will suspend judgment toward a PD component and experiment with it (Rogers and Shoemaker, 1971).

Every conceivable approach has its own proponents, of course, and the choice of one or more of these options is a dynamic, often intuitive, and commonly dramatic and consequential matter.

Especially helpful here is a unique manual designed "to provide effective theories and strategies that will enable the 'doing of good' in execution as well as in intent" (Rothman, et al., 1976:2). Several action principles are explored in depth (Rothman, et al., 1976:7):

- Promoting an innovative service or program, by demonstrating it first with a smaller portion of the target population, then expanding to the larger group.
- Changing the goals of an organization, by introducing new groups into the organization who support those goals *or* by increasing the influence of those groups within the organization who support those goals.

These authors, however, are quite clear about the locus of ultimate responsibility. "The user's intelligence, sensitivity, judgment, creativity, and moral choice are essential, and are in no way mitigated by the relevant social science knowledge that is offered to facilitate implementation" (Rothman, et al., 1976:14-15). Similarly, another manual (Zaltman and Duncan, 1976:190) focuses in a straightforward way on the characteristics of successful change agents. "The best change principles are unlikely to achieve their maximum effect if change agents themselves are inadequate interpersonally or in expertise."

Evaluation

After a PD innovation has been implemented, considerable trial and error data must be assessed before the program becomes stabilized and its full benefits can be realized. Two issues stand out in this regard: "One has to do with whether the change has realized its original purposes; the other, with whether it has caused negative consequences" (Brager and Holloway, 1978:227).

PD evaluation seeks to provide clear statements about what the project sought to accomplish, how it went about accomplishing its objectives, and how one can know whether or not it has accomplished what it claims. Among the standards of comparison employed are questions of how the program compares with its own earlier version (prior to the PD project), how it compares with other similar programs, how it compares with what the project members wanted, and how it compares with ways in which research and experience suggest it should function. Especially helpful is a standardized questionnaire instrument, the *Survey of Organizations*, which enables users to compare their organization with norms on organizational climate, supervisory leadership, peer leadership, group process, job characteristics, and satisfaction (Bowers and Franklin, 1977).

The classical approach, in which the evaluation is based on a post-experimental accounting of the "end results," is now under critical review. Certain PD practitioners urge clients to recognize that a project entails "more 'causes' than can be controlled, more 'effects' during the experimental period and beyond" (Mirvis and Berg, 1977:329). Accordingly, a new model in PD evaluation urges a continuous, rather than a discrete evaluation, stressing that evaluation should be an ongoing and integral aspect of the entire PD scenario.

The new model departs from the traditional format in four other major ways: 1) Overt measures are substituted for the kind of covert measures that can keep clients from knowing they are being evaluated. 2) Experimental understanding gains as much emphasis as does quantitative analysis. 3) No effort is made to mask the fact that "a great deal of human and organizational behavior is neither predictable nor under control" (Mirvis and Berg, 1977:330). 4) Focus is placed on what *is* happening rather than what *has* happened, and how it might have been preferred.

Stabilization

In this phase of the PD process a desired change can finally be institutionalized, albeit "...process does not end there. Forces within the environment and the organization continue to generate tensions for organizational actors—and as old problems are solved, new problems emerge. Thus does the process begin again" (Brager and Holloway, 1978:235). At stake here is the capacity of the PD collaboration (sociologists and clients) to facilitate what Lewin has graphically called the "refreezing process" (Lewin, 1951). After a system has been "unfrozen" and a desired change has occurred, the equivalent of "refreezing" must be secured if this new change pattern is to prevail against forces intent on restoring the earlier status quo.

Resistance to a PD process is quite natural, and PD specialists respond by defining its causes, understanding its varied expression, and suggesting appropriate counteraction. Among its causes, four are especially prominent: 1) inaccurate or insufficient information, 2) derogatory rumors, 3) value clashes with PD preferences, and 4) the fear that PD changes will expose or embarrass one. Appropriate counters include a frontal corrective to misinformation or false rumors, an intense exploration of value differences with key resistors, a smoothing of "ruffled feathers," and/or a strategizing with PD stalwarts (Hausser, et al., 1977:148–49). Forcing the matter is also occasionally necessary, though "forcing will lead to ineffective decisions if it is the dominant mode" (Galbraith, 1973: 62).

Commonly overlooked is the related need for realism about the actual rhythm of the process. While the PD consultant may thrive on change activity, members of the client group commonly waiver in confidence and effort. Accordingly, the consultant must make a sustained effort to reinforce, encourage, and support the morale of his or her collaborators. Providing opportunities to "retreat" for brief periods, or to visit previous successful PD efforts, are typical of the devices that may help revitalize temporary falloffs in morale.

Critical for success in "refreezing" is nurturing interdependence, or linking the PD change with older, well-established organizational entities (as when a change is linked to its clients by initiating a citizen's advisory group). Another important aid involves standardizing the operation of the desired change within the program as soon as possible. To be sure, creating linkages increases the vulnerability of the change to outside influences, and promoting premature standardization can vitiate the full benefit of a really novel change. Both of these risks may be well worth running, however, if a PD effort is to gain a semblance of (temporary) closure.

"Refreezing" has an additional component that some hail as the ultimate measure of the worth of any such venture. This involves the learning of skills from the project that can continue to reinforce it long after the departure of the PD consultant (Margulies and Wallace, 1973). Without this kind of organizational learning, temporary success in the stabilization quest may prove very short-lived. Inertia, opposition, and chance factors are likely to take a heavy toll unless participants become both learners and reinforcers of change.

Some PD specialists find it difficult to separate themselves from the client and turn the PD program over to them. While they know they should feel a sense of pride and accomplishment in every such transfer, the temptation remains to encourage further dependency and a prolonged consultation—a process seldom to the lasting good of either party.

Looking back, it is clear that the stabilization phase makes remarkable demands on a PD specialist, not the least of which is the need to essentially reverse direction:

> In the early stages of a change attempt, their task was to disrupt system stability, creating disequilibrium in forces that impinged on their problem area. In implementation, they began the process of reducing the tension caused by their intervention, an effort that is accelerated in the institutionalization phase. Coming full circle, they seek stability instead of change. (Brager and Holloway, 1979:231)

Versatility and diplomacy are taxed here as seldom elsewhere in the entire PD process.

Unfortunately, the "refreezing" phase remains one of the weakest links in the PD process. Pressed to explain this dilemma, PD specialists often point to inadequate time provisions (Dyer [1977:135], for example, contends that one to three years are required for a team-building PD project), to the common decline in top-level commitment (as in the aftermath of executive turnover), and to the awesome lure of "the path of least resistance" (represented here by business-as-usual practices popular with influential program members before the PD venture in question was ever initiated). Singly, or in combination, these countervailing forces explain much of the uneven and generally disappointing record of PD ventures thus far.

HOW HAS PROGRAM DEVELOPMENT BEEN USED?

While much of the answer to this question has been systematically reviewed above, three brief field reports and a spotlight on innovation in the matter may help underline the indispensability of creativity where PD is concerned.

Golembiewski (1972) was invited to develop a design to meet a particularly conflict-marred situation. A company had created a new post at its headquarters that it filled with a veteran of previous field service. The gentleman's old colleagues in the field, however, rejected him as a "headquarters' man," and fought his recommendations, forcing his removal in less than a year. Golembiewski was asked how the next incumbant might remain in office at least 18 months. His PD analysis led to the suggestion that the job description for the position be rewritten by the six disgruntled field managers themselves, three of whom were candidates for the position and all of whom would be affected in one direct way or another by the outcome. This novel PD design forced the managers to "put themselves in the role of the actor" and weigh the potential impact of their behavior on the new executive. It invited them to rewrite their own parts, head off trouble, and forge new bonds among themselves—all of which seemed to serve all the parties to the situation handsomely (Golembiewski, 1972).

French and Bell, Jr. (1973:5-7) were asked to help a group of strangers form an interdependent team to assist in the start up of a new junior high school. They developed a six-step approach to accomplish this task: 1) They isolated the team away from its normal tasks for a concerted week of PD activities. 2) After an array of emotive get-acquainted activities, they focused the group's attention on the nature of interpersonal communications, improving interpersonal communications skills, and exploring issues of trust, openness, and concern for each other. 3) Next, attention was paid to determining what kind of organization the members wanted to build together, what kind of climate they wanted to have, and how they could build themselves into an effective team (e.g., how the group was going to make decisions as a group). 4) After the week's program three inservice training days were scheduled at two-month intervals to enable the total school staff as a "family group" to look inward at its self and its processes. 5) The following summer a second one-week laboratory was held to sharpen skills in two areas: understanding organization dynamics, and learning how to generate and utilize valid information about the organization climate and culture. 6) In the PD project's second year, several inservice training days were given over to evaluation and reinforcement activities. Team satisfaction was apparently considerable, and the new junior high school was quickly accorded a valuable reputation as a model school that outsiders tagged as a place to transfer into (although turnover remained low among both staff and faculty).

This writer is currently analyzing an effort in Philadelphia between 1966 and 1970 to use citizen participation to liberalize the city's anti-poverty program. Four steps are particularly relevant to weighing what a PD process may actually entail:

1. A small group of grassroots critics of the city hall antipoverty program formed a protest group, the Maximum Participation Movement. At a series of bi-weekly public meetings MPM clarified its mission (ending the alleged patronage control of the OEO-funded local program) and its short-term objectives (earning media exposure of the program, earning an OEO cleanup of the program, etc.).

2. MPM began to publish a brief critique of the weekly meetings of the local antipoverty governing council. This critique was mailed to all media sources, the OEO, and nearly 300 influential Philadelphians.

3. MPM sponsored the only opposition slates ever entered into the city's two annual area-wide elections for neighborhood antipoverty boards.

4. MPM helped persuade OEO to freeze the city's millions of dollars of antipoverty funds for several months until the program's directors signed an extensive reform protocol.

Other activities included clandestine meetings with disgruntled "whistle-blowing" members of the local antipoverty program, and the unnerving discovery that hostile undercover agents were apparently tape recording MPM deliberations in a surreptitious way. Original PD objectives were revised over and again as the entire venture reverberated with fresh challenges and nasty blows.

Given a well-publicized "freeze" of OEO funds for several tense months until the city nominally agreed to the reforms, and given a small number of victories by MPM-backed candidates in the two city-wide elections for Poverty Board seats, this particular PD scenario appears rather successful. The real story, however, is actually quite the opposite. Since MPM could not help its members secure jobs in the local antipoverty program its membership rapidly slipped away. As media interest remains generally short-lived in these matters, MPM could not sustain harsh media attention to the persistent shortcomings of the local program. In addition, since the OEO was short of staff and long on problems, it proved impossible to sustain OEO pressure to effectively police the city's reform protocol after its ceremonial signing. Still, the PD scenario accomplished unprecedented collaboration between middle-class and welfare-class activists, many of whom are still drawing lessons from the entire effort.

These colorful field reports go hand-in-glove with comparatively imaginative PD applications being tried now by enthusiasts for a sweeping new approach, "Authentic Management," which dramatically challenges the status quo in PD implementation.

This approach was designed by Herman and Morehick (1977:211-16) to draw the insights of gestalt psychology into PD practice. Its brash originality is evident in these prescriptions:

> Try saying the unsayable, e.g., "Joe is a pain in the ass." Consider the unconsiderable, e.g., "We ought to change the whole damn distribution system."
>
> Play around more and encourage the client to do as well. Out of loose, unlikely speculation may come some new, real possibilities.
>
> Be willing to scrap ideas, plans, and other things that don't work; don't hang on to protect your image. Chances are people already know you've blown it anyway.
>
> Sometimes help your client to consider giving up.... it really is tremendously useful to have access to your ability to surrender ... the client can stop wasting energy, emotional as well as intellectual, in fruitless internal struggles..., [and] it very frequently provides a surprising basis for a new thrust of productive energy in another direction.
>
> Generally (though there are some exceptions) advice isn't very helpful. People usually have the best answers to their own questions within themselves, and the most useful thing you can do is to help them tune in on their questions within themselves, and the most useful thing you can do is to help them tune in on their own resources. [Italics in original].

PD practitioners may find especially provocative the positive regard here for power rather than gentility, directiveness rather than collaboration, and impulse rather than exclusive reliance on unemotional logic. The gestalt approach, with its unique emphasis on "the vitality and value of negative as well as positive emotions and attributes" (Herman and Morehick, 1977:37), departs sharply from values currently advocated by mainstream human relations approaches, making all the more vital its serious review by interested PD practitioners.

WHAT HAS PROGRAM DEVELOPMENT ACCOMPLISHED?

Beyond the many successful applications of PD, as illustrated by the case studies in the previous section, practitioners of this craft have learned numerous valuable lessons. Several of these are mentioned in the following paragraphs.

First, PD is not welcome everywhere, and this can become a very sticky issue recognized late in preproject negotiations—or worse yet, sometime long after that. Bennis (1969:45-50) urges giving careful attention to the "cultural readiness" of a potential PD host, including the organization's quotient of internal conflict and authoritarianism, too much of which can be fatal to PD possibilities. Possibly the most important factor here is the consultant's personal relationship with the client. "If the relationship is based on fantasy, on unrealistic hopes, or fear or worship or intimidation, then the change agent and/or the client system must seriously re-examine the basis for their joint work" (Bennis, 1969: 46). While a PD project rarely starts on a totally trusting and realistic basis, PD specialists are learning to use initial preproject dialogue with key program personnel to anticipate what may lie ahead. These persons are cautiously assessed and carefully incorporated into the PD process, which is then more likely to accomplish significant reforms.

Second, personal attributes of PD specialists (which is a sensitive issue) are receiving remedial attention from reformers. Bennis (1969:49), for example, has urged practitioners to encourage trust in others and to demonstrate behavioral flexibility. A practitioner should "recognize and come to terms with (as much as humanly possible) his own motivations." Above all, a PD specialist must have the capacity to be what the new program itself promises: "... so much of the change agent's influence grows out of his relationship with the client system and the extent to which he is emulated as a role model that any significant discrepancies between the change agent's actions and his stated values cannot help but create resistance" (Bennis, 1969:50). Although admittedly a tall order, this prescription becomes somewhat more manageable if the practitioner remains "someone with a script of his own and not ... a hack writer who will ghost any script required for the money" (Mangham, 1978:100).

Third, several critical ethical issues within PD are now receiving searching attention from practitioners. Five such situations noted by Walton (1978:122) are these: 1) the practitioner assists an organization whose goals and strategies he morally disapproves, 2) he associates himself with managerial actions of questionable justification and fairness, 3) his interventions employ means or produce consequences not consistent with his own personal values, 4) his actions vis-a-vis his clients violate standards that normally govern the professional-client relationship, and/or 5) his interventions produce consequences not consistent with the values generally attributed to his profession.

Warwick (1978:149,154) takes the matter farther by insisting that any serious ethical analysis must ask: 1) Is it fair that those who already possess power and control wealth have disproportionate access to PD techniques? 2) Are the power consequences acknowledged, or are they masked by benign, neutral language such as "problem solving" and "interpersonal gains"? 3) Do participants in a PD venture really make an informed choice? ("The practitioner who asks no questions about how the recruits were conscripted becomes the amoral 'hired gun' of social science.") He concludes by urging practitioners to delay over their own quandaries and to proceed only with caution and foresight: "If the cost ... is a slower pace of change and even a few lost contracts, so be it" (Warwick, 1978:159).

Fourth, especially controversial are certain time-honored problems inherent in the prescription of the PD specialist as an "actualizer of values" (Solomon, 1971). Practitioners who view PD in this manner emphasize the role tasks of 1) facilitating change in the direction of the client's values (lower turnover, more completion of job training, etc.), and 2) promoting broad humanistic values (encouraging program participants to develop their creative energy, growth, discretion, authenticity, expression of feeling, utilization of the whole personality, etc.). Whereas the first task requires the practitioner to view the client's program in a neutral manner, the second task puts the practitioner in the position of a critic who cannot remain neutral in his evaluation of the client's program. While some PD practitioners believe that the latter evaluative task is inherent in their role, others deny that it involves any such value commitment. Rather, they insist on their capacity to remain neutral, and they reject PD-related humanistic values as "a curious kind of anti-intellectualism nourished by an over-emphasis upon feelings, upon phenomenology, and upon the idiosyncratic as the only basis for true knowledge" (Mangham, 1978:13).

Each PD practitioner must achieve his or her own resolution of this dilemma, recognizing that honor and effectiveness compel an overt declaration of one's values or value-neutral advocacy. Zinn (1971:1) helps clarify this matter and puts it into historical perspective: "In the early sixteenth century Machiavelli and More, in a long-range moral duel, laid out the alternatives for intellectuals of the whole modern era: to serve the Prince with unquestioning efficiency; or to ask why and for what purpose, and who will live and who will die as a result of my efficiency." PD practitioners know they cannot escape responsibility for looking beyond the immediate situation and questioning the moral implications of their work, however sometimes unfashionable and often unsettling that task.

In sum, what sorts of things has PD accomplished to date? A judicious list would include all the features discussed above, plus the fact of its very persistance, which is no small accomplishment considering the unglorious history of short-lived fads in the applied social sciences. Eclectic and programmatic, PD adopts and abandons tools and insights as field tests recommend, thereby opting for timeliness over tradition, and for untidy experiments over neat reliance on less venturesome approaches. PD's accomplishments extend in every direction, including, fortunately, a keen appreciation of the long distance still to go.

WHERE IS PROGRAM DEVELOPMENT GOING?

Optimists in this area are fond of hailing several recent developments, including: the appearance in 1976 of the journal *Sociological Practice*, the creation of Ph.D. programs in applied sociology at the University of Pittsburgh and Washington State University, the insistence of the editors of *The Journal of Applied Behavioral Science* that contributors explicate ethical issues in their case studies, the seeming restoration of sanity in the off-campus use of sensitivity training, and the recent creation of a section on sociological practice in the American Sociological Association (Shostak, 1974b). Some cheer the eclecticism of a new arrival like "authentic management" with its irreverent gestalt approach, even while others see more potential in the contrary paradigm of operant conditioning (Jablonsky and DeVries, 1972).

A small, but hopefully growing, number of practitioners especially appreciate pioneering efforts being made to obtain data on the financial gains actually likely to accrue from a PD intervention. Mirvis and Lawler (1977), for instance, have demonstrated the novel use of a cost accounting system to explain how attitudes (intrinsic motivation, satisfaction) have an important financial impact on absenteeism, turnover, and performance. Future PD undertakings may hinge more and more on the ability to prove achievement of economic gains, as the "bottom line" becomes increasingly crucial in the "Age of Frugality" of the 1980s (Tregoe and Zimmerman, 1980).

Paradoxically, the future of PD efforts may also turn on how much attention is paid to PD failures (Blackler and Brown, 1980; Mangham, 1978:118–19: Porras and Wilkins, 1980; Spergel, 1972; Brill, 1971; Goodman, 1979). Honors here go to a pioneering collection of first-person essays about failures in organizational development and change: "This book is to some extent a reaction against an ethos of success gone berserk. Around us we see a world and a profession that worships success without an appreciation that *success is often born of failure* and that to learn from our failures we must *nurture and support their examination*" (Mirvis and Berg, 1977:xii). Eleven case studies make a prophetic case for the use of "successful failure" in PD campaigns, which is a critical step if PD is to move beyond situations that "promote caution when risk is needed, short-run achievement when long-term persistence is needed, and the disavowal of errors when error-embracing is needed" (Mirvis and Berg, 1977:333).

Fascinating in this connection is the related argument of some PD specialists that what clients take to be organizational problems in need of PD relief are actually problems requiring fundamental changes within the larger social order. To the extent that this is true, PD projects can offer only "band-aid" measures that deal with surface manifestations of the problem rather than with its basic causes (Shostak, 1974a). From this perspective, progress made towards a restructuring of the economic, political, and class structure of the United States, as guided by a reordering of its social priorities, can give practitioners the opportunity to use PD as more than a short-term palliative and temporary pain reliever (Brager and Holloway, 1977:18). Fascinating in this connection is a dramatic new radical critique of PD that has emerged in the early 1980s in British literature. Lambasting PD for serving only the interest of "capital," the critique complains that PD will only support minor adjustments within the existing social order (Bradley and Wilkie, 1980:574–79). While many practitioners would disagree with this scenario, it is clear that questions of ultimate sources, optimum levels of engagement, and fundamental targets and challenges vex many PD practitioners who are obliged to thrash out episodic and situational answers on a project-to-project basis (Shostak, 1966).

Where PD's allies are concerned, it is helpful to note that program development has many boosters outside of sociology, regardless of its checkered past, uneven present record, and long way to go. Typical is this "call to arms": "Perhaps what every corporation (and every other organization) needs is a department of continuous renewal that could review the whole organization as a system in need of continuing innovation" (Gardner, 1965:114). The long-term secular drift in the focus of our native curiosity also seems to favor PD ventures: "... never before in history, in any society, has man in his organizational context been so willingly searched, scrutinized, examined, inspected, or contemplated— for meaning, for purpose, for improvement" (Bennis, 1969:23).

Should enough of us care, and should we soon invest the energy, craft, and creativity appropriate to the task, PD efforts in the 1980s could help programs, their participants, and the social science professions as never before. Program development might yet evolve into a kind of "department of continuous renewal" for us all.

REFERENCES AND SUGGESTED READINGS

Argyris, Chris and Donald Schon. 1974. *Theory in Practice*. San Francisco: Jossey Bass.

Bennis, Warren. 1969. *Organization Development: Its Nature, Origins and Prospects*. Reading, Mass.: Addison-Wesley.

*Bermant, Gordon, Herbert C. Kelman and Donald P. Warwick. 1978. *The Ethics of Social Intervention*. New York: John Wiley & Sons.
  This is a pioneer collection of essays on: behavior modification, encounter groups, organization development, community-controlled educational reform, intervention in community disputes, income maintenance experiments, federally funded housing programs, and family planning programs.

Blackler, F.H.M. and C.A. Brown. 1980. *Whatever Happened to Shell's New Philosophy of Management?* Westmead, G.B.: Teakfield.

Bowers, David G. and Jerome L. Franklin. 1977. *Survey-Guided Development I: Data-Based Organizational Change*. La Jolla, Calif.: University Associates.

Bradley, David A. and Roy Wilkie. 1980. "Radical Organizational Theory—A Critical Comment." *British Journal of Sociology* 31:574–79.

Brager, George and Stephen Holloway. 1978. *Changing Human Service Organizations: Politics and Practice*. New York: The Free Press.

Brill, Harry. 1971. *Why Organizers Fail: The Story of a Rent Strike*. Berkeley: University of California Press.

Dyer, William C. 1976. *Insight to Impact: Strategies for Interpersonal and Organizational Change*. Provo, Utah: Brigham Young University Press.

_____. 1977. *Team Building: Issues and Alternatives*. Reading, Mass.: Addison-Wesley.

French, Wendall L. and Cecil H. Bell, Jr. 1973. *Organization Development: Behavioral Science Interventions for Organization/Improvement.* Englewood Cliffs: Prentice-Hall, Inc.

Galbraith, Jay. 1973. *Designing Complex Organizations.* Reading, Mass.: Addison-Wesley.

Gardner, John W. 1965. *Self-Renewal.* New York: Harper & Row.

Golembiewski, Robert T. 1972. *Renewing Organizations: The Laboratory Approach to Planned Change.* Itasca, Ill.: F.E. Peacock.

Goodenough, W.H. 1974. "On Cultural Theory." *Science,* 186:435–36.

Goodman, Paul S. 1980. *Assessing Organizational Change: The Rushton Quality of Work Experiment.* New York: John Wiley & Sons.

Gould, Tony. 1979. "Reviews in Brief." *New Society* (June 7, 1979):595

Haskell, Thomas L. 1977. *The Emergence of Professional Social Science.* Urbana: University of Illinois Press.

Hausser, D.L., P.A. Pecorella, and A.L. Wissler. 1977. *Guided Development II: A Manual for Consultants.* La Jolla, Calif.: University Associates.

*Herman, Stanley M. and Michael Morehick. 1977. *Authentic Management: A Gestalt Orientation to Organizations and Their Development.* Reading, Mass.: Addision-Wesley.

This work employs a major new perspective to shed fresh and invigorating light on PD topics. It poses a healthy challenge to conventional human relations material.

Jablonsky, S.F. and D.L. DeVries. 1972. "Operant Conditioning Principles Extrapolated to the Theory of Management." *Organizational Behavior and Human Performance,* 7:340–58.

Kold, David A., Irwin M. Rubin and James McIntyre, eds. 1974. *Organizational Psychology—A Book of Readings,* 2nd ed. Englewood Cliffs, N.J.: Prentice-Hall.

Kotter, John P. 1978. *Organizational Dynamics: Diagnosis and Intervention.* Reading, Mass.: Addison-Wesley.

Levinson, Harry. 1972. *Organizational Diagnosis.* Cambridge, Mass.: Harvard University Press.

Lewin, Kurt. 1951. *Field Theory in Social Science.* New York: Harper & Row.

Mangham, I.L. 1978. *Interactions and Interventions in Organizations.* New York: John Wiley & Sons.

March, James G. and Herbert A. Simon. 1958. *Organizations.* New York: John Wiley & Sons.

Margulies, Newton and John Wallace. 1973. *Organizational Change: Techniques and Applications.* Glenview, Ill.: Scott, Foresman.

*Mirvis, Philip H. and David N. Berg. 1977. *Failures in Organization Development and Change.* New York: John Wiley & Sons.

This is a pioneer collection of PD essays that explore failure in entry, change, and diffusion. Rich in candor, counsel, and craft, the book will, one hopes, be followed often by comparable guides from equally forthright, searching professionals.

Mirvis, P.H. and E.E. Lawler III. 1977. "Measuring the Financial Impact of Employee Attitudes," *Journal of Applied Psychology,* 62:1–8.

*Nadler, David A. 1977. *Feedback and Organization Development: Using Data-*

Based Methods. Reading, Mass.: Addison-Wesley.

The book offers a sound combination of analysis and prescriptive detail, complete with helpful tips on application.

Pettigrew, A. 1972. "Information Control as a Power Resource." *Sociology* 6: 187–204.

Pinder, C.C. 1977. "Concerning the Application of Human Motivation Theories in Organizational Settings." *Academy of Management Review* 2:384–97.

Porras, Jerry I. and Alan Wilkins. 1980. "Organizational Development in a Large System: An Empirical Assessment." *The Journal of Applied Behavioral Science* 16 (Oct–Dec):506–34.

Postman, Neil and Charles Weingarten. 1969. *Teaching as a Subversive Activity.* New York: Delacorte.

Rogers, Everett M. and F. Floyd Shoemaker. 1971. *Communication of Innovations: A Cross-Cultural Approach.* New York: The Free Press.

Rothman, Jack, John L. Erlich, and Joseph G. Teresa. 1976. *Promoting Innovation and Change in Organizations and Communities.* New York: John Wiley & Sons.

Shostak, Arthur B., ed. 1966. *Sociology in Action.* Homewood, Ill.: Dorsey.
_____. 1974a. *Modern Social Reform: Solving Today's Social Problems.* New York: MacMillan.
_____. 1974b. *Putting Sociology to Work: Case Studies in the Application of Sociology to Modern Social Problems.* New York: David McKay.

Solomon, L.N. 1971. "Humanism and the Training of Applied Behavioral Scientists." *Journal of Applied Behavioral Science* 7:531–47.

Spergel, Irving A., ed. 1972. *Community Organization. Studies in Constraint.* Beverly Hills, Calif.: Sage.

Tregoe, Benjamin B. and John W. Zimmerman. 1980. *Top Management Strategy: What It Is and How to Make It Work.* New York: Simon & Schuster.

Walton, Richard E. 1978. "Ethical Issues in the Practice of Organization Development." In *The Ethics of Social Intervention,* edited by Gordon Bermant, Herbert C. Kelman, and Donald P. Warwick, pp. 121–46. New York: John Wiley & Sons.

Warwick, Donald P. 1978. "Moral Dilemmas in Organization Development." In *The Ethics of Social Intervention,* edited by Gordon Bermant, Herbert C. Kelman, and Donald P. Warwick, pp. 147–62. New York: John Wiley & Sons.

*Weisbord, David A. 1978. *Organizational Diagnosis: A Workbook of Theory and Practice.* Reading, Mass.: Addison-Wesley.

This combines a first part of exercises with a concluding section of illustrative readings. Refreshing, challenging, and sage throughout, the volume's potential is very considerable.

Zaltman, Gerald and Robert Duncan. 1976. *Strategies for Planned Change.* New York: John Wiley & Sons.

Zander, Alvin F. 1977. *Groups at Work.* San Francisco: Jossey Bass.
_____. 1979. "The Psychology of Group Processes. In *Annual Review of Psychology,* edited by Mark R. Rosenzweig and Lyman W. Porter, pp. 417–51. Palo Alto, Calif.: Annual Reviews.

Zinn, Howard. 1971. *The Politics of History.* Boston: Beacon Press.

4 CONFLICT INTERVENTION

James H. Laue

In the 1960s, protests on behalf of the rights of racial minorities and women, and against the United States' role in the Vietnam War, became a part of the daily news and consciousness of America. The public learned in dramatic fashion what many sociologists had known for some time—that conflict is an ever present and important part of human social life.

Amid these events, social scientists, lawyers, labor mediators, and others began applying and refining a number of strategies for dealing with conflict. These techniques of negotiation, conciliation, mediation, and arbitration are being applied to diverse problems such as racial struggles, school controversies, housing project disputes, political demonstrations, prison uprisings, and environmental contests. The result has been the emergence of the applied field of conflict intervention.

WHAT IS CONFLICT INTERVENTION?

The Meaning of Conflict Intervention

Conflict intervention is the process by which an outside or third party enters into a conflict in order to influence its outcome in a direction that he or she defines as desirable. Because intervention always alters the power configuration of the conflict, all intervenors are advocates—for either a specific party, a particular outcome, or a preferred process of conflict intervention.

The Nature of Social Conflict

Social conflict refers to "a struggle over values and claims to scarce status, power, and resources in which the aims of the opponents are to neutralize, injure, or eliminate their rivals" (Coser, 1968:232). Two or more parties may be involved, and their conflict represents an escalation of the competition that is a part of virtually all social relationships. A crucial distinction must be made between conflicts over *power* (the control of decisions about the allocation of resources) and conflicts over *resources* (goods, services, jobs, facilities, land, etc.). Power conflicts strike more at the structure of the social systems and generally lead to more far-reaching changes than do disputes over who gets how much of a given resource. The basic issue in power disputes concerns the control of the process for determining the allocation of resources in the future (Laue and Cormick, 1978).

The focus of sociology on social structure and patterning is especially relevant to conflict, since conflict is not chaos or the absence of social order. Rather, it is highly patterned, moving through stages and phases, which, if not always precisely predictable, do exhibit considerable orderliness across conflicts. Conflict is a natural and inevitable part of all social life—within and between individuals, families, schools, offices, neighborhoods, communities, and nations. Conflict is not only normal in a vigorous social system, but it also can contribute to individual and social development. Yet, conflict that escalates to violence inflicts hurt on individuals and the whole fabric of society, including physical injury and death to persons, damage to property, and the cultivation of hatred and fear (Mack and Snyder, 1957; Kriesberg, 1973; Williams, 1977).

A major problem facing every group and society is finding ways of constructively managing, regulating, or resolving the inevitable conflicts that arise, while also striking a workable balance between individual rights and collective needs. The extremes of personal anarchy (if there is too little regulation of conflict) and social repression (if there is too much regulation) must be avoided if society is to promote the greatest good for the greatest number. The techniques of conflict intervention are designed to deal with conflict in constructive ways that avoid both those extremes (see Bermant, et al., 1978).

The Many Goals of Conflict Intervenors

It is often mistakenly assumed that "resolution" is the only appropriate approach to conflict. But sociologists have learned that not everyone wants conflict "resolved." Depending on one's perspective and position in the system, there are a number of different approaches to conflict. Establishment parties (e.g., mayors, police chiefs, and college presidents) seem most eager to resolve conflict, for they generally wish to stop it as quickly as possible so that their institutions can "get back to normal." This approach may result in attempts to manage or regulate conflict to keep it within what are defined as appropriate bounds. In its extreme form, these approaches may lead to attempts to repress conflict and suppress the weaker parties involved.

On the other hand, people who want to call attention to and remedy injustices often instigate a conflict or confrontation. When the sheriff in Selma, Alabama accused civil rights demonstrators of "causing problems" by their actions in 1965, movement leader Andrew Young replied: "We are not 'causing' problems; we are just bringing them out in the open. You have been beating blacks in the back of the jail on Saturday night for years. We are simply saying that if you are going to do this now, you'll have to do it during the day, on Main Street, and in front of the television cameras" (Laue, 1965).

From still another perspective, sociologists and other academics may wish to study conflict or to educate people about it, based on their belief that knowledge can lead to more constructive action.

Within these approaches lie a number of specific goals held by individual conflict intervenors. Some may wish to be involved in "peace promotion." Some may seek the goal of preventing violence. Some may wish to achieve social reform, revolution, or social justice. Other intervenors simply take the reduction of social tension as ther major goal.

Whatever the goal, every approach to conflict is a form of advocacy. There are no neutrals. Some intervenors advocate or work on behalf of a particular party, others for a specific type of outcome, still others for good process or "truth." As with all activities of applied sociologists, the very act of being involved—even as a researcher or teacher—means that one has taken a stand and cannot claim to be neutral.

The Development of Conflict Intervention Techniques

Recognition of conflict intervention and its techniques as a "field" that can be studied and applied has emerged only within the last 25 or 30 years. Sociology has played a major role in this development, as evidenced by the writings of Robin Williams (1947), Lewis Coser (1956), and James Coleman (1957), the founding of the Society for the Study of Social Problems and its journal *Social Problems* in 1951, and the establishment of the Center for Research in Conflict Resolution and the *Journal of Conflict Resolution* in 1956.

The development of conflict intervention in the United States can be traced to at least five sources: sociology and other social sciences, labor-management relations, peace research, the racial conflicts of the 1960s, and the court diversion movement of recent years.

The Social Sciences. Social scientists are interested in conflict for many reasons. Marxist theory, which provides the philosophical roots of so much social science, views conflict as the central dynamic in all societies. International, intergroup, and race relations have occupied the interests of social scientists for many years. Sociology was born amid times of revolution and reform in Europe, and sociologists often have been motivated by a desire to promote social change and justice (Laue, 1978)—which usually involve intensive social conflict. Appropriately, at its 1977 annual meeting, the American Sociological Association unanimously supported a resolution calling for the establishment of a United States Academy of Peace and Conflict Resolution.

Labor-Management Relations. Perhaps the best-known forerunner of conflict intervention was the development of collective bargaining and mediation between labor unions and corporate management in the 1920s and 1930s. Since then, a body of theory, a set of techniques, and numerous statutes and agencies supporting this approach to resolving labor-management conflict have developed. The passage of the National Labor Relations Act and the establishment of the Federal Mediation and Conciliation Service in the 1940s helped institutionalize the field. Thousands of labor-management disputes each year now turn to mediation and arbitration for solution.

Peace Research. Beginning with the publication of Lentz' *Towards a Science of Peace* (1955), research dealing with the causes of peace and war has proliferated in the United States and merged with similar traditions in other countries. The current status of the persons and organizations in the field is described more fully later in this chapter and in Chapter 24.

Racial Conflict. Events in Birmingham, Selma, Watts, Detroit, Newark, and other communities dramatically brought the issue of racial conflict to the attention of the U.S. public in the 1960s. The institutional responses to these upheavals included the establishment of the Community Relations Service in the 1964 Civil Rights Act to mediate and conciliate racial disputes, and the revival of human relations commissions in cities and states throughout the country. More recently, the women's rights and antiwar movements have adopted the civil rights movement's confrontation/concession model.

Court Diversion. As the courts became clogged with cases in the 1960s and 1970s, it was clear that litigation is not the best way to resolve many conflicts. It is costly, adversarial, lengthy, and usually leads to a win/lose decisions that is unsatisfactory to one (and often both or all) of the parties involved. Alternative programs for dealing with many types of conflicts arise, literally diverting the process into mediation or conciliation. Prominent examples include juvenile justice procedures in which young offenders go to counseling and community treatment programs rather than to jail, recent developments in adult corrections (Hepburn and Laue, 1980), family and neighborhood dispute mediation centers, and environmental conflicts (Ford Foundation, 1978a).

HOW IS CONFLICT INTERVENTION IMPLEMENTED?

How does conflict intervention work? Is it really possible to manage or direct conflict in a particular direction once it is under way? To answer these questions, we shall examine conflict intervention in terms of the settings in which it takes place, the roles played by intervenors, the skills and techniques they use, preferred personality characteristics of intervenors, and the strengths and problems of conflict intervention.

The Setting for Conflict Intervention

At least three conditions must be met to build a setting for successful conflict intervention: finding the right forum, establishing the legitimacy or credibility of the intervenor, and achieving a willingness to negotiate.

The Right Forum. The conflicting parties must be willing to locate at least part of their relationship in physical and social space. Combat, information sharing, charges and counter charges, position-taking, and compromise-shaping can only take place within a framework of procedures in space and time. Finding the right turf and rules acceptable to all the participants is essential. For some disputes and disputants the forum involves a courtroom and the litigation process, but increasingly this arena is proving unsatisfactory. For other participants informal mediation in the streets is the appropriate forum, and in yet other situations the acceptable forum may be a marathon problem-solving session at a retreat setting.

The Credibility of the Intervenor. Whatever the skills of the would-be intervenor, until he or she is perceived as legitimate by the disputants, there can be no intervention. Except in cases where the power of law or military force makes it possible to intervene, the disputants literally must grant the intervenor the right to enter their conflict. Often a lengthy process of building communication and trust among the parties and the potential intervenor is required. This legitimacy may be based on a number of factors, including the person's position, past experience, reputation, skills, personal style, perceived integrity, etc.

A Willingness to Negotiate. Intervention cannot proceed unless the parties are willing to negotiate their differences. Often the existence of a forum that feels right and an intervenor who seems credible is enough to coax disputants to risk accepting an intervenor. In other situations, one or more of the parties may feel that their interests are best served by refusing to cooperate with any intervention attempts, perhaps believing that they have adequate power to get what they want without the possible buffering effect of outside "do-gooders." Until all the disputants believe it is in their best interests to enter a joint process for solution, constructive intervention is not possible.

Once a setting for intervention has been established, it is probable that all the parties have concluded that some kind of win/win outcome of the conflict is possible and perhaps desirable. Instead of viewing the game as a win/lose contest in which there are clear winners and losers, the disputants come to perceive it as a win/win situation in which every party achieves at least some of its goals.

The Roles of Conflict Intervenors

Laue and Cormick (1978:212–17) have identified five basic roles that are played individually or in combination by intervenors in all conflict situations: Activist, Advocate, Mediator, Researcher, and Enforcer. These roles are differentiated in terms of their organizational and fiscal bases, their relationships to the disputants, and the skills they require.

Persons taking the role of *Activist* are leaders based in one of the conflicting parties, who generally are so strongly identified with that party that they are unable to empathize, negotiate, or compromise with the other party or parties. Skills required include organizing, public speaking, and strategizing. A welfare mother leading a welfare rights protest is a good example. An Activist often faces the charge of "going native" and siding entirely with one party—almost always the out-party. A counterpart, the Reactivist, often is aligned with the more established party in such disputes.

The *Advocate* works on behalf of an interest group in a conflict and is supported either by that group or by an independent, generally sympathetic source. Skills include the ability to promote the party's cause to wider constituencies, serving as a negotiator for the party's interests, and helping achieve conflict termination on what that party defines as good terms. A management consultant is a typical in-party Advocate, while a community organizer is representative of the typical out-party Advocate role.

The role of the *Mediator* is based on a desire for "good process" rather than a preference for any of the parties. A good process usually is defined as one that involves all the stakeholders and leads to a jointly determined, win/win outcome of the conflict. The mediator must be acceptable to all of the parties. Skills include facilitating negotiations, organizing, communicating, seeking additional resources, and packaging settlements.

The *Researcher* has an independent or semi-independent base and may be a social scientist, policy analyst, media representative, lay observer, or monitor. This type of intervenor seeks to provide an objective description of the given conflict situation. Observation, data gathering, writing, and oral communication are some of the requisite skills. Often Researchers perceive themselves as neutral, but they alter the power relationships of any situation by their very presence and may be used by parties on all sides to further their interests.

Operating from an independent power base, the *Enforcer* has the power to impose conditions on conflicting parties irrespective of their wishes. Often the Enforcer is a formal agency of social control—a court, the police, a funding agency, or an arbitrator. Unlike any of the other intervenor roles, the Enforcer brings formal coercive power to the situation, carrying the ability to specify behavior or impose sanctions that may favor the goals of none, some, or all of the parties.

The Skills of Conflict Intervenors

All conflict intervenors must master certain skills to be effective. Eleven types of critical skills are listed in this section, roughly in the order they are—or should be—applied in conflict intervention.

1. *Self-analysis*—the ability to assess one's skills, potentials, limitations, and power within a highly transient social network.
2. *Social analysis*—compiling a comprehensive picture of the social system in which the conflict is set, as well as the history of the conflict, its major actors, and its central issues.
3. *Communication*—the ability to think, speak, and write clearly and the ability to facilitate communication between the disputing parties and with the media.
4. *Organizing*—the ability to organize both small groups of persons and entire interest groups, neighborhoods, or communities.
5. *Providing information*—combining relevant knowledge, communication skills, and good timing to provide information to disputing parties, which is an important source of power for the intervenor and of empowerment for the parties.
6. *Identifying resources*—obtaining outside resources (money, jobs, facilities, etc.) that may aid in successfully terminating a conflict.
7. *Brokering*—putting different entities together under the intervenor's aura of credibility.
8. *Contingency thinking*—the ability to construct a wide range of potential scenarios in a conflict and readiness to operate in any of them.
9. *Planning*—providing such planning skills as sequencing the elements of a solution and developing a timeline for implementing them.
10. *Counseling*—offering good counsel to conflicting decision makers concerning the dilemmas and decisions they face.
11. *Implementing solutions*—helping to shape the details of the solution and assist in its implementation through program development, budgeting, training, and evaluation.

The Major Techniques: Negotiation, Conciliation, Mediation, Arbitration

The major techniques of conflict intervention emerge from the *activities* of a *person or organization* with a cluster of the *skills* named above in a given conflict *situation*. The techniques vary in degree of formality, type of advocacy, and sanctions they carry. There are four major techniques: negotiation, conciliation, mediation, and arbitration. It could be argued that various forms of investigation or fact-finding also deserve to be listed as formal intervention techniques; indeed, the Community Relations Service carries "Assessment" as one of its program categories, and the Federal Mediation and Conciliation Service and most labor mediation agencies do the same with "Fact-Finding."

Negotiation is a technique in which advocates selected by the parties represent their interests in a more-or-less formalized discussion setting, engaging in give-and-take in an attempt to get the best settlement of the disputed issues. Parties agreeing to participate in negotiation recognize that a winner-take-all,

100 percent victory is not possible, and they are willing to make tradeoffs and fashion a jointly acceptable agreement.

Conciliation involves a combination of fact-finding, assisting in negotiations, community organizing, and other activities aimed at finding constructive forums and methods for the parties to use in settling their differences. Strong advocacy may be required on the part of the conciliator if the parties are to be brought into a constructive, win/win process. Conciliation often is viewed as a premediation activity.

Mediation involves a third party (often called a "neutral") who is acceptable at some level by all the disputants and whose major role is to help the negotiations process work. Often parties in conflict turn to mediation when negotiations have broken down or are not seen as yielding a satisfactory solution. The ultimate goal of mediation is to assist the parties in reaching a mutually satisfactory solution to their differences. The mediator carries no formal power or sanctions into the situation; he or she is there because the parties have allowed access.

Arbitration is a technique in which the arbitrator carries sufficient formal power to enforce sanctions on all the parties to the dispute. While many of the arbitrator's activities (fact-finding, facilitating communication, and pacing the discussions, for example) are similar to those used in the other three techniques, there is a major difference: an "award" by the arbitrator is the outcome, rather than a negotiated settlement or joint agreement. When arbitration is applied (as in a labor-management impasse or in litigation), the parties know that they literally have given over some of their decision-making sovereignty to the arbitrator.

Preferred Personality Characteristics of Intervenors

Most of the skills are required in any conflict intervention situation regardless of the role of the intervenor, the type of dispute, or the major technique applied. In addition, personality characteristics and personal style are key factors determining the potential effectiveness of any intervenor. The trick in successful conflict intervention, some would say, lies in getting the disputants to sufficiently identify with the intervenor and invest enough trust so they are willing to be jointly influenced toward a resolution of their differences.

The personality and style of the intervenor are crucial in this process. Intervenors must display flexibility in keeping options open, delaying closure, shifting roles, and considering alternative solutions. They must be able to delay or deny gratification by letting the conflicting parties take credit for any solutions achieved and inhibiting any tendency to "give the right answer" at every turn. They must avoid counterdependence by knowing when not to intervene and when to withdraw from a situation if the parties need to carry it on their own. They must have good "senses"—of humor, timing, and perspective. And because timing is so important in moving conflicts toward termination, intervenors must have the stamina to go without sleep for many hours and to maintain high levels of intensity for weeks or months.

Strengths and Problems of Conflict Intervention

As with any technique, conflict intervention has its strengths and problems, its potentials and limitations. Chief among the concerns of many practitioners and observers is that intervention may simply promote the reduction of tension and a return to the status quo, rather than allow conflict to play itself out and result in needed social change. Out-groups and powerless groups rarely if ever call for conflict intervention or conflict resolution; they want change, justice, or empowerment. If conflict intervention serves only to "get the natives off the street," then only the interests of the elite or agents of social control have been served.

Various forms of conflict intervention can act as a buffer between the parties and prevent the conflict from escalating. Yet, the goal of some parties in a conflict may be to escalate it to the point where the negotiation of change becomes possible. This tactic was dramatically evident at Wounded Knee, South Dakota in 1973 when a number of federal, private, and religious intervenors worked to prevent confrontations and save lives. Yet, some of the more militant leaders of the American Indian Movement were prepared to bear the ultimate escalation to violence and their own death at the hands of the U.S. government, feeling that "a second Wounded Knee massacre" might be needed to awaken the country to the plight of Native Americans.

Cooptation is another potential problem. Strong out-group leaders may be absorbed by establishment representatives in a negotiation or mediation process. They then become incapable of organizing and empowering their own constituents for action. Establishment parties often have the ability to "buy off" protestors with offers of jobs or other rewards.

If the intervenor is sensitive to these inherent problems and limitations, the processes of intervention can work for social justice, empowerment of out-groups, and the facilitation of constructive change. The key is sensitivity to the power dimensions of the situation. Tokenism and cooptation can be avoided if intervenors constantly ask themselves whether their actions are helping to reduce the power disparities between the parties and thus promote joint, win/win outcomes.

HOW HAS CONFLICT INTERVENTION BEEN USED?

Understanding the application of any technique of social intervention calls for an analysis of at least two important questions: 1) To what issues, problems, or concerns of the society is the technique applied? 2) What types of persons and groups utilize the technique, and how widespread is their activity?

Issues and Problems

As the techniques of conflict intervention—negotiation, conciliation, mediation, and arbitration—have developed and become more visible, they have gained increasing use in conflicts at every level of U.S. society and with virtually every issue facing the nation (Ford Foundation, 1978a, 1978b; Laue and Cormick, 1978; Wehr, 1979). Development and application of these techniques is also occurring in a number of European countries and, to a more limited extent, in Asia, Latin America, Africa, and the Pacific Basin (see especially Ford Foundation, 1978b). The following analysis of areas of application ranges roughly from situations where the actors and the impact are limited to a small area and/or number of persons to those where the scope is larger and more general.

Family and Neighborhood Disputes. "Family crisis intervention" has developed as an established field in the mental health disciplines within the last 20 years. Techniques of conciliation and mediation (and sometimes advocacy and arbitration) are applied to family conflicts in group counseling settings by psychiatrists and social workers, and in less controlled settings by police and other officials trained in special units. Nearly one-quarter of all police killed in the line of duty die stepping into a family quarrel. Many police departments, beginning with New York City's Family Crisis Intervention Unit in the late 1960s, have dramatically reduced these figures by training officers in intervention techniques (Bard, 1975). In more structured family counseling situations, many practitioners are using techniques that require intervention with the entire family unit.

Provider–Consumer Disputes. Disputes over the quality of goods or services sold in the private sector have been the object of much attention by private advocacy and mediation groups and, more recently, by public ombudsmen, publicly-financed neighborhood mediation centers, and such state offices as the dispute resolution unit of the Office of the Public Advocate in New Jersey. The sit-in movement at southern lunch counters in the early 1960s was the forerunner, with its focus on refusal of service and other forms of discrimination based on race. But it is the quality of *public services*—and the inability of citizens to receive fast and fair responses to their complaints about such services—that has most often been the stimulus for application of the new conflict intervention techniques. Most prominent among the public sector disputes addressed through mediation and other techniques have been those involving public housing, welfare, public schools, prisons, police services, and health care.

Intra-organizational and Interorganizational Relations. The fields of group dynamics, group leadership, and organizational development long have utilized many of the intervention techniques described here to deal with conflicts within and between organizations (Argyris, 1970; Likert and Likert, 1976). The problems addressed usually focus on communication and information flow rather than power dimensions. The classic example, however, deals directly with power relations: labor-management relations in industry (see Walton and McKersie, 1965 and Simkin, 1971). More than any other issue or problem, the ongoing relations between owners, managers, and workers in U.S. industry have been the focus of application of the formal techniques of mediation and collective bargaining.

Racial and Other Intergroup Conflicts. Racial discrimination and tensions often are involved in provider–consumer disputes. The presence of race-related issues in such disputes tends to heighten the tension and make successful intervention more difficult. Race is a major factor especially in provider–consumer conflicts about school desegregation, welfare services, and inmate rights. Many of the techniques and practitioner agencies described in this chapter were developed in response to broader white–minority conflicts, most of them involving major public services or rights. Chief among them were protests in Birmingham in 1963, Mississippi in 1964, and Selma, Alabama in 1965, which involved voting rights and access to public accommodations. The major racial disorders of the 1960s often involved concerns (however violently manifested) about housing, job programs, and the functioning of the criminal justice system. Massive street demonstrations and hundreds of racial disorders during the 1960s probably provided the most common breeding ground for the development and application of conflict intervention techniques (see Chalmers, 1974). Conflicts surrounding the antiwar movement of the 1970s, the women's movement, and the politicization of other groups (Hispanics and Native Americans, for example) also have been the target of conflict intervention.

Federal–State–Local Relations. Relations between the various levels of government in the United States have increasingly provided an arena for application of conflict intervention techniques. Disputes regarding boundaries of political jurisdictions and service areas now are often negotiated rather than litigated. Conflicts over attempts by the federal government to regulate the activities of state and local governments receiving federal funds have led to mediation and, in some cases, formal arbitration. The most extensive and specific effort in the history of the United States to apply mediation to the formation and implementation of policy among the levels of government has been under way since 1979, with St. Paul, Minnesota, Columbus, Ohio, and Gary, Indiana, serving as initial test cities. Termed the "Negotiated Investment Strategy" and sponsored by the Charles F. Kettering Foundation, the experiment is described in later sections of this chapter.

Environmental Disputes. The increase in public awareness of environmental and energy issues that began in the 1960s brought with it heightened concern for methods of dealing with conflicts in more constructive ways than confrontation and litigation. Shall a dam be built? Must an aluminum smelter be placed near our town? Where can we dispose of radioactive waste from nuclear power plants? Since approximately 1970, a number of attempts have been made to resolve such problems through the application of mediation and other conflict intervention techniques. Application in this area is especially complex, for environmental disputes often involve different ethnic or racial groups, public service institutions, levels of government, and private interest groups—all holding different views of what is best for the environment.

   International Conflicts. The largest of all arenas for conflict—the international system—has been the setting for the application of intervention techniques ranging from informal trade relations to formal diplomacy to world war. Attempts have been made to establish world law. The United Nations provides a formal forum for conflict resolution. The World Court attempts to act as an arbitrator of differences among nations but carries little authority. Beyond these types of formal mechanisms, we find increasing attention to such techniques as mediation and conciliation in international relations. U.S. State Department diplomats recently requested and received training in negotiation from the American Arbitration Association. A number of scholars are actively applying intervention models to specific international disputes (U.S. Commission, 1980). And in the most dramatic application, President Jimmy Carter utilized the "single negotiating text" model in assisting Israel and Egypt in achieving the Camp David accords in 1978.

Scope of the Field in the United States

   Today the formal practice and study of social conflict intervention in the United States is carried on by several thousand persons and several hundred organizations. Uncounted additional thousands of individuals and groups practice such techniques in their daily activities (e.g., as politicians, managers, counselors, community workers and the like) without the conscious sense that they are a part of a "field" called conflict intervention.

   The development of this field has gone through a number of phases. Formalization of collective bargaining, fact-finding, mediation, and arbitration in labor-management relations in the 1930s and 1940s was the first and most thoroughly developed application of conflict intervention techniques. A legal framework and a number of formal organizations and practitioners evolved, as described below. Then came the societal response to the racial conflicts of the 1960s, resulting in the emergence and re-emergence of a number of intervention organizations such as the U.S. Justice Department's Community Relations Service and two private organizations—the Institute for Mediation in New York, and the National Center for Dispute Settlement of the American Arbitration Association based in Washington, D.C. These types of organizations have not achieved the wide-scale acceptance and support accorded the labor-management sector, however, for reasons described later in this section. The "third generation" of the field in the United States began with the emergence since 1975 of hundreds of neighborhood mediation centers to deal with a wide range of local issues without litigation, such as disputes between neighbors over property boundaries and uses, and minor assaults.

   The number of individual and organizational practitioners has grown dramatically in the last few years—largely at the local level, where neighborhood and agency dispute resolution programs have multiplied. But few major agencies have been created since the conflict-ridden 1960s. The scope of the field may be described with reference to several categories: public and private practitioner agencies at all levels of the society, college and university study centers and projects, professional associations and networks, foundations, and individual practitioners.

Public Agencies. The best-known public agency involved in the direct application of conflict intervention techniques is the Federal Mediation and Conciliation Service, established in 1947 to assist in the resolution of labor-management disputes through fact-finding, mediation, and arbitration. The Service has a staff of more than 300 professional mediators, annually receives notice of some 35,000 disputes, and actively intervenes in 10,000 of them (Horvitz, 1980). The other major agency involved at the Federal level is the Community Relations Service (CRS) of the U.S. Department of Justice, created in 1964 to assist communities in resolving disputes related to racial discrimination and conflict. The CRS has a field staff of some 60 persons distributed throughout the ten federal regions in the United States. The agency intervenes through fact-finding, mediation, or conciliation in more than 3,000 disputes involving race and discrimination annually. The preponderance of the problems in recent years has involved the criminal justice system and school desegregation. CRS played extensive roles in attempting to peacefully mediate such situations as the Selma-to-Montgomery March in 1965, the urban racial disorders of the 1960s, the Wounded Knee confrontation in 1973, and the Miami racial problems in the summer of 1980.

Other public organizations applying conflict intervention techniques include state labor-management mediation agencies in the more than 30 states with collective bargaining laws; a number of state, county, and municipal human relations and human rights commissions that include conciliation as part of their mandate; state services such as the dispute resolution section of the Office of the Public Advocate in New Jersey; such criminal justice diversion activities as the Access-to-Justice Project in Philadelphia, the Columbus (Ohio) Night Prosecutor's Office, and the Neighborhood Justice Center in Kansas City; the Office of Collective Bargaining in New York City (supported jointly by the city and public employee unions to deal with public sector labor disputes); and a growing number of special crisis intervention units in police departments throughout the United States. Other nations are also adopting such approaches. Representative programs include the arbitration alternatives in the English court system, the Swedish small claims court, and the Public Office for Legal Information and Conciliation in Hamburg, Germany (Ford Foundation, 1977).

Private Agencies. Beginning in the late 1960s, the American Arbitration Association established the National Center for Dispute Settlement (NCDS), and Automation House in New York formed the Institute for Mediation and Conflict Resolution—both with major grants from the Ford Foundation. The

NCDS later became the office of Community Dispute Services, and the Institute expanded its base of functioning to include training throughout the nation. The Center for Criminal Justice in Washington began in 1973 with the aim of developing inmate grievance procedures in prisons. It became the Center for Community Justice later in the 1970s when it entered the field of student grievance procedures. Another national private agency working in the field is RESOLVE, which is applying mediation techniques to environmental disputes.

Notable among regional and state level activities in the private sector are the Institute for Environmental Mediation in Seattle (which works in the Pacific Northwest and has had notable successes since 1973 in mediating confrontations over environmental issues) and the Rocky Mountain Center for the Environment, which is doing environmental mediation in that area.

The greatest growth in the field is occurring at the local/private level, with literally hundreds of local projects being initiated by churches and synagogues, bar associations, private social agencies, and the like. Many of them deal with interpersonal and neighborhood disputes. They include such efforts as the Community Dispute Settlement Program of Delaware, the Center for Collaborative Planning and Community Service in Boston, the Albany Dispute Resolution Program, the Dispute Settlement Center of Chapel Hill (North Carolina), Dispute Services at Oklahoma State University, Rental Information and Mediation Service in Santa Cruz (California), Community Mediation Service of the Metropolitan Ministry with Women in Washington, D.C., and Neutral Ground in Walla Walla (Washington). The Neighborhood Justice Centers (NJCs) in Atlanta and Los Angeles-Venice are part of the same federally-initiated program as the Kansas City NJC, but they have closer ties to the private sector.

College and University Projects. Another important part of the growing field of conflict intervention is the group of study centers, projects, and institutions in colleges and universities. Most often their focus is on "peace research" or "peace and conflict studies," with primary emphasis on the international level. Some of them engage in direct intervention at the community level, such as the Office of Environment Mediation at the University of Washington, the dispute resolution program run by the Political Science Department at the University of Hawaii, and the Community Conflict Resolution Program at the University of Missouri–St. Louis. For the most part, however, their concern is teaching and training students and community groups. Nearly 100 such units are affiliated in COPRED–the Consortium on Peace Research, Education, and Development.

Professional Associations and Networks. The scope and impact of any field can be partly measured by the extent to which its practitioners organize themselves to share information and further their own interests. COPRED is an example of one important association of practitioners and scholars in this emerging field. The Association of State Mediation Agencies was established in the 1950s to promote interchange and professionalism among these organizations. Newer associations and networks include the Society of Professionals in Dispute Resolution (SPDR or "Spider"), which encompasses persons from a wide variety of perspectives and agencies, and the Citizens' Clearinghouse for Grass Roots Dispute Resolution in Pittsburgh, which maintains up-to-date information on such efforts and works to prevent "over-professionalization" of the field.

Individual Practitioners. Another indication of the maturity and scope of an enterprise is the number of individuals whose efforts can be supported. A small number of private consultants make their living by offering conflict training and intervention services, and many other persons engage in such activities as an adjunct to their regular positions in universities or other organizations.

Private Foundations. Any discussion of the emergence and application of a new technique of social intervention must deal with the bases of its support in the earliest days. Private foundations have played an especially important role regarding conflict intervention. The Ford Foundation has been the most significant institution in the conflict intervention field, providing several million dollars of support since 1968 to the American Arbitration Association and the Institute for Mediation and Conflict Resolution for the development of the field. The Rockefeller, Carnegie, and Arco foundations have added significant sums during the past few years in the area of environmental mediation, Ford, Rockefeller, and Carnegie long have been among the leaders in sponsoring international relations projects related to world peace. One of the most innovative recent applications of conflict intervention techniques—the Negotiated Investment Strategy—is being sponsored by the Kettering Foundation.

WHAT HAS CONFLICT INTERVENTION ACCOMPLISHED?

"But what did it accomplish?" is one of the most difficult questions that may be posed about any social intervention, because it is not possible to compare what would have happened in a specific situation if the technique had not been applied. Would a riot really have occurred if conflict intervenors had *not* been on the scene?

Despite this limitation, it is possible to say that the application of conflict intervention techniques to community and interorganizational disputes during the past 20 to 30 years has yielded some significant accomplishments. But whether these accomplishments are to be praised, damned, or ignored depends largely on one's perspectives regarding the conflicts and problems addressed. Consider peaceful school desegregation, voting rights for southern blacks, or inmate grievance procedures. Are these "accomplishments" or unfortunate outcomes? These and many more results of conflict intervention approaches in specific cases described below can only be judged as positive or negative in the light of some set of values and political interests. The rule of thumb usually is that the party or parties who gained more power or privilege as a result of conflict and intervention tend to define it as a positive outcome, and vice versa!

What Is "Successful" Conflict Intervention?

Simply "putting the lid on" conflict without regard to the power and justice dimensions of the situation does not constitute "successful" conflict intervention. If it is true that some amount of conflict is a normal and healthy expression of problems in the system that demand attention, then successful conflict intervention must attend to those underlying conditions—and not just the surface expression of conflict. In fact, if conflict intervenors' only aim is to reduce the immediate tension and bring things "back to normal," the outcome usually tends to support the status quo organization of power.

A successful outcome of conflict intervention can be said to occur when the intervenor has assisted in achieving a *jointly determined, win/win, lasting resolution of the conflict in which the values of mutual empowerment, social justice, and maximum personal freedom for all the actors are realized*. A tall order! And the dilemma for the potential intervenor is that he or she often never knows whether an outcome meeting these criteria is possible in a given conflict.

The elements of such an outcome are analyzed in greater detail elsewhere (Laue and Cormick, 1978). They include 1) reducing existing disparities in the distribution of power and resources among the parties, 2) a more democratic decision-making process, with at least informal guidelines for constructively dealing with future conflicts, 3) stabilization of relations between the parties, 4) decreasing the parties' dependency on outside intervenors in dealing with conflict, and 5) direct or indirect policy changes that can prevent future injustices and violent conflicts.

As with all social intervention techniques, the intervenor can neither predict nor fully control the impact of his or her intervention. But any decision regarding whether or not to intervene must include an assessment of the chances for achieving what the intervenor defines as a positive outcome.

Examples of the Accomplishments of Conflict Intervention

There is as yet no systematic assessment of the tens of thousands of formal applications of conflict intervention to social disputes in the United States in recent decades. But it is possible to cite examples that skilled intervenors, the parties, and/or researchers believe indicate positive accomplishments resulting from intervention.

Family and Neighborhood Disputes. Court diversion programs in many cities deal predominantly with family quarrels and neighborhood squabbles. One New York program reports resolution without return to the courts in nearly 90 percent of its cases (Ford Foundation, 1978a:19-21). Neighborhood justice centers and other neighborhood or court-based programs report high success rates in assisting family members and neighbors to resolve disputes through mediation and quasiarbitration, avoiding lengthy and expensive court action (*The Mooter*, 1977–80).

Provider–Consumer Disputes. The Tenant Affairs Board in St. Louis, formed in 1969, was one of the first and most heralded models for tenant representation in local public housing authorities. After a serious strain developed between the parties, the tenants' right to be represented in the St. Louis Housing Authority was reestablished through a two-day marathon mediation session (Laue, 1978). In 1969 in New York City, black and Puerto Rican communities were struggling for control of a $3 million per year antipoverty program. When elections and administrative intervention failed to resolve the problem, a multiracial mediation team succeeded after two months of negotiation to achieve a compromise applauded by both sides (Ford Foundation, 1978a:8–10). The Center for Community Justice, meanwhile, has introduced inmate grievance procedures in a number of state prisons. Litigation is reduced and the tone of prison life is enhanced through such procedures (Hepburn and Laue, 1980).

Racial and Intergroup Conflicts. The Community Relations Service of the U.S. government played a major conciliation role during efforts to register black voters in Selma, Alabama and the subsequent voting rights march to Montgomery in 1964. Government personnel served as the only line of communication between local law enforcement officials and Dr. Martin Luther King, Jr. and other civil rights leaders. This was a major development for many of the emerging conflict intervention techniques (Laue, 1965). Chalmers studied the use of negotiation and mediation in a number of racial confrontations in the 1960s. He concluded that third party intervenors played important roles in bringing many of these disputes to a resolution, including helping the parties find terms of agreement, supporting substantive progress for the minority groups, and helping stabilize relationships for further constructive bargaining (Chalmers, 1974:271–73). More recently, a number of urban police departments have established specially trained hostage negotiation units that are reported to be highly successful. The best example is the effort by the Washington, D.C., Police Department to end the building holding and hostage taking by a group of Hanafi Muslims in 1978, in which three days of negotiating culminated in the release of the hostages.

Intra-organizational and Interorganizational Relations. The best-known and most successful application of conflict intervention is in the field of management-labor conflicts. The Federal Mediation and Conciliation Service notes that of the more than 35,000 actual or potential disputes that come to its attention each year, 95 percent are settled without strikes, most of them through direct face-to-face negotiations. The Service has now been named in legislation to help resolve specific problems and monitor implementation, as in the Navaho-Hopi land dispute in the Southwest (Horvitz, 1980). The last decade has witnessed a proliferation of firms and individuals offering services to "reduce conflict," "improve communication," and "teach negotiation" in agencies and organizations. Another development leading to this type of intervention is the growth of "management sciences" in business and public administration, with a focus on managing conflict. Conflict intervention techniques are also being applied to the field of higher education. A Ford Foundation project begun in 1978 is attempting to introduce mediation and conciliation into disputes within and between colleges and universities, as in turf battles over student recruiting activities.

Federal–State–Local Relations. When members of the American Indian Movement occupied Wounded Knee, South Dakota in 1973, an intergovernmental conflict of monumental proportions was touched off, involving federal, state, and local jurisdictions as well as the Pine Ridge Sioux Reservation. While the initial issue was internal to the tribe, the state and federal governments became involved in a struggle for control of decision-making processes regarding the reservation. The Community Relations Service played perhaps the major role in helping avert a second Wounded Knee massacre. In the context of the current debate over the role of government in social service programs and regulatory activities, disputes over benefits, jurisdictions, and interagency relations are reaching mammoth proportions. More and more of these disputes are being handled through administrative tribunals and informal hearing procedures, rather than by going to court (Ford Foundation, 1977). Particularly noteworthy has been an experiment funded by the Kettering Foundation, called the Negotiated Investment Strategy. It has been applied in the cities of St. Paul, Columbus, and Gary. In each case, a team of cabinet-level negotiators was selected by the mayor, the governor, and the president of the Federal Regional Council in the Midwest. Each team developed a formal "investment strategy" that specified jointly agreed upon policy objectives for its community during the coming years, as well as specific action commitments by all three governmental levels and the private sector (*Nation's Cities Weekly*, 1979). These three agreements were all signed in 1980, and requests are pouring in from other cities for information about this approach.

Environmental Disputes. Mediation helped resolve a major environmental dispute in Washington State in the 1970s that involved more than a dozen parties, including farmers, politicians, environmentalists, and corporations. At issue was a plan by the U.S. Army Corps of Engineers to build three massive dams on the river system in the Cascade Mountains east of Seattle. A team of mediators supported by the Ford Foundation worked intensively with the involved parties for nearly two years before reaching an agreement in 1975. The key to this agreement was a recommendation for a total land-use plan for the basin of the major tributary (Ford Foundation, 1978a). A number of organizations, some of them mentioned earlier, now are involved in environmental mediation, including the National Coal Policy Project, the Keystone Radioactive Waste Discussion Group, the Rocky Mountain Center on the Environment at the University of Colorado, the Office of Environmental Mediation at the

University of Washington, and the Western Forest Environmental Discussion Group (Cormick and Lee, 1980).

International Disputes. The most dramatic application of conflict intervention techniques on the international scene was the achievement of the 1978 Camp David accords. This agreement to reduce political tensions in the Middle East was reached by Israel's Prime Minister Begin and Egypt's President Sadat, under the mediation/arbitration of U.S. President Carter. It was a milestone for international conflict intervention because the strategy used by President Carter was borrowed directly from experience at the national level in labor-management bargaining. This strategy used a "single negotiating text" in which staff personnel for the three parties worked in advance on the issues and prepared a broad draft agreement, which became the basis for discussion among the principals at the bargaining table (Livezey, 1979). More recently, the Hostage Mail Exchange Service was established in 1980 by the United Methodist Church and the International Indian Treaty Council to explore intervention possibilities in the Iranian-U.S. hostage situation. The Service established a communication link between the hostages and their families when all other channels had been cut off. When formal diplomatic channels are frozen, this type of "without-portfolio" intervention is essential to maintain enough communication to provide the conflicting parties with enough information and contacts to eventually fashion a settlement (see Fisher 1969).

WHERE IS CONFLICT INTERVENTION GOING?

Growth in the Field of Conflict Intervention

We may predict confidently the continued development and application of nonlitigational techniques for dealing with social conflicts. Litigation—the major forum for dealing with conflicts in the United States—is plainly inappropriate for many types of disputes. This is especially true for disputes between persons and groups who will have to continue to live and work together in an institution after the immediate conflict is resolved. The adversarial process and the win/lose decisions of litigation yield bad feelings that do not promote constructive functioning in organizations and societies.

The court dockets are clogged. Court diversion programs are growing. There is increasing experimentation with conflict intervention techniques, in separation and divorce, prisons, and schools. Literally hundreds of local community and neighborhood dispute resolution centers are being formed, involving thousands of average citizens and specialists.

Problems Facing the Field

Chief among the problems and challenges to be faced by the next generation of conflict intervenors and scholars are the following.

Conceptual Development. There still is a great need to develop firm theoretical foundations for the field and a thorough body of case literature regarding implementation procedures and outcomes of conflict intervention. Smith (1971), Deutsch (1973), Dedring (1976), Williams (1977), and Wehr (1979) have made important recent contributions to this area.

Quality Control. As with any new endeavor, the forms of practice are varied and often unfocused. With the rising popularity of local community and neighborhood dispute resolution centers, growing numbers of well-motivated persons are working in the field who have given relatively little thought to the critical underlying issues of injustice, power, and the ethics of intervention. The quality of intervention therefore varies greatly.

Empowerment Versus Cooling. The "social change vs. social control" argument is phrased most strongly in these terms. Any kind of intervention tends to buffer the immediate situation and reduce the possibility that the outcome will be at the extremes of either repression or revolution. But the uses of intervention for humane purposes may be subverted by intervenors who do not understand that their work may be serving the cause of delaying, diverting, diffusing, or defusing a conflict without attending to its underlying causes.

Funding. Conflict intervention is moving to a stage where more regularized funding will be required if it is to grow and develop. Thus far, foundations and some limited public funding have carried the field. But problems of cooptation and infiltration must be faced if any one funding source becomes too influential in such activities.

Conflict Issues. Conflict intervenors are likely to be called into a broader range of disputes as word of the technique expands. Will they be ready? The 1980s will test the young field as issues of energy, classism, racism, human rights, and the responsibility of the public sector to meet human needs all demand solutions.

Research Prospects

In addition to intensive evaluation of the processes and outcomes of conflict intervention, the following areas present research problems that investigators should address in the 1980s.

- Biological and anthropological bases of violence and aggression.
- The relationship of personality factors to successful intervention.
- The role of the electronic media in conflict intervention—and in promoting violence.
- The state-of-the-art in international, national, and community conflict intervention.
- How the results of peace research can be applied to conflict intervention.
- The processes whereby such techniques can best be promoted and utilized to influence policy decisions.

Will There Be Jobs for Conflict Intervenors?

It appears that there will be substantial opportunities for employment of persons trained in conflict intervention techniques during the coming decades, for as resources become more scarce, conflict increases. Energy scarcity, the elimination of thousands of jobs through new technology, the decreasing availability of cheap land for residential and commercial development, and many other scarcity trends all lead to the prediction that conflicts will abound at all levels of our society and world. A project at Bethel College in Kansas in 1977–78 developed a long list of agencies that hire entry level persons trained in conflict skills. A broader survey would turn up many more organizations seeking persons who know how to deal with conflict constructively.

Will trained intervenors be available? Much depends on the types of facilities and programs available for education and training in this field. The approximately 50 peace and conflict studies programs existing among the 100 institutional members of COPRED are not equipped to train large numbers of persons. There is a serious lack of facilities, funding, and expertise for training in the field. The formation of a United States Academy of Peace for training and research in conflict intervention and peacemaking skills could help answer this need.

Prospects for the United States Academy of Peace

In October 1978 the U.S. Congress authorized formation of a Commission on Proposals for the National Academy of Peace and Conflict Resolution and the last of the nine commissioners was appointed in 1979. Two of the commissioners are sociologists. The Commission was charged with conducting an investigation to determine whether to establish a United States Academy of Peace and Conflict Resolution. This idea first surfaced when Benjamin Rush, a signer of the Declaration of Independence, called for the establishment of a "peace office" in 1789. Since 1935, more than 140 proposals have been introduced in the Congress to establish a department, academy, or office of peace in the federal government.

The Commission operated during 1980, holding 12 hearings nationwide and conducting extensive studies on the state-of-the art of peacemaking and various models for a peace academy. More than 300 persons testified, representing the United Nations, the Foreign Service Institute of the U.S. State Department, the Federal Mediation and Conciliation Service, the Community Relations Service, and numerous private organizations promoting peace including the American Friends Service Committee and local mediation centers throughout the country.

The Commission issued its report to the President and the Congress in 1981 recommending that the country establish the United States Academy of Peace, and legislation to this effect has been introduced into the Congress. The Academy would conduct extensive research and training in the application of such intervention techniques as mediation and conciliation to international conflicts, with attention as well to national and community-level conflicts and their relationship to international peace. There would be a strong focus on extending the training and educational programs of the Academy to states and communities through a decentralized structure, in addition to a central research and training facility.

If the Academy is established, it will mark a major point of maturation for the field of social conflict intervention in the United States. It would become the first such institution in any national government in the world, taking its place in stature with the U.S. Army, Navy, and Air Force academies.

Social conflict intervention—a technique nurtured by sociologists, other social scientists, and practitioners from various disciplines—will then have emerged full-blown as the vehicle for translating the United States' long-published values of peace and peacemaking into the permanent structure of a national institution.

REFERENCES AND SUGGESTED READINGS

Argyris, C. 1970. Management and Organizational Development. New York: McGraw-Hill.

Bard, M. 1975. *The Function of the Police in Crisis Intervention and Conflict Management.* Washington, D.C.: Criminal Justice Associates.

*Bermant, G., H.C. Kelman, and D.P. Warwick. 1978. *The Ethics of Social Intervention.* Washington, D.C.: Hemisphere.
    The authors present analyses of social intervention ranging from one-on-one behavioral modification to community disputes on such national policy issues as family planning and income maintenance. Each section is followed by a critique by an ethicist, and the book concludes with an extensive chapter by the authors that analyzes the materials from the perspective of three critical ethical issues: power, freedom, and accountability.

Chalmers, W.F. 1974. *Racial Negotiations: Potentials and Limitations.* Ann Arbor: University of Michigan-Wayne State University.

Coleman, J.S. 1957. *Community Conflict.* New York: The Free Press.

Cormick, G.W. and K.N. Lee. 1980. "Settling Environmental Disputes: A Conceptual Reconnaissance." Proposal, mimeo. Seattle: University of Washington.

Coser, L.A. 1956. *The Functions of Social Conflict.* New York: The Free Press.
    _____. 1968. "Conflict: Social Aspects." In *International Encyclopedia of the Social Sciences*, Vol. 3, edited by D.L. Stills. New York: Macmillan.

*Dedring, J. 1976. *Recent Advances in Peace and Conflict Research.* Beverly Hills, Calif.: Sage.
    This book is a critical survey of theories, recent research, and case studies in peace, war, conflict, and conflict intervention. Special attention is given to the international system, but the models of conflict and conflict resolution presented are helpful in understanding the national and community levels, as well. There is an extensive bibliography.

*Deutsch, M. 1973. *The Resolution of Conflict.* New Haven, Conn.: Yale University Press.

This book is an analysis, from the perspective of a political scientist, of the ways in which social and political conflicts are resolved. Deutsch develops and applies theories of conflict and includes a section on the role of third parties in conflict resolution.

Fisher, R. 1969. International Conflict for Beginners. New York: Harbor.

Ford Foundation. 1977. Appendix to "Conflict Resolution and Regulation: Another Look." New York.

_____. 1978a. *Mediating Social Conflict.* New York.

_____. 1978b. *New Approaches to Conflict Resolution.* New York.

Hepburn, J.R. and J.H. Laue. 1980. "Prisoner Redress: Analysis of an Inmate Grievance Procedure." *Crime and Delinquency* 26 (Apr):162–78.

Horvitz, W. July 23, 1980. Testimony before the U.S. Commission on Proposals for the National Academy of Peace and Conflict Resolution. Washington, D.C.: *Congressional Record.*

Kriesberg, L. 1973. *The Sociology of Social Conflicts.* Englewood Cliffs, N.J.: Prentice-Hall.

Laue, J.H. 1965. "Field Notes," Community Relations Service. Selma and Montgomery, Ala.

_____. 1978. "Advocacy and Sociology." In *Social Scientists as Advocates,* edited by G.H. Weber and G.J. McCall, pp. 167–99. Beverly Hills, Calif.: Sage.

Laue, J.H. and G.W. Cormick. 1978. "The Ethics of Intervention in Community Disputes." In *The Ethics of Social Intervention,* edited by G. Bermant, H.C. Kelman, and D.P. Warwick, pp. 205–32. Washington, D.C.: Hemisphere.

Lentz, T.F. 1961. *Towards a Science of Peace.* New York: Bookman Associates. (Orgl. 1955).

Likert, R. and J.G. Likert. 1976. *New Ways of Managing Conflict.* New York: McGraw-Hill.

Livezey, Emile Teval. 1979. "Peace Is Not A Competition." *Christian Science Monitor* (Eastern Edition), June 19, 1979.

Mack, R.W. and R.C. Snyder. 1957. "The Analysis of Social Conflict: Toward an Overview and Synthesis." *Journal of Conflict Resolution* 1:212–48.

Nation's Cities Weekly. 1979. "Negotiating the City's Future." November 26, 1979. (Copyright by the Charles F. Kettering Foundation.)

Simkin, W.E. 1971. *Mediation and the Dynamics of Collective Bargaining.* Washington, D.C.: Bureau of National Affairs.

Smith, C.G. 1971. *Conflict Resolution: Contributions of the Behavioral Sciences.* Notre Dame, Ind.: University of Notre Dame Press.

The Mooter, 1977–80. Newsletter, Grassroots Dispute Resolution Clearinghouse. Vol. 1–4. Pittsburgh: American Friends Service Committee.

U.S. Commission on Proposals for the National Academy of Peace and Conflict Resolution. 1980. Testimony at 12 public seminars, March 10–July 23, 1980.

Walton, R.E. and R.B. McKersie. 1965. *A Behavioral Theory of Labor Negotiations.* New York: McGraw-Hill.

*Wehr, P. 1979. *Conflict Regulation.* Boulder, Colo.: Westview.

This volume contains a synthesis of theories, methods, and training materials for persons interested in dealing with social conflict, particularly in organizations. Many of the early trends and developments in conflict intervention are brought together in this book, which grew out of a series of seminars presented nationally for members of the American Association for the Advancement of Science.

Williams, R.M., Jr. 1947. "The Reduction of Intergroup Tensions." *Social Science Research Council Bulletin* 57:1–153.

*_____. 1977. *Mutual Accommodation: Ethnic Conflict and Cooperation.* Minneapolis: University of Minnesota Press.

Williams presents an analysis of a large mass of data on how "workable solutions" have been achieved in a wide variety of conflict situations, most of them directly involving racial or ethnic minorities. The author, famous for his 1947 synthesis of principles in "The Reduction of Intergroup Tensions," offers a number of propositions about "successful" conflict resolution.

5   PROGRAM EVALUATION

Peter H. Rossi and Sonia Rosenbaum

Each year, the federal government spends hundreds of billions of dollars on programs and interventions whose purpose is to ameliorate social and economic problems. Additional sums are spent by governments at state and local levels and, increasingly, by foundations, philanthropies, and international organizations seeking to deal with human miseries on a global scale. From the point of view of the larger society, these expenditures can be seen as societal investments whose return is measured by the effectiveness of programs in realizing their desired ends. Evaluations of programs are thus essential in helping the society make decisions about investments. The ultimate goal of program evaluation, in short, is to aid the larger society in making maximally wise decisions about the allocation of scarce social, economic, and human resources.

WHAT IS PROGRAM EVALUATION?

Program evaluation is the application of social science theory and methods to the design, implementation, and assessment of social policies and social programs. It is intended to aid policy makers in the formulation and implementation of programs that most closely achieve intended aims. Social science theory provides knowledge about social problems and effective treatments to ameliorate such problems. Social science research methods provide the techniques for attaining firm knowledge about program operation.

Specifically, program evaluation provides social science based information on the following broad issues.

1. *Program design and planning.* Has a social problem been correctly identified as to extent and location? Do the ideas underlying the program

correspond to existing social science understanding concerning the problem in question, i.e., is the program theoretically sound? Does the design of the program correspond to its intended goals? Have target populations been correctly identified and located, and has a delivery mechanism specified that shows some promise of reaching the intended targets?

2. *Program monitoring.* How well is a program being implemented? Is it reaching the target units to which it was addressed? Is it providing the services, resources, or other benefits intended in the program design? In short, who is getting what and how?

3. *Outcome assessment.* Is the program effective in achieving its intended goals? Is the program responsible for producing the observed outcomes, or can the results of the program be explained by some alternative process other than the program? Are there unintended side effects of the program?

4. *Economic efficiency.* What are the costs of delivering services and benefits to program participants? Is the program an efficient use of resources compared with alternative uses of resources?

While in principle an evaluation of a specific program might be addressed to all four issues, usually in the sequence shown, in practice an evaluation rarely can address more than one or two. Only for newly contemplated programs that are followed through from initial conceptualization to full implementation is it possible to conduct a comprehensive evaluation that covers all issues. For established programs previously designed and implemented, it is usually possible only to monitor, assess outcomes, and estimate economic efficiency. In this chapter, therefore, we are concerned primarily with those three topics. Issues involved in the design of social programs are discussed in greater detail in Chapter 3 (see also Rossi, Freeman, and Wright, 1979).

Systematic evaluation shares many characteristics with other social science research. It strives to be objective and replicable. That is, it uses techniques that when employed by different observers would produce the same results. It strives also to test its conclusions against alternative explanatory schemes, seeking to rule out competing explanations. To contrast, nonsystematic evaluations tend not to be replicable and often do not rule out competing alternative explanations, and the results tend to depend on the persons conducting the evaluation.

The starting point of any evaluation study is the question of whether or not a particular social program "works." The answer to such a seemingly simple question, however, is complex. For example, to evaluate whether or not an employment training program is working involves deciding what is meant specifically by "working," since such a program may be seen as a means of teaching new occupational skills, or as a method for raising the incomes of poor people, or as a vehicle for providing income support to persons during their training, or even as a means of undercutting radical political activity. Each goal implies different criteria of assessment.

Programs may also be evaluated at different levels. For example, at the planning level, a program may be judged on the basis of whether or not the characteristics, needs, and distribution of its target population are properly defined or known in sufficient detail. A training program aimed at unemployed women may be poorly designed if there are no provisions for child care arrangements or transportation.

At the implementation level, a program may be evaluated as not working because it is not reaching its intended target population, or because its delivery of services is not consistent with the program design. Lack of effectiveness in reaching its intended goals may be due to faulty implementation, and therefore it is essential to undertake monitoring evaluations prior to assessing program impact. Simple accounting of the programs is also essential. How many clients are being served? What services are being provided? What is the cost?

The next level in an evaluation is to assess the outcomes of the program, to document whether the program produces the anticipated change, and to establish that it was in fact the intervention (the program) that produced the outcome and not some other process. Do trainees in fact acquire new job skills? Or is the success of the training program established if the graduates find and maintain jobs during a standard time period? What is the nature of the economy and available employment opportunities? And finally, a program may be working but be economically irrational or inefficient when considered against alternative methods of finding employment.

Not all social programs can be evaluated. The major examples of non-evaluable programs are those whose goals and/or means of reaching these goals are so vaguely stated that clear criteria for judging the success of the program cannot be established. Thus, a program designed to "improve the quality of life" cannot be evaluated without detailed specification of what is meant by "quality of life." Similarly, a program that uses "all possible means" to achieve a given goal cannot be evaluated because the intervention cannot be clearly defined (and hence observed).

Setting goals and specifying the broad outlines of a program are the provinces of policy makers. While evaluators may help policy makers to articulate goals more clearly, the choice among goals and methods is largely a matter of value preference. However, determining whether a particular method will achieve its intended goal is a process of technical judgment in which social science knowledge and theory come into play. This division of labor between the social scientist as evaluator and the policy maker as program designer is what defines program evaluation as an applied social science field.

Program evaluation is an applied social science in the sense that the independent and dependent variables of evaluation research are determined by the policy makers and the nature of the problem being addressed. Thus, samples to be used are determined by the definition of the target population for the program. Any descriptive studies undertaken in a monitoring evaluation must focus on the nature of the services being provided by the program to the appropriate target population. In impact assessments the independent variable is the program or intervention, and desirable outcomes are the dependent variables. Of course, the researcher should anticipate secondary effects and unintended consequences of an intervention, but the central research topics are given in the policy makers' statements of goals and means. The evaluation researcher may have to forego considerable control over the specification of the problem, the variables to be included, and the sample to be used, since these may be determined largely by the program under evaluation.

The requirements of the research setting and the realities of the context may place further restrictions on the evaluation. For example, time, legal, political, or ethical considerations may preclude the use of the most scientifically sound research designs and methodologies. If the findings of an evaluation are to have any effect on policy making or on decisions to modify, expand, or curtail the program, they must be available on time, conducted using politically acceptable techniques, and reported in easily understandable and nontechnical terms.

In short, these distinctive features of evaluation research—how the research problems are defined, how the variables and samples are chosen, how hypotheses are formulated, how the results must be reported, and the usually restricted time frames involved—affect the conditions under which program evaluation takes place. They do not, however, change the logic, methods, and techniques employed. Program evaluation does not use specially devised theories or methods. It is basic social science applied to problems defined politically.

HOW IS PROGRAM EVALUATION IMPLEMENTED?

Assuming that a program has been designed for which there is some theoretical justification and whose goals have been specified clearly enough to develop firm criteria for successful attainment, the main evaluation problems center on what research methods are most likely to provide useful and plausible data concerning program implementation and outcomes.

Methodological Issues in Monitoring Implementation

The aim of program monitoring is to provide information on the following issues.

First, does the program in fact exist? Are services being delivered? While this question may seem obvious to the point of silliness, there is evidence that legislated programs have been diluted to the point of nonexistence by local-level agencies designated to administer the programs (McLaughlin, 1975).

Second, is the intervention being delivered in the form intended? Agencies with delivery missions may transform programs in the implementation process that end up as caricatures of intentions (Kassebaum, Ward, and Wilner, 1971).

Third, is the program being delivered to the specified target population? A training program that recruits skilled persons can hardly be as effective in achieving goals as one that starts with an untrained group. Alternatively, hoping to achieve success, program administrators may "cream" a target population and enroll only those with whom the program will have the easiest time.

The evaluator's answers to these monitoring questions provide information to policy makers and program administrators about whether the program is sufficiently well implemented to justify evaluating its outcomes. Monitoring also provides information that enables planners to redesign programs to accomplish aims.

The methodological issues faced in monitoring evaluations are those facing any descriptive research. Measures should be reliable and valid. Observations should be generalized to a reasonable universe. Specific approaches may vary from qualitative observations and participant observation techniques to highly structured surveys (Wright, 1979). Carefully kept records of clients by program staff have been routine for health interventions, but the use of computerized record keeping systems, known as management information systems, is increasing and generating useful evaluation data.

Monitoring evaluations require data not only on program participants, but also on program dropouts and units who are eligible but nonparticipating. Such cases are important in order to detect whatever participation bias may be present, to help qualify the program impact that is observed subsequently, and to measure more precisely the program costs and benefits. The findings of monitoring evaluations are also useful for program staff in meeting their managerial and accountability responsibilities and in making decisions about program modifications whenever appropriate.

Methodological Issues in Outcome Assessment

Outcome assessment is beset with at least two serious problems. In the first place, a social program should produce effects over and above those that would ordinarily be expected. Thus, a training program designed to increase long-term earnings has to be judged against what participants would have earned without the training. The second problem is that social programs in this historical period are likely to be only slight revisions of existing programs and hence not likely to have very strong effects. For example, any educational reform is not likely to make very much difference in learning, especially as compared to the effects of schooling versus no schooling. Thus, programs have to be evaluated using methods powerful enough to detect weak effects.

The methodological considerations for designing appropriate outcome evaluations have been summarized as problems in attaining several types of validity (Campbell and Stanley, 1966; Cook and Campbell, 1979). Any outcome evaluation, therefore, is judged by its ability to attain findings that are highly valid as described below.

Of primary importance is internal validity, or the degree of certainty that the program produced the observed net outcomes. Internal validity is largely a function of the research design. There is almost universal agreement that the randomized controlled experiment constitutes the ideal model for evaluating the effectiveness of a program, because it is the best research design for reaching conclusions with high internal validity. In a randomized controlled experiment to test the effects of a program, persons or units are randomly assigned to either a participating (experimental) group or a control group. The first receives the intervention and the second does not, so that any differences that are observed after the program between the participating and nonparticipating groups can be inferred to be caused by the program and not by any preconditions or differences between the groups. Randomization assures that the two groups will differ only through the operation of chance processes, and that any differences are not due to systematic selection biases. For example, if program participation is left to those who wish to enroll, there is a strong likelihood that those who seek out the program are more motivated, more able, and capable of improving their condition regardless of the program. The reverse can also occur, when those who choose to participate are the ones who are worse off, with the result that the program is less likely to appear effective.

Campbell and Stanley (1966) have specified potential "threats to internal validity" accompanying a variety of research designs. These constitute possible obstructions to assessing properly the effects of interventions. In addition to self-selection, such threats include past experiences or relatively enduring characteristics of the group studied that make participating groups differ from the comparison group. Internal validity can also be threatened by a wide variety of potentially interfering events that are either contemporaneous with the program or reflect historical trends and that may produce changes that either enhance or mask the effects of the program. Maturational and developmental changes may produce the observed outcomes instead of the program. For example, children ordinarily achieve cognitive gains as a function of growth and maturation. Artifacts of the research procedure may also be responsible for the observed outcomes. In short, threats to internal validity constitute alternative plausible explanations for the observed outcomes of a program. An evaluation design must be able to produce findings that are purged of all such nonprogram influences, so as to produce evidence of program effects that are the *net* of all those contaminating influences.

Randomized controlled experiments are not feasible when 1) a program is already in full operation, 2) when withholding the intervention is legally impossible or unethical if a hardship is created, so that experimental and control groups cannot be constructed through randomization, or 3) when only a short time is available for the research, since a well conducted field experiment may take a number of years to operate and additional years to analyze the results. Hence, many evaluations employ designs that depart in one or more crucial ways from the format of randomized controlled experiments and consequently are not as strong in internal validity. The crucial departures usually involve substituting a control group constructed in some nonrandom way, or controlling variables statistically in attempts to rule out competing explanations through multivariate analyses.

While internal validity is a necessary condition for good evaluation, it is not sufficient. External validity is also necessary if the evaluation results are to be useful for policy making. External validity refers to the generalizability of the results, or the ability of a research design to allow inferences about program effects beyond the specific groups and contexts being tested. For example, a well-executed experimental evaluation of an educational program shown to produce certain achievement gains cannot be generalized to the entire population if it was carried out in a wealthy and innovative school system. The problems posed by threats to the external validity are usually easier to counter than those posed by internal validity, because modern sampling methods have advanced to the point where most of the problems of sampling individuals, households, or organizations have been solved, at least in principle. The main obstacle to the application of powerful and unbiased sampling designs has been cost. The best designs involve methods that insure the selection of each person, household, organization, or other unit from the target population with a known probability. The external validity of evaluations based on such probability samples is high.

A third type of validity, construct validity, refers to the problem of valid measurement. The concepts or constructs involved in both the treatment and outcomes of the program must be validly translated into appropriate research operations resulting in well measured variables. The instruments employed ought to actually measure what is intended.

The final consideration is policy or substantive validity: whether or not a program or treatment effect is large enough to become the basis of policy change. The distinction is between results that are statistically significant (given large enough samples, for example, even small effects are statistically significant) and those that are substantively significant. A small effect such as an earnings increase of $5 per week as a result of a program may not justify the expenditures of funds to produce such a difference. The techniques of cost-benefit and cost-effectiveness analysis may be applied to such considerations. Ultimately such decisions involve making value judgments about the worth of demonstrated effects.

HOW HAS PROGRAM EVALUATION BEEN USED?

Evaluation for Monitoring Program Implementation

The more dramatic monitoring evaluation findings have been instances in which program delivery has failed, or some cases in which the intervention that was planned and mandated never took place. For example, McLaughlin (1975) reviewed the evidence on the implementation of Title I of the Elementary and Secondary Education Act, which allocated billions of dollars yearly to aid local schools in overcoming students' poverty-associated educational deprivations. Local school authorities were often unable to describe their Title I activities in any detail, and few activities could be identified as educational services delivered to school children, although the funds had been expended in the school systems. Similarly, in some cases manpower training programs supposedly in existence during the 1960s did not recruit any persons for training.

The intervention may be diluted so that an insufficient amount of the treatment actually gets delivered—for example, insufficient funds, inadequate services, or just ritual compliance with a regulation. In a program designed to substitute employment for welfare support, jobs were provided that paid less than Aid for Dependent Children (AFDC). Affirmative action laws require organizations to place public advertisements for positions that may have already been filled informally. Or the wrong treatment may be delivered. In an experiment in a California prison to test the effectiveness of group counselling in reducing recidivism, hostile and untrained prison guards had to be used as group leaders instead of group therapists. Other instances in which the delivery of a program violates the program design occur when there is a difference between pilot or test runs of a program and mass production or full program implementation. For example, interventions that might work well in the hands of highly motivated and trained deliverers may end up as failures when put in the hands of a mass delivery system lacking training and motivation, as illustrated by the computer assisted instruction attempted in school systems (Rossi, 1978).

Outcome Evaluation

Outcome evaluation seeks to establish, with as much certainty as possible, whether or not an intervention is producing its intended effects. The policy importance of outcome evaluation is clear and straightforward. Social programs are costly. Hence, decisions concerning their establishment, continuation, expansion, or curtailment have to be made with some care. Knowledge of outcomes and effectiveness can be crucial input for such decisions. Indeed, the trend in current public and private decisions on programs is to require the allocation of a portion of new program resources to outcome evaluation research, as in the "Sunset Laws."

High quality outcome evaluation demands systematic and rigorous effort. The end product must be causal statement of the form, "the intervention program causes (produces) the following outcomes ...." Such research conclusions require ruling out other competing, plausible explanations of the results (or lack of results) of social interventions. We must be as sure as possible that it really was the intervention (program) that produced the observed results, instead of something else unrelated to the program. In short, the internal validity of the evaluation is crucial.

This mandate can be achieved in principle by methods available at our current level of technical skills. However, the realities of the world of social action, including the cooperation of program staff and target participants and the press for timely and unambiguous findings, may preclude the application of well established evaluation procedures. Essentially, the assessment of program outcomes involves comparing information about participants and nonparticipants before and after an intervention. In this section we review some examples of outcome evaluations proceeding from the most to the least rigorous research designs in terms of their ability to provide valid conclusions.

Randomized Experimental Designs. As noted earlier, the best method for insuring valid comparisons between program participants and nonparticipants before and after an intervention involves a randomized controlled experimental design. Some examples follow.

In the 1960s, the California Adult Authority (the agency in charge of prisons) had installed in most state prisons a voluntary group counseling program to help prisoners understand their motivations for criminal activity through participation in weekly group counseling. Presumably the understanding gained would reduce the prisoners' adherence to peer group norms within prison and enhance their ability to adjust to civilian life and thereby succeed on parole.

Taking advantage of a new prison that was to be constructed, evaluators received permission and encouragement from the California prison agency to run a controlled experiment (Kassebaum, Ward, and Wilner, 1971). The prison was built in four more-or-less isolated "quads." Two of the quads were designated to receive varying forms of counseling (small and large group counseling), a third quad was designated as a control with no counseling, and the fourth quad was reserved for special behavior problem prisoners and was excluded from the study. As new prisoners arrived at the prison when it was opened, they were assigned at random to the first three quads.

When prisoners in both the control and experimental groups were released on parole, their parole records for two years beyond release were examined for evidence of adjustment to civilian life. No differences were found among the experimental and control groups. The group counseling interventions were judged a failure.

In the late 1960s, when federal officials concerned with poverty began to consider changing welfare policy to providing some sort of guaranteed annual income for all families, the Office of Economic Opportunity (OEO) launched a large scale field experiment to test one of the crucial issues in such a program (Kershaw and Fair, 1976). Economic theory predicted that the provision of supplementary income payments to poor families would be a work disincentive (i.e., they would reduce efforts to find and hold jobs).

Started in 1968, the experiment was carried on for three years. It was administered by Mathematica, Inc., a research firm in Princeton, New Jersey and by the Institute for Research on Poverty at the University of Wisconsin. The experiment was aimed at a target population of intact families with incomes below 150 percent of the poverty level, whose male heads were between ages 18 and 58. Eight treatments consisted of various combinations of both guarantees, pegged to what was then the current poverty level and the rates at which payments were taxed, or adjusted to earnings received by the families. For example, for a family in one of the treatments with a guaranteed income of 125 percent of the then-current poverty level, if no one in the family had any earnings, the family received that guaranteed amount. However, if that treatment had a tax rate of 50 percent and someone in the family received earned income, payments were reduced at the rate of $.50 for each dollar earned, until the payments were zero. Other treatments consisted of tax rates that ranged from 30 percent to 70 percent and guaranteed levels that varied from 50 percent to 125 percent of the poverty line. A control group consisted of families who did not receive any payments.

The experiment was conducted in four New Jersey cities and one in Pennsylvania. A large household survey identified eligible families, who were invited to participate. Participating families were randomly allocated to one of the experimental groups or the control group. Families in the experimental group reported their earnings each month. If a family's earnings statement indicated eligibility for transfer payments, a check was mailed.

Families were interviewed in great detail prior to enrollment in the program and at the end of each quarter over the three years of the experiment. These interviews generated data on such topics as employment, earnings, consumption, health, and various social psychological factors. These data were then analyzed, along with the monthly earnings reports, to determine whether those receiving payments diminished their work effort (as measured in hours of work, for example) relative to the comparable families in the control group. Results showed a slight work disincentive effect induced by the payments, which was especially strong among secondary earners and whites (as opposed to blacks).

Despite their power, randomized experiments constitute a relatively small proportion of completed evaluations, primarily because the method is feasible only for assessing outcomes of interventions that can be administered on the basis of chance selection to some portions of a target population and withheld from others. Thus, when a policy mandates that those who are eligible become participants, or when a program has been in effect for some time and the evaluator has no option in participation selection, or when there are other political or ethical impediments to randomization, or when the costs of resources and time are too great, other methods may have to be used.

Designs Using Constructed Control Groups

When experimental and control groups cannot be established through randomized assignment, other selection methods may be used to construct control groups. The goal is to identify and measure a group of potential targets for an intervention who are comparable in essential respects to those exposed to that intervention. For example, in an evaluation of the effects of nutritional supplements on intellectual functioning of children, such supplements were given to all children in some villages in a developing country, while observations were also made on children in other villages to whom nutritional supplements were not given (Freeman, et al., 1977).

In another instance, the Education Voucher Demonstration was designed to introduce free enterprise concepts into the educational process (Gramlich and Koshel, 1975). Under the voucher concept, parents freely select a school for their child and receive a credit or voucher equal to the cost of the child's education that is paid directly to the school upon enrollment. It was presumed that this form of school financing would foster competition among the schools and improve the quality of education by making schools more responsive to students' needs. An initial external evaluation at the conclusion of the first year found, however, a relative loss in reading achievement for students in six public schools that participated in the voucher demonstration. A secondary evaluation re-examined these findings from the first year of the voucher demonstration (Wortman, et al., 1978).

Schools were divided into three groups: 1) voucher schools with a traditional academic orientation, 2) voucher schools with an innovative orientation, and 3) nonvoucher comparison schools. These schools were not randomly assigned. The comparison schools were selected from the same districts and were comparable in terms of ethnic and socioeconomic composition, welfare status, etc. The results indicate that the deleterious reading effect of the voucher demonstration was confined to only a few schools with programs featuring nontraditional, innovative curricula.

The major problem with constructed controls is that there can never be any certainty that they are comparable to the program participants in all relevant ways that may affect the results. Other ways to construct comparable controls, therefore, involve matching the program participants with units that have the same characteristics on factors thought to be important in the intervention. For example, in educational research, control groups are often constructed by selecting for each student who participates in a program a "partner" who constitutes the closest possible equivalent in terms of age, sex, family characteristics, test scores, and so on.

Time Series Designs. Another strategy for obtaining control observations can be used when substantial longitudinal (time series) data exist before and after an intervention, so that participants can be used as their own controls. For example, in studies of certain disease control or prevention programs, where time series of vital statistics of known reliability are readily available, the time series design can be applied in assessing program effects. Data on the incidence of the disease can be plotted on a graph that extends back a number of time periods (say, monthly intervals) prior to the introduction of the program and forwards after its introduction for a sufficient period of time. If the program was effective, one would find a drop in the incidence, i.e., an interruption in the time series. Sophisticated statistical methods have been developed for the analysis of time series.

In a typical appropriate application of this approach, the effect of the Massachusetts gun control law that went into effect in 1975 was analyzed (Deutsch and Alt, 1977). The law mandates a one-year minimum sentence on conviction of carrying a firearm without a special license. The incidences in Boston of gun-related offenses of homicide, assault with a gun, and armed robbery were examined for changes in their levels, using data series covering the time prior to, concurrent with, and after the enactment of the law. The evaluation concluded that the gun control law decreased both armed robbery and assault with a gun, although no significant changes in the homicide rate were observed.

The major threats to the validity of time series designs involve the possibility that historical trends or maturational changes in the participants may in fact be responsible for shifts in the time series rather than the program being evaluated. Other interfering events occurring at the same time as the intervention may also produce observed differences before and after the intervention. Therefore, when possible, control observations over the same time period are also used in longitudinal designs.

Statistical Adjustments and Cross-Sectional Designs. In many circumstances, control or comparison groups cannot be constructed and time series data are not available. In particular, when a program has been in operation for some time prior to an evaluation and has had wide coverage of its target population, there is often no alternative to estimating outcomes by using multivariate statistical methods.

Many evaluations are made using cross-sectional designs. Observations are made at a single point in time, contrasting those who have participated in a program with those who have not. Typically, the target population is sampled and a survey is administered to gather information on a large number of possibly confounding variables. Differences between levels of exposure to an intervention are held constant through statistical analyses, as well as other relevant differences between participants and nonparticipants.

An excellent use of a cross-sectional design using existing data was an elaborate attempt to discern whether family planning programs of the federal government had an impact on fertility (Cutright and Jaffe, 1977). Taking advantage of the existence of a survey of all family planning clinics in the United States that included measures of the services delivered in each unit, the authors linked that information to vital statistics for the same areas. The main program variable was rate of enrollment in family planning clinics (constructed from the survey), while the outcome variable was the fertility rate for the same areas (from the vital statistics census, measured in various ways). Statistical controls were introduced for population density, education, migration, marital status, in-school status, race, labor force, age, and parity. The program was found to have fairly strong negative effects on the fertility rates of both white and black married women in all subgroups defined by age and socioeconomic status, after controlling for the other factors. The impact on fertility was found to be proportional to the measured level of activity of the family planning units.

Approximate Methods. Other less rigorous research designs are sometimes used for evaluating outcomes when resources, time, or technical skills preclude the use of the procedures described above. Unfortunately, such designs have many deficiencies because they are typically based on slim data and usually provide no opportunity to rule out contaminating influences that may account for the observed effects. In some situations, however, these less rigorous methods constitute the only possibility for evaluation.

For example, in the 1930s during the New Deal, a series of agricultural reforms were enacted, most of which were short-lived. One of the reforms involved purchasing land and selling it to small farmers for homesteading at very favorable prices and financing terms. A few of these projects were started before protests from establishment agricultural interests brought about a cancellation of the program.

In the 1970s, Salamon (1974) conducted an "evaluation" of the New Deal land resettlement program by examining the current owners of parcels of land that were sold to black tenant farmers in eight land resettlement projects in five states. Land ownership records were searched to determine whether the land in question remained in the hands of persons related to or descended from the families to whom the parcels were originally sold in the 1930s. Salamon concluded that the project was successful in creating a permanent black middle class, since much of the land was still in the hands of the original settlers and their descendants.

Cost-Benefit and Cost-Effectiveness Analyses

Effective programs that can be implemented are clearly desirable, especially if their costs are less than their benefits. The art of making such cost calculations, originally developed for evaluating the efficiency of technical and engineering projects, has been extended, at least conceptually, to social programs.

A comprehensive cost-benefit analysis requires estimates of the benefits of a program, both tangible and intangible, and the costs of undertaking the program, both direct and indirect. Once specified, the benefits and costs are then translated into a common measure, usually (but not necessarily) a monetary unit. The benefits and costs can then be compared, generally by computing either a benefit-to-cost ratio (benefits divided by costs), the net benefits (benefits minus costs), or some other value (internal rate of return) for summarizing the results of the analysis.

Given adequate estimates, cost-benefit results provide a straightforward assessment of economic efficiency that can be used to guide resource allocation decisions with respect to economically desirable options. Although many other factors besides economic efficiency are brought to bear in policy making, planning, and program implementation, considerations of economic efficiency are almost always critical, given the universality of scarce resources.

Cost-benefit analysis requires the adoption of a certain economic perspective. In addition, certain assumptions must be made in order to translate program inputs and outputs into monetary figures. As noted, there is disagreement in the field as to which specific procedures to utilize. Moreover, the assumptions made in developing definitions and measures of costs and benefits strongly influence the resulting conclusions. All the requisite data for cost-benefit calculations are seldom available. Nonetheless, even if specific applications and conclusions can be questioned, one advantage of this approach is that the discipline imposed by cost-benefit analysis forces the evaluator, policy maker, planner, and manager to articulate economic consideration that might otherwise remain implicit or unstated.

Cost-benefit analysis is especially appropriate for technical and industrial projects, where it is reasonable to place a monetary value on benefits as well as costs. Some examples might include engineering projects designed to reduce the cost of electricity to consumers or to increase the ease of transportation with new roads, and irrigation projects to increase crop yields. A monetary estimation of benefits, however, is not possible in many social programs where setting a monetary value on benefits may be virtually impossible, or where, in the best of circumstances, only a portion of the known program outputs may be reasonably valued. For example, it is possible to translate future occupational gains deriving from an educational program into monetary values. But the issues are complex when attempting to monetize the benefits of other social interventions such as fertility control programs or health services projects, since ultimately one has to place a value on human life in order to fully monetize these program benefits.

For these reasons, cost-effectiveness analysis rather than cost-benefit analysis is often seen as the more appropriate technique for resource allocation considerations of social interventions. Cost-effectiveness requires quantifying program costs and benefits, but the benefits do not have to be monetized, only the costs. For example, a free textbook distribution program for rural primary school children could have cost-effectiveness findings expressed as follows: each $325 of total program costs increased reading scores by an average of one grade. For cost-effectiveness analysis, the outputs or benefits are expressed in terms of the actual substantive outcomes rather than in monetary values. A cost-effectiveness analysis allows comparison and ranking of choices among potential programs according to the magnitudes of their effects relative to their costs. (For a more detailed discussion and examples of cost-benefit and cost-effectiveness analyses, see Rossi, Freeman, and Wright, 1979; Ch. 8).

WHAT HAS PROGRAM EVALUATION ACCOMPLISHED?

Program evaluation is intended to provide information useful in the formulation and administration of rational policy. The decision-making process is complicated, and evaluation results are potentially useful at almost every point in this process. In some cases, decision makers and/or program administrators may contract for an evaluation because they need critical input for continuation, modification, or termination of a program. The evaluators may be under pressure to produce information quickly, but they have a receptive audience.

In other situations, however, the parties in the decision-making process may react slowly to evaluation findings. Even more disconcerting is the case where evaluation results are seemingly ignored, despite their potentially valuable and often expensive input. A major reason for ignoring the results of an evaluation is that they are only one of the many elements in decision making.

Many parties are typically involved in social programs. Sponsors, managers, and operators, and sometimes the participants, often have very high stakes in the continuation of a program. The outcomes of a political process may be viewed as balancing the representations of a variety of interested parties. Evaluation information is then simply one more argument for one side or another in this balance. As with other expert witnesses, the evaluator's testimony concerning program effectiveness may be given more weight than uninformed opinion or shrewd guesses, but it does not determine the future of the program.

What have been the roles of evaluation in determining policy decisions? First, evaluations have been useful in deciding technical planning and management questions. Second, evaluations have provided information about program outcomes upon which decision makers have acted. Third, evaluations have had some general impact on decision making by changing the grounds of political argumentation.

Role of Evaluation in Technical Issues

A technical issue is neutral with respect to policy and values. That is, the various parties involved in a social program have no stake in how the issue is decided. For example, it may make little difference to any of the parties in an adult literacy program whether the teaching method relies on recognition of whole words or of individual letters. An evaluation that could prove the clear superiority of one method over the other would have little difficulty affecting decision making. Clearly, there are many technical issues to be resolved in the design, execution, and implementation of social programs. The role that evaluation research can play in deciding such issues is considerable and important.

Evaluation results, especially at the program design stage, have also been used by management to change its focus, implementation methods, or even goals, thereby improving or perhaps salvaging a program that might otherwise have failed. This is most likely to occur when a new intervention contains many components and different means of reaching goals.

One of the clearest examples of the resolution of a technical issue through evaluation research has been the contribution of the income maintenance experiments in setting income reporting periods for households on welfare. Traditional procedures for income reporting called for the upgrading of income reports from recipients, either at their initiative or at periodic—usually semi-annually or annually—reassessments. Careful research during the income maintenance experiments indicates that monthly reporting increases accuracy considerably and makes the payment system more responsive to change in the income status of households. Welfare reform legislation currently being considered by Congress contains provisions for income reporting on a monthly basis, largely influenced by the testimony of researchers who conducted the income maintenance experiments.

Evaluation as Program Validation

There are many reasons why evaluations of program outcomes often find no positive effects. The programs that are tested are sometimes slight alterations or increments to existing programs. Anticipated effects are necessarily slight and therefore hard to detect. In addition, program alterations are usually designed to meet needs of target populations that are harder to reach than the existing program has already been reaching. In general, interventions are more likely to produce measurable effects in situations of high demonstrated need and no competing or existing programs.

In the abstract, it is equally as valid (and from a resource commitment standpoint, important) to evaluate programs with potentially weak and strong effects. However, the long-term influence of evaluation on social program development is enhanced by evaluations with positive findings. In the face of scarce resources for both interventions and evaluations, judicious choices should be made about what programs to evaluate. Evaluators may have a responsibility to influence program planning and design to maximize the opportunities for evidence of positive outcomes, and consequently give less attention to evaluating all outcomes.

Thus, when a program is inherently benign or regarded as intrinsically good, demonstrated effects may not be very important. The obverse also holds. A program that has the potential for inflicting harm should be evaluated with extra care because the risks of accepting such a program when it is in fact not useful are greater (Berk and Rossi, 1976).

Evaluation as General Information on Social Problems

Although the main role of evaluation is to provide information on specific social programs, another role may in the long run be as (if not more) important in the design and implementation of interventions. This role is providing general information on how social programs operate and on their effectiveness. While no well established program that is found to be ineffective may be discontinued, negative evaluation results may affect whether new programs using the same philosophy will be started.

One of the major reasons why employment training programs have been deemphasized is the difficulty of discerning any major effects on either participants or the general unemployment rate. Similarly, 15 years of evaluation research on educational programs has led various governmental groups and foundations to invest in basic research on learning processes, since evaluations of many interventions such as Headstart have shown that such innovations were at best marginal improvements over existing educational practices.

Thus, one of the major lasting effects of evaluation is to increase the sophistication of our knowledge about how social programs operate. This general rise in knowledge has filtered into the administration of social programs, to some degree into legislative bodies, and possibly to a lesser degree to the general public. It has made special inroads into the curricula in universities, and it may well serve as the knowledge base for the decision makers of the future.

WHERE IS PROGRAM EVALUATION GOING?

Program evaluation as an applied social science research activity is still in its formative stage. Its final form as a mature and fully developed science can be only dimly perceived. There are, nonetheless, some recent signs that reveal the likely characteristics of evaluation research in the future.

One of the youthful excesses of program evaluation research was an undue emphasis on program effects and a relative neglect of the policy and societal processes by which these outputs were produced. It is one thing to say that a program has failed to achieve its aims but quite another to say why. More and more, evaluation researchers have come to recognize that there is often a massive slippage between the "program as designed" and the "program as delivered." It is probably this slippage, more than any other single factor, that causes program failures. Because of this recognition, it seems clear that program evaluation in the future will be as concerned with the delivery or implementation of programs as it has in the past been concerned with program effects.

From the start, the idea behind program evaluation was to assess the effects of programs and policies either already in the field or at least in the late design phases. There is increasing recognition that policy experiments can be conducted on a small scale in advance of full-scale program delivery, and that such pilot tests can be useful not only in assessing probable effects but also in making cost-efficient decisions about which policies to introduce. The various income maintenance, housing, health, education, supported work, and other experiments are archetypes of the kinds of predelivery policy experiments that seem likely to grow in frequency and importance. The well-known superiority of experimental methods for assessing causal patterns, and the high costs that often result when policy decisions are made in an information vacuum, suggest strongly that future evaluation research will deal as much with cost-efficiency evaluations of prospective programs as it has thus far dealt with outcome evaluations of ongoing interventions.

More and more, policy makers at all levels are coming to recognize the importance of program evaluation. Recent interest in "Sunset Laws" (whereby programs lacking demonstrable effectiveness are automatically terminated) is testimony to this trend. Enacting legislation for new social programs often contains specific stipulations about program evaluation. In the past, the uncertain legitimacy of applied research in general, and evaluation research in particular, has been one of the barriers to attracting first-rate research talent into this field (Rossi, Wright, and Wright, 1978). The increasing legitimacy given to these activities by both government and academics bodes well for the future of applied social science.

Finally, one of the most distinguishing and remarkable features of program evaluation is its strongly multidisciplinary character. The evaluation of a major social program provides an occasion for researchers from several disciplines to orient their collective intelligence around a common problem and to set aside disciplinary differences in theory, concept, and technique. In this sense, program evaluation—and the broader field of applied social research in general—may present an opportunity, perhaps even a catalyst, for the unification of the social sciences, a goal which has long been sought for but which has, so far, remained elusive.

REFERENCES AND SUGGESTED READINGS

*Anderson, S.B. and S.A. Ball. 1978. *The Profession and Practice of Program Evaluation.* San Francisco: Jossey-Bass.
    This volume is a survey of the types of work done by evaluation researchers and the kinds of training evaluation researchers believe to be needed to practice successfully in that field.
Berk, R. and P.H. Rossi. 1976. "Doing Good or Worse: Evaluation Research Politically Re-Examined." *Social Problems* 23(Feb):337–49.
*Campbell, D.T. and J. Stanley. 1966. *Experimental and Quasi-Experimental Designs for Research.* Chicago: Rand McNally.
    This is a classic discussion of the comparative strengths and weaknesses of a variety of research designs. It contains an extensive discussion of types of validity.
Cook, T.D. and D.T. Campbell. 1979. *Quasi-Experimentation: Design and*

Analysis Issues for Field Settings. Chicago: Rand McNally.

Cutright, P. and F.S. Jaffe. 1977. *Impact of Family Planning Programs on Fertility.* New York: Praeger.

Deutsch, S.J. and F.B. Alt. 1977. "The Effects of Massachusetts Gun Control Law on Gun-Related Crimes in Boston." *Evaluation Quarterly* 1(Nov): 543–67.

Freeman, H.E., R.F. Klein, J. Kagan, and C. Yarborough. 1977. "Relations Between Nutrition and Cognition in Rural Guatemala." *American Journal of Public Health* 67(Mar):233–39.

Gramlich, E.M. and P.P. Koshel. 1975. *Educational Performance Contracting: An Evaluation of an Experiment.* Washington, D.C.: Brookings Institution.

*Guttentag, M. and E. Struening. 1975. *A Handbook of Evaluation Research.* (two volumes) Beverly Hills, Calif.: Sage.

> Encyclopedic in coverage, this volume contains contributions from almost all the leaders in the field of evaluation research applied to most social program areas.

Kassebaum, G., D. Ward, and D. Wilner. 1971. *Prison Treatment and Parole Survival.* New York: John Wiley & Sons.

Kershaw, D. and J. Fair. 1976. *The New Jersey Income Maintenance Experiment.* (Vol. I) New York: Academic Press.

McLaughlin, M. 1975. *Evaluation and Reform: The Elementary and Secondary Education Act of 1965.* Cambridge, Mass.: Ballinger.

*Riecken, H.W. and R.F. Boruch (eds.). 1974. *Social Experimentation: A Method for Planning and Evaluating Social Interventions.* New York: Academic Press.

> The rationale and logic of social experimentation and specifics on how to execute experiments for evaluation is explored in this book. Examples of completed randomized field experiments in many areas are provided.

Rossi, P.H. 1978. "Issues in the Evaluation of Human Services Delivery." *Evaluation Quarterly* 2(Nov):573–99.

*Rossi, P.H., H.E. Freeman, and S.R. Wright. 1979. *Evaluation: A Systematic Approach.* Beverly Hills, Calif.: Sage.

> This work is an introductory survey of evaluation research, liberally supplemented with many examples of researches conducted in the past 20 years. It provides an overview of evaluation research as applied to program design, implementation, impact assessment and cost efficiency.

Rossi, P.H., J.D. Wright, and S.R. Wright. 1978. "The Theory and Practice of Applied Social Research." *Evaluation Quarterly* 2(May):171–92.

Salamon, L.M. 1974. *The Time Dimension in Policy Evaluation: The Case of the New Deal Land Reform Experiments.* Durham, N.C.: Duke University. Center for Urban and Regional Development Policy.

Wortman, P.M., C.S. Reichardt, and R.G. St. Pierre. 1978. "The First Year of the Education Voucher Demonstration: A Secondary Analysis of Student Achievement Test Scores." *Evaluation Quarterly* 2(May):193–214.

Wright, S.R. 1979. *Quantitative Methods and Statistics: A Guide to Social Research.* Beverly Hills, Calif.: Sage.

Part
B

IMPROVING
SOCIAL
INSTITUTIONS

One of Max Weber's principal concerns was to determine how social organizations in modern societies could best function to attain their desired goals. His ideal bureaucratic model of an efficient and effective organization was built around such features as: 1) a formal structure of clearly defined positions and relationships, 2) narrowly and precisely defined tasks and roles, 3) rational procedures such as standard rules and written records, and 4) a centralized hierarchy of authority based on legal principles and expert knowledge.* To a considerable extent, most complex organizations in contemporary societies are molded on this model, while other types of organizations such as the family and the community often incorporate several aspects of it.

In recent years, however, sociologists have begun to question the Weberian model. How applicable or desirable is the model to many of the organizations that comprise the major social institutions of societies? Both the members of these organizations and applied sociologists would like them to function as efficiently and effectively as possible. Weber's basic concern has not been rejected. But many of his prescribed means for improving organizational functioning are no longer accepted uncritically by applied sociologists.

We have learned, for instance, that when structural arrangements are overly formalized they are likely to become rigid and inflexible, making it difficult for the organization to adapt to changing circumstances. Loosely prescribed roles and informal relationships within an organization may be crucial for its survival and functional effectiveness. An overly narrow division of labor can lead to serious problems of task coordination, as well as denying participants a sense of personal fulfillment. Standard operating procedures and endless forms and documents can easily become the dominant concern of organizational members, so that the means become ends in themselves and the organization loses sight of its original goals. Hierarchical authority structures, meanwhile, tend to perpetuate established patterns of inequality among organizational members and to inhibit individual initiative and creativity. Decentralization of decision making may therefore be a vital requirement for organizational viability.

Applied sociologists are now examining critically all the different kinds of organizations that comprise the basic institutions of contemporary societies, in an effort to discover how they can be altered to improve their functioning. They are asking such questions as these: How can informal social arrangements within organizations be promoted and supported? How can role definitions be expanded and enriched? How can operating procedures be kept open and dynamic so that they remain means rather than ends? How can authority be distributed throughout all parts of an organization?

---

*Max Weber, *Economy and Society*, edited by Guenther Roth and Claus Wittich. (Berkeley: University of California Press, 1978), Ch. 11.

These and related questions about improving our social organizations are explored in the chapters in this section—dealing with the institutional spheres of families, neighborhoods and communities, communication networks, complex bureaucracies, and government agencies. In each area, the authors explore the major problems, existing knowledge, current programmatic efforts, functional accomplishments, and future trends that are relevant for applied sociology.

6 FAMILY DYNAMICS

John Scanzoni

Though debate and controversy pervade all areas of applied sociology, none is more fraught with deep feelings and emotions than the realm of family policy. On matters such as the Equal Rights Amendment, daycare centers, or contraception and abortion, opposing groups do not stop at debate. They launch crusades and holy wars to press their goals.

Opponents of changes in long-standing family policies are termed "Traditionals" by Novak (1977), who describes them as being "fiercely traditional ... in matters touching the family." While the United States has never had an explicit federal family policy, all the states have laws governing virtually every aspect of marriage and the family. These laws have typically reflected the influence of the Traditionals, who want no deviation from two centuries of established family policies.

In contrast, Novak applies the term "Progressives" to persons and groups who favor removing as many restrictions as possible governing marriage and family behaviors. Most—although not all—Progressives support policies that enhance the widest possible range of life choices for women, or what Safilios-Rothschild (1974) calls "liberation" social policy. Some Progressives place considerable emphasis on training programs that enable individuals and families to utilize existing social arrangements to their own advantage in the most effective fashion possible. Others favor a structuralist approach that focuses on changing the existing arrangements. Most Progressives realize, however, that effective family policy requires a blend of both programmatic and structuralist strategies.

Throughout this chapter we shall use Novak's terms of Traditionals and Progressives to describe the opposing sides in the controversy over marriage and family policy that is currently being waged throughout the United States. We shall focus on three overlapping family areas: children, adolescents, and adults.

115

Within each area we shall discuss 1) some major problems and issues, 2) current research knowledge concerning those problems, 3) public policies pertaining to each problem, 4) the consequences, if any, of these policies, and 5) future trends we may expect in each area.

WHAT ARE THE PROBLEMS?

Children of Working Mothers

A major review of family policy in the United States argues that "the most familiar" family trend is "the increase in the number of working mothers" (Advisory Committee, 1976:15). Over the last several decades, the proportion of employed mothers (with husbands present) whose children are under age six has risen dramatically. Among women who are single parents, the proportion who work is even higher and increasing even faster. Keniston (1977:5) asserts that "mothers who go off to a job every day are likely to worry about harming their children by neglecting them." He also makes a second generalization, which—like the first—may oversimplify reality: "For many generations in this country, the ideal ... has been the stay-at-home mother, involved full time with her children until they enter school, and, once the children are in the first grade, at home after school waiting for them" (p. 5). That idyllic scene may represent what some Traditionals would like to believe about the past, instead of what actually happened. Kanter (1977) reminds us that prior to industrialization, the great masses of women worked full time alongside their husbands, most of them struggling to eke out a bare existence from the soil. There was no leisure time for "full time mothering." Furthermore, among the social classes that possessed the leisure for full time mothering (the aristocracy, landed gentry, etc.) most women did not do it. They typically employed nannies and tutors and then shipped the children off to boarding school as soon as they were old enough.

With the advent of industrialization, whole families entered the factory system. Gradually, children and then women were edged out of the factories. Consequently, by the early twentieth century, great numbers of middle-class women found themselves with leisure time hitherto unknown except to the upper classes.

Two conditions emerged to fill that time vacuum. First, with the rise of a genuine middle class, many families could afford dwellings that demanded and deserved upkeep—that constantly needed to be painted, scrubbed, and swept. During that era, the idea became widely accepted that housekeeping is women's exclusive responsibility (Safilios-Rothschild, 1974). Furthermore, women's self-respect and social esteem became as dependent on good housekeeping as men's self-respect and esteem were dependent on occupational success.

The second condition that resulted from industrialization was the idea that "only children brought up with twenty-four-hours-per-day care by their natural mothers can have a normal development" (Safilios-Rothschild, 1974:18).

Freudian and other psychoanalytic theories concocted justifications for the belief that mothers should use their newly obtained leisure time to be constantly with their children.

In this area, the issue to which policy should be addressed is two-fold: 1) the working woman's feelings of guilt over alleged neglect of their children, and 2) the alleged harm done to children as a result of the mother's absence.

Children of Single Parents

Related to that two-fold issue is the question of alleged harm done to children who live with only one parent. Recent data reveal that the proportion of children who live with a single parent (usually the mother) has steadily risen over the past several decades (Advisory Committee, 1976:17–20). This trend is due primarily to increasing divorce, but it is also stimulated by the recent growth of illegitimate births. Traditionals tend to seize upon data showing increased solo parenting as evidence that our society is being torn from what they consider its solid foundations of the past. However, Laslett (1977) argues that we must put this matter in historical perspective. He refers to the Traditionals "...tendency ...to look on our own generation as burdened by the problem to an extent never paralleled in the past" (Laslett, 1977:161). He then marshalls data from seventeenth and eighteenth century England showing that there were as many children then without benefit of both parents as there are in the United States today, or about 12 to 15 percent of all children under age 17. The main reason for the solo parent situation then was the high death rate among young parents. Nevertheless, the problem of providing adequate economic and emotional care for the bereft child was as great—or greater—at that time as it is today. And that is the nub of the issue: do children without both parents suffer disadvantages when compared to children from dual-parent homes?

Problems of Adolescents

Shifting the focus from children to adolescents alters the tone of our discussion. Children are typically depicted as relatively helpless and passive. In contrast, adolescents are neither helpless nor passive. The problems that have "grown up" around teenagers reflect their active behavior. Two adolescent problem areas are the related concerns of controlling sexual activity and controlling reproduction, including the issue of illegitimacy (Chilman, 1978). Policy planners concerned with children's well-being believe that society will suffer if children suffer. If a child is prevented from completing all of the schooling of which he or she is capable, that child will be less likely to become a productive adult. The goal, therefore, is to design policy that will relieve children's deprivation and also enable them eventually to do more for society.

When we turn to adolescent sex and reproduction, in contrast, the basic goal is to design policy that will not only assist teenagers, but will simultaneously influence them from doing as little harm as possible *to* society. Observers vary concerning the nature of this "harm," however. Some Traditionals charge that high rates of teenage sexual intercourse "weaken the social fabric" and therefore ought not to be permitted, and by all means not encouraged. Progressives, on the other hand, argue that this charge is vague and unsubstantiated and that, in any case, it is impossible to prevent adolescent coitus simply by condemning it.

Progressives contend that what *is* demonstrable is that increasing numbers of single teenage women are becoming pregnant and having children, and that this pattern is undesirable for the women, their offspring, and the larger society. Progressives then argue that what is needed to deal with this problem is to provide comprehensive programs of sex education to adolescents (including training on how to refuse sex when it is not genuinely desired), as well as unrestricted access to efficient contraceptives and to abortion (Chilman, 1978).

While the Traditionals concur that teenage illegitimacy is a serious problem, they argue that the Progressives' policies would encourage more teens to have coitus more frequently. They believe that this would pose a threat to the fabric of society, even if illegitimacy were reduced substantially.

Problems of Adults

Divorce is the most widely discussed family policy matter in connection with adults. We have known for quite some time that money matters are closely related to divorce patterns. More recently, changes in sex roles have also entered the divorce picture. Therefore, as we focus on policy issues for married adults in terms of divorce, the related questions of money and of sex roles become our concern as well.

WHAT DO WE KNOW?

Children of Working Mothers

Since the issue of women's guilt seems contingent on the matter of damage to children, what is known about "harm to children"? Clarke-Stewart (1977) published an exhaustive review of 350 studies on the characteristics and behavior of family members that affect children's development. Her investigation concluded "that a mother working does not necessarily produce disadvantages for a child" (Keniston, 1977:5).

That conclusion points to a key feature of the Progressives' position: the need for policy directed toward the best ways of caring for children of working parents. It seems rather futile to support ideologies, as done by some Traditionals, aimed at keeping women out of the labor force on the grounds that working "harms" children, since there is no evidence to support that contention.

The other side of the coin is policy aimed at the "guilt issue." More specifically, Safilios-Rothschild (1974:18–19) argues for policy to "liberate women from the motherhood cult." She cites evidence that some women who stay home to care for children would prefer to be working instead. The pressure they experience to conform to unwanted expectations may be detrimental to their mental health. In addition, she reports that "...fulltime housewives spend an average of less than two hours a day in direct interactions with their children....Women who stopped working because they felt it was their 'duty' as good mothers...to take care of their children but who would have liked to work had...difficulties being 'good' mothers....They...had less confidence in their functioning as mothers than working women."

Children of Single Parents

When considering policy for children in solo-parent situations, one must keep in mind the finding that "female-headed single-parent families comprise a substantially larger and increasing proportion of all families at lower income levels" (Advisory Committee, 1976:23). In short, most children in single-parent households are *economically* disadvantaged. There are three reasons for that conclusion.

First, Bane (1976:112) points out that illegitimate children are born more frequently to less-educated women. Second, divorce is more likely to occur among lower-status couples. Third, death rates are also higher among lower-status adults. Therefore, the lower the social status of the child's parents, the more likely the child is to spend all or part of his or her childhood and adolescence in a single-parent household. The critical point that Bane and many others make is that while some children from dual-parent households are indeed economically deprived, the greatest economic suffering occurs among children in solo-parent households.

This situation is further complicated by the factors of the mother's age and her race. Solo parenthood and economic deprivation are most likely to occur among women under age 25, precisely the women who have the greatest numbers of vulnerable children, children who suffer the most from that deprivation (Advisory Committee, 1976:22). And while many white children are economically deprived, the proportion of black children who suffer deprivation is substantially greater. Furthermore, the rate of increase of economic deprivation has recently been greater among blacks than whites (Advisory Committee, 1976:26-32).

While the economic deprivation of children in solo-parent homes is quite evident, it is less certain that these children are deprived emotionally and in other intangible ways. The folk wisdom has been that children require both parents for normal emotional and social development. In planning policy, it is essential to know if that "wisdom" is mythical or true. On the basis of her review of the literature comparing children from divorced marriages with those from intact marriages, Bane (1976:111) was led to "...challenge the popular homily that divorce is disastrous for children. Differences between children... of comparable economic status on school achievement, social adjustment, and delinquent behavior are small or even nonexistent." Therefore, whichever of the three reasons cited above (divorce, death, illegitimacy) is responsible for a child's being in a solo-parent household, there is no evidence to suggest that he or she will suffer intangible damage on that account alone, when compared to children with dual parents at the same class level.

Adolescent Sexuality, Reproduction, and Illegitimacy

As we consider statistics showing increases in illegitimacy, it is vital to keep in mind the historical perspective we used when we looked at children deprived of both parents. Traditionals tend to believe that premarital sex and illegitimacy were "discovered" by contemporary youth and that they are behaving in "new ways" on both counts. Laslett (1977:102) reminds us that in past centuries, "ordinary, modest, conscientious men and women did not spend much of their time describing for the benefit of posterity ... their sexual relationships with ... their spouses-to-be." Laslett's historical research shows that some degree of both premarital sex and illegitimacy have always occurred in Western societies. In the past, illegitimacy rates in Western societies have fluctuated widely. Furthermore, prior to modern methods of efficient record keeping, it was much simpler than it is today to hide premarital conception and illegitimacy.

Based on today's relatively sophisticated counting procedures, demographers conclude that in the United States during 1960 among every 1,000 unmarried women aged 15-19 there were 15.3 illegitimate births. By 1974 that figure had risen 52 percent to 23.2 (Baldwin, 1977:7). But why is illegitimacy a "problem"? The "principle of legitimacy," according to Malinowski, dictates that every child must have a "sociological father" for his or her maximum well-being. However, as we saw earlier, the existing literature suggests that not having a father is by itself no guarantee that a child will be deprived. The principle of "status-adequacy" —or having adequate material provision regardless of its source (Scanzoni and Scanzoni, 1976:161–64)—is far more significant in explaining a child's well being than is the principle of legitimacy. Being born to a teenage woman poses serious hazards for a child because the young mother is ill-equipped economically to care for it. Adolescents who become pregnant and bear a child tend to drop out of school (Baldwin, 1977:20). Regardless of whether these women return to school in later years, while their children are young these mothers lack the training and skills to compete effectively in the job market (Baldwin, 1977:26). If they can find a job, child care costs may devour their earnings, making it difficult for them to provide adequately for their children. Furthermore, there is a tendency for unmarried teenage mothers to have additional illegitimate children (Baldwin, 1977:26-27). Extra mouths to feed strain already limited resources, making the situation even much more punishing for each child in the household.

Viewing that same situation from the mother's perspective, it can be seen that bearing illegitimate children is likely to undermine her "life-chances," or the possibilities for her own social and economic achievement. Her plans to work or go to school must always be contingent on the fact of having had one or more children before she was well established in an occupational pattern. In addition, the evidence shows that black adolescent women are much more likely than white adolescent women to experience an illegitimate birth. The 1974 illegitimacy rate (illegitimate births per 1,000 unmarried women aged 15–19) for blacks was 88.8 as compared to 11.1 for whites (Baldwin, 1977:8). Since blacks are generally less economically well off than whites, black adolescents have fewer life-chances than whites to begin with, and those few life-chances are further minimized by bearing children without adequate means of child support. Additional negative consequences faced by the unwed adolescent mother of any race are a greater likelihood of divorce, a greater risk of suicide, and a greater risk of abusing her child (Baldwin, 1977:27–28).

In spite of these and other risks of early sexual intercourse, a recent national study showed an increase in teenage premarital coitus. For instance, in 1971, 27 percent of never-married women aged 15–19 had experienced sexual intercourse. By 1976, that figure had risen to 35 percent—a 30 percent increase in the prevalence of premarital coitus (Zelnik and Kantner, 1977:56). Obviously, coitus results in illegitimacy only if conception occurs, the woman does not marry, and the pregnancy results in a live birth. A key factor is therefore the degree to which sexually active teens are using contraception.

In 1976 among white women aged 15–19 who had ever had coitus, 27 percent report they "always" used contraceptives, 45 percent report they "sometimes" did, and 28 percent say they "never" did. Among black adolescent women the figures are 24, 33, and 43 percent, respectively (Zelnik and Kantner, 1978a:136). It is not surprising, therefore, that among these three categories of whites, the proportions who report they had ever been pregnant are 11, 23, and 52 percent, respectively. Among blacks, the three figures are 10, 30, and 71 percent, respectively, Zelnik and Kantner (1978a:138) conclude that "those who had used a medical method ... are one-third as likely to become pregnant as those who use a nonmedical method, and one-tenth as likely to get pregnant as those who use no method."

The other factors that affect illegitimacy rates are abortion and marriage. Zelnik and Kantner (1978b:18) report that between 1971 and 1976 there was an increase in abortions among pregnant teenagers. They conclude that because of this increase, pregnant teenage females were less likely to get married in 1976 than 1971. However, the rise in the abortion rate was actually quite modest, with the majority of unwed pregnant teens still carrying their child to full term, which accounts for the increase in illegitimacy.

In addition to the burdens that illegitimacy places on mothers and their children, there are societal costs. Medical costs—including hospitalization—of most teenage illegitimate births are paid from public funds (Baldwin, 1977:28). Nevertheless, Congress recently cut off federal aid for abortions (many states did likewise), even though the cost of an abortion is far less than the medical costs of a full-term pregnancy. A second cost of adolescent motherhood to society is the welfare payments received by many of these women. A New York City study discovered that 55 percent of teenage unwed mothers "were in households receiving public assistance as opposed to 17 percent of the mothers aged 20-23 and 9 percent of those aged 24-29" (Baldwin, 1977:29). As Baldwin (1977:29) concludes, "it is difficult to assess all of the costs [of illegitimacy] that the individual and society must bear.... It is generally agreed that family planning services are ... less expensive than the consequences of pregnancy and childbirth."

Divorce and Role Transitions

Patterns in divorce rates are closely related to economic matters and to sex roles (Scanzoni, 1972). For example, the lower the husband's education or income the more likely he is to experience separation and/or divorce. Furthermore, men who marry prior to age 20, as well as all black men, are also more likely to divorce. Both factors are plainly associated with economic disadvantages. In addition, women with lower-status husbands report less marital satisfaction (Scanzoni, 1975).

The basic reason for these findings is that, according to traditional role expectations, men have "the moral, social, and legal obligation to support all the 'dependent' women and children in their lives" (Safilios-Rothschild, 1974:73). Women with these role expectations look to "their man" to be their provider. To the degree that he fails to fulfill these expectations, disillusionment and disappointment are likely to occur, marital satisfaction declines, and dissolution becomes a stronger possibility. Thus, traditional sex role expectations are ultimately responsible for a large share of the divorces in the United States and in other industrialized societies.

A social policy dilemma becomes apparent as we consider the following scenario. If men have difficulty providing for their families, one solution to their problem is for their wives to alter their sex role behavior and enter the labor force. But Ross and Sawhill (1975) conclude that one of the consequences of women entering the labor force is sometimes to disrupt marriages. Thus, the apparent "solution" to husband economic shortfall becomes part of the "problem" of marital dissolution.

We must be cautious, however, in labeling marital dissolution a "problem." While divorce can be emotionally and financially costly to the parties involved, it can also be of benefit to society. Although Traditionals have long resisted the idea, divorce can function like a boiler's safety valve, enabling individuals who are dissatisfied with their marriages to exit from them in an orderly fashion (Scanzoni, 1979). The history of Western societies has taught us that when divorces are difficult or impossible to obtain, persons who are dissatisfied with their marriage simply desert or maintain extramarital liaisons. If divorce were not permitted, and if it were somehow possible for society to prohibit desertion and extramarital alliances, the institution of marriage would probably undergo violent upheaval much like a boiler exploding. Rheinstein (1972) has demonstrated that strict divorce laws have absolutely no effect on holding down divorce rates. Divorce is not a root problem; it is rather a symptom in part of sex-role problems and related economic matters. Divorce is also a necessary mechanism to facilitate orderly transition from the status of being married to that of being unmarried, and potentially to becoming remarried. Divorce rates, like birth rates, fluctuate through time. While the U.S. divorce rate did double during the late 1960s and early 1970s, it remained fairly stable during the mid and later 1970s (U.S. Department of Health, Education, and Welfare, 1978).

WHAT ARE WE DOING?

Meeting the Needs of Children

As observed earlier, children's well-being is connected to a set of interrelated factors subsumed under economic support, household composition (one or both parents present), and work involvement of parents (one or both parents employed). Since the economic issue is the easiest to identify and document in terms of consequences, most policy suggestions have dealt with this topic. As Keniston (1977:83) states: "Other things being equal, the best way to ensure that a child has a fair chance at the satisfactions and fulfillments of adult life is to ensure that the child is born into a family with a decent income." To achieve "decent" incomes for all families, Keniston suggests a twin program of jobs for all parents "able to work," and income supports "for all families with children."

These twin proposals are at the heart of the "welfare reform" bill that President Carter submitted to Congress in August 1977. Popular stereotypes often characterize the poor as unwilling to work and incapable of doing as effective a job of childrearing as those who are more advantaged. However, "research evidence indicates that the poor do not differ from the non-poor in personality, character and aspirations as much as has been assumed" (Advisory Committee, 1976:46). Where severely disadvantaged people do differ from the more advantaged is in their *expectations* for themselves and their children. That is, persons who have never been able to control the conditions of their own lives to improve their economic situation are hard-pressed to believe that the situation could ever be improved for themselves or their children. Income/jobs policies such as President Carter's turn on that distinction between aspirations and expectations. If the disadvantaged did not aspire to the dominant work ethic and the "American Dream" of upward mobility for themselves and their children, then a case might be made for current welfare policies that do nothing to stimulate fulfillment of the Dream. However, since all levels of American society apparently aspire to this Dream, it makes sense to devise social policies that will encourage fulfillment of the Dream—policies that will create the hope that individuals can *expect* to improve their own and their children's economic situation.

President Carter claims his plan would achieve that goal by providing more job opportunities and requiring all able-bodied persons to work. The only exception would be mothers of preschoolers. Mothers whose "youngest child was between 7 and 14 would have to accept part-time employment while the child was in school and full-time work if adequate day-care facilities were available" (*New York Times*, August 7, 1977:40). When the youngest child reached 14, mothers would be required to work full time. This plan also includes income supports for families in which the adults are unable to work or cannot locate jobs.

Despite the fact that there is no evidence to support the Traditionals' idea that children of working parents suffer hardships, policy questions remain concerning how to provide the best possible care for such children as to ensure their well-being and assuage parental guilts and fears. Safilios-Rothschild (1974:20) remarks that "two basic principles" must govern all such policies. First, both parents (if present) must be defined as equally responsible for the child's development and care. The father is neither more nor less liable for the child's well-being than is the mother. Second, a pregnant working woman or a nursing mother must not be discriminated against in any way regarding her job. Pregnancy, childbirth, and lactation are temporary matters that call for minor alterations in work routines. Employers must deal with those matters in the same fashion that they cope with any other physical condition that causes temporary interruptions in work routines for members of either sex.

Once the first of these basic principles is granted, a variety of policy options are available to complement our current emphasis on providing adequate child care facilities. This current theme is based on "the organization of efficient, well-run, and well-staffed child care centers operating twenty-four yours a day and equipped to accept infants and newborns or sick children ..." (Safilios-Rothschild, 1974:18). It should be apparent that policies promoting greater involvement of fathers in child care do not contradict policies promoting increased day care facilities. For instance, fathers might be held equally responsible with mothers for ensuring that their children get to and from daycare centers, as well as for any other demands that might arise from the child's daycare involvement.

In effect, policies that include both daycare facilities and paternal responsibilities are designed to achieve the twin aims of enabling both parents to participate equally in the labor force and in child care. The presumed benefits of these policies for the child are increased socioeconomic resources from the employed mother and greater socioemotional support from the caregiving father.

Coping with Adolescent Sexuality and Reproduction

The Traditional's reaction to trends in adolescent sexual behavior is to try to persuade them not to have coitus. To Traditionals, increasing rates of coitus are the root problem. Progressives, on the other hand, maintain two policy thrusts, one of which is preventive. Progressives contend that before intercourse occurs and any conceptions result, the community should provide complete and candid discussions of human sexuality to adolescents, along with unrestricted access to effective contraceptives. Their second thrust is ameliorative. If conception does occur, Progressives want to provide services to the adolescent woman (and man) that include unrestricted access to abortion.

Ever since the time of Margaret Sanger (founder of the movement to make contraceptives available to all persons), Progressives have been struggling with Traditionals over these two sets of policies. This struggle has resulted in very slow but steady gains for the Progressives, especially in recent years with regard to the issue of wide-spread contraceptive dissemination.

Coping with Divorce Patterns and Role Transitions

Reference was made earlier to government-sponsored income maintenance experiments. These had several purposes besides meeting children's needs. Since divorce occurs most frequently when the husband's income is low, one of the purposes of those experiments was to determine if infusing dollars into disadvantaged households would reduce marital instability. Since money matters rank as the most frequently reported area of marital conflicts, the experiments sought to reduce the incidence of serious money-related conflicts and thus lessen the likelihood of separation or divorce among these couples.

In contrast to that structuralist strategy, a programmatic approach to reduce divorces would emphasize marriage counseling. Counseling can be preventive or ameliorative. In addition, "family life" courses taught in high schools, colleges, and community settings are intended to prevent divorces. Within those settings, attempts are sometimes made to make persons aware of the significant implications, both for themselves and for their marriages, of the changes in female and male sex roles that are presently occurring throughout U.S. society (Mason, et al., 1976).

WHAT HAVE WE ACCOMPLISHED?

Children

The Advisory Committee (1976:48) concludes that "there is increasing evidence that many of the [family] differences between the poor and non-poor would disappear if the poor had more money and other material resources. What has not been completely established is the effect of increasing family resources on the welfare of children. From available research, however, it is reasonable to infer that the school performance, health, and cognitive development of poor children would probably be significantly improved by more favorable economic circumstances and a generally higher standard of living, which children share with their parents."

The Advisory Committee goes on to argue that the key to children's well-being seems to lie in making it possible for "the family to exert some control over its destiny." The implications of destiny control on child-rearing practices are spelled out in the various investigations conducted by Kohn (1978) and his colleagues, both in the United States and in some European countries. These studies conclude that parents from more-advantaged homes train their children to be self-directed, to be autonomous, to think for themselves, and to "master" their life situations. In contrast, less-advantaged parents are more likely to teach their children to be obedient, to conform, and to be "passive" in the face of life situations. In short, long-standing social arrangements and policies have made it possible for children from more advantaged homes to learn how to achieve in an optimal fashion in modern societies. Goal attainment in such societies is determined primarily by self-direction, autonomy, and initiative. The result is that more-advantaged children tend to maintain their advantage, while less-advantaged children tend to retain their relative disadvantage. Obedience and conformity do not "pay off" in terms of occupational achievement. The question then becomes: what new family policies or arrangements might make it possible for greater numbers of less-advantaged children to become upwardly mobile?

In regard to alternative child-care arrangements, there is unfortunately very little evidence concerning the effects of equal father participation in child-care responsibilities. However, a recent census report reveals that when mothers work, fathers are more likely to care for children than sitters, friends, relatives, or child-care centers (U.S. Bureau of Census, 1976:1).

As to the effects of child-care centers on children, a recent literature survey (Belsky and Steinberg, 1978) shows no significant difference between preschool children reared with their mothers and children who spent their days in superior child care facilities. This comparison took into account such dimensions as intellectual growth, social development, and ability to achieve close relationships with their mothers.

Adolescents

According to Zelnik and Kantner (1978a), a higher proportion of sexually active teenagers were using contraceptives in 1976 than in 1971. The impact of this greater usage of contraceptives has been dramatic. In 1976, for instance, there were 780,000 premarital teenage pregnancies (Zelnik and Kantner, 1978a: 142). However, Zelnik and Kantner (1978a:142) calculate that, since many more teens were sexually active in 1976 than in 1971, if those 1976 active adolescents had not had access to and used contraceptives, there would have been an *additional* 680,000 premarital pregnancies.

This shift in adolescent protection against pregnancy is accompanied by increasing public support for "making birth control devices available to teenage boys and girls." A 1977 Gallup survey reported that 56 percent of all Americans approved of that policy; 35 percent disapproved; and 9 percent had "no opinion."

Moreover, 77 percent of Americans "approve of schools giving courses in sex education," while 69 percent "approved of these courses discussing birth control." In 1965, only 46 percent approved of such discussions (Gallup, 1978:30).

In spite of the fact that public opinion has shifted in the Progressives' direction, Traditionals maintain substantial influence on local school boards. The result is that many schools in the United States offer no sex education at all. And among schools that do, teachers are generally not allowed to deal with "controversial" subjects such as birth control. Furthermore, a recent study observes that public and private services for pregnant teenagers are inadequate (Goldstein and Wallace, 1978). Most notably lacking is full information about and unimpeded access to abortion. Some community facilities, for example, require parental consent before an adolescent is allowed to abort.

Divorce and Role Transitions

The Advisory Committee (1976:47) speculated about the possible alternative impacts of income transfers on family stability. On the one hand, "some [spouses] endure substantial ... conflict ... simply because they cannot afford to maintain separate households...." Consequently, "policies ... making it more feasible for one parent to live and rear children apart from the other parent may lead ... to more divorces and separations, at least in the short run." On the other hand, "minimal levels and security of income may improve the chances that a two-parent family will remain a suitably warm and nurturing environment for children."

Recent data from the experimental income transfer programs have tended to verify the first of these two alternatives. Households receiving income transfers were more prone to marital dissolution than households without them (Hannan, et al., 1977). Nevertheless, there is additional evidence (Hannan, et al., 1978) to suggest that, as the Advisory Committee conjectures, dissolution may be a short-run consequence of severe conflicts that existed prior to the receipt of these monies. More research is needed to determine if, in the long run and under certain conditions, transfer policies might enhance marital stability.

Furthermore, since there is no valid evidence to support the contention that "children of divorce" suffer hardships, there is no reason to restrict income transfers solely because, in the short run, marital instability is increased. We would not want to construct social policy aimed at family economic well-being by building on the false premise that: "If children involved in divorces suffer, we will therefore not contribute to that suffering by carrying out income transfer projects."

There are no systematic data to ascertain how effective either counseling or courses are in reducing marital dissolutions. However, the consensus among many professionals is that few courses come to grips with the issues that are fundamental to contemporary marriage. This deficiency is particularly acute in high schools because of pressures by Traditionals to avoid such topics as contraception, sex roles, cohabitation, and homosexuality. Similarly, counseling efforts are believed to have little effect on marital dissolution rates, either because the people who need counseling the most (the disadvantaged) do not have access to it, or because people wait to seek help until the critical point in their relationship is passed and it is "too late" to implement the changes necessary to maintain it.

WHERE ARE WE GOING?

Research Aimed at Children's Well-Being

Considerable research evidence has demonstrated how vital it is for a child's well-being that he or she learn to be autonomous, to be self-directed, and to possess a sense of mastery. We have also learned that the more advantaged the child's background, the more likely the child is to develop these characteristics. Therefore, one policy option to assist low-income children might be some sort of income transfer program. However, preliminary reports concerning the impacts of such programs on work patterns of adults are inconclusive. One of the prime objectives of the income transfer experiment was to determine if such transfers would influence low-income persons to decrease their work activity. Such a decrease did not occur in the experiment that took place in New Jersey (Lynn, 1977:115–16). However, in the Seattle-Denver experiment, income transfers had the opposite consequence and acted instead as a disincentive to work activity (Spiegelman, 1978). Speculation as to the cause of that latter result centers on the kinds of jobs available in those regions to minimally-educated persons. Because those jobs are menial, uninspiring, unchallenging, and "dead-end," people may understandably choose to live on the income transfers and forego that sort of employment. Whether or not that interpretation is correct, it raises critical questions that need to be investigated in order to devise policies aimed at children's well-being. For example, if providing income to adults does not increase work incentives owing to the character of available employment, it is not likely that those incentives will give the recipients any sense of "mastery" or "control" over their own destinies. They will then not be inclined or able to pass on those orientations to their children. Thus, income transfers may not be likely to provide children with the orientations so critical to personal well-being in an achievement-oriented society.

Both Kohn's (1978) investigations and the results of the income experiments suggest that job status rather than income transfer may be the crucial factor in stimulating mastery, autonomy, and self-direction among adults—and hence among their children. In that regard, certain job training programs have had some "effect on removing persons from poverty" (Levin, 1977:179). Perhaps future job training experiments could be conducted asking such questions as: Does altering the job status of adults increase their sense of mastery, while decreasing their sense of passivity? Does changing the life-situations of adults in this fashion have similar consequences for their children's views of life?

Research Aimed at Responsible Adolescent Sexual Patterns

In formulating policies to cope with adolescent contraception and repro-duction, Luker (1975) argues that making effective contraceptives and abortion easily available to adolescents is merely a necessary first step. She argues that "deciding" to contracept involves complex social behaviors based on inter-locking sets of costs and rewards (Scanzoni, 1975). Zelnik and Kantner (1978a: 140), for instance, report that some unmarried sexually active adolescents actually wanted to become pregnant. And many sexually active women who did not want to become pregnant nevertheless reject contraception. Some policy makers have considered these and similar patterns "nonrational." In contrast, Luker (1975) and others suggest that those patterns appear "nonrational" simply because policy makers do not comprehend the full range of costs and rewards that these women tacitly take into consideration.

Luker's research and policy suggestions revolve around encouraging women and men to make the perceived rewards and costs of sexual activity, contracep-tion, and childbirth more explicit to themselves and to each other. She points out that in U.S. society sexual activity is inseparable from the sex roles ascribed to men and women by virtue of their gender. These sex roles greatly influence adolescent dating games. Since the games reward women for attracting men, a traditional woman may be willing to cement that attraction by consenting to coitus. Even though she (or he) is aware that potentially she is risking pregnancy, that likelihood and its costs seem remote. Moreover, as Luker says, risking pregnancy is like smoking or driving without a seat harness: One cannot be certain the undesirable consequences will actually result.

In short, efficient contraception is primarily a problem of motivation. Therefore, making contraceptives and abortion increasingly accessible to teens is a necessary, but not sufficient, policy. We must simultaneously encourage adolescents to develop more egalitarian sex roles in which personhood rather than sexuality becomes the focus of their relationships. Such programs must include training (especially for women) on how to negotiate assertively for equity. Because so many unmarried adolescents who bear children are econom-ically disadvantaged or black, or both, it becomes a policy imperative to make adolescent females aware of, and have access to, opportunities for major life gratifications other than bearing and caring for children. Therefore, programs must also train adolescents to seek the most demanding and rewarding occupa-tions their native talents permit. At the same time, society must provide the structural opportunities to permit the fulfillment of these aspirations. Other-wise, it will be meaningless to suggest to these adolescents that important grati-fications other than childbearing and caring are available to them.

Research Aimed at More Equitable Marital Patterns

If divorce is in part the result of the traditional sex roles described above, Progressives contend that policies aimed at reducing divorce must take account of those role expectations. One way to do that in a preventive manner is to offer programs to high school students. Since early marriage accounts for a high proportion of divorces, these programs could help eliminate a major factor leading to marital dissolution. Such programs would lay bare the "economic and social realities" of marriage (Safilios-Rothschild, 1974:96–120). Evaluation research should also be conducted to measure the effectiveness of these demonstration programs. The programs would begin by freeing individuals of the notion that "romantic love" is a sufficient reason for marriage. To those feelings must be added candid information about the significant impacts that money has on marriage, as well as information about the relative advantages that husbands and wives have as a result of their differing sex roles. Marriage-information programs for adolescents must transmit the fundamental notion that economics and sex roles tend to overwhelm the importance of "feelings of love" in determining whether or not the couple achieves marital satisfaction and stays together.

Perhaps even more crucial for the success of such preventive programs is conveying the additional notion that each partner brings his or her ideas regarding economic lifestyles, occupational pursuits, and sex roles to the crucial process of negotiation. Although at first many women may allow their husbands' ideas to shape their marriages, there is evidence showing that the longer they are married the more likely women are to think that arrangement unfair (Scanzoni, 1978). What must be conveyed to single women is the determination and skills to negotiate equitable arrangements prior to marriage. They must learn that if they are unable to bargain effectively with a man before marriage, it will be much more difficult to do so afterward when they have relinquished the option of a relatively easy exit from their relationship. Likewise, men must learn to take women seriously and learn how to negotiate with them in order to achieve mutual benefits. Men need to be made aware that an increasing minority of women will no longer settle for arrangements in which men consistently achieve the greater advantage, as was generally the case in the past.

Several decades ago a prominent judge named Ben Lindsey, in an effort to reduce the number of divorce cases, advocated a legalized temporary period of "trial marriage" as a means of enabling persons to "test" whether or not they ought to marry permanently (Chilman, 1978:149). Today, an increasing number of single persons are cohabiting, and the question can be raised as to what effect (if any) that pattern has on divorce rates. We do not presently have extensive data on the consequences of cohabitation, but it is worth noting that during the mid 1970s cohabitation was increasing while the divorce rate leveled off (Glick and Norton, 1977). In contrast to the earlier pattern of marrying at a young age and then later divorcing, some never-married people may be choosing to cohabit as a form of "trial marriage." In addition, men who have been divorced are very likely to cohabit instead of almost immediately remarrying, as once was the case (Glick and Norton, 1977:34). Whether that emerging pattern leads to fewer divorces is still unknown. There is no evidence to suggest that cohabitation fosters effective negotiation or greater equity for women. Nor is there any guarantee that effective negotiation before marriage will ensure effective negotiation later on. Nevertheless, two testable predictions are that 1) couples who begin marriage on an egalitarian basis are likely to maintain that pattern over time, whereas 2) couples who form marriage based on sex-role specialization are likely either to maintain that pattern or later try to renegotiate more egalitarian arrangements.

However, there is no imperative to wait for those results before policy is instituted. If we concur that a worthy societal goal is improving the "quality" of marriages and reducing the likelihood of divorce, we can begin now to design experimental or demonstration programs for singles and marrieds centered on marriage realities. Such policies should operate in conjunction with programs to provide greater educational and occupational opportunities for blacks and women. These policies should stress the point that as women gain greater socio-economic autonomy, they will become more capable of contributing to tangible and intangible male well-being. The eventual outcome of such policies could be greater interdependence between partners and, thus, more stimulating and stable marriages.

Space prohibits us from examining many other areas of applied sociology (e.g., aging, abuse, homosexuality) that pertain to marriage and the family, but the topics discussed here provide a foundation on which the interested reader can explore additional concerns. Essential to an understanding of family social policy, for instance, is the ongoing struggle between Traditionals and Progressives.

A second critical foundation for family policy is the connection between the occupational opportunity structure and marriage and family life. Despite romantic myths to the contrary, socioeconomic factors pervade all aspects of family structure and dynamics.

Sex role issues are another crucial factor in family policy. Like economic factors, they are also ubiquitously interwoven throughout the entire fabric of marriage and family patterns.

Applied sociology attempts to use research findings to solve social problems. But because there is often divergence over the most effective or desirable ways of solving those problems, application of knowledge is not a simple matter. In regard to applied family sociology, there are policy divergences not only between Traditionals and Progressives, but also between the less advantaged and the more advantaged, and between women and men. Nonetheless, we can hope that out of this ferment will arise new family policies that will enhance the quality of family life in the years ahead.

REFERENCES AND SUGGESTED READINGS

Advisory Committee on Child Development. 1976. *Toward a National Policy for Children and Families*. Washington, D.C.: National Academy of Sciences.

*Baldwin, W.H. 1977. "Adolescent Pregnancy and Childbearing—Growing Concerns for Americans." Population Bulletin (31:2). Washington, D.C.: Population Reference Bureau.

The bulletin provides a comprehensive, though brief, survey of the issues surrounding teenage sexual activity.

Bane, M.J. 1976. "Marital Disruption and the Lives of Children." *The Journal of Social Issues* 32:103–18.

Belsky, J. and L.D. Steinberg. 1978. "The Effects of Day Care: A Critical Review." *Child Development* 49:929–49.

Chilman, C.S. 1978. *Adolescent Sexuality in a Changing American Society.* Washington, D.C.: U.S. Government Printing Office.

Clarke-Stewart, A. 1977. *Child Care In The Family: A Review of Research and Some Propositions For Policy.* New York: Academic Press.

Gallup Opinion Index. 1978. "Report No. 156." Princeton, N.J.: American Institute of Public Opinion.

*Glick, P.C. and A.J. Norton. 1977. "Marrying, Divorcing and Living Together in the U.S. Today." Population Bulletin (32:5). Washington, D.C.: National Academy of Sciences.

This bulletin provides a wealth of information regarding contemporary marriage patterns.

Goldstein, H. and H.M. Wallace. 1978. "Services for the Needs of Pregnant Teenagers in Large Cities of the U.S., 1976." *Public Health Reports* 93:46.

Hannan, M.T., N.B. Tuma, and L.P. Groeneveld. 1977. "Income and Marital Events: Evidence from an Income-Maintenance Experiment." *American Journal of Sociology* 82:1186–211.

———. 1978. "Income and Independence Effects on Marital Dissolution: Results from the Seattle and Denver Income-Maintenance Experiments." *American Journal of Sociology* 84:611–33.

Kanter, R.M. 1977. *Work and Family in the United States: A Critical Review and Agenda for Research and Policy.* New York: Russell Sage Foundation.

*Keniston, K. 1977. *All Our Children: The American Family Under Pressure.* New York: Harcourt Brace Jovanovich.

Keniston presents extensive analyses and critiques of various social and economic policies currently being proposed to enhance family life.

Kohn, M. 1978. *Class and Conformity.* Chicago: University of Chicago Press.

Laslett, P. 1977. *Family Life and Illicit Love in Earlier Generations.* New York: Cambridge University Press.

Levin, H.M. 1977. "A Decade of Policy Developments in Improving Education and Training for Low-Income Populations." In *A Decade of Federal Antipoverty Programs*, edited by R.H. Haveman, pp. 123–88. New York: Academic Press.

Lipman-Blumen, J. and J. Bernard. 1979. *Sex Roles and Social Policy: A Complex Social Science Equation.* Beverly Hills, Calif.: Sage.

Luker, K. 1975. *Taking Chances: Abortion and the Decision Not to Contracept.* Berkeley: University of California Press.

Lynn, L.E., Jr. 1977. "A Decade of Policy Developments in the Income Maintenance System." In *A Decade of Federal Antipoverty Programs*, edited by R.H. Haveman, pp. 55–117. New York: Academic Press.

Mason, K.O., J. Czajka, and S. Arber. 1976. "Change in U.S. Women's Sex-Role Attitudes, 1964–1975." *American Sociological Review* 41:573–96.

*Morris, R. 1979. *Social Policy of the American Welfare State*. New York: Harper & Row.

After providing a framework useful to understanding social policy in general, Morris then ties together in systematic fashion several issues relevant to family policy in particular: income maintenance, health, housing, social services, children, and the aged.

*Novak, M. 1977. "The Family Out of Favor." *The Urban and Social Change Review* 10:306.

Sympathetic to the Traditionals' position, Novak tries to show why it is a reasonable posture to take.

Rheinstein, M. 1972. *Marriage Stability, Divorce, and the Law*. Chicago: University of Chicago Press.

Rice, R.M. 1977. *American Family Policy: Content and Context*. New York: Family Service Association.

Ross, H.L. and I.V. Sawhill. 1975. *Time of Transition: The Growth of Families Headed By Women*. Washington, D.C.: The Urban Institute.

*Safilios-Rothschild, C. 1974. *Women and Social Policy*. Englewood Cliffs, N.J.: Prentice-Hall.

This work provides one of the best available syntheses of family social policy and "women's social policy."

Scanzoni, J. 1972. *Sexual Bargaining: Power Politics in American Marriage*. Englewood Cliffs, N.J.: Prentice-Hall.

_____. 1975. *Sex Roles, Life Styles and Childbearing: Changing Patterns in Marriage and Family*. New York: The Free Press.

_____. 1978. *Sex Roles, Women's Work and Marital Conflict: A Study of Family Change*. Lexington, Mass.: D.C. Heath/Lexington Books.

_____. 1979. "An Historical Perspective on Husband-Wife Bargaining Power and Marital Dissolution." In *Divorce and Separation*, edited by George Levinger and Oliver C. Moles. New York: Basic Books.

Scanzoni, L. and J. Scanzoni. 1976. *Men, Women, and Change: A Sociology of Marriage and Family*. New York: McGraw-Hill.

Spiegelman, R.G. 1978. Testimony before a U.S. Senate Subcommittee. Reported in *The Greensboro* (N.C.) *Record*, November 12, 1978.

U.S. Bureau of the Census. 1976. *Current Population Reports*. No. 298 (Oct): 20. Washington, D.C.: U.S. Government Printing Office.

U.S. Department of Health, Education, and Welfare. 1978. "Monthly Vital Statistics Report." No. 27 (Aug 11):5. Washington, D.C.: U.S. Government Printing Office.

Zelnik, M. and J. Kantner. 1977. "Sexual and Contraceptive Experience of Young Unmarried Women in the United States, 1976 and 1971." *Family Planning Perspectives* 9:55–73.

_____. 1978a. "Contraceptive Patterns and Premarital Pregnancy Among Women Aged 15–19 in 1976." *Family Planning Perspectives*, 10:135–43.

_____. 1978b. "First Pregnancies to Women Aged 15–19: 1976 and 1971." *Family Planning Perspectives* 10:11–19.

7   COMMUNITY NETWORKS

Donald I. Warren and Jack Rothman

Applied sociology at the community level draws on a rich tradition of literature whose key rubric of "community organization" encompasses a wide array of strategies and intervention models (Rothman, 1979a). These range from social planning through social action to "local development," which stresses the process of citizen mobilization for self-help and neighborhood revitalization (Warren and Warren, 1977).

While all three of these approaches merit a full discussion, the present chapter focuses on the single theme of local community self-help. We believe that economic constraints and a renewed interest in the importance of locality will increasingly suggest avenues for applied sociology at this grassroots level. Much innovative activity has been occurring in urban and rural settings over the past decade, and we see the coming years fostering further efforts at "community capacity building" and local self-help initiatives.

Locality development can occur in two different ways. One entails the creation of informal helping networks composed of neighbors and friends who extend assistance to one another in coping with the demands and complexities of modern social living. Actions such as lending a hand with babysitting, giving information about community services, or keeping a friend company when he or she is "down" fall into this category. The second component of locality development involves the establishment of voluntary associations, in which residents band together to improve conditions for all people in a geographic area. Voluntary associations, which usually have some degree of formal structure, may tackle such projects as forming a credit union, providing volunteers to enrich a local public school program, or building a playground for young children. Both facets of locality development are encompassed by our framework, but emphasis in this discussion will be on informal helping networks. These are a newer phenomenon, both in the sociological literature and in professional community organization endeavors.

Informal helping networks sometimes become organized into voluntary associations. In many cases, however, mutual problem coping and aid remains at the interpersonal level without any formal community action. In those instances, a critical function of community organization may be the development of appropriate linkages between informal helping networks and the formal agencies mandated to deliver human services.

WHAT ARE THE PROBLEMS?

The Emergence of Locality Development

Until quite recently, human service programs have assumed a continual growth in service demands—the "revolution" of rising quality of life expectations. This situation is likely to change, however, as a result of the anticipated slowing of economic growth in most Western democracies during the remainder of this century. A gap is already opening in many urban communities, in which an almost geometric increase in social needs must vie with restricted resources and capacity for formal services. This discrepancy places severe strains on values of equity, access, and fairness in the delivery of a variety of social and municipal services.

Underlying our argument is a broad assumption about the contours of economic development in the United States during the coming years. This is a prediction of economic constriction. A tightening economic situation will be brought on largely by the dual factors of chronically dwindling oil supplies, coupled with increasing boldness of oil producing nations in their price demands. This situation will be propelled by both objective economic forces and the psychological and political predisposition of the oil producing nations to insist on a larger return for their resources (and a willingness of advanced industrial nations to acquiesce).

Higher oil prices will have an inflationary effect on the economy of the United States and other Western nations for the next decade and possibly until the end of the century. This prediction applies in the event that there are no dramatic breakthroughs in other sources of energy, no drastic military or political initiatives, and no spectacular natural or social disasters or transformations.

Zald's recent analysis of economic aspects of social welfare processes is congruent with our projection.

A moderate prediction would be that until the end of the century [economic] growth rates will be substantially lower than they have been for the past quarter century, unemployment will be higher than it has

> been for the past quarter century.... Thus, we are unlikely to see an
> expanded welfare state fueled out of a burgeoning economy ... the wel-
> fare state in western industrial countries will be in low gear. (Zald, 1977:
> 120, 122)

In a climate of austerity, local communities have two main options. The first is to react with passive resignation, accepting hard conditions fatalistically. The second option is to respond in a determined, self-actualizing way, applying indigenous energies to maximize whatever potentialities exist in the local situation. Classic theorizing by de Tocqueville (1947) and a contemporary variant by Oberschall (1973) both hold that collective participation in community life declines during periods of economic stress. Their view is that an economic downturn produces despair, which in turn leads to inaction. This perspective fails to note, however, that people learn from past organizing activities and can apply this experience to current conditions. It also asks us to believe that a huge middle class accustomed to material comforts will lightly accept a declining standard of living. In contrast, we believe that an active response is plausible, based on long-standing U.S. traditions of local initiative, voluntary action, and optimism (Rothman, 1979b).

Compounding the trend of economic constriction is a second major tendency in U.S. society. This is a populist revolt by "Middle America" against what is perceived as governmental interference and lavish public spending (Warren, 1976). It is related to what Nathan Glazer and others term the "limits" of problem-solving capacity by professionals. Because professionals have lost credibility as experts, local communities have begun to claim a share in decision making that affects indigenous situations. Many localities are arguing that they possess at least some of the expertise needed to cope with contemporary problems, which supports the trend toward local self-help.

The idea that communities are experts in handling their own problems implies that they may not always require professional help. This can more appropriately be described as a continuum of "invoked expertise." At one end of this continuum are problems for which a highly effective technology currently exists. If communities can gain access to that technology, their problems can be largely or totally resolved. Let us call this "high invoked expertise." Examples of such problems might include diagnosing sickle cell anemia or designing a neighborhood traffic pattern.

The opposite end of the continuum consists of countless problems and concerns arising in daily living for which there may not even be common definitions or labels, let alone an established technology. An example would be psychological depression, which people variously describe as feeling low, having the blues, or being lonely. When people are asked how they cope with feeling blue, we find that they often seek companionship within a natural helping system. This is a typical instance of "low invoked expertise," in the sense that interpersonal sharing and sympathy may be the main ingredient for alleviating the problem, regardless of whether the person visits a clinician or simply talks with a friend. In this type of situation—which might also be called "grassroots expertise"—no professional group can claim full technical jurisdiction over the problem. There is also a midpoint on this continuum of invoked expertise. It consists of situations in which a competitive market exists between professionals and grassroots efforts. Drug abuse programs, alcoholism, obesity, smoking, and child discipline all fit into this category of "medium invoked expertise." These problems can be dealt with through multiple strategies involving both informal groups and formal organizations, which give affected individuals several alternative choices of action. Table 7.1 describes these conditions of high, medium, and low invoked expertise in greater detail and gives examples of each situation drawn from health and family issues.

In sum, the scope of local self-help activity is expanding in response to a number of social stimuli. These include the economics of professional resources, increasing problem complexity (which diminishes the credibility of professional expertise), increased capabilities among local populations, and the growth of an ideology that is distrustful of government and favorable to indigenous initiatives.

WHAT DO WE KNOW?

Before proceeding to the application of locality-based social forms, it would be useful to review the literature on "informal community" and local social networks. We will employ a schematic device that we believe permits a cogent summary of these wide-ranging writings in sociology and the other social sciences. Table 7.2 depicts attributes that frequently appear in the literature on local social networks. They represent important modalities around which various typologies—both heuristic and ideal-typical—have been constructed (see, for example, Homans, 1950; Litwak and Zelenyi, 1969; D. Warren, 1975). The rows of the chart list different kinds of informal systems, ranked from a high level of primary group intensity or intimacy to a low level of intensity. In the columns, each type of system is rated as high, variable, or low on ten different dimensions of social ties. The purposes of arraying these systems are to: 1) clarify the confusion that exists in the current literature regarding the concept of "social network," and 2) identify the significant facets of different forms of informal social systems commonly present in urban industrial societies.

Before discussing each of the types of informal systems, four clarifications should be noted. First, these are not pure types. They tend to flow into one another through overlapping memberships and individuals. Second, these types do not exhaust all possible variations. Rather, they are a means of summarizing current conceptualizations and research found in the literature. Third, the social system bonds described, while widely dispersed among various populations and

TABLE 7.1
A Typology of Social Problems Based on the Level of Invoked Expertise

High Expertise (Low Community Variance)	Medium Expertise (Medium Community Variance)	Low Expertise (High Community Variance)
Problem has a well-defined sophisticated technology associated with its detection and resolution, although debate may occur regarding its most efficient solution "design" or engineering.	Problem has an actively developing technology, but with widely varying success levels in application, or competing approaches have similar limited effectiveness. Differing definitions, analytical frameworks, and discipline and specialization origins; various operational "models" are rampant. Little is known about long-term effects of solutions.	Problem either lacks formal recognition in professional taxonomies or is included with other problems. It tends toward diffuse or nonspecific etiology or symptom syndrome. In particular, it lacks a treatment modality or technology that has been well tested, let alone refined.
Problems of social values are minimal; high consensus is present both from experts and nonexperts as to the need for action. Debate centers on the timing, equity, and speed of implementing a solution.	Problems are often in a state of flux and redefinition. The experts can't agree, and formal agencies vie over proper jurisdictional lines. Rival labels are used to describe the seriousness of the issue, although there is widespread recognition that "something" should be done in the short run.	Both initial and ongoing effects are closely tied to traditional social values or norms, which are created and sustained by significant primary groups.
Problem is often identified with a highly specialized field within a profession, and may be treated entirely within the confines of a formal agency.	Nonexpert elements may be significant in symptom remediation and treatment.	Specialized expertise is only ancillary to problem definition and coping. Perception and response are highly idiosyncratic, and not readily visible to formal social institutions. Regulation of behavior depends heavily on shared local values and "moral suasion."
Actions and efforts by nonexperts or advocate groups cannot greatly change the nature of the problem or provide a solution that is at variance with the known data.		

Regardless of the perceived severity of the problem or consensus as to longer run effects as seen by specialists, major social values and the nonuniform character of the problem as experienced by individuals makes concerted formal action of limited value.

Selected Examples of Health and Family Issues

1. Hypertensive heart disease	1. Alcoholism	1. Life cycle role transition (women entering work force after absence, men retiring)
2. Sickle cell anemia	2. Simple depressive psychosis	2. Youth-parent tensions
3. Schizophrenia	3. Job related emotional stress	3. Leisure malaise (due to shortened work week, etc.)
4. Organically based child mental retardation	4. Control of smoking	4. Common cold effects
5. Prenatal child/mother care	5. Obesity	5. Consumer purchases by families (house, furnishings, car, appliances)
6. Cancer detection and treatment	6. Postoperative and general physical therapy	6. Family budgeting
7. Stroke	7. Career selection	7. Postnatal family adjustment
	8. Marital discord	
	9. Family planning	

Source: Donald Warren and David Clifford, "Invoked Expertise and Neighborhood Type: Two Critical Dimensions in the Coordination of Bureaucratic Service Organizations and Primary Groups." Paper read at the annual meeting of the American Sociological Association, 1974.

TABLE 7.2
Varieties of Informal Social Ties (Compared on Ten Dimensions)

	Size	Duration of Membership	Intimacy	Face to Face Contact	Reference Group Identification	Frequency of Interaction	Member Similarity	Shared Values	Central Behavior Setting	Diffuse vs. Problem Specific Interaction
Traditional primary groups	small	high	high	high	high	high	high	high	yes	diffuse
Work groups	small	high	high	high	high	high	variable	high	yes	variable
Close-knit (interlocking) social networks	small	high	high	variable	low	variable	high	high	variable	diffuse
Helping Networks	variable	variable	variable	variable	low	variable	low	low	yes*	specific
Loose-knit (radial) social networks	small	variable	variable	variable	low	variable	low	low	no	specific
Weak ties	large	variable	variable	variable	low	low	low	low	no	variable

Key: high refers to a positive valence on the attribute; variable refers to the indeterminency of that attribute; low means the absence of a positive valence on the attribute.

*Initial contact for referrals is the behavior setting not a necessarily specific individual within it.

Source: Donald I. Warren "Social Bonds in the Urban Community: An Integrative Approach," unpublished paper read at the Eighth World Congress of Sociology. Uppsala Sweden (1978).

ecological settings, are not randomly or equally distributed. Finally, the systems are not mutually distinct in terms of all ten of the characteristics included in the chart.

Traditional Primary Groups

Charles Horton Cooley defined primary groups as possessing an intimate psychological association. Cooley said that in such groups there is "a certain fusion of individuals in a common whole, so that one's very self, for many purposes at least, is the common life and purpose of the group" (Cooley, 1966: 23).

According to Cooley, et al. (1933:208–12), primary groups have basic common properties: 1) face-to-face interaction, 2) diffuse and unspecialized interaction, 3) relative permanence, 4) "sympathy and natural identification for which 'we' is the natural expression," and 5) small size. This definition represents an "ideal type," the elements of which contrast in most respects with properties of secondary or "formal" groups.

George Homans' (1950) analysis of "the human group" added the elements of "sentiment," "activity," and "interaction." Group functioning was found by Homans to require motivation by members to join in activities, which results in interaction among participants and a spiral of continued feedback that sustains these group processes. In Sanders' (1958) social system analysis of community, intimacy is linked to locality or neighborhood. Such spatial anchoring is a major attribute of the traditional primary group as well. Sanders also includes stability, cohesion, and homogeneity of residents as indicators of interpersonal contact. The primary group milieu therefore includes not only the traditional extended family and the more portable nuclear family but also such forms as the parochial neighborhood, the rural village, the commune, and the "Therapeutic Community."

Work Groups

Recognition of informal work groups in occupational settings is a product of the early research by Roethlisberger and Dickson (1939), Mayo (1945), and the later work of their disciples. The industrial work group differs from the traditional primary group only in its shorter duration and frequently narrower scope of interpersonal exchange. Blau and Scotts' description of the research on work groups provides a useful summary:

> The observer painstakingly recorded the overt manifestations of the network of informal relations that developed among the workers. There were distinct patterns of interaction: some workers frequently helped out certain others; games were regularly played at lunchtime which included some workers but not others. Sentiments of liking and respect were expressed primarily toward some group members, while others were not respected and were disliked. These observable aspects of their informal relations divided the workers into two cliques and a few iso-

lates who were not members of either clique. It was among members of the same clique that most friendship ties developed, most games were played, and even most lunchtime conversations took place. While there was some conflict between cliques, there were social bonds that united the entire group and made possible the enforcement of common norms. (Blau and Scott, 1962:91)

Friendship and intimacy is clearly a basis for group solidarity in work groups and a source of internal social regulation for deflecting the demands of management. Seashore (1954) notes in his research on work groups that amount of interaction, length of shared experiences, and small size—but not homogeneity of group members—determine the level of mutual confidence. Table 7.2 indicates that the work groups differ from primary groups in only two respects: they lack diffuse social interaction and homogeneous members.

Although the concept of work groups originated in studies of blue-collar workers, this kind of social tie occurs in many social settings. It can be the basis of neighborhood organization, particularly the heterogeneous forms found in black ghettos (Warren, 1975), as well as voluntary associations and civic groups. For example, Wireman (1976) has described the social relationships among civic activists in two communities as "intimate secondary" group patterns. In terms of our schema, these are work groups located within voluntary associations.

Close-Knit (Interlocking) Social Networks

As described by Bott (1957), Laumann (1966, 1973), and Craven and Wellman (1973), this type of social pattern lacks a self-conscious group identity but includes several other attributes of primary groups. Consisting of reciprocal friendship and kinship linkages, close-knit networks frequently provide critical social support to individuals. Elizabeth Bott (1957:58–60) explains this concept:

It appeared that the external social relationships of all families assumed the form of a *network* rather than the form of an organized group. In an organized group the component individuals make up a larger social whole with common aims, interdependent roles, and a distinctive subculture. In network formation on the other hand only some, not all, of the component individuals have social relationships with one another. . . . In a network the component external units do not make up a larger social whole; they are not surrounded by a common boundary.

Lauman's (1966, 1973) research on urban community social networks builds directly on the work of Bott. This form of social network is also found in Liebow's (1967) analysis of a low-income neighborhood, as well as several descriptions of work and associational settings (Kapferer, 1969; Mitchell, 1969; Milgram, 1970).

Helping/Social Networks

In helping networks, mutual aid is given and/or received with regard to problems confronted in one's daily life. Not all components or "members" of the network are found in a single setting, so that their mobilization as a network depends on activation by one member at a particular locale. What sharply separates this form from the close-knit network is specialization of content, heterogeneous composition, and absence of common values.

This form of social bond lies at the boundary of urban community organization because it is the exchange point between loose- and tight-knit social ties. Its flexibility and adaptability make it an ideal transition system. It provides both a medium for individual problem identification and coping as well as a means of reacting protectively against the general assaults of rapid or unanticipated social change.

Problem-anchored helping networks are heterogeneous in composition and can readily expand in a chain fashion outward to other networks. An individual may therefore belong to several networks simultaneously. These networks are bound together only through a common link of one individual and are not cohesive in any other way. Structurally, such networks are "always there" even if a given individual does not utilize them.

This concept was discussed by Speck and Attneuve (1973) in a mental health context. They describe the creation of a "social web" through the convening in one place of all of an individual's or family friends, neighbors, and kin, as well as mental health professionals. This network of up to 100 persons meets to solve a crisis and return the "patient" to a better mental state. Collins and Pancoast (1974) discuss the utility of "natural helping networks" in facilitating daycare services. Their program identified available helpers who served as key activists in outreach efforts, similar to the "reputational helpers" discussed by Warren (1976).

Loose-Knit (Radial) Social Networks

These networks consist of a heterogeneous sets of individuals who share superficial interactions but lack either a self-perceived common bond or a shared social status. Such social networks may be highly transient and rootless. They function largely as sociability clusterings in work settings and neighborhoods, or as transitional forms of group life. While impermanent and nonintimate, they may over time constitute nascent staging or spawning grounds for significant social groupings approaching the traditional primary group.

Bott (1957) described such groupings as "loose knit networks." Laumann (1966, 1973) uses the term "radial" for such networks, which he identifies in the following manner:

> They may be formed on some more specialized basis.... There is little need for uniformity of opinions across the set of persons inasmuch as

they do not interact with other than ego and he can tailor the interactional exchange to fit a particular dyadic relationship. Consequently the alters *can* be considerably more differentiated or heterogeneous in important social respects although . . . they do not have to be so.

People in radial networks are moreover likely to have a relatively lower affective involvement and commitment to their relations with alters because the set of common interests and concerns is likely to be more severely circumscribed and limited by virtue of the greater likelihood of differing statuses comprising the networks. (Laumann, 1973:114)

Laumann implies that although radial networks are less intimate than close-knit ones, they can be quite significant in contemporary urban society. They are highly flexible and thus adaptive to the demands for geographic and social mobility.

Weak Social Ties

This concept is derived from the work of Granovetter (1973, 1974) and of Duff and Liu (1972). The latter two researchers discovered that neighbors are a major source of information about family planning. Lower-income women in mixed-income neighborhoods shared more information than women in homogeneous middle- or lower-income neighborhoods. The "weak ties of neighborliness between some members of different socioeconomic classes allows new ideas to enter the network of homophilous relationships, where such ideas and information were hitherto unavailable" (Duff and Liu, 1972:366).

In a similar vein, Granovetter (1973:1371) comments that: "Those to whom we are weakly tied are more likely to move in circles different from our own and will thus have access to information different from that which we receive." When people are looking for a new job, he notes that: "In many instances the contact was someone only marginally included in the current methods of contacts, such as an old college friend or a former work mate or employer, with whom sporadic contact has been maintained." Granovetter (1973:1372) also points out that the original relationship was itself weak and "for work related ties respondents almost invariably said they never saw the person in a non-work context." He (1973: 1376) concludes that: "Unlike most models of interpersonal networks, the one presented here is not meant primarily for application to small, face to face groups of institutional settings."

Weak ties lack virtually all of the attributes of the traditional primary group, yet they can be enduring. They can be reactivated by chance or circumstance and can provide useful information and resources over an extended period of time. Through occasional utilization, loose-knit social ties bind together what are otherwise disparate social units and enable individuals to function on a more continuous basis.

This review of the literature has revealed the complexity of the social network concept and the varied ways in which it is employed among different researchers and scholars. The schema of six types of informal social ties that has been offered provides a basis for conceptual clarification. It also indicates the kinds of social integration or cohesion that can occur in a population or a spatially defined community. As this chapter proceeds, our attention will be focused on the problem-anchored helping network, and our applied interest will be in enhancing the problem-solving capability of such social entities.

WHAT ARE WE DOING?

At the present time, many community organization efforts are recognizing the importance of local self-help networks. A number of programs throughout the United States in the health, social service, planning, crime control, and neighborhood redevelopment spheres have attempted to identify and link up with natural/informal helpers. Some programs have developed their own terminology (e.g., "capacity building"), while others use general terms that are likely to cover a variety of activities (e.g., "outreach"). Three major approaches can be identified.

Focus on the Individual Case

With this approach networks and natural helpers are seen as resources for actual or potential clients of a formal agency. An elderly man, for example, may be having trouble caring for himself in his own home but will not have to be institutionalized if some formal supports can be developed. Three subtypes of agency intervention can be delineated: 1) agency staff identify members of the client's family, friendship, or neighborhood network and help them on the client's behalf, 2) agency staff identify specific services that the informal network cannot supply to the client and provide these services without usurping other functions of the natural network, and 3) agency staff refer isolated individuals to ongoing informal networks.

The work of Speck and Attneuve (1973) in regard to convening all members of one's "social support network" is an example of the first category. Some of the activities of the North Shore Child Guidance Center in New York illustrate the second category. It established a Family Life Center to help single parents cope with problems of their adolescent children after a survey showed that natural helpers could not meet this need. The third category is typified by the RSVP program conducted in Chicago by ACTION through the Senior Centers of Metropolitan Chicago that are affiliated with Hull House. This program, which seeks to reduce social isolation among the elderly, utilizes personal calls to elderly people and provides help with routine shopping, errands, and similar activities.

Increase the Capacity of the Informal System as a Whole

In this approach the formal agency does not identify specific clients or "at-risk" groups, but rather attempts to strengthen the community network for the benefits of all members. This could mean reducing residential mobility or supporting family life by modifying work schedules. Many of these efforts involve identifying "key figures" or natural helpers who can influence others in the network.

Some programs provide key figures with information to disseminate to other members of the network. For example, information about health problems and available health services is provided to key figures in a network of mothers who are not prone to seek preventative medical services for their children. Mental health consultation, focusing on specific problems faced by natural helpers as they attempt to assist members of their networks, has been provided by professionals. The National Institute of Mental Health (NIMH) has supported training of bartenders and beauty operators to deal with depression and aid in the referral process. Several projects have offered training to natural helpers in communication skills, crisis intervention techniques, and the use of formal community services (including such technical matters as obtaining home improvement loans).

Toward these ends, partnerships of various kinds have been established between natural helpers who have experienced certain kinds of problems and community institutions such as churches, synagogues, and social clubs. Examples of these efforts include the following: 1) Collins (1973) worked with neighbors who provide neighborhood daycare services for children. 2) Smith (1975) identified central figures who provided services to the elderly within their community. 3) Pancoast (1970) discovered and worked with a natural network of boarding homes for discharged mental patients in an urban poverty area. 4) Silverman (1976) catalyzed the development of an outreach program to the newly bereaved, called the Widow-to-Widow program. 5) Ellis (1972) initiated a program in which elderly people staff after-school activities for children of working mothers. 6) Patterson and Twente (1971) developed mental health services in rural areas using natural helpers and local counselors such as ministers, lawyers, bankers, and county extension agents. 7) Caplan (1976) organized support systems during a time of war and developed a program of professional aid in "supporting the supporters."

Valiance and his colleagues at Pennsylvania State University College of Human Development, in collaboration with the Geisinger Mental Health Center in Danville, are developing an experimental model to identify and train natural caregivers in order to extend preventive mental health manpower and to reduce costs of service delivery. In the first phase, professional educators will teach trainers to train direct service providers. These trainers will in turn train a group of formal and informal helpers in basic helping skills, crisis intervention skills, and life development skills. Finally, these natural helpers will enhance the development of life skills in others in their communities. The goal is to establish an administrative structure within a mental health system that can sustain and expand community helping networks.

Focus on the Community or Neighborhood

Sometimes agencies are less interested in particular individuals, whether they are clients or members of networks, than in improving the general liveability within a geographical area. They may use natural helpers to deal with issues such as neighborhood deterioration or racial tensions. Two different approaches to this practice have been identified. In one, agency staff encourage neighbors to identify common concerns, such as inadequate formal services, and to organize and bring pressure on institutions to improve their services. In the other, agency staff assist natural helpers/neighbors in identifying underutilized resources within the informal system and to develop ways to make better use of them.

The first approach is based on the concept of "indirect" capacity building, or "empowerment," in which an effort is made to consciously inculcate in indigenous populations the ability to influence formal agency services to meet neighborhood needs. One such capacity-building program is the Neighborhood and Family Services Project of the Washington Public Affairs Center of the University of Southern California. This project examined needs and resources from a neighborhood perspective in two ethnic communities in Baltimore and Milwaukee to determine ways of linking professional services to natural helping networks in the neighborhood such as churches, fraternal and social organizations, and natural helpers or "gatekeepers." In each city, the project was designed to work through a local community organization that is representative of, and controlled by, the residents of the community. The objective was to refocus previously fragmented services into a partnership of professional providers and informal helping resources in the community, mediated through a neighborhood organization.

The second approach, a "direct" linkage strategy, is being undertaken by the North Shore Child Guidance Center of Manhasset, New York, which is a community-based mental health facility serving families in seven communities. It is redesigning its programs with the goal of maximizing services while minimizing costs. Their efforts have led to the development of new services to unserved and underserved children and their families, such as child advocates for youthful offenders. A pilot survey was undertaken in one of the communities to examine the needs of women who were single parents. Members of existing formal and informal neighborhood support systems were interviewed, as well as single female heads of households from five different ethnic groups. A professional from the Center helped the community to organize on its own behalf. Volunteers collected data and communicated results to survey participants as well as to a range of other community resources that could play important support roles. The Center is currently planning a Family Life Center, utilizing professional resources in collaboration with neighborhood volunteers, to strengthen the capability of natural helping networks in all seven communities to meet the needs of families undergoing stress.

These developments in local informal networks are part of a broader pattern of neighborhood participation and voluntary association activity. In recent years, there has been a sustained level of grassroots activity of this type. Citizen participation has come to be associated with the decade of the 1960s, but precursors existed before then and other developments have followed into the mid and late 1970s. The frenetic 1960s displayed a vivid mosaic of organization activities: civil rights, black power, American Indian Movement, La Raza, Office of Economic Opportunity, community action, Alinsky, the student movement, the peace movement, Model Cities, welfare rights, feminism, gay liberation, environmental protection, consumer rights, white ethnic activism, political reforms, and so on. Grassroots civic action is often likened to a falling star, reaching its apex in the 1960s and plummeting to earth, burned out and dissipated, with the transition into the 1970s. A closer look reveals that the legacy of the 1960s has been carried forward, not in a spectacular way, but, nevertheless, with vitality and prevalence.

One element of this movement is the inclusion of provisions for citizen involvement in governmental programs of all sorts. A kind of "participation revolution" has been carried out somewhat imperceptibly but at least at the level of formal requirements. The participatory aspects of recent governmental programming have been described by Spergel as follows:

> Federal and state governments now encourage or require citizen partici-
> pation and structures and processes in most of their funded social pro-
> grams, including health, mental health, housing, manpower development,
> education, welfare, aging, economic development, and environmental
> and consumer protection. Recent evidence of federal support for
> community development and the necessity for local participation in
> governmental decision-making and program development is found in
> the State and Local Fiscal Assistance Act (federal revenue-sharing) of
> 1972 and the Housing and Community Development Act of 1974.
> (Spergel, 1977)

An even broader assessment by Wireman which takes into account both governmental factors and general community aspects, describes current grassroots activity in this manner:

> Despite a weakening of citizen input in many programs, new legislation
> in the mid-1970s strengthened the citizens' role in some instances;
> therefore, the situation remained mixed. Changes in Title XX of the
> Social Security Act mandated a period of public review before state
> plans for a variety of social service programs could be adopted. A
> majority of the members of health planning agencies must now be

consumers. Almost nine hundred community action agencies still exist, providing employment, community organizations, and social services. Some citizens continue to be active in decentralized city halls and neighborhood service centers. Others participate in consumer cooperatives or community development corporations in an attempt to make their neighborhoods more self-sufficient economically. Many citizens have turned to mass consumer education or political activities. (Wireman, 1976b)

WHAT HAVE WE ACCOMPLISHED?

The multifaceted interest in strategies using support networks, helping networks, and natural helpers represents a stimulating application of sociological knowledge. At the time of this writing, a major evaluation of "natural helping network projects" is underway by Diane Pancoast and her colleagues at the Regional Research Institute of Portland State University. Results from this effort and a growing number of related studies such as the health and social support studies by Kahn, French, and others at the Survey Research Institute at the University of Michigan, when completed, will undoubtedly help applied sociologists design and implement effective programs.

In the meantime, many policy questions regarding the use of informal community systems and intervention efforts remain unanswered. A number of these issues have recently been discussed in a paper presented by Donald Schon (1977), prepared for the National Institute of Education. In addition, the work of one of the authors of this chapter (Warren, 1976, 1980) reports results from surveys of several neighborhoods and communities on the role of helping networks in coping with problems and promoting individual well being.

In the report of the President's Commission on Mental Health (1978:15), the Task Force on Community Support urged that we "initiate research to increase our knowledge of informal and formal community support systems and networks." This Task Force also recommended that mental health research should include:

.... exchanges of information among lay community groups and mental health professionals about model, ongoing community support programs; ... development, through grants and contracts of demonstration programs with an evaluation component that can identify effective ways to establish linkages between community mental health services and community support systems; and development of research initiatives on the efficacy of social networks as adjuncts to mental health service delivery systems, and on the effects of informal and formal community support systems on the utilization of health and mental health services. (President's Commission on Mental Health, 1978:61)

Figure 7.1 Schematic Depiction of the Relation of Formal and Informal Life Support Systems

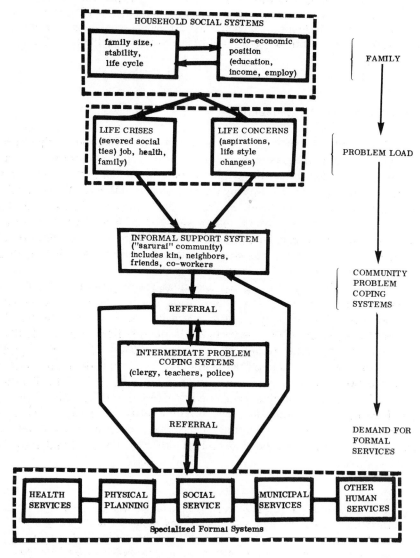

Source: Constructed by the authors.

As researchers and practitioners learn more about the positive functions of informal social support systems in helping people cope with stress and other life concerns, the importance of assuring that public and private agencies offering services are not destroying or discouraging natural support systems becomes increasingly clear. Some functions that are presently performed by formal services may devolve back to informal systems due to rising costs. Hospital stays, for example, are growing shorter, placing a greater burden on informal systems to provide convalescent care. Communities are also being asked to care for chronically disabled persons who were previously institutionalized.

There are weaknesses in natural support systems as well. These systems may be too selective and not include many people who could benefit from and contribute to them. There are undoubtedly many urban neighborhoods in which the residents are quite isolated and cannot rely on a neighborhood based helping system.

WHERE ARE WE GOING?

For applied sociology there is a range of roles and functions related to informal helping networks. Some of the main problems that can be met by such networks include the following:

1. Isolation and loneliness of individuals, particularly in urban settings.
2. Weakening of informal ties and social support systems, especially extended kinship structures.
3. Personal and family problems such as those associated with life crises (loss of a job), life concerns (getting a better education), and life conditions (social isolation).
4. Lack of knowledge of residents of community services and resources, and difficulty in making contact with and using such services and resources.
5. Environmental or structural problems at the local level that affect or cause problems for many individuals, such as uneven distribution of resources or lack of certain services in the community.

Both informal networks and formal service agencies can function to alleviate these problems. Sometimes one or another of these systems is better equipped to deal with the problem. Often some partnership or collaboration between the two is useful. A schematic depiction of the relationships that are involved is given in Figure 7.1.

Several applied research concerns can be identified for each level of analysis in the diagram and for the linkages between each level. For example:

1. What are the existing and emerging patterns of family life and neighborhood structure?

2. What are the existing and emerging life crises, concerns, and situations requiring assistance?
3. What are the existing and emerging patterns of informal support systems, and in what ways might these systems be strengthened?
4. What are the structures and programs of professional service agencies, and how well do they address the problems experienced at the grassroots level?
5. What are the linkages through which informal networks contact the formal service system, and how do agencies reach out to individuals?

A list of specific research tasks for applied sociologists would include the following:

1. Describing and analyzing the networks and natural helpers with which agencies throughout the country are currently working.
2. Describing the models of intervention that have been developed to date and assessing their effectiveness, taking into account the characteristics of the agency, the target population, and the type of community setting.
3. Determining what problems are best handled by informal networks, by formal agencies, and by collaborative endeavor.
4. More generally, designing strategies for increasing awareness in human service agencies of the existence of natural helping networks and for engaging such networks in providing services to individuals, families, and neighborhoods.

The "gatekeeping" role of the neighborhood is vital in this scheme. As we have shown, the nature of the local neighborhood can be defined in terms of its richness or lack of resources for problem solving. Neighborhoods can isolate individuals from the resources of society or to help tie them into these resources.

A basic problem facing the public sector and applied sociology is therefore to diagnose and understand differences in structure and social processes among communities and to identify the human resources and leadership available in local communities, as well as to work collaboratively with them in a variety of different situations (Warren and Warren, 1977).

Some applied action tasks for sociologists are evident. These include aiding in extending services to local people through outreach activities and helping local people make more appropriate use of formal services. The latter involves providing information to natural helpers about available services. Conversely, applied sociologists can help people avoid unnecessary use of formal services by referring clients to natural helpers. This may require providing natural helpers with consultation or training. More broadly, applied sociologists can focus on improving the environmental climate to maximize the effectiveness of informal support networks. This might involve helping people stave off commercial or governmental intrusions that are disruptive or destructive of neighborhood life. Applied sociologists can serve not only as data gatherers in these matters, but as facilitators, implementors, and change agents working collaboratively with social workers, public health personnel, and other human service professionals. Increasingly, applied sociologists will be using the skills of the service provider and social activist as well as those of the analyst. In a period of constricting academic opportunities, this broad conception of the role of applied sociology may represent not only an enlightened perspective but also a requirement for professional survival.

REFERENCES AND SUGGESTED READINGS

Blau, P.M. and W.R. Scott. 1962. *Formal Organizations: A Comparative Approach*. San Francisco: Chandler.

Bott, E. 1957. *Family and Social Network*. New York: The Free Press.

*Caplan, G. 1974. *Support Systems and Community Mental Health: Lectures on Concept Development*. New York: Behavioral Publications.

Caplan presents the theory of social support networks in overcoming personal isolation and achieving mental health. The focus is the application of community resources to the therapeutic repertoire of clinically trained mental health professionals.

_____. 1975. "Support Systems: A Model for Reaching the Population of a Community Mental Health Program." Keynote address at the Kings View Foundation Symposium on Prevention and Indirect Services. Fresno, California. (April 25, 1975.)

_____. 1976. "Organization of Support Systems for Civilian Populations." In *Support Systems for Mutual Help*, edited by G. Caplan and M. Killilen, pp. 273-315. New York: Grune and Stratton.

Collins, A.H. 1973. "Natural Delivery Systems: Accessible Sources of Power for Mental Health." *American Journal of Orthopsychiatry* 43(1):46-52.

*Collins, A.H. and D.I. Pancoast. 1974. *Natural Helping Networks: A Strategy for Prevention*. New York: National Association of Social Workers.

The book develops a social service intervention model in which the neighborhood is a basic link between professional practitioners and the local community. A case review of day care programs using this technique is utilized to illustrate the principles of natural networks. Also a good review of the early social network literature is provided.

Cooley, C.H. 1966. *Social Organization*. New York: Charles Scribner's Sons.

Cooley, C.H., R.C. Angel, and L.J. Carr. 1933. *Introductory Sociology* New York: Charles Scribner's Sons.

Craven, P. and B. Wellman. 1973. "Informal Interpersonal Relations and Social Networks." *Sociological Inquiry* 43:57-88.

de Tocqueville, A. 1947. *Democracy in America*. New York: Oxford University Press.

Duff, W. and W.T. Liu. 1972. "The Strength in Weak Ties." *Public Opinion Quarterly* 36(Fall):361–66.

Ellis, J.B. 1972. "Love to Share: A Community Project Tailored by Oldsters for 'Latch-Key' children." Paper presented at the meeting of the American Orthopsychiatric Association. Detroit.

Fischer, C. and R.M. Jackson. 1976. "Suburbs, Networks, and Attitudes." In *The Changing Face of the Suburbs*, edited by B. Schwartz. Chicago: University of Chicago Press.

Granovetter, M.S. 1973. "The Strength of Weak Ties." *American Journal of Sociology* 78(May):1360–80.

Granovetter, M.S. 1974. "Granovetter Replies to Gans." *American Journal of Sociology* 80(Jan):527–29.

Homans, G.C. 1950. *The Human Group*. New York: Harcourt Brace Jovanovich.

Kapferer, B. 1969. "Norms and Manipulation of Relationships in a Work Context." In *Social Networks in Urban Situations*, edited by J.C. Mitchell. Manchester, England: Manchester University Press.

Laumann, E.O. 1966. *Prestige and Association in the Urban Community*. Indianapolis: Bobbs-Merrill.

_____. 1973. *Bonds of Pluralism*. New York: John Wiley & Sons.

Liebow, E. 1967. *Tally's Corner*. Boston: Little, Brown and Company.

Litwak, E. and I. Zelenyi. 1969. "Primary Group Structures and Their Functions: Kin, Neighbors, and Friends," *American Sociological Review* 34 (Aug):465–81.

Mayo, E. 1945. *The Social Problems of an Industrial Civilization*. New York: Macmillan.

Milgram, S. 1970. "The Experience of Living in Cities." *Science* 167(Mar):1461–68.

*Mitchell, J.C. 1969. *Social Networks in Urban Situations*. Manchester, England: Manchester University Press.

The book is a compendium of studies by urban anthropologists and other urban researchers. It provides the background to later methodological studies and their applications to understanding urban social structure. It develops basic concepts about networks such as range, density, and paths.

Oberschall, A. 1973. *Social Conflict and Social Movements*. Englewood Cliffs, N.J.: Prentice-Hall.

Pancoast, D.I. 1970. "Boarding Home Providers for Released Mental Hospital Patients." Unpublished manuscript.

Patterson, S.L. and E. Twente. 1971. "Older Natural Helpers: Their Characteristics and Patterns of Helping." *Public Welfare* (Fall):400–3.

President's Commission on Mental Health. 1978. *Task Force on Community Support*. Vol. 1, ch. 1.

Roethlisberger, F.J. and W.J. Dickson. 1939. *Management and the Worker: Social Versus Technical Organization in Industry*. Cambridge, Mass.: Harvard University Press.

Rothman, J. 1979. "Three Models of Community Organization Practice, Their Mixing and Phasing." In *Strategies of Community Organization*, edited by Fred M. Cox, et al., pp. 25–45. Itasca, Ill.:F.E. Peacock.

Rothman, J. 1979. "Macro Social Work in a Tightening Economy." *Social Work* 24(Jul):274–81.

Sanders, I.T. 1958. *The Community*. New York: The Ronald Press.

Schon, D. 1977. "Network-Related Intervention." Washington, D.C.: National Institute of Education. Unpublished paper.

Seashore, S.E. 1954. *Group Cohesiveness in the Industrial Work Group*. Ann Arbor: University of Michigan, Survey Research Center.

*Silverman, P.R. 1976. *If You Lift The Load, I Will Lift It Too: A Guide To Developing Widow-to-Widow Programs*. New York: Jewish Funeral Directors of America.

This publication describes a major success story of applying the concept of support systems to the problems of bereavement. It suggests that at several different stages a network of widows creates a natural helping resource.

Smith, S.A. 1975. "Natural Systems and the Elderly: An Unrecognized Resource." Unpublished report. Oregon State Programs in Aging and the School of Social Work, Portland State University.

Speck, R. and C. Attneuve. 1973. *Family Networks: Retribalization and Healing*. New York: Pantheon.

Spergel, I. 1977. "Social Planning and Community Organization: Community Development." *Encyclopedia of Social Work*, 1428–29.

Vallance, T.R., C.E. Young, et al. 1976. "Indigenous Care Giving Networks in Primary Prevention" NIMH Project. Pennsylvania State University, College of Human Development.

Warren, D.I. 1975. *Black Neighborhoods: The Dynamics of Community Power*. Ann Arbor: The University of Michigan Press.

_____. 1976. *The Radical Center: The Politics of Alienation*. Notre Dame, Ind.: University of Notre Dame Press.

_____. 1978. "Social Bonds in the Urban Community: An Integrative Approach." Uppsala, Sweden: Unpublished paper read at the Eighth World Congress of Sociology.

_____. 1980. *Helping Networks: How People Cope with Problems in the Metropolitan Community*. Notre Dame, Ind.: University of Notre Dame Press. Warren reviews the findings of a study in the Detroit metropolitan area in which "recent concerns" and "life crises" are traced over a two-year time span to define the role of neighborhood, municipality, and socioeconomic status on the strength and type of help provided by informal and formal helpers. The author describes a basic theory of "organic" instrumental helping networks versus close-knit social networks.

Warren, D.I. and D. Clifford. 1974. "Invoked Expertise and Neighborhood Type: Two Critical Dimensions in the Coordination of Bureaucratic Service Organizations and Primary Groups." Montreal. Paper read at the annual meeting of the American Sociological Association.

Warren, R.B. and D.I. Warren. 1977. *The Neighborhood Organizer's Handbook*. Notre Dame, Ind.: University of Notre Dame Press.

Wellman, B. 1976. "Urban Connections." University of Toronto. Research Paper #84, Centre for Urban and Community Studies.

Wireman, P. 1976a. "Citizen Participation." *Encyclopedia of Social Work*. New

York: National Association of Social Workers, pp. 178–79.
————.1976b. "Meanings of Community in Modern America." Unpublished
  doctoral dissertation, American University.
Zald, M.N. 1977. "Demographics, Politics and the Future of the Welfare State."
  Social Service Review 59(Mar):120–22.

8 MASS COMMUNICATIONS

Alan Wells

The twentieth century is increasingly a media age. Radio, television, and the press are found throughout the world. In poor countries transistor radios are found in the remotest spots, and in rich countries it is virtually impossible to escape repeated daily contact with a variety of mass media. They are an important part of our environment. Many people spend more time watching television than any other single activity, while others are constantly accompanied by radio music and news bulletins. The media shape our language and our way of thinking and reasoning.

Given the pervasiveness of media in our environment it is perhaps surprising that so little sociological research has been done on this topic. We often take the media—like the air we breathe—for granted. The newest medium, television, has operated extensively for only three decades, and even newer developments like satellites, cable TV, and home video threaten to revolutionize media use. Research and our understanding of the media are hard pressed to keep pace with these developments. Knowledge follows, rather than precedes, media use. The media, therefore, pose serious problems for social scientists.

WHAT ARE THE PROBLEMS?

Sociological interests in mass media range across a broad spectrum of topics dealing with the connections between media and society. Sociologists who seek a general knowledge of society must take mass media into account. At the broadest level, we want to know how media shape the culture and way of life of a population. At a less abstract level, we may be concerned with organizational aspects of the media, such as how the media themselves are organized, how this influences their use, and how they relate to other organizations (financial, political, religious, military, and so on). Knowledge of such linkages is essential

157

to our understanding of social structure. Most sociological attention, however, has focused on the individual level, examining the characteristics of the audience and how the media effect, shape, influence, and change people.

Questions about mass media problems are different for more- and less-developed nations. In the more-developed countries, for example, we want to know whether the mass media are being used to further cultural goals. Are they producing a mass society, mindless consumerism, or a desensitized audience? Do they promote the values their audience would rationally dictate? To what degree are the media propaganda channels; do we need propaganda; what are the political impacts of the media? Are minority cultures adequately served and what is the effect of media on their cultures? To what degree are the media responsible for what some people see as a crisis in culture?

While these questions also apply to the less-developed nations, a further set of problems are crucial in these countries. Are the media the bearers of cultural disruption—Westernization—that is not essential for economic growth? Can the media provide shortcuts to literacy, health care, better technologies, population control, and so on, without destroying indigenous cultures? Can they, in sum, help provide a better life for the world's impoverished populations?

Organizational problems of the media have received relatively little attention by sociologists, although a broad literature of research findings on complex organizations is applicable in some respects. Problems include the types of organization that prevail and how these organizations affect media content. What are the linkages between media and other organizations? In the United States how do corporate interlocks effect media use? Or, in countries with state controlled media, how do intragovernmental conflicts influence media use? How do other organizations or individuals gain media access? Overall, how can the media be paid for, and who should control them?

The social psychological problems are concerned with the communication process, the characteristics of audiences, and the impact of media messages on their receivers. What are the difficulties in accurately relaying a message over a mass medium, and how do misunderstandings occur? Why do some people prefer one medium over another, use media more or less than others, and show differing degrees of attention and retention? How do media affect our thinking, change and shape our minds, often without our full consciousness? What, then, are the media's personal impacts on their audience?

Because of the pervasiveness of the media in modern societies, sociologists are increasingly concerned with these cultural, organizational, and social psychological questions. While much is yet to be learned, we have a broad basis for our understanding.

WHAT DO WE KNOW?

While the general problems of the mass media apply to both printed and electronic forms, attention here will be focused on the latter. This is partly because there is a massive literature on the printed media that cannot be easily summarized, and also because applied work apparently favors the new electronic media. More is expected of them as agents of change. Indeed, one basic fact is that when radio and television are available they are usually more popular with general audiences than print media.

Mass Media, Mass Society, and Mass Culture

During the last two centuries so many changes have taken place in Western societies that many social scientists claim we now have a qualitatively unique form of organization, often referred to as mass society. With the democratic revolutions in the United States and France at the end of the eighteenth century, men (and later both sexes) came to be viewed increasingly as political equals regardless of social status. The Industrial Revolution of the nineteenth century destroyed the old aristocratic order in Europe and the nascent one in the United States. Although industrialization shattered the economic basis of the old middle class, advanced industry did not lead to a simple division of society into impoverished workers and rich owners as Karl Marx had predicted. Because industrial society required a wide range of skills, class divisions were no longer clearly discernible. A job could not provide concrete social identity, for one was no longer simply an aristocrat or a peasant, a capitalist or a proletarian. The nation or the state became the primary source of self-identification. In this sense society became more of a homogeneous mass.

Industrialization also gave rise to the explosive growth of cities, and cheap transportation between them facilitated the establishment of national markets. Regional differences became less significant, and the new urban man, with his standardized, mass-produced possessions and uniform environment, became more like his fellow citizens than ever before. Mass society is characterized by bigness, standardization, increased density of settlements, and formal equality of individuals. The mass media are a product of this mass society, and they in turn produce a standard product for their audiences. It is often argued that the development of mass society leads to a homogenization of culture—the arts, values, and overall lifestyle of the population—which is in part due to the media's impact. Proponents of this view point out that the media constantly need material for their mass audiences. To fill pages and airwaves they borrow and popularize work meant for more refined tastes. (A record album entitled "Beethoven's Greatest Hits" comes readily to mind.) Artists themselves are tempted by the lucrative popular market, and artistic standards are undermined. The criteria of excellence becomes: "If it sells, it's good."

Of course, uniformity of culture is a matter of degree, since no audience is entirely homogeneous, and distinct social groups still exist. Ethnic groups, youth, and college-educated "highbrows," for example, often support their own specialized media.

Survey research carried out by Bradley Greenberg and Brenda Dervin (1970) further indicates that we must modify our views on the pervasiveness of the general mass media. Their study shows that the amount of media exposure as well as the tastes of the poor are in many ways more homogeneous than those of the general population. The poor watch more television and choose the most popular programs and are less open to such specialized media as magazines and newspapers. Since the media habits of the black and white poor do not vary much, the pattern of varied tastes and exposure has been attributed more to class characteristics, such as income levels and occupations, than to race. But at all social class levels the long-run historical trend seems to be toward increasing cultural uniformity.

Herbert Schiller (1971) has examined the uses of the media in industrial societies. Commercial "messages" and the increasing use of advertising skills in political management, he claims, constitute a form of mind management. Schiller skillfully ties this theme in with social and cultural changes taking place in the rich nations. The growth of an educated "information" work force and corporate consolidation has made mind management a priority. While the mass working class is already saturated with consumer values, he argues, it is now necessary to manipulate the new industrial intelligentsia that might question the status quo.

The age of mass media has coincided historically with a vast increase in the use and importance of propaganda. This is by no means accidental. The mass media inevitably speak for a select number of people who control the key means of persuasion in society. In modern societies people are expected to have opinions on a wide range of topics and, according to Jacques Ellul have a strong need for propaganda.

> The public will accept news if it is arranged in a comprehensive system, and if it does not speak only to the intelligence but to the "heart." This means, precisely, that the public wants propaganda, and if the State does not wish to leave it to a party, which will provide explanations for everything (i.e., the truth), it must itself make propaganda. Thus, the democratic state, even if it does not want to, becomes a propagandist state because of the need to dispense information. (Ellul, 1966:250)

The news in the press and electronic media serves this purpose.

Because there are often discrepancies between the government's interpretation of events and that offered by the mass media—neither of which is necessarily compatible with public opinion—the United States is internally vulnerable to credibility gaps. This, of course, is normal in a democracy. But, as Ellul has pointed out, competition in the Cold War—clearly a contest heavily dependent on propaganda—demands a united voice, which is the antithesis of democracy. Modern countries are engaged in international propaganda. The United States, as will be discussed later, operates the U.S. Information Service and Radio Free Europe, and the Soviet Union, Britain, France, and Germany are similarly active in overseas communication.

Terence Qualter (1962) has outlined the main techniques of propaganda. His definition of the term, like Ellul's, goes beyond that of most laymen, who tend to see propaganda as persuasive lies told by some person or organization they don't like (e.g., communist propaganda, Republican propaganda as interpreted by Democrats, and vice versa). To Qualter, propaganda is any message that "works on the minds of other men, seeking to influence their attitudes and thereby their actions." Thus, propaganda may be political, commercial (advertising), religious, etc. It may be good, evil, or neutral. Those who know the techniques readily switch from one type of persuasion to another, thus justifying the utility of this broad definition. For example, skilled advertisers may handle not only consumer goods but also religious revivals, political campaigns, and the type of national "image making" that is directed at foreign countries.

Robert Cirino (1971) has investigated propaganda in the U.S. media. Contrary to the claims of conservatives in government, he concludes that the media are inherently conservative and represent the views of the establishment. Cirino, who has amassed considerable evidence supporting this position, points out that the media label leftist viewpoints as propaganda but do not label their own bias. We are seldom aware of the status quo viewpoint of our own press, or of the way in which sports entertainment—the Super Bowl for example—is turned into a nationalist celebration (Real, 1975).

News is one of the prime areas for propaganda, despite claims of objectivity (Tuchman, 1972). Network news, like other programming, revolves around commercial imperatives. Newscasters have been promoted as entertainment stars, and the news in general is treated as just one more program in which to set advertisements. Epstein (1973) conducted the first "inside" study of network news. While he did not fault the system as a whole, he did find built-in biases in network news. The news production process originates in New York City and stresses only big city news. The network newsmen must "create" news, and their need for visual material has placed emphasis on violent and sensational events. Epstein suggests organizational changes that would remedy some of these built-in biases. The networks could regionalize their evening news, increase their news staffs, utilize a string of local reporters (as do the wire services), and deemphasize violence. But, as Epstein notes, these steps would hurt the networks financially. Despite such criticism, numerous polls indicate that TV anchormen have high credibility—above that of politicians—and that network news is the public's first choice for information.

We know that the instruments of mass communication in the modern world have an enormous potential for shaping politics. This is particularly obvious in totalitarian societies, where the media are under direct political control. Misuses in our own society are less obvious but real enough, and in recent years public concern has grown over such issues as political bias and control, the effect of the media on political campaigns, and the long-range implications for the political system.

Perhaps the most important political effect of the media is an "unseen" one, their ability to "set the agenda" of public debate. This ability, claim McCombs and Shaw (1976), is shared by politicians, news reporters, and editors working together. They decide what is "newsworthy," along with the reporters and editors of the wire services.

The news and public issues that are exposed by these organizations constitute a large degree of what we know of politics. Sidney Kraus (1973) has summarized what contemporary research findings show about the ways in which the media shape political opinions and actions. Because young voters today, unlike their parents, have grown up with television, they are much more likely to have learned political concepts from that medium. Not only has television brought them direct political information, it has also shaped their view of the country and of the world. That view is both more sophisticated and less optimistic than that of their elders. Kraus concludes that since much research still ignores the possibility that the media are important in forming political beliefs, more research and reevaluation are called for.

Organization of the Media

We know surprisingly little about the organization of mass media and their interrelation with other organizations, despite the political influence this may have on content and audience effects. We do know that a number of different organizational forms are possible, including state control, public nonprofit corporations (with or without state partnership), and private corporations. The United States has generally opted for the latter.

Prior to the introduction of television, radio in the United States was dominated by national networks and programmed for mass audiences. Now, however, radio is a diversified medium with more specialized audiences. Most stations are run as local, profit-making ventures, often linked to larger financial corporations. They are devoted primarily to entertainment (DeFleur and Ball-Rokeach, 1975). In poor countries, radio is often still geared to national audiences and is widely considered a powerful educational medium.

Television reaches more than 97 percent of all U.S. households, who average about six hours per day of viewing time. From the outset, television broadcasting in the United States has been overwhelmingly a commercial undertaking, even though the airwaves are recognized by law, if not by the industry, to be public property. The Federal Communications Commission has weak regulating authority over the medium's operators.

Television was a $4.1 billion industry by 1975 with an income of $780 million. More than $300 million went to the three networks: NBC, CBS, and ABC. These networks are not autonomous entrepreneurial establishments in any real sense. NBC is a subsidiary of RCA as are Hertz, Banquet and Oriel Foods, Random House, RCA records, and others. CBS's "family" is reported to include Creative Playthings (toys), book publisher Holt, Rinehart, and Winston, and CBS records. ABC-TV is a part of the larger ABC-Paramount organization. Banks have heavy stock participation in all three (Pearce, 1976). The impact of these financial ties has not been fully understood or researched.

We do know that the organizational form of commercial television demands that network programs meet financial rather than artistic criteria. These programs generate a large audience that can be sold to advertisers. Soap operas, game shows, and situation comedies are cheap to produce but hold mass audiences, with possibly serious cultural impact (Goldsen, 1977).

Public television in the United States is clearly overshadowed by commercial interests. The noncommercial network, PBS, runs many cultural and general interest programs in addition to daytime school programming. Public stations however, have continuous financial difficulties and must rely on private contributions and a limited amount of tax money (Cater and Nyhan, 1976). Many of public TV's successful programs, therefore, are imported. They are high-budget programs produced, for the most part, by the British Broadcasting Corporation and rented for a fraction of their production costs. At present, PBS cannot finance a full schedule of quality programming.

Social Psychology of Mass Media

The study of mass communication by social scientists has been overwhelmingly concerned with social psychological questions about the ways in which the media influence their audience. What follows is a summary of the most reliable knowledge established by empirical research over several decades about the basic communication process, information flow, and the capabilities of messages to change the opinions and behavior of their audiences.

Wilbur Schramm (1955) has outlined the basic model of communication used by researchers. Information held by the sender is "coded," that is, an idea is put into words, print, or film. This message is then sent out as a "signal." If it is received by an audience, it may be "decoded" and reinterpreted as an idea. Only then is the information received. A break may occur at every link in this chain. The intended meaning may not be conveyed in the coding process, the signal may be faulty and hence not received, the decoder may infer meanings other than those intended and, finally, the message may be rejected by the receiver. Schramm outlines the conditions under which such breakdowns can be avoided. In mass communications the sender is an organization, while the receivers are individuals. Unlike face-to-face communication, there is no real feedback enabling the receiver to become the sender, and the communicator has no immediate cues to indicate whether his message has been received as intended.

In Schramm's communication scheme the sender must sift his information before he codes a message. He selects from all the information available to him only those elements that he wants to convey. If he is a newspaperman or a TV newsman, he will probably rely on a wire service for information. The content of the wire he receives is a product of several editorial stages. The field reporter is selective in what he reports; then regional and national wire editors decide which incoming news items to pass on. Any person who serves this editing and condemning function may be called a "gatekeeper." David White (1950) examined in detail the way one of these men, a newspaper wire editor, went about his task. His decisions were highly subjective, reflecting his own values and prejudices rather than those of his audience or the intrinsic "newsworthiness" of the items he selected. This subjectivity no doubt affects all "gatekeepers" to a degree. The functions of "gatekeepers" are basic to our understanding of the media (Bass, 1969).

At the other end of the communication chain, mass media messages often do not go directly to the target audience. Instead, there is what has been termed a "two-step flow" of information (Katz and Lazarsfeld, 1955; Katz, 1957). The message transmitted by the mass media is picked up by "opinion leaders" who pass it on to the mass population. This idea has generated considerable interest among communication researchers. Irving L. Allen (1969), for example, has shown that knowledge of public affairs is greater among those who talk about the news than among those who silently absorb it from the media. Apparently interpersonal contacts reinforce mass-directed messages. Other researchers who set out to test the two-step flow hypothesis were less convinced of its validity, however (Troldahl, 1966-67; Greenberg, 1964). People today may well be turning more and more to the media rather than to other individuals, not only for technical information, but for news of political and social issues as well. The media appear to have a more direct effect on us than ever before.

Gerhart Wiebe (1969-70) attempted to explain why the audience for banal television programs continues to be very large. He claims that such programs serve the psychological needs of the mass audience because they do not make intellectually demanding appeals for change, nor do they present unfamiliar subject matter that would require concentrated attention. These programs are geared to existing values and sentiments. The effect of such media content, however, is probably less innocuous than Wieber implies. There is considerable hidden bias in even the tamest program.

Leon Festinger (1964) has usefully summarized existing knowledge of the relations of opinions to behavior change. He notes that researchers overly concerned with opinion change have often simply assumed that behavior is consequently modified. When both opinion and behavior change are measured the results are often different. A new opinion may be insufficiently internalized to modify behavior. Thus, the espousal of "correct" opinions on race may not change the actual behavior of whites toward minorities. In fact, subsequent behavior may be even more strongly opposed to the new opinion. Festinger gives as an example an experiment in which subjects were given instructions on dental hygiene. The subjects who received the harshest message had the largest change in attitude but the smallest change in subsequent behavior. The strong message may be convincing at first but later rejected if it doesn't fit the recipient's existing cognitive structure. In addition, Festinger noted that a new attitude must be reinforced by external support.

Raymond Bauer (1964) has also investigated the autonomy of audiences. He summarizes many of the findings of communications research and detects two conflicting traditions: a social model, which stresses media exploitation of a preponderantly passive audience, and a scientific model, which emphasizes the transactional nature of communications. Although Bauer prefers the latter view, evidence for the former can scarcely be denied. A way to synthesize the two should be on the agenda for future research.

We have, therefore, a broad base of knowledge about the mass media and their social effects. This knowledge shapes the applied research efforts currently in progress.

WHAT ARE WE DOING?

In recent years considerable attention has been given to applied research on the mass media. This research has been directed to the evaluation of media effects, particularly the effects of violence, the handling of sex roles, and the media's effect on children. Some research has also been conducted on the planning and production stage of programming, most notably in the Children's Television Workshop's productions *Sesame Street* and *The Electric Company* and in educational TV generally (Mendelsohn, 1969). Research inputs have been used in regulating the media and in international propaganda. In poor countries very large "action research" projects in literacy, development, and family planning have been conducted.

Media research has covered the full range of tasks attributed to applied sociology by DeMartini (1979) and Lazarsfeld and Reitz (1975). Media researchers have been active in the formation of public policy—for example, in the conduct of research for presidential commissions (Komarovsky, 1975)—although their recommendations are often ignored. Thus the Kerner Commission on violence (Baker and Ball, 1969), the Commission on Obscenity and Pornography (*Report*, 1970), and the Surgeon General's Advisory Committee on Television and Social Behavior (1972) all conducted and collected research findings. Their recommendations for socially constructive program changes, however, have had little direct impact, as we will see in the following section.

Broadcasters, especially outside the United States, feel the need to conduct research prior to production (Ono, 1974), and the U.S. networks employ in-house research staffs. There have been conflicts between researchers and industry representatives in policy research (Paisley, 1972), and the academic researcher clearly loses some autonomy when serving in an applied capacity. Several prominent researchers were barred from participation in the Surgeon General's study by network vetos (Baffey and Walsh, 1970). Nevertheless, interest in active applied research involvement continues (Annenberg, 1977). In-house research is often conducted primarily to justify existing media practices and counter outside critics. To answer its critics, CBS has conducted large scale social surveys to show, for example, the positive rather than antisocial learning of children viewing its entertainment programming (Child Research Service, 1975).

Applied research and expert testimony have been employed in the regulation of the media. Self-regulation by professional codes of ethics (for example, the National Association of Broadcasters broadcasting code) has not been highly successful in maintaining standards (Persky, 1977). The media are subject to the pressures of critics, press councils, and public opinion. The latter includes both fragmented audience response and the coordinated complaints of citizens' pressure groups. These citizens groups—for example, Action for Children's Television (ACT) and the Office of Communication of the United Church of Christ (which has systematically monitored television programs)—generate and employ much media research findings in their lobbying. They have been most successful when they have mobilized a public, and then put pressure on regulatory and legal agencies rather than directly on the broadcaster.

The mass media are regulated by many different government agencies. The basic guidelines come from the executive branch of government and congressional legislation. On a day-to-day basis, both the Justice Department and the Federal Trade Commission are involved with law enforcement. But the most important regulatory agency is the Federal Communications Commission. The FCC has authority to license the more than 7,000 radio and television broadcasting stations in the United States. The license renewal process that stations must undergo every three years is a forum for pressure groups. The FCC also holds public hearings in developing legislative proposals and framing its own policies such as the "fairness doctrine," or the rules governing fair advertising, political campaigning and viewpoints, and right to reply to personal attacks.

The FCC is neither a large nor an activist body (Johnson, 1970), and it often must be pushed into action. While the FCC has been an advocate of limiting cross-media ownership (for example, a newspaper owning a television station), it formulated a rule in 1975 exempting existing cross ownership (Gormley, 1977). A pressure group, the National Citizens Committee for Broadcasting, successfully contested the FCC's rule in 1977 before the U.S. Court of Appeals. Evidence like that collected by Gormley (1977) on the limitation of news sources in cross ownership is highly useful in such litigation.

Media research, particularly as it relates to successful propaganda, is widely employed in international communication. The United States Information Agency's task is to aid U.S. foreign policy through information and advisory services and by influencing public opinion overseas. The agency staff of over 9,000 persons provides numerous services. USIA's operations are very diffuse, including staffing 168 overseas posts, maintaining libraries, distributing subsidized textbooks, publishing magazines, running "binational centers," and promoting all official large-scale exhibitions abroad. The Agency produces a daily news teletype as well as film and television program services for foreign media. Its most direct impact, however, occurs through the Voice of America radio network. VOA has more than 100 transmitters world wide, broadcasting 858 hours per week in 36 languages to an estimated audience of more than 50 million people (U.S. Information Agency, 1973). The U.S. government also operates several formerly clandestine radio stations (see U.S. Senate, 1971, 1972) including Radio Free Europe and Radio Liberty beamed to the communist bloc. Both the VOA and RFE conduct audience research to gauge their effectiveness. RFE, for example, has polled listeners and nonlisteners in Poland to determine program effects on political attitudes (Radio Free Europe, 1976).

Large scale research and development programs in poor countries have built on experiences gained in the 1950s and 1960s (Lerner and Schramm, 1967). The focus of many projects has been the diffusion of innovations (Rogers and Shoemaker, 1971) and attitude change in the least-developed sections of poor societies (Rogers, 1969). Programs have been aimed at changes in agriculture, health, family planning, literacy, and formal education. These range from introducing new seed and planting methods of crops in India, radio forums for small farm information in Jordan and India, and mobile information teams promoting public health in the Philippines and South Korea to television literacy programming in many less-developed countries (Schramm, 1964).

WHAT HAVE WE ACCOMPLISHED?

The results of applied media research are not, of course, always decisive, nor are policy implications necessarily heeded. But such research is not without impact, at least in directing public attention to the issues.

Racism and Sexism

The relation of mass media to sexism and racism in American society is a complex issue. It can be approached by asking, first, how the media cover different racial and ethnic minorities and the sexes and, second, how these groups should be treated if the media are to help build a more egalitarian society. Media coverage raises both quantitative and qualitative issues. How much time is given to the various groups, and what type of coverage are they given? A related question is whether the media employ and promote women and minorities on the same basis as white males?

Charlotte O'Kelly and Linda Bloomquist (1976) did a content analysis of network programming and found that both women and blacks were stereotyped and underrepresented. More exposure, therefore, would not necessarily change people's attitudes on racism and sexism.

When the "white" media attempt to reduce racism, their effort can backfire. *All in the Family*, the highly popular TV program, was supposed to reduce racism, and it won an NAACP award for its contribution to race relations. Neil Vidmar and Milton Rokeach (1974) studied the effects of Archie Bunker's bigotry. Their findings suggest a negative outcome—that lovable Archie wins supporters and reinforces the racism of the bigots in his audience. Because of its controversial nature, this program has generated a large body of research (Surlin, 1976).

In regard to sexism in the media, Helen Franzwa (1974) has analyzed women's magazine fiction. She concludes that, despite the increasing number of women in the work force, they are usually portrayed as docile homebodies, housewives, and mothers. Alternatively, they play negative sex roles in which their lives revolve around the absence of men; they are presented as sad or comic husband-seeking singles, widows, and divorcees, or as aging spinsters. Similar results have been found for television (Long and Simon, 1974; Guttman, 1973; Levenson, 1975). Women are seldom portrayed as individuals with independent lives and careers of their own. Above all, the media treat women as sex objects, typified by the illustrations, if not always the text, of *Playboy* and scarcely less subtly by advertising copy.

Even public television is afflicted by this problem. Muriel Cantor (1977) reports that although the treatment of women in public broadcasting is better than on commercial television, there is much room for improvement. This holds true for programs aimed at adults and even in children's programming, an area where public television is often thought to be uniquely enlightened. The Task Force on Women in Public Broadcasting (Isher and Cantor, 1975) also found evidence of discriminatory employment practices in public broadcasting. The recommendations by the Task Force to the PBS have stimulated some changes in employment, but none as yet in programming. Women are still seen, Cantor concludes, as a special group rather than an integral part of the population involved in all social and political issues.

Violence

While scholarly research concludes that most pornography is basically harmless (*Report*, 1970), research on violence indicates the opposite. The media portrayal of violence has powerful and harmful effects. (For a discussion of this seeming contradiction in the effects of media, see Dienstbier, 1977.) Neither finding has been readily accepted by policy makers.

Academic researchers have investigated the effects of violent television programs on children and have helped precipitate the current debate on the subject. Albert Bandura's (1963) laboratory research, for example, has shown that viewing violence reduces inhibitions on aggressive behavior and teaches children aggression. This apparently also holds true for adults. Most TV viewers know how to commit murder, elementary forms of torture, and other crimes, even if they don't practice them. The mass media effects, together with novels and handed-down nursery tales and folklore, are perhaps more important in the formation of a climate of violence than in triggering it directly. The networks, of course, claim that their programming is not harmful, and both NBC and ABC have sponsored research (Goldsen, 1971; Milavsky and Barton, 1972) presumably in the hope of supporting their position. Other researchers (Feshback and Singer, 1971; Kaplan and Singer, 1976) have attempted to refute the argument that violent programming *directly* affects behavior.

The Surgeon General's Scientific Advisory Committee on Television and Social Behavior (1972) was formed to study TV programming and its effect on children. The study convinced the Surgeon General that television violence is indeed harmful. His research director, Eli Rubinstein (1974, 1976), has argued that it is now time for action: we should learn how to produce socially constructive programming for children. Bogart (1972:973) argues that the Committee's study was not needed because there was already enough evidence of the effects of violence, but he concurs on the need for action.

The most prominent investigator of TV violence today, the person credited with putting the networks "under fire" as never before, is George Gerbner (1975). Using methods contested by the networks, he and his associates have devised a "TV violence profile" of the year's programming, which they publish annually. The networks have responded with annual violence reports of their own (Klapper, 1977). Gerbner claims that high audience consumption leads to the development of a "mean world" view, in which heavy viewers "see the real world as more dangerous and frightening than those who watch very little." They are "less trustful of their fellow citizens and more fearful of the real world" (Gerbner and Gross, 1976:41). In summarizing the antiviolence movement to date, Gerbner (1975) finds that it has often missed what is to him the main point: TV violence is probably not presented by "corporate America" to stimulate off-screen violence, but to use symbolic violence for social control. TV violence is not the precursor of more violence, but of ultimate oppression.

Social Change in Less-Developed Countries

Change programs in poor countries have had mixed results, but they have usually provided less impact than their design called for. In the process, much has been learned about how and how not to use mass media. Schramm (1977) warns of the care necessary in choosing the appropriate medium for the job. All too often the most sophisticated news medium, such as satellite TV, is chosen over more suitable indigenous media. Rogers and Adhikarya (1978) have evaluated recent research findings and project experience. They claim that the communication part of the projects in agriculture, literacy, hygiene, and so on, is too often not an integral part of the project design. Feedback, or two-way communication, is often nonexistent or neglected, and audience characteristics are often slighted. Before major changes can occur, there must usually be broad structural changes. This is a major political constraint for field projects. For example, programs often aid rich farmers in rural projects, and the poor correctly discern that the program is not for them.

Birth control programs are similarly most successful with audiences (usually the more affluent) who are predisposed to family limitation from the outset. Rogers (1973) has made a comprehensive survey of national family planning programs and numerous research findings, including several hundred "KAP" studies (almost half in India). KAP studies measure knowledge of, attitude toward, and practice of birth control. Most studies show that while knowledge can be readily disseminated through mass media, attitudes and especially practices are much more difficult to change. Indeed, Rogers concludes that population programs that rely on diffusion of information and media persuasion cannot be successful in reducing population unless they are part of a much broader population policy.

WHERE ARE WE GOING?

Applied communication research faces a number of new challenges. In poor countries social needs are likely to perpetuate mass programs that use media research. The problem in these programs is to avoid the failures of the past. Even a well codified body of knowledge from previous programs cannot alone ensure success. A village in Mexico is not the same as one in India. But after taking local conditions into account, a set of generalized principles, some of which are now available, would clearly be useful. Project organization structures, political influences, and researcher authority will continue to be problems. Applied research, as in the past, will often go unheeded, especially when it conflicts with bureaucratic or political ideologies.

In the United States a new type of "action" research may grow. Particularly in issue areas like violence and sexism, the results are already clear. We know that the media exploit violence successfully because it holds audiences. We know that media programs are often sexist and insensitive to minorities. The problem is what to do next. In television the question is how to make the networks pay for their antisocial programming. This is now being attempted through applied sociology in support of legal briefs and regulatory hearings and through mass mobilization and politicization of citizen pressure groups. Until the commercial imperatives of network television are challenged, however, it is unlikely that even sustained pressure group activity can make social uplift, aesthetics, or even intelligence the prime consideration in programming.

Before this action research can be launched, the mass media are likely to be revolutionized by the spread of existing technology. Satellites and cable systems, for example, can greatly increase the number of television channels. These technologies drastically fragment audiences and could shatter the financial base of network television. Recent profit taking in the face of declining audiences may indicate that the networks know the end is in sight. Home video is also spreading rapidly, and the combined new technologies could make two-way communication a reality, the newspaper obsolete, and mass audiences a part of history.

These new developments will pose the greatest challenge for applied media research. Mass audience characteristics will be of declining importance, but the opportunities for research on effects via two-way communication will become increasingly possible. Who will sponsor such research and who will finance the emerging fragmented media system will be our most immediate problems.

REFERENCES AND SUGGESTED READINGS

Allen, I.L. 1969. "Social Relations and the Two-Step Flow: A Defense of the Tradition." *Journalism Quarterly* 46(Autumn):492–98.

Annenberg School of Communication. 1977. *Social Research and Broadcasting*, Proceedings of a symposium. University of Southern California, Los Angeles (August).

Baffey, P.M. and J. Walsh. 1970. "Study of TV Violence: Seven Top Researchers Blackballed from Panel." *Science* 22(May):949–52.

Baker, R.K. and S.J. Ball. 1969. *Mass Media and Violence, A Staff Report to the National Commission on the Causes and Prevention of Violence*. Washington, D.C.: U.S. Government Printing Office.

Bandura, A. 1963. "What TV Violence Can Do to Your Child." *Look*, October 22, 1963, pp. 46–52.

Bass, A.Z. 1969. "Refining the 'Gatekeeper' Concept." *Journalism Quarterly* 46(Spring):69–72.

Bauer, R. 1964. "The Obstinate Audience." *American Psychologist* 19(May): 319–28.

Bogart, L. 1972–73. "Warning: The Surgeon General has determined that TV violence is moderately dangerous to your child's mental health." *Public Opinion Quarterly* 36(4):491–521.

Cantor, M.A. 1977. "Women in Public Broadcasting." *Journal of Communications* 27(Winter):14–19.

Cater, D. and Michael J. Nyhan, eds. 1976. *The Future of Public Broadcasting*. New York: Praeger.

Child Research Service. 1975. *A Study of Message Received by Children Who Viewed an Episode of "The Harlem Globetrotters Popcorn Machine."* New York: Columbia Broadcasting System, Office of Social Research.

Cirino, R. 1971. *Don't Blame the People*. New York: Random House.

DeFleur, M.L. and S. Ball-Rokeach. 1975. *Theories of Mass Communication*. New York: Longman.

DeMartini, J.R. 1979. "Applied Sociology: An Attempt at Clarification and Assessment." *Teaching Sociology*, 6(July):331–54.

*Dennis, E.E. 1978. *The Media Society*. Dubuque, Iowa: William C. Brown.
This is a basic text on the relation of mass media and society (primarily in the United States). It draws extensively on media research findings. Its three sections are on the impact of media, their operation, and criticism. These include treatment of policy topics and applied research.

Dienstbier, R.A. 1977. "Sex and Violence: Can Research Have It Both Ways?" *Journal of Communication* 27(Summer):176–88.

Ellul, J. 1966. Konrad Kellen and Jean Lerner, trans. *Propaganda*. New York: Alfred A. Knopf.

Epstein, E.J. 1973. "The Selection of Reality." *The New Yorker*, March 3, 1973, pp. 41–77.

Feshback, S. and R.D. Singer. 1971. *Television and Aggression*. San Francisco: Jossey-Bass.

Festinger, L. 1964. "Behavioral Support for Opinion Change." *Public Opinion Quarterly* 29(Fall):404–17.

Franzwa, H. 1974. "Working Women in Fact and Fiction." *Journal of Communication* 24(Spring):104–09.

Gerbner, G. 1975. "Scenario for Violence." *Human Behavior* (Oct):65–69.

*Gerbner, G., ed. 1977. *Mass Media Policies in Changing Cultures*. New York: John Wiley & Sons.
The 25 essays in this volume were selected to provide a "multinational comparative perspective" to aid communication policy makers. They are divided into three sections: international trends, Third World media, and new developments in theory and research.

Gerbner, G. and L. Gross. 1976. "The Scary World of TV's Heavy Viewer." *Psychology Today*, 9(Apr):41–45.

Goldsen, R.K. 1971. "NBC's Make-Believe Research on TV Violence." *Transaction* 8(Oct):29–35.

———. 1977. *The Show and Tell Machine*. New York: The Dial Press.

Gormley, W.T. 1977. "How Cross-Ownership Affects News Gathering." *Columbia Journalism Review* 16(June):38–46.

Greenberg, B.S. 1964. "Person-to-person Communication in the Diffusion of News Events." *Journalism Quarterly* 41(Autumn):489–94.

Greenberg, B.S. and B. Dervin. 1970. "Mass Communication Among the Urban Poor." *Public Opinion Quarterly* 35(Summer):224–36.

Guttman, J. 1973. "Self-Concepts and Television Viewing Among Women." *Public Opinion Quarterly* 38(Fall):388–97.

Haden-Guest, A. 1977. "The Man Who's Killing TV Violence." *New York*, July 11, 1977, pp. 33–36.

Isher, C. and M.G. Cantor. 1975. *Report on the Task Force on Women in Public Broadcasting*. Washington, D.C.: Corporation for Public Broadcasting.

*Jamison, D.T. and E.G. McAnany. 1978. *Radio for Education and Development*. Beverly Hills, Calif.: Sage.
The book gives a summary of the use of radio in low-income countries. It focuses on radio's use in formal education and development communica-

tion, what has been learned, and how the medium could be used. The constraints to new radio strategies are also considered.

Johnson, N. 1970. *How to Talk Back to Your Television Set*. New York: Bantam.

Kaplan, R.M. and R.D. Singer. 1976. "Television Violence and Viewer Aggression: A Re-examination of the Evidence." *Journal of Social Issues* 32:35–70.

Katz, E. 1957. "The Two-Step Flow of Communication: An Up-to-Date Report on an Hypothesis." *Public Opinion Quarterly* 21(Spring):61–78.

Katz, E. and P.F. Lazarsfeld. 1955. *Personal Influence*. Glencoe, Ill.: Free Press.

Klapper, J.T. 1977. *Network Prime-Time Violence Tabulations for the 1976–77 Season*. New York: Columbia Broadcasting System, Office of Social Research. (May 6).

Komarovsky, M., ed. 1975. *Sociology and Public Policy: The Case of Presidential Commissions*. New York: Elsevier.

Kraus, S. 1973. "Mass Communication and Political Socialization." *Quarterly Journal of Speech*, 59(Dec):390–400.

Lazarsfeld, P.F. and J.G. Reitz. 1975. *An Introduction to Applied Sociology*. New York: Elsevier.

Lerner, D. and W. Schramm, eds. 1967. *Communication and Change in Developing Countries*. Honolulu: East-West Center Press.

Levenson, Richard M. 1975. "From Olive Oyl to Sweet Polly Purebread: Sex Role Stereotypes and Televised Cartoons." *Journal of Popular Culture* 9(Winter):561–73.

Long, Michele L. and R.J. Simon. 1974. "The Roles and Statuses of Women on Children's and Family TV Programs." *Journalism Quarterly* 51(Spring): 107–10.

McCombs, M.E. and D.L. Shaw. 1976. "Structuring the 'Unseen Environment'." *Journal of Communication* 26(Spring):18–22.

Mendelsohn, H. 1969. "What to Say to Whom in Social Amelioration Programming." *Educational Broadcasting Review* 3:19–26.

Milavsky, J.R. and A.H. Barton. 1972. "In Defense of NBC Violence." *Transaction* 9(Jan):30–31.

O'Kelly, C.G. and L.E. Bloomquist. 1976. "Women and Blacks on TV." *Journal of Communication* 26(Autumn):179–184.

Ono, K. 1974. "How Research Can Help Broadcasters." *Media Asia* 1:17–21.

Paisley, M.B. 1972. *Social Policy Research and the Realities of the System: Violence Done to TV Research*. Stanford, Calif.: Stanford University, California Institute for Communication Research.

Pearce, A. 1976. "The TV Networks: A Primer." *Journal of Communication* 26(Autumn):54–59.

Persky, J. 1977. "Self-Regulation of Broadcasting—Does It Exist?" *Journal of Communication* 27(Spring):118–21.

Qualter, Terence H. 1962. *Propaganda and Psychological Warfare*. New York: Random House.

Radio Free Europe, Audience and Public Opinion Research Department. 1976. *Party Preferences in Poland, 1968–1975* (January).

Real, M.R. 1975. "Super Bowl: Mythic Spectacle." *Journal of Communication* 25(Winter):31–43.

Report of the Commission on Obscenity and Pornography. 1970. New York: Bantam.

Rogers, E.M. 1969. *Modernization Among Peasants: The Impact of Communication.* New York: Holt, Rinehart and Winston.

*_____. 1973. *Communication Strategies for Family Planning.* New York: The Free Press.

Rogers gives a comprehensive evaluation of population programs worldwide and of the role of communication. The book suggests strategies to improve communication aimed at change. They are based on communication theory and numerous population research findings, including the author's studies in Asia and recent information from China.

Rogers, E.M. and R. Adhikarya. 1978. "Communication and Equitable Development: Narrowing the Socio-economic Benefits Gap." *Media Asia* 5:3–10.

Rogers, E.M. and F.F. Shoemaker. 1971. *Communication of Innovations.* 2nd ed. New York: The Free Press.

Rubinstein, E.A. 1974. "The TV Violence Report: What's Next?" *Journal of Communication* 24(Winter):80–88.

_____. 1976. "Warning: Surgeon General's Research Program May be Dangerous to Preconceived Notions." *Journal of Social Issues* 32:18–34.

Schiller, H.I. 1971. "Mind Management: Mass Media in the Advanced Industrial State." *Quarterly Review of Economics and Business* 11(Spring):39–52.

Schramm, W. 1955. *The Process and Effects of Mass Communication.* Urbana: University of Illinois Press.

_____. 1964. *Mass Media and National Development.* Stanford, Calif.: Stanford University Press.

*_____. 1977. *Big Media, Little Media.* Beverly Hills, Calif.: Sage.

Schramm deals with the full range of audio-visual media used in education in developed and less-developed countries. The book provides an inventory of research and field experience in utilizing media. It evaluates school supplement and extension, nonformal education, and national education reform projects in general.

Surgeon General's Scientific Advisory Committee on Television and Social Behavior. 1972. *Television and Growing Up: The Impact of Televised Violence.* Washington, D.C.: U.S. Government Printing Office.

Surlin, S.H. 1976. "Five Years of 'All in the Family': A Summary of Empirical Research Generated by the Program." *Mass Communication Review* 3 (Summer):2–6.

Troldahl, V.C. 1966–67. "A Field Test of a Modified 'Two-Step Flow of Communication' Model." *Public Opinion Quarterly* 3(Winter):609–23.

Tuchman, G. 1972. "Objectivity as Strategic Ritual: An Examination of Newsmen's Notions of Objectivity." *American Journal of Sociology* 77(Jan): 660–76.

U.S. Congress, Senate. 1971, 1972. *Hearings before the Senate Foreign Relations Committee,* first session on S. 18 and S. 1936, (May 24, 1971) and second session on S. 3645 (June 6 and 7, 1972).

U.S. Information Agency, Office of Public Information. 1973. *The Voice of America in Brief* (July).

Vidmar, N. and M. Rokeach. 1974. "Archie Bunker's Bigotry." *Journal of Communication* 24(Winter):36–47.

Wiebe, G.D. 1969–70. "Two Psychological Factors in Media Audience Behavior." *Public Opinion Quarterly* 34(Winter):523–36.

White, D.M. 1950. "The 'Gate-Keeper': A Case Study in the Selection of News." *Journalism Quarterly* 27(Fall):383–90.

9 BUREAUCRATIC FUNCTIONING

Richard H. Hall

Do bureaucracies ever function well? This question can be asked of businesses, government agencies, hospitals, universities, police departments, labor unions, religious bodies, and all other complex organizations. This chapter examines the functioning of bureaucratic organizations from the applied perspective of how to improve that functioning, so that organizations will more effectively serve their intended purposes. The focus of this discussion is entirely on bureaucratic organizations as social entities; it does not deal with the ways in which individuals participate in organizations. That closely related and equally important problem will be treated in Chapter 13.

This analysis of bureaucratic organizations rests on two fundamental assumptions: 1) All organizations are bureaucratized to some degree, although bureaucratization is usually more evident in large, complex organizations. 2) These complex social entities can be examined apart from the characteristics and behavior of their individual members. While this may offend some people's sensitivities regarding the worth of each individual, it should be understood at the outset that a dominant characteristic of bureaucracies is that they are designed to persist through time despite continual turnover of their members. Thus, General Electric or the University of Minnesota retain their basic forms and actions through many generations of students, professors, executives, and other personnel. As we will see, however, maintaining this process is one of the main problems of bureaucratic functioning.

WHAT ARE THE PROBLEMS?

The basic and inescapable problem of bureaucratic functioning is that complex organizations dominate modern society. We live in an "organizationally dense" (Hall, 1977) system. It requires little imagination to make this point real. If we think about our own lives, very little (some would say nothing) is accomplished outside of an organizational framework. Our work, our education, and our play are largely accomplished within organizational settings. Leisure perhaps best illustrate this fact, since most people like to think of these activities as chosen through one's own free will. Our particular leisure activities may well be self-chosen, but certainly the form and fashionability of leisure is markedly affected by the media and corporate advertising.

The current high level of interest in jogging and running serves as a good case in point. While the decision to take up this activity may be made in the privacy of one's own room, it undoubtedly has been influenced by many organizations such as governmental health agencies, media popularization of the phenomenon, and corporate advertising campaigns. Once one begins to run, organizations really take over, specifying uniform types of shoes and clothing. If one really becomes serious about this lonely sport, it is possible to join a jogging club or even participate in highly organized sponsored races such as the Boston or New York Marathon. In 1978 the latter event drew some 11,000 participants and an estimated 2 million spectators. This activity requires extensive bureaucratic functioning, including organizing the event itself, arranging for the police department to cordon off streets, obtaining city government recognition and payment for services, and ensuring media coverage.

The point of this example is to demonstrate that bureaucratic functioning is a pervasive social issue. Even the most intimate aspects of our lives, such as sexual attraction or falling in love, are organizationally influenced. Organizations influence the criteria determining the attractiveness of a potential partner, and they can even enhance or prohibit the development of romance. Organizations are thus a dominant force in the lives of everyone. Only the hermit can truly escape.

Moreover, we have thus far only seen the proverbial tip of the iceberg. Organizations are also dominant wielders of power in society. Modern corporations, particularly financial institutions, control the wealth of the nation. Government is composed of independently operating or loosely coupled organizations that have power over some aspects of the private sector and certainly over the actions of individuals. The federal government can pass and enforce laws such as school desegregation requirements that directly affect states and municipalities. To this power of corporations and government agencies, we can add that of other organizational sectors of the society such as universities, labor unions, and professional associations. When society is viewed in this way, it is obvious that organizations are the dominant power wielders.

The distribution and use of power is the dominant problem of bureaucratic functioning. It is also the one that is least likely to be approached by applied sociologists, since it is difficult both to conceptualize and to treat. These power arrangements are so strong that they can often perpetuate themselves indefinitely.

The organizational problems with which applied sociology typically deals are of lesser magnitude, but they are not insignificant. Before turning to them, however, two issues must be addressed. The first issue involves types of organizations. Business corporations, labor unions, government agencies, and hospitals are all classified as formal organizations by sociologists. Nevertheless, it does not take an organizational analyst to realize that there are some important differences among such organizations. Without going into the complexities of organizational typologies, we can make the assumption that organizations with similar tasks are probably rather similar in other respects. Thus, an organization that is predominantly administrative, such as the U.S. Department of Commerce, is probably similar to a private corporation that is also predominantly administrative, such as a bank. To make matters more complicated, all organizations are differentiated into various departments or other subunits, so that the research department of a corporation resembles a university department more than it does the production department in the same corporation. We will attempt to keep these distinctions clear in the analysis that follows. This second issue involves levels of analysis. As suggested above, when examining organizations we can focus on the total entity, on major subunits such as departments, or on smaller units such as branches or working groups within the organization. These various levels of analysis may or may not share common characteristics. Again, we will attempt to specify the level of analysis throughout the discussion that follows.

The Problem of Effectiveness

What, then, are the organizational problems with which applied organizational sociology deals? Foremost among these is organizational effectiveness. This may seem to be a rather dry topic, suggesting images of annual reports, profit and loss statements, and accounting procedures. It becomes a much more exciting issue, however, when we ask the question: effectiveness for whom? Very different answers emerge, depending on whether we take the viewpoint of customers, clients, workers, managers, or the whole society. For instance, a particular practice might be quite profitable for an organization and yet be extremely dangerous for its customers, workers, or society. The use of nuclear reactors to generate electricity is a relevant example.

This effectiveness problem is complicated by the fact that almost all organizations have multiple goals or effectiveness criteria. Business firms may simultaneously seek to survive and grow, make a short-term or long-term profit, produce quality products, and be socially responsible. Success in one of these efforts may, nevertheless, work against success in another. These multiple goals of business firms also occur in the public sector. And they are particularly evident among organizations that provide human services, since these services may contain several contradictory elements and provide no clear indicators of whether or not the services provide any benefits to the clients.

Adding to the problematic nature of organizational effectiveness is the fact that within organizations there are likely to be disputes over which kind of activities are most appropriate. All organizations can be viewed as political entities containing several interested parties vying for power. The dominant coalitions that emerge through this process commonly impose their interests on the entire organization and define its major actions (Pennings and Goodman, 1977).

On top of all of this is the problem of measuring effectiveness. How does an organization know if it has been or is going to be effective? There are no easy answers here, since searches for universal indicators of effectiveness have proven fruitless. Probably the most intelligent approach to effectiveness is to realize that the question of overall organizational effectiveness is irrelevant. We can then concentrate on more specific effectiveness indicators, recognizing that organizations are constantly attempting to accomplish multiple and often contradictory objectives. Despite all these problems, effectiveness remains the principal problem for organizations and the public.

The Problem of Change

A second organizational problem is related to effectiveness but is more specific. Why do some organizations adapt successfully to changing situations while others do not? This is a complicated issue. Organizations, like individuals, are not islands unto themselves. They all exist within social environments comprised of other organizations, individuals, constituent groups, and the broad sweep of social change. The dominant contemporary model of organizations is that of an open system, in which organizations must adjust to a range of environmental pressures while at the same time attempting to accomplish their goals.

This open system model is useful, but it does not sensitize us to the fact that organizations are variously affected by their environments. Some organizations are more fragile than others. Small and new organizations are most susceptible to environmental influences than are large and old organizations. Moreover, small and new organizations are often in competition with large and old organizations, which is a particular kind of environmental influence that frequently leads to organizational failure. Large organizations, whether in the public or the private sector, are more able to withstand environmental pressures because of their greater resources.

A large organization is also more likely to be able to manipulate the environment to its advantage, which is another point ignored by the open system model. For example, large business corporations normally have numerous linkages with major financial institutions (Allen, 1974). This provides them with easier access to capital than smaller organizations without this access. It is not just large size, of course, that "buffers" organizations from their environments. It has been found, for instance, that links between the ethical drug industry and organized medicine have helped ensure the passage of legislation favorable to the continued profitability of drug firms (Hirsch, 1975). Such linkages are not limited to the private sector, since, as will be indicated in a later section, the success of government programs is similarly tied to environmental manipulation.

Not all change or adaptation in organizations is caused by external events. Organizations can innovate on their own. Ideas for change can be developed at any level in an organization, although the implementation of change must be accompanied by support from personnel at or near the top of the organization. We will therefore examine those internal factors that appear to affect the capability of organizations to sustain change.

The Problem of Responsiveness

The final organizational problem is also related to effectiveness but turns the issue in a different direction. How can organizations be made more responsive to public and private needs? As suggested in the discussion of effectiveness, multiple public and private demands often impinge on organizations. The issue here is how bureaucracies can be made more responsive to their constituents. Must responsiveness be obtained through forced compliance, as when government policies require consumer protection or affirmative action? Or can organizations develop voluntary programs to deal with constituent groups? These questions revolve around the issue of organizational change. Ideas from both outside or inside an organization must make their way through the organization to the point where operating policies are made more responsive to currently unmet constituent needs.

A basic difficulty here is that organizations are inherently resistant to change, because of the nature of organizational power arrangements. The people in positions of power within an organization have a vested interest in maintaining their positions and their accompanying privileges. Unless faced with a serious crisis, there is little impetus for them to seek change. Nonetheless, change is possible through two basic processes. First, despite the inherent resistance to change, organizational decision makers frequently "scan" the horizon of the organization to see if there are impending problems or opportunities. When these are perceived, some shifts in the organization will often be made. Such shifts will be made on the basis of the "bounded rationality" (Simon, 1957) that surrounds any organizational decision. This term refers to the fact that organizational decision makers never operate with full knowledge of the situation or complete predictability about the outcomes of their decisions. They may, however, attempt to implement change, so long as their positions are not threatened.

The second process of change occurs when the political situation within the organization is altered. Power coalitions may shift, or new power elements may enter the organization. It is not uncommon, for example, for university departments to undergo a major change in focus as younger, more research-oriented faculty members gain ascendance over an "old guard." Both processes of change, nevertheless, take place within the context of the ongoing organization. Change does not just occur as a result of an external mandate ordering a change, or as an outgrowth of some "better idea" that is immediately grasped by all members of the organization.

WHAT DO WE KNOW?

Effectiveness

In the area of organizational effectiveness our present knowledge is both definitive and vague. On the definitive side, Weick (1977:193) summarizes Steers' (1975) conclusions that the effective organization is "flexible and productive, satisfies its members, is profitable, acquires resources, minimizes strain, controls the environment, develops, is efficient, retains employees, grows, is integrated, communicates openly, and survives." This is a nice prescription, but it is unfortunately quite vague about how an organization achieves effectiveness. What strategies lead to these conditions? The prescription also contains some glaring contradictions, which become evident when one considers various pairs of effectiveness criteria, such as productivity and satisfaction. If there is a push for production, satisfaction may go down. If satisfaction is encouraged, production may go down. This linkage between production and satisfaction continues to puzzle researchers, some of whom believe that satisfaction leads to productivity, others of whom believe that productivity leads to satisfaction, while still others look for independent causal factors.

The practical problems encountered when trying to understand organizational effectiveness are nicely illustrated by Sapolsky's (1972) analysis of the U.S. Navy's Polaris missile system. This nuclear ballistic missile, which is launched from a submerged submarine, was developed in the late 1950s and 1960s. By the standards of the Navy, the Congress, the administrations, the media, and the public, the development of the Polaris weapon system was an unqualified success. It was produced on time and at costs lower than had been budgeted. Much of the success of the Polaris development program was initially attributed to its use of PERT (Program Evaluation and Review Technique), which is a computer-based research and development planning, scheduling, and control device. As a consequence, PERT became an important management tool in both industry and government. In reality, however, PERT was a myth, at least for the development of the Polaris system. Although adopted as a managerial philosophy, it was never put into practice with the Polaris program.

Basically, the managers of the Polaris program were able to convince Congress and the Navy that it had a highly effective management device, and they were therefore allowed to conduct their development program without outside interference. In addition, this and other programs were "the beneficiaries of an unusual convergence between technological opportunities and a consensus on national needs..." (Sapolsky, 1972:241). In essence, the Polaris system was developed with a highly supportive environment. The program managers convinced the relevant components of their environment (Congress and the Navy) that they were operating in an effective manner, which in turn led to continued financial and political support. In addition, the Polaris program also adopted some other highly effective policies, including disciplined flexibility, decentralization, and competition.

The Polaris program was effective. Its effectiveness was the consequence of fortuitous timing, policies such as decentralization, and the capacity to convince its relevant environment that it was successful. What does this tell us? In the first place, timing is largely uncontrollable by most organizations, except with very limited innovations in which some time planning is possible. Second, policies such as decentralization must be viewed in a contingent model. That is, decentralization will be effective only under certain conditions. It is not a universal panacea. Finally, the capability to influence the relevant environment is crucial for organizational effectiveness. In a very real sense, effectiveness is in the minds of the beholders. The ways in which reality is constructed by significant elements of the environment is a crucial determinant of effectiveness, since these outside groups can frequently grant or withhold resources and label the organization as successful or unsuccessful. As a footnote to all of this, Sapolsky (1972) notes that the management techniques designed during the Polaris program, when applied in other developmental efforts, often limited the effectiveness of those programs.

Our knowledge about organizational effectiveness is not certain. The most we can presently say is that organizations must acquire sufficient resources such as money, personnel (and clients, where relevant), and general environmental support in order to meet basic operating constraints (Pennings and Goodman, 1977). Once these operating constraints are met, effectiveness is commonly judged on the extent to which organizational goals are met.

Change

Our knowledge of adaptation and change is also characterized by some uncertainty. Much of this is due to the fact that research on organizational change has tended to confuse the various stages of the change process. In Zaltman, Duncan, and Holbek's (1973) view, there are two major change stages. The first is the "initiation" stage, in which the organization seeks knowledge and awareness of change possibilities, forms attitudes about the potential change, and makes a decision in regard to the change. This is followed by the "implementation" stage, in which a change is introduced on a trial basis and then later sustained as an ongoing part of the organization. The reason for distinguishing between the two stages is that the organizational characteristics necessary for success in each stage are different. The initiation stage requires flexibility and the capability to explore a variety of ideas. Implementation, in contrast, requires greater centralization and less flexibility and experimentation among organizational subunits.

To carry out this two-stage process of organizational change, an organization must be designed for initial flexibility, but later it must impose relatively tight control over its components as the change is implemented. This can be a demanding task, since organizations strongly resist alterations in their basic form.

Several techniques have been developed to facilitate the process of organizational change. The major one at the present time is organizational development (OD). According to Bennis (1969:2), this is "a complex educational strategy intended to change the beliefs, attitudes, values, and structures of organizations so that they can better adapt to new technologies, markets, challenges, and the dizzying rate of change itself." As will be discussed in more detail in the next section, organizational development has become something of a social movement. The basic notion is that intervention strategies can lead organizational personnel into new understanding of, and relationships with, themselves, other members, and the total organization. OD has not been an unqualified success (Mirvis and Berg, 1977). Without going into details here, we have discovered that OD efforts can be thwarted by 1) economic or other external threats to an organization that make it impossible for the organization to do more than struggle for survival, 2) resistance on the part of organizational members to any kind of change, 3) an emphasis on changing individual attitudes without coming to grips with the context in which individuals work, and 4) the presence of powerful individuals and groups within organizations who are opposed to the changes being attempted. In a nutshell, organizations and their members resist change. Their dominant tendency is to perpetuate established patterns, regardless of whether or not they are as functionally effective as any potential alternatives, because these patterns reinforce members' expectations and give them a sense of stability and security.

Responsiveness

On the topic of organizational responsiveness to social needs, relatively little is known, since the question is not often asked by social researchers. We can begin by noting that organizations tend to act in their own self interest. At times, this can bring them into close contact with elements of the public who may subsequently exercise more influence on the organization than was originally intended. The classic study of this process is Selznick's *TVA and the Grass Roots*. The Tennessee Valley Authority was formed in 'the 1930s, under President Roosevelt's New Deal administration, for flood control and the generation of electricity.

The TVA had an immense impact on the physical environment of the region. The surrounding social environment was also altered, but, as this occurred, TVA was simultaneously transformed. This reciprocal flow of social influence occurred through "co-optation" of TVA's social environment, or the "process of absorbing new elements into the leadership or policy-determining structure of an organization as a means of averting threats to its stability or existence" (Selznick, 1966:13). Two major groups were brought into TVA's decentralized decision-making process. These were the agricultural extension divisions of the local land grant colleges and the American Farm Bureau Federation. This co-optation accomplished its intended purpose of blunting any potential opposition from these parties. It also reduced the power of organizations that were excluded from the TVA decision-making apparatus, such as other agricultural associations (composed primarily of small farmers) and local black colleges. (The Farm Bureau was jealous of its special position with the TVA and opposed including all other farm organizations.) As a result of this co-optation process, the TVA became increasingly responsive to the needs of its most powerful constituents, who increasingly shaped TVA policy. Moreover, as pressures for soil conservation diminished in importance, the TVA became involved in strip mining with the major coal companies in the area. Once again, a powerful segment of the public was served by TVA while other segments were ignored.

What can be learned from this? Organizations are responsive to public needs when those needs are represented by other organizations with strong economic, political, or social power bases. Organizations will seldom act on the basis of pure altruism. Because they seek to function in a manner that will maximize their own interests and benefits, organizations are most responsive to other organized segments of the society.

WHAT ARE WE DOING?

This is a complex question since "we" refers to a variety of social and behavioral sciences, management and administrative scientists, and practitioners in a range of organizational settings. A bit of history may help to understand this wide array of efforts.

Organizational analysis emerged as a distinct approach early in the twentieth century with the "classical" works of Taylor, Fayol, Mooney, Gulick, and Urwick. These were management-oriented theories (as are most current approaches), largely concerned with techniques such as work simplification or employee incentives for controlling workers and increasing productivity.

A very different approach entered the scene during the 1930s through the work of Barnard and Mayo. This "human relations" approach to organizations views workers as being capable of cooperative action and as having social needs that they seek to fulfill on the job. This new perspective, which produced a major shift in managerial theory, can be traced through numerous attempts to raise the motivation and satisfaction of workers. Much of the impetus for the approach came from extensive experiments at the Hawthorne plant of the Western Electric Company. Both the interpretation of the results (Carey, 1967) and the very nature of the results themselves (Franke and Kaul, 1978) have since been thrown into serious question, but the ideas of human relations management linger on.

There have been other shifts in the approaches people take to organizations, including the current emphases on the contingent effects of technological and environmental impacts on organizations. Nevertheless, most attempts to change organizations are linked to the classical and human relations approaches. By and large, all attempts to change organizations come from management, and almost all of the work carried out by social scientists and consultants shares this orientation.

Effectiveness and Change

In the following discussion, we will combine the topics of organizational effectiveness and organizational change, since almost all change efforts are directed toward increasing effectiveness. Our stance will be relatively critical, since many change efforts have not yielded the results their advocates hoped for.

One major type of change effort, which might be termed "management rationalization," is derived from classical theory. The PERT program of the Polaris project illustrates this approach in its effort to control the weapons development process. Another example is Management by Objectives (MBO). MBO is intended both to specify organizational objectives and to assess the accomplishments of organizational subunits according to how well they meet those objectives (Drucker, 1973). It is also concerned with the attitudes of management during this process. MBO has been described as 1) a systems approach to managing an organization, where those accountable for directing the organization first determine where they want to take the organization, 2) a process requiring and encouraging all key administrative personnel to contribute their maximum to achieving the overall objectives, 3) an effort to blend and balance the goals of all key personnel, and 4) an evaluation mechanism (McConskey, 1973).

A key to MBO is the nature of the organization's objectives. "What will objectives look like? They should be tangible, measurable, and verifiable! That means that, wherever possible, we should avoid qualitative objectives and substitute in their place quantifiable statements. For example, a quantitative objective might be to 'initiate a direct check purchase-order system for all orders under $500 by December 31,' or 'to increase donations next year by 15 percent'" (Robbins, 1976:139).

This sounds fine and has worked in many situations, but it contains several critical problems. A major one is that translating some kinds of objectives into quantifiable statements reduces them to trivia. This is particularly true with human services, where a qualitative objective like "providing humane treatment" is hard to quantify. It is certainly possible to spell out elements of humane treatment in quantitative terms, but these are often the least important elements of the service being rendered, so that while the trees are being counted the forest is missed.

A second problem lies in the nature of the power structure within the organization. Such a program requires commitment from top management, as Robbins (140) notes. But to be effective, it also requires supportive responses from those at all lower levels in the organization. Without such responses, MBO cannot produce organizational change.

There is still another problem with MBO. Tosi, et al. (1976) point out that most studies have reported positive behavioral and attitudinal results on the part of management. However, these studies have generally relied on just two measurements—before and after the MBO program—and have uncritically attributed all observed attitude changes to the program. In contrast, Tosi, et al. measured the effects of an MBO program at three different time periods. Their research revealed some improvement of goal clarity, superior-subordinate relationships, rewards linked to performance, orientation toward MBO, and job satisfaction. They carefully noted, however, that these results might also have been caused by either simple mood changes on the part of managers or the impact of extraneous external events on the organization. Even more important was the fact that, over time, perceived success in goal attainment tended to be inversely associated with other aspects of the MBO program. This raises the serious question of whether or not MBO is actually an organizational change tool. Although it may change management practices and orientations, its effectiveness in improving organizational performance appears questionable, and its effects on non-management personnel appear to be unknown.

A second major type of organizational change effort is Organizational Development (OD), which emerged from the human relations tradition. Like MBO, OD is management oriented. OD has become a big business in its own right. Strauss (1976:617) notes that by 1969, "one firm, Scientific Methods, Inc., numbered among its clients forty-five of the top one hundred U.S. corporations, conducted courses on every continent, and projected profits of $1.1 million...; and by 1973 there were an estimated 500 to 1,000 external OD consultants in the United States alone."

OD is an attempt to bring about "*planned change*, a coordinated attack on organizational interpersonal problems. In Argyris's (1971) terms, it is designed to generate 'valid information' which will help the organization make 'free choices' which will in turn assist not just the solution of immediate problems, but also in the strengthening of problem solving ability" (Strauss, 1976:618).

The origins of OD lie in a training technique known as T groups. The emphasis in T groups is on experiential learning and the development of interpersonal competence. T-group training has been applied to such diverse topics as job-related problems, women's consciousness-raising sessions, Alcoholics Anonymous, and marital relations. The T-group approach has been criticized, however, for the intense stress it can place on participants, and for its failure to demonstrate that the learning acquired in the group situation can be carried back to the job or other spheres of life.

OD differs from T groups in that its emphasis is on the organization rather than individuals. According to Strauss (1976:628-29), "OD *claims* to be a systems approach: its objective is planned, managed change, and a coordinated attack on organizational problems. OD *presumably* deals not just with attitudes, structure, technology, or behavior alone, but with a combination of these (Friedlander and Brown, 1974). In *principle* it is concerned not just with the problems of a single department or a single organizational level, but the organization as a whole. (The italicized qualifiers are justified because OD often fails to live up to its promise and noninterpersonal aspects of the system tend to be slighted.)"

A straightforward example of an OD program, provided by Zaltman and Duncan involves a Chicago-area school district.

> The program was designed to provide administrators and faculty with information about their problems, allowing them to diagnose and ultimately remedy those problems. The procedure involved four stages. First, survey data on work attitudes were collected from faculty and principals. Questionnaire items focused on issues such as task relations between school and district personnel, special services, professional and nonprofessional work loads, materials and equipment, student needs, etc. These data were given to school personnel to provide an objective basis for problem and need identification.

> Next, task-oriented meetings focused on problem analysis and solution generation were held by the principals and teachers. These groups were encouraged to generate and analyze a number of alternatives prior to selecting a final solution. Once a solution was determined, a timetable was developed for its implementation.

> Following the problem solving meetings, a program was undertaken to implement the suggested solutions. Teams of faculty and administrators used special documents to facilitate the communications, sanctioning, and implementation of recommended changes. Finally, the program included a self-monitoring feature that allowed each group of teachers and principals to evaluate the success of the program. (Zaltman and Duncan, 1977:125–26)

This relatively simple OD program was apparently successful. A more complex form of OD, which failed, occurred in the U.S. State Department. It is described by Crockett (1977), an administrative official within the State Department who attempted to implement a program known as ACORD (Action Program of Organizational Development). ACORD involved 1) the elimination of several levels of hierarchy between the top and the bottom, 2) training centering on T-group concepts, 3) team building among executive work groups in training sessions designed to allow the members of the group to understand each other better and to operate better as a group, 4) team building downward, in which administrators took their subordinates with them to a training and team building, 5) an external consulting team which was designed to assist in the training and team-building, 6) internal change agents, who were designated as internal consultants, and 7) research and publication efforts designed to determine the outcomes of the process.

This was OD in one of its fullest forms. What were the results? Crockett concluded that in the short run there were some improvements (as well as some failures), but that in the long run most things returned to their former status. Part of the failure of this OD program may have been due to the fact that Crockett left the State Department, but he also offers some additional reasons for the failure. Perhaps the major one was that changing a number of organizational activities did not change the behavior of the people involved. The training and team building apparently did not have lasting effects on the participants. In addition, the program may have attempted too much. Another critical factor was lack of strong support from top officials. The State Department is an exceptionally traditional organization, especially as reflected among its foreign service officers. Such a setting is hardly conducive to major changes, particularly when people's positions and values are threatened. This is a basic problem commonly faced by OD: "It's ok, as long as my position is not threatened."

What can we conclude about OD? In his comprehensive review of the pros and cons of OD, Strauss (1976:672) states that: *"under some circumstances, OD can lead to lasting organizational gain."* He suggests that OD has the greatest likelihood of being successful over time when emphasis is placed on changing the structure of the organization, such as job responsibilities, rather than simply training individuals. OD also requires the commitment of the total hierarchy within the organization, or belief in the utility of the OD effort. The unanswered question here is how such belief is to be created? In addition, Bowers and Hausser (1977) found that the success of OD efforts depends heavily on the type of work group involved. All of these factors lead to the conclusion that OD has only limited applicability as a change process. If the organization is willing to be changed and has adequate resources to support the program, the outcomes may be 1) managers who are somewhat more capable of understanding their subordinates, and 2) decision making that is based on slightly improved analytic skills (Strauss, 1976:675).

Responsiveness

Turning to organizational responsiveness, we find a state of some confusion which is caused, in large part, by the variety of efforts organizations have made to be responsive or to avoid responsiveness. This topic can be approached best by dividing organizations into private and public sectors, since public responsiveness is presumably more critical for organizations that are intended to serve public interests (Blau and Scott, 1962).

Organizations in the private sector, such as business firms, vary considerably in their need to be responsive to the public. Some firms—particularly those that deal exclusively with other organizations—have virtually no need to concern themselves with the responsiveness of their outputs to public demands. An example would be coal companies, whose output goes almost entirely to other organizations such as steel companies. While these companies may well face

threats from environmentalists, there is virtually no need for them to be responsive to the public.

At the other extreme are organizations that are almost totally subject to the
whims of the public, such as popular entertainment business and the mass media,
where rapid shifts occur in styles and tastes. Since public demand is critical for
these businesses, they often take various kinds of direct actions toward the public. These actions include: 1) monitoring the environment through such techniques as marketing research and demographic analysis, which are attempts to
predict the size of the potential market and the range of likely tastes within that
market. 2) Attempts to reduce the uncertainty in their environment. For example,
Hirsch (1975) has shown that the pharmaceutical industry enlisted the help of
organized medicine in assuring the passage of laws that allowed firms to influence
drug pricing, distribution patterns, patent and copyright laws, and public opinion
leaders. 3) Engage in illegal acts toward the same ends. 4) Use advertising to
increase demand for their products, thus making their markets more secure.
5) Press for the passage of regulatory laws that can be used to protect the
industry from the public.

In a pure capitalistic system, business firms respond to public pressures by
successfully meeting demands. Those that don't go out of business. Our current
economic system differs considerably from this model, however, since businesses
commonly attempt to create markets for their products and services. More
important, they often look to government to keep them solvent during financially
difficult periods (Lockheed and Penn-Central) and to provide protective legislation. All of these efforts are perfectly reasonable and rational from the perspective of the businesses involved.

Business firms that deal with the public must also contend with public
interest associations such as Ralph Nader's consumer protection organization
and the numerous environmental protection organizations. Many large business
firms at first tended to ignore these groups, and when Nader first attacked
General Motors, it responded by trying to discredit him through hints of homosexuality rather than deal with the issues he raised. As the consumer and environmental movements have grown in strength and effectiveness, however, businesses
have begun to give serious attention to their demands. And as these organizations have secured the passage of legislation governing corporate activities,
business firms have been forced to become responsive to public demands.

Lest this analysis be viewed as entirely antibusiness, it should be pointed out
that business firms vary widely in their responsiveness to public needs. Some opt
to keep their corporate headquarters and other operations in central cities, while
others flee to the suburbs, which eliminates jobs for innercity residents while
simultaneously increasing the city's financial burden for public services. Businesses also vary in their philanthropic efforts and other public interest concerns.
The factors that create these differences among organizations are not known,
but they may be linked to the manner in which corporate officers are involved in

or isolated from the social fabric of the communities in which their organizations are located.

When the analysis shifts to the public sector, the picture is not greatly different. Katz, et al. (1975) studied the reactions of individuals who had had contacts with a range of governmental programs in the human services, such as manpower training, veteran's programs, welfare services, and medical services. By and large, these respondents were reasonably satisfied with the services they had received. A critical factor here is that agency officials receive feedback from their clients concerning the effectiveness of their services. As noted by these researchers: "To achieve the optimization . . . requires more than the good intentions of agency administrators. It calls for feedback cycles to furnish information about the specifics of agency functioning and to provide penalties and rewards for different types of performance. The feedback can be from the clientele to higher levels in government who can then exert pressure to improve matters" (Katz et al., 1975:195).

Serious problems often occur in these organizations when such feedback is absent or inadequate: "In the absence of adequate feedback about basic objectives, lower level administrators are inclined to be motivated by two considerations: (1) How can the operation be run smoothly with as few embarrassing and difficult problems as possible for agency officials? (2) How can the agency achieve some limited objectives which will ensure some palpable success? (Katz, et al., 1975:195). What is being suggested here is that lower level personnel—those who have direct contacts with clients and their immediate supervisors—can protect themselves at the expense of providing adequate client services. This often involves dealing only with clients for whom "success" is relatively certain, while passing over the really difficult cases. In this manner, the operations of the agency are deflected away from its basic objectives.

Katz and his collaborators are essentially calling for increased input on the part of the clients who receive social services. The issue then becomes how to organize the clients, which creates its own set of problems. For example, in the State of New York there is a well-organized client group concerned with the problem of mental retardation. This advocate group is composed primarily of relatives and friends of persons afflicted with learning disabilities. In contrast, persons suffering from mental illness do not have such a well-organized set of advocates. The consequence of this is more intense lobbying on behalf of the mentally retarded and more feedback to the facilities that treat them. As a result, one client group is benefiting at the expense of another, since the resources to be shared among these programs are clearly not infinite.

Public organizations, like those in the private sector, are responsive to the needs of the public insofar as those needs are articulated through the basic political process surrounding all organizations. In other words, all organizations are affected by pressures from other organizations. Public responsiveness must therefore be viewed in terms of interorganizational pressures that must be considered by individuals in organizational decision-making positions.

WHAT HAVE WE ACCOMPLISHED?

As might be expected from the discussion thus far, accomplishments are difficult to evaluate. In a very real sense, the analysis of organizations could replace economics as the "dismal science," since there is little evidence that much has been changed. The very nature of organizations augurs against change. Organizations develop rules and procedures and hierarchical arrangements for the specific purpose of erecting obstacles to change. They want the behavior of individuals to be predictable and not shift as different persons come in and out of jobs. They also seek to "buffer" their central operations or core technology from shifts in the environment. In short, organizations seek stability and security.

This tendency is exemplified in Kanter's (1977) excellent analysis of a large industrial conglomerate in the United States. Discussing the managers of the firm, she notes that: "Managers at Indsco had to look the part. They were not exactly cut out of the same mold like paper dolls, but the similarities in appearance were striking. Even this relatively trivial matter revealed the extent of conformity pressures on managers. Not that there were formal dress rules in this enlightened company, like the legendary IBM uniforms, but there was an informal understanding all the same. The norms were unmistakable after a visitor saw enough managers, invariably white and male, with a certain shiny, clean-cut look. The only beards, even after beards became merely daring rather than radical, were the results of vacation-time experiments on camping trips, except (it was said) for a few in R & D—'but we know that scientists do strange things,' a sales manager commented" (Kanter, 1977:47). This conformity in dress is an extension of the similarity in background shared by the managers. Even the secretaries were largely cut from the same mold; "The first fact about the several thousand secretaries at Indsco was that they were all women, except for two men at headquarters who were classified as typists. If they entered at the bottom, Indsco secretaries were generally hired out of high school or a secretarial finishing school like Katherine Gibbs. There was a tendency in corporate headquarters to recruit from parochial schools, which meant that a very high proportion of secretaries were white and accustomed to hierarchical discipline" (Kanter, 1977:70).

Why this emphasis on conformity? Is it an expression of an antifeminine or antiminority bias? Kanter believes not. Instead, she traces it to the need by the organization to reduce uncertainty, increase discretion, and ensure trust and mutual understanding. By hiring persons with similar backgrounds, trust and discretion were more assured than if new and potentially disturbing types of individuals were introduced.

Lest the reader think that this is just an instance in the backwaters of the business world, let us consider an alternative way in which trust and discretion can be secured. Many readers of this book will be students in sociology or practicing sociologists. Most of the instructors in those courses, and many practicing sociologists, have a Ph.D. degree. The requirement of advanced degrees is another mechanism that organizations use to insure that individuals performing crucial functions will understand and trust one another.

The point is that organizations normally manage to continue functioning in the face of constant external and internal pressures. They are highly resistant to change. If this point is not understood, too much can be made of change strategies, and bureaucracies can be viewed as far too "dynamic." Having noted this, what can be said about accomplishments of applied sociology in the areas of organizational effectiveness, change, and responsiveness?

Effectiveness

With regard to effectiveness, several points can be highlighted. First, it is now well recognized that all organizations have multiple and frequently conflicting goals. This often leads to internal conflicts over goal priorities, which can contribute to organizational change. Second, we know that it is folly to attempt to analyze the effectiveness of any organization. Instead, we must measure effectiveness on all the criteria related to organizational survival and multiple goal attainment. Third, we know that organizations exist in an environment. Organizations attempt to manipulate this environment to their own advantage and succeed in this endeavor to varying degrees. Nevertheless, environmental pressures always remain an active force in the operations of all organizations. Finally, and perhaps most importantly, we know there is not one best way to organize.

As stressed by Lawrence and Lorsch (1967) a contingency approach to organizational effectiveness is now the dominant mode of analysis in this area. The idea of contingency rests on the fact that organizations must respond to their environments. These environments include all of the various social pressures that have previously been described, plus technological developments concerning organizational operations. The most effective organizations are those whose structures and processes are most congruent with external and internal demands. For example, if an organization operates an area in which there is a great deal of scientific and technological development, it must contain units that can keep up with these developments. These R & D units are usually structured differently from production units, with the result that conflicts often arise. Similarly, if an organization is staffed by people with high levels of professional training or strong desires and abilities to determine their own modes of organizing, the effective organization is one that does not try to impose heavy bureaucratic rules on its personnel. Our knowledge about effectiveness thus incorporates the basic notion of organizations acting within their environments, but adds a concern with human relations. At the same time, we also know that highly routine matters in organizations staffed by persons who do not seek expanded responsibilities or enlarged jobs are best handled through more traditional or bureaucratic procedures.

This last generalization might not seem to be a major accomplishment, since it seems to suggest that some people will always be satisfied with dull, routine work. We can state this point in a positive manner, however, by noting that if and when people come to organizations demanding greater responsibility in terms of self-determination and job content, then organizations will have to respond by debureaucratizing. Recognition of this fact, accompanied by the expanded opportunities for assuming responsibilities within organizations, will definitely be an accomplishment.

Change

Turning to organizational change, quite a bit has been accomplished. Despite the evident drawbacks and ethical issues surrounding change strategies such as OD, we do know that certain strategies work under certain conditions. Zaltman and Duncan (1977) have catalogued the issues surrounding organizational change quite thoroughly, and it is impossible to discuss all of their conclusions here. One conclusion is inescapable, however. Organizational change is a political process. Those who exercise power in organizations have an overriding role in the success or failure of OD efforts, and political processes govern the outcome of efforts to restructure organizations. Radical changes—such as replacing those in power with another group—can be accomplished only if those who seek power can amass more resources than can those presently in power. This can be done either by creating a coalition of forces within the organization, or by bringing in additional resources from outside the organization. Note that in the case of the failure of OD in the State Department (Crockett, 1977), it was the power of tradition and the hierarchy that defeated the effort.

Another example of the crucial role of power can be seen in Kanter's (1977) analysis of the role of women and minority group members in Indsco. Female managers and nonwhites were largely "tokens" in the organization, and did not fit into the traditional categories of individuals who were believed to be trustworthy and discrete. Kanter (1977:267) argues that the way to improve this situation is to employ power to "*enhance opportunity, empower,* and *balance* the *numbers* of socially different people." She carefully points out, however, that her proposals involve organizational reform, not revolutionary change. A revolutionary might likely oppose strategies that would temporarily alleviate harmful conditions and instead support the "positive value of present suffering in heightening radical consciousness" (Kanter, 1977:286-87). Kanter argues strongly against this stance by noting that it is not those in power who suffer, but rather those without power—the token women and token minorities. She is, thus, arguing for change from within the organization, brought about by pressures originating outside the organization. This is a useful summary of what has been accomplished thus far in regard to organizational change.

Responsiveness

Turning to organizational responsiveness, we must begin with the same conclusion we have been stressing throughout this section. Organizations will normally tend to continue functioning in their usual manner, even when they are supposed to be responsive to the public. This conclusion is buttressed by Warren, et al.'s (1974) analysis of the organizations and interorganizational linkages existing within nine cities. Their study dealt with the ways in which organizations concerned about urban problems responded to increased demands for citizen participation. Those demands were primarily an outgrowth of the widespread urban disorders during the late 1960s and early 1970s. Federal programs such as the War on Poverty and Model Cities contained strong mandates for citizen participation, to be accomplished largely through existing agencies.

Warren and his collaborators argue that a major factor contributing to the failure of these "liberal reform" efforts was the unchangeable nature of the agencies involved. An additional source of this failure was the absence of any substantial change—such as income redistribution—in the social structure surrounding poverty. Instead, the reform programs emphasized "cooperation and contest that is confined to the norms that preserve the existing organizational configuration; types of interaction that the community decision organizations can control; coordination that is much more extensive and much less productive than it is generally thought to be; gross and secondary innovation, defined and confined by organizational viability considerations and by prevalent professional technologies; gross and secondary responsiveness, confined largely to issues of what services will be delivered, to whom, and how, but not including changes in the institutional structure that produces and sustains poverty; a conception of poverty area residents as agency clients and agency constituencies, but not as citizens to whom agencies are directly responsible" (Warren, et al., 1974:180-81).

These authors conclude that the principal way in which changes in organizational responsiveness will be brought about is through political action, in which organized groups fight for new policies—as in the case of "taxpayers' revolts." This is our conclusion also, given what we know about organizations and why they change. Unless the force for change comes through organized political action, little is likely to be accomplished. How to achieve participation in organized political action remains problematic.

WHERE ARE WE GOING?

The answer to this final question is brief and should already be evident. *We are going where we have been.* The very nature of organizations forces us to this conclusion, whether we are concerned with effectiveness, change, or responsiveness. We will undoubtedly continue to attempt OD or similar efforts based on some sort of contingency model that takes critical environmental factors into account. The emphasis will probably continue to be at the managerial level and will probably continue to focus on individual changes rather than structural alterations. Part of the reason for this focus is that applied sociologists have not suggested viable alternatives to the existing system. We have analyzed and criticized, but we have not provided alternative solutions to the crucial problems of bureaucratic functioning.

REFERENCES AND SUGGESTED READINGS

Allen, M.P. 1974. "The Structure of Interorganizational Elite Cooptations: Interlocking Corporate Directorates." *American Sociological Review* 39 (June):393–406.

Argyris, C. 1971. *Management and Organizational Development*. New York: McGraw-Hill.

Bennis, W.G. 1969. *Organizational Development: Its Nature, Origin, and Prospects*. Reading, Mass.: Addison-Wesley.

Blau, P.M. and W.R. Scott. 1962. *Formal Organizations*. San Francisco: Chandler.

Bowers, D.G. and D.L. Hausser. 1977. "Work Group Type and Intervention Effects in Organizational Development." *Administrative Science Quarterly* 22(Mar):76–94.

Carey, A. 1967. "The Hawthorne Studies: A Radical Criticism." *American Sociological Review* 32(June):403–16.

Crockett, W. 1977. "Introducing Change to a Government Agency." In *Failures in Organizational Development and Change*, edited by Philip H. Mirvis and David N. Berg. New York: John Wiley & Sons.

Drucker, P.F. 1973. *The Practice of Management*. New York: Harper & Row.

Franke, R.H. and J.D. Kaul. 1978. "The Hawthorne Experiments: First Statistical Interpretation." *American Sociological Review* 43(Oct):623–42.

Friedlander, F. and L.D. Brown. 1974. "Organizational Development." In *Annual Review of Psychology, Vol. 25*, edited by M. Rosenzweig and L.W. Porter, pp. 313–41. Palo Alto, Calif.: Annual Reviews.

Hall, R.H. 1977. *Organizations: Structure and Process*. Englewood Cliffs, N.J.: Prentice-Hall.

Hirsch, P.M. 1975. "Organizational Effectiveness and the Institutional Environment." *Administrative Science Quarterly* 20:327–44.

*Kanter, R.M. 1977. *Men and Women of the Corporation*. New York: Basic Books. Kanter provides an analysis of the management personnel, their wives, and their secretaries in a large industrial firm. Kanter demonstrates the manner in which the types of personnel working in the organization and corporate policies interact to maintain stability in the organization. The analysis also focuses on the problems faced by women and minority group members in such situations.

*Katz, D., B.A. Gutek, R.L. Kahn, and E. Barton. 1975. *Bureaucratic Encounters: A Pilot Study in the Evaluation of Government Services.* Ann Arbor: University of Michigan, Institute for Social Research.
The study is an analysis of the public's responses, based on a national survey, to services received from government agencies in areas of health, welfare, employment, and retirement. Most of the respondents were relatively satisfied with the services they received. Less satisfaction was noted with a comparison group of social control agencies.

*Lawrence, P.R. and J.W. Lorsch. 1967. *Organizations and Environment: Managing Differentiation and Integration.* Cambridge, Mass.: Harvard Graduate School of Business Administration.
This book examines organizations within three industries. The most effective business firms differed in their structure and operations across industrial types. This has been the cornerstone of the development of contingency theory of organizations and has moved the analysis of organizations away from looking for the one best way to organize.

McConskey, D.D. 1973. "Applying Management by Objectives to Non-Profit Organizations," *SAM Advanced Management Journal* 38(Jan):10-20.

*Mirvis, P.H. and D.N. Berg. 1977. *Failures in Organizational Development and Change.* New York: John Wiley & Sons.
As the title suggests, this is an analysis of organizational development programs that were not successful. While critical of OD, the study pinpoints the conditions under which organizational change can be accomplished and where there is likely to be blockage.

Pennings, J.M. and P.S. Goodman. 1977. "Toward a Workable Framework." In *New Perspectives on Organizational Performance,* edited by P.S. Goodman, J.M. Pennings, and Associates. San Francisco: Jossey-Bass.

Robbins, S.P. 1976. *The Administrative Process: Integrating Theory and Practice.* Englewood Cliffs, N.J.: Prentice-Hall.

*Sapolsky, H.M. 1972. *The Polaris System Development: Bureaucratic and Programmatic Success in Government.* Cambridge, Mass.: Harvard University Press.
Sapolsky demonstrates the manner in which organizations must cope with and attempt to control their environments. While an initial examination of the development of the Polaris missile system would suggest that it was a highly rational program development and implementation process, its success actually depended on convincing Congress and the Navy that it was successful.

Selznick, P. 1966. *TVA and the Grass Roots.* New York: Harper Torchbook Edition.

Simon, H.A. 1957. *Administrative Behavior.* 2nd ed. New York: Macmillan.

Steers, R.M. 1975. "Problems in the Measurement of Organizational Effectiveness." *Administrative Science Quarterly* 29(Dec):546-58.

Strauss, G. 1976. "Organizational Development." In *Handbook of Work, Organization, and Society,* edited by R. Dubin. Chicago: Rand McNally.

Tosi, H., J. Hunter, R. Chesser, J.R. Tarter, and S. Carroll. 1976. "How Real are

Changes Produced by Management by Objectives." *Administrative Science Quarterly* 21(June):276–306.

*Warren, R.L., S.M. Rose, and A.F. Bergunder, 1974. *The Structure of Urban Reform*. Lexington, Mass.: Lexington Books.

The book examines organizations that are ostensibly committed to social reform. The authors find that these urban agencies do not want to eliminate poverty, since that would eliminate the agencies. The study also examines linkages among these organizations.

Weick, K.E. 1977. "Re-Punctuating the Problem." In *New Perspectives on Organizational Performance*, edited by P.S. Goodman, J.M. Pennings, and Associates. San Francisco: Jossey-Bass.

Zaltman, G., R. Duncan, and J. Holbek. 1973. *Innovations and Organizations*. New York: John Wiley & Sons.

Zaltman, G. and R. Duncan. 1977. *Strategies for Planned Change*. New York: John Wiley & Sons.

10 STATE PERFORMANCE

Edward W. Lehman

The modern democratic state is in trouble—some would even apply the diagnosis of "crisis." We are told that 1) today's regimes are too strong *or* too weak, 2) they meddle too much *or* do too little, 3) they are dominated by powerful elites *or* stymied by excessive dispersions of power, and 4) they manage to fool most of the people most of the time *or* face massive erosions of public confidence. That these laments are plagued by contradictions seems self-evident. Yet closer inspection reveals a more consistent picture of the dilemmas of contemporary politics. This chapter attempts to flesh out that picture by suggesting ways of estimating state performances and assessing prospects for enhanced political viability. It focuses on the United States, although much of this discussion also applies to the other advanced liberal democracies.

WHAT ARE THE PROBLEMS?

The preceding four pairs of complaints are not so contradictory as they first seem. One reason is that apparent polar opposites actually may point to different facets of political life. Comparison of the complaints that regimes are too strong and that they are too weak provides the clearest instance of this polarity. Acceptance of one grievance appears to require the rejection of the other. Warning about strong regimes is perhaps the most widely voiced lament in the present era. Office seekers and incumbents alike flail "big government" and urge "cutbacks" and "give backs."

Yet worry over faltering regimes does not necessarily refute alarms of "big government." The prime culprits in this complaint are interest groups and political parties that lack sufficient support among the public to allow political authorities to govern effectively. Morris Janowitz (1978:546) discerns a gradual

198

emergence in the post-World War II period of weak political regimes in Western democracies, because of "new forms of dispersion of political power which lead to the inability to create meaningful majorities which can effectively govern." Thus, fears of "big government" and weak regimes are not logically antithetical and may, in fact, be complementary. The former worries about the state's intrusion into everyday life, while the latter decries the inability to mobilize public support for authorities.

These first two fears are voiced by many different groups. In fact, what appears to be the same complaint may be pushed by competing forces. Although the enemies of "big government" cover the entire political spectrum, closer scrutiny reveals different concrete grievances. Paul Starr (1975:17) notes that "while left and right seem equally dissatisfied with government, they tend to have different parts of it in mind. On one side, the characteristic targets are the CIA and FBI; on the other, HEW and the regulatory agencies." On the other hand, those who decry inefficient political mobilization are often liberal scholars concerned with citizen participation, the democratic party system, and electoral politics. Some of these thinkers have discerned a depoliticization of the U.S. public since 1952 and an erosion of citizen identification with the two major parties, which has precipitated a crisis or "decomposition" of the two party system (Burnham, 1970, 1975; Janowitz, 1978; Nie, et al., 1976).

Similar points can be made about the cries that the state meddles too much and does too little. Fear of meddling can be seen as an expression of concern over "big government." Worry that regimes are not doing enough may be viewed as dissatisfaction with how demands are processed from the public to political authorities. This pair of grievances has further implications, however. Free and Cantril (1967) and Ladd (1978) have found that public opinion favors the general principle of reduced government and, at the same time, demands more specific services. For example, Ladd reports that while the public agrees (72 percent versus 28 percent) that the government is too strong, it also emphatically favors national health insurance (67 percent versus 33 percent). Enough public support exists for a broad array of programs to hearten the most ardent Great Society enthusiast. Missing at the present time, however, are the ability to mold diverse demands together into an overall agenda and the capacity to join the scattered constituencies backing specific demands. This absence of linkages among demands and constituencies generates considerable public discontent with the performance of the authorities. That discontent finds expression in the simultaneous cry that the government interferes too much (in areas of demand by others) but does too little (in areas of interest to me).

The potential incompatibility among policies favored by different groups is particularly worrisome. While it is true that skillfull political managers have forged workable coalitions in the past, and may do so again, tension among problems and priorities, nevertheless, has a life of its own. People and groups can be maneuvered into political coalitions, but the major problems on the political horizon cannot be so readily reconciled. Values tied to the solution of one set of problems are at odds with the values underlying others. More concretely, when we tackle one goal, the amount of resources available for dealing with others inevitably diminishes. That lack of fit among looming crises has been described in several ways.

Charles Lindblom (1977) captured one aspect of this clash in the title of his recent book, *Politics and Markets*. Mature nation-states are confronted by two principal alternative ways of coping with the potential disasters of the late twentieth century. Either they can rely on centralized authority to guide the public (a political strategy), or they can use incentives, particularly monetary ones, as coordination mechanisms for dealing with the trials that lie ahead (a market strategy). Historically, market systems have been associated with capitalism, although socialist market systems are a possibility (as in Yugoslavia). Capitalist market systems have thus far proven more efficient than socialist political systems in producing and allocating valued goods and services, but they are poor vehicles for decisive change and do much better at "muddling through."

National democratic systems have only arisen under capitalism, but Lindblom questions whether this historical relationship between capitalism and democracy is necessary. He answers that capitalism is now a barrier to further democratization. The main stumbling block is the role of the business elite. Government officials in liberal democracies depend on business because the most important day-to-day economic activities are carried out by corporations, not by state functionaries. Yet, economic success is a responsibility of the state, and a faltering economy is often the central issue that brings down a government. Consequently, the state attempts to win the cooperation of the business elite by granting it special privileges such as protected markets, tax advantages, direct access to high government officials, and so on. The liberal democratic state, Lindblom argues, knows it must meet business demands to insure economic stability and growth and thus slants power in favor of the corporation. Lindblom (1977:356) concludes: "The large private corporation fits oddly into democratic theory and vision. Indeed, it does not fit."

A second way of portraying the clash over differing approaches to contemporary problems is to speak of a conflict of core values. Difficulties are seen as reflections of (at least partially) contradictory themes in a society's overriding culture. Lipset (1963:99-204), for example, argues that the seeming complementary values of achievement and equality that characterize U.S. society are also in conflict. He holds that values that endorse rewarding people for their accomplishments may collide with those that proclaim that all persons must be respected as human beings and that differentials among them should be reduced. Each of these themes is a permanent feature of our society and the tensions they arouse are reduced only because, at any given time, one is more highly regarded than the other. Lipset believes that alternation between the two values tends to coincide with liberal and conservative phases in U.S. party politics.

As will be argued later, political analysis advances when we descend from the clouds of value analysis and talk instead about the central goal conflicts of the modern state (Lehman, 1972, 1977). The language of achievement versus equality tends to create a fuzzy image of the state's key performance dilemmas. Focusing on goals yields a fuller picture of the crises that beset our policy. Concern with values, moreover, creates the misleading impression that the dilemmas can be reduced to the clash of two abstract alternatives. In reality, the concrete political situation is much more complex.

The complaint that power is either too dispersed throughout society or too concentrated in the hands of an elite appears to be another oddly matched pair of diagnoses. We could treat this set as a manifestation of the well-worn Pluralist-Power Elite debate (as summarized by Prewitt and Stone, 1973). The Pluralist perspective sees the political process as shaped mainly by the competition of roughly equal interest groups; the Power Elite perspective asserts that political decisions are dominated by a few powerful, yet shadowy, elites. A new element has been added to this debate, however, by Janowitz's (1978) previously noted complaints about weak political regimes. His charge that the political marketplace has become so choked by mutually crippling pressure groups that effective government is impossible has severe implications for Pluralism. It moves the once optimistic Pluralistic tradition closer to the pessimistic Power Elite perspective, since both orientations now assume a crisis exists.

Increasing numbers of social scientists now reject the either/or style of the old Pluralism-Power Elite debate, however. There is growing recognition that not all political sectors have the same patterns of power. It may be, for instance, that the debate over national health policy is more "pluralistic," while the formation of foreign policy is more "elitist." Moreover, Lindblom (who is a product of the Pluralist tradition) has made a cogent case for the thesis that business inevitably dominates economic policy in capitalist society. Thus, the two orientations of an "excessive" dispersion of power versus the overweening impact of a few elites may not be so antithetical as they looked a decade ago.

The final pair of complaints noted in the opening paragraph can be treated under the heading of a "crisis of legitimacy." The propounders of this diagnosis often trace their intellectual roots to Karl Marx, although the imagery they use owes more to Max Weber. The notion of a crisis of political legitimacy focuses mainly on the advanced capitalist nation-states and is the latest in a series of long expected "final upheavals" of the system. Herbert Marcuse (1964) represents a "negative" version of this approach. He argued that the "repressive tolerance" of capitalist democracy seduces all except those at the very edge of society (e.g., blacks, the lumpenproletariat). In this respect he can be seen as an "anticrisis theorist." Yet, for Marcuse the pervasive legitimacy of capitalism is inauthentic and smothering, for it perverts people's real biological, psychological, and moral needs.

Habermas (1975), O'Connor (1973), and Wolfe (1977) have focused more overtly on legitimation crises. These theorists see the current crisis of capitalism as deepening and irreversible because the prime goal of the state is to abet the "ruling class" in extending its position of privilege, primarily by promoting economic growth and capital accumulation. At the same time, the state must assuage the masses with more social benefits in order to provide the system with a modicum of "legitimacy." The growing inability of the state simultaneously to purchase adequate levels of capital accumulation and legitimacy has been called "legitimation crisis" by Habermas, "limits of legitimacy" by Wolfe, and the "fiscal crisis of the state" by O'Connor. We face crisis, they predict, because the state must give priority to capital accumulation. Cutbacks in social programs are inevitable and thus will undermine the willingness of the masses to endorse the system.

The concept of "legitimation crisis" helps us see the common concerns of Marcuse, Habermas, O'Connor, and Wolfe that lie beneath their surface differences and sheds some light on today's political malaise. Nevertheless, the theme has drawbacks as a diagnostic tool. To begin with, those who loosely adopt Weber's terminology often equate legitimacy with all types of political support, including support for particular incumbents or regimes (e.g., Nixon or the Carter administration) as well as approval of entire systems of government (e.g., the U.S. or the Soviet system).

A more important impediment stems from the use of "legitimation crisis" as an axis along which to study the crises of modern political life. It suffers from the deficiencies of a high level of abstraction that relies on the language of culture and values. As indicated previously, such approaches reduce the complexities of political organization to one or a few polar alternatives. As expressed by Janowitz (1978:9) "the crisis of political legitimacy . . . is an ideological slogan which distorts and oversimplifies sociological investigation of modern political institutions."

The preceding summary of the key complaints about the state has attempted to show that they overlap and complement one another more than we usually assume. The principal missing element is a larger "context" in which to place these complaints. Such a context will enable us to appreciate what we know and don't know about the crises of the state, as well as what has and can be done about the problems facing democratic governments. This larger context is a sociological perspective on the nature of the state and political viability. A significant portion of that perspective is theoretical in nature and, hence, provides a basis for examining the inner logic of the complaints noted above. A theoretical grasp of the dimensions of political life is indispensable for forming consistent hypotheses about political crises as well as for laying the groundwork for the empirical study of the state's problems.

WHAT DO WE KNOW?

Society, Polity, and State

Recent advances in macrosociological theory have helped clarify the relationship among state, polity, and society (Etzioni, 1968; Gouldner, 1970; Kornhauser, 1959; Lehman, 1977). Indeed, the debate over the relation of political units to society has diminished since Lipset (1959:21-41) argued that political structures and processes do not form a separate entity, but rather are a *segment of society*. Political units are part of a larger entity and the relationship is that of a part to a whole. This part/whole terminology does not suggest that society "determines" political life. Society is seen as a system of "Chinese nesting boxes" (Parsons, 1967:322) in which the largest unit (society as the suprasystem) contains many smaller ones (e.g., the political and economic sectors as subsystems). The overall traits of a society limit the forms that political institutions can assume, however. For example, the overarching nature of medieval Europe encouraged feudal political institutions. At the same time, of course, feudal political arrangements affected the tone of the entire medieval society.

The relationship between the state and the political system also becomes clearer using part/whole language. The political system—or *polity* for short—is society's system of political power. The concept of political power refers to a society's potential for setting, pursuing, and implementing collective goals despite resistance. Societies vary in their degree of specialization in political power, and a hallmark of advanced societies is the structural separation of political power from intermember power (Gamson, 1968; Lehman, 1977). Intermember power refers to the immemorial struggles over scarce resources that have marked all human societies. If political power is to guide society, specialized structures must develop and penetrate the system of intermember power to check the drift to ever greater differentials in privilege.

While the concept of *polity* refers to the overall system of political power, the *state* is part of the polity. The state is often the most critical component of the political system, but it is not coextensive with it.

What is a state? Max Weber (1947:156) defined it as that agency that successfully claims a monopoly of the legitimate means of violence over a given territory. With some modification, this definition is acceptable to most students of political behavior (Runciman, 1969:35-42). It can be clarified in two ways, however. First, the distinguishing feature of the state is in its wielding of political power. The responsibility for setting, pursuing, and implementing collective goals in a given territory is the hallmark of the state. Monopoly of legitimate violence is but a secondary characteristic. Access to coercive resources may serve as the ultimate backing for political power, but it is neither the state's defining element nor the only type of resource it needs.

Second, Weber's definition encourages a constricted view of the state, which often equates it with the executive branch of a national government. The state consists of a larger web of political power, however. Ralph Miliband (1969:49–53) criticizes those who equate the state with the national executive. He argues that the state has six branches: the government, the administration, the military and police, the judiciary, the subcentral government, and the parliamentary assemblies.

The government or national executive, says Miliband (1969:42) is often confused with the state because "it is government which speaks on the state's behalf." The administrative component of the state today encompasses agencies "often related to particular ministerial departments, or enjoying a greater or lesser degree of autonomy—public corporations, central banks, regulatory commissions, etc.—and concerned with the management of the economic, social, cultural, and other activities in which the state is now directly or indirectly involved" (Miliband, 1969:52).

The third element of the state includes the armed forces as well as the paramilitary, security, and police forces, "which together form the branch of it mainly concerned with the 'management of violence'" (Miliband, 1969:51). Both the administrative and military elements are constitutionally subordinate to the governmental branch. However, their actual degree of subordination varies from state to state and from era to era. The judiciary, on the other hand, is usually expected to stand apart. Miliband (1969:52) says that "it is not the formal constitutional duty of judges, at least in Western-type political systems, to serve the purposes of their governments. They are constitutionally independent of the political executive and protected from it by security of tenure and other guarantees." Of course, how free a judicial branch actually is from executive domination also varies by period and by polity.

Miliband's (1969:52) fifth component contains the units of subcentral government. In some political systems (such as in France) this element is an extension of the national executive and the administrative branch, "the latter's antennae or tentacles." In other systems with federal patterns (the United States, Canada, West Germany, and Switzerland) the subcentral governments enjoy considerable autonomy.

Miliband's final element of the state is the parliamentary assembly. Like the subcentral governments, the relationship of assemblies to the national executive is a mixture of conflict and cooperation. This ambivalence exists for both the progovernment and antigovernment sides of the aisle. Opposition parties are not wholly uncooperative, for in entering legislative competition they make the ongoing political game possible. At the same time, government parties rarely give blanket support to the national executive.

Miliband's list is not logically exhaustive nor is it intended to tell us how these six elements are organized to constitute a state. The state may contain other elements, such as *the* Party in totalitarian systems. Moreover, the "character" of a state derives less from its elements taken singly than from the network of relationships among them. Merely knowing which elements exist tells us little about the organization of the state. States range from monocratically organized systems in which one of the elements (usually the national executive but sometimes others such as the military) exercises extensive domination all the way to systems of "state feudalism" in which the branches maintain considerable independence in most or all of their activities.

The polity is not the same as the state. The enveloping system of political power embraces more than Miliband's six elements or any other such bodies we might add to his list. The concept of "state" focuses attention only on the legal agents of political power. Of course, the state is charged with political control, but who are the targets of control? The concept of polity helps us locate the political roles that are lodged elsewhere in a society. The modern world is noted for the multiplication of specialized political roles among both individuals and groups. Such roles have long been recognized among economic actors, but today even such actors as research institutes, hospitals, and universities play them.

How do we identify political roles? Three factors are crucial: two have to do with the state's capacity for control, and the third with the political influence of the targets of that control. Social actors tend to have political roles when: 1) they are recipients of the state's commands, and 2) these commands require significant role performances from them. Thus, the modern state's penetration of economics, health, education, and welfare is constantly creating new political roles. Social actors also tend to develop political roles when they struggle to influence state policy. Universal suffrage has been a major impetus for the rise of political roles. The targets of "downward" control processes and the initiators of "upward" influence efforts have been treated under the rubric of "citizenship" by T.H. Marshall (1950). He saw a continuous extension of the citizenship role in the modern world largely as a result of 1) the penetration of the state into previously "nonpolitical" sectors, and 2) the expansion of democracy, which permits more groups to engage in politics.

The polity is not a fixed segment of society, but a constantly expanding one. The bureaucratic elaboration of the state is one of the causes of this trend that has received the most attention. But the expansion of political roles throughout the rest of society is equally important. Many critics attack "big government," yet few are willing to reduce their own citizenship roles. In any event, no diminution of the state or of citizen roles appears likely in the foreseeable future.

Dimensions of Crisis: Ingredients of Viability

Sociological theory also enables us to identify the main factors that determine the success or failure of modern polities. The elements of this theory provide us with a firm handle for mastering the logic of the crises discussed in the opening section. It matters very little whether we open by asking about the crises of the state or the ingredients of political viability. Crises are merely diminutions of viability; viability is the ability to surmount crises.

A viable political system has three main ingredients (Lehman, 1977:129-82). First, it needs an effective state to impose political control. Effectiveness speaks of an ability to attain goals. Second, the system must efficiently incorporate political influence. The question of efficiency points to the fact that a polity depends on contributions from key societal groups, but that those contributions must not drain off resources needed for essential goal attainment activities. Third, a polity must possess legitimate "rules of the game." Groups must not only know how to play the political game, but must also view the rules as integrated, plausible, and morally appropriate. Low legitimacy poses severe problems for a polity (Weber, 1960:4-13). Weak or illegitimate rules foster a lack of trust in the state's commands and tend to provoke coercive sanctions, which further erode effective political control. Moreover, a state that emphasizes coercion too much increases alienation and encourages the public to perform only minimal citizen roles. Mobilization efforts based on even greater coercive sanctions tend to exacerbate the situation and to weaken the efficient flow of political influences even further.

Effective Political Control: The Need for Payoff

In contemporary polities, effectiveness is the pivotal ingredient of viability. A modern polity can hobble along for a time without efficient influence and with low legitimacy, but it cannot survive without some payoff to its citizens. Lipset (1959:81-82) notes that effectiveness is sometimes a substitute for legitimacy in the short run and its generator in the long run. He suggests that the republics set up in Germany and Austria after World War I survived through the 1920s, despite their weak legitimacy, because they were perceived as effective. Powerful groups went along with the rules of the game as long as the new states, which many despised, provided political, social, and economic amenities. Similarly, Lipset (1963:45-60) argues that the United States coped with the absence of pervasive legitimacy during its infancy partly because the union demonstrated effectiveness. It provided a payoff in terms of economic goods and a rising living standard. Tangible results allowed the new nation time to sink its moral roots and to build a reservoir of legitimacy.

Each of our original four pairs of complaints contains grievances about the modern state's capacity to provide satisfactory levels of payoff. The "big government" versus weak regimes pair focuses specifically on the problem of what the state can deliver. This theme also occurs in the other three pairs, however. In fact, the final pair—which appears initially to be concerned with the "spiritual" subject of the crisis of legitimacy—ends as a critique of the modern state's ability to provide contradictory services.

To a large degree, the crisis in effectiveness reflects the state's need to pursue multiple—and potentially conflicting—goals. As indicated above, this dilemma has too often been couched in terms of two polar alternatives that make the issue seem to be "merely" a clash of abstract values. Lipset (1963) spoke in this vein when he used the terms of achievement versus equality (see also Milner, 1972; Nisbet, 1974). More recently, the neo-Marxist James O'Connor (1973) has employed the terminology of capital accumulation versus legitimacy, which allows him to move the issue into the context of societal structure. The gap between the state's expenditures and revenues that is the inevitable result of pursuing both capital accumulation and legitimacy constitutes "the fiscal crisis of the capitalist state." Daniel Bell (1974) applied O'Connor's insight to all industrial societies under the rubric of "equity versus efficiency," while I have discussed the effectiveness crisis in terms of economic growth versus more equality (Lehman, 1977:134-36).

Economic growth requires the accumulation of capital. Emphasis is put on such assets as factories, buildings, machinery, and transportation facilities, all of which generate revenue. While every segment of society may benefit from economic expansion, the most privileged (the business elites) tend to be the chief beneficiaries. Hence, this goal is likely to exacerbate inequality. Lindblom's previously mentioned point about the state's dependence on the corporate sector explains why this occurs. At the very least, capital accumulation widens the relative gap between groups at the top and those near the bottom, even if the absolute wealth of each increases.

Programs for economic growth tend to clash with the interests of those advocating more equality. Conflict is particularly intense when choices must be made concerning the allocation of limited state resources. The debate over ways to overcome recession and unemployment reflects this clash, with some arguing for the stimulation of capital accumulation and others calling for improved benefits for the less privileged.

Economic growth, however, is a requisite for dispensing assets more equally. Capital formation fuels social services by providing the revenues (through surpluses and taxation) that pay for improved education, welfare, and health care. Moreover, an argument can be made for the long-range economic advantages of a better-educated, healthier, and happier public. But, in the short run, social services yield no profits; hospitals do not pay for themselves the way factories or dams do. When inflation and recession slow capital accumulation, more than economic growth is impeded. The fiscal basis for more equality is also weakened.

Economic growth and more equality hardly tell the entire story about the polity's effectiveness problems, however. Two other major goals complicate matters further: national defense and quality of life.

The boundaries of the modern state were shaped primarily by the physical limits of its military prowess (Poggi, 1978). Even today a state's official borders reflect its capacity for "national security" more than the scope of its economic, cultural, and linguistic penetration. Indeed, military prowess remains the major element in the relations among nation-states, although the deployment of nuclear weapons has produced an unprecedented threshold for violence in international relations and, thus, has raised questions about the role of military force in the future (presuming a nuclear holocaust can be avoided).

Under the impact of two World Wars and the Korean and Vietnam wars, the United States has constructed a permanent military establishment unthinkable in the nineteenth century. This system has become the principal rival of domestic programs for governmental appropriations. Radicals have argued that the existence of a "military-industrial complex" serves as an underpinning for economic growth, so that defense and capital accumulation go hand-in-hand rather than being antagonistic goals. Recent empirical work, however, suggests that the ties between the military and business are far from monolithic. A small segment of the corporate elite profits excessively from swelling military appropriations, but the overall economy does not (Lieberson, 1971; Szymanski, 1973; Tucker, 1971; Weidenbaum, 1969). A bloated military budget may be a threat to capitalism. Certainly, no one doubts the conflict between the goals of military spending and more equality—although we tend to forget that federal welfare expenditures have risen far more sharply in the past two decades than the proportion of the budget devoted to defense (Moore, 1972:108-11).

Quality of life is the latest entry into the national goals sweepstakes. The past ten years have witnessed the rise of a myriad of "environmental" issues such as: opposition to nuclear power plants; cries for pollution and toxic substance controls; concern for forests, parks, and wildlife; and demands for auto safety. The Chase Manhattan Bank has estimated that the quality of life agenda would cost at least $100 billion per year (Butcher, 1978). Quality of life poses a challenge to the advocates of economic growth because the costs of items such as auto safety and pollution equipment are regarded as inflationary as well as "nonproductive." Moreover, quality of life goals drain funds away from investments in new plants and equipment needed for economic growth. The proponents of more equality are also coming to recognize that environmental programs may siphon off funds from social programs and, thus, benefit the affluent and the suburban more than the poor and the urban.

In short, the modern polity's effectiveness crisis cannot be adequately described in terms of polar opposites. Four problem areas impose themselves on the state's agenda: economic growth, more equality, national defense, and quality of life. In isolation, each is desirable. Yet, a major initiative in favor of any one of them lessens the chances that the others will be dealt with satisfactorily.

Efficient Political Influence

The topic of efficient influence focuses on processes through which the public funnels inputs to the state. Social scientists suggest that these inputs are of two types: confidence and demand (Parsons, 1967; Easton, 1965). Confidence refers to broad endorsements of political authorities, particularly the national executive. When granted, confidence confers a "zone of indifference" so that the state does not have to sell each directive or to expend inordinate resources to obtain acquiescence. Political commentators point to this phenomenon when they say that a newly elected government has a "mandate" or is in a "honeymoon period."

Confidence should not be confused with legitimacy, although the two are related. Confidence points to the credibility of officeholders. Legitimacy refers to the degree of moral approval for the rules of the game, apart from the incumbents. For example, confidence in the Truman, Johnson, and Nixon administrations dipped sharply during their last year in office (1952, 1968, and 1974), but moral acceptance of the U.S. political system remained relatively high. Legitimacy provides a foundation for confidence but cannot guarantee it. Conversely, a series of governments whose credibility is weak is likely to set off an erosion of legitimacy.

The core issue concerning demand is how adept various groups are in channeling their desires upward and having them acted upon by the state. Demand and confidence are linked. Groups with less access to the state are also likely to have less confidence in it. In democratic systems, nevertheless, demands tend to be broad enough so that confidence does not rest on the satisfaction of each petition. Confidence slips only when a group senses that many of its demands are being evaded.

The most formidable obstacle to efficient political influence in democratic society is the persistence of unresponsiveness in the polity. Responsiveness refers to how closely the state's means and goals coincide with the demands of the various segments of society. (For a detailed analysis of responsiveness, see Etzioni, 1968:430-548.) Unresponsiveness in contemporary U.S. society has two bases: unequal influence and the "decomposition" of the two party system. The first of these factors has been the key complaint of the Power Elite school; the second has become the lament of pessimistic Pluralists like Janowitz.

Unequal influence refers to the differential ability of groups to affect the state. Less privileged people are poorer not only financially but also in such matters as health, education, self-respect, and administrative skills. They may care deeply about societal problems, but they have few assets to expend on something as "extraneous" to everyday survival as politics. This condition of few surplus resources and little experience in mobilizing them reverberates to the level of interest groups. Not much money, time, or ability are available to nurture these organizations. Consequently, the less privileged have fewer interest groups of their own, while those that do exist do not represent their true interests. Statistically, this means that the ratio of potential to actual political participants decreases as one moves down the stratification hierarchy (Milbrath and Goel, 1977), since for less privileged people the cost of exerting political influence is very great relative to the resources they have on hand. Low political mobilization is quite "rational" for these groups, as Anthony Downs (1957:237-73) has noted. Yet, it is a narrow and costly rationality for the less privileged and for the viability of the entire polity.

"Decomposition" is a way of stating that the U.S. two party system is in trouble. Parties have been the key mechanism in liberal democracies for processing demand and confidence from the public and its interest groups to the state. The U.S. system has traditionally consisted of "parties of representation" (Neumann, 1956:403-5; Lipset, 1959:85-87; Lehman, 1977:155-61). Such parties pursue adherents wherever they can find them. Their passion is for electoral victory, not saving souls or transforming society. Success is more important to them than ideological purity. Rather than presiding over a circumscribed constituency, parties of representation try to widen their base of support by attracting new adherents. They "bargain policies for votes" (Lipset 1968:397). In any given election, a party of representation is well advised "not to try to convert a sizeable number of those disposed to vote for its opponent but to do everything possible to get out the vote among its own supporters" (Lipset 1968: 390). At the same time, parties of representation are marked by their continuing effort to reach electoral victory even if this means sacrificing ideological purity.

The party systems of mature democracies are tending to become increasingly representational in character. Universal suffrage has been crucial here. The pressures to win and hold large bodies of voters have made parties more flexible, less dogmatic, and more tolerant of diversity. This is true even of many of the so-called parties of "democratic integration" such as European Catholic and social democratic parties. In West Germany, the Christian Democrats and Social Democrats resemble the Conservative-Labour and Republican-Democratic splits in Britain and the United States more closely than did their sectarian predecessors in the Weimar Republic. All this has pushed political debate toward the center. To optimize their political advantage, parties eschew sectarian appeals to the extreme right or left out of fear of losing supporters in the middle.

Walter D. Burnham (1970, 1975) has described the current U.S. situation as "decomposition" of the party system and "depoliticization" of the electorate. Janowitz (1978:101-13), in his review of the data on U.S. political participation, finds that while decomposition has accelerated since 1952, depoliticization has not. To refute alleged depoliticization, he notes, a long-term increase in electoral turnout (from 41.0 percent of eligible voters in the 1920 presidential campaign to 62.8 percent in 1960). Even recent turnout rates (55.7 percent in 1972 and 53.3 percent in 1976) have been roughly the same as those in FDR's four campaigns and the Truman election of 1948. Moreover, public interest in political issues and involvement in political activities has risen sharply since 1952.

On the other hand, the decomposition of the party system has proceeded at a gallop, according to Janowitz. He believes that the most direct manifestations of decomposition are the increase in the proportion of citizens who describe themselves as "independent," sudden shifts in voter preferences from one election to the next, and ticket splitting within elections.

What has this done to the party of representation system in the United states? Nie, et al. argue that:

These changes add up to an "individuation" of American political life
.... [R]egion, class, religion are still associated with party affiliation,

but not as closely as they once were. Nor does party affiliation predict political behavior well; fewer have such affiliation and fewer of those with such affiliation follow it. The individual voter evaluates candidates on the basis of information and impressions conveyed by the mass media, and then votes on that basis....Elections turn more on the short-term forces in the election—the candidates and the issues as they come across to the electorate through the media....It is certainly likely to mean a less predictable electoral process (Nie, et al., 1976:347-48).

In short, today's two party system no longer processes either confidence or demand efficiently. Politicians without predictable party anchorage seem immoral and opportunistic. Robert Lekachman (1979:A23) calls them a "despised species:....Lacking firm principles of their own (a prerequisite for election), bombarded by conflicting claims, they improvise, swing from anti-inflationary to anti-unemployment initiatives and back again before either affliction is more than slightly ameliorated, and avoid painful choices as long as possible by yielding to the threats of those who scream loudest." He might add that this failing is due less to a rise in individual perfidy than to a decline in the efficiency of our two party system.

Legitimate Political Institutions

Legitimacy is an important ingredient of political viability but in a very different way than effectiveness and efficiency. Effective political control and efficient political influence concern processes within political structures. They refer to the actions and interactions among the men, women, and groups that make up the polity. Legitimacy is part of the *political culture* and points not to the networks of relations among political actors but to the *patterns of beliefs, values, and sentiments used by members of a polity to orient themselves to political life.* In theoretical terms, political culture is logically separate from political structures (Lehman 1977:20-40).

Legitimacy is generally important for political viability, but its specific effects are indirect, partly because of its "external" status. Legitimacy is generally important because a political culture includes more than rules of the political game. The public needs a working consensus about what authorities and potential partisans are likely to do. But orderly political life demands more than rules, for they do not contain a moral imperative capable of fostering compliance. Workable rules must be associated with symbols that endow them with moral worth. These latter symbols are called legitimations.

Weber's (1947:324-406) classification of doctrines of legitimation still provides the best perspective. Rules of the game are routinely legitimated by either: 1) a body of "sacred" symbols viewed as the product of immemorial lore—traditional legitimation, or 2) a set of abstract criteria perceived as rational, from which lower-level directives are felt to be logically derived—rational-legal legitimation. Weber's third type, charismatic legitimation, is the antithesis of the other two because it arises when routine doctrines lose their moral appeal.

Political institutions in premodern societies tend to be legitimated by traditional themes, but in the modern world legitimacy can be ranged on a continuum from traditional to rational-legal. Societies whose ultimate moral appeals are to written constitutions are characterized by legitimacy near the rational-legal end of the continuum. The United States is an example, although the Constitution is not without sacred strands. When doctrines give ultimate authority to a revolutionary ideology (as in the Soviet Union) or to a social unit that is "above the fray" (such as the British monarchy), we have a good indication that legitimation retains more traditional elements. However, both these cases include more rational-legal components than most premodern political societies.

The impact of legitimacy on viability is indirect, not only because it is logically external to political structure, but also because political culture tends to change slowly. The search for potent levers of societal transformation, therefore, should not look to the realm of culture. A strategy focusing on culture is urged by those who diagnose our current political malaise as a "crisis of legitimacy," "adversary culture," "moral decline," or "failure of nerve." Yet, given the glacial movement of culture, this approach calls for no significant change in our lifetimes. How seriously should we take calls for "spiritual rebirth" as the method of grappling with the problems outlined at the outset? These crises do have "moral" dimensions, but they can only be treated when the polity is made more effective and efficient.

The indirect contribution of legitimacy to political viability takes two main forms. First, legitimacy provides the moral frame within which citizens judge political events. Little research has been done on how modern citizens use doctrines of legitimation to evaluate political experiences—both those that they encounter directly and those that reach them through the mass media. We can hypothesize, however, that the more political events are framed in rational-legal terms, the more grueling and volatile the public's judgments of authorities are likely to be. A traditional frame of reference, on the other hand, yields judgments that are more generous to authorities and less changeable.

If this hypothesis is valid, the United States and other advanced polities are faced with more grueling and volatile judgments because of the importance of rational-legal legitimations. A positive view of rationality and state activism is a distinctive feature of such polities. This frame of reference treats social problems as susceptible to easy political remedies, which in turn leads to a heightened demand for payoff. Consequently, modern polities often find it difficult to keep pace with demands. Although the relative ineffectiveness of the state may also contribute to this open-ended type of the political agenda, it is certainly stimulated by rational-legal legitimation. In the short run, the ensuing discontent leads only to the withdrawal of confidence in particular leaders. If the process goes unchecked, the moral worth of the political order may be called into question.

In advanced polities, therefore, failure to deliver expected payoffs is very likely to be intertwined with legitimacy and to weaken it.

The second indirect contribution of legitimacy to viability is via its "structural manifestations." Key political activities are highly sensitive to levels of legitimacy. Indeed, such "structural manifestations" are litmus tests of the level of moral worth attributed to the political order. Generally speaking, when moral approval for a polity is high, problems of succession and the circulation of political factions are handled fairly easily. For example, Lyndon Johnson's smooth assumption of office following John F. Kennedy's assassination in November 1963 was considered normal by Americans, even with the emotional turmoil of the moment. In fact, there was nothing natural or normal about it. Johnson had been peripheral to the power centers of the administration. Robert F. Kennedy, not Johnson, had been the second most powerful figure. Johnson's succession presaged the political decline of the Attorney General and his allies. Yet, the succession was never in doubt, nor was it challenged.

The ability to call upon third parties to support political actions is another structural manifestation of legitimacy. All else being equal, as third-party backing increases, political control grows in effectiveness and political influence becomes more efficient. The ability to count on allies reduces the risk that initiatives will be resisted. As a result, the state's ability to guide society expands. The U.S. Civil War demonstrated that a regime cannot automatically count on crucial third party support. Conversely, the presence of powerful forces that recognize a group's right to exert political influence inhibits those who might impede political participation. Support for the right of black Americans to participate in the political process shows how a structural manifestation of legitimacy may increase the efficiency of a group's political influence.

WHAT ARE WE DOING?

To date, there has been little systematic application of social science knowledge to the major dilemmas of political viability. To the extent that the ingredients of viability have been examined, attention has been focused primarily on problems of effectiveness. Far less effort has been expended on applying practical knowledge to questions of efficiency and legitimacy. This is not hard to understand, since the question of effective political control asks about the ability of political authorities to guide society. The topics of efficiency and legitimacy, on the other hand, are not central features of political authorities' official duties, although they sporadically try to manipulate both factors to mobilize support for themselves and the system.

The modern state's efforts at more effective control have reached the point that awareness of the potential strains among its four crucial goals (economic growth, more equality, national defense, and quality of life) is commonplace. Very little, however, has been accomplished in the task of assigning priorities among these goals to allow for better long-range planning. The fiscal limits constraining the state (which became so visible in the 1970s) require a clearer ranking of these goals because not enough economic and noneconomic resources are available to maximize pursuit of all four simultaneously. If we fail to prioritize our goals, we will likely be even less successful in attaining any of them during the 1980s than we have seen in the past. That is, if we continue to "muddle through" with ad hoc policy decisions (which has been the hallmark of democratic polities), economic growth, equality, national security and quality of life will all be impaired.

At this time, the prime contender for top priority is economic growth. In part, this is a reflection of the surge in conservative political mood currently marking most Western democratic societies. As fear of "big government" has grown, overt resentment of "big business" has slackened. Another, probably more important, factor has been sputtering economic performance since the late 1960s. Chronic "stagflation"—episodic bouts of simultaneous inflation and recession—has made the public less optimistic about the economic future and more hesitant about diverting resources from economic growth to other goals. Polls report that citizens are now far more concerned about economic growth than about equality, quality of life, and even national defense. Certainly, political authorities seem more interested in maintaining the good will of the business elite whom they regard as the guarantors of prosperity.

Two areas in particular are touted as critical entry points for state intervention on behalf of economic growth. One is encouragement of investment; the other is expanded research and development. Stimulation of investments is vital because, according to *Time* (1979:36): "during the 25 years up to 1973, business spending on new plants added about 3% a year to the nation's capital base—plants and machines—but since then the total has risen only some 1.75% a year." Outdated plants and machinery stifle operating efficiency and productivity and, thus, serve as drags on a society's economic potential.

In 1964 U.S. spending on research and development was approximately 3 percent of the gross national product. By 1978 the figure had dropped to 2 percent. One consequence has been that the number of U.S. patents issued to American citizens and corporations has dipped by 25 percent since 1971, while the number issued to foreigners has jumped by 14 percent. Unless a stimulus for new technological innovations is provided, it is argued, economic growth suffers (*Time*, 1979:36). The call for innovation in the area of new energy sources has received particular attention in the past few years.

It can be argued, of course, that single-minded concentration on such a narrow band of economic objectives may be counterproductive. From this perspective, the pursuit of economic growth through capital accumulation ought not to occur at the expense of social and welfare services, nor ought it further to erode the quality of the environment. Advocates of national defense have entered the fray as well. After a period of quiesence following the Vietnam war, the military establishment and its supporters now are making a renewed effort for national priority. They point to a burgeoning Soviet arms budget and its invasion of Afghanistan and claim that unless the United States acts soon we will be in a position of decisive military inferiority by the mid 1980s. It goes without saying that these military estimates are disputed by those who argue that comparisons of current military spending levels are a tricky matter and that present gross spending levels are poor guides for estimating military balances, both now and in the future.

The inability to assign consistent priorities among competing national goals is due in part to the crisis in efficient political influence. The "decomposition" of the two party system makes successful societal guidance more difficult. Inefficient influence mechanisms also encourage the growth of single-issue pressure groups (Right to Life, anti-Panama Canal treaty, etc.), which further undermines the stability of the two party system. The result has been weak regimes that may not be able to make the big decisions needed in the decade ahead.

WHAT HAVE WE ACCOMPLISHED?

Increased awareness of the dilemmas facing modern polities has not been matched by enhanced political viability. Political problems such as the "energy crisis" still explode suddenly and are treated in a crisis atmosphere. Moreover, problems related to political effectiveness are still handled one at a time with little consideration to how any one set of resolutions impinges on other problems and goals. Since the dilemmas of efficient influence and legitimate rules of the game are by their nature less susceptible to direct state intervention, it is safe to say that nothing at all has been accomplished in regard to these ingredients of political viability.

WHERE ARE WE GOING?

The several crises of the state are not a hodgepodge of random or contradictory laments. Our four pairs of problems form a more coherent picture of the crises of the state when framed in terms of effective political control, efficient influence, and legitimate institutions. Effectiveness stands out as the most important of the ingredients for the reasons I have detailed. However, problems of efficiency and legitimacy cannot be ignored, for that would lead to misunderstandings of such complaints as the "meddling of big government."

In fact, when issues of political effectiveness are treated in isolation they appear to be the most manageable of the three types of problems. Relatively noncontroversial principles are available for promoting more effective policy formation, although their introduction into the governmental process has been very slow. Moreover, the need to set priorities among the goals of economic growth, greater equality, quality of life, and national defense—and to stick with these choices—is not an insurmountable task. Such changes would enhance the state's capacity for comprehensive decision making and allow it to deal more systematically with the ominous problems of the late twentieth century. Formidable as these concrete issues (e.g., energy shortages, pollution, inflation, poverty, Soviet-U.S. rivalries) are today, techniques and know-how for coping with all of them and mastering some of them are within our grasp.

The critical issue, rather, is how efforts at enhanced political effectiveness mesh with prevailing modes of political influence and, in the long run, how this interaction affects the legitimacy of the political system. Enhanced political effectiveness requires a greater capacity for comprehensive planning than most democratic polities now possess. Is the need for greater coordination compatible with democratic mechanisms of influence? Some commentators think not (for example, see Heilbroner, 1974). They argue that the decisive leadership demanded by looming crises is antithetical to the piecemeal style of democracy. They fear that mounting problems and fumbling regimes will make the temptations of totalitarianism irresistible. For instance, are the members of Congress who must run for reelection every two years really capable of the "hard" decisions necessary for a successful long-term energy policy? The present inefficiencies of democratic influence that were detailed earlier make matters even graver. The persistence of unequal influence and the trend toward party system decomposition increase the risks that leaders will be unable to solicit support from a working majority of the citizens. As a consequence, the state will be deprived of the capacity to guide the society in a way that allows us to deal adequately with the major items on the political agenda. Under the impact of these factors it is problematic whether democratic institutions can retain their legitimacy. Elites and the general public, yearning for strong leadership, may abandon the rules of the game that permit opposition and rally behind a "strong man," or a "revolutionary vanguard," who promises greater effectiveness.

What lies ahead, in other words, is more than a test of the state's capacity to provide payoffs more effectively. The deeper question is whether the crises of the state can be mastered within the framework of democratic institutions in which significant portions of the public can continue to place their trust. Predictions are difficult, but without doubt democratic systems are heading toward a period of major trial in which their endurance will be severely challenged. The most optimistic thing I can say is that the outcome is still in doubt. Democracy may yet survive in a more effective, efficient, and legitimate form.

REFERENCES AND SUGGESTED READINGS

Bell, D. 1974. "The Public Household." *The Public Interest* 37(Fall):29–68.
Burnham, W.D. 1970. *Critical Elections and the Mainsprings of American Politics.* New York: W.W. Norton.

_____. 1975. "American Parties in the 1970's: Beyond Party?" In *The Future of Political Parties, Sage Electoral Studies Yearbook,* Vol. I., edited by Louis Massel and Paul M. Sacks, pp. 238–77. Beverly Hills, Calif.: Sage.

Butcher, W.D. 1978. "The Stifling Costs of Regulation." *Business Week,* November 6, 1978, p. 22 et seq.

Downs, A. 1957. *An Economic Theory of Democracy.* New York: Harper & Row.

Easton, D. 1965. *A Systems Analysis of Political Life.* New York: John Wiley & Sons.

*Etzioni, A. 1968. *The Active Society: A Theory of Societal and Political Processes.* New York: The Free Press.

Etzioni provides an indispensable analysis of the underpinnings of contemporary macrosociological theory. Etzioni believes that we have entered the "postmodern" era, and he examines the factors fostering societal guidance in this context. He explores the types of knowledge, power, and consensus-building arrangements needed for an "active society."

Free, L. and H. Cantril. 1967. *The Political Beliefs of Americans: A Study of Public Opinion.* New Brunswick, N.J.: Rutgers University Press.

Gamson, W.A. 1968. *Power and Discontent.* Homewood, Ill.: Dorsey.

Gouldner, A.W. 1970. *The Coming Crisis in Western Sociology.* New York: Basic Books.

Habermas, J. 1975. *Legitimational Crisis.* Boston: Beacon Press.

Heilbroner, R.L. 1974. *An Inquiry with the Human Prospect.* New York: W.W. Norton.

Kornhauser, W. 1959. *The Politics of Mass Society.* New York: The Free Press.

*Janowitz, M. 1978. *The Last Half-Century: Societal Change and Politics in America.* Chicago: University of Chicago Press.

The book is an analysis of the last 50 years of U.S. political life. Janowitz is particularly concerned with the reasons for flattering regimes in the United States and the rest of the Western world. In the course of his analysis he provides the most up-to-date and comprehensive summary of research on the contemporary United States, including such topics as political participation, inequality, the military, the changing organization of work and community life, the roles of the mass media and agencies of social control, as well as the impact of behavioral science knowledge.

Ladd, E.V., Jr. 1978. "What the Voters Really Want," *Fortune,* December 18, 1978, pp. 40–44 et seq.

Lehman, E.W. 1972. "On the Concept of Political Culture: A Theoretical Reassessment," *Social Forces* 50(Mar):361–70.

_____. 1977. *Political Society: A Macrosociology of Politics.* New York: Columbia University Press.

Lekachman, R. 1979. "More Means Less" *The New York Times,* September 5, 1979, p. A23.

Lieberson, S. 1971. "An Empirical Study of Military–Industrial Linkages." *American Journal of Sociology* 76(Jan):562–84.

*Lindblom, C.E. 1977. *Politics and Markets: The World's Political Economic Systems.* New York: Basic Books.

This work presents an analysis of the two main ways that economic life in advanced societies can be organized: via politics or markets. Lindblom inquires into the ability of each to balance the needs of economic growth, more equality, and the furtherance of democracy and liberty. He finds that significant, although different, constraints operate in both systems.

Lipset, S.M. 1959. *Political Man: The Social Bases of Politics.* Garden City, N.Y.: Doubleday.

_____. 1963. *The First New-Nation: The United States in Historical and Comparative Perspective.* New York: Basic Books.

_____. 1968. *Revolution and Counterrevolution: Change and Persistence in Social Structures.* New York: Basic Books.

Marcuse, H. 1964. *One Dimensional Man.* Boston: Beacon Press.

Marshall, T.H. 1950. *Citizenship and Social Class.* London: Cambridge University Press.

Milbrath, L.W. and M.L. Goel. 1977. *Political Participation: How and Why do People get involved in Politics?,* 2d ed. Chicago: Rand McNally.

Miliband, Ralph. 1969. *The State in Capitalist Society.* New York: Basic Books.

Milner, M., Jr. 1972. *The Illusion of Equality: The Effects of Education on Opportunity, Inequality and Social Conflict.* San Francisco: Jossey-Bass.

*Moore, B., Jr. 1972. *Reflections on the Causes of Human Misery and Upon Certain Proposals to Eliminate Them.* Boston: Beacon Press.

In an analysis of what constitutes a "decent society" and whether it is obtainable, Moore asks us to let the political chips fall where they will. "There is no innate guarantee that valid social science analysis will always yield conclusions favorable to the humanitarian impulse...." The book concludes with an analysis of the United States as a "predatory democracy."

Neumann, S. 1956. "Toward a Comparative Study of Political Parties." In *Modern Political Parties,* edited by Sigmund Neumann, pp. 395–421. Chicago: University of Chicago Press.

Nie, N.H., S. Verba, and J.R. Petrocik. 1976. *The Changing American Voter.* Cambridge, Mass.: Harvard University Press.

Nisbet, R.A. 1974. "The Pursuit of Equality." *The Public Interest* 34(Winter): 103–20.

O'Connor, J. 1973. *The Fiscal Crisis of the State.* New York: St. Martin's Press.

Parsons, T. 1967. *Sociological Theory and Modern Society.* New York: The Free Press.

*Poggi, G. 1978. *The Development of the Modern State: A Sociological Introduction.* Stanford, Calif.: Stanford University Press.

In analysis of the formation of the state as we know it today, Poggi relies both on a variety of social theories and on data based on Western European history. The final chapter offers Poggi's perspective on the crisis of the modern state.

Prewitt, K. and A. Stone. 1973. *The Ruling Elites: Elite Theory, Power and American Democracy.* New York: Harper & Row.

Runciman, W.G. 1969. *Social Science and Political Theory,* 2d ed. London: Cambridge University Press.

Starr, P. 1975. "Politics Against Government." *New Republic* 173(Dec 27):19–23.

Szymanski, A. 1973. "Military Spending and Economic Stagnation." *American Journal of Sociology* 79(July):1–14.

Time. 1979. "To Set the Economy Right." August 27, 1979, pp. 24–36.

Tucker, R.W. 1971. *The Radical Left and American Foreign Policy.* Baltimore: The Johns Hopkins University Press.

Weber, M. 1947. *The Theory of Social and Economic Organization.* New York: Oxford University Press.

_____. 1960. "The Three Types of Legitimate Rule," Pp. 4–13 in Amitai Etzioni (ed.) *Complex Organizations: A Sociological Reader.* New York: Holt, Rinehart and Winston.

Weidenbaum, M.L. 1969. *The Modern Public Sector.* New York: Basic Books.

Wolfe, A. 1977. *The Limits of Legitimacy: Political Contradictions of Contemporary Capitalism,* New York: The Free Press.

Part
C

REDUCING SOCIAL INEQUITIES

A few years ago, Herbert Gans wrote that "America is heading for more equality of results, by which I mean a greater similarity in income and political influence among income, occupational, racial, ethnic, and age groups and the sexes."* He went on to argue that we are presently in the midst of an "equality revolution" in which all forms of economic, social, and political inequality are slowly being eliminated. The equality revolution offers applied sociologists innumerable opportunities for both studying and participating in one of the major trends in contemporary societies.

Western social philosophy has long viewed equality as a moral imperative, but usually it has been conceptualized as equal opportunities for all. "Everyone should have a fair and equal chance at the starting line of life and not be handicapped by family background, mental or physical capabilities, ethnicity, or sex." This is an admirable goal, which we are still far from attaining. But no matter how equal people are at the beginning of the race, some will inevitably finish far ahead of others. "That is their just reward for superior effort," assert some observers, while others with a more fatalistic perspective say "that's life."

Gans believes, however, that we should strive for as much equality at the finish line as possible—which he calls "equality of results"—and that we are slowly achieving this goal. Many other sociologists disagree with his empirical observations, if not his normative goal. In the contemporary United States, more than 10 percent of the population still lives in abject poverty, while 20 percent own over three-fourths of all personal wealth. Nor have most members of the working class experienced "embourgeoisement" in either their wealth or life styles. In the political realm, numerous observers contend that most citizens exercise virtually no influence on government and that people are increasingly becoming aware of this fact. At work, most large organizations are built around a centralized hierarchy of authority that leaves ordinary workers—blue-collar and white-collar—with little control over their job activities. Racial and other ethnic cleavages stubbornly refuse to disappear and remain bases for marked social inequality. Women have discovered that suffrage and education have not given them equal power and status with men. Finally, the discrimination experienced by older citizens in our society is slowly coming to light. With gross inequality continuing to pervade all these realms of social life, what can applied sociologists possibly do to alter the situation? That is the central concern of the following chapters.

One way of lessening the pessimism that frequently results from these efforts is to strive for equity rather than equality. In an equitable situation there is a range of outcomes or statuses, but they are kept within tolerable limits. Anyone who gets too far ahead of the accepted limits is restrained, while anyone

*Herbert J. Gans, *More Equality* (New York: Random House, 1973, p. 3).

223

who falls too far behind is helped to catch up. Inequality remains, but the race is seen as fair for everyone, and the results are tolerable to all. Creating equity may not be as exciting as demanding equality for all, but it is much more readily attainable.

11 SOCIOECONOMIC STATUS

Jonathan H. Turner and James R. Kluegel

Only recently has U.S. society recognized inequality of socioeconomic status as a "social problem." Just two decades ago, spurred by works such as Harrington's *Other America* (1962), we first began to realize that a sizeable minority of Americans (25 to 30 million) were poor. And only then did we take any large scale, tax-supported actions to reduce this condition.

WHAT ARE THE PROBLEMS?

The dual concerns of understanding what is responsible for this widespread poverty and deciding how it might be eliminated are the major challenges for applied sociology in the area of socioeconomic inequality. There is also a third aspect of socioeconomic inequality that some (but far fewer than the majority of Americans) consider problematic. This is the fact that a small elite class controls most of the scarce resources in U.S. society. Later in this chapter we will argue that the failure of most Americans to view the concentration of wealth as a social problem presents an important barrier to solving the problems of poverty and inequality of opportunity.

Understanding and solving problems of socioeconomic inequality require several related activities by applied sociologists: 1) providing an accurate reading of the state of inequality in the United States, 2) attempting to understand why problematical aspects of inequality arise and persist, 3) designing programs to resolve problems of socioeconomic inequality, and 4) judging the success of these programs.

WHAT DO WE KNOW?

The extent of inequality in both the distribution of scarce resources and opportunities for attaining desired positions are two characteristics that tell us much about a society. We begin with an examination of inequality in the distribution of scarce resources and then look at what we know about unequal opportunities.

The Unequal Distribution of Scarce Resources in the United States

The issue of inequality turns on the question of how unevenly scarce and valuable resources are distributed among the members of a society. In general, there are three basic resources: 1) income and wealth, 2) prestige, and 3) power. We begin our analysis of inequality by examining how unequally these three resources are distributed in the United States.

Figure 11.1 Distribution of Wealth by Wealth Fifths

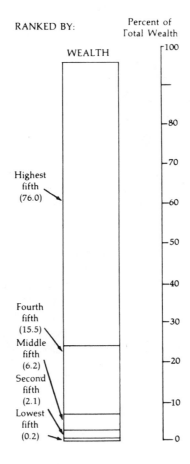

Source: Executive Office of the President: Office of Management and Budget, *Social Indicators 1973* (Washington, D.C.: Government Printing Office, 1973), p. 164.

Income and Wealth Inequality. Figure 11.1 shows the distribution of wealth by wealth fifths in the United States in 1962 (Turner and Starnes, 1976). A word of explanation on wealth and wealth fifths is necessary in order to interpret the table. Wealth is defined as people's total assets (that is, everything they own that can be converted into money). In addition to providing a source of income, wealth is a major source of power in capitalistic economies. A "wealth fifth" is a statistical category that is created by rank ordering all the adults in a country by their total wealth and then dividing that ranking into five equal-size categories. The wealthiest 20 percent of the population comprises the top wealth fifth, the next 20 percent is the fourth wealth fifth, and so on.

As is seen in this table, there was considerable wealth inequality in 1962 (this was the last year that comprehensive data on wealth inequalities were made available by the U.S. government, an interesting fact in itself). At that time, 20 percent of the population held 76 percent of all wealth, whereas 60 percent of the population (the bottom, second, and middle fifths) possessed less than 10 percent of all assets in the United States. To the best of our knowledge, this same distribution exists today.

Even more revealing is the concentration of wealth in the hands of the top 1 percent of the population. In Table 11.1, we estimate from a variety of sources the concentration of total wealth among the top 1 percent of wealth holders between 1810–1969. Throughout that time period, this tiny proportion of the population has held about one-quarter of all wealth in the United States. (Turner and Starnes, 1977:19).

Turning to income, or money earned in a given year, the pattern of inequality is given in Table 11.2. Income fifths are calculated in the same way as wealth fifths. This table reveals less inequality in income distribution than in wealth distribution, which is to be expected since wealth represents the accumulated and inherited consequences of years of income inequality. Income inequalities over a number of years are presented because the federal government regularly reports these data (it is interesting that the government reports only those data that show less inequality). The distribution of income has remained fairly constant over the years, with the bottom fifth of the population receiving around 5–6 percent of all income and the top receiving about 40 percent of all income in a given year. Thus, even though there is less income than wealth inequality, this form of economic inequality is still quite marked.

Prestige inequality. Prestige can be defined as the amount of esteem, deference, or social honor that people receive from others. While the wealthy and powerful are held in high esteem in our society, the poor are strongly stigmatized and punitively viewed (Feagin, 1975). They are often characterized as lazy, indolent, and amoral. For the majority of Americans, prestige is derived from one's occupation. Studies of occupational prestige (Hodge, et al., 1964; Blau and Duncan, 1967; Treiman, 1977) show that occupations involving high levels of education are consistently given high prestige. And when an occupation is associated with high income and/or power it is given even more prestige.

TABLE 11.1
Share of Wealth Held by Richest 1 Percent, United States

Year	Percentage of Wealth Held	By 1 Percent of:
1810	21.0	U.S. families
1860	24.0	U.S. families
1900	26.0–31.0	U.S. families
1922	31.6	U.S. adults
1929	36.3	U.S. adults
1933	28.3	U.S. adults
1939	30.6	U.S. adults
1945	23.3	U.S. adults
1949	20.8	U.S. adults
1953	27.5	U.S. adults
1956	26.0	U.S. adults
1958	26.9	U.S. adults
1962	27.4	U.S. adults
1965	29.2	U.S. adults
1969	24.9	U.S. adults

Sources: For 1810, 1860, and 1900, Robert E. Gallman. "Trends in the Size Distribution of Wealth in the Nineteenth Century." In *Six Papers on the Size Distribution of Wealth and Income,* edited by Lee Soltow, p. 6. New York: National Bureau of Economic Research, 1969.

For 1922, 1929, 1933, 1939, 1945, 1949, and 1956, Robert J. Lampman. *The Share of Top Wealthholders,* p. 204. In *National Wealth 1922–1956.* New York: National Bureau of Economic Research, 1962.

For 1953, 1958, 1962, 1965, and 1969, James D. Smith and Stephen D. Franklin. "The Concentration of Personel Wealth, 1922–1969," *American Economic Review* 64 (May 1974): 162–67, at p. 166.

Note: Smith and Franklin report that data for 1962, 1965, and 1969 were adjusted to achieve statistical comparability with the earlier 1953 and 1958 data. The result sacrifices their best estimates for the later years in the interest of consistency and, they note, produces a downward bias in their best estimates of wealth concentration. The bias is estimated to be 10 to 15 percent. Thus, the actual concentration of wealth in the years 1962, 1965, and 1969 could run as high as 32.2 percent, 34.8 percent, and 29.8 percent, respectively.

TABLE 11.2

Percentage Share of Money Income, Before Taxes, Received by Each Income Fifth

Year	Lowest Fifth	Fourth Fifth	Middle Fifth	Second Fifth	Highest Fifth	Top 5 Percent
1973	5.5	11.9	17.5	24.0	41.1	15.5
1972	5.4	11.9	17.5	23.9	41.4	15.9
1971	5.5	11.9	17.4	23.7	41.6	15.7
1970	5.5	12.0	17.4	23.5	41.6	14.4
1969	5.6	12.3	17.6	23.5	41.0	14.0
1968	5.7	12.4	17.7	23.7	40.6	14.0
1967	5.4	12.2	17.5	23.7	41.2	15.3
1966	5.5	12.4	17.7	23.7	40.7	14.8
1965	5.3	12.1	17.7	23.7	41.3	15.8
1964	5.2	12.0	17.7	.24.0	41.1	15.7
1963	5.1	12.0	17.6	23.9	41.4	16.0
1962	5.1	12.0	17.5	23.7	41.7	16.3
1961	4.8	11.7	17.4	23.6	42.6	17.1
1960	4.9	12.0	17.6	23.6	42.0	16.8
1959	5.0	12.1	17.7	23.7	41.4	16.3
1958	4.7	11.0	16.3	22.5	45.5	20.0
1957	4.7	11.1	16.3	22.4	45.5	20.2
1956	4.8	11.3	16.3	22.3	45.3	20.2
1955	4.8	11.3	16.4	22.3	45.2	20.3
1954	4.8	11.1	16.4	22.5	45.2	20.3
1953	4.9	11.3	16.6	22.5	44.7	19.9
1952	4.9	11.4	16.6	22.4	44.7	20.5
1951	5.0	11.3	16.5	22.3	44.9	20.7
1950	4.5	12.0	17.4	23.5	42.6	17.0
1949	3.2	10.5	17.1	24.2	45.0	18.3
1948	3.4	10.7	17.1	23.9	44.9	18.7

TABLE 11.2 (continued)
Percentage Share of Money Income, Before Taxes,
Received by Each Income Fifth

Year	Lowest Fifth	Fourth Fifth	Middle Fifth	Second Fifth	Highest Fifth	Top 5 Percent
1947	5.0	11.8	17.0	23.1	43.0	17.2
1946	5.0	11.1	16.0	21.8	46.1	21.3
1945	3.8	11.0	17.2	24.0	44.0	17.6
1944	4.9	10.9	16.2	22.2	45.8	20.7
1941	4.1	9.5	15.3	22.3	48.8	24.0
1935–36	4.1	9.2	14.1	20.9	51.7	26.5
1929	(12.5)		13.8	19.3	54.4	30.0

Sources: U.S. Bureau of the Census. *Current Population Reports.* Series P-60, No. 85, Table 14 for the years 1947, 1950, and 1959–1971. Washington, D.C.: Government Printing Office, 1972.

Edward C. Budd, "Postwar Changes in the Size Distribution of Income in the U.S." *American Economic Review* 60 (May 1970): 247-60, Table 6, p. 255 for the years 1945, 1948, and 1949.

U.S. Bureau of the Census, *Income Distribution in the United States* (a 1960 Census Monograph), by Herman P. Miller, p. 21 for the years 1929, 1935-1936, 1941, 1944, 1946, and 1951-1958. Washington, D.C.: Government Printing Office, 1966. Data from the latter source were gathered by the Office of Business Economics.

Power Inequality. The existence of power is often hidden and its use is frequently covert. How, then, can we assess the distribution of this important resource? At best, we can only guess at the distribution, as is done in Table 11.3. Variables that might affect the distribution of power are listed on the left side, while in the body of the table three income categories are assessed in terms of their respective degrees of power. This table is basically only an educated guess, but it summarizes the results of numerous studies on the power of various segments of U.S. society (Turner and Starnes, 1976:83; Turner, 1977:343).

What can we conclude about the distribution of scarce resources in the United States? First, there is enormous inequality in the distributions of wealth, income, prestige, and power. Second, there is a high correlation between these different types of resources, so that persons who rank high in one are also likely to be high in other areas. Conversely, those who are low in one area will typically be low in the others. Third, this correlation between status dimensions allows us to distinguish at least three broad socioeconomic classes: 1) the very

TABLE 11.3
Variables Influencing the Distribution of Power

	The Poor (bottom income fifth)	The Middle Class (middle income fifths)	The Rich (portion of top income fifth)
Size of population	large	quite large	relatively small
Distribution of population	rural and urban, large mass in cores of large cities	urban, large mass in suburbs of large cities	rural and urban, relatively high degree of dispersion
Level of organization	low, fragmented	high: unions, professional associations, corporations, and trade associations	high: corporations and trade associations
Type of organization	fragmented, decentralized, loosely coordinated national confederations	high centralized, tightly coordinated national con-federations	highly centralized, overt and covert confederations
Financial resources	meager	great	very great
Lobbying tradition	short	long	long
Established influence channels	few	many	many
Total power	little	considerable	great

rich, powerful, and prestigeful, 2) the middle mass, and 3) the poor, powerless, and stigmatized. We might want to make finer distinctions within the middle mass, since they comprise the bulk of the population, but for general purposes these distinctions will suffice.

Unequal Opportunities in the United States

The existence of poverty amid widespread affluence and the concentration of wealth among so few persons are two aspects of socioeconomic inequality that many people find highly troubling. To fully understand the unequal distribution of resources, however, we must also ask how the opportunities to acquire these resources are distributed among Americans? If opportunities to acquire wealth, income, and positions of influence and prestige are equally available to all, then the existing patterns of inequality may be viewed as at least partially justified. Even if the "game" of resource distribution does result in sharp status inequalities, with equality of opportunities one can at least assume that the game is being played fairly.

In the last 20 years a large body of writing and research on the opportunity structure in our society has accumulated through the study of social mobility (Blau and Duncan, 1967; Jencks, 1972; Featherman and Hauser, 1978). Two resources—occupation (prestige or status) and income—have been the most frequent concerns of these studies of social mobility. Occupational mobility is a common area of study for those interested in the structure of opportunities (Featherman and Hauser, 1978), because occupation is thought to be the best single measure of overall resource position (Duncan, et al., 1972). One's occupation is normally closely related to one's share of income obtained, prestige received, and influence.

The research on occupational mobility provides a fairly complete picture of the structure of opportunities within the U.S. middle mass, but both the rich and the poor tend to be overlooked. The rich are overlooked because their principal source of wealth is not the performance of an occupation, but the ownership and management of wealth. The poor are often underrepresented in this research because they are frequently unemployed. Although we can make general statements about mobility into and out of the wealthy and poverty classes, these topics have not received adequate research attention by applied sociologists.

Research on social mobility in the United States suggests that white males have experienced a modified version of "the American Dream," but that this "Dream" has been closed to minorities and women. We shall first sketch the mobility picture for white men and then the contrasting pictures for minorities and women.

Occupational Mobility Among White Males. A high proportion of the male population has been mobile, with upward movement predominating over downward movement by a ratio of roughly three to one (Featherman and Hauser,

1978). Higher education plays an important part in promoting upward mobility, in accord with the American belief that position should be based on achieved merit (Featherman and Hauser, 1978). Other aspects of the mobility picture, however, do not fit well with our conception of the United States as the land of opportunity:

1. Most mobility takes place within the middle mass. Furthermore, within this middle mass, mobility into and out of the upper middle class (defined by holding professional and managerial occupations) is restricted (Featherman and Hauser, 1978).

2. The very rich and the very poor are the most likely to remain in the class into which they are born. A high percentage of the wealthy derive their position from inheritance, and there is little mobility into this class (Brittain, 1978). There are also apparent restrictions on mobility out of poverty (Schiller, 1970).

3. The higher the socioeconomic status of one's parents, the greater one's own chance to achieve high status (Jencks, 1972; Featherman and Hauser, 1978). High status parents can provide their children with greater opportunities for advanced education, as well as directly transferring wealth and prestige to them.

These generalizations reveal that there is not equality of opportunity even for white men. In spite of this fact, the mobility structure for white males approximates a "best of both worlds" condition. On the one hand, it enables socioeconomically advantaged families to pass on many of their privileges to their children. On the other hand, it presents to the middle mass a reasonable hope for upward mobility. Technological change has spurred rapid growth in the number of high status (principally professional and managerial level) jobs over the last several generations (Hauser, et al., 1975). The volume of upward mobility created by such change (commonly called structural mobility) has accommodated the twin desires to pass on privilege to one's offspring and to better one's own position.

Occupational Mobility Among Minorities and Females. The opportunity structures for minorities and women show some similarities, but they are different enough to require separate discussion. We shall focus first on the circumstance of minorities, and specifically on blacks since they constitute the largest minority. Recent evidence shows that the circumstances of Mexican Americans, the second largest minority, are substantially similar to (but in some ways worse than) those of blacks (Featherman and Hauser, 1978).

The socioeconomic statuses of blacks are, on the average, markedly lower than those of whites. The black unemployment rate (approximately 13 percent) is roughly twice as high as for the white rate (approximately 6.6 percent) at the present time (U.S. Bureau of the Census, 1977:389). Employed blacks, in comparison to whites, are disproportionately found in semi-skilled and unskilled jobs and are highly underrepresented in high-status professional and managerial occupations (U.S. Bureau of the Census, 1977). And black earnings average only 70 percent of white earnings (Haworth, et al., 1975). Although the fact of lower socioeconomic statuses among blacks is not disputed, the explanation of who or what is responsible for this racial discrepancy is a matter of continuing controversy. Explanations for the black-white gap in socioeconomic status have ranged from racial differences in intelligence (for a discussion of this issue see Loehlin, Lindzey, and Spuhler, 1975) to the argument that racial discrimination is an inherent feature of capitalistic economies (Gordon, 1972). In general, however, the bulk of the literature on this topic that has accumulated in recent years indicates that no single factor can account for these racial differences.

Two characteristics of the opportunity structure for women are highly salient. First, women are predominantly found in sex-segregated occupations, within the middle of the status hierarchy. For example, approximately one-third of all women in the employed labor force are found in the three occupations of secretary (or related occupation), nurse, and elementary or secondary school teacher (U.S. Bureau of the Census, 1977). Women are as poorly represented in managerial and high-status professional occupations (doctors, college professors, and lawyers) as are blacks. Second, women receive lower pay than men for jobs that are at least nominally the same. On the average, full-time employed women receive about three-fourths of the earnings of men.

WHAT ARE WE DOING?

Efforts to deal with the marked inequalities of socioeconomic resource distribution and opportunities in the United States have focused on two areas: 1) antipoverty programs, and 2) legal efforts to ensure equality of opportunity by race and sex. There has been no serious effort to redistribute wealth, nor any effort to equalize the opportunity to achieve positions of control over substantial wealth. We will first discuss legal efforts to ensure equality of opportunity and then examine antipoverty programs.

Programs for Equality of Opportunity

Programs to equalize opportunity are of two kinds. One type consists of programs to equalize human capital, most often education but also attitudes and skills relevent to employment. Several of these programs were developed in conjunction with antipoverty efforts, and they will be discussed subsequently. The bulk of this effort has gone into programs to equalize educational opportunity, involving federal aid for schools, bussing programs, and so on. Since these programs are discussed in other chapters of this book, we will not examine them here.

The second type of equal opportunity program pertains to discrimination in employment, and is popularly referred to as affirmative action. In contrast to poverty or educational opportunity programs, government efforts to equalize occupational opportunities have been quite passive. Aside from a few programs specifically designed to improve job opportunities for minorities—such as the much touted but ill-fated black capitalism effort—the federal government has acted primarily as a legal watchdog in this area.

The Equal Employment Opportunity Commission (EEOC), established under the provisions of Title VII of the Civil Rights Act of 1964, is the government agency charged with administering federal efforts to prevent discrimination in employment. Initially the EEOC was charged with the responsibility of investigating complaints of job discrimination and promoting voluntary conciliation of alleged discriminatory practices, but the Commission was given no legal standing or enforcement sanctions. In 1968, Executive Order 11246 gave some power to the EEOC by requiring firms to establish an affirmative action program in order to receive government contracts over $10,000. Since failure to comply with affirmative action guidelines could result in a loss of government business, and since many major corporations do substantial work under government contracts, E.O. 11246 gave the EEOC a potentially powerful sanction—even though it has rarely been used.

The EEOC also issued guidelines for compliance with the antidiscrimination provisions of Title VII and its subsequent amendments. These guidelines have no legal standing, but they do influence employers who receive government contracts and wish to comply with the affirmative action provision of E.O. 11246. The major role of the EEOC, in short, is advisory. Any legal action against an employer for discriminatory practices must be initiated by an individual, not the EEOC.

Given its task, the EEOC has been inadequately funded (receiving only about $90 million in 1978), with predictable consequences. It has been beset with organizational problems stemming from the need to coordinate the activities of some 20-odd agencies responsible for various parts of the antidiscrimination effort. It also has built up a serious backlog of unresolved cases, totaling over 130,000 in 1977 (Mossberg, 1977). Complainants do have the option of bypassing the EEOC and suing employers directly, but the cost and time this requires undoubtedly discourages many individuals.

Poverty Programs

Historically, care of the poor in the United States was considered a local community problem and was left to private charities and local government (Turner and Starnes, 1976; Piven and Cloward, 1971; Seligman, 1970). During the depression of the 1930s, however, this pattern was altered. The Social Security

Act of 1935 initiated the basic structure of welfare in the United States, but it was not until after World War II that the federal responsibility for relief giving achieved a coherent profile.

Between 1945 and the early 1960s, public assistance programs were not guided by social science research. As a result, subsequent assistance programs, which have utilized social science knowledge, have operated under contraints inherited from the initial approaches to the problem. These constraints include (Turner, 1977:223-51): 1) a set of cultural beliefs that hold the poor responsible for their poverty, seeing poverty as individual failure rather than as a problem created by the structure of the society, 2) another set of beliefs that stresses (a) the importance of maintaining the sanctity of private enterprise and competition when assisting the poor, (b) the need to maintain incentives for the poor to work rather than seek public doles, and (c) the necessity for monitoring the poor who receive assistance in order to keep them from becoming "chronic charity cases," 3) a set of policies that makes public assistance conditional, specifying that only certain categories of poor are eligible for assistance and that the poor must constantly prove their need, 4) a set of structural relations among local, state, and federal governments that places considerable discretion in the hands of local administrators, creating wide disparity in public assistance programs among states and communities, and 5) a related set of structural relations in which diverse, overlapping, and often competitive public agencies at the federal, state, and local level all exercise jurisdiction over poverty programs. All efforts to help the poor have operated under these constraints, few of which have any firm basis in sociological knowledge. Rather, these constraints reflect the moral values of the general public and those legislators and administrators who, over the years, have created the complex and diverse system of public assistance in the United States.

The major period of growth in efforts to eliminate poverty in this country occurred between 1965 and the present. Moreover, to at least some extent, social scientists have made inputs into various programs, although always under the constraints mentioned above. Three general approaches to poverty have been taken during the past 15 years: 1) the War on Poverty, 2) the creation and extension of special programs, such as Food Stamps and Medicare, and 3) the growth in the public welfare system. A fourth approach, which has only been tried on an experimental basis, is income maintenance, which is often termed "a negative income tax" or "guaranteed annual income." These four approaches represent the sum of what is now being done about poverty in the United States. Each is worthy of more detailed examination (Turner, 1977; Haveman, 1977).

The War on Poverty. The War on Poverty was initially conceptualized in the 1960s under President Kennedy and then implemented under President Johnson. Its basic approach involved the creation of a central federal agency—the Office of Economic Opportunity (OEO)—to oversee and coordinate the diverse agencies and programs in the federal government dealing with poverty and to act as a liaison between local agencies and the federal government. The Office of Economic Opportunity was also to work with Congress in assessing the impact of legislation for eliminating poverty. The War on Poverty was to be "fought" on three fronts: 1) Stimulate the economy in ways that would increase the demand for labor, for it was believed that subsidies to private industry would "trickle down" to the poor in the form of new job opportunities. 2) Increase the labor skills of the poor by (a) creating special programs for youth in communities and schools that would allow the poor to increase their educational attainment, and (b) establishing job training and counseling programs for those already in the labor market. 3) Provide community services, such as legal aid, child care, job counseling, credit counseling, and similar services needed by, but previously unavailable to, the poor.

From its inception, the War on Poverty encountered a number of problems that have plagued almost all federal programs (Turner, 1977). First, the OEO immediately became embroiled in conflicts among federal agencies in the departments of Health, Education and Welfare, Labor and Agriculture, all of which had overlapping poverty programs. Second, OEO initially chose to bypass state government and local welfare offices in administering its programs, with the result that it was thrown into competition and conflict with these levels of government and their alternative assistance agencies. Third, the War on Poverty was underfinanced and reached only a few targeted populations, primarily urban blacks, with the result that the majority of the poor (who are white and often live in rural environments) were unaffected. Other poor populations, such as Hispanics, were similarly unaffected until quite recently. Fourth, the efforts to stimulate the economy often resulted in high profits for industries and secure wages for the affluent, but few permanent jobs "trickled down" to the poor. Fifth, the school programs—such as Operation Head Start, Upward Bound, vocational training programs, and school breakfast and lunch programs—all encountered resistance from the educational bureaucracy. More importantly, the effectiveness of these programs in increasing the cognitive skills and achievement levels of the poor could not be conclusively documented (Levin, 1977). Sixth, the nonschool programs—such as the Job Corps and Neighborhood Youth Corps—were raked by defections of poor youth, charges of inefficiency and graft, and a failure to find permanent jobs for their members in the private economic sector. Seventh, the local community service agencies established by OEO were charged with graft and corruption and were viewed as instigators of the urban riots in the late 1960s. Eighth, the War never attacked directly the major source of poverty, which is inequality in the distribution of wealth and income, as shown in Tables 11.1–11.3.

Evaluating the total impact of the War on Poverty is difficult, because the criteria for assessing success or failure are unclear, The War did reach some poor; it did provide many needed services; it did improve the diet of many poor children; it did train some youth for the job market; and it may have helped some children improve their level of educational attainment. At best, however, the War reached only a small minority of poor; its costs were often seen as excessive in comparison with its lack of demonstrated effectiveness; and its constant conflicts with federal agencies, state governments, and local establishments diverted many of the resources into a "War on Bureaucracy" rather than poverty. Thus, by the 1970s, the War on Poverty was, like its counterpart in Vietnam, simply abandoned. Although OEO still exists in skeletal and residual form, most people would agree that, while a number of important battles were won, the overall War was lost.

The Welfare System. The welfare system in this society is currently a categorical "grants and aids" system in which the federal government makes monies (which usually must be matched) available to the states for certain types of poor, such as mothers with dependent children, the blind, the handicapped, and the unemployed. It was not until the early 1960s that unemployed single males, or even heads of families, were included in the federal categories. The last 15 years, however, have seen the extension of welfare to many more categories of poor. And in some states, such as New York, California, and Massachusetts, the categories and associated benefits extend beyond those of the federal government. Nevertheless, because much of the welfare money is generated by state and county taxes (and in a few cases by city taxes), welfare is financed and administered differently in various states. Some states take advantage of matching monies for a limited number of categories of the poor, while others have many categories and generous benefits. The result is that aid varies widely from state to state, and because welfare is administered by county or city governments, the benefits even vary from area to area within a single state (Piven and Cloward, 1971).

During the 1940s, 1950s, and early 1960s there were many abuses of welfare recipients by local welfare agencies. These included: constant monitoring of recipients, arbitrary decisions concerning eligibility without the right of appeal, and midnight raids to check on the sexual and moral habits of welfare mothers. Many of these abuses have been curtailed, but for a long time they discouraged countless eligible people from applying for welfare. Even today, the formality, surveillance, and constant need to prove eligibility tend to discourage many people from seeking welfare assistance. By some estimates, only half of those eligible for welfare actually receive any benefits (Turner, 1977).

The welfare system was never intended to be a permanent income maintenance system for individuals or families, even though many categories of poor, such as the handicapped and aged, have chronic needs for aid. The system works to discourage recipients by keeping benefits low, typically below prevailing wages for unskilled menial labor. Because the system is decentralized, local agencies can induce or even force recipients to enter the menial-wage job market by keeping benefits low or by cutting them off when welfare administrators decide that work is available. The result is that the poor remain poor by virtue of low benefits and are kept as a reserve labor pool for affluent sectors of the economy that may require cheap, temporary labor (Piven and Cloward, 1971; Turner and Starnes, 1976). In this way, the welfare system sometimes operates as a subsidy to employers by maintaining a labor force that can be called upon when needed and then discarded back to the welfare rolls. Employers in need of domestics, seasonal agriculture workers, temporary work crews, and the like, can thus avoid paying high wages or the typical benefits (retirement, workman's compensation, etc.) that go with full-time employment.

Special Aid Programs. A number of programs for the poor have been initiated independently of either the War on Poverty or the welfare system, although some of them have eventually been incorporated into the welfare system or OEO (Haveman, 1977). The Food Stamp program, Medicare, housing rent subsidies, public housing, direct rural loans, low interest loans for college, unemployment insurance, old age and survivor's benefits, aid to the blind, benefits for the handicapped, and food supplements are prominent examples of these programs. Emanating from the federal government and often requiring matching monies from state and local governments, such special programs have expanded greatly in the last 15 years. Some of them, like Food Stamps and Medicare, have become multibillion dollar programs (Davis, 1977).

All of these programs help the poor by reducing the amount of money they have to pay for certain vital services such as food, rent, and medical care. They do not directly increase the incomes of the poor, however, nor do they provide ways of securing a steady income. They provide for important and immediate needs, but they do not help people move permanently out of poverty. In fact, they often increase people's dependence on the services of the federal government, thereby discouraging efforts by the poor to enter the labor market (which is justifiably perceived as a not very pleasant place by the unskilled poor) for fear of losing these special sources of aid.

The Guaranteed Income Alternative. While the specifics of various proposals vary, the guaranteed annual income alternative to the welfare system and the collage of special aid programs involves a number of unique features (Turner, 1977:240–45). First, for all families, and perhaps for unattached individuals, a minimum income floor would be established. All families would be guaranteed a certain level of income, consisting of both cash and in-kind services such as food stamps and Medicare. Second, if poor people receive some pay from work, their income would be supplemented at least up to the income floor, and in most proposals the supplementary benefits would extend beyond the income floor at a diminishing rate, as an inducement to work. Third, depending on the proposal, those who cannot work, such as the aged, blind, and severely handicapped, would continue to receive their aid through a revamped welfare system that would administer, on a standardized basis in all states, the current plethora of special categorical grants and aids.

The advantage of the guaranteed income is that the aid system in the United States would be greatly simplified. Many of the special programs, lodged in diverse federal, state, and local agencies, could be eliminated. OEO could be completely dismantled. The welfare bureaucracy could return to its original function of providing aid to the indigent and needy rather than to the unemployed. The entire aid system would be more equitable, since benefits would be the same across the nation. The burden of income maintenance would be taken off local and state budgets and put in the federal budget (and hence be financed by the progressive federal income tax rather than by regressive sales and property taxes).

A number of problems would occur with such an income maintenance program, however. First, it would likely be more expensive than the current system, especially if income guarantees were tied to actual costs of living (Lynn, 1977:117). Second, many commentators feel that incentives to work or to seek further job training would be eliminated for the poor, with the result that they could become welfare burdens. Third, the procedures for monitoring eligibility would likely create yet another public bureaucracy overseeing the poor. Fourth, since aid levels would probably be lower than the actual cost of living and since many other in-kind programs would be cut back or eliminated with the income guarantee program, the actual plight of the poor might not be improved and might even worsen.

In recent years, there have been a number of income maintenance pilot programs employing the guaranteed income approach (Lynn, 1977:114-17). The findings of these experiments are far from clear, but two results seem evident: 1) On the surface, the system does seem to cost more. However, the hidden costs of the overlapping aid programs of OEO, various executive agencies, and the welfare establishment are not accurately calculated, so that it is not clear if an income maintenance system would cost more if these other aid programs were drastically cut back or eliminated. 2) With a guaranteed income, work incentives do not appear to be seriously eroded. In fact, individuals who are not forced to grab the first job that comes along appear to hold out for better paying jobs with more security and fringe benefits, thus making them less likely to need income supplements in the future. And for those who do withdraw from the labor market, such as mothers with young children, it is questionable whether they should have been in the labor market in the first place.

Although a number of income guarantee proposals have been put forward by two presidents and many high-level federal administrators, these proposals all suffer from deficiencies (Turner, 1977:242). One obvious deficiency is that the proposed income guarantee is only about one-half the actual cost of living (as set by the Labor Department, whose figure is always low). Another deficiency is the inclusion of a work requirement, which defeats the purpose of the income guarantee and throws the program back to welfare agencies who would have to monitor the work eligibility of each recipient. Thus, should an income guarantee program be implemented, it might retain the worst features of the current system—low benefits, forced inducements to work, and constant monitoring of the poor—which would undermine the intended benefits of such a program such as simplification, equity, and true income maintenance.

WHAT HAVE WE ACCOMPLISHED?

Accomplishments for the Disadvantaged

Since 1965, when the War on Poverty was initiated and other aid programs began to expand, the proportion of the population with annual incomes below the official poverty level has decreased from around 20 percent to 11 percent (Lynn, 1977:88-89). Such figures are somewhat illusionary, however. The official poverty level is low, so that even though many families have risen above that level, they are far from affluent. Moreover, the poor have not gained relative to the rest of the population, but have actually fallen further behind. As Table 11.2 emphasizes, their share of the total income has not increased dramatically, and relative to the rest of the population, whose living standards have risen, the poor have not closed the gap in cash income.

The poor have, however, made gains in terms of income in-kind, such as provided by the Food Stamps, Surplus Food, Medicare, and Medicaid programs (Lynn, 1977:95-96). Moreover, data on the income of the poor are distorted by the recent increase in the aged population, whose income may be low (and hence place them in the poverty category) but whose wealth assets (house, cars, savings, etc.) distinguish them from the poor.

What can we conclude about the effectiveness of programs to eliminate poverty? The safest conclusion is that abject deprivation, in which people do not have adequate shelter, medical care, or food supplies, has declined significantly—perhaps by one-half. But relative to the general population's increasing level of affluence, the poor have not made great strides.

Moreover, progress in reducing poverty and equalizing opportunities has been severely limited by the prevailing distribution of economic and political power. By attempting to improve the individual capabilities of the poor or to conciliate complaints of individual discrimination against corporations, current programs favor solutions that fall within the bounds of the prevailing economic structure. No program has seriously addressed such questions as these: Why is the low-wage sector so large? What mechanisms permit white males to so thoroughly control positions of economic and political power? How might this situation be changed? If applied sociology is to move beyond ad hoc solutions to current problems of socioeconomic inequality, it must address the validity of prevailing assumptions about the workings of the U.S. economy and also be aware of the structural and cultural barriers to changing patterns of inequality.

Accomplishments for the Affluent

A prevailing assumption of U.S. economics is that wealth must be controlled by a small group of individuals if it is to best serve the goal of economic growth. If wealth is widely dispersed it will presumably be used to purchase consumer goods and will not be reinvested to create further wealth. Although there is no evidence to support this assumption (see Gans, 1973 for a discussion of this issue), governmental actions continue to encourage the concentration of wealth and its perpetuation in families across generations. The government subsidizes the wealthy in four basic ways: government contracts, price supports, export-import subsidies, and tax expenditures.

Government Contracts. The tax revenues of the federal government are spent in both the labor and commodities markets. As a result, the government provides employment, both directly and indirectly, for certain categories of workers and gives business (and hence profits) to those corporations that produce services and commodities required by government. Government expenditures can, thus, be viewed as a subsidy to certain industries and workers in much the same way that welfare and various special programs represent a subsidy to the poor. But there are important differences. Government contracts typically go to large corporations that are top heavy in management and that employ workers who are members of unions and professional associations. These subsidies largely go to the segment of U.S. workers who are already the most privileged.

The major difference between subsidies to the rich and those to the poor is that the former involve 1) high cash benefits, 2) more secure and permanent benefits, 3) numerous in-kind benefits (such as expense accounts, government cars, etc.), and 4) the prestige that comes with a full-time job and the capacity to purchase symbols of affluence. Analytically, there is little difference between subsidies to the affluent and poor—both involve use of tax monies to create benefits—but those that go to the poor often do not involve the prestige and satisfaction that come with full-time employment, nor do they represent high levels of cash or in-kind benefits. In this way, income, wealth, prestige, and power inequalities are perpetuated by the manner in which the government spends its monies in the labor and commodities markets.

Government Price Supports. The federal government regulates, both directly and indirectly, the prices of many commodities in the market, particularly dairy and agricultural products. This regulation is often very complex, but it revolves around two types of effort: 1) manipulation of supply and demand, and 2) direct regulation of prices (such as interstate hauling rates, utilities, telephone rates, etc.). In either case, governmental policies are typically aimed at keeping profit levels at an adequate level for owners of regulated corporations and at maintaining favorable employment levels in specific industries. As a result, these policies benefit industries that can provide essential goods and services, employ large numbers of organized workers, and exert political influence to receive favorable price regulation. Thus, the price regulation practices of government operate, in most instances, to preserve the pattern of inequality delineated in Tables 11.1–11.3.

Export-Import Subsidies. The federal government regulates the prices of goods by controlling the volume of export and import commodities. Such policies protect corporations that compete with corporations in other countries. Such regulation is highly selective, however, favoring protection of those industries, such as steel, cars, and textiles, that cannot always compete with overseas companies. It also encourages exports (and, hence, higher domestic prices and profits) by those industries, such as agriculture, computers, and aerospace, in which domestic corporations can compete effectively. The result is that large corporations, employing large numbers of organized workers, receive a subsidy (either market protection or expansion) that protects profits and salaries. Such corporations do not typically employ the poor, although the poor may be forced to pay higher prices for manufactured goods.

Tax Expenditures. The most expensive federal subsidies, which account for the largest share of the unequal distribution of money, are the tax expenditures of government. A tax expenditure is the difference between the amount of tax that should be collected before various deductions, exclusions, credits, and special rates are taken into account and the actual amount of tax paid. For example, all corporations are supposed to pay a flat 48 percent on net profits. In fact, most pay around 30 percent, and some, such as the oil companies, around 5 percent. This average difference of 18 percent represents an expenditure by government for corporations and, as such, is a subsidy (Turner and Starnes, 1976:89-121).

As Table 11.4 underscores, such tax expenditures work in favor of those in higher income brackets. For various income groupings, from those under $3,000 to those over $1 million, the amount of money that each can avoid paying in taxes by virtue of deductions, credits, special rates, shelters, loopholes, and the like is viewed as a payment by the government. As can be seen, the higher the income bracket, the greater the payment. A similar table could be constructed for corporations, with large corporations in certain favored industries, such as oil, receiving the largest payments, and small, family-run corporations receiving the smallest payment.

In sum, inequality in the United States is maintained by a dual system of federal programs: 1) those for the poor, such as the War on Poverty, special aid programs, and the welfare system and 2) those for the affluent, such as tax expenditures, export-import policies, price regulations, and market activities. The combined effect of these two types of governmental systems is to perpetuate the current unequal distribution of scarce resources in this society.

Structural Barriers to Changing Patterns of Inequality

As Table 11.3 underscores, the poor are not in a position to exert great political influence. They are not well organized; they have few financial resources; they do not have established influence channels or a lobbying tradition; and they are subject to many unfavorable beliefs. In contrast, the affluent constitute the majority; they have unions, associations, and organizations to lobby for their interests; as working, tax-paying citizens they are defined as culturally "desirable"; and wealthy persons have the resources and influence channels to exert a considerable influence on political decisions. Any policy recommen-

TABLE 11.4
Average Yearly Tax Expenditure Payment in 1972
for Selected Income Groups

Income Group	Average Payment
Under $3,000	$ 15.00
$3,000–$5,000	$ 143.00
$5,000–$10,000	$ 286.00
$10,000–$15,000	$ 411.00
$15,000–$20,000	$ 600.00
$20,000–$25,000	$ 871.00
$25,000–$50,000	$ 1,729.00
$50,000–$100,00	$ 5,896.00
$100,000–$500,000	$ 29,503.00
$500,000–$1,000,000	$216,751.00
Over $1,000,000	$726,198.00

Source: Stanley S. Surrey. *Pathways to Tax Reform,* Cambridge, Mass.: Harvard University Press, 1973, p. 71. Copyright © 1973 by Harvard University Press.

dations by sociologists for reducing socioeconomic inequality and improving the situation of the poor must confront these political barriers. Such structural obstacles are legitimated by cultural beliefs, which create additional barriers to applied action programs.

Cultural Barriers to Reducing Inequality
Cultural beliefs in the United States operate to legitimate the dual subsidy systems to the affluent and poor. They also stigmatize the poor, which makes it easier to maintain them at the edge of deprivation. We can isolate four of these cultural beliefs supporting socioeconomic inequality (Turner and Starnes, 1976: 151–59; Turner, 1977:213–14): national interest beliefs, "trickle-down" beliefs, the work ethic, and the charity ethic.

National Interest Beliefs. If a government activity can be defined as being in "the national interest," it can be made to seem legitimate. This tactic is frequently employed to justify tax expenditures, market subsidies, import-export quotas and tariffs, and the letting of noncompetitive governmental contracts.

"Trickle-Down" Beliefs. Subsidies to large corporations, stockholders, and wage earners are also legitimated by "trickle-down" beliefs. The basic idea here is that money trickles down to the poor, creating jobs. If corporate investment is subsidized, then new jobs are supposedly created. Or if wage earners have money, their purchases will generate further economic expansion and jobs.

The Work Ethic. Americans firmly believe that income should come from work. Income acquired in other ways is viewed as tainted, and its recipient is held in low esteem. The poor who received governmental aid are, thus, stigmatized by the general population.

The Charity Ethic. Americans believe that charity is sometimes a necessity, but it should be given only when there is no work alternative. Moreover, charity must be temporary, unless people are to become dependent on public aid and lose their desire to work.

The "culture of inequality" in the United States, thus, makes subsidies to the rich and affluent seem proper, while public aid to the poor appears tainted. These beliefs also prevent detailed scrutiny of the rich and affluent in terms of "eligibility" and "incentives," but they have legitimated a welfare system that constantly checks up on the needs and eligibility of the poor, while seeking to maintain work incentives. Applied sociology must, therefore, understand the ways in which these powerful beliefs operate and recognize that they will be a continual source of resistance to eliminating the basic structural patterns that generate socioeconomic inequality in the United States.

WHERE ARE WE GOING?

As we have emphasized, the phenomena associated with socioeconomic status—the existence of a large poverty sector, unequal opportunities, and the control of resources by a small segment of the population—pose difficult challenges for applied sociology. Past efforts at dealing with poverty have focused primarily on the psychological deficiencies of the poor (lack of motivation, cognitive skill, beliefs, job skills, etc.) and on their immediate social conditions (ghetto life and the associated lack of community agencies, medical care, proper diets, etc.). We have assumed that by changing the attributes of the poor and their immediate environment the poor will have greater chances for upward mobility into the blue- and white-collar classes. In this way, poverty in the United States can supposedly be eliminated.

The major deficiency in these efforts is that they tend to ignore the overall structure of socioeconomic inequality, as well as the political and cultural conditions supporting this inequality. This structure and its sociocultural supports affects not just the poor, but all segments of society. The rich and affluent are able to transmit their privileges, whereas the less affluent will have great difficulty becoming socially mobile. If we truly wish to reduce socioeconomic inequalities, eliminate abject poverty, and increase opportunities for all citizens to realize their full potential, then current programs are not likely to be noticeably successful.

Without dramatic reductions in income and wealth inequalities, and without a corresponding change in basic cultural beliefs, present conditions will prevail. But to recognize the problem and its causes does not automatically suggest effective solutions. How are income and wealth to be redistributed? How are well-entrenched cultural beliefs to be changed? How are opportunities to be made more equal? How are those individuals with personal handicaps stemming from their social background to be changed in ways that will facilitate their educational and occupational attainment? Such questions are not easily answered. More importantly, any proposed answer will encounter severe resistance from those who believe that their benefits from the current system are threatened. In addition, any innovative program always will have unanticipated consequences that will create new problems and/or subvert its goals.

The challenge of applied sociology is to go beyond the bounds of current accommodative programs by seeking answers to these difficult questions. If applied sociologists continue to accept the current constraints imposed by the initial establishment of public assistance, the uninformed biases of politicians, and inaccurate cultural beliefs, they will remain apologists for a system of resource distribution that is not only unequal but also morally inequitable.

REFERENCES AND SUGGESTED READINGS

Blau, P.M. and O.D. Duncan. 1967. *The American Occupational Structure*. New York: John Wiley & Sons.

Brittain, J.A. 1978. *Inheritance and the Inequality of Material Wealth*. Washington, D.C.: The Brookings Institution.

Davis, K. 1977. "A Decade of Policy Developments in Providing Health Care for Low-Income Families." In *A Decade of Federal Antipoverty Programs*, edited by R.H. Haveman, pp. 197–232. New York: Academic Press.

Duncan, O.D., D.L. Featherman, and B. Duncan. 1972. *Socioeconomic Background and Achievement*. New York: Seminar Press.

Feagin, J.R. 1975. *Subordinating the Poor*. Englewood Cliffs, N.J.: Prentice-Hall.

Featherman, D.L. and R.M. Hauser. 1978. *Opportunity and Change*. New York: Academic Press.

*Gans, H.S. 1973. *More Equality*. New York: Vintage Books.
    In a discussion of programs and issues concerning income and wealth inequality in the United States, Gans argues that practical policies can be developed to reduce the range of inequality in U.S. society.

Gordon, D.M. 1972. *Theories of Poverty and Underemployment*. Lexington, Mass.: D.C. Heath/Lexington Books.

Harrington, M. 1962. *The Other America: Poverty in the United States*. Baltimore, Md.: Penguin Books.

Hauser, R.M., P.J. Dickinson, H.P. Travis, and J.M. Koffel. 1975. "Structural Change in Occupational Mobility Among Men in the United States." *American Sociological Review* 40:585-98.

*Haveman, R.H. 1977. "Introduction: Poverty and Social Policy in the 1960's and 1970's: An Overview and Some Speculations." In *A Decade of Federal Antipoverty Programs*, edited by R.H. Haveman, pp. 1-20. New York: Academic Press.

Several chapters in this book examine the range of government programs currently dealing with aspects of poverty and evaluate the success and failure of these programs.

Haworth, J.G., J. Gwartney, and C. Haworth. 1975. "Earnings, Productivity and Changes in Employment Discrimination During the 1960's." *American Economic Review* 68:158-68.

Hodge, R.W., P.M. Siegel, and P.H. Rossi. 1964. "Occupational Prestige in the United States, 1925-1963." *American Journal of Sociology* 70:286-302.

*Jencks, C.S. 1972. *Inequality: A Reassessment of the Effect of Family and Schooling in America*. New York: Basic Books.

Jencks provides a thorough review of research on the role of schools in governmental antipoverty programs and critiques U.S. social policy in this area.

Levin, H.M. 1977. "A Decade of Policy Developments in Improving Education and Training for Low-Income Populations." In *A Decade of Federal Antipoverty Programs*, edited by R.H. Haveman, pp. 123-88. New York: Academic Press.

Loehlin, J.C., G. Lindzey, and J.N. Spuhler. 1975. *Race Differences in Intelligence*. San Francisco: W.H. Freedman.

Lynn, L.E., Jr. 1977. "A Decade of Policy Developments in the Income-Maintenance System." In *A Decade of Federal Antipoverty Programs*, edited by R.H. Haveman, pp. 55-117. New York: Academic Press.

Mossberg. W.S. 1977. "Carter's Reorganization Plan Worries Them; Changes Pledged by EEOC's Chief." *Wall Street Journal*, August 26, 1977, p. 1.

*Piven, F.F. and R.A. Cloward. 1971. *Regulating the Poor: The Functions of Public Welfare*. New York: Random House.

This book reviews the history of U.S. poverty policy and describes the consequences of this history for current policy.

Schiller, B.R. 1970. "Stratified Opportunities: The Essence of the 'Vicious Cycle'." *American Journal of Sociology* 76:426-42.

Seligman, B.B. 1970. *Permanent Poverty: An American Syndrome*. Chicago: Quadrangle Books.

Treiman, D.J. 1977. *Occupational Prestige in Comparative Perspective*. New York: Academic Press.

Turner, J.H. 1977. *Social Problems in America*. New York: Harper & Row.

*Turner, J.H. and C.E. Starnes. 1976. *Inequality: Privilege and Poverty in America*. Pacific Palisades, Calif.: Goodyear.

Basic statistics on the distribution of income and wealth are examined in this work. The role of power and cultural beliefs in supporting inequality is discussed. The twin social policies of welfare (government aid for the poor) and wealthfare (government aid for the wealthy) are contrasted.

U.S. Bureau of the Census. 1977. *Statistical Abstracts of the United States: 1977.* Washington, D.C.: U.S. Government Printing Office.

12   RACIAL INEQUALITY

Howard H. Garrison

In the past decade there has been a growing consensus among researchers that the problems of racial inequality are structural in nature. Most racial minority groups became a part of the U.S. society through conquests, enslavement, or subjugation, and shortly thereafter social institutions began to emerge to maintain the pattern of racial domination (Jacobs and Landau, 1971; Blauner, 1972). While racial oppression underwent periods of greater and lesser intensity (see Woodward, 1974), major social mechanisms for maintaining racial inequality persisted. The system of de jure segregation, only recently dismantled, is the most obvious example of government efforts to maintain inequality. But other mechanisms were equally effective. School desegregation suits in the North have demonstrated that patterns of segregation in many northern school districts were no less deliberate than those in the South (U.S. Commission on Civil Rights, 1976:6). In addition to official government actions, a host of established practices had an enormous impact on racial inequality. Hiring policies in the public and private sectors limited employment opportunities for members of minority groups, while real estate associations threw their weight behind a variety of programs designed to maintain residential segregation (Yinger, 1975). Today, the legislated forms of separation are gone, but discrimination still remains and, along with indirect and institutional factors like intergenerational status transmission, contributes to the persistence of racial inequality.

WHAT ARE THE PROBLEMS?

As America enters the 1980s it is hard to find an area of national concern where race is not an issue. Racial inequality is pervasive across subjects and over

---

*The opinions expressed in this paper are solely those of the author and do not represent the views of the U.S. Commission on Civil Rights.

time. In almost every measure of well-being racial disparities appear: health, education, occupation, employment, income, and housing.

Health

Life expectancy and mortality rates are commonly used to compare the well-being and general living conditions of two or more populations. In the United States black-white comparisons yield a stark picture of racial inequality. In 1974 the infant mortality rate for nonwhites was 24.9 per 1,000 live births, while for whites it was 14.8, 59 percent of the nonwhite rate. The ratio of nonwhite to white infant mortality has been stable since 1940 (U.S. Department of Commerce, 1977: 193). Life expectancy at age 20 also varies by race. In 1950 20-year-old white males could expect to live an additional 50 years, while for nonwhite males of the same age this figure was 44 years. Male life expectancies at age 20 have been fairly stable since 1950. White women 20 years of age could expect to live an additional 55 years in 1950, but black women only 47 additional years. Life expectancies increased for women of both groups by 1970—whites by almost three years and nonwhites by five years—reducing the female disparity from eight years to six (U.S. Department of Commerce, 1977:191).

Education

Racial disparities still exist in education. In 1955 21 percent of the white youth 18–19 years of age were enrolled in college, while only 6 percent of the nonwhites were enrolled, which is a white-nonwhite ratio of over three to one. By 1975 white enrollment rates rose to 38 percent, while black rates reached 25 percent (U.S. Department of Commerce, 1977:301). While a disparity still exists, the gap has been dramatically reduced. A sustained effort such as the one to achieve equal educational opportunity can have an impact on racial inequality.

Progress was made in school desegregation as well as in educational attainment. However, this reduction in segregation was largely confined to southern schools where the desegregation effort first began. In 1967 the typical black student in a large central city school district in the south went to a school that was 14 percent white. This figure rose to 42 percent by 1974. A typical black student in a large central city school district in the north went to a school that was 25 percent white in 1967. By 1974 this percentage had risen only three points to 28 percent (Farley, 1978:26-27).

Occupation and Employment

While there are some moderately encouraging trends in education, comparable reductions in employment and earnings disparities have not been observed. In studies of employment, occupational attainment, and earnings (Masters, 1975; Featherman and Hauser, 1976), racial disparities remain after controlling for a number of individual attributes and background characteristics. While these and other studies report some reduction in inequality during the last 15 years, substantial differences remain (see also Farley and Hermalin, 1972; Farley 1977).

A recent study conducted by the U.S. Commission on Civil Rights (1978b) revealed that the pattern of inequality between blacks and whites is found among other minorities as well. The unemployment rates of "majority" (white, non-Hispanic) males and females were significantly lower than those of most minority groups in 1960, 1970, and 1976.

The Commission's study also revealed that members of minority groups are likely to be employed in different occupations than members of the majority group. These occupational disparities reflect differences in rank as well as category. In 1960 only Chinese American males had occupational prestige scores as high as majority males. The prestige scores of American Indians, Mexican Americans, Filipino Americans, and Puerto Ricans were substantially lower. By 1976 all racial minority groups improved their position relative to majority males, but prestige scores of blacks, Mexican Americans, and Puerto Ricans were only four-fifths of majority males' prestige scores. For women the prestige gap is also large. In 1960 majority females had higher prestige scores than all other groups. By 1976 the prestige disparity was reduced for all groups, although Mexican American, Puerto Rican, and black women still had occupational prestige scores below those of majority women.

Earnings

Comparisons of majority and minority earnings for 1959 indicate that majority males and females, on the average, earned more than minority males and females. The gap was reduced by 1975, but American Indian, black, Mexican American, and Puerto Rican males still earned less than three-fourths of white male earnings (U.S. Commission on Civil Rights, 1978b:54). A large portion of the earnings gap remains when adjustments are made for differences in occupational prestige, age, education, weeks worked, hours worked, and average income for the respondent's state of residence.

While studies may differ in their assessment of the degree of earnings inequality among the racial groups, the existence of a racial disparity is a consistent finding. Studies that compare young people, control for family composition, or are restricted to employed persons find less inequality and more convergence over time than studies that include older persons and the unemployed and examine families without regard to their composition and employment status. This disparity occurs because the gains made by the employed have been offset by higher rates of unemployment. In addition, working women earn less than working men, and the more rapid increase of minority households headed by a single female means that the burden of sex discrimination falls disproportionately on minority families.

Housing

Inequalities remain in consumption and life style as well as in earnings. High and persistent levels of residential segregation by race are documented in several empirical studies (Sorensen, et al., 1975; Van Valey, et al., 1977). These high levels of segregation are not merely the reflection of income or status differences. Research has shown that the segregation of black and white professionals is much greater than that between white professionals and white laborers (Simkus, 1978). Studies have also shown that other socioeconomic factors cannot explain residential segregation (Taueber and Taueber, 1965; Wilson and Taueber, 1978).

WHAT DO WE KNOW?

This discussion views racial inequality as a structural problem and will emphasize the attempts to change social (as opposed to personal) relationships. However, this focus has not always been dominant; one of the oldest research traditions in the field is the study of prejudice.

Reducing Prejudice

There is a large body of research that seeks to define the conditions under which interracial contact leads to a reduction in prejudice (Simpson and Yinger, 1972:673-84). However, since racial inequality in the United States involves more than prejudice, research on the modification of attitudes has limited the potential for reducing racial inequality. Moreover, it would be grossly unfair to harness policies designed to promote the well-being of racial minorities to the attitudes of white Americans. Had this been the case in the past, very little progress would have been made in school desegregation. Jacobson (1978) has shown that attitudes toward school desegregation and bussing became more favorable after court orders than before. This and other research suggests that attitudes often conform to an accomplished fact (Pettigrew, 1971:274-85). Finally, much of the theoretical and empirical discussion of the "contact hypothesis" seems to be in agreement with Allport's (1954) view that contact must be between persons of equal status in order to reduce prejudice. The equal status requirement suggests that positive intergroup contact is more likely to be a consequence than a cause of racial equality.

A series of laboratory studies by Cohen (1975) illustrate how the larger social context conditions interracial contacts. In work groups made up of black and white students of comparable socioeconomic status there was a tendency for white students to dominate, even when there was no objective basis to assume greater competence. This pattern was identified as a consequence of expectations of greater competence for members of the higher-status group. These expectations, however, can be modified by equal-status experience. In a school setting, interracial classes taught by interracial teaching teams in a noncompetitive atmosphere proved successful. Cohen concludes that equal socioeconomic status may not be sufficient for achieving Allport's equal status requirement; previous expectations are also important in the shaping of interracial interaction. Understanding the way in which interactions are structured by status relationships and expectations helps to explain why some previous contact situations have not always produced improved race relations. While contact situations are not the key to racial equality, studies of contact situations may be useful in facilitating other programs and policies.

The Research Context

The study of racial inequality as a structural problem entails some unique limitations. Unlike individuals, families, or organizations, which may on occasion voluntarily place themselves under the care of experts, no society has ever presented its structural alignments to social scientists for manipulation. Despite the frequent claim in newspaper editorials that sociologists and other social scientists are toying with the fabric of U.S. society, sociologists can claim neither credit nor responsibility for the programs, which (with one or two exceptions) are certainly not experiments.

The civil rights initiatives were directed at specific agencies (e.g., the courts, Congress, the president) and the responses were subject to the constraints of the agencies' scope and mission. Programs were initiated, not as major efforts to reduce racial inequality, but rather as specific remedies for specific situations. School desegregation suits produced desegregation plans on a district-by-district basis, employment discrimination suits apply to particular companies, and executive orders refer to specified agencies or governmental actions. From a research perspective, these partial and piecemeal programs hardly provide a firm basis for analysis. Programs were established as remedies and few had built-in evaluation components. Furthermore, the variety of programs, the uniqueness of the situations covered, and the resulting small number of comparable cases frustrates ex post facto evaluation.

Education

Recently, most applied sociological research on race relations has focused on schools. In part, this is due to the fact that school desegregation was given a high priority by the civil rights movement and, consequently, public schools were the first major social institution in which the goal of racial equality was upheld. Research on school desegregation can be divided into two areas: studies of the amount of school desegregation, and studies of the effects of school desegregation.

In both the North and the South, studies of school desegregation efforts have shown litigation to be the most successful method of achieving effective school desegregation. "Free choice" plans, administrative sanctions, local initiatives, and legislative actions have produced modest results (Orfield, 1978). The emergence of litigation as the principal stimulus for desegregation and the absence of other successful approaches (especially in large metropolitan areas) limits the contribution of social research in the area of "how to motivate desegregation."

The social, political, and administrative contexts become crucial once desegregation is ordered. Orfield (1978) suggests that local leaders, especially elected representatives, must support the plan and must not offer false and divisive hopes to the electorate. In many cases the problems associated with desegregation can be attributed to last ditch plans prepared by reluctant administrators. These plans, when properly prepared, should include funding for initial costs of desegregation: busses, program changes, counseling, etc. Failure to provide for these expenditures may force the tightening of budgets and lead to the elimination of other programs, resulting in the decline of educational programs that the opponents of bussing fear. To keep this self-fulfilling prophecy from coming to pass, funding for desegregation, both for initial and long-term requirements, should be sought in advance of implementation.

There is a large body of research that measures the effects of school desegregation. These studies fall into three main categories: 1) studies of aspiration and achievement, 2) studies of intergroup relations (chiefly attitudes, with some studies of behavior), and 3) studies of "white flight." In each area, some studies report positive effects, others find negative effects, and still others discover no change. While the debate over effects still rages, two points are helpful in understanding the controversy.

First, over a decade of research has shown that "school effects" are small. Studies have attempted to specify the impact of various school "inputs" (funding, facilities, teacher training, etc.) and school composition or "context" (race, socioeconomic status, ability, etc.) on student performance. While some studies have found statistically significant results, they are without exception small, both in absolute terms and in comparison with individual-level attributes. One reason for the failure of schools to have a more determinate role in shaping student life chances is suggested by Hauser, et al. (1976:322). In a study of Wisconsin high school graduates, they find that most of the variation in career outcomes occurs within schools rather than between schools. Once relevant social and psychological variables are controlled, school differences explain only 2 percent of the variation in outcomes. These results, the authors caution, do not speak to the possible influence of schools, but, rather, to the impact of schools as they are currently organized. Elizabeth Cohen makes a similar point in reference to school desegregation:

> ...trying to change the status order of an entire society by a superficial change in the racial composition of an organization which has traditionally reflected faithfully the power and status order in society at large is not an easy thing to do....(Cohen, 1975:299)

While it may be naive to expect massive effects by changing school composition alone, the absence of dramatic, easily obtained results should not be interpreted as a failure of desegregation.

A second factor also contributes to the confusion over the results of desegregation. Design flaws in many studies have hindered the identification of those desegregation situations that produce the most beneficial results. Cohen (1975) noted several of these: 1) the absence of control groups, 2) the use of cross-sectional rather than longitudinal data, 3) the use of short-time periods between measurements in studies that do use longitudinal data, 4) different measures of achievement or prejudice, and 5) the absence of rigorous controls for social standing, racial composition of the classroom, and prior desegregation experience.

In addition to, and perhaps underlying, the specific flaws are theoretical deficiencies that inhibit development of a definitive body of desegregation research (Cohen, 1975). Widely different levels of desegregation (including token desegregation) in a variety of settings (ranging from hostile to strongly supportive communities) have been examined for the benefits of desegregation. Until conditions necessary for success are coherently stated, much of the research on the effects of school desegregation will remain unsuited for either cumulation or comparison.

As a consequence of these methodological and theoretical limitations, the research literature is composed of a host of conflicting and uncomparable studies (Weinberg, 1975; St. John, 1975). From this quagmire of data some researchers draw more optimistic assessments than others. For example, researchers have reported improved performance by minority students and improved race relations, but the gains in achievement have not been dramatic. This is also true of studies reporting negative effects.

The most controversial "effect" of school desegregation is the charge that it leads to "white flight" in which white parents, seeking to avoid having their children attend school with blacks, either send their children to private schools or move to suburban districts. In a research report that sparked a heated debate, Coleman, et al. concluded that

> The emerging problem of school segregation in large cities is a problem of metropolitan area residential segregation, black central cities and white suburbs, brought about by a loss of white from the central cities. The loss is intensified by extensive school desegregation in those cities, but in cities with high proportions of blacks and predominantly white suburbs, it proceeds at a relatively rapid rate with or without desegregation. (Coleman, et al., 1975:80)

The debate ultimately moved beyond the reported research and the controversy escalated as probussing and antibussing forces reacted to perceived implications of the report. Much of the debate came to center not on the actual research, but on remarks by Coleman and his critics in press interviews and statements of opinion.

There was, however, substantial and significant sociological criticism of the Coleman, et al. study (see the January-February 1976 issue of *Social Policy* for several comments and reanalyses). Critics pointed to the inadequacies of the sample, the short time span covered, the lack of control for the source of the desegregation action, and deficiencies in the models used to estimate "white flight," particularly the failure to assess the impact of other factors leading to white and black suburbanization. Some of the analyses contradicted or modified the conclusions of Coleman and his colleagues (Farley, 1976). Others argued that "white flight" was only an immediate and limited reaction to the initial desegregation order and was unlikely to have major long-term effects on district racial composition.

Beyond the furor that followed the escalation of this controversy, the amount of attention given to the "white flight" debate is unfortunate for two reasons. First, it is largely irrelevant to the future of desegregation, since it is ordered on the basis of constitutional and legal principles, not sociological research. Second, the question "Does 'white flight' result from bussing?" directs attention away from the more fruitful policy issue of "How can resegregation be minimized?"

While some researchers suggest that recent attempts at school desegregation have produced results that are contrary to its initial goals, others have argued that integration has not failed because it has not really been attempted. Integration is seen as more than just the reassignment of pupils. Many of the desegregation efforts have been limited and half-hearted. There is a strong possibility that with large-scale implementation the results may· be different. The research on school desegregation does not provide a firm basis for guiding policy. School desegregation was not implemented in a manner suitable for experimental design, and attempts to study the process ex post facto have been plagued by design flaws and theoretical inadequacies. Thus, instead of a set of proven principles we have only suggestions for improving the outcomes of desegregation that are based as much on past mistakes as on successes. From the experience in Boston it is clear that in the absence of strong community leadership, community polarization over school desegregation can spill over into the schools and exacerbate the difficulties of desegregation.

Currently, there exist several lists of "dos and don'ts" for successful desegregation. In their summary of research findings, Henderson and Von Euler (1979) suggest that a social class mix, including some upper-status students, helps students believe that they can succeed and that their fate has not been abandoned. Younger students are thought to adjust better to desegregation than older students. Classroom desegregation is recommended and faculty/staff desegregation is encouraged in order to provide role models for both majority and minority students. Curriculum changes to include elements of minority group culture are recommended, along with inservice training to prepare teachers for the new task. Gay (1978) suggests that these innovations include self-analysis, information about the new students' culture and history, and techniques for teaching heterogeneous groups of students. In a list that includes many of the same recommendations, Orfield (1975) also emphasizes the role of the school principal in setting the tone for desegregation, providing leadership, and resolving conflict. Weinberg (1975) suggests that the achievement of minorities is greatest in those desegregated schools with inservice training for teachers, higher-status students, classroom desegregation as well as school desegregation, no rigid ability grouping (especially for the earliest grades), desegregation at the earliest grades, no racial hostility, and a supportive community.

Despite all the controversy, at least one prominent observer feels that school desegregation offers the best chance for building a bridge across the racial gulf in the foreseeable future (Orfield, 1978:455). Other forms of discrimination, such as residential segregation and employment and earnings disparities, may prove even harder to remedy. To the public, the order sometimes seems reversed. Farley (1978:41) reports that many survey respondents view residential desegregation as a possible key to school desegregation without "bussing." But demographers who study the issue are generally pessimistic about its prospects, in large part because the chance of major changes in patterns of residential segregation is slim.

Housing

Several factors contribute to the difficulty of eliminating residential segregation. First, there are few tools with which to combat housing discrimination. Primary responsibility for enforcing Title VIII, the Fair Housing section of the 1968 Civil Rights Act, rests with the Department of Housing and Urban Development (HUD). Most of HUD's actions are based on formal complaints. This case-by-case approach, even when successful, is extremely slow. HUD has no real enforcement power other than cutting off funds if the target of the complaint is receiving HUD assistance. Cases that cannot be settled by HUD conciliation efforts are turned over to the Justice Department for prosecution.

Second, the use of existing remedies has been rare and the penalties have been mild. HUD has been criticized for taking too long with its conciliation efforts and being too slow to turn cases over to the Justice Department (U.S. Commission on Civil Rights, 1974:330–31). In 1973 only 58 suits to end housing discrimination were filed by the Justice Department. In that year, suits against apartment owners covered about 33,000 rental units (U.S. Commission, 1974: 126). Since the law went into effect, a total of only 300 suits have been filed (Babcock, 1980).

Other institutional factors serve to reinforce current patterns of residential segregation. Tax incentives for new homes (built largely in the suburbs) serve to discourage white home buyers from purchasing older homes in the central city. Black suburbanization, on the other hand, may be severely curtailed by the rapid rise in housing costs. Rising real estate prices give increased equity to current home owners and limit the ability of many renters (disproportionately members of minority groups) to purchase housing. Finally, since residential moves are individual actions and relatively infrequent, even major changes in the destinations of black and white "movers" would not rapidly alter the city–suburb imbalance (Frey, 1978) or immediately alter the pattern of residential segregation.

Orfield (1978) suggests that none of the proposals for accelerating the recent small declines in residential segregation are likely to have an impact in the near future. Proposals for dispersing low income housing have had little political support, often meeting with strong opposition in the communities mentioned. The campaign against exclusionary zoning practices has produced few gains. Thus far only two municipalities have been challenged by the Justice Department in land use cases. Orfield (1978) suggests that to change residence patterns, a massive campaign of sanctions and incentives would be necessary.

Most sociological research on residential segregation has been descriptive. Some work has been done on attitudes of residents in racially changing neighborhoods, but the absence of major residential desegregation programs and the rarity of stable integrated neighborhoods (Orfield, 1978:439), naturally occurring or by design, severely restricts the potential of applied sociological research in this area.

Employment and Income

The effort to eliminate labor market discrimination differs in two important respects from the school desegregation efforts. First, in school desegregation cases entire districts were the targets of administrative and legal actions. In employment, discrimination issues may involve individuals and each "victory" involves a smaller number of beneficiaries. Second, the initial policies aimed at ending labor market discrimination were adopted a decade after the 1954 Brown v. School Board decision. Title VII of the 1964 Civil Rights Act outlawed a variety of discriminatory employment practices and created the Equal Employment Opportunity Commission (EEOC), and the 1972 amendments to this act gave the EEOC the power to go into court when conciliation fails (U.S. General Accounting Office, 1978:5). While the school desegregation process began slowly, the later initiation of equal employment policy means that the procedures needed to enforce, mold, and refine these policies are not as well established.

Research on employment policy has also lagged behind research on school desegregation policy. There are currently two types of studies in this area: a body of research that seeks to evaluate the general impact of the 1960s programs, and an emerging body of research focusing on specific policies and government actions.

Masters' (1975) research is an example of the former. His time-series analysis of the nonwhite–white median income ratio sought to determine if the 1964 Civil Rights Act had an effect. Controlling for the impact of changes in the gross national product and the unemployment rate, Masters found that the nonwhite–white income ratio was significantly lower and stable before 1964 and that it rose rapidly after 1964. Masters was unable to determine whether the observed effects were due to the legislation itself or to changes in the sociopolitical environment that enabled the legislation to be passed. The latter interpretation is consistent with Gunnar Myrdal's view that the status of blacks in the United States would improve when whites changed their attitudes toward blacks.

McCrone and Hardy (1978) suggest that Masters' focus on 1964 may be premature, noting that the law did not go into effect until 1965. When 1965 is used as the focal point Masters' conclusions are still supported. They emphasize, however, that the effects of the Equal Employment Opportunity (EEO) legislation have not been very large in comparison with the effects of changes in the gross national product and the unemployment rate. Furthermore, when the time-series analysis is done separately for geographic regions, the trend found in the national sample is evident only in the South. The other regions do not show major differences in the pre-EEO and post-EEO periods.

Burstein (1979) adds further refinement to Masters' model. First, he includes survey data on attitudes toward equal employment opportunity for blacks in order to test directly Myrdal's hypothesis about the role of white attitudes in the drive for racial equality. Second, the analysis makes a more realistic attempt to assess the impact of EEO laws by including annual measures of EEO litigation outcomes, EEOC budget, and the number of actionable charges based on race processed by the EEOC. Finally, Burstein controls for skill or productivity differences by including the ratio of black to white median education at each point in time. All three sets of variables (attitudes, EEO activities, and education ratio) have an effect on the relative income of nonwhite men. However, given the strong interrelationships between all these variables, it was impossible to completely disentangle their effects. It is important to note, however, that when attitudes toward race are included in the model the EEO variables still have an effect, suggesting that not all of the change in relative incomes found by Masters and others is due to attitude change. Some income change appears to be a result of the initiation and enforcement of EEO programs.

These studies documenting broad national trends have been performed at a high level of aggregation. In contrast, the studies of school desegregation are much more highly developed, despite their own serious flaws. The school studies typically contain more precise specifications of the treatments and more control variables. Recently, however, social scientists (especially economists) have begun to do more research on specific programs using characteristics of firms such as size or percent minority as control variables. One program that has been studied in this manner is the affirmative action requirement for contractors doing business with the federal government.

In 1965 President Johnson issued Executive Order 11246 requiring all federal contractors to take affirmative action in the hiring of minorities. In recent years compliance review procedures have been instituted. Studies of the effects of these programs differ in their samples and use of control variables. Goldstein and Smith (1976:531) find small but significant improvements in relative wages for black males. Gains have been greater in firms with government contracts than in firms without contracts, and even greater gains are found in those firms that are subject to compliance review. The relationship between contract status and black employment gains is also noted by Heckman and Wolpin (1976). However, their study of a single labor market failed to find any substantial effects of compliance reviews. Studies are mixed in their findings on the impact of contractor status on the employment and earnings of women and nonblack minority groups, however. This may be due to the time periods examined. The initial focus of the civil rights movement was on black-white inequality, and concerns with gender inequities and the plight of nonblack minority groups are relatively recent. As the scope of the civil rights effort expands, a broader pattern of program effects may likely be observed.

WHAT ARE WE DOING?

The major policy initiatives in the area of racial inequality have stemmed from the actions of the civil rights movement. Social scientists have played a much smaller role in this movement than the critics of desegregation would have the public believe. Most of the significant changes in the areas of race relations, school desegregation, and civil rights legislation during the 1960s, as well as the establishment of affirmative action programs, were the result of major political initiatives on the part of minority groups and their allies. While this coalition included social scientists, it would be wrong to credit them with the establishment of these programs. In the effort to alter the historical pattern of racial inequality in the United States, sociologists have primarily played a variety of supporting roles: publicizing, advising, and evaluating.

Publicizing

One of the major tasks performed by sociologists is documenting the need for change. This monitoring activity occurs in a variety of settings, including universities, government agencies, and private institutions. Among the university researchers, the demographic analyses of the Tauebers, Farley, and others are often cited as evidence of racial inequality in the United States. Government agencies like the Bureau of Labor Statistics and the U.S. Commission on Civil Rights monitor racial inequality in their regulation publications and in special reports. Civil rights organizations also maintain research staffs and sponsor sociological research. The National Urban League publishes a widely cited annual review (*The State of Black America*), a research journal (the *Urban League Review*), and special studies. Contract research firms like RAND and The National Opinion Research Center (NORC) have also done studies assessing racial inequality. Recently, minority operated firms like ASIAN, Inc. (Asian American Service Institute for Assistance to Neighborhoods) have become active in monitoring racial inequality.

There has also been a move beyond documentation of problems and the need for change. Recognizing the policy impact of the major opinion polls like the Harris and the Gallup polls, three black organizations announced their own attitude surveys. The NAACP plans to poll its own membership, while the National Urban League and Data Black, a private organization, announced national surveys of black Americans. Dr. Kenneth B. Clark, one of the founders of Data Black, notes the danger of generalizing about blacks from the 150 to 200 blacks usually included in the national samples (Dionne, 1980). In addition to the problem of sampling error and accuracy of estimates, a small sample does not permit the examination of subgroups in order to assess the diversity of black opinion. All black samples also enable the surveys to focus on topics of special interest to blacks.

Advising

Sociologists have been less prominent in designing programs once the need for them has been established. This is because most plans are limited at the time of their inception by the political opposition and restricted in implementation by the authority of the agencies involved. With the major program features determined in the political area, there is usually little room for "scientific" input. In the area of race relations, like most areas of applied sociology, research does not have a direct and immediate effect on public policy. Several writers conclude that policy makers are more apt to respond to sociological theory and general knowledge than to sophisticated studies. When studies are used, it is more often to support a decision already made than to reach one (Semas, 1977). This suggests a time lag in the impact of sociological research. Ideas must first gain widespread professional acceptance before they are useful in the policy arena. The popularization and increasing public sensitivity to general sociological concepts like racism, institutional discrimination, ethnicity, and cultural pluralism has probably had more policy impact than any specific investigation. This indirect role of sociological research is unlikely to change dramatically. However, in some areas of program implementation technical social research may play a larger and more direct role. The greatest potential for this role appears to be in connection with school desegregation plans, when courts that are charged with reviewing or designing programs may seek the expertise of social scientists.

Evaluating

Despite the lack of direct sociological impact on the design of programs, sociologists have been extensively involved in program evaluation. While studies of school desegregation are probably the most numerous, evaluations of specific agencies by internal staff or outside investigators are becoming more common. In the early 1970s, the U.S. army engaged a contract research firm to evaluate its race relations programs (Hiett, et al., 1974) and to develop measures of racial discrimination in the army (Nordlie, 1974). Using ratios of the observed number of blacks in specific positions to the expected number of blacks, the Nordlie (1974:62) report concluded that the "tendency for blacks to occupy the lower ranks disproportionately to the higher ranks is still present, but less than it once was in the Army." The study recommended that a regular system of evaluation be established, and in 1976 the army began publishing a report called the Annual Assessment of Race Relations and Equal Opportunity Programs. While not as extensive as the recommended evaluation, the Annual Assessments do provide considerable descriptive data on the distribution of women and minorities in military grades and programs. The U.S. Army Research Institute has also produced a series of reports evaluating the racial climate in the Army and its race relations training programs.

With the increased use of statistical evidence in court cases, sociologists as well as statisticians are preparing and evaluating data for presentation in court. Recently, the courts have become much more sophisticated in their treatment of statistical issues, methodological criteria, and theoretical concerns. In Castenada v. Partida—a case involving the selection of Mexican Americans for jury duty—the court ruled that differences between expected and observed values greater than two standard deviations would be sufficient evidence to reject the hypothesis that the jury selection was random. In Albermarle Paper Co. v. Moody, the court relied on the .05 level of significance for interpreting correlations. In both cases reference was made to prevailing social science standards and conventions. Issues of proper comparison and relevant control variables are also pertinent in court. As a result, social scientists are increasingly becoming involved in the legal system, especially in discrimination cases. Individual social scientists are called on for testimony, government agencies charged with enforcement are hiring social scientists and statisticians to work on the presentation of evidence, and private consulting firms are offering litigation support services that include statistical and sociological expertise.

The role of social scientists in legal proceedings has been debated ever since the 1954 Supreme Court decision in the Brown school desegregation case. There has been disagreement over the proper role of social science in discrimination cases (Clark, 1976), as well as disagreement over whether social science evidence supports particular policies. Much of the controversy, however, stems from a misconception of the actual role of social science in the legal system. Social science evidence played a minor role in the Brown case; the much discussed research citations appeared in a footnote (number 11) and were used to support the decision, not to reach it. As one federal judge remarked recently, there is a "... misunderstanding of the very limited consideration given to social science evidence in court deliberation and the limited role such evidence plays in the outcome. Far more important than social science evidence in policy cases, e.g., a school desegregation case, is the basic law which has been referred to" (Doyle, 1976: 12). Social science evidence is useful in establishing the existence of discrimination, designing remedies, and guiding implementation. This means that for legal issues, social science is far more relevant to questions of "what exists" and "how to resolve it" than to debates over "should we do this?"

WHAT HAVE WE ACCOMPLISHED?

Optimistic evaluations of the current status of minority groups (Glazer, 1976; Wilson, 1976) have drawn critical reactions from both the academic community and civil rights activists (Willie, 1979). The controversy centers in part on whether one is willing to accept the removal of barriers or the reduction of racial disparities as the criterion of equality. In terms of intergroup disparities, progress has been modest, especially in light of what remains to be done.

Furthermore, it is difficult to isolate the role of sociologists from that of other actors in the civil rights movement. In documenting racial disparities sociologists have helped to focus attention on discrimination and minority group disadvantages and have helped demonstrate a need for action. In this general way sociologists have contributed to progress in the reduction of racial inequality.

Two specific contributions of social science research have been particularly useful in this regard. First, the use of statistical data on minorities has provided a basis for legitimating demands for action. Second, the logic of social science research has helped to focus attention on equality of outcomes as a legitimate public concern. This focus has helped to maintain a concern with racial inequality even though many of the grosser forms of racial discrimination have been eliminated, and it has helped to guide the search for the sources of remaining inequality.

Statistical Documentation

The ubiquitous presence of income and other statistical data (often reported by race, sex, and other demographic variables) obscures the fact that this is a recent innovation and at one time represented a controversial departure from existing policy. The addition of an income question to the 1940 census generated heated opposition in Congress. One southern congressman opposed the inclusion of items on income and years of schooling because he feared that these "socialistic New Deal inquiries" would be used in attempts to achieve racial equality (Hauser, 1975:3). As it turned out, he was in some ways correct; the data and the studies they generated have been important tools for supporting the movement toward racial equality.

In their roles as advisors, consumers, and lobbyists, social scientists have exerted considerable influence in creating and expanding the federal government's statistical programs. Items have been added to the census and new sources of data have been established. Special purpose surveys on health, fertility, and housing, as well as surveys specifically designed to investigate racial inequality (e.g., the 1965 Equality of Educational Opportunity Survey and the regular Office for Civil Rights Survey of Elementary and Secondary Schools), have been important in documenting inequality in the United States. Analysis of these data has been greatly enhanced by the creation and distribution of public use tapes. Welfare measures like the unemployment indexes and Mollie Orshansky's poverty index

(1965) have been politically useful. Concern with the quality of the statistical data led to the creation of social science advisory panels like the President's Committee to Appraise Employment and Unemployment Statistics (the Gordon Commission) in 1961 and the National Commission on Employment and Unemployment Statistics (the Levitan Commission) in 1978. The Levitan Commission report included several specific recommendations to improve the quality and quantity of statistical data on minority groups.

Evaluation Research

In the assessment of programs and policies the role of applied sociology has also been rather modest. This has been due, in part, to the modest nature of the programs. There is a growing evaluation literature on the effects of school desegregation, but the limited degree of school desegregation is a more fundamental concern in the assessment of inequality. Several guides to more effective school desegregation are beginning to appear. Unfortunately, they may be of limited use since some of the crucial variables (student socioeconomic status and school racial composition) may not be manipulable in the context of existing school districts and current court rulings.

The evaluation of affirmative action programs is currently constrained by their limited adoption. Until they are more pervasive it would be premature to pass judgment on their ultimate possibilities for success. In other areas, accomplishments are even more modest. Short of massive government intervention, few viable proposals exist for altering residential segregation, and researchers express pessimism about the likelihood of significant change in the foreseeable future (Orfield, 1978:90–91; Frey, 1978). Unfortunately, given the existing racial disparities and the continuing need for action, the catalogue of accomplishments is far shorter than the list of continuing problems.

WHERE ARE WE GOING?

In the past, policies designed to alter racial inequality have been shaped largely by political forces. Government programs and social science research have been guided by social movements, and the 1980s are likely to see a continuation of this pattern. But two major factors may shape the direction of civil rights activity in the 1980s: the fate of affirmative action programs and the political/ethnic composition of the civil rights movement.

Affirmative Action Programs

The limited success of indirect strategies (such as programs concentrating on education) in eliminating labor market inequality has led to an emphasis on direct efforts to increase the hiring and promotion of minority persons. These affirmative action strategies—labeled "quotas" by their opponents—have been challenged in print (Glazer, 1976) and in court (Weber v. Kaiser). In the Weber case, the Supreme Court ruled that Kaiser's affirmative action program did not violate Title VII of the 1964 Civil Rights Act. But affirmative action programs remain controversial and voluntary plans have not been widely initiated. Successful implementation of affirmative action strategies could provide an effective mechanism for reducing racial inequality, and their proliferation would provide a major channel for research. Legal challenges to the federal government's minority contractor program have been launched and are likely to continue until there is a definitive court ruling. Restriction of affirmative action programs would be a serious setback and would require a major reevaluation of efforts to eliminate inequality. Applied research and program development in this area will, therefore, be shaped by the political and legal actions of the 1980s.

Changing Composition of the Civil Rights Movement

Following the lead of the black civil rights movement of the 1960s, the 1970s saw a rise in organized activity by Hispanics, Native Americans, and other minority groups. Americans of Hispanic origin—represented by groups like the Mexican American Legal Defense and Education Fund (MALDEF) and the League of United Latin American Citizens (LULAC)—have become increasingly important in the civil rights arena, and in recent years government agencies have become more sensitive to the concerns of Hispanics. Federal data collection and statistical analyses provide one example of this phenomenon. Prior to 1973, data on Hispanic unemployment was not regularly collected by the federal government. In hearings before the Congress, Hispanic organizations and individuals noted that lack of data seriously restricted the government's ability to understand and remedy the difficult social and economic conditions facing Hispanics (U.S. Commission on Civil Rights, 1978a:1–4). These hearings led to the passage of Public Law 94-311, which calls for expanded collection, analysis, and publication of the data on the social and economic conditions of Hispanic Americans. These data may then be used to demonstrate the need for programs and policies.

Hispanics are not the only group seeking to bring their plight to the attention of the U.S. public. Asian Americans, long regarded as a successful "model" minority group, have begun to document the discrimination that they face and to assert parallels between their situation and that of blacks and Hispanics (Cabezas, 1979; Cabezas and Yee, 1977). These and other political campaigns have generated a trend toward broader coverage of racial minorities in government programs. Affirmative action programs have been expanded to include nonblack minorities (U.S. Department of the Army, 1979:1), and researchers have begun to devote more attention to other minority groups (Bean and Frisbie, 1978).

The increased diversity of actors in the civil rights movement, along with heightened awareness of discrimination against women, the aged, and the handicapped, complicates the civil rights picture. On one hand, it offers a broader base upon which claims to equity can be made. On the other hand, it may result in competition for the limited resources devoted to reducing inequality. It is also possible that a tremendous expansion of the concept of "disadvantaged" may trivialize it and reduce the justification for action by bringing under the disadvantaged label many persons who have many social advantages based on other statuses or family connections. In any event, programs and policies for the 1980s will most likely be shaped by a variety of minority groups either cooperating or competing with one another. Certainly some new issues will emerge, particularly those connected with the special needs of the newly mobilized minorities. For example, Hispanic groups have become increasingly vocal about immigration policy and the treatment of undocumented residents (illegal aliens).

While major policies will be determined by the success of civil rights activities, several trends are likely to continue. The use of quantitative data in litigation will probably continue to expand and become more sophisticated. Education and school desegregation will still be important concerns, but it is likely that labor market issues will become the major focus of political activity and research. The rejection of cross-district bussing in Miliken v. Bradley limits the possibility of instituting massive school desegregation in large metropolitan areas. This limitation, along with the modest relationship between education and earnings, suggests that the labor market itself is the most effective forum for reducing socioeconomic inequality among racial and ethnic groups.

REFERENCES AND SUGGESTED READINGS

Allport, Gordon W. 1954. *The Nature of Prejudice.* Cambridge, Mass: Addison-Wesley.

Babcock, Charles R. 1980. "U.S. to Check on Bias in Local Zoning." *Washington Post*, January 18, p. A2.

*Bean, Frank D. and W. Parker Frisbie, eds. 1978. *The Demography of Racial and Ethnic Groups.* New York: Academic Press.

Twelve careful quantitative analyses of policy and policy-relevant issues by leading demographers are collected in this volume. They provide current information on patterns of migration and segregation and ethnic differences in fertility, mortality, and labor force participation. Several studies contain data on Hispanic and other nonblack minorities.

Blauner, Robert. 1972. *Racial Oppression in America.* New York: Harper & Row.

Burstein, Paul. 1979. "Equal Employment Opportunity Legislation and the Income of Women and Nonwhites." *American Journal of Sociology* 44 (June): 367–91.

Cabezas, Amado Y. 1979. "Disadvantaged Employment Status of Asian and Pacific Americans." In *Civil Rights Issues of Asian and Pacific Americans: Myths and Realities*, edited by the U.S. Commission on Civil Rights, pp. 434–44. Washington, D.C.: U.S. Government Printing Office.

Cabezas, Amado Y. and Harold T. Yee. 1977. *Discriminatory Employment of*

Asian Americans: Private Industry in the San Francisco-Oakland SMSA. San Francisco: ASIAN, Inc.

Clark, Kenneth B. 1976. "Social Science, Constitutional Rights, and the Courts." In *Education, Social Science and the Judicial Process: An International Symposium*, edited by National Institute of Education, United States Department of Health, Education, and Welfare, pp. 3–9. Washington, D.C.: U.S. Government Printing Office.

Cohen, Elizabeth. 1975. "The Effects of Desegregation on Race Relations." *Law and Contemporary Problems* 39:271–99.

Coleman, James S., Sara D. Kelly, and John A. Moore. 1975. *Trends in School Segregation, 1968–1973.* Washington, D.C.: Urban Institute.

Dionne, E.J., Jr. 1980. "Pollsters Do Their Number on What Black America Thinks." *New York Times*, January 20, p. 20E.

Doyle, Willie E. 1976. "Can Social Science Evidence Be Used in Judicial Decision Making?" In *Education, Social Science and the Judicial Process: An International Symposium*, edited by the National Institute of Education, U.S. Department of Health, Education, and Welfare, pp. 11–17. Washington, D.C.: U.S. Government Printing Office.

Farley, Reynolds. 1976. "Is Coleman Right?" *Social Policy* 6 (Jan/Feb):14–23.

_____. 1977. "Trends in Racial Inequalities: Have the Gains of the 1960s Disappeared in the 1970s?" *American Sociological Review,* 42 (April):189–209.

_____. 1978. "School Integration in the United States." In *The Demography of Racial and Ethnic Groups*, edited by Frank D. Bean and W. Parker Frisbie, pp. 5–50. New York: Academic Press.

Farley, Reynolds and Albert Hermalin. 1972. "The 1960s: A Decade of Progress for Blacks?" *Demography* 9 (August):359–70.

Featherman, David, and Robert M. Hauser. 1976. "Change in the Socioeconomic Stratification of the Races, 1962–1973." *American Journal of Sociology* 82 (Nov):621–51.

Frey, William H. 1978. "Black Movement to the Suburbs: Potentials and Prospects for Metropolitan-wide Integration." In *The Demography of Racial and Ethnic Groups*, edited by Frank D. Bean and W. Parker Frisbie, pp. 79–117. New York: Academic Press.

Gay, Geneva. 1978. "Multicultural Preparation and Teacher Effectiveness in Desegregated Schools." *Theory Into Practice*, 17; 149–56.

Glazer, N. 1976. *Affirmative Discrimination: Ethnic Inequality and Public Policy.* New York: Basic Books.

Goldstein, Morris and Robert S. Smith. 1976. "The Estimated Impact of the Antidiscrimination Programs Aimed at Federal Contractors." *Industrial and Labor Relations Review* 29 (July):523–43.

Hauser, Philip M. 1975. *Social Statistics in Use.* New York: Russell Sage Foundation.

Hauser, Robert M., William H. Sewell, and Duane F. Alwin. 1976. "High School Effects on Achievement." In *Schooling and Achievement in American Society,* edited by William H. Sewell, Robert M. Hauser and David L. Featherman, pp. 309–41. New York: Academic Press.

Heckman, James and Kenneth Wolpin. 1976. "Does the Contract Compliance Program Work? An Analysis of Chicago Data." *Industrial and Labor Relations Review* 29 (July):544–64.

Henderson, Ronald D. and Mary Von Euler. 1979. "What Research and Experience Teach Us About Desegregating Large Northern Cities." *Clearinghouse for Civil Rights Research* 7 (Spring):2–14.

Hiett, Robert L., Robin S. McBride, and Byron G. Fiman. 1974. *Measuring the Impact of Race Relations Programs in the Military*. McLean, Va.: Human Sciences Research.

Jacobs, Paul and Saul Landau, with Eve Pell. 1971. *To Serve the Devil. Volume 1: Natives and Slaves*. New York: Vintage Books.

Jacobson, Cardell K. 1978. "Desegregation Rulings and Public Attitude Changes: White Resistance or Resignation?" *American Journal of Sociology* 84 (Nov): 698–705.

*Masters, Stanley. 1975. *Black-White Income Differentials: Empirical Studies and Policy Implications*. New York: Academic Press.

Masters examines the effects of migration, residential segregation, productivity and discrimination on black-white income differentials in a series of quantitative studies. References to both sociological and economic research, plus a strong emphasis on policy (including a test of the liberal, conservative, and radical policy perspectives), distinguish this book from similar undertakings.

McCrone, Donald and Richard Hardy. 1978. "Civil Rights Policies and the Achievement of Racial Economic Equality, 1948–1975." *American Journal of Political Science* 22:1–17.

Nordlie, Peter G. 1974. *Measuring Changes in Institutional Racism in the Army*. McLean, Va.: Human Sciences Research.

Orfield, Gary. 1975. "How to Make School Desegregation Work: The Adaptation of Schools to Their Newly Desegregated Student Bodies." *Law and Contemporary Problems* 39:314–40.

*_____. 1978. *Must We Bus?* Washington, D.C.: The Brookings Institute.

A comprehensive review of the legal, residential, and political context of school desegregation leads Orfield to conclude that bussing is the only practical solution. This is a cogent and well substantiated argument for a policy that has too few public champions.

Orshansky, Mollie. 1965. "Counting the Poor: Another Look at the Poverty Profile." *Social Security Bulletin* 28 (Jan):3–29.

Pettigrew, Thomas F. 1971. *Racially Separate or Together*. New York: McGraw-Hill.

*St. John, Nancy H. 1975. *School Desegregation. Outcomes for Children*. New York: John Wiley & Sons.

This review of over 120 studies of school desegregation provides a valuable summary of previous research and serves as a useful guide for future investigation. From the inconsistent and often conflicting reports of various researchers, the author presents a coherent picture of school desegregation as a multifaceted phenomenon, the outcomes of which are conditioned by children's needs and methods of implementation.

Semas, Phillip W. 1977. "How Influential is Sociology?" *The Chronicle of Higher Education* (Sept 26):4.

Simkus, Albert A. 1978. "Residential Segregation by Occupation and Race." *American Sociological Review*, 43 (Feb):81–92.

Simpson, George E. and J. Milton Yinger. 1972. *Racial and Cultural Minorities: An Analysis of Prejudice and Discrimination.* 4th revised ed. New York: Harper & Row.

Sorensen, Annemette, Karl E. Taueber, and Leslie J. Hollingsworth, Jr. 1975. "Indexes of Racial Residential Segregation for 109 Cities in the U.S., 1940–1970." *Sociological Focus* 8 (Apr):125–42.

Taueber, Karl E. and Alma F. Taueber. 1965. *Negroes in Cities.* Chicago: Aldine.

U.S. Bureau of the Census. 1977. *Social Indicators: 1976.* Washington, D.C. U.S. Government Printing Office.

U.S. Commission on Civil Rights. 1974. *The Federal Civil Rights Enforcement Effort–1974, Volume II, To Provide...For Fair Housing.* Washington, D.C.: U.S. Government Printing Office.

_____. 1976. *Fulfilling the Letter and Spirit of the Law: Desegregation of the Nation's Public Schools.* Washington, D.C.: U.S. Government Printing Office.

_____. 1978a. *Improving Hispanic Unemployment Data: The Department of Labor's Continuing Obligation.* Washington, D.C.: U.S. Government Printing Office.

_____. 1978b. *Social Indicators of Equality for Women and Minorities.* This report provides data on education, employment, income, and housing for men and women in seven minority groups (American Indians, Alaskan natives, blacks, Mexican Americans, Japanese Americans, Chinese Americans, Pilipino Americans, and Puerto Ricans) and for white non-Hispanic men and women. Social indicators (ratios of minority group scores to white non-Hispanic male scores) are derived from the 1960 and 1970 census and the 1976 Survey of Income and Education. This informative report is one of the few studies to provide extensive data on nonblack minorities.

U.S. Department of the Army. 1979. *Race Relations and Equal Opportunity: Annual Assessment of Programs.* Washington, D.C.: U.S. Government Printing Office.

U.S. Department of Commerce, Bureau of the Census and Office of Federal Statistical Policy and Standards. 1977. *Social Indicators, 1976.* Washington, D.C.: U.S. Government Printing Office.

U.S. General Accounting Office. 1978. *A Compilation of Federal Laws and Executive Orders for Nondiscrimination and Equal Opportunity Programs.*

Van Valey, Thomas, Wade C. Roof, and Jerome E. Wilcox. 1977. "Trends in Residential Segregation, 1960–1970." *American Journal of Sociology* 82 (Jan):326–44.

Weinberg, Meyer. 1975. "The Relationship Between School Desegregation and Academic Achievement." *Law and Contemporary Problems* 39:240–70.

Willie, Charles V., ed. 1979. *Caste and Class Controversy.* Bayside, N.Y.: General Hall.

Wilson, Franklin D. and Karl E. Taueber. 1978. "Residential and School Segregation: Some Tests of Their Association." In *The Demography of Racial and Ethnic Groups*, edited by Frank D. Bean and W. Parker Frisbie, pp. 51–78. New York: Academic Press.

Wilson, William J. 1976. *The Declining Significance of Race*. Chicago: University of Chicago Press.

Woodward, C. Vann. 1974. *The Strange Career of Jim Crow, 3rd revised ed.* New York: Oxford University Press.

Yinger, John. 1975. "An Analysis of Discrimination by Real Estate Brokers." Madison: University of Wisconsin, Discussion Paper 252–75, Institute for Research on Poverty.

13 WORK ROLES

Edward Gross

To examine work is to examine society. Studies of social trends often consist largely of studies of occupational trends. And often great shifts in the structure of a society reflect new modes of work: computerization of simple jobs, immigration of new workers into countries for "temporary work" that stretches into years, and new modes of work organization, such as multinational firms that operate in several countries. Clearly, when work effects reach out into so many functional areas, it is hardly surprising that work becomes a major concern of government and planning bodies, and hence a legitimate interest for an applied sociology.

WHAT ARE THE PROBLEMS?

There appear to be six main problems raised by work in modern society. First, although every generation (at least since Plato) has produced prophets who claim that we are about to enter an era when the shuttles will run themselves and men and women will frolic about all day, there is no society on the horizon, including the most industrially advanced and leisure prone, that is anywhere near such a goal. Work for pay remains the only important and widely approved way of attaining an acceptable standard of living and style of life for most persons. Hence, the first problem is finding work for persons that pays them enough to enable them to live a comfortable life with dignity in their society. The labor force continues to expand in all countries—indeed the "developing" countries are developing in precisely that direction—and the needs of all persons for accelerating quantities of food, materials, energy, and products creates a growing need for more, not less work. At the same time, industrialized countries experience a continuing problem of unemployment and underemployment.

271

Second, perhaps because work has religious routes in the Florentine conception of the craftsman or because it still absorbs so much of our waking life, it is difficult for persons to treat their work lightly and see it simply as no more than a living. The kind of work that a person does is still a basic answer to the question: Who am I? As long as this is the case, it remains essential that persons be able to describe their work to their friends, families, and themselves with a sense of pride. This brings us to the second problem. Much work in modern society is demeaning, degrading, or just plain boring—something to be got through as quickly as possible. This problem is a major focus of the search for a better quality of life in industry. Although surveys have shown that the vast majority of workers say they are "satisfied" with their jobs, this response appears often to be a matter of making the best of things, given their few alternatives. If allowed to start over, many would choose a different job.

The third major problem revolves around increasing female employment. Not only has there been an increase in the number and proportion of females employed in the United States and elsewhere, but there has also been a shift in the attitude both of men and women toward female employment. Of course women in all societies have always worked. But the classic pattern has been for women to work temporarily (before marriage) or to serve as aides or adjuncts to men, providing "social-emotional" supports to the serious task-instrumental work that men performed. Women are now a permanent part of the labor force (though still dropping out some in their late 20s and 30s if they marry), and the women's liberation movement has initiated a battle for total equality with men—for the top positions in education, industry, the professions, and all other areas of work.

Fourth, closely related to the problems presented by increasing female employment are the inroads the civil rights movement has made in the field of employment. Here women join forces with blacks, Chicanos, Puerto Ricans, and other minorities in combatting discrimination in employment. Most of the public attention in the United States has focused on blacks, who have pioneered tactics of civil disobedience and confrontation and have attempted to develop a distinctive black subculture. Universities have been major targets of efforts to increase enrollment, and there is impressive evidence of progress in this realm. This battle is far from won, and efforts are continuing to pass appropriate legislation and make use of the courts. There is evidence that the income of black families has risen strikingly, so that among married couples, both of whom work, average income now exceeds that of comparable white couples (Wattenberg and Scammon, 1973). Yet poverty and high rates of unemployment for persons with little education remains severe among blacks.

Fifth, the traditional approach of the aggrieved worker has been unionization. Unions in the United States, in contrast to their European and Japanese counterparts, have tended to emphasize "business unionism," or a concern with wages and working conditions rather than with changing society. This in turn has led to corruption in the unions, with workers often being little concerned with how the union was run as long as it continued to provide them with financial benefits. The issue of democracy in the union, while a focus of Congressional investigating committees, has been of little concern to rank-and-file members, who are often apathetic about issues, rarely turn out for business meetings, and often complain of "compulsory unionism." Yet these same apathetic people will, when called upon, go out on costly strikes that sometimes extend for months. The overall position of the union movement has been the topic of much specu- lation. Some observers see it as having come to an end, while others see it as sim- ply getting ready for new inroads into government employees and university fac- ulties. We are even seeing strikes by firemen, policemen, and other public service workers.

A final issue concerns socialization into work. Classic functional theory in sociology asserts that positions have to be differentially rewarded in order to attract persons to the more difficult and important positions and to motivate them to perform as needed. Although controversy has continued to swirl around the theory, it remains true that matching persons to jobs is a never ending prob- lem. Education has been held out as the high road to upward mobility, and there is no question that the economic returns from education have been impressive in the past. Recently, many students have become "turned off" from schooling and have sought fulfillment in life styles requiring little formal education. The great majority of people continue to seek a rich life, however, the major road to which continues to be higher education. When they enter the labor force, persons have to be socialized to the demands of particular jobs and organizations. Although university training will already have accomplished much of that socialization, each job and organization has its own demands, values, and peculiarities. A major concern of the applied study of work deals with how this socialization process goes on, how much of it is "engineered" by employing organizations, and how much is within the control of individual workers.

In sum, the major work problems in contemporary society revolve around providing employment, making work meaningful and satisfying, satisfying the just expectations of women and minorities, organizing the work force, and social- izing persons into the work world.

WHAT DO WE KNOW?

Social research on applied problems of work is often relevant to more than one of the above problems. But it can be arranged under seven broad headings.

Predominance of large-scale organizations

The fundamental fact about work in Western industrial society (and increas- ingly elsewhere) is that it is carried out in large, complex, bureaucratic organizations. Whether we speak of producing goods or services, healing the sick, educating the young, protecting society against its enemies (internal or external), seeking recreation, celebrating high talent (in sport, theater, or the arts), serving the religious needs of persons, or bringing in the news, the typical approach is to form an organization and assign it the task of meeting those needs. In spite of the many critics of bureaucracies and in spite of the attempt of some to form utopian alternatives, there does not seem to be any other organizational form that offers even the slightest possibility of competition with them. The predominance of the large-scale organization is suggested in Table 13.1. If we look down the left side of the table, we see that small organizations (those with nine or fewer employees) clearly predominate. Many of these are family enterprises or those employing only a helper or two—by any definition a small concern. Yet such concerns, when taken together, make up over three-fourths of all establishments represented in this compilation. At the other end, we can see that large establishments are quite small in number. If we liberally call an establishment with 100 or more employees "large," then all such establishments together make up only 2 percent of the total. One might be inclined, then, to characterize the United States (as Napoleon once characterized England) as a "nation of small shopkeepers." Yet this conclusion would be misleading. For if we turn to the columns on the right side of the table, the employment picture tells quite a different story. All of the small establishments taken together account for only 16 percent of all employment. At the other end, the little group of large establishments account for 46 percent of all employment. In sum, we can say that although the typical establishment is small, the typical employee works for a large organization.

Most occupations are, therefore, practiced in large-scale organizations. This is also true of the professions. The physician in private practice who sees one patient at a time may often provide a model for other professions, but this is actually a rare phenomenon in professional practice. In contrast, social workers, reporters, accountants, architects, clergymen, airplane pilots, engineers, nurses, dieticians, funeral directors, professors, home economists, lawyers (in law offices or corporations), scientists, librarians, personnel workers, and teachers all typically work in organizations, often large ones. That fact often gives rise to conflict between the members of an occupation and the administrators of the organization in which they work to determine how the workers should conduct themselves. Organizations may seek ways of mitigating this conflict, such as putting professionals in charge of themselves (a chemist heads the research division of an oil refinery, a Ph.D. is president of a university), but still the conflict seems endemic. In factories, it often takes the form of conflict between staff and line persons.

Occupational Trends

Much sociological knowledge of occupations comes from studies of occupational trends. The two major conclusions of this research, shown in Table 13.2, are that there has been a great increase in white-collar workers, who now make

Table 13.1

Distribution of Employment and Establishments by Employment--Size Class, 1975

Employment-Size Class	Establishments		Employment	
Number of employees	*number*	*percent*	*number*	*percent*
1–4	2,427,415	59.0	4,602,891	7.6
5–9	744,681	18.1	5,269,099	8.7
10–19	460,797	11.2	6,540,951	10.8
20–49	300,340	7.3	9,387,476	15.5
50–99	98,743	2.4	6,904,337	11.4
100–249	53,486	1.3	8,055,060	13.3
250–499	16,457	.4	5,632,486	9.3
500–999	8,229	.2	4,845,149	8.0
1,000 or more	4,114	.1	9,326,912	15.4
Total	4,114,262	100	60,564,361	100

Source: U.S. Bureau of the Census. *County Business Patterns.* Washington, D.C.: U.S. Government Printing Office, 1975, p. XLX. Not included are: Government Employees, Self-Employed persons, Farm Workers and certain Domestic Service Workers and Railroad Employees.

up over half of all employed persons, and a profound decline in farm occupations. The latter trend reflects the enormous increase in agricultural productivity, as well as movement from farms to cities. At the same time, although the number of farmers is now very much reduced from what it was in the last century when the whole society was rural, farmers are now powerful and visible enough to be able to exert considerable political influence. They represent the only occupation represented in the U.S. Cabinet, and we have witnessed several recent attempts to organize farm unions and farm laborers.

The increase in white-collar workers is, in itself, rather misleading. Such data have provided statistical grist for the claim by Bell (1973) that the United States is the first "postindustrial society." He points out that most countries in the world are still dependent on extractive industries (agriculture, mining, fishing, forestry), productivity is low, and there are wide swings in income as prices fluctuate. In Western and Northern Europe, Japan, and the Soviet Union, the majority of workers are involved in manufacturing. "The United States today is the only nation in the world in which the service sector accounts for more than half the total employment and more than half the Gross National Product" (Bell, 1973:

Table 13.2

Major Occupation Groups of the Experienced Civilian Labor Force, 1900 to 1978

	1900	1920	1940	1960*	1978 (April)
			percentages		
White Collar	17.6	24.9	31.1	40.0	50.2
Professional	4.3	5.4	7.5	10.4	15.3
Managerial	5.8	6.6	7.3	8.4	10.7
Clerical	3.0	8.0	9.6	13.9	17.8
Sales	4.5	4.9	6.7	7.1	6.3
Manual	35.8	40.2	39.8	37.5	33.3
Crafts	10.5	13.0	12.0	13.9	13.0
Operators	12.8	15.6	18.4	18.0	15.4
Labor	12.5	11.6	9.4	5.5	4.9
Service	9.0	7.8	11.7	11.6	13.7
Farm	37.5	27.0	17.4	6.1	2.8
Farmers	19.8	15.3	10.4	3.7	1.5
Farm Labor	17.7	11.7	7.0	2.4	1.3
Total (*in thousands*)	29,030	42,206	51,742	67,990	93,180

*1970 classification

Source: Calculated from *Historical Statistics of the United States: Colonial Times to 1970.* U.S. Bureau of the Census. Washington, D.C.: U.S. Government Printing Office, 1975, pp. 139–140 and *Employment and Earnings,* 25(May 1978):34.

15). However, as he notes, the term "services" is misleading, for agrarian societies often have high proportions of persons involved in personal services. He excludes personal services from this category, focusing instead on health, education, research, and government—a new intelligentsia.

    Bell's (1973) conclusions must be amended to take account of sex differences in occupational distributions, however. Among male workers, even in 1978, manual workers, not white-collar workers, account for the greatest proportion of employed. It is true that the proportion of professionals have gone up, so that they now constitute one-seventh of all male employment, but craftsmen and semiskilled operators make up over one-fourth of the total. It is only among women that the trends that Bell thinks so important are most manifest. White-collar workers make up approximately two-thirds of their numbers, although over one-third of them are in clerical jobs. Hence, we must conclude that if we are on our way to becoming a postindustrial society, it is women who are leading the way, often by doing the dull jobs of key punching, typing, and other routine tasks of the new intellectual technology. Women also loom large in the professions, especially such fields as nursing, teaching, librarianship, and social work.

Another prominent trend has been the great growth in professionals, not only in numbers, but also in the emergence of new professions in public health, accounting, and government-related fields. Government now employs some 15 million persons, but the great preponderance of them (over 12 million) are found in state and local government, where high proportions work in education and health and hospitals. The less than three million civilian federal employees are heavily concentrated in national defense and the postal service, and these numbers have shown almost no change since 1970. Most of the growth has occurred, then, in state and local government. Also noteworthy is the continuation of operatives as a sizable occupational category among women, as well as a very slight decline in the proportion of service workers. There has been a strong decline in household workers, but it has been heavily offset by the increase in personal service occupations in laundries and drycleaning, beauty shops, and food-service operations.

Unemployment has fluctuated over the years, settling down in recent years to 6 or 7 percent of the labor force, but the internal variations in this rate are more important. The unemployment rate is very low (under 3 percent) for whites, especially those in their 30s and 40s. For blacks in these age brackets the figure is under 5 percent, but the rate is much higher among both white and black teenagers. For those 16–17 years of age, the rate is close to one-fifth among whites and approaches one-half among blacks. Even the lowest unemployment figures we have (under 3 percent) are quite unacceptable in other countries, where anything above 1 percent is considered intolerable.

Female Discrimination

While female employment has increased to the point where women now make up about 40 percent of the labor force, they are still the most occupationally segregated of all minority groups (Gross, 1968). This segregation takes two major forms: limitation to a small set of occupations, and concentration in lesser paying and relatively powerless positions within work organizations. Most of the segregation that women experience is structural in nature. That is, little of it can be traced to individual attitudes toward women, and we do not get far if we look for a conspiracy on the part of employers (Blaxall and Reagan, 1976). Rather, the source must be sought in a number of deep-seated practices that are taken for granted in society. One of these is childhood socialization to female roles. Those roles, exemplified in story and myth, paint a picture of women as dependent, warm, and sensitive, winning their way through cajoling and "wiles" (Epstein, 1970). Men, on the other hand, are depicted as aggressive, persistent, and emotionless, or at least keeping emotions under control. A second source occurs in the job search, where the "old-boy network" further excludes women. If a woman seeks a position in the professions, she is likely to encounter assumptions about "proper" female specialties such as pediatrics or public health in medicine, or family or real estate in law. In organizations, she meets beliefs that men (and women) do not want to work under a female boss, but if she works hard to prove herself, that may be counted against her ("she's too aggressive"). A study by Simmons, et al. (1975) of discrimination in the American Telephone and Telegraph Company found that over 90 percent of all jobs were over 90 percent male or 90 percent female. A third pattern of discrimination occurs when females seek to enter traditionally male jobs. They are likely to encounter subtle resistance in the form of "male" talk—rude sex jokes, recounting of male triumphs over females, or other concentration on male pursuits (Spradley and Mann, 1975; Meara, 1974; Kanter, 1977).

The net result of these forces is that women are concentrated in a very small number of occupations. About one-half of all employed women are in about 20 occupations, and one-fourth of them are either secretaries, household workers, bookkeepers, elementary school teachers, or waitresses (Blau, 1975). Such segregation has been present since at least 1900 (Gross, 1968). Women are severely underrepresented in the professions and are restricted mainly to nursing, social work, librarianship, and teaching. Such discrimination is not biological, as seen in international comparisons. As Galenson (1973) points out, the proportion of women in medicine in the United States is lower than in most other industrialized countries. Women are also a rarity in management. In federal employment, women work almost entirely at GS levels of 11 and below (Waldman and McEaddy, 1974). At the very highest levels of private industry, only one woman is presently (as of 1978) the chief executive of one of the 500 largest companies in the United States. In fact, *Fortune* magazine was able to find only ten women in positions that were even close to the top within the 1,300 companies it surveyed (Robertson, 1978). Clearly women's liberation has a long way to go.

Occupational Status

A major area of research has dealt with the ways in which different forms of work are evaluated, especially as measured by money and prestige. Yet, we are far from a simple theory to account for differential pay. Functional theory attributes these differences to the "importance" of the work and the scarcity of qualified candidates, but such factors do not explain why collecting garbage pays about the same as teaching the young. Power and market position seem to be major variables here. The reward for an activity depends in part on what employers can be required to pay. A service that is in great demand places those who supply it in a position to demand high pay. If the service is also of an emergency nature, those who provide it (such as doctors, lawyers, plumbers, and TV repairpersons) can earn more than those who supply services that can be postponed (such as architects, librarians, researchers, gardeners, and drapery cleaners). On the other hand, if demand is low, no matter how skilled the practitioner (bell casters, magicians), the pay will be low or nonexistent unless the work is treated as a performance.

Prestige may also be convertible into money, through a connection with advertising or business (as is often the case with sports heroes or other celebrities), or direct association with an organization that can determine salaries (as seems to be the case with top executives in many businesses) (Broom and Cushing, 1977). Other important variables affecting income include tradition and work-group controls, the extent of fringe benefits offered, and many intangible benefits associated with a job.

Another frequently used criterion for ranking occupations is their prestige. The most carefully studied scale for ranking occupational prestige was developed by North and Hatt in 1947 and replicated in 1963 (Hodge, et al., 1964). Government positions consistently scored high on this scale and appear to be still rising. Managers and officials were not far behind professional and semiprofessional workers. White-collar workers were rated above skilled craftsmen, although the latter often earn slightly more—which is perhaps a relic of their past closeness to power, or perhaps a remnant of the old "clean v. dirty" distinction. Farmers and farm managers fall about at the middle of the prestige ranking, far above many urban occupations. And even farmhands tie with bartenders for occupational prestige.

The most important finding of this research, however, was the remarkable stability of the prestige rankings over both time and space. As concluded by a prestige study going back 50 years "... there have been no substantial changes in occupational prestige in the United States since 1925" (Hodge, et al., 1964: 246). There is also a striking similarity in occupational prestige rankings across industrialized countries (Inkeles and Rossi, 1956), although most of these studies have used very broad occupational categories. Such stability clearly reflects the presence of powerful stabilizing forces—such as education, functional importance, and monetary rewards—that operate in all industrial countries and that change very slowly. Any sudden shifts in these forces would produce status inconsistencies, career breaks, and other problems that could lead to vast changes in society.

Inheritance and Mobility

Studies of occupational mobility have generally found that the most common pattern is for sons to be in the same occupational category (professional, managerial, clerical, craft, etc.) as their fathers. Inheritance is much more common in some occupations than in others, however, It is particularly high among professionals, proprietors, protective service workers, farmers, and unskilled laborers. In contrast, it is quite low among domestic and personal service workers. Occupational inheritance may be either transmitted or coerced. The son of a physician may follow in his father's footsteps because his father has socialized him to the norms of that profession at an early age, facilitated his entrance into medical school, and helped set him up an office. On the other hand, the son of a migratory laborer may follow in his father's footsteps because of a lack of education, a need to help out the family from an early age, and a lack of employable skills. Both occupations will show a high level of occupational inheritance but for very different reasons. Parents may also transmit concrete occupational benefits to their children, such as ownership of a business, farmland, a business reputation, or a set of clients or customers. Children of factory workers or professionals, in contrast, may receive only a set of attitudes or orientations from their parents.

Social class may act as a selective force at all ages, but it is especially influential through its impact on the educational system (Blau and Duncan, 1967). A father may influence his son not only directly, through placement or sponsorship, but also indirectly by influencing the amount of education he obtains and, hence, the kind of job he gets. On the one hand, education is clearly the major avenue of entrance to high-status occupations and to the upper levels of bureaucracies. On the other hand, the evidence also shows that the educational system itself is heavily stratified and, hence, helps to reproduce the social class system of the society. There is strong evidence that teachers encourage and favor students with middle-class hopes and appropriate life styles (Rist, 1970), which tends to shunt working-class and lower-class children into vocational or manual arts curriculums. Colleges and universities are also stratified in all countries. (Gross, 1981), so that careers are often determined by which school one attends. In the United States, with some 2,700 institutions of higher learning, ten universities receive one-fourth of all federal research and development money, and over two-thirds of the money goes to 100 universities and colleges. Anyone contemplating a research career must attend a major university for graduate training, since that is where the adequate laboratories and the leading researchers are to be found. The professors there also have much to say about placement of students in top jobs.

In spite of these powerful stratificational forces, however, stratification does not appear to be increasing over time (Blau and Duncan, 1967). It is about as easy for a son or daughter to move up (or down) now as it was a generation ago, and that pattern has persisted for many years (Rogoff, 1953).

Such studies focus on individual mobility. At the same time, a major form of mobility consists of the rise of whole occupations or classes in prestige or power, often as a result of major technological changes. For instance, recent vast changes in the computer industry and health-distribution systems have provided many people with more mobility opportunities than they ever dreamed of. On the other hand, persons in declining fields such as public school teaching and traditional clerical work (adding up figures, taking inventory, sending out bills) often find upward mobility to be virtually impossible. Whatever the actual opportunities, however, the United States continues to celebrate the possibility of moving up, even though mobility is no greater here than in most other industrialized countries.

Socialization

Recent interest in adult socialization (Kohn and Schooler, 1978) has sought to isolate those special features (outside of childhoood socialization) that affect the entry of persons into occupational and organizational roles. Those features can be described as four processes (Caplow, 1964). First, the new occupational recruit must acquire basic skills and abilities, either in school or on the job. Most on-the-job training is very inadequate, however, primarily because learning takes time away from job performance. Hence, many workers never learn their jobs very well. Especially critical in occupational training is learning tricks of the trade that can save a person from his or her own mistakes, or that save time or energy. In firefighting, for example, one learns not to look up when ascending a ladder (lest sparks or burning material get into one's eyes) and to put on one's helmet before buttoning one's coat (lest it fall off by accident while mounting the engine) (Matthews, 1950). Also important is learning the social skills needed to get along with other workers or with clients and customers. One learns what is considered a proper day's work, whom it is safe to talk to, and what one can talk about.

Second, occupational socialization teaches how to view oneself with a new self-image. Becker and Carper (1956) have shown how beginning physiology students gradually come to see themselves as budding scientists. Engineers, on the other hand, may come to see themselves as potential managers. Such self conceptions may be especially important in the arts and in sports. Third, as one moves up the occupational ladder, old involvements must be sacrificed and new ones acquired, which many people are not willing to do. Sometimes these shifts are enforced through drastic mortification processes, as in military academies, monasteries, or mental institutions (Goffman, 1957). Finally, one must discover how one's colleagues view the world and what is worth pursuing. Simpson (1967) has described how nurses shift from a lay conception of their job ("helping people") to a technical orientation. Instead of discussing the severity of a patient's suffering, they talk about the severity of his illness or the rarity of his disease. These matters are often highly subtle and are communicated indirectly.

The occupational socialization process is highly interwoven with the process of selecting new recruits. Many occupations seek to reduce the amount of required socialization by selecting persons who will be easy to socialize or who have already been socialized in other organizations. Many professions, for example, attempt to select entrants whose parents are professionals and, hence, have already taught them many professional values and norms. It is difficult to separate the effects of selection from socialization. Studies in prisons and universities and schools suggest that both processes always occur, although selection is more prevalent in prisons and socialization is important in universities and schools (Rosenbaum, 1976). Little is known about other occupations or organizations, however.

Colleague Groups and Controls

Much research has focused on how occupational behavior is controlled. A major technique is peer pressure by colleagues, but it requires identification with colleagues and, hence, is found most commonly in the professions and in the higher reaches of management. Building colleagueship involves the following three major processes: 1) Controlling the entry of new members and promoting occupational consciousness by developing an image of the occupation as a unique and exclusive purveyor of essential services. Such identification is often aided if members can be taught to believe they are under attack (e.g., chiropractors), or if they have deviant hours or life styles (jazz pianists, printers). 2) Forming informal associations and communities among the persons in an occupation. 3) Establishing norms or rules of the game to control competition among members, which has frequently been noted in studies of "restriction of output." These colleague controls can be upset as new workers enter a field, however, and programs such as affirmative action and other moves to equalize opportunity can completely overturn them. Yet, informal groups continue to perform many essential functions, including providing protection and assistance to members, communicating essential information, and controlling peer behavior.

As noted earlier, unions in the United States have tended to focus on wages and working conditions, eschewing the political goals of unions in other countries. After early opposition, labor unions in this country grew steadily—often with the aid of legislation—so that they now represent around one-fourth of the labor force, although that figure has not changed much in the last 25 years. Some attempts have recently been made to unionize white-collar workers, with middling success, and there have been notable advances among municipal employees, government workers, teachers, and even college and university faculties, as well as some initial attempts to unionize military personnel. The appeals of unionization remain strong, including grievance processes, the ability to strike for wage increases, cost-of-living escalator clauses in some contracts, and, for a few persons, new careers in the union movement. Unions are particularly strong in certain key industries—such as automaking, steel, and transportation—and strikes by those key unions can bring whole sectors of the economy to a halt. Unions will undoubtedly continue to be an important part of the occupational scene for the foreseeable future.

WHAT ARE WE DOING?

Our review of major research finding has pointed out powerful forces that sift and sort persons in their work careers. Some of them seem so powerful that one might despair of ever developing an effective applied occupational sociology. But a number of important efforts to control some of those forces are being undertaken.

Organizational Programs

First, the importance of large-scale organizations as work settings has been recognized and become the object of numerous training programs. Life in an organization means occupying a position in a hierarchy of authority. An important part of such training—one the job, in workshops, and at organizational retreats—therefore, deals with handling and adjusting to authority. In addition, attempts have been made to actually restructure organizations so as to make them more egalitarian.

Second, because an increasing number of persons are associating themselves with large organizations as protection against the vicissitudes of life, many occupations are almost disappearing into the maw of organizations. As a consequence, government programs have been introduced to protect workers' investments in pension programs and to provide legal recourse for persons claiming adverse or inequitable treatment by organizations.

Third, since the majority of persons in large organizations often do not experience their major friendships and intimate relationships at work (Dubin, 1956), many people in organizations are learning to handle one another in impersonal ways. This enables them to maintain effective role distance and to carry out relatively meaningless jobs with recognition that such work is temporary, or not an essential part of one's self.

Fourth, organizations are set up to reduce uncertainty by routinizing processes. Hence, socialization to work norms means learning to work by routine, and not to see such routine as an affront to one's dignity. Creative persons discover that only in organizations do they have the facilities and collaborators that are essential for the development of effective new ideas.

Finally, employees recognize that not all movement is upward, that there will be lateral shifts, and eventually, for most, downward drops. Organizations seek to manage demotion by creating special jobs, routing persons off to branches, "kicking persons upstairs," and similar techniques. Organizations find such practices highly functional, since younger persons on their way up are often concerned with how they will be treated as they grow older.

Expanding Professionalization

As noted previously, one of the fastest growing occupational categories is the professions. This is partly a functional response to societal needs, spurred by the growth of science and knowledge; but that hardly explains why nonscientific professions such as the ministry and law are also growing. And it only partly explains the growth of such professions as social work and accounting, in which professionalization takes the form of systematizing a body of practice that has grown up over a long period of time. Much of the trend toward expanding professionalization is a deliberate attempt by occupations to claim the mantle of professionalism because of its clear benefits. If an occupation validates its right to be called a profession, it becomes a monopoly in the public interest. The members acquire the right to label others incompetents or quacks, to regulate competition, and to control entry. They can set qualifications for recruits and standards for training and, hence, determine who their future colleagues will be. Professionals can control the price of their services and influence occupational work conditions through legislation.

To obtain such benefits, many occupations are strenuously pressing their claims to professional status. Would-be professions often rename themselves in the effort to upgrade their public image. Commercial artists, appraisers, landscape planners, highway officers, morticians, photographers, piano teachers, radio and television announcers, court reporters, travel agents, librarians, chiropractors, opticians, and public relations workers are all claiming that they offer an honorable self-denying service that deserves professional recognition and protection by legislation. As Wilensky (1964) has noted, however, only a small number of them will actually succeed, partly from public opposition and partly because the established professions resist allowing new ones to compete with them.

Manpower Planning and Training

As government constantly seeks to enlarge its role in directing the economic and social shape of society, it often attempts to affect occupational trends by influencing occupational choice, training, and the structure of job opportunities. In particular, much concern has focused on unemployment. An important controversy revolves about the two major approaches to reducing this problem. The structural approach maintains that unemployment can be reduced only if attention is given to the fact that a high proportion of the unemployed do not have sufficient education or the necessary training to fill available jobs. Workers often have to be relocated from depressed areas, or the areas themselves have to be rebuilt. The aggregate demand approach, in contrast, maintains that the basic problem is lack of sufficient consumer demand. Hence, what is needed are measures to increase demand such as a tax cut or a drop in interest rates. With an increase in demand, more opportunities for employment will open up, and industrial managers will be forced by labor shortages to hire persons lacking required skills and to provide whatever training they need. Recent events tend to support both positions to some extent, though the problem of "fine tuning" the economy seems to resist the valiant attempts of government advisors.

A major focus of training and placement programs has been blacks and other minorities, especially youths, among whom unemployment is especially high. In addition, special attempts are being made to reduce discrimination through civil rights legislation, through the Office of Contract Compliance, which oversees government contracts, and through strong affirmative action programs, which have required all recipients of federal funds to demonstrate progress in increasing minority employment (Levitan and Zickler, 1974).

Increasing Female Involvement in Work

As women have moved into employment they have met stiff resistance, particularly as they have sought more prestigious positions. But important efforts are being made to improve this situation. Barriers created by restrictive legislation are being attacked, and as of this writing a final attempt is being made to pass an Equal Rights Amendment to the U.S. Constitution. Much of this effort is being made by women themselves. Two obvious developments that have had major impacts on this struggle are the reduction in family size and the postponement of marriage. These trends have probably done more than anything else to increase the freedom of women to pursue occupational careers. Another important development has been the push for "part-time careers," or legitimizing part-time work on a regular basis, which has particular appeal to women with children. A related approach has been job sharing, in which one person fills a position in the morning or on certain days, and another person fills it in the afternoon or on other days. Many firms are also adopting "flexitime" as an attempt to reduce the commuter rush. This procedure requires all workers to be present during a specified period each day, such as from 10 to 3. Each person can then choose when to work the remaining three hours, so that her work day might be from 7 to 3, from 8 to 4, from 9 to 5, or from 10 to 6. Such flexibility allows women to make daycare arrangements more easily or adjust their schedules to those of their husbands.

Within large-scale organizations, the problems encountered by women are more serious, especially by those who seek executive positions. In the past most women were not even considered for these positions or were quickly passed over, on the tacit assumption that they would be unwilling to move to another city, or were tied to their husband's job. At the present time, however, the increased looseness of family ties, as well as shifts in managerial attitudes, are altering these practices, so that many promotion committees are beginning to seriously consider women for influential positions.

Changes in Approaches to Training and Counseling

Vocational guidance counselors and others concerned with training and counseling have been adopting new approaches that take seriously the nature of occupational careers. In the past, much counseling focused on providing occupational information and carrying out aptitude tests. Such work, while valuable, was often limited to the children of middle-class parents, who needed such information the least. New counseling approaches reach out to youths who are not in school and tend to be more realistic and social in nature. Jobs are increasingly analyzed not merely in terms of content, but also in terms of role relationships. For example, a counselor may draw up a chart listing the key persons whom job incumbents must satisfy, including those who evaluate their work, those who depend on it, and those on whom they depend for satisfactory job accomplishment. In a factory, these may include certain fellow workers, the foreman, workers in other shops, one's own supervisor, and perhaps a helper. In a restaurant, customers are a major element in this role set. In the professions, the chart will include clients, other professionals with whom one works directly, and all the members of that profession whom one regards as a reference group. This kind of role analysis was carried out by Kahn and his associates (1964) in a study of organizational stress. They found that role conflict was experienced by about one-half of all the workers surveyed.

Counselors are also becoming far more concerned with people's entire careers, particularly as large numbers of women between the ages 35 and 55 are returning to the labor force. It is now recognized that most persons will hold a succession of jobs during their lifetime. Consequently, the "fit" between a person's aptitudes and his or her first job should not be so tight that it incapacitates him or her from taking advantage of later job opportunities. Instead, socialization to a set of flexible work attitudes may be more functional for the individual. In addition, the traditional emphasis on skill preparation is undergoing searching reexamination. Since much training takes place on the job, the most enduring effects of vocational schools and even graduate or professional schools may lie in the values they inculcate, rather than the specific skills they transmit, many of which will be out of date before very long. Another related trend is the "new careers" movement (Pearl and Riessman, 1965). Its purpose is to supplement the efforts of professionals by providing aides to teachers, health professionals, lawyers, and many others. The new careers movement emphasizes the value of these aides to professionals and seeks to establish such positions as recognized occupations. It also encourages these aides, if they wish, to upgrade their position by taking further training and even professional education. Encouraging minority persons to enter such employment may be particularly beneficial both to them and to clients. A Chicano teacher's aide can relate more easily to a Chicano child who is having difficulty in school, can more easily gain entry into the child's community or family, and can act as an effective link between the child and the school.

Involvement of Workers

A final applied development is the current attempt to involve workers more directly in decision making and work planning. We shall not deal here with worker democracy programs, such as workers' councils in Yugoslavia, Germany, and Israel. Instead, we will focus on job redesign. In an effort to make dull work more interesting and meaningful, a variety of approaches have been tried (*Work in America*, 1973).

These new approaches include job rotation (moving a worker from one job position to another), job enlargement (grouping together several previously unrelated tasks), and job enrichment. The latter approach seeks to reverse the trend to minute division of labor, which in many cases has gone so far that jobs have become over fragmented. For example, a worker may be allowed to prepare his materials, set up his machine, repair output that is unsatisfactory, and perform simple repairs on the machine. In addition, a work group may plan the whole work operation, subject only to broad managerial guidelines or quotas. Such programs have attracted much public attention, but very few workers have had any real experience with them. Nevertheless, they represent a potential that may grow in the future. An example is the program at Indiana Bell Telephone for "humanizing" the dull task of preparing telephone directories. In the past, each worker performed a different task—one person noted the needed change (in address, number, etc.), a second person prepared the material, a third typed it or put it into the computer, and a fourth checked it for accuracy. Such work was subject to continuous errors that remained egregiously wrong for a whole year until the next directory came out. The company decided to assign all of the tasks involved in preparing a telephone directory for a small town to one person and to give her full responsibility for that directory. This procedure helped give workers a sense of responsibility and increased their interest and involvement in their work. Similar programs have been introduced into assembly lines in the Swedish Volvo and Saab-Scandia plants, with impressive achievements. Productivity goals have been met or exceeded, unplanned stoppages have been reduced, costs have been lowered, and workers have gained greater job variety and satisfaction, opportunities to learn new skills, and ability to cope with absences of others. The claimed results are often so impressive that one wonders why these experiments have not been more widely adopted.

WHAT HAVE WE ACCOMPLISHED?

The world of work is presently in a period of rapid transition, and the final outcomes of most of these efforts are not yet clear. A number of apparent results can be mentioned, however.

Role of Government in Work

Perhaps the most notable result is acceptance of governmental responsibility for overall direction of the work world. Although the United States still remains committed to employment through private enterprise, the government is no longer a mere arbiter or guarantor of contracts. It makes its own contracts, is a major employer, and actively regulates the shape of the occupational world. Although there is continued criticism of this government role, there seems to be no prospect that it will be reduced. Moreover, minority groups are increasingly insisting that pursuing their legitimate goals requires not simply competitive interaction in the marketplace, but also legislation and court action to further their interests.

Governmental Programs

General acceptance of the government role does not mean that all or even most of its programs are successful. We are currently in the midst of backlash from the promises and hopes of the Great Society and the War on Poverty of the

1960s and early 1970s. Having been promised so much, many persons have become disillusioned with the very slow progress that has been made. Yet such pessimism is surely a passing phase, for we are learning from our mistakes. For example, the New Careers movement has been, on the whole, a failure. As Ritzer (1977) notes, this was partly because its true motives were hidden. The primary goal of this program was to defuse a potentially explosive situation created by minority group revolts. Hence, its designers never expected much to come from it. Furthermore, the jobs given to indigenous persons often lacked serious content—teacher's aides sometimes merely tied children's shoelaces or took attendance. Nonprofessionals who sought to upgrade their skills often met opposition from the professionals involved, and frequently no training programs were established for them. Many professionals, faced with an army of indigenous helpers, felt that they were being forced to become administrators and to neglect their professional work. But in spite of this experience, the basic model has been established and seems to offer genuine possibilities. The New Careers concept seems to be an idea whose time has come.

Prospects of Deprofessionalization

Although the number of professionals is steadily increasing, and although many other occupations are seeking professional status, an opposing process is also occurring that may limit these trends. Haug and Sussman (1969) have pointed to several developments that are whittling away the authority of professionals. Clients have grown increasingly likely to question assumptions by professionals, especially when these clients are organized, as in the case of blacks, students, women, and industrial workers. Many professionals have suffered erosion of their job skills because of computerization and other innovations that make them more dependent on lower-ranking persons and make parts of their jobs more routine. Many of the intangible aspects of professional practice (a bedside manner, or a winning personality) are frequently also possessed by paraprofessionals and aides —sometimes to a greater degree than by professionals. Clients have also become more sophisticated consumers and have acquired advocates to represent their interests, as witnessed in the rash of malpractice suits and other legal actions against professions that have emerged in recent years. Finally, much professional practice now takes place in large organizations, where professionals must justify their claims before the searching demands of hierarchical superiors as well as fellow professionals. Professionalization goes on, but many traditional professions are experiencing routinization and loss of functions in their work.

Strains in Occupational Autonomy

All occupations seek autonomy in order to increase the power of their members. The professions have been the most successful in exploiting their position, but craft workers, managers, proprietors, and salespersons are also seeking greater autonomy, and they have secured some measure of it. At the same time, many occupations have experienced increasing pressures in recent years to serve society and clients more adequately. These pressures come from the setting of work in large organizations, from organized and well-educated clients, from other occupations, from consumer movements, and from legislative action.

In centers designed to help youth and others—such as the Youth Opportunity Centers in the recent past and the CETA (Comprehensive Employment and Training Act) program at present—large proportions of the clients are blacks, Puerto Ricans, Native Americans, migrants, and other distinct groups. The bureaucratic governmental approach does not relate well to them. They are highly suspicious of such institutions, and "explanations" of unemployment in terms of "automation" or other broad social processes are regarded as dodges, especially when they are rejected for jobs for which they feel qualified. Many clients perceive the counselor as a policeman, as "Charley," rather than a person who can be helpful. In many cases, the claims of counselors that they can be trusted turn out to be illusory when their files are subpoenaed by the courts and confessions of crimes are brought to light. In many cases, simply getting to the client requires active community intervention, which is an activity for which counselors, psychologists, psychiatrists, and similar professionals are not trained. Clients may also be organized or represented in class-action suits by activist attorneys. As a result, occupations find themselves in antagonistic roles vis-a-vis one another, with consequent increasing sensitivity of occupations to interoccupational relations and the emergence of interoccupational politics.

Fate of Minorities

The work world is a major arena in which many minority groups—blacks, women, Chicanos, Latinos, Native Americans—seek to improve their lot in society. While gains in the work world do not necessarily lend to improved opportunities in education, housing, civil rights, and politics, they are important goals in their own right and often do reflect improvements in other areas. Yet, it is very difficult to sum up the results of these efforts, since they vary enormously. Blacks pioneered in tactics of civil disobedience and protective legislation, whereas women and Native Americans have only become active rather recently.

Although women might be expected to encounter few obstacles, compared to the deep-seated prejudice faced by blacks and others, their gains have not been impressive. Women experience many special problems related to work. For example, it is estimated that one in seven families is now headed by a woman (Johnson, 1978), and half of these women are in the labor force. Such families are more likely than two-adult families to have children under age 18 and to have very low incomes. In 1976, one-third of those families was living below the officially defined poverty level, compared to only 6 percent of intact families. The income differential between men and women also appears to be increasing. In 1955 women's wages were 64 percent of men's; by 1969 they had dropped to 60.5 percent (Katzell and Byham, 1972); and by 1975 the gap had increased further to 57 percent. Although many more women are now working, they are more likely than men to be employed in lower paying, labor-intensive industries in service or clerical jobs (*Women Today,* 1975:5).

The situation for Native Americans is perhaps too early to assess, especially since they appear to be using different approaches than other minorities, such as a search for land rights, treaty rights, and fishing quotas.

Among blacks the situation is hard to measure because it is mixed. At the risk of some oversimplification, we can summarize the main findings as follows. The overall picture of black economic advance is impressive. The median income of black males is now 73 percent of white males, and for black females it is practically equal to white females, regardless of whether they work part time or full time. Blacks are moving rapidly into both the professions and many crafts, and these gains did not erode during the recession of the early 1970s. Especially impressive are the gains made by black women. In fact, Freeman (1978) states that the main obstacle black women face in the job market is now gender rather than racial discrimination. These gains are not equally distributed among blacks, however. The major gains have been made by better educated and more qualified blacks and by those from more advantaged family backgrounds. A study using 1962 data (Freeman, 1978) found that parents played only a minor role in black economic achievement. If one was black, the socioeconomic status of one's parents did not matter much; all blacks encountered discrimination in the labor market. This has recently changed, however, so that parental socioeconomic status now does influence job attainment among blacks. As a result, blacks from low status homes are now particularly likely to suffer in the job market, so that their experience is almost opposite to their more fortunate brothers and sisters. Overall, job market discrimination has declined, but this has benefitted young blacks from deprived families very little. More importantly, the burden falls especially heavily on older blacks who are experienceing not only whatever discrimination currently remains, but also the effects of past differential treatment. In addition to large wage differentials, they are experiencing an actual decline in labor force participation. One implication of this fact is that merely ending discrimination will not bring job and income parity as long as family background continues to affect opportunities. In this sense, blacks now face many of the same problems as whites from poor family backgrounds, though much more severely.

Meaningful Work

Lastly, we can ask whether the recent attempts to humanize work have been successful, or are likely to be so in the future. In this realm we face an exaggeration of expectations. Enthusiastic writings and careless use of the term "experiment" have given a false picture of actual experience. Many of the positive effects of these efforts can be attributed not to increased humanization, but to tighter control by peer pressure (Tausky, 1978:104ff). When workers are told they can organize their work "as they please," this is often an invitation for the more persuasive and domineering among them to take over. Bureaucratic work situations often provide protections for individuals from arbitrary decisions, such as grievance procedures and unions. But when one is faced with strong peer pressures, it is more difficult to resist. For instance, a person may be more hesitant to be late for work because his peers will pour out their scorn on him. When workers are given responsibility for a whole job (such as compiling a telephone directory), they may experience increased pride. But it is also much easier to check up on who is responsible for any errors that do occur. Hence, it is not surprising that such persons experience both a greater sense of responsibility and a greater feeling of stress. And in many cases, gains in productivity have resulted in the all-too-obvious solution of laying off workers.

On the whole, as Strauss (1974) points out, most studies in this area have extolled these "experiments" rather than carefully evaluating them. Most such efforts in the United States have occurred in small, nonunion plants, have involved careful selection of participants, and have received much favorable publicity. Nevertheless, turnover and absenteeism do seem to decline, and work quality (when measured) does seem to increase. The results are quite mixed in regard to amount of production, and worker motivation does not appear to be affected. Some workers do benefit from these programs, but they are less appealing to workers concerned mainly with income or other instrumental needs. There is no question that increasing numbers of workers want more challenging and interesting work. But the long arm of the wage remains, and challenging work does not appeal to many people unless it also pays well. In fact, if workers are given more challenging work or more responsibility, a frequent and predictable consequence is that they will demand and expect more money.

WHERE ARE WE GOING?

Work remains the main preoccupation of most persons. It ties individuals into society, as Freud pointed out long ago, and it remains the major way in which people seek a dignified and satisfying life. Experiments will go on, but so will work—we are in no danger of being superceded by robots. The study of work will continue to provide a revealing insight into how well society is functioning and how well persons live.

REFERENCES AND SUGGESTED READINGS

Becker, Howard S. and James W. Carper. 1956. "The Development of Identification with an Occupation." *American Journal of Sociology* 61:289–98.

*Bell, Daniel. 1973. *The Coming of Post-Industrial Society*. New York: Basic Books.

Bell presents a sophisticated and well-documented argument that the United States (and presumably other industrial societies) is changing into a "service"-oriented society, dominated by a technological intelligentsia.

Blaxall, Martha and Barbara R. Reagan, eds. 1976. *Women and the Workplace: The implications of Occupational Segregation.* Chicago: University of Chicago Press.

Blau, Francine D. 1975. "Women in the Labor Force: An Overview." In *Women: A Feminist Perspective,* edited by Jo Freeman. Palo Alto, Calif.: Mayfield.

*Blau, Peter M. and Otis Dudley Duncan. 1967. *The American Occupational Structure.* New York: John Wiley & Sons.

This is the definitive work on the structure of U.S. occupations. It focuses on the national society rather than on particular occupations, and attempts to shed light on trends in occupational mobility and social stratification. A major finding is that the effects of education can be separated from those of parental status.

Broom, Leonard and Robert G. Cushing. 1977. "A Modest Test of an Immodest Theory: The Functional Theory of Stratification." *American Sociological Review* 42:157–69.

Caplow, Theodore. 1964. *Principles of Organization.* New York: Harcourt Brace Jovanovich.

Dubin, Robert. 1956. "Industrial Workers' Worlds: A Study of the Central-Life Interests' of Industrial Workers." *Social Problems* 3:131–42.

Epstein, Cynthia F. 1970. *Woman's Place Options and Limits in Professional Careers.* Berkeley: University of California Press.

Freeman, Richard. 1978. "Black Economic Progress Since 1964." *The Public Interest* 52:52–68.

Galenson, Marjorie. 1973. *Women and Work: An International Comparison.* Ithaca, N.Y.: Cornell University Press.

Goffman, Erving. 1957. "The Characteristics of Total Institutions." In *Symposium on Preventive and Social Psychiatry,* pp. 43–84. Washington, D.C.: Walter Reed Army Institute of Research.

Gross, Edward. 1968. "Plua Ca Change...? The Sexual Structure of Occupations Over Time." *Social Problems* 16:198–208.

_____. 1981. "Interuniversity Systems: Problems in the Control of Competition Among Educational Institutions in Australia." In *The Sociology of Higher Education: The Australian Experience,* edited by Edward Gross and John Western. Brisbane, Australia: University of Queensland Press, in press.

Haug, Marie and Marvin Sussman. 1969. "Professional Autonomy and the Revolt of the Client." *Social Problems* 17:153–61.

Hodge, Robert W., Paul M. Siegel, and Peter H. Rossi. 1964. "Occupational Prestige in the United States, 1925–63." *American Journal of Sociology* LXX (Nov):290–92.

Inkeles, Alex and Peter H. Rossi. 1956. "National Comparisons of Occupational Prestige." *American Journal of Sociology* 61:329–39.

Johnson, Beverly L. 1978. "Women who head families: their numbers rise, income lags." *Monthly Labor Review* 101:32–37.

Kahn, R.L., D.M. Wolfe, R.P. Wuinn, J.D. Snoek, and R.E. Rosenthal. 1964. *Organizational Stress: Studies in Role Conflict and Ambiguity.* New York: John Wiley & Sons.

*Kanter, Rosabeth Moss. 1977. *Men and Women of the Corporation.* New York: Basic Books.

Kanter provides a major contribution to understanding the careers of women (and other minority groups) in large-scale organizations. The author shows that structural constraints (opportunity, power, and "numbers") account for much of the behavior of women (and men) in subordinate positions.

Katzell, M.E. and W.C. Byham. 1972. *Women and the Work Force.* New York: Behavioral Publications.

Kohn, Melvin L. and Carmi Schooler. 1978. "The Reciprocal Effects of the Substantive Complexity of Work and Intellectual Flexibility: A Longitudinal Assessment." *American Journal of Sociology* 84:24–52.

Levitan, Sar A. and Joyce K. Zickler. 1974. *The Quest for a Federal Manpower Partnership.* Cambridge, Mass.: Harvard University Press.

Mathews, T.J. 1950. *The Urban Fire Station: A Sociological Analysis of an Occupation.* Unpublished M.A. thesis, Department of Sociology, Washington State University, Pullman.

Meara, Hannah. 1974. "Honor in Dirty Work: The Case of American Meat Cutters and Turkish Butchers." *Sociology of Work and Occupations* 1:259–83.

Pearl, A. and F. Riessman. 1965. *New Careers for the Poor.* New York: John Wiley & Sons.

Reiss, Albert J. 1961. *Occupations and Social Status.* New York: The Free Press.

Rist, Ray C. 1970. "Student Social Class and Teacher Expectations: The Self-Fulfilling Prophecy in Ghetto Education." *Harvard Educational Review* 41:411–51.

*Ritzer, George. 1977. *Working.* Englewood Cliffs, N.J.: Prentice-Hall.

An up-to-date, carefully referenced statement of present research on the sociology of occupations. The author does not hesitate to state his own views on controversial issues, providing for lively debate and a stimulating treatment of the literature.

Robertson, Wyndham. 1978. "The Top Women in Big Business." *Fortune,* July 17, 1978, pp. 56–62.

Rogoff, N. 1953. *Recent Trends in Occupational Mobility.* Glencoe, Ill.: Free Press.

Rosenbaum, James E. 1976. *Making Inequality: The Hidden Curriculum of Tracking.* New York: John Wiley & Sons.

Simmons, Adele, and others. 1975. *Exploitation From 9 to 5.* Lexington, Mass.: Lexington Books.

Simpson, I.H. 1967. "Patterns of Socialization into the Professions: the case of student nurses." *Sociological Inquiry* 37:47–53.

Spradley, James P. and Brenda J. Mann. 1975. *The Cocktail Waitress: Woman's Work in a Man's World.* New York: John Wiley & Sons.

Strauss, George. 1974. "Job Satisfaction, Motivation, and Job Redesign." In *Organizational Behavior: Research and Issues,* edited by Arnold S. Tannenbaum, George Strauss, Raymond E. Miles, and Charles C. Snow, pp. 66–86. Madison, Wis.: Industrial Relations Research Association.

*Tausky, Curt. 1978. *Work Organizations: Major Theoretical Prospectives.* Itasca, Ill.: F.E. Peacock.

This is a brief and well-written introduction to organizations as settings within which occupations are practiced. It is particularly useful for its readable treatment of competing theories and for a critique of "putting meaning into work" experiments.

Waldman, Elizabeth and Beverly J. McEaddy. 1974. "Where Women Work—An Analysis by Industry and Occupation." *Monthly Labor Review* 97:3–13.

Wattenberg, Ben J. and R.M. Scammon. 1973. "Black Progress and Liberal Rhetoric." *Commentary* 55:35–44.

Wilensky, Harold L. 1964. "The Professionalization of Everyone?" *American Journal of Sociology* 70:137–58.

Women Today. 1975. November 24, 1975.

Work in America. 1973. Cambridge, Mass.: M.I.T. Press.

14 GENDER ROLES

Judy Corder-Bolz

"I am free. I make decisions and act based on my best judgment, and I am judged by my performance. The fact that I am a woman (or a man) has little bearing on the course I take in life. Twenty years ago people were much more restricted by their gender, but things are different now."

To the individual who might make such a statement, a sociologist might reply: "Yes, in some respects things are different. Old roles and expectations are being broken down and new ones swiftly created. Our femaleness or maleness and the roles our society attributes to males and females (gender roles) will, however, have a profound effect on the course of our lives."

Research in the social sciences has advanced a growing recognition that gender roles are an important influence in most aspects of human life. This chapter will examine the advances in applied sociology that are relevant to gender roles in this society; the first step in the examination involves discussion of some of the problems that are currently being addressed.

WHAT ARE THE PROBLEMS?

What problems do gender roles create for individuals? Before we explore these, it should be noted that our knowledge about many aspects of gender roles is quite spotty. Some areas have been well researched, while others have not been addressed at all. In applied sociology, as in all of the social sciences, research programs are not only influenced by the interests of social scientists, but are also greatly affected by the availability of government or private funding. Among social scientists, there is an increasing awareness that gender has rarely been given adequate attention in their research. In addition, the recent resurgence of the women's movement has heightened public awareness of the pervasive effects of gender-role typing. This awareness has led to federal legislation against discrimination on the basis of sex, especially in education and employment.

Applied sociology is now treating numerous issues related to gender roles, which range from broad institutional and societal topics to individualistic, psychological problems. It would be impossible to outline all of these issues in an entire book, much less one chapter, but we can attempt to convey some idea of their variety. The following list itemizes a few of the problem areas currently being addressed by applied sociologists which will *not* be included here. It begins with individual psychological issues and progresses to institutional and societal issues.

At the individual end of the spectrum, major gender-role problems being addressed in applied sociology include:

1. Causes and effects of *anxiety about mathematics* (more frequently found in women than in men) and ways of reducing this anxiety so as to open many formerly inaccessible occupations to women.
2. Relationship of gender roles to *self-concepts* and the impact of strategies such as assertiveness training and competency building on this relationship.
3. Relationship of gender roles to treatment and outcome during *psychological* therapy.
4. *Effects of mass media,* especially television, on the development of gender-role attitudes.
5. Relationship of gender roles and occupational stress to the differential in *male/female life expectancy.*
6. *Double standard of aging* with respect to gender roles and its relationship to psychological health.
7. Relationship of gender roles and gender-role attitudes to *teenage pregnancy.*

At the institutional, societal end of the spectrum, some of the major gender-role problems currently being addressed in applied sociology include:

1. Discrimination in *obtaining credit* on the basis of gender.
2. Economic impact of *dual-worker* families.
3. Gender roles and the increase in *women's crimes.*
4. The problem of sex-differential treatment in *juvenile, civil, criminal, and family court cases.*
5. Sex-differential treatment in the *military.*
6. Problems of women in *the ministry* and the relationship of organized religion to definitions of gender roles.
7. Differences in *political participation* of males and females, both in the voting process and in public office.

This chapter examines gender-role problems in three major areas: education, employment, and the family. It discusses what is known, what is being done, and what has been done; it also suggests some possible future directions.

Education

In education, three gender-role problems of particular concern to applied sociologists are 1) gender-role stereotypes in textbooks, 2) the effects of two structural features in schools—the delegation of authority and operational methods—on perpetuating gender-role stereotypes, and 3) gender-stereotypic career and vocational counseling.

Education contributes to the perpetuation of gender roles portrayed in textbooks and other course materials and frequently encourages stereotypic gender attitudes (Saario, Jacklin, and Tittle, 1973). For instance, women in textbooks are typically portrayed as passive, dependent, warm, caring, and enacting home-related roles. Men, on the other hand, are portrayed as aggressive, independent, active, and not enacting home-related roles. Women are also underrepresented in most books. Although these textbook stereotypes may not be overwhelmingly significant in themselves, they can be important in reinforcing similar messages from other sources.

A number of structural features in public education contribute to the formation of gender-role attitudes in children. Two of these are discussed herein. One such structuralistic feature is evident in the differential delegation of authority in schools: in elementary schools, most teachers are female (83 percent) and most principals are male (80 percent) (U.S. Equal Employment Opportunity Commission, 1977). The male is, therefore, the dominant authority figure, the individual with ultimate authority in the enforcement of school rules. In secondary schools, an even higher proportion of principals are male (89 percent), although teachers are about equally male and female (46 percent are female) (U.S. Equal Employment Opportunity Commission, 1977). However, department heads are more likely to be male, except in traditionally female-dominated areas such as home economics.

The second structural feature in schools of concern here is inherent in its methods of operation. Behavioral requirements, specific learning methods, and kinds of skills taught are unfavorable to males, especially in elementary education. On the average, it is more difficult for boys than for girls to sit still and remain quiet. Boys are, thus, more likely to be labeled as discipline problems. Reading, writing, and spelling are the focus of learning activities in elementary grades; and the emphasis is on learning by manipulating verbal symbols. Boys often learn better, however, from visual information and experimentation rather than from such manipulation, and are, therefore, at a relative disadvantage with respect to fine motor coordination. As a result, boys fill remedial reading classes, don't learn to spell, and are classified as dyslexic or learning disabled four times more often than girls.

Boys are nine times more likely than girls to be labeled hyperactive, even though they may be just distractable and disruptive and not unusually active (McGuinness, 1979).

Schools reinforce gender-role stereotypes, and sex discrimination in education has an important impact on future employment via gender-stereotypic career and vocational counseling in schools. Females are often encouraged to prepare for jobs typically held by women (which are thought to combine well with family responsibilities) and discouraged from preparing for jobs typically held by males. Women's aptitudes and interests are, thus, translated into traditional "female" job orientations. Conversely, males are encouraged to prepare for jobs typically held by men (with no consideration of how such jobs might affect family responsibilities), and their aptitudes and interests are translated into "male" job orientations (Vetter, 1978). Thus, both males and females may be channeled away from jobs for which they are suited in terms of aptitude and interest. Males are sometimes steered away from jobs for which they are suited either because women generally hold these jobs and/or because the economic rewards associated with these jobs are considered inadequate to support a family. For example, males may be ridiculed for being interested in elementary teaching or nursing. And no male is allowed to consider not working and being supported by someone else. On the other hand, females are often steered into less lucrative and prestigious careers, e.g., becoming a nurse rather than a physician.

The principal challenge in education is how to change educational institutions, practices, and materials to eliminate gender-role stereotypes and offer male and female students equal educational experiences.

Employment

Regarding employment, three closely interrelated issues in applied sociology have been selected for this chapter: 1) the dual male/female labor market, 2) the male/female income differences in the labor market, and 3) the impact of affirmative action on employment and income patterns.

As referred to above, gender differences in career and vocational counseling and educational attainment contribute to the perpetuation of a dual male/female labor force. Some jobs are held almost entirely by males and others almost entirely by females. For example, 79 percent of all clerical workers in 1977 were female, but only 5 percent of all craft workers were female; 78 percent of all nonfarm managers and administrators were male, but only 38 percent of retail sales workers were male (U.S. Department of Labor, 1976). Recent data on the occupational aspirations of adolescents indicate that the dual nature of the labor force is likely to continue because most adolescents aspire and expect to attain jobs that are usually held by persons of their own sex (Tully, et al., 1978; Rosen and Aneshensel, 1978; Corder-Bolz and Stephan, 1979). This separation has a number of problematic consequences. First, men and women tend to be restricted in their choice of jobs because of what is considered appropriate for each gender. Second, women continue to be concentrated in lower-status and lower-paying jobs than men, perpetuating male/female income differences.

The dual labor force is not the only factor contributing to male/female differences in income. Females typically earn less than males, even when men and women have the same job. On the average, a fully-employed woman with a high school degree earns less money than a fully-employed man who has not completed elementary school (U.S. Department of Labor, 1976a). Recent data also indicate that in most occupations this income differential has been widening since 1960. The ratio of female to male earnings has actually declined during this period (Burstein, 1979; U.S. Bureau of the Census, 1979). These differences in income were a major factor in leading the Women's Bureau of the U.S. Department of Labor to conclude: "Poverty is a woman's issue. It has become a woman's issue because increasing proportions of women live at or below the poverty level, and because child care responsibilities, lack of training for well-paid jobs, and discrimination hinder women's efforts to become economically self-sufficient" (1978a). These income differentials also mean that total family income for dual-worker families is less than it might otherwise be, thus keeping their standard of living lower than if a wife earned as much as her husband in a similar job. Finally, these income differentials violate a norm of fairness in our society that individuals who do the same work should get the same pay.

In the United States, a considerable amount of recent legislation has been aimed at making equal pay for equal work a reality. From these legislative efforts to eliminate sex and race discrimination in employment and resultant governmental programs, the concept of "affirmative action" has slowly evolved. Affirmative action is positive action to remove "artificial, arbitrary, and unnecessary barriers to employment when the barriers operate invidiously to discriminate on the basis of racial and other impermissible classifications" (Hall and Albrecht, 1979). Some of this action has been court ordered, some voluntary. The opposite side of this coin is the concept of reverse discrimination, which refers to affirmative actions that seek to favor a group formerly discriminated against. Litigation based on both concepts—affirmative action and reverse discrimination—has been undertaken, and judicial decisions favoring both concepts have been upheld.

Recent data from the U.S. Department of Labor and the Bureau of the Census indicate that affirmative action programs have not been effective in the sense that, since their inception, females have lost ground to males in terms of both income and entry into male-dominated occupations (Burstein, 1979; U.S. Bureau of the Census, 1979). Since affirmative action programs are intended to ensure equal employment opportunities and equal pay for equal work, the problems inherent in their failure are the same as those inherent in the dual male/female labor force and in male/female differences in income.

Thus, the main objectives in employment should be to eliminate the dual labor force and to ensure equal pay for equal work through successful affirmative action and similar programs.

Family

Because of the family's relationship to other institutions—especially work—two of the three issues to be discussed here deal with the link between family and work: 1) the effects of family/work arrangements on the mental health and satisfaction of both males and females, and 2) the problems of dual-worker families. The third issue deals with the differential impact of divorce on males and females in terms of economic issues and child custody.

As more and more women enter the labor force, concomitant interest in the relationship between work and the family continues to grow. In the past it was usually assumed that women were responsible for the family and men for work outside the home; these two institutions were viewed as different worlds with little overlap, so that little attention was accorded their interrelationships. In recent years, however, rapid increase in the number of two-worker families (especially those with children at home) and in the number of divorces (creating more single-parent families) have led to a concern about the family in relation to employment and economic security.

In 1963 Betty Friedan's book *The Feminine Mystique* suggested the possibility that being a housewife might not be the most satisfying kind of life for all women. Since then, feminist attention to female work roles has led to the claim that the women's movement devalues the housewife role. Consequently, in recent years a number of empirical studies have compared the marital satisfaction and general mental health of women who work outside the home with those who do not, and many popular articles and books have also discussed this topic (e.g., Bernard, 1972; Glenn, 1975; Ferree, 1976; Fidell and Prather, 1976). Generally, this research has focused on problems related to the roles of housewife versus employed wife, particularly on the mental health of wives, the differential marital satisfaction of husbands and wives, and the well-being of children, as these relate to both role situations.

Much of the literature on the role of the housewife compares and contrasts these women with those employed outside the home, while the literature on dual-worker families is, instead, singularly addressed to the problems and advantages of this rapidly increasing nontraditional family structure. These latter studies include such topics as managing child care, handling domestic necessities, changes in the division of household labor (or the lack of them), and changes in decision-making processes in the family. For example, how do dual-worker families make decisions about moving when two careers must be considered, or how do couples decide who leaves work to take care of a family emergency? In general, applied sociologists studying this area are seeking to discover how the family can best be changed to accommodate the needs of dual-worker couples.

Another family issue involves the impact of increasing divorce rates. A critical problem in this area is how to provide economic security for women who have been housewives all their lives, who, after divorce, are left in middle age with no husband to support them and no marketable skills with which to support themselves. Such women are referred to as "displaced homemakers." Questions are also being raised about the award of child support and alimony. Formerly, alimony and child support were paid by males; these responsibilities had been chiefly delegated to men not only because the husband was more likely to be employed and paid a better salary, but also because it was customary for the wife to be awarded custody of the children. Men are now questioning this almost automatic award of child custody to women.

Thus, the main problems in the area of gender roles and the family concern reducing strains on the family produced by societal gender-role definitions, dual employment, and gender-role bias in decisions and outcomes related to divorce. The following section will summarize major research findings on each of the problems identified in the preceding paragraphs.

WHAT DO WE KNOW?

Education

By now there is thorough documentation that many of the books read by pre-school children, as well as the textbooks used in schools (including college) underrepresent females and present stereotypic images of males and females (Weitzman, Eifler, Hokada, and Ross, 1972; Saario, et al., 1973; Women on Words and Images, 1972). Other studies have emphasized that in many books—especially in high school and college texts—women's contributions to society are either treated superficially, or ignored, particularly in history and government texts (MacLeod and Silverman, 1973; Trecker, 1974). The point made by many researchers is that the images portrayed in most of these books do not reflect reality (Saario, et al., 1973). All females are not docile, perpetually cheerful housewives, and all males are not aggressive, unemotional workers. This narrow view of reality can limit the possibilities that children perceive for themselves and may well create unrealistic expectations for themselves and others based on stereotypes of what males and females are like.

The evidence concerning the impact of stereotypic textbooks is less convincing. Generally, it is assumed that children give special weight to things they read in textbooks, and that the texts provide one additional piece of stereotypic information. Although documentation of this is limited, some studies suggest that these assumptions are accurate. For example, Schneider and Hacker (1973) found that, for the majority of college students in their study, the term "man" meant "male" and not "human being."

With regard to gender-role stereotypes being perpetuated by the structure of the school, existing data are primarily inferential. The fact that males usually hold major authority positions in schools is well documented. And Gross and Trask (1976) found that there were significant differences in the career patterns of male and female school administrators. These differential roles of men and women in the school structure provide information about gender roles for children seeking to learn what it means to be male or female (Kohlberg, 1966; Maccoby and Jacklin, 1974). In addition, research indicates that such role models are important, especially for females who aspire to nontraditional occupations. Models of females in authority positions are often missing in schools, including most colleges (Astin, 1967; Almquist and Angrist, 1970, 1971; Tangri, 1972). This means, too, that males have few role models if they choose to become elementary school teachers or pursue some other line of work in which they would work with small children.

There has been a great deal of research on the impact of school structure on male and female students. In one of the earliest studies of this kind, Meyer and Thompson (1956) found that males were reprimanded more than females. Sears and Feldman (1966), however, reviewed the available literature and concluded that, while males are reprimanded more than females, they also receive more positive attention. The research data show that girls typically do better in school than boys, in part because they are more conforming and in part because the structure of the elementary classroom is more developmentally suited for girls than for boys (Torrence, 1965; McGuinness, 1979). On the other hand, school structure tends to stifle creativity in females and does not provide the developmental help they need to excel in mathematics (Torrence, 1965; McGuinness, 1979). Recently, the focus of research in this area has been on the desirability of a flexible structure that maximizes the chances of all students to develop to their fullest potential.

Career and vocational counseling is another important way in which education helps perpetuate traditional gender roles. As early as the second grade, and continuing through college, males and females aspire to and expect to attain different kinds of occupations (Almquist and Angrist, 1971; Tully, et al., 1976; Corder-Bolz, 1979). Males aspire to jobs typically held by men, and females to jobs that women usually hold. Males and females also have different expectations about the necessity of work in their future. Males are much more likely than females to expect to work at a job all their lives, yet the data show that nine out of ten females will also work during their lifetimes—mostly out of economic necessity (U.S. Department of Labor, 1976). Research data reveal that guidance counselors and interest inventories often reinforce stereotypic expectations about jobs and work, even though such expectations may not be realistic or may have adverse consequences for one's future financial security (Tittle, 1974; Vetter, 1978). The practice in many high schools and vocational schools of forbidding or discouraging females from taking male-dominated industrial arts classes means that females are rather effectively banned from many lucrative skilled trades (Roby, 1976; MacManus, 1977; Schenk, 1977). The vocational counseling and guidance process also often fails to give adequate consideration to individual differences, in values, motivation, interests, and skills. For example, there are numerous examples of adolescent females being channeled into nursing or bookkeeping rather than accounting and medicine because the former careers are considered appropriate for females. Yet, an individual female may well be sufficiently motivated, interested, and able to become a doctor or an accountant. Males also tend to be excluded from some occupations through the same processes. They are discouraged from taking such courses as office practices, home economics, and child care and development. Counselors tend to push males who are interested in medicine toward medical school even if their talents and interests (including feelings about educational investments) indicate that nursing school would be more appropriate.

Through these processes, both males and females are consistently channeled in directions that tend to perpetuate gender differences and inequality in employment.

Employment

Available data show that the dual nature of the labor force is changing very little. This is not surprising when one examines other relevant data on factors affecting entry into the labor force. As mentioned previously, adolescents aspire to and expect to have jobs generally held by people of their own gender. The career and vocational counseling and guidance process reinforces this tendency. There have been some recent changes, but these tend to be in the direction of males entering traditionally female-dominated occupations. For example, males now constitute 52 percent of all secondary teachers, and their numbers are increasing in the fields of social work, nursing, and library science. With these few exceptions, the pertinent data indicate that the dual nature of the labor force will in all likelihood continue (Gottfredson, 1978).

Differences in pay for males and females are in part due to the continued existence of the dual labor force. Women are concentrated in the lower-status, lower-paying jobs within each general occupational category. For example, in the professional category, males are doctors and lawyers, while females are teachers and nurses. In the sales category, males are in wholesale and manufacturing sales, while females are in retail sales (which is much less lucrative work). Male/female wage differentials for individuals employed in the same job also persist (Burstein, 1979; U.S. Bureau of the Census, 1979). In 1974 women who worked year-round at full-time jobs earned only 57 cents for every dollar earned by men. This is in part due to the dual labor force (U.S. Department of Labor, 1976). The remaining wage differentials cannot be entirely attributed to individual worker characteristics such as age, education, and work experience, however, Consequently, Almquist (1977) concluded that employer discrimination must also be an important factor. A wealth of data suggests various factors that might lead an employer to discriminate against female employees: 1) many male managers hold attitudes that impede female employees' success (Bass, Krusel, and Alexander, 1979; Tully, et al., 1978), 2) women are often excluded from informal networks that enhance a worker's probability of success (Albrecht, 1976), 3) commonly held stereotypic attitudes about women (e.g., that women are not free to travel) lead to assumptions that exclude women from opportunities to succeed (Tully, et al., 1978; Gordon and Strober, 1975), 4) the different management styles of men and women tend to be detrimental to the success of women (Gordon and Strober, 1975), and 5) men do not like to interact with competent women (Hagen and Kahn, 1975).

Since both the dual labor market and differential income for males and females are prime targets of affirmative action, the data concerning these problems also explain the overall failure of affirmative action programs nationwide. Some kinds of progress, however, have been made. For example, the proportion of women in accounting, public administration, and law is increasing, as is the proportion of men in nursing, library science, social work, and elementary education. But even with these changes, employed women in the United States are, on the average, experiencing greater income differentials (U.S. Bureau of the Census, 1979). Even in the federal civil service—the primary enforcer of affirmative action—income inequality between men and women still exists (Taylor, 1979). Questions are now being raised about why affirmative action is not working and what can be done to make it more effective (Burstein, 1979; Hall and Albrecht, 1979).

Family

Traditional sociological literature on the family has largely ignored the noneconomic role of the father and the economic role of the mother in the family. More attention is now being given, however, to the work role for women and the parent role for men. For example, Jessie Bernard (1972) suggested in *The Future of Marriage* that being a housewife is not an ideal role and can literally "make women sick." Since the publication of that book, a number of other studies have compared wives who work outside the home with those who do not. For example, University of Oregon researchers found that housewives have a 50 percent greater chance of contracting cancer than women in general and twice the chance of working women (*Wall Street Journal,* 1978a). Also, Ferree (1976) found that working-class women with jobs are happier and feel more competent than working-class housewives. However, when Fidell and Prather (1976) studied working-class, middle-class, and upper-middle-class wives who did and did not work outside the home, they found that the happiness of a housewife varies according to circumstances. Upper-middle-class housewives were the happiest and healthiest, while working-class women who wanted to work but were unemployed were the least happy and healthy.

Increasingly, research is also examining the physical and psychological costs to males who must be the sole support of their families. For example, Harrison (1978) argues that growing differentials in life expectancy between men and women in the United States are at least in part related to strains inherent in the male role: the drive to be successful in a job, the imperative to provide economic security for a family, the need to be unemotional, etc. More and more attention is now being given to the effects of the father's work on the children and on marital satisfaction, such as the costs of rigidly defined male gender roles and job demands that limit the amount of time men spend with their wives and children (Polatnick, 1975; Pleck, 1976).

As an outgrowth of these studies, some writers (Bernard, 1972; Scanzoni, 1972; Harrison, 1978) have concluded the family provider and domestic family roles should be shared by both partners, and that both of these roles need redefinition (Pleck, 1976).

At present, a great deal is being written about the two-worker family, which is becoming more and more common (Hayghe, 1976). This literature deals with various kinds of stress encountered by such families, especially with regard to managing a household and providing child care. Lack of adequate daycare and after-school care for children is a major problem, and parents are usually compelled to devise their own solutions. But even the best solution can fail in the event of an emergency involving either the child or the caretaker.

Much of the research on two-worker families has focused on dual-career families in which both the husband and the wife have demanding professions such as law, medicine, or academics. One common finding of this research is that, even in dual-career families, household maintenance and care of the children are primarily the responsibility of the wife, with the husband merely helping her (Epstein, 1971; Rapoport and Rapoport, 1971; Working Family Project, 1978). In other words, traditional division of labor still exists in most of these households, and what shifts do occur are mainly in the direction of women doing tasks typically designated as male responsibilities. Dworkin and Chafetz (1979) concluded: "Men and women are 'liberated' from their traditional, stereotypical household roles when men allow it." What is needed is a systematic study of the effects of division of labor on marital satisfaction, on the careers of spouses, and on the children of dual-worker families. It is often assumed that spouses—especially wives—should be unhappy with the traditional division of labor when they are also working outside the home, but this assumption has yet to be examined.

The changing structure of U.S. families, caused by rising divorce rates and increasing numbers of working women, led the Social Security Administration to conduct a study entitled "Social Security and the Changing Roles of Men and Women." This report identified gaps in Social Security coverage for women, especially after divorce. Some examples of the inequities discovered are that 1) a housewife must be married at least ten years in order to gain any benefits from her husband's Social Security, 2) married women employees receive substantially lower benefits than men, 3) widowed homemakers under 60 can rarely receive benefits, 4) there are serious gaps in disability protection for homemakers, 5) benefits are greater for one-worker than for two-worker households, 6) the benefits for aged widows are inadequate, 7) no benefits are available for disabled widows, and 8) benefits are not provided for children of deceased homemakers (U.S. Department of Health, Education, and Welfare, 1979).

The explanation given for these inequities is that the current system is based on assumptions that are no longer accurate. For example, the present system assumes that husbands work and support their wives and families, and that only death intervenes. Therefore, survivor benefits for wives are not a problem. But middle-aged women (in their 40s and 50s) who are divorced and have been housewives all of their lives often do not receive their husbands' Social Security benefits and do not have any of their own. This is a contributing factor to the dilemma of displaced homemakers. In addition, these women frequently have no recent labor force experience, which, in combination with their age, makes finding jobs extremely difficult. This situation has spawned a heated discussion over the idea of paying housewives salaries. Because they would be earning money, homemakers could then build Social Security credits, as well as increase their self-esteem and their status in the eyes of their families. A multitude of problems are involved in determining the value of housework, however. For one, most homemakers work more than a 40-hour week. Moreover, it would be enormously difficult to evaluate some of the contributions they make to their families, such as providing emotional support or psychological counseling.

As the divorce rate continues to increase, so does social research on divorce and its impact. For example, some recent studies have looked at the effects of divorce on contacts between fathers and their children, given that courts almost always award child custody to the mother. Hetherington, et al. (1976) showed that over time divorced fathers tend to have less and less contact with their children, even when they live in the same town. And several recent publications have been aimed at helping fathers maintain a good relationship with their children after divorce (Atkin and Rubin, 1978). Black (1979) has suggested that two important aspects that have not been adequately examined are the definition of "divorced father" or "part-time father" and the societal sanctions and supports for this role. It may be that there are simply few social sanctions against *not* maintaining contact with children, and few social supports for doing so.

The percentage of fathers with custody of their children is increasing, although in 1975 the figure was still only about 8 percent. There is a clear link between gender-role attitudes and court decisions in this area. Issues of alimony and child support as well as custody are now being raised, especially in the courts. But little research has been done to 1) document the outcome of alimony and child support decisions when the husband and wife have similar salaries, 2) examine the impact of court decisions about alimony, child support, and child custody on the individuals involved, or 3) determine the effects on children of being raised by a father as a single parent. Most available research data have focused on child support and its payment or nonpayment by fathers.

WHAT ARE WE DOING?

Education

Sexism in textbooks is being combatted by researchers who testify at state textbook hearings, thus bringing the issue to public attention. Another common tactic is lobbying against publishers. Both of these tactics have pointed out the potential economic disadvantages of sexist books, which has led to some changes. An additional tactic is training teachers how to use sexist textbooks and other materials in a nonsexist way. This involves making them aware of sexism and giving them suggestions for countering it. For example, Weitzman and Rizzo (1974) in *Biased Textbooks: Action Steps You Can Take* suggested such actions as 1) having teachers point out racist or sexist biases in books or materials, 2) developing classroom activities around identifying bias found in books, television, etc., and 3) assigning student papers, themes, or other activities on topics or persons not usually covered in textbooks or materials.

Efforts have also been made to develop nonsexist curricula for schools. A number of schools now use training films and other materials to sensitize teachers to potential sexism in their teaching methods, the textbooks they assign, and the contents of their courses. One of the principle aims of these efforts is to reduce sex-role stereotyping without substituting other stereotypes—neither suggesting that women should work nor that they should *not* work, or that men should have nontraditional jobs or that they should *not* (Office of Education, 1978).

Gender inequality in the distribution of jobs within schools is being addressed by affirmative action programs. Title IX of the Education Amendments requires public schools to evaluate themselves in terms of the sex fairness of their programs and practices and to correct all identified deficiencies. Finally, there has been federal funding to set up training programs aimed at helping women and minorities learn the skills necessary to move into high level research and development and management positions in educational institutions.

Some changes are being instituted to alter school structures. Open classrooms allow male and female students more freedom of movement and, therefore, more opportunity to learn and explore while moving around. While there has been no change in the emphasis on reading and writing skills (which boys are less prepared to learn at an early age), there has been increased sensitivity to the impact of labeling children as slow or hyperactive and a greater attempt to integrate these children into regular classes, together with giving them special help. These changes benefit both males and females, in that passivity is reduced and independence and creativity encouraged.

There has recently been a push by the Department of Labor and the Office of Education to develop career counseling and vocational education programs that are nonsexist and that encourage both males and females to develop their unique aptitudes and interests, even if this takes them into nontraditional areas. A number of programs around the country have attacked this issue in different ways. These include 1) developing materials and strategies to help students understand and deal with the limiting effects of sex-role stereotypes on their future plans, 2) compiling nonstereotyped career and job information to be used by counselors, vocational education teachers, and career development centers, 3) gathering materials to be used by teachers and counselors for nontraditional career education in secondary schools, 4) establishing programs to encourage females to select nontraditional educational and career goals, and 5) making teachers aware of their own gender biases and how to overcome them (Office of Education, 1978).

Employment

In employment, we are still at the stage of conducting research to determine why pay differentials in the dual labor market persist and why affirmative action has thus far been largely ineffective.

In regard to the dual labor force, it has been noted that an important factor is the very traditional expectations that adolescents have about the jobs they want and will obtain. To a large extent, these expectations are a result of early gender-role socialization. The above mentioned programs in vocational and career counseling can therefore be very significant, since they can make adolescents more aware of the alternatives provided by nontraditional jobs. It is hoped that such programs will eventually minimize labor force inequities for both males and females. Demonstration projects and training are also commonly used to bring about these changes, as are outreach models designed to attract females into training for nontraditional jobs. For example, both Denver and Boston have instituted demonstration projects to channel females into traditionally male-dominated skilled crafts (Women's Bureau of the Department of Labor, 1976). These efforts involve outreach components to attract females into the projects, training programs to give them the technical and social skills necessary to function in such jobs, and placement services.

In addition, companies are increasingly offering training sessions to help their managers and first-line supervisors learn to deal with female employees and the reactions of male employees to female co-workers when females enter male-dominated occupations. This training helps to ease the transition period for both male and female employees, many of whom have had little or no experience with opposite sex co-workers.

To some extent, the efforts mentioned above are related to the issue of pay differences, since they encourage females to enter occupations in which they will be paid more than they would in traditional female occupations. These efforts do not, however, address the issue of how women can be successful once they acquire these jobs, or how to deal with situations in which they are paid less than males with similar jobs. Few systematic programs have been developed to deal with these problems. Affirmative action continues to be mandated, and the Equal Employment Opportunity Commission continues to function, occasionally bringing lawsuits and occasionally winning them. But as the data indicate, these efforts have been insufficient to stem the trend toward greater, not lesser, differentials in pay between men and women, even though they may rectify the problem for specific groups of people.

Family

Research data suggest that appropriate activities regarding family/work arrangements and familial well-being should be directed toward the creation of an environment in which couples choose the arrangements best suited for them, without the constraints of rigid gender roles. Although at present there are very few systematic programs to help individuals achieve this goal, some related efforts are underway. Schools and youth-serving organizations are beginning to provide classes and programs aimed at exposing adolescents to a wide range of potential family/work arrangements, as well as teaching them about life style options and their consequences. These efforts should help males and females make life choices that provide greater satisfaction and better mental health.

Again, little is being done about the problems of dual-worker families, even though it is acknowledged that there is a rapid and projected continued increase in this phenomenon. As mentioned previously, a major problem for dual-worker families is daycare, yet there has been almost no increase in public-supported daycare programs over the past few years. In fact, demand has so exceeded supply that most daycare centers, both public and private, have long waiting lists. Parent co-ops are being formed in some parts of the country, but these tend to be limited to people who have jobs with very flexible time schedules. There have been virtually no efforts to promote or fund demonstration projects for community-supported daycare facilities.

Programs to help working couples manage domestic duties (including child care) are rare, probably because this is viewed as a problem for individual couples —even though millions of couples need this kind of help. Even popular literature dealing with the problems of dual-worker families (e.g., Bird, 1979; Hall and Hall, 1979) gives few suggestions for managing the stress of time constraints in dual-worker households. One might logically expect that studies have been done on the effects of dual employment on children, but very little research has broached in this area. An exception to this deficit is that some companies are experimenting with flexible hours for employees, which makes it easier for working couples to integrate their domestic duties—especially child care—with their work schedules. It was estimated that in 1976 about 300,000 persons in the United States were on some form of flexible work schedule (*New York Times,* 1976). Although this is a sizeable number of people, it, nonetheless, represents only a small proportion of all workers in this country.

A number of programs have been created to help individuals after divorce. Most of these are for women and children, such as the demonstration projects to help displaced homemakers that are funded by the U.S. Department of Labor. Such programs are primarily intended to help women find suitable jobs by assessing their skills, building their self-confidence, helping them translate their home-making experiences into job-related qualifications, and providing them with job counseling.

The Social Security report mentioned earlier recommended changes in the Social Security laws to give greater financial protection to housewives by recognizing their contributions to family incomes. As also mentioned, there has been considerable discussion about paying housewives salaries, letting them set up retirement accounts, or otherwise giving them some kind of financial security in return for their work.

Programs dealing with divorce and fathers primarily involve lobbying efforts to change court policies in awarding custody, alimony, and child support. Currently, joint custody is being advocated in many places (Stack, 1976) and is becoming increasingly popular in some parts of the country. In addition, some organizations have been established that provide support for divorced fathers trying to maintain contact with their children.

WHAT HAVE WE ACCOMPLISHED?

In general, the answer to this question is either "it is too soon to tell" or "not very much." But social change, especially involving such firmly held values as those relating to gender roles, is bound to be slow to evolve. Any progress, therefore, is notable. Moreover, many of the programs discussed above are relatively new. In several areas—such as new patterns of division of labor in the household or how to make affirmative action effective—there is little or no relevant information upon which to design programs. In other areas—such as the difficulties divorced fathers have in maintaining contact with their children—virtually no programmatic efforts have been made. In other areas, programs have been initiated but have not been adequately evaluated. But sometimes the answer to the question of what we have accomplished is simply "greater public awareness" —and that is a place to start.

Education

Some publishers have recently developed guidelines for nonsexist language that have been widely distributed, although this has not prevented some authors from excluding females in certain contexts in their books, or even from treating them in a derogatory manner. Economic incentives, however, have at least made some publishers more aware of the potential costs of stereotyping, and they are beginning to employ reviewers to examine texts for stereotyping or unequal treatment of males and females. Recently published textbooks have changed somewhat, although the probable majority of texts used in schools still portray traditional gender stereotypes, underrepresent the role of women in history and government, and use the generic terms "man" and "he"—simply because they are older books.

A number of changes have also occurred in educational administration and employment. While their numbers are still proportionately small, more women are now serving as principals, deans, administrators, and college presidents than ever before (*PEER*, 1979). There are also more female college professors, although they are still primarily in lower level positions (Patterson and Engelberg, 1978). And increasing numbers of males are being employed as teachers in public schools. Overall, however, the traditional pattern of males and females in education and its administration has not been extensively altered.

Many public schools now have far greater flexibility in providing children with individualized learning environments. In some states, recent legislation has mandated that special education students (predominately males) must be kept in the classroom with other children rather than being separated from them. While the success of this approach is yet unproven, it could have great benefits for the children involved by eliminating the ill effects of labeling and segregation.

Most of the nonsexist programs in vocational and career counseling are too new to evaluate. Their mere existence, however, is a major accomplishment. And there is some evidence indicating that these programs have been at least moderately effective thus far. For example, more females are currently enrolled in male-dominated vocational education courses (*PEER*, 1979). A trend for females to seek less gender-stereotyped jobs is evident, but it is not clear how many of these females will be able to actually secure good jobs in traditionally male-dominated occupations.

Employment

Data presented above indicated that there has been little change in the dual male/female labor force. Recent data on enrollment in professional schools, however (e.g., medicine, law, and public administration), as well as in vocational education courses (e.g., industrial arts, carpentry, and drafting) indicate that increasing numbers of women are preparing for jobs in male-dominated occupations.

Demonstration projects such as the Minority Women Employment Project (U.S. Department of Labor, 1978) and the outreach programs in Denver and Boston (U.S. Department of Labor, 1978b, 1978c) have been able to place women in nontraditional jobs, both in professional and managerial positions (MWEP), as well as in blue-collar occupations (Denver and Boston).

In spite of these accomplishments, programs to reduce wage differentials between women and men have been unsuccessful. Movement of females into male-dominated occupations and of males into female-dominated ones does not automatically insure equal pay for male and female workers. Affirmative action deals with both employment and wage differences but has only been mildly successful with regard to employment and abysmally unsuccessful with regard to reduction of wage differentials between men and women.

Family

The reasons for so little change having been effected in the family may lie in the reluctance of the government to intervene, together with insufficient public demand to induce the government to do so. Two conspicuous exceptions are the programs cited above for displaced homemakers and the Social Security Administration's recommendations.

The impact of family/work relationships on mental health and marital satisfaction is the most difficult factor to assess in this area. It is, therefore, not surprising that little has been accomplished or even attempted here. However, public awareness of the value of housewives and their housework is increasing, there is now some pertinent literature for both housewives and working wives, and there have been more and more organized efforts to affirm the value of being "just a wife."

Since there are presently no programs dealing with the problems of dual-worker families, there have been no accomplishments in this area. Child-care facilities remain patently inadequate. Some corporations have established on-site child care programs and are experimenting with flexible work schedules to allow parents to meet family needs. More and more companies are allowing paternity leave as well as maternity leave (*Wall Street Journal,* 1979a). And there is growing public awareness of the special needs of people with this kind of family structure. Popular magazines have published articles on dual-worker families, and more books on the subject are being published (e.g., Hall and Hall, 1979; Bird, 1979).

With regard to the impact of divorce, the Social Security Administration report has not yet been acted upon by Congress (Gordon, 1978). Nothing has yet been realized in terms of salaries for housewives, but legislation to provide them with some kinds of economic security has been proposed (*Wall Street Journal,* 1979b). The Women's Bureau of the Department of Labor has sponsored programs for displaced homemakers that provide help to women in finding employment. The programs are so recent, however, that data on the numbers of women helped and the effectiveness of the programs are not yet available.

Little has been achieved for divorced fathers and their children, except that their problems have received some treatment in popular literature and media, thereby becoming somewhat better known to the public. In California, priority is no longer automatically given to mothers in custody cases, but this is not true in most states. As mentioned earlier, the percentage of fathers being granted custody of their children is increasing, albeit very slowly. The major accomplishments in paternal custody have been in proposed legislation to equalize the treatment of males and females in divorce cases and in increased public awareness of the dilemma of divorced fathers and their children.

WHERE ARE WE GOING?

There are several ways to approach this question. One interpretation might be, "Where should we be going?" and another, "Where are we going based on what has already begun to happen?" In this section, emphasis will be placed upon where we can realistically expect to go, given what is happening at the present.

Education

Since pressures are being brought to bear on publishers and writers to modify their textbooks, gender biases therein should be largely eliminated within the next decade. With regard to curricula, the most appropriate place to concentrate future efforts would be in preservice and inservice teacher training, since teachers have considerable control over what is taught and how it is taught. It is crucial, therefore, to convince teachers of the importance of gender-fair education, as well as of the importance of flexibility in classroom structure and instructional methods such as individualized instruction. The differential impact of the education process on male and female students should thereby be significantly reduced.

School counselor training is another crucial issue. Counseling courses and materials should be developed to help adolescents with their life plans. Career and vocational counseling should be extended to help students choose jobs or careers that are consistent with their own values, family plans, and personal interests and abilities. The realities of the labor market should be portrayed by giving students as much information as possible about projected supply and demand in various occupations, comparative data on probable incomes, and necessary preparation and training for various jobs. This kind of counseling could be far more realistic and much less gender-biased than many contemporary methods. Career and vocational counseling, by encouraging females to seek more meaningful and lucrative employment, could play a vital role in attracting them to formerly male-dominated areas of the labor force.

Employment

The most obvious need in this area is for programs that would remove structural, attitudinal, and normative barriers that lead males and females to enter sex-typed occupations, that perpetuate differential opportunities for success for males and females once they are employed, and that shield the injustice of differential wages for males and females who have the same jobs. As previously stated, attempts to correct these biases have thus far been quite unsuccessful. This is probably because these structural barriers in employment are so thoroughly entrenched that it is enormously difficult to devise an effective strategy to combat them. Kanter (1977) has suggested that, if women and minorities are ever to obtain equal opportunities, work organizations must ultimately change their basic structures. She also insists that any organizational changes that would benefit women would also benefit men. After examining the potential problems associated with such changes, however, she foresaw slight hope of significant change in the near future.

Legislation against discrimination cannot work by itself. Better programs and techniques must be developed to support such legislation. One possible avenue of approach would be to explore ways of demonstrating that discrimination is not economically sound labor practice. Another would be to draw attention to what happens to men and women once they enter work organizations. Yet another would be to design more extensive programs to help women move into nontraditional positions within work organizations.

Family

Many predictions are presently being made about the future of the family in our society. Although it is still a fundamental social institution, its structure is slowly changing. Divorce has become far more prevalent, and dual-worker families are expected to increase over the next decade. More women should learn how to convert their family and domestic experiences into marketable labor skills, so that, in the event of divorce, for example, the economic consequences would be less acute. It seems likely that women will begin to perceive the homemaker role as a deliberate choice of life style rather than as a preordained fate.

Scanzoni (1972) has argued that as women become economically equal to men they will also become equal partners in marriage. Bernard (1972) proposed that role sharing will be a crucial element in viable marriages in the future. These analyses suggest that working couples will begin to experience more and more job-related stress, as well as share more domestic duties and child-care responsibilities. As the proportion of dual-worker families increases, there will likely be even greater demand for child-care facilities. Government subsidies for child-care programs, as well as government-supported studies to determine how quality programs can be provided, will become an absolute necessity in the future. But it would seem that such measures will be taken only when this problem has reached crisis proportions.

More fathers will gain custody of their children after divorce. This may be caused in part by career women becoming less reluctant to relinquish their custody rights as mothers. Moreover, joint custody will become more prevalent.

More research will be needed on how parent/child interactions can be maximized after divorce, both for parents and for their children. Programs in this area will also be needed for parents and children.

In summation, this chapter has touched on just a few of the multitude of gender-role issues in applied sociology. We have, however, discussed at length three major societal institutions—education, employment, and the family—and have attempted to address both their interrelatedness and certain contemporary gender-role phenomena effecting them. As we have seen, changes in gender-role attitudes are being brought to bear on these institutions, which, over time, can be expected to influence the full range of male and female roles in our society.

REFERENCES AND SUGGESTED READINGS

Albrecht, S.L. 1976. "Informal Networks" *Women in Management, Proceedings of The Conference.* Austin, Tex.: University of Texas, School of Social Work, Center for Social Work Research. Human Services Monograph Series.

Almquist, E. 1977. "Women in the Labor Force." *Signs* 2:843–55.

Almquist, E.M. and S.S. Angrist. 1970. "Career Salience and Atypicality of Occupational Choice Among Women." *Journal of Marriage and the Family* 32:242–49.

_____. 1971. "Role Model Influence on College Women's Career Aspirations." *Merrill-Palmer Quarterly of Behavior and Development* 17:263–97.

Astin, H. 1967. "Factors Associated with the Participation of the Woman Doctorate in the Labor Force." *Personnel and Guidance Journal* 46:240–46.

Atkin, E. and E. Rubin. 1978. *Part-Time Father: A Guide For the Divorced Father.* New York: Vanguard Press.

Bass, M.M., J. Krusel, and R.A. Alexander. 1979. "Male Managers' Attitudes Toward Working Women." In *Women in the Professions: What's All the Fuss About,* edited by L.S. Fidell and J. DeLamater, pp. 63–78. Beverly Hills, Calif.: Sage.

Bernard, Jessie. 1972. *The Future of Marriage.* New York: World Bantam.

Bird, Caroline. 1979. *The Two-Paycheck Family.* New York: Rawson, Wade.

Black, Josie. 1979. Personal communication.

Burstein, Paul. 1979. "Equal Employment Opportunity Legislation and the Income of Women and Non-Whites." *American Sociological Review* 44 (June): 367–91.

Campbell, P. 1978. "Sex Stereotyping in Education." Instructional modules. Atlanta: Georgia State University.

*Cassetty, Judith. 1979. *Child Support and Public Policy.* Lexington, Mass.: D.C. Heath.

Cassetty examines the history of child support and its current status in the United States and then looks at theory, models, and data related to child support payment levels. The author also examines normative issues related to reform and then makes policy recommendations. The book is a good example of using data to arrive at gender-relevant policy recommendations.

Corder-Bolz, J. and C. Stephan. 1979. "Predictors of Females' Aspirations and Expectations for Combining Labor Force Participation and Motherhood." Paper read at the American Sociological Association meetings. Boston.

Corder-Bolz, J. 1979. "Sex Roles and Occupational Aspirations." Washington, D.C.: Unpublished report to the National Institute of Education.

Dworkin, R.J. and J.S. Chafetz. 1979. "The Mop and the Mower: A Study of the Division of Household Labor in White, Middle-Class Families." Paper read at the Southwestern Sociological Association meetings. Ft. Worth, Texas (March).

Epstein, C.F. 1971. *Woman's Place: Options and Limits in Professional Careers.* Berkeley: University of California Press.

Ferree, M.M. 1976. "Working Class Jobs: Housework and Paid Work As Sources of Satisfaction." *Social Problems* 23:431–42.

Fidell, L. and J. Prather. 1976. "The Confused American Housewife." *Psychology Today,* September, 1976.

Friedan, Betty. 1963. *The Feminine Mystique.* New York: W.W. Norton.

Glenn, Norval. 1975. "The Contribution of Marriage to the Psychological Well-Being of Males and Females." *Journal of Marriage and the Family* 37 (Aug): 594–600.

Gordon, F.E. and M.H. Strober. 1975. *Bringing Women Into Management.* New York: McGraw-Hill.

Gordon, Nancy M. 1978. "The Treatment of Women under Social Security." Washington, D.C.: U.S. Commission on Civil Rights.

Gottfredson, L.S. 1978. "Race and Sex Differences in Occupational Aspirations: Their Development and Consequences for Occupational Segregation." Report No. 254. Baltimore: Johns Hopkins University, Center for Social Organization of Schools.

Gross, Neal and Anne E. Trask. 1976. *The Sex Factor and the Management of Schools.* New York: John Wiley & Sons.

Hagen, R.L. and A. Kahn. 1975. "Discrimination Against Competent Women." *Journal of Applied Social Psychology* 5 (Oct):362–76.

Hall, Francine and Maryanne Albrecht. 1979. *The Management of Affirmative Action.* Santa Monica, Calif.: Goodyear.

Hall, Francine S. and Douglas T. Hall. 1979. *The Two-Career Couple.* Reading, Mass.: Addison-Wesley.

Harrison, James. 1978. "Warning: The Male Sex Role May be Dangerous to Your Health." *Journal of Social Issues* 34:65–85.

Hayghe, Howard. 1976. "Families and the Rise of Working Wives: An Overview." *Monthly Labor Review* 99(5):12–19.

Hetherington, E.M., M. Cox, and R. Cox. 1976. "The Aftermath of Divorce." Read at the annual meeting of the American Psychological Association. Washington, D.C.

*Kanter, Rosabeth. 1977. *Men and Women of the Corporation.* New York: Basic Books.

Kanter reports the results of a case study of a corporation. Researcher reaches theoretical conclusions and then specifies the policy implications of her research for the future of men and, especially, women in corporations.

Kohlberg, Lawrence. 1977. "A Cognitive-Developmental Analysis of Children's Sex-Role Concepts and Attitudes." In *The Development of Sex Differences,* edited by E.E. Maccoby, pp. 82–172. Stanford, Calif.: Stanford University Press.

Looft, W.R. 1971. "Sex Differences in the Expression of Vocational Aspirations by Elementary School Children." *Developmental Psychology* 5:366.

Maccoby, Eleanor and C. Jacklin. 1974. *The Development of Sex Differences* Stanford, Calif.: Stanford University Press.

MacLeod, J. and S. Silverman. 1973. "You Won't Do: What Textbooks on U.S. Government Teach High School Girls." Pittsburgh: KNOW.

MacManus, S.A. and N.R. Van Hightower. 1977. "The Impact of Federally Funded Vocational Education Programs on Women: Present Patterns and Future Implications." Paper presented at the annual meeting of the American Political Science Association. Washington, D.C. (September).

McGuinness, Diane. 1979. "How Schools Discriminate Against Boys." *Human Nature,* February, pp. 82–88.

Meyer, W.J. and G.C. Thompson. 1956. "Sex Differences in the Distribution of Teacher Approval and Disapproval among Sixth Grade Children." *Journal of Educational Psychology* 47:385–96.

New York Times. 1976. Section D 17, IV, January 4, 1976.

Patterson, M. and L. Engelberg. 1978. "Women in Male-Dominated Professions." In *Women Working,* edited by A.H. Stromberg and S. Harkess, pp. 266–92. Palo Alto, Calif.: Mayfield.

PEER Perspective. 1979. "PEER Names Best, Worst States on Sex Bias." 5(Sept): 1,3.

Pleck, Joseph H. 1976. "The Male Sex Role: Definitions, Problems, and Sources of Change." *Journal of Social Issues* 32:155–64.

Polatnick, Margaret. 1975. "Why Men Don't Rear Children: A Power Analysis." In *Sex: Male/Gender: Masculine,* edited by J.W. Petras, pp. 199–235. Port Washington, N.Y.: Alfred.

Rapoport, R. and R. Rapoport. 1971. *Dual Career Families.* Baltimore: Penguin Books.

Rosen, B.C. and C.S. Aneshensel. 1978. "Sex Differences in the Educational and Occupational Expectation Process." *Social Forces* 57:164–86.

Saario, T.N., C.N. Jacklin, and C.K. Tittle. 1973. "Sex-Role Stereotyping in the Public Schools." *Harvard Educational Review* 43:386–416.

*Sargent, Alice. 1977. *Beyond Sex Roles.* St. Paul: West.
The book contains a variety of information on gender roles, including: 1) exercises to isolate gender-role stereotypes and change them, 2) exercises related to gender roles and life planning, 3) articles by men and women working in the area of gender roles, and 4) articles on gender-roles and organizations, education, and law.

Scanzoni, J. 1972. *Sexual Bargaining.* Englewood Cliffs, N.J.: Prentice-Hall.

Schenk, J.P. 1977. "Sex Fairness in Vocational Education." Columbus, Ohio: The Ohio State University, ERIC Clearinghouse on Career Education (Information Services 120: ERIC ED 149189).

Schneider, Joe W. and S.L. Hacker. 1973. "Sex Role Imagery and Use of the Generic Man in Introductory Texts." *The American Sociologist* 8:12–18.

Sears, Pauline and D. Feldman. 1966. "Teacher Interactions wtih Boys and Girls." *The National Elementary Principal* 46 (Nov):31.

Sexton, Patricia. 1969. *The Feminized Male.* New York: Vintage Books.

*Sprung, B., ed. 1978. *Perspectives on Non-Sexist Childhood Education.* New York: Teachers College Press, Columbia University.

This book is a collection of articles examining the problems, the research, and some techniques for nonsexist early childhood education.

Stack, C.B. 1976. "Who Owns the Child? Divorce and Child Custody Decisions in Middle Class Families." *Social Problems* 23:505–15.

*Stromberg, A.H. and S. Harkess, eds. 1978. *Women Working: Theories and Facts in Perspective.* Palo Alto, Calif.: Mayfield.

The work contains articles on many of the issues discussed in this chapter: wage differentials, work, home and family (for women), women in male-dominated professions, and housewives as workers. There is one chapter on policy implications. This book focuses almost entirely on women.

Tangri, S.S. 1972. "Determinants of Occupational Role Innovation among College Women." *Journal of Social Issues* 28:177–99.

Taylor, Patricia A. 1979. "Incomes Inequality in the Federal Civilian Government." *American Sociological Review* 44 (June):468–79.

Tittle, Carol Kehr. 1974. "Sex Bias in Educational Measurement: Fact or Fiction." *Measurement and Evaluation in Guidance*, 6 (Jan):818–23.

Torrence, E.P. 1965. *Rewarding Creative Behavior: Experiment in Classroom Creativity.* Englewood Cliffs, N.J.: Prentice-Hall.

Trecker, Janice L. 1974. "Women in U.S. History High-School Textbooks." In *And Jill Came Tumbling After: Sexism in American Education*, edited by J. Stacey, S. Bereaud and J. Daniels, pp. 249–68. New York: Dell.

Tully, J.C., S.L. Albrecht, W. Markham, and C.M. Bonjean. 1978. "Attitudinal Factors in Sex Discrimination." Unpublished paper.

Tully, J.C., C. Stephan, and B. Chance. 1976. "The Status and Sex Typed Dimensions of Occupational Aspirations." *Social Science Quarterly* 56: 638–49.

U.S. Bureau of the Census. 1979. "Money Income in 1977 of Families and Persons in the United States." *Current Population Reports.* Series P-60, No. 118. Washington, D.C.: U.S. Government Printing Office.

U.S. Department of Health, Education, and Welfare, Office of Education. 1978. "Women's Educational Equity Act Program, Annual Report." Washington, D.C.: U.S. Government Printing Office.

U.S. Department of Health, Education and Welfare. 1979. "Social Security and the Changing Roles of Men and Women." Washington, D.C.: U.S. Government Printing Office.

U.S. Department of Labor, Employment, and Training Administration. 1978. "Placing Minority Women in Professional Jobs." Washington, D.C.: U.S. Government Printing Office.

U.S. Department of Labor, Women's Bureau, 1976. "The Earnings Gap Between Women and Men." Washington, D.C.: U.S. Government Printing Office.

___. 1978a. "Employment and Economic Issues of Low-Income Women: Report on a Project." Washington, D.C.: U.S. Government Printing Office.

___. 1978b. "Women in Nontraditional Jobs: A Program Model, Boston: Nontraditional Occupations Program for Women." Washington, D.C.: U.S. Government Printing Office.

___. 1978c. "Women in Nontraditional Jobs: A Program Model, Denver: Better Jobs for Women." Washington, D.C.: U.S. Government Printing Office.

U.S. Equal Employment Opportunities Commission. 1977. "Employment Opportunity in the Schools." Washington, D.C.: U.S. Government Printing Office.

Vetter, Louise. 1978. "Career Counseling for Women." In *Counseling Women*, edited by L.W. Harmon, J.M. Birk, L.E. Fitzgerald and M.F. Tanney, pp. 75–93. Monterey, Calif.: Brooks/Cole.

Wall Street Journal. 1978a. "Dangerous Occupation." Labor Letter, August 1, p. 1.

___. 1978b. "Divorce Laws." May 31, p. 6.

___. 1979a. "AT & T Paternity Leave." April 23, p. 5.

___. 1979b. "Homemakers Retirement Accounts." February 21, p. 1.

___. 1979c. "News From the Front." May 8, p. 26.

Weitzman, L., D. Eifler, E. Hokada, and C. Ross. 1972. "Sex-Role Socialization in Picture Books for Pre-School Children." *American Journal of Sociology* 77:1125–50.

Weitzman, Lenore J. and Diane Rizzo. 1974. "Biased Textbooks: A Research Perspective and Action Steps You Can Take." Washington, D.C.: National Foundation for the Improvement of Education.

Women on Words and Images, 1972. *Dick and Jane as Victims: Sex Stereotyping in Children's Readers.* Princeton, N.J.: Women on Words and Images.

Working Family Project. 1978. "Parenting." In *Working Couples*, edited by R. Rapoport, R. Rapoport and J. Bumstead, pp. 78–88. New York: Harper & Row.

15 AGE DISCRIMINATION

Robert C. Atchley

Our lives are profoundly affected at any given time by our chronological age. Age is a major attribute for deciding where someone fits or doesn't fit in the organization of society. As youngsters we are often constrained by not having attained various ages of eligibility. As we grow older we may find ourselves disqualified by virtue of advanced age. In both cases, age alone is used to exclude people arbitrarily from various kinds of participation. While there has been some effort to address the issue of age discrimination against the young, the greatest attention has been paid to the causes and consequences of age discrimination against the old, and by far the greatest efforts have been made to combat age discrimination directed at middle-aged and older people in the United States. Accordingly, that will be the focus of this chapter.

WHAT ARE THE PROBLEMS?

In the context of social inequality, the aged seem to reap a bitter harvest. All of the sources of economic, educational, and occupational inequality that present problems for the general population—discrimination according to social class, ethnicity, race, and sex—are carried over from the middle age into later maturity and old age. And older people face the additional burden of ageism and age discrimination. Age discrimination represents the main new source of inequality that people experience as they move through middle age into their later years.

Ageism, or age prejudice, is an unfavorable attitude toward aging and older people. It is based on mistaken beliefs that aging makes people unattractive, unintelligent, asexual, unemployable, and "senile"—that aging is a one-way process having no positive features (Comfort, 1976). *Age discrimination* refers to treatment of people in some unjustly negative way solely on the basis of their chronological age. Age discrimination has important consequences. It affects the informal interactions and opportunities of older people and often finds its way into social policies and regulations. A frequent result is the exclusion of older people from opportunities to serve or be served.

Age discrimination denies people access to jobs, and this is perhaps its most significant outcome. But as we shall see, it also negatively influences the probability that individuals will be served by various social institutions, particularly those concerned with health and social welfare. In just about every social institution except the family, age discrimination produces a withdrawal of social support from older people. Older people are denied not only paid jobs but meaningful unpaid volunteer work as well. Educational institutions neglect the needs and interests of older people. Churches and religious denominations often offer lip service to the spiritual needs of their elderly members but fall far short when it comes to delivery. Current approaches to the creation of housing ignore the needs of middle-income retired persons. Planning of health care emphasizes care of acute diseases rather than the chronic diseases that are more prevalent among the old. Unconscious devaluation of the capacities and needs of older people occurs in practically every arena, as does the resultant discrimination.

For administrators and policy makers, ageism tends to act as a set of blinders that prevents the older population from being seen as it actually is—an extremely heterogeneous population with a wide diversity of capacities, interests, and needs. The result is programs and policies designed to meet the needs of the frail, dependent elderly and which ignore the needs of the able-bodied, independent elderly who constitute three-fourths of the older population (Atchley, 1980). The results for society are social policies, laws, and programs that waste both human resources and public money.

For sociologists, ageism and age discrimination are interesting because, unlike other sources of inequality, they cut across all social strata to affect everyone who lives long enough. Aging is the only social process that produces automatic downward social mobility for the vast majority. Only unusually capable or unusually powerful older people escape the effects of age discrimination. Yet, the study of ageism and age discrimination by sociologists is in its infancy, particularly in comparison to other types of prejudice and discrimination. This is unfortunate because ageism is unlike other kinds of prejudice.

This chapter deals with the origins of age discrimination, the extent of it, what is being done to combat it, how successful these efforts have been, and what needs to be done next.

WHAT DO WE KNOW?

Origins of Age Discrimination

That aging is mainly a matter of decrement and that older people are less desirable than younger ones as functioning members of society are ideas that have been around at least since the time of Aristotle (Hendricks and Hendricks, 1977–

78). It is commonly assumed that "back then" aging and the aged were not devalued whereas now they are. However, recent work by Laslett (1976), Auchenbaum and Kusnerz (1978), and others has shown that ideas about aging have never been uniformly either positive or negative, and that historically the situation of the aged in most cultures has been ambiguous and attitudes about aging have been ambivalent (Simmons, 1960). This historical work is important because it points out that ageism has been part of the culture of all large-scale societies since well before the industrial revolution. It is not a recent development. Neither is age discrimination.

The roots of age discrimination both now and in the past lie in cultural beliefs about the adverse impact of aging on physical and mental functioning. Beliefs are assertions about what is true that are accepted and acted upon as true. They are seldom put to the test by the public except in the most haphazard and unreliable manner. Beliefs are simply believed. Whether a belief is widely held or not has nothing to do with its accuracy. Often our cultural beliefs about the causes and consequences of aging have turned out, when tested, to be either substantially incorrect or so oversimplified as to be misleading. For example, it is widely held that retirement increased the suicide rate, yet the overwhelming weight of evidence refutes this proposition (Atchley, 1980).

Beliefs are used to make inferences, draw conclusions, and make decisions. If our beliefs are faulty, our conclusions, inferences, and decisions are likely to be faulty as well. It is important, therefore, to examine what research has uncovered concerning both the content and accuracy of beliefs about aging and the aged.

Harris and Associates (1975) compared what the general public believed to be the most serious problems of older people with what older people actually experienced. The general public substantially overestimated the prevalence of problems such as poor health, inadequate incomes, loneliness, and feelings of not being needed. The image that "most people over 65" have numerous problems is a double-edged sword. On the one hand, it garners political support for programs serving older Americans, but, on the other hand, it perpetuates the stereotype of later life as an unattractive life stage.

Jacob Tuckman and his associates (Tuckman and Lorge, 1953a, 1953b, 1953c, 1956, 1958a, 1958b; Tuckman and Lavell, 1957) developed a scale that they used to measure beliefs about aging in a wide variety of samples. They found that the general public's beliefs about aging and the aged were accurate about as often as they were inaccurate. But inaccurate beliefs were generally negative. Older Americans were seen as conservative, lonely, forgetful, and often at loose ends. In addition, Axelrod and Eisdorfer (1961) found that the older the "stimulus category" rated using the Tuckman-Lorge scale, the greater the percentage of people who applied inaccurate negative beliefs to that category of older persons. For example, people at age 65 were much more frequently seen as preoccupied with the past, slow moving, poorly coordinated, worried, and mentally slow compared to people at age 55.

The semantic differential technique taps beliefs by presenting a standardized set of 20 bipolar adjectives such as happy-sad, relaxed-tense, active-passive, and healthy-sick to respondents who are asked to rate various categories of people. Eisdorfer and Altrocchi (1961) found that compared to the "average adult," both "older men" and "older women" were negatively evaluated by college students. Collette-Pratt (1976) found that older adults were negatively evaluated by adults of all ages in terms of aging's influence on productivity, achievement, independence, and especially health.

Beliefs about the capacities of older workers compared to their younger counterparts are particularly relevant to older people in the labor force. Rosen and Jerdee (1976a) found that prospective business managers rated older workers (age 60) lower than younger workers (age 30) on productivity, efficiency, motivation, ability to work under pressure, and creativity. Older workers were also seen as more accident-prone and as having less potential. Not only were they seen as being less eager, but also as unreceptive to new ideas, less capable of learning, less adaptable, less versatile, more rigid, and more dogmatic, On the plus side, older workers were seen as more reliable, dependable, and trustworthy, and less likely to miss work for personal reasons. No age differences were seen in the area of interpersonal skills.

Inaccurate negative beliefs about aging and the aged bolster the idea that the later stages of life are not desirable and that older people are not preferable as associates or friends. Harris and Associates (1975) found that a large majority of their national sample saw the 20s to the 40s as the most desirable ages. Those who preferred later ages did so because to them later life represented reduced responsibilities and increased enjoyment. People who rejected the 60s and 70s as desirable ages did so because they correlated these ages with poor health, disability, and financial worries.

Seefeldt, et al. (1977) used drawings to get at children's preferences to be with men of different ages. These preschool to sixth-grade children's attitudes may reflect general likes and dislikes stripped of social checks and balances. Nearly 60 percent chose the youngest man to be with, and 20 percent chose the oldest. These preferences were related to perceptions (beliefs) about aging and the aged. These children felt that aging was a time of poor health. They saw the oldest man as not doing much for them, and when they were asked to describe what they would do with the oldest man they tended to describe helping behavior such as "get his glasses" or "help him clean" or "carry things for him." This predisposition to dislike aging and the oldest man relative to the others seems to be related to how the children would come out in exchange relations. They saw themselves as giving more and getting less from the oldest man. These findings are consistent with several prior studies (Hickey, Hickey, and Kalish, 1968; Hickey and Kalish, 1968).

In sum, older people in general are seen as being in poor health, physically frail and inept, conservative and rigid, forgetful and dependent. In relation to jobs, older workers are seen as less able to learn, less productive, less efficient, less creative, and lacking in achievement motivation. No doubt these job-related beliefs are derived mainly from beliefs about the effects of physical aging.

Even though there are positive beliefs that personl warmth and wisdom increase with age, they tend to be offset by the disqualifying character of our negative beliefs about physical aging. Just how accurate are these disqualifying beliefs?

The weight of the evidence shows that less than one-fifth of the population age 65 and over fits any one of the negative beliefs cited above, and the proportion who exhibit a majority of these characteristics is quite small, probably no more than 10 percent. About 14 percent have disabilities that limit the amount or kind of activities they can do (Wilder, 1971). In terms of characteristics such as physical coordination, physical work capacity, memory, creativity, rigidity, and motivation, the range of individual variation is so great that chronological age is a very poor predictor (Fozard and Carr, 1972; Botwinick, 1978; Atchley, 1980). Aging does not have a predictable effect. Some people become more capable with age, some stay about the same, and others show declines in capacity. It appears that those who experience decline serious enough to affect their social functioning are a small minority until at least age 75, at which point the rate of increase in physical or mental disability quickens. This pattern occurs because the body's various physical systems continue to operate satisfactorily in the vast majority of people until after age 75 (Finch and Hayflick, 1977). In fact, most people die without *ever* experiencing socially limiting disability. Compared to middle-aged and younger workers, older workers have been shown to be as productive, as efficient, and more dependable (Sheppard, 1970). Certainly the available knowledge about the effects of physical aging cannot be used to justify treating older people as incapable. Instead, such treatment has been justified on the grounds of inaccurate beliefs.

Types and Prevalence of Age Discrimination

Age discrimination occurs in employment, in the delivery of social services, in opportunities for volunteer service, and in many other areas of life. Kasschau (1977) found that, among adults age 45 and over, age discrimination was thought to be more common than was racial discrimination. This was true even among blacks, although the difference was small. Just over 17 percent of Kasschau's respondents said they had experienced age discrimination personally, 30 percent said that friends had experienced age discrimination, and 85 percent thought that age discrimination was common.

There can be no doubt that many older adults in the labor force face age discrimination in both hiring and retention. There was a time when such age discrimination was blatant. Job vacancy announcements often specified a range of ages that would be acceptable, implying that people not in that age range need not apply. In 1965, more than half of all private employers in states without age discrimination legislation admitted that they used age limits in their hiring practices (Sheppard, 1969). Since the Age Discrimination in Employment Act (ADEA) was passed in 1967, age discrimination in employment has become more subtle. Because employers can no longer overtly cite age as a disqualification, it is difficult to assess the extent of discrimination in employment. Yet, it is possible to assemble a few clues.

Sheppard (1970) reported the results of a study of the age distribution of Packard employees who were hired by the "Big Three" automakers following the permanent Packard shutdown in 1956. Fifty-eight percent of those under 45 were hired by the Big Three, compared to 30 percent of those age 45 to 54 and only 15 percent of those age 55 and over. Among skilled workers, all of those under 40 found new jobs (usually at the same or higher pay), while 38 percent of those who were 40 or over became long-term unemployed, and those who did land new jobs experienced a sizeable reduction in pay. Eighty percent of Packard's employees were age 45 to 64 at the time of the shutdown. Parnes and King (1977) found that "displaced" middle-aged and older workers eventually found other employment, but usually at lower-status, lower-paying jobs compared to the ones they had lost, while younger workers tended to maintain or improve their position.

Older workers are more likely to be selected for layoffs (Sheppard, 1976; Parnes and King, 1977). Those who are laid off in middle age or later tend to work in trade or manufacturing jobs, to have less desirable jobs, to work for small business, to have no pension coverage, and to work for nonunionized firms (Parnes and King, 1977). Those who experience downward occupational mobility are frequently displaced from professional and managerial positions (Parnes and King, 1977).

Sheppard (1969) found that employment agencies behaved as if age were a disqualification. While older jobless workers sought help from employment agencies as often as younger workers did, the older workers received less attention. A smaller percentage were referred to employers for job interviews, given tests or counseling, or referred for vocational training. More than half of the older clients received no assistance from the employment agencies compared to less than 20 percent of the younger clients.

Rosen and Jerdee (1976b) presented a group of business students with a set of management exercises involving memos that required personnel decisions. The six cases involved: 1) a recently-hired but truculent shipping-room employee, 2) a candidate for a marketing job that needed "fresh solutions," 3) a candidate for a position that required the ability to make quick decisions under stress, 4) a request for transfer to a higher paying but more physically demanding job, 5) a request from a production staff employee to attend a conference on "new theories and research relevant to production systems," and 6) a request for a decision whether to terminate or retrain a computer programmer whose skills were obsolete due to changes in computer operations. They manipulated the age of the focal person in each memo by referring to the person as "younger" or "older" and, in four cases, including a personnel file that contained a photograph. Each participant received only one version of the six cases in order to make manipulation of age unobtrusive.

The results were as predictable as they were discouraging for older workers. The older shipping room employee was not expected to be able to change his behavior, and most participants thought he should be replaced. The younger employee was expected to be able to change, and most felt that a talking-to would solve the problem. Only 24 percent recommended promotion if they reviewed the older candidate for the marketing job, while 54 percent who reviewed the younger candidate recommended promotion, even though both candidates had identical qualifications.

The older candidate also came off worse for the risk-taking job. Twenty-five percent who reviewed the younger applicant recommended selection, but only 13 percent of those who reviewed the older one did. The older worker (age 56) who wanted a transfer to a more physically demanding job was significantly more likely to have his request denied. The older production staff employee was significantly more likely to get turned down on his request to attend a conference to update his knowledge. The older computer programmer was less likely to be retrained and more likely to be replaced.

Rosen and Jerdee concluded that the participants' assumptions about the physical, mental, and emotional characteristics of older workers produced managerial decisions that were obviously contrary to the well-being and career progress of older employees. Decisions about hiring, retention, correction, training, and retraining all suffered purely because of the age of the focal person.

While the above data suggest that age discrimination is a sizable factor in hiring and retention, it could be argued that older age is related to having outdated skills and more obsolete education, compared to people of younger ages. While there is some truth to this contention, studies that have controlled for skill level and education still found substantial age discrimination (Sheppard, 1969, 1970). There is also some evidence that the job search behavior of unemployed older workers is not as far-ranging or as intense as that of the younger unemployed (Sheppard, 1969). Because older workers tend to perceive age discrimination as common, it is likely that some do not try as hard as younger workers to find new jobs. But this does not discount the finding that younger employees referred to employers by state employment agencies were much more likely to be hired than were older workers so referred (Sheppard, 1969).

This evidence of age discrimination in employment is supported by Kasschau's (1976) research on perceived age discrimination among aerospace employees. Half of her sample said they had experienced age discrimination in finding a job, job advancement, or holding a job. Forty percent also viewed mandatory retirement as age discrimination in employment. Kasschau concluded that the strongest discriminatory pressure was felt at ages 55 to 59. The aerospace industry is characterized by a great deal of job mobility at all occupational levels as employees follow the ebb and flow of contracts and production demand. As such, there is probably more potential for age discrimination than might occur in other industries, simply because of the greater number of employment decisions to be made. And, as would be expected, the experience of age discrimination is widespread in that industry.

In 1975 over $7 million was paid by employers to over 2,400 workers as a result of law suits charging violations of the ADEA (DeLury, 1976). There is reason to believe that these cases pursued by the Department of Labor represent merely the tip of the iceberg regarding age discrimination. Department of Labor compliance officers were able to check only a handful of the one million establishments covered by ADEA. In addition, ADEA does not cover small businesses with fewer than 20 employees, and these employers are most likely to lay off mature workers. Finally, the fact that age discrimination is very difficult to document means that suits are brought only in the minority of cases for which there is sufficient proof. Thus, while the exact prevalence of age discrimination in employment is unknown, the evidence suggests that it is very common.

Age discrimination can also take the form of unequal treatment by public agencies. A study done by the U.S. Commission on Civil Rights (1977) found that age discrimination was present in numerous federally funded programs—community mental health centers, legal services, vocational rehabilitation, social services to low income individuals and families, employment and training services, the Food Stamp program, Medicaid, and vocational education. This problem existed in all regions of the country.

The older the people involved, the more likely they are to experience discrimination from public agencies. In addition, age discrimination was often compounded by discrimination on the basis of race, sex, national origin, or handicap status. The Commission on Civil Rights concluded that much of this discrimination stemmed from a narrow interpretation of the goals of legislation. For example, community health centers generally interpreted "preventive health care" as applying only to children and adolescents. Directors of employment programs saw their most appropriate clients to be males aged 22 to 44. Even age 22 was too old as far as some job training programs were concerned.

The Commission also found that state legislatures sometimes converted federal programs designed to serve all Americans into categorical programs aimed at specific age groups. For example, the State of Missouri passed a strong child abuse and neglect law—a worthy goal. But the state provided no funds to carry it out. Instead, federal funds for social services to everyone were earmarked to support the child abuse program, and as a result most cities in the state discounted their adult protective services programs. In many cases where states or local governments were responsible for defining the population eligible for federal programs, age discrimination resulted. For example, several states excluded older people from vocational rehabilitation programs because they were not of "employable age."

Age discrimination sometimes occurred when services were provided under contract with agencies that limited the ages of people they would serve. For example, a general social services contract with a child welfare agency was unlikely to result in social services to older adults. The Commission also found that outreach efforts were often aimed at specific age groups, which lessened the probability that other age groups would find out about programs for which they were eligible.

The Commission also concluded that general age discrimination in the public and private job market was an important underlying factor in age discrimination in employment, training, and vocational rehabilitation programs. So long as older people are denied jobs, agencies see little value in preparing them for jobs.

Age discrimination occurs whenever human beings are avoided or excluded in everyday activities because they are "the wrong age." Older people sometimes must literally intrude into various spheres of daily life in order to make people aware that they have something to offer. Most older people are not willing to fight for this recognition and, as a result, there is a great deal of age segregation in their activities and interactions. Only in the family do older people usually escape this sort of informal age discrimination.

Equally important is the impact of age discrimination on opportunities for beginning or continuing participation in various organizations. The stigma of implied inability and the resulting discrimination sometimes extend beyond paying jobs into volunteer jobs and other types of participation. Organizations created for older adults offer an alternative to those who have been rejected by organizations in the "main stream" but at the cost of age segregation. While many older adults prefer association mainly with their age peers, those who do not often find themselves without choices. Research on age discrimination in nonjob organizational settings is greatly needed.

WHAT ARE WE DOING?

Changing Age Prejudice

Attitudes and beliefs about aging have probably always had an ambivalent quality. Most people accept the idea that the scope of experience that comes with age may be a prerequisite for wisdom, and that having made one's fame and fortune can free people to be more supportive of those coming along. But at the same time, they also do not see these positive changes as always happening. And there still remain strong reservations that biological aging has inevitable physical and mental effects that offset the advantages of wisdom and warmth. As we saw earlier, these negative reservations, groundless as they may be, serve as the underpinnings of age prejudice and discrimination.

It is somewhat puzzling that the vast majority of the public's stated attitudes and beliefs about aging can be positive, and yet those used as a basis for action tend to be negative. Part of the answer to this anomaly may lie in the perceived threat that aging represents to American values. Rokeach (1973) found that family security, personal freedom, and contentment were major values for Americans, and all of these values could possibly be affected by one's own aging, the aging of family members, or the aging of society as a whole. In addition, the negative stereotypes of aging are seen as particularly threatening to high productivity and efficiency—keystone values that serve as guiding principles for formal organizations.

Yet, the choice may not be in deciding whether older people as a category are unable to work. Instead, the choice may be whether, in a society with a glut of labor, it is worth trying to identify those older people who are able to work. The issue involves the proportion of older people who are capable of working. If the common view is that most older people are incapable, then an obvious conclusion is that it may not be worth trying to find those who are capable and to continue to employ them. (This is as seen from the vantage point of the public good rather than that of what may be good for individuals.) If, on the other hand, the vast majority of older people are seen as capable, then there is no reason to exclude them wholesale from the labor force.

The public dialogue surrounding the evolution of programs to serve the aged has had an unfortunate side effect of reinforcing negative stereotypes of the aged as dependent, incapable, and needy. At the same time, ordinary, capable older persons have remained relatively invisible, of no interest to the media, to human services agencies, or to legislators. Over 70 percent of the elderly are ambulatory, physically independent people who live in ordinary communities. We do not see them precisely because they are not that distinguishable from other adults. In order to change the image of aging, the public must come to recognize that incapable older people are a small minority. They must come to see that the active, interesting, involved older person is the rule rather than the exception.

There are signs that this is happening. For example, television has historically been negative toward aging (Aronoff, 1974; Harris and Feinberg, 1977). But in 1979, prime time television series reflected a move toward a more balanced view. Older continuing characters represented 12 percent of all continuing characters, which is an accurate reflection of the proportion of older people in the population. Furthermore, adults of a wide variety of ages were shown working together in numerous occupational settings. When older adults worked with young and middle-aged adults, the older adults were portrayed in responsible positions that emphasized their experience and leadership potentials, while young adults were shown as less world-wise but eager and aggressive. Mature and older adults were being shown as able to run if necessary, as interested in romance, and as capable human beings (Atchley, 1980). Television has had little difficulty making middle-aged and older characters seem heroic. It is not an unrealistic premise.

In addition, public affairs and talk shows generally present older people who are quite capable. Older people on talk shows tend to be influential business leaders, prominent politicians, respected actors, or creative artists (Harris and Feinberg, 1977). The late 1970s saw the development of two public affairs shows specifically dealing with positive aspects of aging, *Over Easy* and *Prime Time.*

Thus, there are increasingly frequent messages in the media that most older people are not frail or incapable and that older people are quite able to make positive contributions to society. There is a growing recognition that the quality and fibre of a person says more about his or her potential contribution than does age. As the older population becomes more affluent and well-educated, we can expect the volume of these messages to increase. And presumably at some point there will be a turnaround in public acceptance of the negative stereotypes of aging.

Organizations of older persons also sometimes make concerted efforts to combat ageism. The Gray Panthers are an example. While relatively small in membership compared to other organizations of older people, the Gray Panthers have leaders who have been very effective in raising the national consciousness about ageism. Such efforts usually emphasize the desire and capacity of large numbers of older people to continue to be involved and productive participants in society.

Combating Age Discrimination

Age discrimination is being fought primarily through legislation and the courts. The Age Discrimination Act of 1975 and the Age Discrimination in Employment Act of 1967 are the major legislative efforts to reduce age discrimination.

The Age Discrimination Act (ADA) of 1975, amended in 1978, is a civil-rights-type statute that prohibits age discrimination in any program that receives federal funds. As cited earlier, the Commission on Civil Rights found age discrimination in all of the ten largest federal aid programs. Thus, the need for this legislation is clear, and potentially it could have wide-ranging effects.

Any law is only as strong as its enforcement, however, especially if the statute is controversial. In this case, the Department of Health, Education, and Welfare (HEW) was the linchpin for enforcement of ADA because HEW was given the responsibility to interpret which exceptions to ADA were to be allowed. For example, the original legislation states that programs making age distinctions "under the authority of any law" are exempt from ADA. HEW decided to allow all state statutes and local ordinances to qualify under the "any law" exception, despite the fact that the Commission on Civil Rights study showed that state and local governments were often responsible for creating regulations (laws and ordinances) that diverted program efforts away from older people. Former Secretary of HEW Joseph Califano has said that allowing state and local governments to enact exceptions to federal civil rights legislation does not make sense (Howard, 1979), yet HEW continued throughout 1979 to allow this to happen.

Despite this and other enforcement questions, the fact that all federal agencies were required to develop and submit to HEW by the end of 1979 a plan for implementing ADA, and the fact that all agencies employing 15 or more people and receiving federal funds must certify by June 8, 1981, that they are complying with ADA will produce heightened sensitivity to age discrimination. It will be some time before the full effects of ADA are known, but if its enforcement parallels the legislation protecting the handicapped from discrimination, the effects could be sizable.

The Age Discrimination in Employment Act of 1967 is designed to promote employment of older persons based on their ability rather than their age and to prohibit "arbitrary" age discrimination in employment. Specifically, ADEA prohibits refusal to hire, discharge, discriminatory treatment during employment, advertisements reflecting age preference, refusal of employment agencies to refer clients because of their age, discriminatory treatment by labor unions, and retaliation against employees who assert their rights under the Act.

The only exception to ADEA is cases in which age is a "bona fide occupational qualification." In court tests of this exception, a policy of not hiring bus drivers over age 35 was upheld by an appeals court, presumably to protect the public, and the U.S. Supreme Court upheld the forced retirement of a highway patrol officer on grounds that law enforcement duties require physical capacities beyond those of a 50-year-old man. These court decisions are on shaky ground in terms of the scientific evidence that can be mustered to support them, and they illustrate graphically the fact that courts often operate to justify common prejudices and the resultant discrimination. In the case of the bus company, no evidence was offered that bus drivers trained after age 35 were less safe than those trained at an earlier age. The court merely accepted the company's assertion that this was true. The Supreme Court upheld the dismissal of a highway patrolman who had just been pronounced physically fit for duty of the highway patrol's own physician. Following the intent of ADEA, it seems imperative that courts require scientific evidence of age-related changes that interfere with job performance before certifying age-based employment policies as "bona fide." In addition, the burden of proof should be on the employer to provide such evidence. In other words, age categories of people should be presumed able until proven otherwise.

The original ADEA allowed mandatory retirement if it was tied to the provisions of a pension plan and provided no coverage beyond age 64. The 1978 amendments to ADEA raised the mandatory retirement age to 70 for the vast majority of jobs and eliminated mandatory retirement in federal jobs altogether.

Combating age discrimination in public programs has also been a priority of the largest organizations of older people—the National Council of Senior Citizens (3 million members) and the National Retired Teachers Association/American Association of Retired Persons (6 million combined membership, jointly administered). These organizations employ skilled lobbyists to insure that Congress and the administration set aside appropriate program funds for older people. The National Council on Aging, a group made up of agencies serving older people, pursues similar goals.

WHAT HAVE WE ACCOMPLISHED?

From 1967 until July of 1979, enforcement of ADEA was the responsibility of the Wage and Hour Division of the Department of Labor. Complaints under ADEA gradually increased from 1,000 in 1969 to just over 5,000 in 1977. Department of Labor investigators found that in 1978 over 4,000 people were owed more than $14 million by over 700 employers who had violated ADEA. Of these cases, about a third were settled by agreement with employers and the other two-thirds were referred for litigation. Yet, these cases probably represent only a small proportion of potential complaints of age discrimination. For one thing, employees tend to be poorly informed about what ADEA prohibits and how to claim their rights under the Act. For another, ADEA compliance officers are able to check only a small percentage of establishments covered by ADEA. Finally, ADEA does not apply to small businesses with fewer than 20 employees, and these are precisely the employers most likely to lay off or terminate mature workers (Parnes and King, 1977).

In July 1979 enforcement responsibilities for ADEA were transferred to the Equal Employment Opportunities Commission (EEOC), an arm of the Department of Justice. Many Labor Department staffers were transferred to EEOC, including some compliance officers and some legal staff. While EEOC has a strong commitment to enforcement of ADEA, it remains to be seen whether the shift in locus of enforcement responsibility will cause at least a temporary slowdown in enforcement activity.

Organized advocates of older people have been very successful in getting federal program dollars earmarked for these persons, at least compared with the attention being paid to other disadvantaged groups. For example, during the decade of the 1970s federal program dollars aimed at the poor and at minorities decreased substantially, while dollars going to programs for older people experienced a sizeable increase. This suggests that because aging cuts across social lines it has a high level of legitimacy to the public, to legislators, and to administrators that can be exploited by advocates of the elderly. However, there certainly are limits to how much the public is willing to do for older people, and we may become more aware of those limits in the 1980s.

WHERE ARE WE GOING?

The past 15 years have seen changes that have reduced public support of ageism and age discrimination. New emphases in the mass media have increased the visibility of capable older people. Legislation such as ADA and ADEA, while limited, has provided legal tools for combating age discrimination. The more individual victories that occur in the courtroom arena, and the more publicity these victories receive, the more likely it is that employers will begin to see age discrimination as a risky practice. Older people's advocates have been successful in increasing federal, state, and local efforts on behalf of the aged. We can, therefore, expect some continued improvement as a result of the inertia of current trends.

However, there are population changes in the offing that may accelerate this process. Since 1957, the birth rate in the United States has fallen substantially. Barring an unforeseen economic boom, fertility is likely to remain low. Reduced pressure of young people coming into the labor force means reduced pressure to get people out through retirement. By 1990 the major problem facing employers is likely to be "how do we get workers entitled to retirement to stay on?" rather than "how can we encourage more retirements at earlier ages." Increased difficulty in funding retirement income programs will also exert pressure to find ways of encouraging older workers to remain employed.

There is an interesting fact about age discrimination in employment. When we can't afford it, we drop it. For example, age discrimination was rampant during the depression years of the 1930s. But during World War II, when labor was in short supply because of the demands of the war effort, large-scale testing programs were developed and used to get older people back to work and to match their skills to appropriate jobs (McFarland, 1973). This same pattern occurred in Britain (Phillipson, n.d.). The point is that our basic ambivalence about aging allows us to emphasize either the positive or the negative, depending on our current objectives. And while legislation against using negative beliefs helps, it still depends on the current social climate for the support necessary to enforce it.

Fortunately for those who will experience aging in the United States over the next 30 years, most signs point to societal pressures toward less age discrimination in employment. In the interim, however, older people and their advocates need to be well-acquainted with ADA and ADEA and how to claim their rights under law.

Age discrimination in public programs will be reduced more slowly, if at all. The growing numbers of elderly will definitely have an effect. For example, community mental health centers currently provide very few outpatient services to older people. Extending service to the current older population seems like a costly and impossible job. When the older population is increased by 50 percent (as it will in the next 20 years), it will seem even more costly and impossible.

Age discrimination in informal settings should lessen as awareness of the capabilities of the well elderly penetrates public opinion and beliefs. Yet this too is apt to be a slow process.

One hopes the future will also involve more input from sociology about the process of age discrimination and how it can be influenced. This will require much greater effort by sociologists interested in basic and applied research on age discrimination. It is ironic that although discrimination in general is an area that rests solidly within the boundaries of sociology, sociologists have contributed very little of what we know about age discrimination. Obviously, this represents both a great opportunity and a great challenge for future directions in applied sociological research and practice.

REFERENCES AND SUGGESTED READINGS

Auchenbaum, W.A. and P.A. Kusnerz. 1978. *Images of Old Age in America, 1970 to the Present.* Ann Arbor: University of Michigan/Wayne State University, Institute of Gerontology.

Aronoff, C. 1974. "Old age in prime time." *Journal of Communication* 24:86–87.

*Atchley, R.C. 1980. *The Social Forces in Later Life,* 3rd ed. Belmont, Calif.: Wadsworth.

Atchley provides an overview of what is known about aging in general. See especially the chapters on age discrimination, employment, and social inequality.

Axelrod, S. and C. Eisdorfer. 1961. "Attitudes toward old people: An empirical analysis of the stimulus-group validity of the Tuckman-Lorge questionnaire." *Journal of Gerontology* 16:75–80.

Botwinick, J. 1978. *Aging and Behavior,* 2nd ed. New York: Springer.

Collette-Pratt, C. 1976. "Attitudinal predictors of devaluation of old age in multigenerational sample." *Journal of Gerontology* 31:193–97.

Comfort, A. 1976. "Age prejudice in America." *Social Policy* 7:3–8.

Delury, B.E. 1976. "The age discrimination in employment act: Background and highlights from recent cases." *Industrial Gerontology* 3:37–40.

Eisdorfer, C. and J. Altrocchi. 1961. "A comparison of attitudes toward old age and mental illness." *Journal of Gerontology* 16:340–43.

Finch, C.E. and L. Hayflick, eds. 1977. *Handbook of the Biology of Aging.* New York: Van Nostrand Reinhold.

Fozard, J.L. and G.D. Carr. 1972. "Age differences and psychological estimates of abilities and skill." *Industrial Gerontology* 13:75–96.

Harris, A.J. and J.F. Feinberg. 1977. "Television and aging: Is what you see what you get?" *Gerontologist* 17:464–67.

Harris, L. and Associates. 1975. *The Myth and Reality of Aging in America.* Washington, D.C.: National Council on Aging.

Hendricks, J. and C.D. Hendricks. 1977–1978. "The age old question of old age; was it really so much better when?" *International Journal of Aging and Human Development* 8:138–54.

Hickey, T., L.A. Hickey, and R.A. Kalish. 1968. "Children's perceptions of the elderly." *Journal of Genetic Psychology* 112:227–35.

Hickey, T. and R.A. Kalish. 1968. "Young people's perceptions of adults." *Journal of Gerontology* 23:215–19.

Howard, E.F. 1979. "Public policy report." *Perspective on Aging* (July/Aug): 26–8.

Kasschau, P.L. 1976. "Perceived age discrimination in a sample of aerospace employees." *Gerontologist* 16:166–73.

_____. 1977. "Age and race discrimination reported by middle-aged and older persons." *Social Forces* 55(3):728–42.

Laslett, P. 1976. "Societal development and aging." In *Handbook of Aging and the Social Sciences,* edited by R.H. Binstock and E. Shanas, pp. 87–116. New York: Van Nostrand Reinhold.

McFarland, R.A. 1973. "The need for functional age measures in industrial gerontology." *Industrial Gerontology* 19:1–19.

*Parnes, H.S. and R. King. 1977. "Middle-aged job losers." *Industrial Gerontology* 4:77–96.
   This article gives an excellent account of the subtleties of age discrimination in employment.

Phillipson, C. n.d. *The Emergence of Retirement.* Durham, England: University of Durham.

Rokeach, M. 1973. *The Nature of Human Values.* New York: The Free Press.

*Rosen, B. and T.H. Jerdee. 1976a. "The nature of job-related stereotypes." *Journal of Applied Psychology* 61:180–83.
   This is a well-done research report that details the *content* of age prejudice as it applies to jobs.

* _____. 1976b. "The influence of age stereotypes on managerial decision." *Journal of Applied Psychology* 61:428–32.
   This is a well-done research report that documents the kinds of decisions that produce age discrimination in employment.

Seefeldt, C., R.K. Jantz, A. Galper, and K. Serock. 1977. "Using pictures to explore children's attitudes toward the elderly." *Gerontologist* 17:506–12.

Sheppard, H.L. 1969. "Aging and manpower development." In *Aging and Society, Volume Two: Aging and the Professions,* edited by M.W. Riley, et al., pp. 161–200. New York: Russell Sage Foundation.

_____. 1970. *Industrial Gerontology.* Cambridge, Mass.: Schenkman.

_____. 1976. "Work and retirement." In *Handbook of Aging and the Social Sciences,* edited by R.H. Binstock and E. Shanas, pp. 286–309. New York: Van Nostrand Reinhold.

Simmons, L.W. 1960. "Aging in preindustrial societies." In *Handbook of Social Gerontology,* edited by C. Tibbitts, pp. 62–91. Chicago: University of Chicago Press.

Tuckman, J. and M. Lavell. 1957. "Self-classification as old or not old." *Geriatrics* 12:666–67.

Tuckman, J. and I. Lorge. 1953a. "Attitudes toward old people." *Journal of Social Psychology* 37:249–60.

_____. 1953b. *Retirement and the Industrial Worker: Prospect and Reality.* New York: Columbia University Teachers College.

_____. 1953c. "When aging begins and stereotypes about aging." *Journal of Gerontology* 8:489–92.

_____. 1956. "Perceptive stereotypes about life adjustments." *Journal of Social Psychology* 43:239–45.

_____. 1958a. "Attitudes toward aging of individuals with experiences with the aged." *Journal of Genetic Psychology* 87:199–204.

_____. 1958b. "The projection of personal symptoms into stereotypes about aging." *Journal of Gerontology* 13:70–73.

*U.S. Commission on Civil Rights. 1977. *The Age Discrimination Study.* Washington, D.C.: U.S. Commission on Civil Rights.

This is a comprehensive study of age discrimination in the delivery of services to the elderly by public agencies.

Wilder, C.S. 1971. "Chronic conditions and limitations of activity and mobility. United States, July 1975 to June 1967." *Vital and Health Statistics,* Series 10, No. 61. Washington, D.C.: U.S. Government Printing Office.

Part
D

PROVIDING
SOCIAL
SERVICES

As modern societies pass into the postindustrial stage of development, they are faced with a critical challenge: how to satisfy the rising welfare expectations of citizens. Daniel Bell has argued that "A post-industrial society is based on services.... If an industrial society is defined by the quanitity of goods as marking a standard of living, the post-industrial society is defined by the quality of life as measured by the services and amenities—health, education, recreation, and the arts—which are deemed desirable and possible for anyone."* Increasingly these and other services are viewed as rights of citizenship rather than as discretionary gifts bestowed by a benevolent government. Accordingly, the quality and the availability of services become highly charged public issues.

A society's ability to provide services to its citizens is subject to several constraints. First, every government sets priorities for spending the funds it has available. For most modern societies the highest priority appears to be defense, resulting in large expenditures on weapons and the military. Services such as health and education account for a considerably smaller share of the national budget. Second, citizens are divided into a variety of interest groups that frequently make conflicting demands for services. Thus, the elderly and the poor may argue for improved health and legal services, while younger people and the wealthy may emphasize the need for quality education or better recreational facilities. Third, there is often disagreement over what are minimum standards for services. For example, citizens may push for free medical and dental care, while public officials staunchly oppose "give away" programs. Finally, the provision of public services is often questioned because of its presumed effects on recipients. Do people feel patronized? If citizens are given "too much," do they lose individual initiative? Are persons who receive some services (e.g., welfare payments) stigmatized by those who do not?

The growing demand for services and the constraints affecting their availability raise a number of important questions about programs for service delivery, many of which have been addressed by applied sociologists. What are the goals of social programs and are these goals being achieved? Are there better ways to deliver services? Are the people who really need particular services actually getting them? If not, why? Are the needs of some groups being overlooked, whether inadvertently or on purpose?

In each of the following chapters the authors examine the adequacy of service delivery programs in the areas of education, health, mental health, the law, and leisure. Emphasis is placed on what is being done now and what changes can be expected in the future. As demands for more and better services increase,

---

*Daniel Bell, *The Coming of Post-Industrial Society: A Venture in Social Forecasting* (New York: Basic Books, 1973), p. 127.

these issues will become even more critical. As Bell has suggested, judgments about our standard of living have come to be equated with the quality of services provided. If these services fall short of the public's expectations, confidence in government cannot be maintained. The result would be a serious threat to the stability of government and, in the end, the continuity of social order.

16 EDUCATIONAL SERVICES

Donald A. Hansen and Vicky A. Johnson

The recent history of applied sociology in education is rather dramatic, as academic histories go. Once the poorest of stepchildren to both disciplines of education and sociology, the field was showered with attention in the 1960s and sparkled with excitement. But this was no Cinderella story: by the end of the 1970s a general discouragement had displaced optimism; certainty had turned to cynicism. But hopefulness also could be seen, in diverse efforts to restructure basic understandings about the production and application of sociological knowledge.

In earlier decades, sociologists had visited educational areas with something of the sense of missionaries, offering enlightenment on problems that from a distance appeared quite simple. But in the 1960s some sociologists began to "go native," discovering in schooling cultures the full range of problems in theory and method that plague sociologists in general. In schooling those problems are particularly troublesome, for within education there is an immediacy that forces the continual revision of hypotheses and theoretical abstractions. There is also an unusual sweep of relevant experience, demanding perspectives that link the everyday details of individual lives and classroom interactions to the complexities of organizational structures and to larger contexts of political and socioeconomic change.

WHAT ARE THE PROBLEMS?

Recognition of the complexities of a sociological perspective on education has increased rapidly during the past 20 years, as sociologists joined educators, school administrators, and teachers in efforts to identify the processes and outcomes of massive schooling programs and projects. To date, the sociologist's

341

main contribution appears to have been to raise new questions, casting veils of uncertainty over what had previously been accepted as obvious. Far less has been accomplished toward establishing a viable perspective on education in the United States or identifying reasonable alternatives to faulted programs.

"Taking" and "Making" Problems

In part, the limited contributions of U.S. sociologists may be due to their overriding concern with problem areas that have been identified for them by educators. Sociologists have turned so energetically to the practicalities of U.S. education, as defined by educators, that the recent history of the area might be characterized as a period of "taking" schooling problems, that is, accepting as problematic those conditions that teachers, administrators, and politicians have identified as educational problems. In this role, the sociologist acts as a skilled technician, a troubleshooter, a potentially valuable consultant for the solution of large- and small-scale organizational problems. An optimistic image of the sociologist as the "deliverer of educational services" has emerged and dominated the field through the 1960s and 1970s.

In the following sections, we consider several of the problems addressed in this spirit in recent years, the knowledge that has resulted, and some of the reasons so little work of practical value has yet been accomplished. The final section gives a brief account of a more recent thrust in the sociology of education, toward "making" problems in education. That thrust is toward critical explorations of the processes and structures of education, placed within larger social, political, economic, and cultural contexts.

Of the diverse problems that sociologists have taken from educators, few are so compelling or persistent as those concerning school achievement and inequalities in school performance. Although a wide diversity of problem areas addressed by sociologists will be mentioned in this chapter, and although numerous sociological efforts to address practical problems of education will be illustrated, the area of inequality will serve as our primary vehicle for considering sociological services to education.

Problems of Inequality: Heredity and Motivation

At the center of the concern for inequality is the long-familiar relation between years of schooling and differences in the achievement of blacks and whites. Why do black students, particularly those in urban poverty areas, fall further behind with each year of schooling? The answers have been simple and convincing, at least to those who propose them. Some, noting that even at early ages blacks score lower than whites on achievement and ability tests, argue that there are racial differences in inherited intelligence, and these differences more than anything else explain the racial character of social class in advanced countries. Through natural selection, for which schools often provide an arena, the less able are relegated to the lower social-economic levels of society. Clearly, not all blacks are less able than whites, but proportionately more are, hence the racial character of social stratification (Herrnstein, 1973).

Few sociologists have found such genetic theories palatable. But the addition of another ingredient appears to heighten sociological appetites, particularly among persons who trained in this field in the 1940s, 1950s, and early 1960s. That ingredient is motivation. Combined with ability, motivation provides an image of a "meritocracy" in which "IQ plus effort" determines one's position in the society. This perspective assumes a functional image of society, in which rewards are distributed to qualified people to ensure that they will adequately perform roles that are necessary for system functioning. Schools are seen as mechanisms for producing and transmitting knowledge, and for selecting and sorting individuals according to their abilities and motivation (Clark, 1962; Dreeben, 1968). From this perspective, educational inequalities are only partially due to differences in schooling characteristics, which are themselves formed and transformed in response to the needs of the larger system. Far more important are the characteristics of the students themselves.

In contrast, many who hold a more radical perspective argue almost the reverse. They insist that the basic cause of inequality is the schooling processes, in which some activities and characteristics are rewarded and others are discouraged or even punished. Changing the schools, thus, could produce quite different patternings of inequality (Bowles and Gintis, 1976; Levitas, 1974).

Problems of Inequality: Interactional and Contextual Variables

To most sociologists, the matter is not so clear. There seems to be a far more complex pattern of interaction between students, schools, and larger social processes. The emphasis on "motivation," for example, has led some sociologists to examine various influences on the individual, including one's aspirations, needs to achieve, and willingness to delay gratification; parental expectations and peer group pressures; the competitive handicaps of a "culture of poverty"; the deprivations of a "poverty of culture" (Sewell and Hauser, 1975; Valentine 1968). Within the school, attention has focused on the quality of faculty, educational resources, counseling processes and recordkeeping, the authority of teachers, and differences in teaching styles and expectations (Cicourel and Kitsuse, 1963; Coleman, et al., 1966; Hurn, 1978; Rist, 1970). Attention has turned, too, to classroom processes and curricular organization, evaluation, and flexibility (MacKay, 1974; Young, 1971). Often stimulated by controversies over bussing, studies also have been conducted on characteristics of student populations. Of particular concern has been the question of an optimal mixture of whites and nonwhites, while secondary concerns have included sex, age, and socioeconomic status compositions (Alexander and Eckland, 1975; Eggleston, 1977; Wilson, 1969).

Many other practical problems of schooling have captured the attention of sociologists, such as school unrest, violence and truancy, and changing patterns of relaxation and sexual enjoyment among the young (Chesler and Crowfoot, 1975; Spady, 1974). Other less dramatic but profoundly important issues have been recognized by sociologists. Most notable: problems of administrative controls and their relationship to schooling processes; problems of bureaucratic growth and unresponsiveness; problems of the influence of school boards and other governing bodies and of their vulnerability to other sectors of society; problems of taxpayer resistance and public support; problems of political involvement in schooling matters and educational decisions (Bidwell, 1965; Corwin, 1974; Rist and Anson, 1977).

Concerned with the role of schools in furthering social equity and justice, sociologists have joined other researchers in efforts to establish the correlates of educational inequalities, and to identify the linkages between school achievement and linguistic ability, value, and motivation (Bernstein, 1973, 1974, 1976; Entwistle, 1970). A whole range of problems concerning multicultural and multilingual schooling has forced its attention on the sociology of education (Baratz and Baratz, 1970; Lightfoot, 1978). At the same time, the politics of schooling have grown undeniably troublesome, highlighting still other problems of control in administering programs of affirmative action, compensatory education, bussing, and voucher systems (Carnoy and Levin, 1976; Coleman, et al., 1977).

The Problem of Educational Problems

The many problem areas that sociologists of education have taken from educators are diverse in nature and scope, but they can be represented by a single sensitizing question: *Who* learns *what* in what *kinds of settings* and with what *individual and social consequences?* Each component of this question involves a variety of related issues. For example, the question, "Who learns?" directs attention to the characteristics of the individual learner, such as ability, aspirations, and self-esteem. When these personal characteristics are related to learning, another set of concerns is emphasized, dealing with who brings to schooling the ability, aspirations, and esteem that contribute to success. Do these students come from one type of family rather than another? From one socioeconomic grouping more than another? From one form of peer group culture rather than another?

Similarly, the question "What is learned?" may first draw attention to the success rates of different students with various components of the curriculum. Other topics quickly arise, however. If we note, for instance, that girls excel in the liberal arts while boys generally do better at mathematics and physical sciences, we might ask: Why is it so easy to divide contemporary U.S. curricula into such categories? What characteristics of the curricula are being offered in our schools? How do they relate to genetic and cultural differences between the sexes? How are they influenced by the special qualities of teachers, classrooms, schools, and communities? Who has made the decisions that resulted in these curricula?

Still other questions are raised by those who take a more critical perspective. What sort of ideological or value commitments are implied in the curriculum, and how might these values be related to the social involvement of the decision makers? How are these value positions in the curricula related to social, economic, and political conditions in U.S. society? How have they changed over the past decades and centuries? How might they now be altered, and what character might they have in coming decades and centuries. This list also goes on. And so might the lists of questions that relate to each of the other components of the initial "sensitizing" question.

By comparison, an answer to the question "What do we know?" is fairly straightforward. It is also fairly discouraging.

WHAT DO WE KNOW?

Faced with such arrays of complex questions, it may be difficult to imagine a sociologist approaching educational services with any degree of assurance. Nonetheless, in the early and mid 1960s the writings of sociologists often showed optimism and self-confident zeal. A decade later, however, the optimism had given way to discouragement and modesty marked by a self-admitted impotence. Most sociologists of education were forced to confess that, beyond certain specific and delimited accomplishments, they had been able to contribute little to the workings of our educational system or the larger society. Some insights had been gained, but they were not as clear as had once been expected, and they seemed to have few or no implications for policies and programs. Once unities of thought and confidence dominated the field; now it was beset with diversity and uncertainty.

From Unity to Uncertainty

In earlier decades, sociological propositions about the relationship of schooling to social inequalities seemed almost self-obvious and came close to attaining the status of "sociological truth." Although the themes varied, it was widely held that education offered both individuals and groups mobility routes to higher status. If education itself wasn't the great melting pot, it served as one of the active ingredients for breaking down inequalities and social barriers. The sources of inequality lay elsewhere: rooted in our histories and perpetuated by ignorance, intolerance, fear, and self-centeredness. Education could combat all of these, not only among the uneducated, but also by teaching the advantaged greater tolerance and appreciation for the human qualities of those who had been locked by history into disadvantaged positions.

In this liberal sociological image, the schools were cast in something of a heroic role. In real life, however, the hero was quixotic, constantly missing opportunities, mistaking enemies, and faltering and failing in every effort. Rather than eradicating inequalities in society, the schools seemed to be failing the advantaged as well as the disadvantaged. By the 1960s more cynical sociologists were heard to say that the one saving grace of schools was that they did their job so poorly.

More optimistic sociologists saw the schools as basically sound, but in need of help to fulfill their enormous potentials. The strengths and defects of U.S. education were to be placed in perspective by comparing it with educational systems in other countries, which invariably were seen as less successful in meeting far milder challenges.

Despite these differing views, there was general consensus in the 1950s and 1960s that education could help produce equality. Empirical data seemed to support that argument. For example, both historical and contemporary statistical evidence continues to support the generalization that the relationship between social class and schooling is declining in industrial societies. One's social class is no longer the major determinant of the amount of education one's children will receive; entry into school is no longer the privilege of only the elite; success in school increasingly depends on one's merit and effort and decreasingly on one's family connections; occupational success increasingly depends on one's success in school. This liberal perspective—buttressed by data showing that amount of schooling is in turn directly related to one's later income and occupational status—suggests that the gross disadvantages suffered by blacks, Chicanos, and other minority group members will be reduced if only we can identify the necessary selection, curricular and evaluation procedures. Although some sociologists dissented from this stance, unity outweighed diversity and conviction overwhelmed uncertainty.

Today, the imbalances have reversed. What appeared to be firm sociological generalizations have been called into question. For example, the declining relationship between schooling and social class may pertain only to traditional conceptions of class in Western society. This trend may mask the rise of new systems of stratification in which the fortunes of birth play an important, though different, part in the educational and occupational attainments of children. It is possible, for instance, that the social and cultural positionings that parents provide their children may be far more important for educational careers than in the past. These differences lie not in status or material advantages, but in cultural exposures such as habits, tastes, styles of peer interaction, and community involvements. It is also possible that interpersonal qualities of family life may be far more important today for individual success in school and continuation to higher levels of education.

Such alternatives to the liberal visions of the mid-century United States suggest that an answer to a question "What do we know about the schools and social structures?" depends upon who is asked. Collectively, sociologists don't seem to know what they know. It may be that in a few years sociological opinion will again coalesce in an accepted interpretation, but recent years have clearly been marked more by diversity than unity.

The Promise in Uncertainty

The diversity has considerable merit, however. Most importantly, it encourages a rethinking of ideas about the relationships between individual characteristics, schooling, and the larger social order. Recent efforts to more adequately conceptualize those relationships have suggested promising modifications of established perspectives, while at the same time calling into question other, more restricted, approaches to the study of what goes on within schools. To accurately understand the relationship of schools to the larger society, it is now being argued, we must more fully understand schooling processes themselves.

Boocock (1972:311-12; see also Boocock, 1976:10-16) for example, argues that the school displays a number of characteristics as a social system that prevent it from being as effective as it might be. These include:

1. A reward system based on individual competition in which there are no winners and many losers and that generates peer resistance to high-level performance, discourages motivation for cooperative learning among students, and encourages cheating.

2. Control by the teacher, encouraging passivity in students, and a definition of the student role that is incongruent with other roles that may be more attractive to the young.

3. A definition of schooling success that is very limited in its range of intellectual approaches and styles.

4. An obscurity of the "meaningful connections" between schooling and future possibilities.

5. A tendency to regard at least some students as members of typified subgroups or categories, which may encourage them to fulfill low expectations.

Other sociologists have grown increasingly concerned about the nature of the curriculum, the ways in which it is structured, and the social, political, and economic influences on the structuring processes (Keddie, 1971; Mehan, 1979). Still others have returned to the comparatively well-developed area of educational organization, to ask once again how organizational processes and structures affect what is learned by the individual and by categories of individuals, and how these structures and processes may influence teachers' attitudes, behaviors, and classroom relationships (Corwin, 1974; Goodwin, 1977).

As concern for the relationship of schools to larger structures forces attention to what goes on in schools, this "internal" attention simultaneously forces attention "outward" to the larger society. To date, despite considerable research effort and more considerable polemics, there is little direct support for "within-school" explanations of unequal performance. In a recent review, Christopher

Hurn notes the lack of empirical evidence for what have been taken as "plausible explanations":

> We simply cannot say that if schools had higher expectations for the performance of lower class students that the performance of these students would improve. We cannot say that if tracking were abolished, then differences among students in their performance would diminish. Nor finally, can we argue that the presence of a student subculture hostile to academic performance is a major explanation of why students of underprivileged origins do poorly in school. In some schools any or all of these arguments may be correct, but little evidence shows that they hold for most schools. (Hurn, 1978:163)

In earlier times, most sociologists might have responded to such discouraging comments about within-school explanations by turning their attention to characteristics of individual students, pointing to the persistent and impressive correlations between achievement and such factors as level of aspiration, level of self-esteem, sense of environmental control, tolerance for ambiguity, and delayed gratification. In the current discourse, such explanations appear glib and superficial, in part because measures of these factors are so often situationally relative. A student may report or exhibit low self-esteem or a sense of control in some classroom situations but not in others.

Out of this sociological confusion and discord still other possibilities are emerging. Perhaps most promising is increased concern for the *linkages* between schooling and other social structures that are salient in the student's life. Many years ago, in an attempt to identify the causes of rebellion in the high school, Stinchcombe (1964) emphasized the importance of the "articulation" between what a student experiences in school and what he or she expects to experience in the workplace after leaving school. The broader implications of Stinchcombe's work were ignored until quite recently, however. For instance, "mis-articulations" may contribute to the lower overall achievement levels of minority students or the lower achievement of females in courses that are closely related to the job requirements of industry and commerce. It might be expected that in the 1980s these speculative discussions that emerged in the 1970s will take form in empirical research.

The issues discussed here are but a few of the many topics that are currently emerging. They speak to both the poverty and the possibilities of our current sociological knowledge about schooling and education. As a gross generalization, it seems that the answer to the question, "What do we know?" must be "very little." But we do know enough to continue to explore.

This lack of specific knowledge about schooling in social, cultural, and political contexts may have deterred many sociologists from attempting to deliver educational services to schools and policy makers. It has contributed to the current disinterest among policy makers and school administrators in sociological contributions. Nonetheless, in recent decades, a sizable and growing number of sociologists has been employed in delivering educational services at all levels, from the classroom to state and federal administrative and decision-making bodies.

WHAT ARE WE DOING?

It is fortunate that, in attempting to deliver services to education, sociologists are not limited to the knowledge base provided by the sociology of education per se. Few areas of sociology have been as pressured for policy-relevant statements as has the sociology of education in recent years, and few have been so volatile in their responses. In part, this is due to the political vulnerability of the sociology of education and to the absence of strong traditions of research and theory in the field.

The sociologist who delivers educational services is able to turn to the rich literature on organizational structures and change, on bureaucratic decision making, on collective behavior, on the sociological and social-psychological contexts and consequences of intra group conflict, and to a diversity of other areas. Throughout the 1960s, armed with the conceptual tools and commitments of their liberal traditions, sociologists became involved as never before or since in policy formation, program implementation, and evaluation. With unprecedented interest, politicians and administrators invited the cooperation of sociologists on problems of school integration, bussing, alternative education, student activism and violence, and schooling governance. In more recent years, sociologists have continued their involvement in these debates, as well as in questions of life-long learning, voucher plans, and career development.

The promise of the sociological tradition has proved elusive, however. When wielded by skillful craftsmen, sociological theories offer sensitizing interpretations of educational problems. Nevertheless, sociological research seems to approach those interpretations eliptically, and to ignore altogether the bedrock question of what should be done. By the mid 1970s, a theme that promised to dominate discussion in the 1980s became well-established as sociologists again began to ask why sociological research is of so little use to educational policies and programs.

Part of the answer was to be found in the poverty of research and theory that is specific to the sociological understanding of education. In the 1970s, however, another awareness grew: sociological theory and research in general have far less to offer applied sociology than previously had been thought. That awareness drew closer attention to the basic assumption and methods of sociological inquiry.

Questions of Relevance and Application

The reason sociological literature offers little of practical use to education is basically simple: sociologists rarely point their research toward policy implications, interventions, or innovations. To be sure, a great deal—perhaps the heavy majority—of sociological research on schooling is "relevant" in the sense that it speaks to pressing practical problems of human development, social control, organization, and change. But even among those who identify themselves as "applied" sociologists—an identification inherent in the term "sociologist of education"—few seriously consider "application" in their research designs.

The assumption is widely shared in the field that relevance automatically begets application. That assumption seems particularly compelling when the subject studied is currently a "hot issue." "To be utterly cynical," James Davis (1975:235) writes, "I will hazard the guess that if this article on ethnicity and educational plans had been about the difference in path coefficients between students at Andover and Exeter, it might not have been printed. The referees would have (justifiably) said, 'so what?'"

Beyond this, sociologists tend to choose variables that defy manipulation, such as socioeconomic status, IQ, and aspirations. This emphasis may be encouraged by the "intellectual folkways" of sociology that favor relevance but are prejudiced against pragmatic content. These folkways can be especially troublesome for sociologists of education, particularly if they are in positions where their academic qualifications are judged by peers in terms of adherence to currently prestigeful modes of sociological inquiry, rather than on the basis of their contributions to educational policy and programs.

Questions of Methodology

Statistical and methodological problems also plague the sociological researcher, some of which must be related to the strength of substantive theories. Research in the sociology of education rarely yields correlations beyond the .3 or .4 level, and the call to action is hardly justified when one's findings at best account for 10 or 15 percent of the variance in the subject under study (cf., Davis, 1975).

Stronger correlations would be of only limited use to those who would provide educational services, however. An even more basic problem haunts the sociologist's quantitative research: to date it has been *primarily* correlational. The beginning methodology student quickly learns that "correlation is not causation," but the exigencies of research and the traditions of inquiry in sociology have continued to support correlation as the primary method of inquiry. Yet, it allows only the most uncertain of policy implications ("Years of schooling relates positively to income; let's keep everyone in school and we'll all be rich!").

In recent applications, correlation techniques have acquired considerable sophistication—in multivariate regressions, path analyses, and contextual analyses —so that we might now speak of a "second generation of statistical techniques."

The computer made possible the development and gives promise of facilitating even more sophisticated procedures. To some researchers such developments are exhilarating and point toward models in which causal direction can be detected. To more cynical observers—especially those who are more dedicated to "qualitative" methods—the most sophisticated of these techniques remains simple correlation, and more complex techniques not only distort the reality of the area being investigated, but also create a false image of it.

Whatever the validity of such claims and charges, the basic criticism remains: correlational techniques yield legitimate policy implications only in the very "long run," if at all. To most administrators and policy makers, however, when it comes to application, the short run is the only run, from which the "long run" slowly emerges.

Concerned about such problems, some sociologists have called for increased attentions to observational and other field methodologies; others urge experimental and quasi-experimental designs. Their proposals deserve attention, but the problems of sociological inquiry in education do not stop with methodology.

Questions of Policy Implication

Even when sociological research—correlational, experimental, or observational—is linked to sensitive and informed interpretation, policy and program possibilities may be difficult to identify. Even when identified, they may be almost impossible to apply.

To illustrate this, consider the research of Stinchcombe (1964), mentioned above, which generated the "articulation hypothesis" that unless youth see schools as instrumental in solving occupational identity crises, rebellion and alienation will follow. Strangely, this compelling hypothesis has led to virtually no significant research that would further our understanding of the relationship of schools to the workplace. Even if it had, Entwistle (1975) points out, it is unlikely that either schools or business firms would have been able or inclined to alter their processes to incorporate the findings of that research. On the one hand, there seems to be little compelling reason for business firms to be greatly concerned with what goes on in schools, since both research and practical experience shows little relationship between schooling achievements and success on the job. On the other hand, teachers, counselors, and administrators in schools tend to be unacquainted with the world of business and often are withdrawn from or actively hostile to it.

It is also interesting, Entwistle (1975) notes, that other policy implications that could be drawn from the Stinchcombe research have not been identified, much less acted on. One is that, since schools do not help solve the occupational identity crises for all students, other institutions must help in the process. In part, indifference to such implications may be related to processes analogous to the attempts to limit the labor supply by immigration restrictions. The progressive exclusion of the young from the labor market is directly in the interest of older members of the labor force and, thus, likely to be supported not only by business management, but also by labor unions and political leaders.

Such possibilities, although interpretive and speculative, again highlight a pervasive deficiency noted earlier. In our efforts to provide sociological services to education, we offer little understanding of the processes and problems of applying knowledge within larger sociological and political contexts. In short, however profound the implications of our research literature, it rarely offers evidence or even speculation on the viability of policy or programmatic changes, or even suggests policy changes that might be considered.

The Question of Politics in the Profession

It is important to recognize that what is done in the sociology of education today is not simply a matter of expediency, nor simply a matter of following established traditions of research. It is both of these things, but it is far more. In more general perspectives, much of what is going in the sociology of education can be recognized as politically motivated or constrained. This is particularly true if "politics" is taken in a broad sense to include not only governmental processes, but also the processes of influence, manipulation, and control within the educational profession and within the universities and organizations where sociologists of education work. Thus, "What we are doing" is determined not just by professional folkways, but also in an important way by the structures of rewards and constraints that confront the participants.

Most simply, the current politics of the sociology of education, of sociology in general, and of universities and their departments, discourage attention to immediate or short-term policy implications and program intervention. Arguments can be made in support of these existing structures of possibilities and rewards, emphasizing the importance of inquiry free from the pressures and constraints of local and national politics and vested interests. But clearly, these structures add heavily to the already extreme tension between the effort to understand schooling and the effort to change it. The individual who attempts to pursue both simultaneously may experience frustration and impotence, especially if he or she works in a traditional academic organization.

A short-term, practical resolution might be to reaffirm the distinction between "knowledge production" and "knowledge application," recognize both as academically legitimate, and encourage both equally with organizational and professional rewards. Realistically, we are far from such a resolution. As long as the current priorities in the politics of organizations and professions continue, policy implications and applications will be thwarted, confounding efforts to change the answers we can bring to the question that follows.

WHAT HAVE WE ACCOMPLISHED?

By now the answer is clear: the recent years of sociological involvement in educational issues have yielded little in terms of policy development, program implementation, and evaluation. As the activism of the 1960s gave way to the recessions and retrenchments of the 1970s, program after program was called into question and pronounced a failure, and the confidence that had only recently grown among those who applied their sociology to educational problems gave way to disillusionment.

The most compelling example is seen in the well-documented history of schooling programs designed to reduce social inequalities. In these programs sociologists serve not only as researchers, but also as consultants, evaluators, monitors, and policy advocates. Their roles are often dramatic and politically volatile; they also may be professionally risky. The sociologist who advocates social policy almost inevitably becomes involved in controversy, not only with political actors of contrary opinion but also with other sociologists.

In these exchanges it is not only the sociologists' recommendations that come under attack, but also the interpretations that led to those recommendations, the data on which the interpretations are based, the methodologies that generated the data, and so forth. In a fairly recent example, James Coleman and his collaborators delivered a paper to the 1975 (see Coleman, 1976) meeting of the American Educational Research Association that was interpreted as favoring the end of court-ordered bussing as a means of desegregating urban schools. His statements offered particularly dramatic news, since throughout the 1960s his research, more than any other, had served those who advocated bussing. By the mid 1970s, Coleman had generated what he saw as solid research evidence for the conclusion that enforced bussing accelerates a "white flight" to the suburbs.

The treatment of Coleman's statements in the news media generated considerable criticism, much of it from sociologists who advocated court-ordered bussing (Pettigrew and Green, 1976). The exchanges were bitter, and the relationships between the policy advocates were further strained by the careless treatment they received in the press. If the public images of sociology suffered, however, other consequences were more productive. The public debate heightened awareness of the need to more carefully consider the organizational and policy contexts of the sociologist's research, interpretations, and advocacies.

Part of the sense of futility conveyed by the bussing example may be due to a failure to apply sociological insights to the structures in which the sociologist works. The frustrating career of program failure itself needs to be better understood. Consider Corwin's description of the major failures and modest successes of the Teacher Corps:

The federal program attempted to cooperate with relatively autonomous local organizations to bring about reform from within the established system by adding resources to the present system and making minor adjustments in it. But strong opposition, nationally and locally, prevented the program from receiving the full share of authorized funding; structural concessions were made to local organizations, giving them greater freedom to run the program, and in many instances to go against the policy and purposes of the legislation. On the local level, the program had to face the reality of strong opposition by organizations and professions whose established positions might be threatened by visible accomplishment of the program's goals; the resources available to the federal program were too little and too thinly disbursed to make a striking impact. . . . In short, this program demonstrated the tendency of such organizations to remain prisoners of the coalition of conflicting forces that created them. . . . I suspect that many of these same observations—the frustrating obstacles the Teacher Corps encountered at each turn, and the subsequent goal displacement, co-optation, and disillusionment of its participants—could be made with equal validity about a host of other government programs. . . . (Corwin, 1972:441–54)

To put this another way: One of the most important lessons reaffirmed by the recurrent history of faulted dreams is that innovation in education is not simply an educational process, but also a political process, involving diversities of actors, at a variety of levels, exerting and withholding influence and participation in a multitude of ways. It is clear that such processes cannot be understood at less than the institutional level, which places the interaction between program strategies and the situations into which they are introduced within larger contexts of political, economic, and cultural processes.

From this perspective, another source of the sociologist's sense of failure is seen to be rooted in the inflated hopes of the 1960s. If the unreality of earlier expectations is accepted, more modest accomplishments come into focus. Most importantly, it can be recognized that the past 20 years have witnessed considerable advances in sociological perspectives on schooling and a general acceptance of sociological questions that in earlier decades was lacking. Through the frustrations of failure, sociologists have gained more appreciation of the possibilities and problems of introducing intentional change into schools and of using schools as a vehicle for introducing change into the larger society.

WHERE ARE WE GOING?

At the beginning of the 1980s, the malaise of recent years seems to be lifting. Again it is being said that we simply have not been asking the right questions in the right ways, and confidence is reviving that at last the right questions and methods might be identified. The optimism that some had lost (see Cohen, 1974) is gaining stronger appeal.

A Spectrum of Perspectives

The vision of a theoretically sophisticated applied sociology of education is now shared widely by those who see themselves on the frontiers of their field. The specifics of their visions differ dramatically, however. By the turn of the 1980s, diverse lines of thought could be seen where 20 years earlier had stood a monolith of conventional agreements, contested by only minor deviationists.

This energetic diversity can be seen in a spectrum of alternatives to mid-century liberal agreements about the relationship of schooling to social structure. The subtleties of this spectrum cannot be explored here, but its diversity can be suggested briefly in five differing hues.

First, at one extreme of the spectrum are those who continue to see schooling as a potent agent of social change, in the traditions of liberal reform that dominated sociological thinking about education in the early decades of this century. Although few, if any, sociologists would go so far as their optimistic predecessors, the belief in the power of the schools to enlighten and thereby change society remains popular in sociological traditions.

Second, many who continue to believe in the possibilities of schooling take a less extreme position, arguing that schools serve as an equalizer in an otherwise extremely unequal society. The schools, by themselves, may not have the power and influence to bring about the end of inequality, but they can and do mitigate what might otherwise degenerate into a castelike system. Support for this position is offered by Barbara Heyns' (1978) argument that it is not schooling, but outside influences that foster inequalities and learning between children of various social classes.

Third, in contrast to the above two positions, which continue to see the schools, in varying degrees, as potential agents of change, some sociologists argue that even though schools may alter some things, they do not produce structural change. Schools are seen as merely "interrupters." In the first two positions, schools are seen as playing a part in shaping the structural relationships of the larger society by reducing inequality and eliminating the racial character of inequality.

The image of schools as interrupters holds that they do not contribute to the reduction of racial inequality through structural change. Instead, they reduce the tensions of racial relationships, encourage tolerance, and help blur racial distinctions. In the long run, perhaps, such changes in social interaction may contribute to structural changes, as the lessons learned in schools are brought into the larger social life. Even if such long-run changes do occur, however, they are too complex and multicausal to be of concern to policy-oriented researchers, theorists, or practitioners.

Fourth, in the last two segments of the spectrum, schooling is seen neither as an agent of change nor as an interrupter, but as an agent of social and cultural reproduction. Sorting and selecting are not the simple, functionally rational processes that join individual ability to social needs. Rather, they serve as mechanisms for reproducing failure. Schools are arenas in which the existing and emerging inequalities of the larger society are transmitted to the younger generation.

If the schools give an appearance of attempting to alter social relationships or structures, it is only because these relationships and structures have already begun to change in the larger society. Early in this century, for example, when schools began to emphasize the importance of individuality and the inherent value of each individual, they were simply responding to changing socioeconomic pressures and transitions in the larger political economy. So, too, the accelerating emphases on "merit" in recent decades is seen as a response to the demands, enticements, and sanctions of the larger corporate economy. When old prejudices and distinctions are derided and discouraged, new ones subtly develop.

Finally, at the extreme "reproduction" end of the spectrum, other sociologists argue that schools are active producers of social and cultural inequalities. They not only transmit current structures, but anticipate and encourage the emergence of new ones. They serve both to perpetuate class inequalities and to help generate new forms of inequalities. In particular, the curricula are socially and psychologically constructed to serve the advantaged. In this critical perspective, direct linkages are drawn between schools and the elites of society. The schools are seen as instruments of the political-economic system that variably encourages success or failures, depending on one's race, sex, and socioeconomic status. Schools, in short, create and perpetuate social and cultural domination. Not only are students indoctrinated into conformity to the dominant culture (or "socialized," as less radical sociologists would term it), they are lured into ideological commitments that make not only effort and loyalty but also deprivation and failure appear reasonable, even to those who fail.

This radical image is most easily illustrated by considering what happens as educational systems are transported from a "developed" culture to a less-developed one. It might be argued that this is simply an example of schooling being used in the services of, say, international corporate interests. Far more may be involved, however. Professors and teachers are strategically located to identify the compatibilities of their "industrialized" understandings with the changing culture of the developing nation. In their work, educators, thereby, actively participate in the creation of understandings that support new forms of inequality that will endure far beyond their lessons.

"Making" Problems: Perspectives on Credentialing

The spectrum of current arguments illustrates the willingness of sociologists to "take" problems from educators, ranging over an impressive and demanding array of challenges. It also displays another theme that has in recent years reemerged in the sociology of education. Rather than simply "taking" problems, some sociologists have set out to "make" problems for education. In this role, they ally themselves with the classical traditions of critical sociology and—when they attempt to develop activist programs of social and political change—of radical sociology.

The more radical themes are now well-established in the sociology of education, particularly among those in the last two segments of the spectrum. These themes did not initially arise within U.S. sociology, however, but were stimulated by the history of U.S. education and by the "New Sociology of Education" that emerged in the late 1960s in England.

These efforts may be most readily appreciated in the contrast between Randall Collins' (1979) critical-radical interpretation of education and the critical-conservative interpretations of Daniel Bell (1973). Both writers attempt to "make" rather than "take" educational problems, but there the similarity ends.

Following the traditions of Marx, Weber, and Mannheim, Bell links historical interpretations of political, economic, and cultural development to analyses of contemporary patternings of behavior, in an effort to identify the complex structures and processes that will dominate the twenty-first century. In his view, the cultural contradictions of capitalism have contributed to mutations in our forms of social stratification. Increasingly in recent decades we have seen the emergence of what will be the most fundamental value of the postindustrial society: technical skill. In earlier centuries of Western society, property had played this fulcrum role, but it is now being taken over by science and technology.

Substantively, however, Bell is far from Marx, or even Weber. We are moving rapidly into an age of meritocracy, he argues. If we are wise and industrious, we can mold our future into a "just meritocracy" in which material inequalities are minimized, in which all individuals are afforded dignity, and in which the most meritorious and industrious leaders are given motivating rewards primarily through prestige deservedly enjoyed. In Bell's image education plays a critical role, for it is a vehicle whereby the able and motivated are able to hone the skills that are needed at all occupational levels in the postindustrial society.

Collins finds little evidence to support this "technical-skills" interpretation of education, except perhaps at the most basic levels where it provides literacy and numeracy. Beyond those levels, Collins argues, education serves primarily to provide credentials, which are used in the working world as devices for organizational politics and control. This is familiar in critical-radical arguments, but Collins carries it further in a dramatic extension that begs for comparative research. Why, he asks, has educational credentialing expanded so rapidly in the United States, and why is there such a strong link between this credentialing and occupational divisioning, that is, between education and the stratification of U.S. society? Collins notes that the Soviet Union is somewhat comparable to the United States in this respect, both of which differ from England, Germany, and, until recently, France, where small, elitist, educational systems separate the advantaged student from the rest at a relatively early age.

The key to the difference, Collins' argues, is the existence of sizable ethnic minorities or multiple ethnic groups in the Soviet Union and the United States. The "credentialing boom," seen most early and dramatically in the United States and now a general feature of Western industrialized societies, is a response to the threat posed by the mobilization of distinct cultural groups. This leads the dominant ethnic groups to look increasingly to educational credentials as a means of assuring their offspring more desired professional and elite positions in society. By contrast, where traditional class stratification remains unchallenged by ethnic minorities, a small and elitist educational system remains.

The expansion of education, in this image, has little or perhaps negative effect on the distribution of wealth, power, and prestige in society. As credentialing advances, the credentials required for jobs rise even though there is little change in job content. Consequently, one must work harder and harder and harder to remain in the same place. And those who are disadvantaged, including most ethnic minorities, must work harder and longer to acquire the same positions they might have gained in earlier decades with less effort. Those who do not participate in this race fall even further behind. (For further discussions of credentialing and qualifications, see Dore, 1976).

The Research Potentials of Critical Theory: One Example

Both Bell's and Collins' theses have compelling implications, and both have stimulated strong criticism. Regardless of the validity of either argument, both have considerable potential for applied sociology because of the discussions they occasion and the reconceptualization they encourage. As these reconceptualizations are brought into research and compete with one another in rigorous inquiry, otherwise neglected limits and possibilities of schooling in complex societies may be explored. Such explorations are important at any phase of development in applied sociology. At a time such as this, marked by professional uncertainties and despair, they are invaluable. They offer productive alternatives to either a retreat into "pure" theory and research or a theoretical immersion in everyday minutea.

It can be argued, for example, that the stereotypical image of a "conspiracy of the advantaged" is not necessary for Collins' thesis. Assuming that people are relatively rational and self-interested—and interested in the life of one's offspring—highly individualistic decisions by the advantaged could lead to the same structuring of society as would a "conspiracy" of the advantaged. Those who have the necessary resources and are aware of the working of their society may simply make individual decisions about options to pursue, qualities to encourage, and programs to support in order to give advantage to themselves and their offspring. Education is then seen as a new property of middle class—

a new medium of individual entrepeneurship—which remains very much a mechanism for reproducing culture and renewing ethnic stratification from generation to generation.

Any effort to "manipulate" the child's environment must take such possibilities into account, for they suggest that fundamental importance of the relation between schooling and other sectors of society, especially the economy and the family. In earlier decades, for example, it was assumed that, essentially, "schooling is schooling." Regardless of whatever changes of emphasis occurred in curriculums or styles of teaching, education was seen as a more-or-less unchanging process. Given this assumption, discussions of family-school-work relationships took a fairly uniform character: families "socialize," schools "educate," and the economy "employs."

Families, in this view, are of primary importance during the early years for assimilating the child into the culture. With each successive year of schooling, the family becomes less and less relevant, while the school takes on the role of training the child away from family relationships and toward the working world that will be entered upon graduation. During the school years, this image suggests, the family is something of an adversary of schooling, but an impotent one. In the battle to influence the ideas and values of the child, the school has the more powerful weapons, and if it were not for the incompetence of teachers and school bureaucracies, there would be little question of the outcome.

In recent years, however, this image of the relationship of family, schooling, and work has been called into question. The possibility has been raised that the family continues to exert considerable influence on what is learned in school, shaping and limiting the schooling experiences of the child through adolescence—perhaps as actively and powerfully as schooling experiences shape and constrain the child's experiences in the home. The influence of schooling and workplace are also interactive. The myths, realities, and anticipations of job demands and opportunities help to shape and constrain classroom behavior and learnings.

For example, a child's openness to new ideas in the classroom and his or her ability to deal with the complexities and ambiguities of student-teacher relations may be influenced by similarities and differences of home and classroom in their structures of social relationships, their modes of decision making and communication, and their orientation toward others as persons or as position holders. In contemporary industrialized societies, this may mean that class-situated differences in family relationships interact with organizationally-situated differences in schooling to perpetuate social inequalities.

If such critical theses were substantiated, new possibilities and constraints on manipulative interventions might be identified; fewer efforts at educational reform might unintentionally serve the interests of maintaining the status quo; and the possibilities of turning the interactive influences of family, school, and workplace toward structural change might be explored. In short, the linkage of

Collin's interpretative theory with empirical research—even in this delimited areas—might help us identify some possibilities for and limits of educational and social reform.

In recent years, U.S. scholars have begun to explore these possibilities (Hansen, 1980; Lightfoot, 1978), but this work has been carried furthest by Bernstein and his colleagues in England (Bernstein 1973, 1974, 1976). In a 20-year program of research and theory construction of unusual continuity, they first explored differences in the abilities encouraged by working-class and middle-class families, seeking to identify those that best suit middle-class children for the requirements of higher levels of education and employment. These differences were then related to patterns of family relationships that tend to predominate in various classes and to the ways in which these patterns encourage development in children, preparing them unequally for education and occupation. The Bernstein analyses currently involve the ways in which recent structural changes in schooling further enhance the probabilities of success of middle-class children and further disadvantage lower-class children. Bernstein's continuing explorations are impressive, not only for their creative energies, but also for their persistance in the face of methodological problems, theoretical inconsistencies, and often hostile critics. Most important, they are a response to Cohen's (1974) plea that we "start to learn how to manipulate the social system to the learner's advantage."

Coda

The image of sociology in education that has been offered in this chapter may strike the reader as profoundly pessimistic. The field has been characterized as ineffectual in the face of pervasive and compelling educational problems; its record of practical accomplishments is overbalanced by its record of failures; its methods of inquiry and the structures of reward that support them are seen as ill-suited to policy or program application. But the field also has been presented as irritated with fundamental questionings, rich in methodological innovations, heated with competing perspectives, and alive to substantive possibilities that are being ignored in areas that enjoy a state of professional confidence and accepted wisdom.

REFERENCES AND SUGGESTED READINGS

Alexander, K. and B. Eckland. 1975. "Contextual Effects in the High School Attainment Process." *American Sociological Review* 40:402–16.

Baratz, S. and J. Baratz. 1970. "Early Childhood Intervention: The Social Science Base of Institutional Racism." *Harvard Educational Review* 40:29–50.

Bell, D. 1973. *The Coming of Post-Industrial Society*. New York: Basic Books.

Bernstein, B., ed. 1973, 1974, 1976 (three volumes). *Class, Codes and Control*. London: Routledge and Kegan Paul.

_____. 1974. "Sociology and the Sociology of Education: A Brief Account." In *Approaches to Sociology,* edited by J. Rex, pp. 145–49. London: Routledge and Kegan Paul.

Bidwell, C.E. 1965. "The School as a Formal Organization." In *Handbook of Organization,* edited by James G. Marsh, pp. 972–1022. Chicago: Rand McNally.

Boocock, S. 1972. *An Introduction to The Sociology of Learning.* Boston: Houghton Mifflin.

_____. 1976. *Students, Schools, and Educational Policy.* New York: Aspen Systems.

Bowles, S. and H. Gintis. 1976. *Schooling in Capitalist America: Educational Reform and the Contradictions of Economic Life.* New York: Basic Books.

Carnoy, M. and H. Levin. 1976. *The Limits of Educational Reform.* New York: David McKay.

Chesler, M. and J. Crowfoot. 1975. "Sociologists in the Public Schools: Problems and Roles in Crisis Management." In *Proceedings of the National Invitational Conference on School Sociologists,* edited by A.J. Schwartz, pp. 5–105. Los Angeles: University of Southern California.

Cicourel, A. and J. Kitsuse. 1963. *The Educational Decision-Makers.* Indianapolis: Bobbs-Merrill.

Clark, B. 1962, *Educating the Expert Society.* San Francisco: Chandler.

Cohen, E. 1974. "An Experimental Approach to School Effects." In *Sociology of the School and Schooling,* edited by D. O'Shea, pp. 220–33. Washington, D.C.: National Institute of Education.

Coleman, J. 1976 "Response to Professors Pettigrew and Green." *Harvard Educational Review* 46:217–24.

Coleman, J., J.E. Campbell, L. Hobson, J. McPartland, A. Mood, F. Weinfield, and R. York. 1966. *Equality of Educational Opportunity.* Washington, D.C.: U.S. Government Printing Office.

Coleman, J., and others. 1977. *Parents, Teachers, and Children.* San Francisco: Institute for Contemporary Studies.

Collins, R. 1979. *The Credential Society: An Historical Sociology of Education and Stratification.* New York: Academic Press.

Corwin, R. 1972. "Strategies for Organizational Innovation." *American Sociological Review* 37:441–54.

_____. 1974. *Education in Crisis: A Sociological Analysis of Schools and Universities in Transition.* New York: John Wiley & Sons.

Davis, J. 1975. "On the Remarkable Absence of Nonacademic Implications in Academic Research: An Example for Ethic Studies." In *Social Policy and Sociology,* edited by N. Demerath, O. Larsen, and K. Schuessler, pp. 233–41. New York: Academic Press.

Dore, R. 1976. *The Diploma Disease.* Berkeley: University of California Press.

Dreeben, R. 1968. *On What Is Learned in School.* New York: Addison-Wesley.

Eggleston, J. 1977. *The Ecology of the School.* London: Methuen.

Entwistle, D. 1970. "Semantic Systems of Children: Some Assessments of Social Class and Ethnic Differences." In *Language and Poverty: Perspectives on a Theme,* edited by F. Williams, pp. 243–59. Chicago: Markham.

_____. 1975. "Sociological Understanding Versus Policy Design and Interven-
tion: The Adolescent Crisis," In *Social Policy and Sociology,* edited by N.
Demerath, O. Larsen, and K. Schuessler, pp. 243–59. New York: Academic
Press.

*Goodwin, D. 1977. *Delivering Educational Services: Urban Schools and School-
ing Policy.* New York: Teachers College Press.

This book is an inquiry into the classroom attitudes of teachers that bear
on the daily delivery of educational services and the implications of these
attitudes for policy makers.

Hansen, D. 1980. "Family Structures and the Effects of Schooling in a New
Zealand Suburb." *Journal of Comparative Family Research* (in press).

Herrnstein, R.J. 1973. *I.Q. in the Meritocracy.* Boston: Little, Brown.

*Heyns, Barbara. 1978. *Summer Learning and the Effects of Schooling.* New York:
Academic Press.

Heyns' work is an exemplary linkage of theoretical argument and quantitative data analysis, offering challenging alternatives to accepted perspectives
on schooling effects.

*Hurn, C. 1978. *The Limits and Possibilities of Schooling.* Boston: Allyn & Bacon.

Hurn presents a lucid overview of major themes and tensions in contemporary sociologies of education, arguing that the current intensity of radical and functional commitments thwarts inquiry into the possibilities
of schooling.

*Karabel, J. and A.H. Halsey. 1977. "Educational Research: A Review and Inter-
pretation." In *Power and Ideology in Education,* edited by J. Karabel and
A.H. Halsey, pp. 1–85. New York: Oxford University Press.

This is a cogent assessment of movements of thought and research since
1960, contrasting functionalism, human capital theories, methodological
empiricism, conflict theories, interactionist traditions, and the "new sociology" of education.

Keddie, N. 1971. "Classroom Knowledge." In *Knowledge and Control,* edited by
M.F.D. Young, pp. 133–60. London: Collier-Macmillan.

Levitas, M. 1974. *Marxist Perspective in the Sociology of Education.* London:
Routledge and Kegan Paul.

*Lightfoot, S. 1978. *Worlds Apart: Relationships Between Families and Schools,*
New York: Basic Books.

The author presents an eloquent discussion of the complex relationship of
families and schools, intended in part, to provide a corrective to the mis-
perceptions generated by social science traditions.

MacKay, R. 1974. "Standardized Tests: Objective/Objectified Measures of Competence." In *Language Use and School Performance,* edited by A. Cicourel,
et al., pp. 218–87. New York: Academic Press.

*Mehan, H. 1979. *Learning Lessons: Social Organization in the Classroom.* Cambridge, Mass.: Harvard University Press.

An articulate argument for "constitutive ethnography" as an alternative to
traditional approaches to the study of schooling effects is presented.

Pettigrew, T. and R. Green 1976. "School Desegregation in Large Cities: A Critique of the Coleman 'White Flight' Thesis." *Harvard Educational Review* 46:1–53.

Rist, R. 1970. "Social Class and Teacher Expectations: The Self-Fulfilling Prophecy in Ghetto Education." *Harvard Educational Review* 40:411–51.

Rist, R. and R. Anson. 1977. *Education, Social Science, and the Judicial Process.* New York: Teachers College Press.

Sewell, W. and R. Hauser. 1975. *Education, Occupation and Earnings.* New York: Academic Press.

Spady, W.G. 1974. "The Authority System of the School and Student Unrest: A Theoretical Exploration." In *Uses of the Sociology of Education,* edited by C. Wayne Gordon, pp. 36–37. Chicago: National Society for the Study of Education.

Stinchcombe, A. 1964. *Rebellion in a High School.* Chicago: Quandrangle Books.

Valentine, C. 1968. *Culture and Poverty: Critique and Counter Proposals.* Chicago: University of Chicago Press.

Wexler, P. 1976. *Sociology of Education: Beyond Equality.* Indianapolis: Bobbs-Merrill.

Wilson, A. 1969. *The Consequences of Segregation: Academic Achievement in a Northern Community.* Berkeley, Calif.: Glendessary Press.

Young, M.F.D. 1971. "An Approach to the Study of Curricula as Socially Organized Knowledge." In *Knowledge and Control,* edited by M.F.D. Young, pp. 19–47. London: Collier-Macmillan.

17 HEALTH SERVICES

Gary L. Albrecht

The sociological study of health has a deep intellectual tradition rooted in such classics as Durkheim's *Suicide* (1951), which examined the effect of societal integration on differential suicide rates in late nineteenth century France. Early sociologists raised important theoretical questions about the influence of society on health that also had extensive applied consequences. During the ensuing years, some sociologists continued the tradition of studying the effects of social structure on health and the distribution of illness, while others focused on the organization of medicine and delivery of health services designed to ameliorate health problems. Although each approach has had its impassioned advocates, the two are not mutually exclusive and both contribute enormously to our understanding of the place of health in society. The applied study of health services arises from the later tradition.

The delivery of health services is a social problem expressed in the meaning of, cost of, access to, quality of, and need for medical care. While heterogenous in content, research on health services is designed to provide knowledge about the structure, processes, or effects of personal health services (Institute of Medicine, 1979:14). In recent years, health services research has converged on five major issues: 1) providing access to quality medical care, 2) coordinating the delivery of services to those in need, 3) designing new forms for delivering medical care, 4) integrating the fragmented parts of the delivery system, and 5) improving its efficiency and effectiveness (Mechanic, 1975). This discussion is limited to health services for physical conditions, since mental health services are considered in the following chapter.

WHAT ARE THE PROBLEMS?

While health is a universally desired commodity, we are not quite certain what health is or who can deliver it. Many people, for example, feel healthy when they have serious pathophysiological conditions, whereas others consume care when they have no observable medical symptoms. According to the medical model and the Parsonian conception of the sick role (Parsons, 1951:428–79), physicians are the only professionals qualified to diagnose and treat patients. Nevertheless, many individuals suffering pain and discomfort obtain more relief from chiropractors and faith healers than from traditional physicians.

Health has been marketed as a fundamental right of every human being that can be delivered by the medical profession. The expression of this ideology is embodied in the World Health Organization (WHO) definition of health: Health is a state of complete physical, mental, and social well-being and not merely the absence of disease or infirmity. Physicians are quick to point out, however, that no one can identify or deliver this product. Instead, doctors assert that they can deliver medical care for certain pathophysiological conditions. Expectations for an optimal quality of life cannot be met by the medical profession or perhaps anyone else. Nor is there any guarantee that possession of health will insure happiness. Consequently, health services can be viewed best as a business that delivers medical care to a public at a price and not as a gratuitous institution that promises health and happiness.

The health of a population of people is measured best by indexes of mortality, morbidity, and physical functioning. These indicators measure the causes of death, types and severity of illness, and levels of physical functioning that a population experiences. For example, functional indicators assess whether individuals are able to bathe, dress, walk, and work without assistance. The impact of health services is determined by the extent to which medical interventions produce desired changes in mortality, morbidity, and functional levels. Health services traditionally were directed at acute care problems, but more attention is now being given to prevention and long-term care and consequent changes in health status over time.

Changing Disease Patterns

The effective delivery of health services is dependent on the specific target population and the distribution of disease in that population. Both the epidemiological and demographic transitions have had dramatic effects on the health of the United States population. The epidemiological transition refers to the change in the disease structure from communicable and infectious diseases to chronic illness that has resulted from public health measures and medical intervention. The major causes of mortality and morbidity in 1900 in the United States were pneumonia, tuberculosis, and gastrointestinal problems, but by 1940 these causes had changed to heart disease, cancer, and stroke. Concomitant with these changes in the disease structure was the demographic transition, as death rates dropped and, later, birth rates fell due to birth control technology and voluntary choice to have fewer children. The result is an aging population with longer life expectancies and chronic illness problems. In contrast, the traditional medical system was designed for acute, primary care and not for rehabilitation (Margolis, 1979).

The health services system is, therefore, presently being asked to supply more than medical care; it is expected to improve the quality of life of those with chronic illness (Gerson, 1976).

The Cost/Access/Quality of Care Conundrum

The most pervasive and difficult problem in health services today is the attempt to provide high-quality medical care to every citizen at a reasonable price. While most observers would agree with the goal, they recognize also that increased access to and quality of medical care raises its costs. The public and the government are no longer able to meet these costs at present levels of taxation and insurance premiums. That is one of the major reasons why large public hospitals like Cook County (Chicago) and Los Angeles General that service the poor and minorities are in danger of bankruptcy. Over the last five years the costs of medical care have been rising faster than inflation and people's ability to pay for services, so that national health expenditures now constitute about 9 percent of the gross national product or $180 billion a year (Gibson and Fisher, 1978). The subsequent pressures to reduce medical care costs are intense. The critical problem is how to do this without also reducing the quality of and access to care.

In some ways, these pressures have forced a salutory reexamination of the medical care system. High costs and scarcity have raised questions concerning the efficacy of medical care in terms of improved health status (Rice and Wilson, 1976). Physicians traditionally have concentrated on the quality of care, as typically expressed by the accuracy of diagnoses and the appropriateness of treatment. The difficulty of delivering quality health care is compounded by its two principal goals: processing cases and changing the patient (Hasenfeld, 1972). Accuracy of diagnosis and appropriateness of treatment as judged by peers are well suited to processing cases, but they do not pertain directly to improved health status. Doctors extoll the quality of care delivered by pointing to qualifications of medical staff, type of intensive care, length of stay, number of treatments provided, and level of medical technology used. Yet, as we are beginning to discover, these measures of the medical care process may not be strongly related to the health status outcome of those treated. In other words, many expensive, popular, medically-intensive treatments may not be particularly effective.

Access to medical care has been a long-standing concern of sociologists. Until the 1960s there were serious inequities in access to medical care in the United States. At that time, the higher the income of the family, the better the access. Improvements in employee benefits, increased Social Security benefits, and the passage of Medicare-Medicaid legislation in 1965–1966 dramatically changed this relationship by providing better care to the poor, elderly, and disabled. The gap in access between the haves and have-nots gradually decreased from the 1960s to the present, so that there is now reasonable equity in the system except for rural areas and the inner cities (Andersen and Aday, 1978a). Whether improved access to care implies positive changes in health status is a persisting question, however.

While quality of care and access are important issues, cost containment consumes the attention of those in the medical care business. Because of the nature of the problem, economists in the highest levels of government and industry continue to debate over the best strategies for controlling the inflationary costs of health care and the Social Security system (Golden, 1980). One powerful group argues for limiting unnecessary surgery (Pauly, 1979), monitoring the influx of foreign medical graduates into the physician manpower pool (Williams and Brook, 1975), and regulating the cost and implementation of medical technology (Iglehart, 1977). Others, like Friedman and Friedman (1980), advocate a free market approach to the supply of medical services whereby consumer demand will regulate the costs of care. Regardless of the economic theory invoked, most cost containment strategies are focused on the organization and delivery of medical care, on planning and development, and on reimbursement mechanisms. None of these strategies have been particularly effective. The most promising approaches to cost containment appear to be: 1) "Programs which encourage increased responsibility on the part of individuals for their health, 2) attempts to set limits on total resources [allocated to health care] to force decision makers to choose between alternatives, and 3) structural factors like health maintenance organizations, external review, and reimbursement schemes that provide incentives for efficient medical practice" (Newman, et al., 1979). Despite these creative endeavors, however, the difficult tradeoffs between cost, access, and quality persist.

Need, Demand, and Availability of Services

National health insurance is touted as a mechanism to guarantee quality medical care for all. Yet, regardless of the funding scheme, the fit between need, demand, and availability of services causes problems. People who consume health care are not necessarily those most in need of services, for ability to pay is one of the key determinants of consumption (Donabedian, 1976). Therefore, those with comprehensive private health insurance and those on Medicare and Medicaid are most likely to consume health care if it is available. The overutilizers are those who have the time, money, and inclination to consume medical care. The underutilizers are those who do not have access or resources or who do not perceive themselves to have a health problem. In fact, many people have serious health problems that they do not recognize, while others run for help frequently without any symptoms. This anomaly results in many illegal aliens, working poor, and medically naive individuals not receiving needed medical care. Likewise, medical services frequently are not available in the poor neighborhoods and rural areas where they are needed. Finally, use of medical care services does not guarantee improved health status (Diehr, et al., 1979).

The Intent versus the Outcome of the System

Numerous social critics, including Illich (1976), Krause (1977), and Carlson (1975), have pointed out that the medical care system in some instances not only lacks efficacy but actually produces consequences detrimental to the person seeking help. While hospitalization, for example, places patients where they can be helped, it also exposes them to the risk of malpractice and hospital contacted infections. Access to fully prepaid medical care in Seattle for the poor actually resulted in deteriorated health status after one year of observation (Diehr, et al., 1979). Furthermore, those who do not qualify for Medicare because their incomes slightly surpass the government minimum standard—they have been called the "working poor"—have their own special problems: They earn too much to qualify for Medicare but not enough to pay for their own care or to purchase adequate insurance. Finally, knowledge of and treatment for medical problems such as hypertension may not result in uniformly improved health status (Alderman and Schoenbaum, 1976), since the treatment may be only partially effective. Thus, intensive screening for some conditions does not make good sense.

Who Benefits from the Present Delivery System?

Analyses of health services delivery often overlook the political interests of the principal parties involved. In studying the best form of medical care delivery we should examine who stands to benefit from particular organizational forms. In the United States—where medicine is increasingly operated like a large, for-profit, bureaucratic business—the major interest groups are the hospitals, medical suppliers, doctors, other health professionals, pharmaceutical companies, insurance businesses, federal government, and consumers. These lobbies are so powerful that any form of medical care delivery has to take them into account or fail to meet its objectives.

Social Control and Regulation

From the advent of Franklin Roosevelt's first term in 1932, there has been increasing government intervention in health services. Today, government regulation ranges from equal opportunity employment practices to licensing of professionals and certification of hospitals. Professional Standards Review Organizations (PSRO) are government designated organizations designed to formulate areawide health plans and to control the number of new hospital beds and the type of medical technology in an area. The federal government also regulates professional manpower by specifying the number of foreign medical graduates who can enter and practice in this country. The massive bureaucracy created by these regulatory agencies is directed at controlling medical costs, but the cost of regulation appears to equal or exceed the savings realized. From a sociological perspective, this amount of government regulation raises questions about the social control of medicine. Whereas Freidson (1970) argued that doctors control the practice of medicine, recent analysis indicates that government bureaucracies are determining the types and forms of medical care (Mechanic, 1976).

Accountability

Because of the emphasis on controlling costs while delivering quality medical care to those in need, increasing attention is being given to making doctors, patients, and hospitals accountable for the services delivered and the costs of care. This focus has led to a plethora of cost/benefit studies of medical practice that attempt to evaluate the effectiveness of outcomes in terms of money and resource investments. The notion of accountability is being extended from the cost/benefits of surgery (Bunker, et al., 1977), to the cost effectiveness of different medical care organizations. A positive result of this attention to accountability has been a renewed look at health outcomes. Observers are demanding behavioral results for the resources spent, since medical care is likely to be rationed in the future (Mechanic, 1979). How are we to get the largest bang for the health dollar?

The Limitations of Medical Care

The assumption that increased amounts of medical care produce corresponding positive changes in health status does not seem supported. Many health problems are more a function of life style than of disease processes. Alcohol consumption, drug use, smoking, and overeating are just a few examples of activities related to serious health problems that are not easily controlled by the medical care system. The problem of infant mortality in the inner city offers another striking example. The infant mortality rate of minorities living on the west side of Chicago is 38 per 1,000 live births, which is considerably higher than that for whites. Attempts to lower this rate have been unsuccessful because many of these infant deaths are due to causes like adolescent pregnancy, battered children and battered pregnant mothers, poor nutrition, and lack of prenatal care that are not under the control of the medical system. In these instances, medicine is blamed for results that it cannot alter.

The Self-Care Movement

Disenchantment with the traditional medical care system has led many consumers to seek out helping groups designed to support individuals with similar ailments. These groups include Alcoholics Anonymous, hospices for the dying, Emphysema Anonymous, and Weight Watchers. While these self-help groups assist individuals in need to acquire knowledge, share resources, provide support, and make medicine more humane, they also threaten the knowledge and authority of the medical profession. In some instances, the self-help groups have been effective, as in reducing dependence on alcohol. In other cases, such as rapid weight loss through fad diets, there have been serious deleterious consequences.

WHAT DO WE KNOW?

The Relationship Between Diagnosis, Treatment, and Benefits

Medical care, insurance, and health benefits are based on physicians' diagnoses, yet the patients' social behavior and role performance are not related closely to these medical judgments. Insurance companies and the Social Security Administration calculate benefits based on these same diagnoses. This medical care and reimbursement system does not reward the patient for performance, but rather encourages a labeling process that does not have a strong behavioral basis. Some people continue to function independently even though they have serious pathophysiological conditions, while others behave dependently even when there is nothing debilitating about their health status.

This variability in diagnosis and functional performance has led to an emphasis on quality of life indicators and functional performance scales that focus attention on the health outcome rather than on the diagnosis. Functional life scales measure an individual's ability to perform independently such daily activities as dressing, bathing, eating, and communicating, as well as social roles such as working and parenting. Medical care systems are being designed that examine program cost effectiveness based on these behavioral outcome criteria. This approach to medical care delivery accountability ties medical treatment to the performance of social roles.

Chronic Diseases are a Function of Life Style

The major causes of death and illness in the United States—heart disease, cancer, stroke, and diabetes—are clearly a result of life style. High cholesterol diets, salt intake, and stress are related positively to hypertension, which is judged to be the direct cause of 60,000 deaths a year and an indirect influence on the more than 1.5 million strokes and heart attacks suffered by Americans each year (Knowles, 1977). Obesity is a predisposing factor for diabetes, heart disease, strokes, cancer of the gastrointestinal tract, degenerative arthritis, and disease of the liver. Yet, the Public Health Service estimates that 16 percent of Americans under the age of 30 are obese and 40 percent of the entire population are at least 20 pounds over their ideal weight (Stachnik, 1980). While these facts attest to the consequences of eating too much food, nutritional information also suggests that the quality and preparation of food have far-reaching health consequences. Ingestion of "junk food" laced with chemical preservatives, coloring, and artificial sweeteners, soft drinks containing caffeine, and undue boiling and frying of food are related to different forms of heart disease, cancer, and vitamin deficiency (Turner, 1970; Wood, 1979:57–102).

The recent "Surgeon General's Report on Smoking and Health" argues that smoking or even being near smokers is predictive of lung and heart disease. Cigarette consumption in this country is increasing at 3.5 percent a year. While adult males are smoking less, the high risk groups of industrial workers, pregnant women, and teenagers have not significantly reduced their consumption. The major causes of death and disability for young adults are suicide, homicide, automobile accidents, and drug or alcohol related incidents. Few of these problems are treated effectively by the medical care system, since their causes lie principally in the individual's life style.

The Medical Model and the Sick Role

U.S. health services are delivered within the context of the medical model and the sick role. The medical model influences every aspect of the delivery process from seeking help and presenting complaints to treatment philosophy and responsibility for outcome. This model is based on the assumptions that illness is 1) nonvoluntary, 2) organically based, 3) behaviorly defined as sickness only if it falls below some socially defined minimum standard of acceptability, and 4) properly treated only by physicians. As a consequence, the medical profession—through its monopoly over expertise, the delivery system, and medical technology—controls the ways in which health services are structured and used. According to the traditional conception of the sick role, the doctor additionally dominates the physician-patient relationship, so that the consumer is cast in a dependent, accepting position. This vesting of considerable power in physicians leaves them relatively unaccountable.

The professional dominance and inconsistent performance of physicians raises genuine concerns about the return on investment in the $180 billion medical care business, doctors' claims of expertise and self-regulation, the physician's interest in the patient, and the place of democratic values in medicine (Strosberg, 1977). Popular dissatisfaction with the current form of medical practice has led to consumer activism, aggressive patient involvement in their own health care, and redefinition of the physician's role. The degree of external pressure placed on physicians and the organizational skills of consumers and helping professionals determine the acceptance or rejection of paraprofessionals such as physicians' assistants, Medex, certified nurse midwives, pediatric nurse practitioners, and physical therapists in private practice (Record and Greenlick, 1975). Therefore, the effective use of new health paraprofessionals and a redefined doctor-patient relationship is largely dependent on physicians relinquishing the medical model and the traditional concept of the sick role.

Primary and Secondary Deviation

Labeling is one of the dominant themes in the sociology of health. The emphasis of labeling is on the process by which certain individuals such as alcoholics and cancer victims become defined and treated as deviant. According to this perspective, deviance lies not in the act itself but in the reaction of individuals to the act. Labeling is, therefore, sometimes called societal reaction theory. There is considerable evidence that labeling affects the ways in which the mentally ill, alcoholics, and the physically disabled are identified and treated and the ways in which they respond to rehabilitation efforts (Mercer, 1973; Scheff, 1974). Yet, there also is evidence that labeling has little effect on health status or future acceptance of the labeled person by the family or community (Gove and Howell, 1974; Gove, 1975).

Labeling, or secondary deviation, is predicated on a societal reaction to some observed deviant behavior, sometimes called primary deviation. While the emphasis on the labeling effects of medical diagnosis and treatment are important, many patients do suffer serious pathophysiological conditions. In other words, not all illness is a result of societal reaction. For this reason, health service researchers are refocusing attention on primary deviations or pathophysiological conditions and downplaying the effects of labeling on patient behaviors that are a complication of the more serious, underlying problem (McKeown, 1979).

Technology

Medicine has become caught in the technological imperative of using increasingly sophisticated instruments and techniques without evaluating fully the effectiveness or cost of the treatment. Given this caution, the impact of technology on health status is staggering. Public health measures such as sanitation, mosquito abatement, and vaccination have brought most of the major communicable diseases under control worldwide. In fact, smallpox has been virtually eradicated, except for those viruses kept in laboratories for experimental purposes. Techniques like renal dialysis, organ transplant operations, coronary bypass surgery, and computer tomography (CT) scanning have made new levels of diagnosis and treatment available that are less intrusive and more accurate, while reducing pain and extending lives (Altman and Blendon, 1979). Biochemical discoveries like interferon to treat specific forms of cancer may lead to a whole new set of technologies for biochemically treating and altering disease processes.

Health management technologies are often as impressive as medical and surgical techniques. Medical centers are combining to form multiple hospital systems that share laundry, food, maintenance, and accounting services. These inventive organizational arrangements provide new economies of scale. Most medical care delivery institutions are implementing computerized information systems that permit better financial control and patient record keeping and also build a useful data base for research. These computerized systems reduce the need for patient records, make patient data readily available to staff members working on a case wherever they may be located, and control treatment and medication regimens. A team approach to patient care that revolves around a physician and a nurse practitioner is another innovation that ensures better coordination of complex treatments. New organizational developments aimed at integrating and coordinating medical care are illustrated by spinal cord injury systems that keep track of the patient from point of injury to helicopter or ambulance to a tertiary-care, spinal cord injury center and on through rehabilitation to follow-up in the home. This kind of comprehensive integrated system is designed to speed the patient through the system in a humane but efficient manner. The results are encouraging. Costs are reduced and mortality and morbidity reduced for individuals in these comprehensive systems. Finally, there are effective outpatient technologies such as home nursing care for the homebound, meals on wheels for the elderly, and visiting physical therapists for the disabled that have moved medical care outside the hospital and also reduced costs.

Health Knowledge versus Behavior

There is a clear but complex relationship between knowledge about health practices and changes in health behavior. The significant reduction during the last ten years in the proportion of the adult population who smoke cigarettes can be attributed to increased public information on the relationship between smoking and cancer. At the same time, many people who know about this relationship continue to smoke or stop only to begin again (Elinson and Wilson, 1978). These behavior patterns are replicated by people with weight, alcohol, and diet problems. The Health Belief model developed by Rosenstock (1966) and elaborated by Becker (1974) attempts to explain the effects of health beliefs on altered health behaviors.

According to this model, preventive health behavior is dependent upon an individual's perceptions that he or she is personally susceptible and that contracting a disease would result in severe consequences. A key assumption of the model is that disease onset would be avoided or severely reduced if specific preventive actions were taken. The relationship between individual perceptions and health beliefs is modified by demographic, social psychological, and social structural variables such as age, race, social class, peer pressure, and knowledge about the disease. In addition, individual action, according to Rosenstock, is contingent on specific cues like mass media campaigns or the advice of others. These situational cues are necessary to overcome the expense, inconvenience, or pain of the health intervention. While useful, the Health Belief model is most applicable to preventive situations in which the individual can act voluntarily.

Utilization of medical care services is even more complex than taking preventive action. Ronald Andersen and his colleagues (Andersen and Aday, 1978b) have developed an analytic model to explain health service utilization. This model suggests a sequence of predisposing, enabling, and illness variables that predict the number of times that individuals will visit a physician. Predisposing variables such as age, race, and education influence enabling variables like family income and insurance and illness variables like symptoms and perceived health. These three sets of variables, in turn, determine the individual's physician visits. The work of Andersen and his colleagues over the last ten years shows that access to medical care has become more equitable with the advent of Medicare and Medicaid. Remaining inequities in the health services system can be addressed by providing familiar sources of care to those who are not covered adequately by insurance or who do not use available services. This research provides support for health maintenance organizations and regular physician contacts in outpatient clinics.

The Organization of Health Services

Traditionally, medical care has been delivered by a physician in a private office or community hospital. As a result of specialization, the high cost of equipment, and a desire for a more stable personal life, many doctors have been forming group practices in which medical care is delivered by a collaborative group of peers (Freidson, 1975). Although the average size hospital in the United States remains about 50 beds (Longest, 1979), multiple hospital systems are being formed to take advantage of the cost efficiencies of shared services and the quality of care available in large, more specialized facilities. These multiple hospital systems are found in rural areas where disparate small or medium sized institutions band together under one centralized professional administration and medical staff, or in large urban areas where numerous tertiary care facilities are constructed contiguous to each other.

With aging populations suffering from chronic illnesses, the United States and other industrial countries are developing new forms of integrated long-term care. Nursing homes have become a growth industry providing different levels of care, depending on the patient's level of physical and social dependency. Other services are delivered on an outpatient basis or in the patient's home by "meals on wheels" staff, visiting nurses, and physical therapists. Hospitals are moving aggressively into outpatient services to compete with freestanding, established outpatient clinics run by such organizations as Easter Seal.

Related to these new organizational forms is the health maintenance organization concept that grew with the Kaiser model to emphasize preventive health practices in a prepaid group practice. Most care is delivered on an outpatient basis. Theoretically, costs are held down through prevention, early detection, and quick treatment. Under this model, patients bear more responsibility for their own health status than they did under the traditional medical model. These new organizational forms promise individualized care at a competitive price.

Costs of Care

Costs are the dominant issue in health services today. Intervention by the federal government during the last 15 years has resulted in dramatic changes in the U.S. medical economy. The extensive benefits of Medicare and Medicaid to the poor and the elderly definitely have improved access, but have cost large amounts of money. Concurrent with increased benefits, astounding advances in scientific knowledge and medical technology have raised consumer expectations and resulted in increases in third party payment mechanisms (Rice, 1976). Inflation, government subsidies, and the rising costs of more specialized medicine also have contributed to the high cost of medical care.

Economists have demonstrated that rising doctor fees are due largely to a lack of incentives among physicians to hold down charges. The three predominant payment methods for physicians are fee-for-service, capitation (where fees are calculated on the number of members served), and salary. The majority of U.S. doctors work on a fee-for-service basis that offers few incentives to the physician to control prices (Gabel and Redisch, 1979). This payment system has been perpetuated by government health plans and private insurance companies. The subsequent absence of risk sharing promotes expensive and specialized institutional care. Strategies designed to control physician changes by structuring fee schedules to reflect the costs of producing services in an efficient and competent manner, controlling utilization, and linking annual fee increases to the average rate of growth in physicians' incomes appear to work (Holahan, et al., 1979).

The costs of care seem best controlled when the doctor, the consumer, and the payer of health services all share the costs and the risks. For example, low income participants in prepaid group practices consumed less medical care than a similar population under Medicaid (Johnson and Azevedo, 1979), and prepaid groups also demonstrated savings to the Medicare program (Weil, 1976). These findings suggest that the payment mechanisms for and social control of medical care need to be seriously reconsidered to produce more cost-effective and humane care systems.

WHAT ARE WE DOING?

Identifying the Problems

Until recently, the emphasis in U.S. medicine was on improving the quality of care through improved technologies, increased specialization, and extensive research into disease processes. While these advances have been useful, many remaining problems in medical care delivery appear to be more sociological and management-related than medical in nature. For years the consuming public operated on the assumption that "the doctor knows best" and that, consequently, health problems could best be solved by the medical profession. Additional assumptions expressing an underlying trust in the medical model and the power of the physician implied that doctors always worked in the best interest of the patient and that medicine is best practiced through not-for-profit institutions. The work of sociologists and medical economists, however, has seriously questioned these assumptions. For example, Freidson (1975) and Millman (1978) demonstrate that despite good intentions, doctors sometimes do make mistakes, act in their own self-interest, are not fully effective as self-regulators, and frequently confront problems that do not have medical solutions.

The sociological and management nature of current health problems is reflected in recent reports of the United States Public Health Service (1978, 1979), indicating that:

1. Despite increased mortality due to lung cancer and chronic respiratory diseases directly related to smoking, 42 percent of men and 32 percent of women smoke.

2. A substantial proportion of young children are not protected against childhood diseases such as rubella for which there is a vaccine, and 10 percent of adults have not been immunized.

3. Although there is a clear correlation between prenatal care and the health of a child, only 77 percent of all women and 59 percent of black women experiencing live births see a physician during the first three months of pregnancy.

4. Infant mortality rates for blacks remain much higher than for whites —23.6 versus 12.3 infant deaths per 1,000 live births.

5. Many people do not receive or use adequate dental care.

6. Social class continues to influence the need for medical care, with the poor reporting more illness and disability than the nonpoor.

7. About 27 million people live in locations designated as primary medical care manpower shortage areas.

8. A proliferation of technology and specialized manpower across the country has created duplication of services and unnecessary surgery problems.

9. The cost of medical care has more than doubled since 1970 and is rising faster than most other goods and services in the economy.

The Surgeon General of the United States (1979) responded to these problems by setting five national health goals to be achieved by 1990 that are coordinated with the life cycle. These goals are to: 1) improve infant health and reduce infant mortality by 35 percent to nine deaths for 1,000 live births, 2) improve child health, foster optimal childhood development through better nutrition and control of child abuse, and reduce deaths due to accidents and injuries, 3) improve the health habits and reduce the death rates of adolescents and young adults by controlling motor vehicle accidents, drug and alcohol abuse, and adolescent pregnancies, 4) improve the health of adults through diet, control of smoking and alcohol use, and environmental controls, and 5) extend life and reduce the number of days of restricted activity for the elderly by controlling influenza and pneumonia and reducing social and psychological dependency and institutionalization. Having identified the problems and set health goals, intervention methods become a cause of concern.

The Medical Care Delivery System

Sociological research on the deleterious consequences of institutionalization (Goffman, 1961; Mercer, 1973; Millman, 1978) and rising hospital costs has focused attention on outpatient care in satellite offices and in the home. This reorganization of medical care delivery has encouraged independent new health paraprofessionals such as physicians' assistants and support personnel such as physical therapists to work outside hospitals on a fee-for-service basis and has returned some medical care to the home. A corresponding concern with unnecessary surgery has begun to stress the use of less intrusive and intensive treatments, reserving surgery as a last resort.

The regulatory effects of health systems agencies and "certificate of need" legislation are limiting the proliferation and duplicate medical technologies and the number of hospital beds in a community. Since there is a financial incentive for hospitals to fill all of their beds, large urban areas are typically overbedded and poor areas often do not have sufficient beds. Health systems agencies are attempting to relieve this maldistribution problem by making hospitals formally justify all additional beds. Physicians are being recruited into underserved areas through the Public Health Service and by incentive systems such as extra pay and guaranteed vacations (Hyman, 1975). Coordination of care is being accomplished through integrated care systems such as specialized spinal cord injury systems that continually monitor patient care.

Compliance

While considerable attention has been given during the last decade to making medical care equitably accessible to all citizens, current efforts are devoted to understanding and improving patient compliance with sound medical advice. Successful prevention of and treatment for known diseases is contingent on individual cooperation. Recent research (Hayes-Bautista, 1976a, 1976b) suggests that compliance with medical advice is highly dependent on doctor-patient interaction. For example, Albrecht (1977) argues that diagnosis and treatment are often negotiated between the doctor and the patient and that compliance will not occur unless they understand and agree with one another. Svarstad (1976) adds that compliance implies a feedback process in which the patient is able to discuss treatment and outcome throughout the course of the medical care. Use of this behavioral information is improving both the utilization of prevention measures and compliance rates.

A growing appreciation of the causes and consequences of chronic illness has focused attention on the cumulative effects of life style on health. A better understanding of this relationship is sought in programs supported by the Public Health Service (1979) designed to control the incidence, prevalence, and disabling effects of diabetes, stroke, coronary heart, and lung disease through better nutrition, changes in diet, smoking cessation, reduction in obesity, and physical exercise. These prescriptions are reflected not only in sound exercise programs sponsored by employers and changes in restaurant menus and food preparation, but also in fads such as extreme diets and life style conversions such as leaving the city to work on a farm.

Cost–Benefit Analysis

Questions about the efficacy of medical care (Illich, 1976; Krause, 1977) and competition for the health care dollar have made cost–benefit analysis a popular tool in the medical care business. Cost effectiveness is the general goal of this approach that examines the relative costs of producing a predetermined health outcome. For example, McPherson and Fox (1977) examined radical mastectomy, local removal of the tumor, and radiotherapy as alternative treatments for breast cancer. They concluded that, to the extent that treatments are expensive, intensive, and painful and that a large proportion of the women with this disease die from it, the most preferred treatments are not cost beneficial. The general effect of cost–benefit analysis in health services is to question unsubstantiated "common knowledge and practice" and inhibit unnecessary surgery and heroic medical treatments.

The Role of Sociologists

Sociologists are playing an essential role in the development of these trends in U.S. medical practice by examining the organization of the medical care delivery system, the health professions, the social meaning of medicine and health, and the outcomes of care. Sociologists are instrumental in documenting the need for equitable access to health care and in suggesting ways in which access might be improved. Freidson (1970) and Bucher and Stelling (1977) have demonstrated how sociological analyses of the medical profession contribute to our understanding of professions and occupations and suggest changes in training and practice. Mechanic (1979) and Anderson (1972) have contributed institutional analyses of organized medicine that question the purpose, structure, and operation of the entire system. In this context, sociologists serve as social critics of the medical establishment by pointing out the consequences of various courses of action. On another level, these sociologists add to our knowledge of occupations, professions, and institutions by analyzing the evolving structures, processes, and outcomes of a complex human service delivery business.

Other sociologists (Gibson, et al., 1970; Shortell, 1973) are more interested in the manner and effectiveness with which medical care is delivered. The thrust of this work is on intervention effectiveness. For example, Maiman, et al. (1979) showed how personal phone calls from a nurse educator encouraging informed self-treatment were effective in achieving a short-term reduction in emergency department visits for asthma. Sociologists, then, are active in developing theory and enhancing practice in the medical care delivery business.

WHAT HAVE WE ACCOMPLISHED?

Access to Medical Care

The principal contribution of sociology to medicine has been to emphasize that the delivery of medical care is a social activity. During the 1960s, sociologists pointed to the obvious social inequities in the delivery of medical care. Medicine at that time was a privilege of the middle and upper classes; the poor and elderly often went without. Medicare and Medicaid, improved private insurance plans, and modifications in the medical care delivery system were dramatic attempts to relieve these inequities. Since 1963 access to medical care has improved for the general U.S. population and become increasingly equitable (Andersen and Aday, 1978a). In 1963 the inequities were apparent. While 69 percent of the white population saw a physician in 1963, only 49 percent of the blacks had the same experience. This discrepancy was also reflected in social class differences. In 1963, 70 percent of the high-income group visited a physician, while only 55 percent of the low-income group enjoyed the same opportunity. Since 1963, the picture has remarkably changed. In 1976, 76 percent of the population (74 percent black and 77 percent white, 79 percent of the upper-income and 73 percent of the low-income groups) saw a physician at least once.

A careful analysis of these data reveals that the main determinants to medical care are social class, insurance, and availability of physicians (Andersen and Aday, 1978a, 1978b). The most noticeable changes in improved access have been in the inner city. Although access to and use of medical services have improved and become more equitable, similar changes in access to dental care have not occurred. While 49 percent of the population saw a dentist in 1976, this statistic has not changed much since 1963. In addition, only 34 percent of the low-income group saw a dentist in 1976, when 62 percent of the high-income group had a visit. This overall underutilization of and inequity in the use of dental services results from lack of dental insurance (only 18 percent of the population has dental insurance) and insufficient disposable income to purchase these services.

Quality of Care

Improved access has been accompanied by better quality care. Nurse practitioners are bringing humane care back to the patient. Life saving technologies such as renal dialysis and transplants designed to prolong the life of the terminally ill are available to many. Coronary bypass surgery, for all of the criticism it has received, does seem to relieve the pain of angina. Biomedical breakthroughs like interferon offer hope for cancer victims. Organizational innovations such as multiple hospital systems and computerized information systems provide improved coordination of care and quality control. Hospices even offer the terminally ill a humane way to die. The lesson we have learned is that the wholesale infusion of money and technology into the medical care system did improve access to and the quality of care, but it also drove costs to the point where health care will have to be rationed like other high demand commodities.

The Cost of Care

There is no doubt that mortality and morbidity rates have been decreasing as a result of public health measures, better nutrition, biological adaptation, and medical intervention. For example, life expectancy calculated at birth in Sweden increased from 30 to 40 years in 1700 to 72 years for males and 77 years for females. Death rates in England and Wales dropped 100 percent from 1700 to 1971 (McKeown, 1979:31). Morbidity rates have also showed comparable declines.

Chen and Wagner (1978) argue that the decline in age-adjusted death rates from 12.5 per 1,000 population in 1930 to 6.7 in 1975 is due principally to medical advances resulting from biomedical research. McKeown (1979), however, disputes this type of argument, pointing out that decreases in mortality and morbidity began before the application of most modern biomedical innovations and that the declines are more likely due to public health measures, biological adaptation, and improved nutrition. Regardless of the explanation, the health of the country has improved because of advances in medical knowledge. Unfortunately, the cost of many interventions is astronomical. For example, Cullen, et al. (1976) indicate that the average hospitalization charge for 226 critically ill postoperative patients at Massachusetts General Hospital was $14,304 per patient in 1972! Furthermore, at the end of one month, 123 (54 percent) of the patients had died. The authors proceeded to raise serious questions about the return on investment for some interventions.

Certainly, the health of the nation has improved partially as a result of health services, but the critical question remains: Can we afford to provide extremely high quality care to every citizen? The answer probably is no. Attention, therefore, must be given to the incredibly difficult task of rationing medical care. Accountability is one such form of rationing.

Accountability

Regardless of intent, the provision of access and technology does not necessarily improve the health of the nation. We are learning to be more modest in our claims and to be more accountable. We realize that it is easier to criticize than to make the system work to the satisfaction of all. Accountability is a common theme. The consumer-taxpayer is asking pointedly, "What am I getting for my investment?" The hospital is being forced either to be more accountable for services delivered and costs charged or face the threat of increased government regulation. Health professionals are being asked to demonstrate that high-cost screening techniques, extensive laboratory tests, and intensive treatments are necessary and effective before they are employed extensively. Consumers have been notified that they cannot live a reckless life with impunity. Risk exposure to diseases and health problems have their consequences. The patient who appears at a doctor's office with chronic lung disease and hypertension after 20 years of smoking and overeating will not have his demand to "make me like new" satisfied. Sociologists have underscored that health is a joint venture between the provider of services, the taxpayers, government, society, and consumers. We all share in this negotiated process.

WHERE ARE WE GOING?

Needed Research

While sociologists have studied and criticized health professionals and the larger delivery system, they have often not given due credit to the people and institutions that have changed our lives dramatically. Many sociologists have assumed that the government and medical professionals have more control over their work than is actually the case. Further research needs to be done on the social, political, economic, and ethical constraints that affect the delivery of medical care. For example, how strongly should we encourage adolescent women to practice birth control and have abortions, and how forcefully should we compel pregnant women to get prenatal and postnatal care in the interest of reducing infant mortality? These are difficult questions that indicate the constraints on the medical care system.

Sociologists have also made considerable contributions to our knowledge of medical care delivery from the societal and institutional perspective, but they have given insufficient attention to the patient-consumer. Contrary to past interpretations of the sick role, the patient-consumer is not caught in a passive, powerless role. In fact, numerous social movements are drawing attention to the power of the consumer. The disabled are forcing themselves into the mainstream of society by demanding architectural and social access. The chronically ill have organized themselves into self-help groups for the problem drinkers, mentally retarded, ostomy patients, and cancer victims. Critically ill persons are asking to be allowed to die with dignity. Finally, the consumer is demanding that medical care providers justify their charges and account for the services they deliver. This activity is a vastly understudied area.

There is, likewise, a need to study the content and interaction of therapy. Typically, sociologists examine the number and type of therapy units provided to a patient without examining what goes on during the encounter. For example, when a patient sees a doctor about chest pains, what transpires? Do they spend time talking about football or the stock market? Do they directly address the problem? Is there mutual understanding and expectations? What occurs during surgery or drug therapy? These questions and their outcomes are not well studied.

Finally, sociologists are just beginning to examine the humaneness of medicine. What values underlie contemporary medical practice and who is to make final judgments? These issues have given rise to the subfield of bioethics that is concerned with therapeutic abortion, genetic mutation, euthanasia, malpractice, and the dignity of life. These problems raise questions about the basic social values of our society.

Prospects for Sociologists

While prognostication in any field is inaccurate at best, there are clear indications in the labor market that sociologists increasingly will be moving outside universities to work for government, consulting firms, research organizations, and for-profit businesses. In these new roles, sociologists will be asked to be less speculative and more specific in delivering a final product that has some utility. This is not to say that all science must have immediate application, but that the measure of a discipline is determined partially by its ability to explain and predict in problem areas with direct societal consequences.

Sociologists of health have an opportunity to show how high technology can be delivered effectively in human services. Just as health problems are social in nature, so are the solutions. Sociologists will make continued contributions to medicine by addressing the social context and content of medical care delivery transactions between health providers and consumers. This form of sociology already is being practiced in prestigious medical centers like the Mayo Clinic (Chaska, 1977). The success of this diffusion of manpower will rest on the ability of professionals to retain their disciplinary identity while asking telling questions and on the institutional support they receive to pursue important questions.

The medical care delivery system will certainly benefit from increased interaction between medical professionals and behavioral scientists, for the health problems confronting the country are both medical and behavioral in nature. This increased collaboration promises to produce better solutions to persistent problems and to delineate the limitations of each discipline in addressing critical health care issues.

REFERENCES AND SUGGESTED READINGS

Albrecht, Gary L. 1977. "The Negotiated Diagnosis and Treatment of Occlusal Problems." *Social Science and Medicine* 11:277–83.

Alderman, Michael H. and Ellie E. Schoenbaum. 1976. "Hypertension Control Among Employed Persons in New York City." *Milbank Memorial Fund Quarterly* 53:367–78.

Altman, Stuart and Robert Blendon, eds. 1979. *Medical Technology: The Culprit Behind Health Care Costs?* Washington, D.C.: U.S. Department of Health, Education, and Welfare.

Andersen, Ronald and LuAnn Aday. 1978a. *The Robert Wood Johnson Foundation Special Report.* Princeton, N.J.: Robert Wood Johnson Foundation.

* _____. 1978b. "Access to Medical Care in the U.S.: Realized and Potential." *Medical Care* 7:533–46.

This recent article contains an exposition of Andersen's behavioral model of health services utilization, which is tested on a large national sample. The authors show that equity of access has improved and offer suggestions to achieve greater equity in the medical care system.

Anderson, Odin. 1972. *Health Care: Can There be Equity?* New York: John Wiley & Sons.

Becker, Marshall H., ed. 1974. *The Health Belief Model and Personal Health Behavior.* San Francisco: Society for Public Health Education.

Bucher, Rue and Joan G. Stelling. 1977. *Becoming Professional.* Beverly Hills, Calif.: Sage.

Bunker, John P., Benjamin A. Barnes, and Frederick Mosteller. 1977. *Costs, Risks and Benefits of Surgery.* New York: Oxford University Press.

Carlson, Rick. 1975. *The End of Medicine.* New York: John Wiley & Sons.

Chaska, Norma L. 1977. "Medical Sociology for Whom?" *Mayo Clinic Proceedings* 52:813–18.

Chen, Milton M. and Douglas P. Wagner. 1978. "Gains in Mortality from Biomedical Research 1930–1975: An Initial Assessment." *Social Science and Medicine* 12C:73–81.

Cullen, David J., Linda C. Ferrara, Burton Briggs, Peter F. Walker, and John Gilbert. 1976. "Survival, Hospitalization Charges and Follow-up Results in Critically Ill Patients." *The New England Journal of Medicine* 224:982–87.

*Davis, Alan G. 1979. "An Unequivocal Change of Policy: Prevention, Health and Medical Sociology." *Social Science and Medicine* 13A:129–37.

Davis questions some of the basic assumptions of medical care delivery. He concludes that: the medical model is limited because it ignores the social context of the system; reorganization of the system does not necessarily lead to better care; medical professionals do not always act in the best interest of the consumer; much behavior in everyday life has been "medicalized"; and, medical care will become community care.

*Diehr, Paula K., William C. Richardson, Stephen M. Shortell and James P. Lo Gerfo. 1979. "Increased Access to Medical Care: The Impact on Health." *Medical Care* 17:989–99.

This article questions the assumption that improved access translates into improved health status. In a controlled study, poor people in an experimental group with unlimited access to care through prepaid insurance actually reported a decrease in health status after one year, while poor people without prepaid insurance showed better health status than the treatment group.

Donabedian, Avedis. 1976. "Issues in National Health Insurance." *American Journal of Public Health* 66:345–50.

Durkheim, Emile. 1951. *Suicide: A Study in Sociology,* translated by John A. Spaulding and George Simpson. Glencoe, Ill.: Free Press. (Originally published in 1897.)

Elinson, Jack and Ronald W. Wilson. 1978. "Prevention." In *Health: United States, 1978,* edited by U.S. Department of Health, Education and Welfare, Public Health Service. Washington, D.C.: U.S. Government Printing Office.

Freidson, Eliot. 1970. *Profession of Medicine.* New York: Dodd, Mead.

_____. 1975. *Doctoring Together: A Study of Professional Social Control.* New York: Elsevier.

Friedman, Milton and Rose Friedman. 1980. *Free to Choose: A Personal Statement.* New York: Harcourt Brace Jovanovich.

Gabel, Jon R. and Michael A. Redisch. 1979. "Alternative Physician Payment Methods: Incentives, Efficiency, and National Health Insurance." *Milbank Memorial Fund Quarterly* 57:38–59.

Gerson, Elihu M. 1976. "On Quality of Life." *American Sociological Review* 41:793–806.

Gibson, Geoffrey, George Bugbee, and Odin W. Anderson. 1970. *Emergency Medical Services in the Chicago Area.* Chicago: University of Chicago, Center for Health Administration Studies.

Gibson, Robert M. and Charles R. Fisher. 1978. "National Health Expenditures, Fiscal Year 1977." *Social Security Bulletin* 41:3–20.

Goffman, E. 1961. *Asylums: Essays on the Social Situation of Mental Patients and Other Inmates.* New York: Doubleday.

Golden, Soma. 1980. "Superstar of the New Economists." *New York Times Magazine,* March 23, 1980, pp. 30–33, 91–95.

Gove, Walter R. 1975. *The Labelling of Deviance.* New York: Halsted Press.

Gove, Walter R. and Patrick Howell. 1974. "Individual Resources and Mental Hospitalization: A Comparison and Evaluation of the Societal Reaction and Psychiatric Perspectives." *American Sociological Review* 39:86–100.

Hasenfeld, Yeheskel. 1972. "People Processing Organizations." *American Sociological Review* 37:256–63.

Hayes-Bautista, David. 1976a. "Termination of the Patient-Practitioner Relationship: Divorce, Patient Style." *Journal of Health and Social Behavior* 17: 12–22.

_____. 1976b. "Modifying the Treatment: Patient Compliance, Patient Control and Medical Care." *Social Science and Medicine* 10:233–38.

Holahan, John, Jack Hadley, William Scanlon, Robert Lee, and James Bluck. 1979. "Paying for Physician Services under Medicare and Medicaid. *Milbank Memorial Fund Quarterly* 57:183–211.

Hyman, Herbert H. 1975. *Health Planning: A Systematic Approach.* Germantown, Md.: Aspen Systems.

Iglehart, John K. 1977. "The Cost and Regulation of Medical Technology: Future Policy Directions." *Milbank Memorial Fund Quarterly* 55:25–59.

Illich, Ivan. 1976. *Medical Nemesis.* New York: Random House.

Institute of Medicine. 1979. *Health Services Research.* Washington, D.C.: National Academy of Sciences.

Johnson, Richard E. and Daniel J. Azevedo. 1979. "Comparing the Medical Utilization and Expenditures of Low Income Health Plan Enrollees with Medicaid Recipients and with Low Income Enrollees having Medicaid Eligibility." *Medical Care* 9:953–66.

Knowles, John. 1977. "The Responsibility of the Individual." In *Doing Better and Feeling Worse: Health in the United States,* edited by John Knowles, pp. 1–8. New York: W.W. Norton.

Krause, Elliott. 1977. *Power and Illness.* New York: Elsevier.

Longest, Beaufort B., Jr. 1979. "The U.S. Health Care System." In *Health, Illness and Medicine,* edited by Gary L. Albrecht and Paul C. Higgins, pp. 341–69. Chicago: Rand McNally.

Maiman, Lois, Lawrence Green, Geoffrey Gibson, and Ellen MacKenzie. 1979. "Education for Self-Treatment by Asthmatics." *Journal of the American Medical Association* 18:1919–22.

Margolis, Emmanuel. 1979. "Changing Disease Patterns, Changing Values: Problems of Geriatric Care in the U.S.A., An Outsider's View." *Medical Care* 17:1119–30.

McKeown, Thomas. 1979. *The Role of Medicine.* Princeton, N.J.: Princeton University Press.

McPherson, Klim and Maurice S. Fox. 1977. "Treatment of Breast Cancer." In *Costs, Risks, and Benefits of Surgery,* edited by John P. Bunker, Benjamin A. Barnes and Frederick Mosteller, pp. 308–22. New York: Oxford University Press.

Mechanic, David. 1975. "Ideology, Medical Technology, and Health Care Organization in Modern Nations." *American Journal of Public Health* 65:241–47.

_____. 1976. *The Growth of Bureaucratic Medicine.* New York: John Wiley & Sons.

*_____. 1979. *Future Issues in Health Care.* New York: The Free Press.

This book is an excellent analytical discussion of the dilemmas encountered in the medical-care delivery system. Mechanic discusses implicit rationing of services involving limiting the resources available for health care and explicit rationing involving administrative decisions regarding limitations on what services will be provided or covered under health insurance.

Mercer, Jane R. 1973. *Labelling the Mentally Retarded.* Berkeley: University of California Press.

Millman, Marcia. 1978. *The Unkindest Cut.* New York: Morrow.

*Newman, John F., William B. Elliott, James O. Gibbs, and Helen C. Gift. 1979. "Attempts to Control Health Care Costs: The United States Experience." *Social Science and Medicine* 13A:529–40.

This article analyzes the attempts to control health care costs and why most efforts have failed. The authors then suggest promising mechanisms for controlling costs without seriously limiting access to those in need and without compromising acceptable quality of care.

Parsons, Talcott. 1951. *The Social System.* Glencoe, Ill.: Free Press.

Pauly, Mark V. 1979. "What is Unnecessary Surgery?" *Milbank Memorial Quarterly* 57:95–117.

Record, Jane Cassels and Mervyn R. Greenlick. 1975. "New Health Professionals and the Physician Role: An Hypothesis from Kaiser Experience." *Public Health Reports* 90:241–46.

Rice, Dorothy P. and Douglas Wilson. 1976. "The American Medical Economy: Problems and Perspectives." *Journal of Health Politics, Policy and Law* 1:151–72.

Rosenstock, Irwin. 1966. "Why People Use Health Services." *Milbank Memorial Fund Quarterly* 44:94–127.

Scheff, Thomas G. 1974. "The Labelling Theory of Mental Illness." *American Sociological Review* 39:444–52.

Shortell, Stephan M. 1973. "Patterns of Referral Among Internists in Private Practice." *Journal of Health and Social Behavior* 14:335–48.

Stachnik, Thomas J. 1980. "Priorities for Psychology in Medical Education and Health Care Delivery." *American Psychologist* 35:8–15.

Strosberg, Martin, Charles Levine, and Alfred Manet. 1977. "Technology and the Governance of the Health Care Industry: The Dilemma of Reform." *Journal of Health Politics, Policy and Law* 2:212–26.

Surgeon General of the United States. 1979. "Health People: The Surgeon General's Report on Health Promotion and Disease Prevention." Washington, D.C.: U.S. Department of Health, Education, and Welfare.

Svarstad, Bonnie L. 1976. "Physician-Patient Communication and Patient Conformity with Medical Advice." In *The Growth of Bureaucratic Medicine,* edited by David Mechanic, pp. 220–38. New York: John Wiley & Sons.

Turner, James. 1970. *The Chemical Feast.* New York: Grossman.

U.S. Public Health Service. 1978. *Health: United States, 1978.* Washington, D.C.: U.S. Department of Health, Education, and Welfare.

_____. 1979. *Health: United States, 1979.* Washington, D.C.: U.S. Department of Health, Education, and Welfare.

Weil, Peter. 1976. "Comparative Costs to the Medicare Program of Seven Prepaid Group Practices and Controls." *Milbank Memorial Fund Quarterly* 54: 339–65.

Williams, Kathleen N. and Robert H. Brook. 1975. "Foreign Medical Graduates and Their Impact on the Quality of Medical Care in the United States." *Milbank Memorial Fund Quarterly* 53:549–81.

Wood, Corinne Shear. 1979. *Human Sickness and Health.* Palo Alto, Calif.: Mayfield.

18 MENTAL HEALTH SERVICES

John A. Clausen

Theories about the influence of modern society and social change on the mental health of the population were put forth by physicians and social philosophers long before the discipline of sociology was established. Most early research on the sociological aspects of mental illness was based either on case histories or on examination of records of institutions that harbored the mentally ill. In the United States prior to the passage of the Mental Health Act in 1946 mental illness was, by and large, a problem for the states. It was a problem that most states handled in the late nineteenth and early twentieth centuries by building large asylums, often in remote places, where the mentally ill could be hidden away. Only when this mode of societal defense mechanism was challenged by our military experience in World War II and the federal government both proposed reform and came to the aid of the states did we begin to examine our mental hospitals and the possibility of providing more adequate services. Sociology played a minor role in the initial challenge but a substantial role in raising and helping to answer some of the questions basic to a sound national policy and to the design of effective programs.

Sociological research on mental disorder and on mental health services may be carried out under a variety of auspices and for a variety of purposes. We must recognize at the outset that the dividing line between basic and applied research in this area cannot be drawn easily. Goffman's (1961) seminal research on the character of total institutions, for example, was designed as a contribution to sociological theory, but its impact on professions in the field of mental health policy and planning was probably equally great. So we shall be less concerned with research auspices and aims than with the potential contribution that any given study may make to the planning, development, and evaluation of mental health services.

WHAT ARE THE PROBLEMS?

The provision of mental health services requires that we know something of the prevalence and incidence of mental disorders (in other words, the level of need for services), the readiness of members of the population to use various types of services, and the potential effectiveness of alternative approaches to providing service. Sociologists can also contribute greatly to the field of mental health by identifying sources of stress and other threats to mental health in the life experiences of members of various cultural and income groups. Such data are useful for social planning and for public health approaches to minimizing the amount of mental disorder. Moreover, the responses of persons close to the emotionally distressed individual will themselves influence the magnitude of such distress and its resulting impairment. Systematic research may indicate what kinds of response are likely to exacerbate symptoms or to increase the probability of long-term impairment. Before examining what we know in each of these broad areas, it may be useful to pose some of the questions that face sociologists working in the field of mental health.

Assessment of the Need for Services

We all suffer occasionally from emotional upset, feelings of tension and anxiety, or psychophysiological symptoms such as headaches, sweating palms, trembling hands, etc. Unless such problems are persistent and unusually severe, however, we can usually handle them without help. Where does one draw the line between normal problems of living and emotional problems in need of treatment? How can we best measure emotional distress or mental disorder in the population at large?

Federal policy at present is to provide an integrated package of community mental health facilities, including inpatient and outpatient services, within local communities or catchment areas containing roughly 100,000 persons. How should the boundaries of such areas be set? It would seem to make sense to incorporate in a given service area population groups that have somewhat similar problems and needs, so that the services can be tailored specifically for them. The delineation of boundaries for catchment areas is an obvious task for social scientists.

A related question bears upon the kinds of services that are most appropriate for particular population groups. What sociocultural features influence the effectiveness of alternative service strategies? While there may be certain common denominators in treating severe mental disorder, impairment as a consequence of emotional problems may take many forms and respond to may different kinds of intervention. For example, job training, situational change, or the provision of social support may be more important than insight therapy for persons in particular sociocultural circumstances.

Once services are in place, there is the task of making them maximally available. Can sociological research help locate persons in need of service, insure that the available services are appropriate to them, and then assist in making those services socially and culturally acceptable?

Public Attitudes Toward Mental Disorder and Mental Health Services

A major difference between mental disorder and most other serious illnesses is that neither the potential patient nor those close to him or her may be aware they are confronting mental illness. The definition of a health problem largely determines what one does about that problem. What social and cultural patterns facilitate early recognition and referral for treatment? To what extent are persons in need of help (or their families) aware of the existence of potential helping services in their own community? Are there resistances against using particular types of facilities? Is there a fear of stigmatization if psychiatric services are used?

There are many potential gatekeepers to mental health services. How well informed are the clergy, general medical practitioners, the police, and other agents of the community about the nature of mental disorder, the best means of dealing with it, and the existing facilities in the community?

Planning and Organizing New Services

To be effective, mental health services cannot simply be imposed upon the community. In planning facilities, how can the local population and indigenous leaders be brought into the planning process? What kinds of services already exist, and how can new services best be planned to supplement rather than duplicate those already existing? Is there still a place for the long-term mental hospital? What organizational features and policies can enhance its usefulness, and what features may be potentially antitherapeutic?

Minimizing Stress and Maximizing Support

Effective psychological functioning seems to require both a reasonably high level of self-esteem and freedom from physical and social stresses that threaten the stability of basic life satisfactions. What conditions that impinge upon a given population or subgroup within it are likely to cause low self-esteem or to threaten the stability of everyday life and close personal ties? How can persons who are peripheral to integrated social networks be given the necessary support to cope with life change and stress?

No one sociologist can attempt to answer all these questions, but all of them are relevant to the provision of mental health services in at least some circumstances. Fortunately, almost all these questions have been addressed to some degree, so we have clues as to how they may be answered.

WHAT DO WE KNOW?

Extent and Nature of Mental Health Problems

Information about the incidence and prevalence of various types of mental disorders comes from two basic sources. The first is information derived from services actually provided, indicating 1) the number of patients coming into treatment during a given period (incidence), 2) the number in treatment at any given time (treated prevalence), and 3) the duration of treatment or of impairment, classified by the specific type of symptom presented (diagnosis). Such data are essential if we are to know something about the features and processes of psychopathology, for only as patients are studied in clinical perspective can reliable and valid diagnoses be made and the course of various disorders charted. But information about persons under treatment cannot tell us anything about the overall need for treatment services.

The second basic source of information is systematic studies of cross sections of the population that assess the incidence and prevalence of varying degrees of emotional discomfort, psychophysiological symptoms, and/or role impairment. Perhaps the best known, and certainly one of the most ambitious, efforts of this sort was the Midtown Manhattan Study by Srole and his associates (1962). This research found that roughly a sixth of the population reported psychophysiological and psychological symptoms or interpersonal problems that were severe enough to cause some impairment of functioning. This is very close to the estimate of the President's Commission on Mental Health, which reported in 1978 that at any given time perhaps 15 percent of the U.S. population is in need of mental health services. Yet, the proportion of the population actually seen in mental health facilities in the most recent years for which data are available was substantially smaller—3 percent, or some 6.7 million persons. Of these, roughly 1.5 million were hospitalized and the rest were treated in outpatient services of one kind or another. (Information about treated mental illness is regularly published by the Division of Biometry and Epidemiology of the National Institute of Mental Health and is an invaluable source of data for the mental health researcher.)

The most serious mental disorder, in terms of prevalence, duration, and degree of impairment, is schizophrenia. Approximately 2 million Americans are estimated to display the schizophrenic syndrome (profound thought disorders, including delusions and/or hallucinations, social withdrawal, and bizarre behavior) at one time or another, and often recurrently. While some sociologists and even a few psychiatrists do not regard schizophrenia as a disease and criticize the sloppiness of diagnostic classifications made in everyday psychiatric practice, more rigorous methods of assessment are sufficiently reliable to make the diagnosis of schizophrenia at least as defensible as many of the classifications made by sociologists (World Health Organization, 1973).

Episodes of severe depression occur with even higher incidence than schizophrenia, though for the most part they are of shorter duration and, therefore, less prevalent at any given time. So-called bipolar or manic depressive psychosis occurs with substantially less frequency, but it is markedly disruptive of functioning and role relationships. We know that these disorders are distributed somewhat unevenly in the population, and, as we shall see, sociologists have played a major role in trying to establish the sociocultural correlates of such disorders.

For data on the incidence and prevalence of diagnosed mental illness, we must rely almost exclusively on data from the records of treatment facilities. Systematic studies of population cross sections do not provide sufficient information about the individuals interviewed, (most of whom have not sought help for psychological problems) to permit a diagnosis in most instances, even though some symptoms are reported. Attempts to establish the true incidence of mental illness are also enormously complicated by the fact that acknowledgement of one's psychological discomfort is socially patterned, as are the forms that symptoms take. The literature on assessments of mental illness across cultures and subcultures has been thoroughly reviewed by Dohrenwend (1975), who also summarized the main findings that had emerged by the mid 1970s.

Cross-national and cross-time comparisons of rates of treated mental disorder are markedly influenced by the availability of treatment facilities and the policies governing the use of such facilities. In the United States, for example, state mental hospitals were for more than a century used as custodial caretakers for the mentally ill. Schizophrenic and senile patients were particularly unlikely to be returned to the community once they had been hospitalized. The resident population in our state hospitals approached 600,000 in 1955, when a combination of circumstances—drug therapy, improved staffing, changed administrative policies—reversed a century-long trend toward ever increasing hospital populations (Clausen, 1976).

Today state hospitals contain only about a third of their previous patient loads, and the average length of the stay for even chronic patients is much shorter. Can we assume that senile patients are now being cared for in the community? We would be deceived if we thought so. Although these persons are not now counted among the residents of mental hospitals, many of them can be found in nursing homes and other custodial institutions largely operated on a for-profit basis. Census data on persons in institutions show an increase in the number of residents in such institutions far greater than the decline in residents in state mental hospitals. Thus, any attempt to assess trends in the number of persons in treatment (or custody) for psychiatric problems must take into account alternative ways of defining and handling people impaired by such problems.

Another approach to assessing the need for services is to interview key persons in existing community agencies concerning the extent to which they encounter clients with apparent psychiatric disabilities. Welfare agencies, courts, schools, lawyers, physicians, and clergymen are especially likely to deal with persons and families who are struggling with mental disorder, either because the disorder leads to failures in role performance or because these gatekeepers are sought out by persons with problems. In areas where specialized psychiatric services are sparse, these agencies and gatekeepers must often use stopgap methods. If they can be induced to maintain systematic records of all instances over a period of time in which they would like to make psychiatric referrals, such records would provide a useful estimate of the potential demand for services (Warheit, et al., 1975).

Whenever one relies on informants who are not psychiatrically sophisticated, however, there is a danger that they will identify persons who give them trouble (or who in general make trouble), rather than persons who are themselves troubled. Often, of course, the two groups overlap, but many accurately disturbed persons are withdrawn and/or depressed and do not come to the attention of existing community agencies.

Even when assessments are made by psychiatrists or other specialists, it is sometimes difficult to distinguish between persons who lack certain basic social competences because they are never afforded the opportunity to acquire them and those who are incompetent because they are suffering from a severe mental disorder. Lack of social and occupational skills is likely to lead to low self-esteem and feelings of being unable to cope with life. Adequate assessment of the need for mental health services must deal with such issues, as well as with severe mental disorder, but must not confuse the two (Mechanic, 1969).

Sociocultural Correlates of Mental Disorder

Despite the difficulties confronted in attempting to assess the incidence and prevalence of mental disorder, there is enough consistency across existing studies for us to make a number of generalizations with a good deal of confidence. Members of the working class, and particularly the lower working class, present far more symptoms of psychological discomfort than do members of the middle and upper classes, and lower-class persons are substantially more likely to be hospitalized for mental disorder. Schizophrenia, for example, is more prevalent in the lower class than in the upper middle class, and schizophrenic patients tend to be treated differently according to their social class background (Hollingshead and Redlich, 1958; Kohn, 1973). Evidence for a genetic factor in schizophrenia is now overwhelmingly strong, but it appears that socioenvironmental factors are important both in the precipitation of schizophrenia and in the course of the illness (Brown, et al., 1972).

How does one explain the greater prevalence of symptoms of psychological distress and of schizophrenia at the lower levels of social status? Social status is associated with so many variations in life experience that one is tempted to say that almost any social circumstance assumed to have a bearing on psychological well-being can be invoked to explain the effects of social class. These might include socialization and personality development in early years, the impact of social stresses and unpleasant life changes, the lack of resources for coping with stressful changes, and the lack of integration into stable and supportive relational networks.

The lower-class child is more likely than the middle-class child to encounter a diversity of standards and an inadequate or at least less coherent orientation to the world. Lower-class parents provide less successful and less self-confident models for emulation, and their children are less likely to experience a sense of efficacy in dealing with the social environment. Lower-class children are more likely to experience failure and rejection in school and in the larger community. Modes of coping and defending are more likely to include escape and denial in the lower class. Thus, social class tends to have substantial influence on one's personality. At the same time, we must recognize that this tendency is not destiny. Many working-class parents are competent, effective persons, able to give their children not only love but a set of consistent standards and a sense of their own potential for mastery. And some middle-class parents fail to give any of these ingredients to their children. So it is not class per se that makes for personal vulnerability, but certain patterns of socialization that tend to be class linked but are not necessarily so.

This appears to be true of stress and life change also. Lower-class persons and families are more subject to the vicissitudes of social change and economic swings, although sources of life stress are to be found at all levels of society. The literature on the effects of social stresses on psychological distress and mental disorder has been growing by leaps and bounds but shows many inconsistencies concerning the linkage between social status and life stress (Dohrenwend and Dohrenwend, 1974). In general, however, it appears that while stresses from all forms of life changes do not differ greatly by social class, those that have strongly negative connotations are more frequent in the lower working class. For example, Brown and his co-workers in London (Brown, et al., 1976) found that working-class women were subject to many more stressful events involving their husbands, children, and housing than were middle-class women. Moreover, such stresses were associated with a high incidence of episodes of depression.

Is stress inevitably followed by symptoms or illness? Not necessarily. Along with an interest in stress has come an interest in modes of coping and in the importance of social supports. Persons who are well integrated into supportive social networks appear to be much better able to withstand stressful events without serious psychological consequences (Lin, et al., 1979). And again we find a linkage with social status. Upper-status persons tend to be more closely tied into enduring relationships and satisfying social roles. Such roles and relationships moderate the effects of life stress and promote more effective coping.

Space does not permit fuller examination of the ways in which sociocultural backgrounds and life patterns may influence the frequency of psychiatric disorder, but it is clear that much further research is called for and that sociologists will have an important role in such research. Some of the most significant studies conducted thus far, such as that of Brown and his associates (1976), have involved sociologists working closely with psychiatrists attached to community mental health facilities that provide access to carefully assessed groups of patients as well as community samples.

Sociocultural Orientations Toward Mental Disorder and Sources of Help

Throughout recorded history, it would appear that persons whom we would today regard as mentally ill have been regarded with fear and loathing. To be "crazy," or to act like a "mad man," connotes markedly devalued behavior that is commonly stigmatized. It is not surprising, then, that numerous studies using different techniques have found that the topic of mental disorder is disturbing to many persons (Clausen and Huffine, 1975). Not only the mentally ill but also those who serve them (psychiatrists and personnel of mental hospitals in particular) are regarded negatively by many persons. What is perhaps more surprising is that most members of the general public do not recognize mental illness when confronted by it, either in the form of brief descriptions of persons suffering from mental disorders or actual encounters with mental illness in a family member. Insofar as a stereotype of mental illness exists, it appears to consist of inexplicable bizarre, disruptive, and threatening behavior. But even when a person's behavior approximates the stereotype, family and close associates tend to find some other explanation for that behavior (Yarrow, et al., 1955).

Consider the implications of this two-pronged finding that 1) instances of mental disorder are often not recognized as such and, 2) mental disorder is stigmatized, with the stigma extending to those who treat mental disorder. If one does not recognize the nature of the problem confronted, one does not know to whom one can turn. And even when a correct definition occurs, both the patient and his or her family may hesitate to seek help from mental health services.

In general, favorable attitudes toward the use of psychiatric services increase with rising educational level, and better educated persons tend to be much more aware of the existence of psychiatric services within the community (Gurin, et al., 1960). Nevertheless, a good many studies have found that only a small segment of the population is aware of the location of mental health facilities within their local communities. In some instances, not even physicians in the community are well informed about available resources for treating mental disorder, although physicians are generally much better informed today than they were a decade or two ago. The general practitioner appears to be the primary gatekeeper to securing psychiatric aid for severe mental disorder. This has been true for the middle-class population for some time and seems now to be true for the working-class population as well (Shepherd, et al., 1966).

The Impact of Mental Illness on Patient and Family

Whether or not social processes and cultural orientations affect the occurrence of mental illness, the experience of even a brief episode of severe mental disorder is likely to have long-term consequences for both patient and family. The disruptive influence of paranoid delusions (which accompany many mental disorders), rage, or severe depression can tear apart the most cohesive family. Uncertainty about the former patient's continued functioning after termination of treatment can lead to pronounced insecurity even when interpersonal relationships have not been severely strained. The former patient may also experience that insecurity in its most frightening form: Will I lose control again, and, if so, what may I do?

Our knowledge in this area is extremely limited. There have been many short-term follow-up studies to ascertain what patient characteristics and treatment regimes are associated with the most favorable outcomes but relatively few long-term studies of patients and their families. To begin with one of the most obvious findings of past research, long-term outcome is related to diagnosis and to the age of onset of severe symptoms. Persons who manifest the basic thought disorder of schizophrenia in adolescence, for example, and who have been constricted in their relationships with others, tend to be the most chronically impaired in later life, even though they may be able to function episodically in certain types of social roles.

The person who develops schizophrenia prior to having acquired occupational skills and experience faces a tremendous obstacle to the achievement of full adult competence. Schizophrenia also tends to create a severe deficit in one's ability to relate to others, especially persons of the opposite sex. This is most true of male schizophrenics, of whom only about a third ever marry. Indeed, the ability to enjoy a heterosexual relationship is perhaps the best single indicator of a favorable prognosis in schizophrenia (Garmezy, 1968).

Men who have married and achieved a measure of occupational competence prior to experiencing an episode of schizophrenia are much less likely to be chronically disabled than are those whose breakdown comes in adolescence. Long-term longitudinal research by Huffine and Clausen (1979), for example, revealed that among a group of hospitalized men, most of whom had been diagnosed as schizophrenic and whose initial breakdown occurred after several years of marriage, about three-fifths had resumed stable careers after hospitalization and were functioning effectively in occupational roles 15 to 20 years later. While stable occupational performance was most often found in the absence of persistent symptoms, it was even more closely associated with competent job performance prior to initial hospitalization.

The subsequent life experience of women who develop schizophrenia is less predictable from their heterosexual histories, though it is certainly related to previously acquired social skills. In the research mentioned above, married schizophrenic women had experienced many more recurrent episodes of treatment than had the men, though here again most of them were functioning in the community 15 to 20 years later.

The long-term consequences of an episode of depression appear to be much less severe than those of schizophrenia for the patient and his or her career, and if recurrences do occur they tend to be less chronically persistent. Manic-depressive or bipolar psychoses, on the other hand, are likely to recur, and when they do they often wreak havoc on the family (Goffman, 1961). Apart from their episodes of acute disturbance, however, these patients appear to be unimpaired and are often extremely productive.

Many marriages remain intact despite the experience of mental illness by one spouse, but, in general, mental illness in either a child or a spouse severely stresses the marital tie. Are there ways of helping families to cope with the problem of mental illness? One might think that psychiatric services should be oriented to the needs of the family, but in general they are not. Much lip service is paid to the importance of the family, both as a source of stress and as a potential support system, but when the resources of treatment personnel are stretched thin, the family receives little help (Clausen and Huffine, 1975).

We know a little, then, about how life careers are influenced by the contingencies of mental disorder, but we need to know a good deal more if we are to plan appropriate mental health services that will soften the blow of mental disorder.

Preventing Mental Illness

An ounce of prevention is said to be worth a pound of cure. The great gains in longevity enjoyed by Western nations up to the time of World War II were brought about almost exclusively by better public health practices that prevented many diseases, rather than because of improved medical care. Indeed, an eminent leader in the field of public health has estimated that the gains to health in the coming decade that could result from renunciation of tobacco by the U.S. public would be greater than anything that could be accomplished by doubling the amount of money spent on health care.

Can mental illness be prevented? We certainly know enough about the consequences of certain types of experiences to say that if we could prevent those experiences or provide greater support to people who go through them, it should be possible to reduce markedly the anxiety and psychophysiological symptoms that impair so many persons. Quite possibly a substantial proportion of severe psychotic episodes might also be prevented, though here we are on somewhat less firm ground. For example, studies of attachment behavior in young children, as well as of children who were separated from their primary caretakers after they had formed firm attachments, have revealed that separation can be a source of lasting anxiety unless consistent nurturant care can be provided to the child. The human infant's basic need for love and consistent care cannot be far behind its need for food and physical comfort. Without such loving and care, the child cannot establish a trusting relationship with others. And without trust, there can be no self-confidence. It is beyond the scope of this chapter to suggest how preventive health services might be developed, but the President's Commission has assigned a task force to work on the topic, and it will undoubtedly engage the attention of many social scientists in the future.

In recent years, much attention has been given to identifying so-called "high risk" types of people, especially children who seem to be especially vulnerable to schizophrenia or other serious behavior disorders. To the extent that one can identify such children early in life—perhaps in the classroom, perhaps in the family—and can provide special attention for them, there is hope of diminishing their vulnerability (Garmezy, 1974a and b). There is now sufficient evidence of genetic vulnerability to schizophrenia to suggest that children of schizophrenic parents are at high risk, as are those from families in which there is an established history of schizophrenia. The risk appears to be much greater in matings of two persons whose family lines both contain schizophrenia, so that one element in preventive services will certainly be genetic counseling (Worden, et al., 1976).

Recent studies of the effects of life change and stress upon psychiatric symptoms suggest that stress itself may be less important than the supports available to those who undergo such experiences. As already noted, persons from the upper and middle classes have far more resources for dealing with stress, including sources of personal support and economic resources. Persons who are isolated from others, either because of their own personality problems or for other reasons, are quite vulnerable to mental disorders. This is especially true of older people who have outlived those nearest and dearest to them. Here again, sociologists (e.g., Lowenthal, 1964) have provided important basic data useful for mental health planning.

WHAT ARE WE DOING?

Development and Evaluation of Services

What have we learned from past research concerning problematic aspects of psychiatric facilities and about the methods for assessing their effectiveness? Perhaps the greatest contributions here have come from research that was less oriented to the needs of the field of mental health than to the study of social institutions and organizations. Early studies of the mental hospital (Belknap, 1956; Goffman, 1961; Stanton and Schwartz, 1954) and of processes related to admission to and release from mental hospitals (Scheff, 1964; Rosenhan, 1973) revealed that stereotypic views and routinized treatment of mental patients were far more prevalent in psychiatric settings than in the general community. Having to deal almost exclusively with psychotic patients, especially chronic patients who have succumbed to "institutionalization" as a way of existence, can be a profoundly discouraging occupation. Documentation of the effects of such discouragement, nevertheless, came as a shock to many people who had accepted the state mental hospital as the necessary if not ideal cornerstone of our institutional arrangements for caring for the mentally ill.

Research demonstrated that even in the best-staffed and best-equipped hospitals, the staff seldom listened to what patients said outside of therapy periods, and that much of what happened in the hospital might be considered antitherapeutic. Hearings to assess the need for hospitalization were superficial and so routinized that they gave patients little opportunity to present their own views.

Determination of the need for commitment depended more on the patient's being represented by an attorney than upon his or her psychiatric condition (Scheff, 1964). Once in the hospital, the patient became an "inmate," stripped of the badges of his or her identity, regimented in daily activities or all but abandoned on the back wards (Goffman, 1961). This picture of the mental hospital helped to explain the finding, based on studies of large numbers of hospitalized patients, that those who remained in the hospital for two years or more were extremely unlikely to be released thereafter. The mental hospital was largely the creator of the chronic mental patient.

This solid evidence that our hospitals for the long-term care of the mentally ill were to a large degree self-defeating helped to bring about a shift to community care for the mentally ill through the enactment of federal legislation providing aid to the states for community mental health centers. But such aid, and the establishment of many such clinical centers, has not been a panacea. Many persons in need of services do not receive appropriate care. Often there is no agreement as to what would be appropriate services.

Community Mental Health Centers

Federal involvement in mental health services, especially after the passage of the Community Mental Health Centers Act in 1963, has called for the planning of new services, provided in the community, and (one hopes) the evaluation of the effectiveness of psychiatric services. But establishment of a national policy and provision of funds for implementing that policy does not necessarily lead to systematic development of the policy in institutional forms that are viable. Nor do they necessarily entail implementation of the policy at the state and local level. The ultimate objective of the Community Mental Health Centers Act was to establish a network of comprehensive community mental health programs throughout the nation that would integrate and coordinate comprehensive services at the local level, so as to keep patients close to their environment and to maintain their links with family and community. Five essential types of service were to be provided by every center, including: 1) inpatient services offering a 24-hour care for treatment of acute disorder, 2) outpatient services, 3) partial hospitalization services, such as day care, night care, and weekend care, 4) emergency services 24 hours per day, and 5) consultation and education services available to community agencies and professional personnel. It was further envisioned that persons qualified to carry out research and evaluation would be added to the staffs of most community mental health centers.

Both planning and evaluation at the state and local levels have left much to be desired. Existing state agencies that administer health programs or are responsible for mental hospitals often vie for control of the funds available for community mental health purposes. It is not surprising, then, that planning has frequently been haphazard, with considerable duplication of effort on the one hand and enormous gaps on the other, and that evaluations have been at best fragmentary and inadequate. The recent report of the President's Commission on Mental Health (1978) gives some notion of the complexity of the problem and of the needs that exist.

The Role of Social Scientsits

In many ways, sociologists have been the not-so-loyal opposition to those who hold the reins of policy and administration in the field of mental health. This has been especially true in the case of sociological studies of the mental hospital, which have focused on the underside of hospital operations. But it has also been true of analyses of the processes of commitment and diagnosis. Sociological examinations of the nature of mental disorder and its treatment tend to reject traditional psychiatric perspectives. The medical model of mental illness seems much too narrow a formulation to fit much of the aberrant behavior and psychologic discomfort found in all societies (Sells, 1968).

Has the critical stance of many sociologists working in this field precluded the acceptance of sociological contributions to the field? Hardly at all, if the roles currently being played by sociologists are any criterion. Many of the most outstanding psychiatric administrators and clinicians have welcomed the new perspectives brought by social scientists and have invited them to participate more fully in planning and policy development. Sociologists were heavily involved in the work of the President's Commission on Mental Health, in some cases serving as coordinators of the panels that carried out the work of that Commission. Rather than being unwelcome, sociologists have at times been confronted with unrealistically high expectations concerning the contributions they could make to the field of mental health.

In any event, sociologists have provided valuable information for more effective planning in the field of mental health. They have collaborated with psychiatrists not only to assess the prevalence of symptoms of mental disorder in the population, but also to examine how social class and other social attributes influence the utilization of services by persons in need of help and to evaluate the actual services provided by various types of mental health facilities. Sociologists tend to be sought out for their methodological sophistication in studying behavior in social contexts as well as social institutions and social processes. They have also brought helpful theoretical formulations to bear on psychiatric problems.

Many of the studies cited in this chapter are a product of collaboration between social scientists and psychiatrists. Especially in the United States and Great Britain, such collaborative effort has had great payoffs. Wing and Brown (1970), for example, studied the social climates in rehabilitative efforts of three mental hospitals in Great Britain to ascertain the circumstances under which schizophrenic patients made the most progress. By identifying conditions that led patients to become passive and withdrawn, they were able to propose ways of redesigning programs to make them more effective. In another collaborative effort, Brown and Harris (1978) investigated the social origins of depression. After discovering that episodes of depression were much more likely to occur among working-class women than among middle-class women, this team set out to ascertain what kinds of experiences resulted in depression and what kinds of social relationships and activities tended to insulate or innoculate people against depression. This research, conducted in a community mental health center in a borough of London, affords many clues for developing preventive services and identifying those who are most vulnerable to severe depression.

Increasingly, sociologists are securing regular positions within departments of psychiatry and in mental health centers. Their primary responsibility is commonly for research, but some are centrally involved in planning and determining policy. As the demand for trained sociologists has increased, a number of training programs have been developed at both the predoctoral and postdoctoral levels to provide the kind of educational, research and field placement experiences that will greatly enhance the ability of sociologists to address the problem of mental disorder.

WHAT HAVE WE ACCOMPLISHED?

Effectiveness of Community Mental Health Centers

Our accomplishments in this area to date have not been great, but we have gained considerable experience at the local level that can be useful in subsequent planning and research. We have learned, both from mistakes that have been made and from a few well-developed programs, some of the costs and benefits of involving local community residents in the process of planning mental health services. Especially in the case of services for minority groups whose cultural norms and needs for services are often quite different from those of the white middle class, it is imperative that local leaders be involved in the planning process if a projected facility is to be perceived as a positive resource in the community. It is true that local citizens may have unrealistic expectations and little understanding of the services that professionals have to offer, but it is equally true that if local leaders are not given a realistic understanding of what is feasible and if professionals do not listen to their reports of local needs, there is little chance for a successful service relationship. It is not easy to achieve consensus when participants start with very different conceptions of reality and desired ends, but a measure of consensus can usually be attained if professionals sincerely seek to understand the local community and its problems. The services of social scientists, especially if their background is similar to that of local residents, can be invaluable in achieving this goal.

The costs and benefits of involving the local community in the planning and evaluation of health care services are difficult to assess systematically. But in the area of alternatives to hospital care for the seriously mentally ill several studies have provided us with a good deal of solid knowledge. For example, Pasamanick and his associates (1967) carried out an experimental study of hospital versus community care with some 152 schizophrenic patients. Patients were randomly assigned to three groups whose treatments were 1) home care with drug therapy, 2) home care with a placebo instead of an active drug, and 3) hospital care. When followed up six to 30 months after entering the program, 77 percent of the first group and 34 percent of the second group remained continuously outside the hospital, saving many thousands of dollars in hospital costs. This research proved the feasibility of maintaining schizophrenic patients in the community, at lower cost and presumably greater satisfaction for the patients than if they had been hospitalized. Nevertheless, sociological assessments of the families of these patients revealed substantial costs to family members in terms of upset, interference of the patient with family and work routines, and general worry and strain among other family members. Moreover, long-term outcomes appear to be as good and possibly better for those patients who were hospitalized. The most effective mode of dealing with severe mental illness may well entail short-term hospitalization followed by outpatient treatment.

Mechanic (1969:108-16) has suggested that with chronic patients who have been hospitalized for a long period, an educational model may be more appropriate than the medical model of therapy. He enlisted schizophrenic patients in a British hospital to carry out clerical tasks in connection with a research project and found that they were careful workers and received much gratification from their involvement. Having a chance to use one's skills and abilities—thereby gaining a feeling that one can make a contribution—is as important to mental patients as to everyone else. Moreover, even chronic patients do have useful skills and abilities if these can only be mobilized.

Needed Research

There are many types and levels of evaluation. Highly sophisticated research is needed to establish the therapeutic effectiveness of new drugs and other procedures, but often rather simple studies can produce very useful information in a given situation. All clinical facilities keep records, but a surprising number of them never study those records. Much can be learned by coding and tabulating just the attributes of persons who present themselves for service. Staff members have impressions of their clientele and of the services they provide, but those impressions are often drastically wrong. In one case, the social service department of a large public mental hospital reported that "most" of the families of patients were visited at home during the patient's stay or shortly thereafter. A check of records (confirmed by interviews with family members) revealed that "most" was actually less than 5 percent. In such instances, operational myths need to be examined and general policies reviewed.

Case records can be analyzed for evidence of differential use of a service by subgroups of the population, for information about referral processes, and for an indication of the characteristics of patients or families who either drop out early or are forever using services. Such information is not a basis for evaluating out-comes, but it does permit some understanding of what makes certain services problematic.

Outcome studies, whether for the evaluation of service modalities or simply to understand what happens to patients after treatment, have been carried out very frequently by sociologists (Angrist, et al., 1968; Freeman and Simmons, 1963; Myers and Bean, 1968). From such research we know something about the extent to which needs for treatment are recurrent and the circumstances under which patients are most likely to be retained in the community after re-lease from hospitalization. In general, the more hospitalizations a patient has experienced, the greater the likelihood of return to the hospital. But one of the most exciting findings of recent years—which a number of research teams in several countries are now seeking to replicate—deals with the consequences of patient-family interaction patterns in influencing the ability of previously hos-pitalized schizophrenic patients to function in the community. Brown, et al. (1972) found that if family members tend to be overly involved with the patient and to express emotionally-toned critical comments about the patient prior to his or her return from the hospital, the patient is much less likely to be able to remain at home through the first year after release from the hospital. The pres-ence of what Brown has called "expressed emotion," seems devastating to the patient unless he or she is heavily drugged.

Contribution by Sociologists

The major contributions and accomplishments of sociologists working in the field of mental health have been derived from the general perspectives of socio-logical and social-psychological theory and from research that has focused upon many critical issues in the field. Sociologists and social psychologists have pro-vided the first systematic data on attitudes toward mental disorder and mental health services. Sociologists have been in the forefront in devising techniques for assessing mental health in the general population, going beyond reliance on data derived from treatment services. Sociologists and anthropologists have studied the organization and dynamics of mental hospitals and have helped to make the large "total institution" that was our dominant treatment modality prior to World War II now largely a thing of the past.

Social science research provided much of the documentation on which cur-rent governmental planning is based. This is not to claim that the community mental health program is a direct outcome of social science research, far from it. But applied social science research has had a direct impact on policy makers in this area.

In the process of conducting research on many facets of the mental health field, sociologists have also developed a number of technical skills and improved conceptualizations. Research on the effects of social stressors and social supports, for example, has led to a marked increase in conceptual and methodological sophistication. We have become aware of the inadequacies of institutional records and official statistics on treated mental illness, and we have learned how to supplement these records and statistics with systematic data collection. In short, applied sociologists have begun to learn how to be full participants in the planning, development, and evaluation of mental health services.

WHERE ARE WE GOING?

We can predict with some assurance that sociologists will continue to play a very important role in mental health research, both basic and applied. As the number of community mental health centers securing federal funding increases and budgetary costs mount, there will be an expanding need for data on program effectiveness. The enormous costs for personnel and plant can only be justified if it can be demonstrated that human suffering is being diminished and personal effectiveness increased. It must be demonstrated that persons suffering from severe or chronic mental disorder are receiving better care at less cost through these centers than could be provided in a hospital setting. And it must be demonstrated that all segments of the population are being served by community mental health centers.

Ultimately, one might expect that every community mental health center will have qualified social scientists on its staff, both to carry out research and to participate in policy making and program implementation. Already a number of eminent psychiatrists have had a significant amount of training in sociology or in other social sciences and are eager to incorporate social scientists into their staffs. We may expect that more sociologists will prepare themselves for work in the mental health field, not only by mastering basic sociological theory and methods and the sociology of mental health and illness, but also by learning enough about clinical operations to be able to bring sociological skills to bear on planning and evaluating those operations. It is easy to sound grandiose when talking about such possibilities, but the magnitude of the tasks remaining to be tackled is sufficient to humble even those with grandiose ideas. Perhaps it will suffice to say that there are extraordinary opportunities for sociologists to apply their skills in the field of mental health.

REFERENCES AND SUGGESTED READINGS

Angrist, S.S., M. Lifton, S. Dinitz, and B. Pasamanick. 1968. *Women After Treatment: A Study of Mental Patients and Their Normal Neighbors.* New York: Appleton-Century-Crofts.

Belknap, I. 1956. *Human Problems of a State Mental Hospital.* New York: McGraw-Hill.

*Brown, G.W. and T. Harris. 1978. *Social Origins of Depression* New York: The Free Press.

The authors present the full report of a very exciting and methodologically exemplary study of the impact of life events and the protective value of social supports in relation to the experiencing of depressive episodes among women in a borough of London.

Brown, G.W., M.N. Bhrolchain, and T. Harris. 1976. "Social Class and Psychiatric Disturbance Among Women in an Urban Population." *Sociology* 9:226–54.

Brown, G.W., J.L. Birley, and J.K. Wing. 1972. "Influence of Family Life on the Course of Schizophrenic Disorders: A Replication." *British Journal of Psychiatry* 121:241.

Clausen, J.A. 1976. "Mental Disorders." In *Contemporary Social Problems,* 4th ed., edited by R.K. Merton and R. Nisbet, pp. 105–39. New York: Harcourt Brace Jovanovich.

Clausen, J.A. and C.L. Huffine. 1975. "Sociocultural and Social Psychological Factors Affecting Social Responses to Mental Disorder." *Journal of Health and Social Behavior* 16:405–20.

Dohrenwend, B.S. and B.P. Dohrenwend, eds. 1974. *Stressful Life Events: Their Nature and Effect.* New York: John Wiley & Sons.

Dohrenwend, B.P. 1975. "Sociocultural and Social Psychological Factors in the Genesis of Mental Disorders." *Journal of Health and Social Behavior* 16:365–92.

Freeman, H.E. and O.G. Simmons. 1963. *The Mental Patient Comes Home.* New York: John Wiley & Sons.

Garmezy, N. 1968. "Process and Reactive Schizophrenia: Some Conceptions and Issues." In *The Role and Methodology of Classification in Psychiatry and Psychopathology,* edited by M. Katz, pp. 419–66. Washington, D.C.: U.S. Government Printing Office.

_____. 1974a. "Children at Risk: The Search for the Antecedents of Schizophrenia. Part I, Conceptual Models and Research Methods." *Schizophrenia Bulletin* 8:14–90.

_____. 1974b. "Children at Risk: The Search for the Antecedents of Schizophrenia. Part II, On-going Research Programs, Issues and Intervention." *Schizophrenia Bulletin* 9:55–125.

Goffman, E. 1961. *Asylums: Essays on the Social Situation of Mental Patients and Other Inmates.* New York: Doubleday.

Gurin, G., T. Zaroff, and S. Seld. *Americans View Their Mental Health: A Nationwide Interview Survey.* New York: Basic Books.

Hollingshead, A. and F.C. Redlich. 1958. *Social Class and Mental Illness.* New York: John Wiley & Sons.

Huffine, C.L. and J.A. Clausen. 1979. "Madness and Work: Short and Long Term Effects of Mental Illness on Occupational Careers." *Social Forces* 57:1049.

Kohn, M.L. 1973. "Social Class and Schizophrenia. A Critical Review and a Reformulation." *Schizophrenia Bulletin* 7:60–79.

Lin, N., R.S. Simeone, W.N. Ensel, and W. Kuo. 1979. "Social Support, Stressful Life Events, and Illness: A Model and an Empirical Test." *Journal of Health and Social Behavior* 20:108–19.

Lowenthal, M.F. 1964. *Lives in Distress: The Paths of the Elderly to the Psychiatric Ward.* New York: Basic Books.

*Mechanic, D. 1969. *Mental Health and Social Policy.* Englewood Cliffs, N.J.: Prentice-Hall.

This slim volume gives a good overview of the issues that must be dealt with in developing more comprehensive mental health services. It also provides a sociological perspective and some cogent criticisms of existing policies and services.

Myers, J.B. and L. Bean. 1968. *A Decade Later: A Follow-up of Social Class and Mental Illness.* New York: John Wiley & Sons.

Pasamanick, B., F. Scarpitti, and S. Dinitz. 1967. *Schizophrenics in the Community: An Experiment in the Prevention of Hospitalization.* New York: Appleton-Century-Crofts.

*President's Commission on Mental Health. 1978. *Report to the President from the President's Commission on Mental Health and Appendices, Volumes 2, 3, and 4, Task Panel Reports to the President's Commission on Mental Health.* Washington, D.C.: U.S. Government Printing Office.

Volume 1 provides an overview of the findings of the Commission and its recommendations; Volume 2 presents back-up data on the nature and scope of the problems of mental health and on mental health service delivery, personnel, and costs; Volume 3 examines mental health needs, with particular attention to special populations such as children, rural residents, veterans, minorities, etc.; Volume 4 deals with legal and ethical issues, research prevention, and public attitudes. Most of the Task Panel reports contain summaries and bibliographies, affording a comprehensive view of the issues of the field.

Rosenhan, D.L. 1973. "On Being Sane in Insane Places." *Science* 179:250–58.

Scheff, T.J. 1964. "Social Conditions for Rationality: How Urban and Rural Courts Deal with the Mentally Ill." *American Behavioral Scientist* 8:21–24.

Segal, S.P. and U. Aviram. 1978. *The Mentally Ill in Community-Based Sheltered Care.* New York: John Wiley & Sons.

Sells, S.B. 1968. *The Definition and Measurement of Mental Health.* Washington, D.C.: U.S. Government Printing Office.

Shepherd, M., B. Cooper, A.C. Brown and G. Kalton. 1966. *Psychiatric Illness in General Practice.* London: Oxford University Press.

*Srole, L., T.S. Langner, S.T. Michael, M.K. Opler, and T.A.C. Rennie. 1962. *Mental Health in the Metropolis: The Midtown Manhattan Study.* New York: McGraw-Hill.

Intensive interviews with 1,600 New Yorkers provided material for psychiatric ratings of symptoms and impairment. This most ambitious and influential study provided the first thorough documentation of the extent of untreated psychological discomfort and has served as a model for much subsequent research.

Stanton, A.H. and M.S. Schwartz. 1954. *The Mental Hospital.* New York: Basic Books.

*Warheit, G.J., R.A. Bell, and J.J. Schwab. 1975. *Planning for Change: Needs Assessment Approaches.* Gainesville: University of Florida, Department of Psychiatry.

> This is a very helpful manual on how to carry out research to assess needs of service. It discusses suggested approaches and even includes sample instruments for field use by the social scientist.

Wing, J.I. and G.W. Brown. 1970. *Institutionalism and Schizophrenia.* London: Cambridge University Press.

Worden, F.C., B. Childs, S. Matthysse, and E. Gershon. 1976. "Frontiers of Psychiatric Genetics." *Neurosciences Research Program Bulletin* 14: entire issue.

World Health Organization. 1973. *Report of the International Pilot Project of Schizophrenia, Volume 1.* Geneva, Switzerland: World Health Organization.

Yarrow, M.R., C.G. Schwartz, H.S. Murphy, and L.C. Deasy. 1955. "The Psychological Meaning of Mental Illness." *Journal of Social Issues* 11:12–24.

19 LEGAL SERVICES

Richard L. Abel

Legal services are qualitatively different from the other social services discussed in this section. Physical and mental health, education, and leisure are important roughly in proportion to their quality and quantity. In seeking to improve the educational, medical, and recreational services available to disadvantaged groups, the fact that these services are unequally distributed throughout the population does not diminish the quality of whatever services are enjoyed. Equality of services may also be a goal, but it is an independent goal. This is not true of legal services. The role of the lawyer is to mediate conflict: to avoid, prepare for, engage in, and resolve disputes. This role presupposes an adversary. Consequently, the services of a lawyer are valuable only if they are roughly equal, in quality and quantity, to the services possessed by adversaries. Indeed, legal services that are consistently inferior may be worse than no services at all, since both adversary and arbiter are often more solicitous toward an unrepresented party than they are toward one who is inadequately represented.

WHAT ARE THE PROBLEMS?

Achieving Legal Equality

Equality in the distribution of legal services has a value beyond that of enhancing the welfare of the unrepresented or underrepresented. The very integrity of the U.S. legal system as an adversary system depends upon equal representation of all parties. The legitimacy of contemporary law rests on the assumption that optimally efficient allocations of scarce resources are produced by parties who freely negotiate with each other on the basis of equal information about the law and equal competence to use it. The adversarial model of litigation—whether in a civil action or a criminal prosecution—is grounded upon the belief that fac-

407

tual truth and fidelity to substantive and procedural rules are best achieved by partisan struggle between equal opponents, which at a minimum means opponents who are equally represented. Moreover, the theory of democratic pluralism assumes that all citizens are equally able to influence the making and application of laws. Given the influence of lawyers in U.S. politics, that assumption requires equal representation by lawyers before both the legislature and the executive at all levels of government.

Virtually every problem in the area of legal services is related to this central issue of equality. To what extent does the existing distribution satisfy the fundamental criteria of justice? What reforms have been proposed or attempted to achieve that ideal? How successful have they been? To answer these questions it is necessary to specify more precisely what we mean by equality of legal services.

Barriers to Legal Equality

A preliminary question is whether the parties who confront each other—either in face-to-face negotiation or before a third party such as a judge, arbitrator, or mediator—represent all the interests affected by the controversy? If there are other interests, is their failure to participate a function of inadequate resources, lack of information, or insufficient organization, and how can these deficiencies be remedied? In addition to these obstacles to effective participation in the adversary process, inherent in the parties themselves, others derive from the composition and structure of the legal profession. Lawyers, as professionals, tend to belong to the upper socioeconomic strata and most are white males. As a consequence, they are socially quite distant from the poor and from minorities and often far more comfortable with corporate executives or wealthy individuals. Lawyers tend to share the political outlook of the latter two categories, which may affect their readiness to represent the disadvantaged and their effectiveness in doing so.

Although the legal profession is relatively homogeneous when contrasted with the general population, internally it is highly stratified. These status distinctions closely reflect the clientele a lawyer represents. Differences in the size, wealth, power, and social status of clients are reproduced in a hierarchy of lawyers ranging from the senior partners of large corporate firms to the sole practitioner handling the personal problems of individuals (Heinz and Laumann, 1978). These extremes differ greatly in expertise, resources, and influence. Consequently, equality of representation is as much a question of who is representing the party as of whether the party is being represented at all. Differences in the quality of legal representation are equally important in evaluating reforms that consciously seek to achieve the adversarial ideal. Thus, it is essential to look at the backgrounds and training of lawyers, at the way in which they are organized, and at the sources and extent of their funding—in comparison to those of their adversaries—when assessing the adequacy of services provided to the unrepresented or underrepresented.

Finally, although these problems are posed most starkly in litigation, where the parties confront each other in the midst of controversy, they are even more important outside that context. Do the parties have, or can they be given, equal access to, and power within, those institutions that formulate the rules governing future controversies? These institutions include not only legislatures but also courts and administrative agencies in their rule-making capacities. And do the parties have, or can they be given, equal competence to take advantage of existing rules in planning transactions and anticipating future controversies? The following discussion will explore these questions: How unequal is the present structure of legal representation? What efforts are being made to equalize it? How successful are they? What needs to be done?

WHAT DO WE KNOW?

The Legal Profession

The total inadequacy of the legal services available to the poor—or even to middle-class individuals (Cheatham, 1963; Christensen, 1970)—has been documented repeatedly for more than half a century (Smith, 1919). When Smith published his landmark book in 1919, there were only 62 full-time legal aid attorneys in the entire country, located in 42 cities, with a total budget of less than $200,000, handling little more than 100,000 cases a year (Johnson, 1974:6). Although Smith's book stimulated considerable growth in the legal aid funded by municipalities and charitable organizations, prior to the advent of the federal Legal Services Program in the Office of Economic Opportunity (the War on Poverty) in 1965, there were only 236 legal aid organizations with a total budget of less than $4 million.

> This amounted to less than two-tenths of 1 percent of the nation's total annual expenditure for the service of lawyers... to provide representation for the more than one-fourth of the nation's population unable to afford a lawyer when they needed one. Expressed in other terms, the equivalent of 400 full-time lawyers were available to serve almost 50 million Americans (a ratio of one lawyer for 120,000 persons) as compared with almost 250,000 full-time attorneys to take care of the remaining 140 million (a ratio of one lawyer for every 560 persons). (Johnson, 1974:9)

To obtain a better understanding of the growth of subsidized legal services, it is necessary to view them against the background of the market for private legal services. How many lawyers are there? We do not really know. The last comprehensive survey, completed in 1971, revealed something under 400,000 lawyers (Sikes, et al., 1972; see also Grossblatt and Sikes, 1973). But the past decade has witnessed a phenomenal rise in law school enrollments, from 43,700 in 1960 to 106,000 in 1973. And there has been a concomitant increase of 91 percent in annual admissions to the bar between 1970 and 1975 (York and Hale, 1973; Rudd and White, 1974; White, 1975). We know little about the causes of this growth, however. Is it due primarily to a decline in other professional employment opportunities; to the rapid increase in lawyers' incomes, from a law firm starting salary of $7,000 in 1965 to more than $30,000 today (compare Pashigian, 1977, 1978 with Weinfield, 1949, 1952); or to a vision of law as an avenue of social change, which strongly attracted college students of the late 1960s and early 1970s (Stevens, 1973; Erlanger and Klegon, 1978)? Moreover, little information is available on where potential lawyers come from, why they enter the profession, what form and subject matter of legal practice they choose, or how they are distributed geographically (Blaine, 1976; Ramey, 1978).

The starting point for such an understanding is the sociography of the profession. Existing overviews are unsatisfactory because they are merely anecdotal (Mayer, 1967) or were commissioned by the organized bar and offer little more than an official whitewash of the profession (Blaustein and Porter, 1954). However, two excellent studies of legal practice—one conducted in New York City, which has the largest concentration of lawyers in the country (Carlin, 1966), and the other in Prairie City, a small Midwestern city (Handler, 1967)—allow us to explore the influence of social environment on the structure of legal practice and the behavior of lawyers. Lawyers in New York are more specialized (70 percent devote more than half their time to one area, compared with 17 percent in Prairie City). Their clientele is heavily oriented toward business organizations (70 percent compared with 57 percent in Prairie City). As a consequence, they tend to practice in larger firms (21 percent are in firms of more than 15 lawyers, whereas no firm in Prairie City is that large). On the other hand, more lawyers in New York City practice by themselves (47 percent). As a result, the New York bar is highly stratified by national origin, religion, clientele, subject matter, organization of practice, service rendered, fora in which lawyers appear, and income. Indeed, there are two professional organizations in the city, representing the split between elite lawyers and the rest of the bar. In Prairie City, by contrast, the bar is both small and relatively homogeneous along each of these variables. Carlin and Handler agree, on the basis of their independent studies, that these structural differences are largely responsible for the fact that lawyers in New York violate the rules of professional ethics far more often than do those in Prairie City.

Relationships between lawyers and clients may be even more significant than social environment in determining the ethical behavior of lawyers. Here it is necessary to distinguish between sole or small firm practitioners serving individual or small business clients and large firms representing corporate or wealthy individual clients.

Sole and Small-Firm Practice

Let us begin with sole and small-firm practitioners. It is helpful to separate the problems that occur in acquiring clients from those that arise once the lawyer-client relationship has been established. To quote Karl Llewellyn's colorful language:

> The canons of ethics on business-getting are still built in terms of a town of twenty-five thousand... a town where reputation speaks itself from mouth to mouth, even on the other side of the railroad track; and the reputation not only of the oldster, but of the youngster. (Llewellyn, 1933:115)

Until very recently, lawyers were prohibited from actively seeking business. They could not advertise their services, approach individuals they knew were in need of representation, or even offer advice gratuitously. Yet, lawyers obviously need business to survive, and the public needs lawyers. Often the gap is bridged by contacts growing out of kinship or friendship. Numerous studies have shown that this kind of personal mediation is the most common means by which an individual finds a lawyer (Curran, 1977:201). But, as Llewellyn (1933) observed, these contacts are less widely enjoyed in large cities and are least available to those segments of the population—the poor and minorities—whose members have been systematically excluded from the legal profession. Nor are lawyer and client frequently brought together by prior contact, for two reasons: 1) the legal problems of individuals are typically one-shot, nonrecurring affairs, such as, car accidents, wills, residential land transactions, and divorces; 2) individuals prefer not to return to lawyers they have previously used (Curran, 1977:191). The consequence of this dilemma is that sole and small-firm practitioners serving an individual clientele regularly engage in behavior that skirts, or openly flouts, the rules of professional conduct. They may exchange favors with those in a position to steer business to them, such as real estate brokers, insurance adjusters, trust companies, or doctors. They may purchase clients on a piecework basis, paying commissions to police, bail bondsmen, auto mechanics and tow truck operators, ambulance drivers, used car dealers, and nurses and hospital attendants. They may even employ full-time "investigators," whose actual job is to solicit clients (Carlin, 1962; Reichstein, 1965). The Supreme Court recently found state regulation of lawyer advertising unconstitutional (*Bates* v. *State Bar of Arizona,* 1977) but upheld state regulation of lawyer solicitation (*Ohralik* v. *Ohio State Bar Association,* 1978). Research is needed on the impact of liberalized rules concerning advertising and on the empirical bases for, and consequences of, the continued ban on solicitation.

Other kinds of problems arise once the solo or small-firm lawyer and the individual client have been brought together. This relationship is structurally unequal. The lawyer is usually better educated and always possesses superior technical expertise. He often enjoys a higher social status than the client. He is personally uninvolved and faces a situation that is routine. By contrast, the client is in the midst of a crisis, or he would not have sought legal advice in the first place: his family is dissolving, he is physically injured or financially at risk, or he is threatened with punishment by the state. When the interests of lawyer and client diverge, those of the lawyer are likely to prevail. And despite the fact that the adversary system is predicated on the total fidelity of lawyer to client, such conflicts are structurally inevitable. The contingent fee system, by giving the attorney a share in his client's recovery in a personal injury claim, may appear to unite the interests of lawyer and client, but in fact the lawyer's hourly earnings decline the more time he invests in the case. Thus, the lawyer will seek a quick settlement at a lower figure, even though his client might be better served by a more intransigent bargaining posture or by going to trial (Rosenthal, 1974). Furthermore, the client is interested in maximizing the outcome in *this* case, which is typically his only pending involvement with the legal system. He wants the highest possible payment for his injuries, the lowest possible liability for alimony and support, or the most lenient punishment. The lawyer, however, is interested in preserving his relationship with other actors whom he confronts repeatedly, such as the insurance adjuster with whom he settles many claims (Ross, 1970), the prosecutor with whom he bargains many pleas (Blumberg, 1967; Alschuler, 1975), and the domestic relations attorney with whom he may be paired in the next divorce case (O'Gorman, 1963). Given the capacity of the lawyer to dominate the client, these latter considerations are likely to prevail. In Marc Galanter's (1974) very useful terminology, the one-shot client is at a structural disadvantage when dealing with the repeat-player lawyer. A critical question, therefore, is how the relationship between lawyer and client can be equalized? Will this require educating clients, aggregating clients, interposing intermediaries, giving clients more legal rights, encouraging clients to obtain second opinions, or curtailing the need for professional representation and advice?

Large Firms

The ethical problems that afflict the large-firm lawyer and his corporate client are in many ways the obverse of the tendency of the sole or small-firm practitioner to dominate his client. Prior to 1900 there were no partnerships with more than five lawyers. Today firms of 50 or 100 lawyers can be found in dozens of U.S. cities, and a handful have more than 200 (Bernstein, 1978). This transformation is the product of several factors: growth in the size and complexity of industrial, financial, and service enterprises; the advantages of specialization and economies of scale; and the capacity of partners to increase their earnings by hiring salaried associates. But though the "law factories" of Wall Street and other U.S. financial districts are huge when contrasted with their historical antecedents or with their counterparts in other countries, they are miniscule compared to the wealth and power of their clients. Furthermore, these large firms are dependent on their clients to an unprecedented degree. They achieve economies of scale by using paraprofessionals, office machines (increasingly computerized), and salaried lawyers, which constitute an enormous overhead. To sustain this burden they must be able to rely on a high and constant volume of business, which only the largest corporate clients can provide (Smigel, 1969). Consequently, the law firm cannot afford to alienate its corporate client. Indeed, it often seeks to cement this relationship by 1) placing some of its (less talented) associates in the office of house counsel of the corporation, 2) having partners sit on the board of directors of the corporation, 3) acquiring familiarity with the affairs of the corporation (as well as physical possession of its files), each of which would be very expensive for another firm to reproduce, and 4) hiring relatives of corporate executives. The consequence of such actions is an extraordinarily intimate bond (often expressed by sharing an office building) that is practically never severed (Hoffman, 1973). For the law firm's partners, however, this also imposes an inability to blow the whistle, to exercise independent judgment about the behavior of its corporate client, or to withdraw from representation where the client refuses to follow legal advice or persists in illegal conduct. These problems are particularly acute for those Washington law firms that represent corporate clients before federal regulatory agencies (Goulden, 1972; Green, 1975) and for lawyers employed as house counsel within corporations (Donnell, 1970).

Large firms are structurally dependent upon their corporate clients, but this institutional relationship must also be reproduced in individual lawyers. Because there is relatively little lateral entry, such firms acquire new lawyers by carefully selecting new associates, socializing them during a lengthy and intense apprenticeship, and finally offering partnership only to those who have been adequately socialized. In fact, this process begins even earlier. Ascriptive criteria for entry into law school exclude much of the population (women and minorities were barred by rule or practice until very recently and even now are admitted only in token numbers), and law firms prefer the graduates of private secondary schools, ivy league colleges, and elite law schools (Smigel, 1969). Those who are selected as associates have learned to place corporations and taxation at the top of their ranking of legal subjects, through the bias inherent in the law school curriculum (Erlanger and Klegon, 1978; Nader, 1970; Seligman, 1978), and have come to define all legal questions as technical through participation in a socratic dialogue that compels them to argue both sides of every issue without making any ethical judgment (Kennedy, 1970; Taylor, 1975; Rathjen, 1976).

The law firm then subjects its associates—already in their middle to late 20s—to another five to ten years of enforced immaturity (older law graduates are rejected as insufficiently malleable). Salaries, though high, are a fraction of what partners earn (as little as one-fifth) because the extraordinary incomes of partners are produced by billing the time of associates at three times the rate the associates themselves are paid. Associates have no say about what they will be paid, are uncertain whether they will receive raises, and are kept in ignorance of what their peers are making. The price of these privileges is a work load whose burden is legendary. Indeed, associates compete with each other about who stays latest at night and gives up most weekends, in a parody of the puritan ethic—conspicuous production as the prerequisite for conspicuous consumption. Nor do they have any control over the kind of work they do or the clients for whom they work. The associate is generally given relatively little responsibility and is constantly evaluated by the partners (a relationship that is totally one-sided) but is often kept ignorant of the judgment rendered. These two forms of dependence—in wages and work—are mirrored throughout the law firm in the size and location of offices, forms of address, and patterns of socialization. At the same time, the subordination experienced by the associate is partly compensated by his superior status in relation to others in the firm (paraprofessionals, secretaries, and younger associates) and in the larger society. After this lengthy and arduous apprenticeship only about two of every ten beginning associates are offered partnerships (Smigel, 1969). Acknowledged as adults only in their late 30s or early 40s, partners are extraordinarily loyal to the firm, as demonstrated by their ability to divide up partnership earnings in shares that may differ dramatically, without resort to a formal agreement. Both partners and associates in such a firm are unlikely to raise, or even perceive, moral issues arising out of its representation of corporate clients.

Professional Stratification

Our discussion of ethical issues encountered in various forms of law practice suggests another major problem. The legal profession is highly stratified and, like all forms of stratification in a society legitimated by an egalitarian ideology, such a hierarchy must be justified. Two mechanisms justify the stratification of lawyers. The first is meritocracy, as institutionalized through the educational system. At every stage of his educational career, the professional options of the potential lawyer are narrowed by decisions—both individual and institutional—concerning which schools he attends and how his performance is evaluated. Although these decisions are rationalized in terms of inclination, ability, and achievement, ascriptive criteria of sex, race, religion, national origin, and class strongly influence both entry into secondary school, college, and law school and performance at each level, as well as on standardized tests (Stevens, 1973; Ladinsky, 1963; Lortie, 1959; Auerbach, 1974; Warkov, 1965). The location of each school in the educational hierarchy and the student's performance at each stage significantly affect the range of employment opportunities available upon graduation. Furthermore, there is relatively little upward career mobility between major strata of the legal profession after the first job has been obtained (Carlin, 1966).

A second, less obvious, mechanism for justifying differentials in wealth, status, and power among lawyers is the entire system of professional ethics. These rules are formulated (if not formally promulgated) by bar associations dominated by elite lawyers (Auerbach, 1974; Gilb, 1966; Tisher, et al., 1977). As a consequence, they focus on behavior that is problematic for low status lawyers—such as obtaining business through advertising, or solicitation and mishandling client funds—rather than on the ethical dilemmas of the elite—such as using undue influence, engaging in deliberate delay, or failing to disclose client improprieties or withdraw from representation. Because the substantive rules are biased, they can be applied evenhandedly and yet so stigmatize the lower strata that the distribution of privilege within the profession appears to be simply a reflection of moral stature (Carlin, 1966). This latent function of the disciplinary process assumes additional prominence when contrasted with its total failure to control the unethical behavior of the bar (Carlin, 1966), or to insure a minimum standard of competence (Marks and Cathcart, 1974; Rosenthal, 1976; Carlson, 1976).

WHAT ARE WE DOING AND WHAT HAVE WE ACCOMPLISHED?

Legal Maldistribution

Because maldistribution is the single most important problem in the area of legal services, most reform efforts have been directed toward ameliorating it. Such reforms necessarily start with an attempt to map the nature and magnitude of the maldistribution. Who presently uses legal services, in what amounts, and for what purposes? Do people differ in the extent to which they perceive a given problem as legal? How does past use affect the likelihood of future use? How do clients find the lawyers they use? How satisfied are they with the services they obtain and how likely are they to return to the same lawyer in the future?

The most recent and sophisticated effort to answer these questions (Curran, 1977) begins by documenting the extent to which various segments of the population differ in perceiving a given experience as a problem, an obvious prerequisite to defining the problem as legal. Thus, men perceive consumer problems more often than do women, despite the fact that women make more purchases. Whites perceive legal problems more often than do minorities in situations where the incidence of the problematic event is approximately equal across races—as in automobile accidents and other injuries, or the disposition of property after death. Once the problem is perceived, there are further differences in taking any action in response to it, and especially in consulting a lawyer. The differentials at each of these stages are cumulative and produce a pattern of lawyer use that varies directly and strongly with income, education, and being white. Perhaps almost as significant as these differences is the extraordinarily low level of lawyer use by most individuals throughout the society. One third of the population has never used a lawyer, and another third has used a lawyer only once. Two lessons can be drawn from these data. First, the distribution of legal services clearly reflects, and presumably also contributes to, the fundamental inequalities of U.S. society. Second, there appears to be a substantial "unmet need" among the public for more legal services (it is not surprising that this latter discovery coincides with the overproduction of recent law graduates).

Although the legal profession commonly explains and justifies this pattern of lawyer use as simply its response to public needs, sociologists have demurred (Marks, 1976; Mayhew and Reiss, 1969; Mayhew, 1975). That 40 percent of the caseload of legal aid offices in the United States (and many European countries, as reported by Cappelletti, et al., 1975) is devoted to divorce does not mean that nearly half the legal needs of the poor are confined to family matters. Rather, the poor have learned to use legal aid offices for divorce because that is the principal service those offices provide (Mayhew, 1975). Where legal services are not subsidized by charity or the state, lawyers have structured them to maximize their control over a market that can be exploited for profit (Larson, 1977). Thus, lawyers commonly offer advice and representation 1) in the transfer of property (residential land transactions, wills and estates, contracts, including labor contracts), 2) in situations where physical and mental integrity is treated as a form of property (compensation for injuries), and 3) where the individual is threatened with the loss of life, liberty, or property (criminal defense, opposition to state regulation). But whenever the existing distribution of legal services is attributable to the actions of lawyers (whether or not consciously motivated), efforts to redistribute legal services will necessarily acquire political significance. The questions to be asked, therefore, are these: How are we to understand the numerous recent efforts to redistribute legal services? How do they serve the interests of the legal profession (or certain portions of it) or those of other powerful political actors? And what kinds of redistribution would advance other goals? The following pages describe four current efforts to redistribute legal services.

Governmental Action

The most substantial redistributive effort thus far is the Legal Services Corporation (formerly the OEO Legal Services Program), whose budget is now close to a quarter billion dollars a year. This program has pursued three potentially conflicting objectives: 1) providing the poor with representation in the kinds of problems for which middle-class people routinely use lawyers, 2) challenging substantive and procedural rules that operate to the disadvantage of the poor, and 3) organizing the poor to enhance their political, social, and economic power. There is considerable disagreement about whether each goal should be sought, the priority that should be assigned to it, and whether it is attainable. Legal services lawyers have argued that the "need" of the poor for routine representation (in uncontested divorces or landlord-tenant disputes, for example) can never be met with the available resources and that, in any case, to do so would not break the circle of poverty (Rothstein, 1974; Silver, 1969). Furthermore, many have observed that legal services lawyers "burn out" if restricted to routine matters and can only sustain their commitment to the hard and often frustrating task of representing the poor if they are able to transform individual problems into larger issues, thereby endowing the rare victory with greater significance (Katz, 1978). But there is debate whether litigation, the principal strategy of poverty lawyers, can ever result in substantial redistribution (compare Johnson, 1974 with Hazard, 1969, 1970a, 1970b). It is also clear that the energetic efforts by poverty lawyers to promote legal change and organize the poor (Wexler, 1970) aroused vigorous opposition by conservative lawyers and politicians (Agnew, 1972; Stumpf, 1975). This led to the Legal Services Corporation Act of 1974, which severely curtailed both the legal and the political activities of its lawyers. Because the program is still quite young, it has not yet been adequately evaluated (Champagne, 1974, 1976; Cole and Greenberger, 1973), but the Corporation is presently devoting substantial efforts to self-evaluation, and especially to a comparison of its delivery system with some of the alternatives discussed below.

Programs for delivering legal services to the unrepresented or underrepresented can be analyzed in terms of many variables, but one of the most significant is whether lawyers are full-time specialists in providing the redistributed service or are primarily engaged in other activities. Thus, we can contrast the public defender with the private attorney appointed by the court to provide criminal defense in a specific case, "closed-panel" prepaid legal service plans with "open-panel" plans (see below), and public interest law firms with the pro bono activities of the private bar. The counterpart of the "staffed offices" of the Legal Services Corporation that provide legal aid to the poor is judicare (a neologism borrowed from medicare), which reimburses members of the private bar on a piecework basis for services rendered to qualified clients. Although judicare has only been tried as a pilot project in two states, it has considerable potential significance because: 1) that project was extensively described (Brakel, 1974), 2) the Legal Services Corporation is required by law to choose some mix of staffed offices, judicare, and other alternatives, and 3) judicare is the prevailing form of legal aid in much of Europe (Cappelletti, et al., 1975).

Comparisons of staffed office with judicare delivery systems employ a number of criteria. First, the eligibility standards of the two systems are pushed in opposite directions. Staffed offices are under pressure from the private bar to keep their standards low and not accept clients who might possibly be able to afford a private attorney. Staffed office attorneys may share that inclination, both because their lawyers are ideologically committed to serving the very poor (Finman, 1971) and because they operate under constant caseload pressures. Private attorneys reimbursed under judicare, on the other hand, tend to construe eligibility liberally to justify state payment for clients who could not otherwise retain them. Considerations of geographic accessibility favor judicare in rural areas where the poor are too few and too thinly scattered to justify a full-time attorney, whereas staffed offices are preferable in cities since private lawyers are rarely located in poor communities (Fisher and Ivie, 1971). And although data are not available on the kinds of problems handled, it seems plausible that private attorneys would assimilate the needs of their judicare clients to those of their paying clients, whereas staffed office specialists would focus on legal problems that are distinctive to the poor. One indication of such a bias may be the fact that only 5 to 10 percent of eligible families used judicare each year, whereas 20 percent of the eligible population used staffed offices in the comparison communities (Brakel, 1974:55, 58).

One of the primary advantages claimed for judicare is that it gives poor clients the same right to choose a lawyer that is enjoyed by those who can afford to pay. Yet, this argument is suspect on several grounds: First, it is advanced by lawyers, who have an interest in being chosen, and not by clients. Second, until very recently the organized bar systematically denied all potential clients the information they would need about cost and quality in order to make an intelligent choice. Third, legal services lawyers are selected—not by clients, it is true, but by the experienced directors of staffed offices from among the many highly qualified aspirants to those jobs. Furthermore, there is evidence that the choice judicare ostensibly offers poor people is significantly curtailed by the attorneys chosen. Of the 57 lawyers approached by judicare clients, 36 turned down at least one case for reasons that are inherent in the use of private practitioners to serve the poor: 1) conflict of interest (the private bar necessarily represents the principal adversaries of the poor), 2) too busy or fee too low (judicare clients invariably pay less than private clients), 3) the problem is diagnosed as not legal or beyond the lawyer's competence, or 4) the claim is seen as unmeritorious or unlikely to succeed (private lawyers often take a narrow, traditional, unsympathetic view of the legal problems of the poor and lack the necessary competence to deal with their problems). These same reasons explain why private lawyers who did accept poor clients engaged in virtually no appellate litigation directed toward changing the laws that disadvantage the poor, in sharp contrast to staffed office lawyers. The finding that judicare clients are substantially more satisfied with their attorneys than staffed office clients are with theirs must therefore be qualified by Brakel's (1974) failure to inquire about the responses of those clients who were turned down. It seems to reflect the form of the services provided rather than their substance. But perhaps most significant is the relative cost of the two systems: judicare attorneys are almost twice as expensive as their staffed office counterparts, by the most conservative estimates. Yet, because each system has advantages and disadvantages, a mix of the two might well be desirable and, indeed, allow them to compete, thus permitting a market test of the questions posed above. Furthermore, it would enable those staffed office lawyers, who no longer wish to make the financial and psychological sacrifices inherent in full-time representation of the poor, to serve some poor clients through judicare, thus using the expertise they acquired to fulfill the ideological commitment they developed (Handler, et al., 1978).

Prepaid Legal Service Plans

Many of these same issues arise in comparisons among prepaid legal service plans (Pfennigstorf and Kimball, 1977; Deitch and Weinstein, 1976). Just as staffed office legal services and judicare have their equivalents in systems for delivering medical care (the free clinic and medicare), so prepaid legal service plans for working-class and middle-class individuals can be analogized to health maintenance organizations (closed-panel plans) and insurance schemes of the

Blue Cross type (open-panel plans). (A third arrangement—numerous but not otherwise significant—is the group plan without prepayment, which serves merely to channel prospective clients to lawyers enrolled in the plan through claims that the cost of an initial consultation or of certain routine services has been reduced.) All prepaid plans offer members two advantages: they spread routine costs over time and unforeseen risks over the entire population of subscribers. But beyond that there are significant differences. Not surprisingly, the organized bar has energetically favored open-panel plans, which allow all lawyers to work for members and be reimbursed by the plan, over closed-panel plans, whose benefits are concentrated among the small number of lawyers who belong to the plan. Nevertheless, the efforts of the American Bar Association and state bars to promulgate and enforce discriminatory rules of professional conduct that would give open-panel plans a competitive advantage were attacked by the U.S. Department of Justice as violations of the antitrust laws and were ultimately abandoned.

Although comprehensive data are unavailable, nearly a million people are probably covered by prepaid plans today, and this number can be expected to increase substantially in the next decade. The following discussion of variations among plans is extrapolated from the only detailed study, which describes the open-panel plan serving the Laborers International Union, Local 229, of Shreveport, Louisiana (Marks, et al., 1974). Open and closed, first of all, should be seen as end points on a continuum. The most open plan would be a legal insurance policy that reimbursed the member who retained any qualified lawyer; the most closed plan would require its members to use the services of a single specified lawyer. Shreveport falls toward the open end of this continuum, allowing participants to use any member of the local bar association. In practice, however, the 60 consultations that occurred during the first year of the plan were concentrated among 32 of the 268 members of the bar, and one-sixth of these were handled by the lawyer who represented the union. Thus, Shreveport actually functioned more like the majority of plans, which are structurally closed. Every plan delimits its coverage in terms of the type of case handled (representation of plaintiffs in personal injury matters is often excluded because of the availability of private counsel through a contingent fee arrangement), the number of hours of work that will be reimbursed, or the services that will be performed (litigation, counseling, negotiation). Open plans leave the negotiation of fees to the individual client, which means that they do not alter the existing structure of fees. Closed plans can bind participating lawyers to a fee schedule that reflects the enhanced bargaining power of the members as a collectivity. Lawyers in closed-panel plans can also engage in preventive law, giving lectures to members and disseminating educational materials.

What are the consequences of such plans for their members? One would expect lawyer use to increase, for several reasons. First, some economic barriers are eliminated—barriers the public commonly exaggerates because it overestimates the cost of many routine legal services. Second, the problem of finding a lawyer is alleviated because the plan, whether nominally open or structurally closed, directs members to lawyers. Shreveport did exhibit an increase in lawyer use of more than 50 percent during the first year, but this extraordinary change must be qualified in two respects: 1) the frequency of use began, and therefore ended, at a very low level (10.3 and 16.3 percent of the eligible population), 2) the increase was largely limited to those who had used lawyers before. Nevertheless, many members felt a new sense of entitlement to use lawyers, as well as greater confidence in asserting their legal rights without representation because they knew they could call upon a lawyer if necessary. Many questions remain unanswered about both the Shreveport plan and its relative merits when compared to other plans. What kinds of cases are brought to plan lawyers? How perceptive are those lawyers in seeing new legal issues? How aggressive are they in pursuing changes in legal rules that will benefit plan members? Do legal plans, like medical plans, experience problems with trivial complaints or abusive demands by members or with fraudulent claims or unnecessary services performed by lawyers? Which plans are best able to take advantage of efficiencies of scale, employing paraprofessionals and following routinized procedures so as to reduce costs? Which plans encourage the development of expertise in the problems unique to their members?

Charitable Redistribution

This third mechanism for redressing the imbalance of legal representation can be evaluated in terms of the same variables used to analyze governmental redistribution and prepaid legal services. Again, the most important distinction is whether the lawyer is functioning as a full-time specialist or a part-time generalist. At one extreme of this continuum is the public interest law firm, supported largely by foundation grants (Handler, et al., 1978; Weisbrod, et al., 1978; Council for Public Interest Law, 1976). At the other extreme is the private practitioner, either solo or firm, who occasionally represents a client without fee or at a reduced fee (Lochner, 1975; Maddi and Merrill, 1971; Marks, et al., 1972; Handler, et al., 1978). There are also numerous intermediate arrangements: mixed law firms that support their representation of public interests through paying work for a carefully chosen private clientele, branch offices in poor neighborhoods staffed either by a single large private firm (Ashman, 1972) or by lawyer time contributed by many different firms and supplemented from other sources (Rosenthal, et al., 1971), and varying degrees of commitment to handling cases referred by a clearinghouse, often sponsored by a bar association.

Starting at the lower end of this continuum, it is important to recognize how minimal the legal services are that the private bar renders "pro bono publico." Three studies, employing different methodologies and sampling different populations at different times, have come to similar conclusions. About one-third of the bar donates no time at all (Maddi and Merrill, 1971; Lochner, 1975; Handler, et al., 1978), and the annual average for the bar as a whole is three cases (Lochner, 1975) or 27 hours (Handler, et al., 1978). Most of these cases are handled very cursorily: 40 percent in less than five hours and another 20 percent in less than ten (Lochner, 1975). The lawyer writes a letter, drafts a document, offers advice, or makes a phone call, but litigates in less than a fifth of the cases (Handler, et al., 1978). These clients constitute not only a small fraction, but also a very select subgroup, of the needy population. Only those who know lawyers, or have acquaintances who do, can even seek such assistance. This excludes ethnic minorities (because of their underrepresentation within the profession), the extremes of youth and age, and the very poor. Lawyers then make a further selection, discouraging the more deviant among potential clients—who may be most in need of representation (Maddi and Merrill, 1971)—and accepting those who offer the greatest possibility of becoming paying clients in the future (Lochner, 1975). Similar considerations govern the representation of groups: churches and women's clubs often receive pro bono services but not organizations dedicated to social change (Handler, et al., 1978). Finally, private attorneys normally represent nonpaying and low-paying clients in the same kinds of cases they routinely handle for paying clients—primarily family, criminal, housing, and consumer disputes—and do not devote themselves to test cases intended to establish new legal rights.

At the opposite extreme of the continuum, public interest law firms are far more ambitious in their activities but numerically almost insignificant. Recent studies have estimated that there are presently 70 to 80 such firms employing fewer than 500 lawyers and endowed with an aggregate annual budget of 30 to 40 million dollars, or about one-tenth of 1 percent of the profession and of private sector expenditures on legal services (Council on Public Interest Law, 1976; Weisbrod, et al., 1978). These firms are committed to using law as an instrument of social change. Indeed, the need to demonstrate that commitment effectively disables them from providing routine legal services. But structural constraints severely limit the ways in which they can pursue their goal. First, because they are funded by nonprofit foundations, the tax status of their benefactors prevents them from engaging in political activity such as lobbying or elections. In addition, the relative youthfulness and inexperience of public interest lawyers, and their short time-horizon, impatience for change, and predilection for a principled adversarial strategy, lead them to prefer litigation as a modus operandi. Yet, changes within the judicial and administrative arenas can often be reversed through legislative action. Finally, the continued funding of public interest law is extremely problematic. The Ford Foundation, which has provided much of this financial support, intends to withdraw most of its funding within the next few years. Current efforts are directed toward creating a statutory right to recover the costs of litigation (including lawyers' fees) from an adversary. However, this is not only politically doubtful but also will discourage litigation that is uncertain to succeed or involves a relatively impecunious adversary.

Legal services supported by charitable sources (foundations, financial sacrifices by private lawyers, or reimbursement extracted from adversaries) have grown dramatically during the last decade. Yet, we still know relatively little about such endeavors, and what we do know is subject to change, given their indefinite future. Comparisons between the different ways in which these legal services are structured may help to guide further research. What are the sources and magnitude of financial support? How does this constrain their activities? Are there differences in the competence of lawyers working within different structures, perhaps associated with their degree of specialization? What clients are served? What kinds of cases are handled for them? What services are performed and what strategies used? What are the relative costs of the different structures? How are the activities justified, and how do they help to legitimate both the legal profession and the larger legal system and society?

Removing Restraints

This fourth set of changes redistributes legal services by relaxing or eliminating some of the many restraints that the legal profession has laboriously erected during the past century in an effort to achieve market control (Larson, 1977). As those restraints have gradually been abolished, lawyers have become more competitive, actively disseminating the information consumers need to make intelligent choices when purchasing legal services, specializing and advertising that specialization, and creating new structures for delivering their services. In addition, other occupations are challenging the monopoly of lawyers, and individuals are increasingly performing legal services themselves. The most significant blow to professional control of the market for legal services was the decision by the United States Supreme Court in *Bates v. State Bar of Arizona* (1977), which ended what had been an almost total prohibition of lawyer advertising. Although the precise boundaries of constitutionally protected advertising will not be clear until more cases are decided, attorneys can advertise areas of specialization, hours, and the cost of routine services. A majority of states have already liberalized their rules of professional conduct to conform, more or less, to the spirit of the new rulings (Muris and McChesney, 1979). An important question for future research will be the impact that different forms of advertising have on the distribution of legal services. A number of states have also created procedures for certifying lawyers in various specialties. This development simultaneously threatens the unity of the bar while allowing members of the new specialties to strengthen their control of a narrower market (*Virginia Law Review*, 1975; Zehnle, 1975; cf. Laumann and Heinz, 1977). Professional control over the cost of legal services has also been weakened by a Supreme Court decision that state and local bar associations violate federal antitrust law when they promulgate and enforce minimum fee schedules (*Goldfarb* v. *Virginia State Bar*, 1975). The price competition that these decisions permit is likely to lead to increased use of paraprofessionals (Brickman, 1971). Finally, the professional monopoly that lawyers have long maintained through civil actions and criminal prosecutions against the "unauthorized practice of law" is currently being challenged by the federal government, by other competing occupations, and by individuals who want to represent themselves (*Yale Law Journal,* 1976; Ziegler and Hermann, 1972).

Legal Clinics

The significance of these diverse efforts to redistribute legal services is most evident when they converge in the growth of a new structure for delivering legal services to individuals, such as the legal clinic (Downey, 1977; Muris and McChesney, 1979). A legal clinic is a profit-making law firm (in contrast to a legal services office) that offers its services to the general public (in contrast to a prepaid plan) without any charitable motive (in contrast to public interest law firms and pro bono activities). It seeks to achieve high volume through massive advertising. The legal clinic of Jacoby and Meyers in Los Angeles, for instance, spent $300,000 on press and electronic media advertising in the first half of 1978 and obtained 2,500 new clients a month (Muris and McChesney, 1979). Volume enables the clinic to take advantage of economies of scale in its operations. It can specialize, use systems management procedures, including prepared forms and electronic data processing, and substitute paraprofessionals for lawyers (Jacoby and Meyers have a ratio of .6 paraprofessionals per lawyer compared with the nationwide average of .07 for sole practitioners serving a comparable clientele). The consequence is a cost savings as high as 50 percent, which is reflected in lower prices. Jacoby and Meyers charge $100 for an uncontested divorce, compared with a northern California average of $270; the Baltimore clinic of Cawley, Schmidt, and Sharrow charges $150, compared with a local average of $344. Reduced prices can, obviously, be used in subsequent advertising to increase volume still further. Finally, the quality of service provided by clinics appears to be superior to that offered by comparable lawyers in more traditional practices, whether quality is measured by the frequency of mechanical errors, the level of client satisfaction, or the size of recoveries (Muris and McChesney, 1979).

Clinics exemplify the potential impact of changes in the structure of the market for legal services. Concentration is rapidly increasing, both among suppliers (in "law factories," multistate firms, offices of house counsel, and legal clinics) and among purchasers (unions and other groups of subscribers to prepaid plans and public interest member organizations like the Sierra Club). Just as corporate law firms have grown phenomenally during the last decade and now are establishing branch offices in many cities, here and abroad, clinics may expand even faster. Jacoby and Meyers has increased from three offices in Los Angeles in 1975 (before the liberalization of rules about advertising) to 35 offices in California and New York in 1979. Smaller firms and sole practitioners cannot achieve the volume necessary to permit economies of scale and investment in advertising, which produce even greater volume. Inevitably they will lose business to clinics. Through aggressive advertising and price cutting, clinics are extending legal services to new consumers who previously were ignorant of their value or unable to afford them. This phenomenon is so new that it has hardly been studied. We need a great deal of research to understand the evolution of clinics, the kind, cost, and quality of services they render, and the clients they reach.

WHERE ARE WE GOING?

The legal profession has undergone extraordinary changes during the last decade. These have included the multiplication and growth of corporate law firms, the expansion of legal education, the entry of minorities and women into the profession in substantial numbers, and the development of new delivery systems through government subsidization for the poor, insurance for the middle class, charitable support for the representation of inchoate interests, and increased market competition. None of these phenomena is adequately understood, and we have not even begun to explore their interrelationships and overall impact. To what extent do they express the restructuring of career opportunities in an economy that is still experiencing a rapid shift from production to service and, simultaneously, suffering from stagflation? Among the endless possibilities for research, several areas should be emphasized.

What changes can we expect in the personnel of the legal profession? Two issues stand out. First, what are the prospects for achieving representation of women and minorities proportionate to ther numbers in society? This question is particularly acute in light of the decision of the United States Supreme Court in *University of California Regents* v. *Bakke* (1978), limiting inverse discrimination in admission to public professional schools. Second, will there be a continuation of the trend toward the proletarianization of professionals? Recent years have seen an enormous increase in the proportion of lawyers who are employees rather than independent professionals, growth in the size of the organizations that employ them, rising unemployment and underemployment among professionals, declining salaries at the base of the profession, loss of control over the substance and pace of work, and a concomitant growth of unions and other employee organizations. The impact of these trends for the legal profession and its clients is likely to be profound.

We need to devote less research to the lower, often deviant, strata of the profession and those that serve the lower strata of society and give more attention to elite lawyers. Aside from one dated study of Wall Street lawyers (Smigel, 1959), we have only anecdotal information about how the elite of the bar serve their corporate clients. We need to know the extent to which, and the circumstances under which, lawyers exercise independent moral judgment about their own conduct and that of their colleagues and clients. What role do lawyers play in implementing or frustrating the enormous regulatory apparatus through which big government purports to control big business?

Finally, we need to look at the array of mechanisms for redistributing legal services and ask what impact they are likely to have (Abel, 1979). Can they achieve procedural justice—formal equality in adversarial proceedings, in planning, and in negotiation? Can they contribute to furthering substantive justice—social, political, and economic equality? If the answer to either, or both, of these questions is negative, what explains the continued attention paid to such redistributions? Do they assist in legitimating the legal system or the larger society? And what changes in the structure of legal services might have more significant impact? Can lawyers help to organize those who are socially, politically, or economically powerless, or disaggregate those who are powerful? These last questions are both the most important and the least studied issues in the sociology of law.

REFERENCES AND SUGGESTED READINGS

Abel, R.L. 1979. "Socializing the Legal Profession: Can Redistributing Lawyers' Services Achieve Social Justice?" *Law and Policy Quarterly* 1 (Jan):5–51.
*Abel-Smith, B. and R. Stevens. 1967. *Lawyers and the Courts: A Sociological Study of the English Legal System, 1750–1965.* London: Heinemann.
   A comparative perspective is essential for understanding legal services in the United States, and perhaps the most useful is that offered by the English legal system, from which ours derives.
Agnew, S.T. 1972. "What's Wrong with the Legal Services Program." *American Bar Association Journal* 58 (Sept):930–32.
Alschuler, A.W. 1975. "The Defense Attorney's Role in Plea Bargaining." *Yale Law Journal* 84 (May):1179–314.
Ashman, A. 1972. *The New Private Practice: A Study of Piper & Marbury's Neighborhood Law Office.* Chicago: National Legal Aid and Defender Association.
Auerbach, J.S. 1974. *Unequal Justice: Lawyers and Social Change in Modern America.* New York: Oxford University Press.
Bates v. *State Bar of Arizona.* 1977. 433 U.S. 350.
Bernstein, P.W. 1978. "The Wall Street Lawyers Are Thriving on Change." *Fortune,* March 13, pp. 104–12.
Blaine, W.L. 1976. *Where to Practice Law in California: Statistics of Lawyers' Work.* Berkeley, Calif.: Continuing Education for the Bar.
Blaustein, A.P. and C.O. Porter. 1954. *The American Lawyer: A Summary of the Survey of the Legal Profession.* Chicago: The University of Chicago Press.
Blumberg, A.S. 1967. *Criminal Justice.* Chicago: Quadrangle Books.
Brakel, S.J. 1974. *Judicare: Public Funds, Private Lawyers, and Poor People.* Chicago: American Bar Foundation.
Brickman, L.J. 1971. "Expansion of the Lawyering Process Through a New Delivery System: The Emergence and State of Legal Paraprofessionalism." *Columbia Law Review* 71 (Nov):1153–255.

*Brickman, L., and R.O. Lempert, eds. 1976. "Delivery of Legal Services." *Law & Society Review* 11 (Special):167–415.

This issue consists of seven papers and the transcript of a conference on legal services, with a ten-page agenda of "questions for research" and a lengthy bibliography covering many of the issues raised above.

Cappelletti, M., J. Gordley, and E. Johnson, Jr. 1975. *Toward Equal Justice: A Comparative Study of Legal Aid in Modern Societies* (text and materials). Milano: Giuffre and Dobbs Ferry, N.Y.:Oceana.

*Carlin, J. 1962. *Lawyers on Their Own: A Study of Individual Practitioners in Chicago.* New Brunswick, N.J.: Rutgers University Press.

This is the best ethnography of working lawyers presently available, illuminating the ethical problems created by the rules of professional conduct.

_____. 1966. *Lawyers' Ethics: A Survey of the New York City Bar.* New York: Russell Sage Foundation.

Carlson, R.J. 1976. "Measuring the Quality of Legal Services: An Idea Whose Time Has Not Yet Come." *Law & Society Review* 11 (Special):287–317.

Champagne, A. 1974. "An Evaluation of the Effectiveness of the OEO Legal Services Program." *Urban Affairs Quarterly* 9 (June):466–89.

_____. 1976. *Legal Services: An Exploratory Study of Effectiveness.* Sage Professional Papers in Administrative and Policy Studies No. 03-028. Beverly Hills, Calif.: Sage.

Cheatham, E.E. 1963. *A Lawyer When Needed.* New York: Columbia University Press.

Christensen, B.F. 1970. *Lawyers for People of Moderate Means: Some Problems of Availability of Legal Services.* Chicago: American Bar Foundation.

Cole, G.F. and H.L. Greenberger. 1973. "Staff Attorneys vs. Judicare: A Cost Analysis." *Journal of Urban Law* 50 (May):705–16.

Council for Public Interest Law. 1976. *Balancing the Scales of Justice: Financing Public Interest Law in America.* Washington, D.C.: Council for Public Interest Law.

Curran, B.A. 1977. *The Legal Needs of the Public: The Final Report of a National Survey.* Chicago: American Bar Foundation.

Deitch, L. and D. Weinstein. 1976. *Prepaid Legal Services: Socioeconomic Impacts.* Lexington, Mass.: Lexington Books.

Donnell, J.D. 1970. *The Corporate Counsel: A Role Study.* Bloomington: Indiana University Bureau of Business Research.

Downey, C.E. 1977. "Clinics: The State of the Art," *Juris Doctor* 7 (Sept):21–25.

Erlanger, H.S. and D.A. Klegon. 1978. "Socialization Effects of Professional School: The Law School Experience and Student Orientations to Public Interest Concerns." *Law & Society Review* 13 (1):11–35.

Finman, T. 1971. "OEO Legal Service Programs and the Pursuit of Social Change: The Relationship Between Program Ideology and Program Performance." *Wisconsin Law Review* 1971:1001–84.

Fisher, K.P. and C.C. Ivie. 1971. *Franchising Justice: The Office of Economic Opportunity Legal Services Program and Traditional Legal Aid.* Chicago: American Bar Foundation.

Galanter, M. 1974. "Why the 'Haves' Come Out Ahead: Speculations on the Limits of Legal Change." *Law & Society Review* 9 (Fall):95–160.

Gilb, C.L. 1966. *Hidden Hierarchies: The Professions and Government.* New York: Harper & Row.

Goldfarb v. *Virginia State Bar.* 1975. 421 U.S. 773.

Goulden, J.C. 1972. *The Superlawyers: The Small and Powerful World of the Great Washington Law Firms.* New York: Weybright and Talley.

Green, M.J. 1975. *The Other Government: The Unseen Power of Washington Lawyers.* New York: Grossman.

Grossblatt, M. and B.H. Sikes, eds. 1973. *Women Lawyers: Supplementary Data to the 1971 Lawyer Statistical Report.* Chicago: American Bar Foundation.

*Handler, J.F. 1967. *The Lawyer and His Community: The Practicing Bar in a Middle-sized City.* Madison: University of Wisconsin Press.

  Handler presents a comprehensive study of legal services, public interest law firms, and the pro bono activities of the private bar, using survey research and extensive interviews.

Handler, J.F., E.J. Hollingsworth, and H.S. Erlanger. 1978. *Lawyers and the Pursuit of Legal Rights.* New York: Academic Press.

Hazard, G.C., Jr. 1969. "Social Justice Through Civil Justice." *University of Chicago Law Review* 36 (Summer):699–712.

_____. 1970a. "Law Reforming in the Anti-poverty Effort." *University of Chicago Law Review* 37 (Winter):242–55.

_____. 1970b. "Legal Problems Peculiar to the Poor." *Journal of Social Issues* 26:47–57.

Heinz, J.P. and E.O. Laumann. 1978. "The Legal Profession: Client Interests, Professional Roles, and Social Hierarchies." *Michigan Law Review* 76: 1112–43.

Hoffman, P. 1973. *Lions in the Street: The Inside Story of the Great Wall Street Law Firms.* New York: Saturday Review Press.

Johnson, E., Jr. 1974. *Justice and Reform: The Formative Years of the OEO Legal Services Program.* New York: Russell Sage Foundation.

Katz, J. 1978. "Lawyers For the Poor in Transition: Involvement, Reform, and the Turnover Problem in the Legal Services Program." *Law & Society Review* 12 (Winter):275–300.

Kennedy, D. 1970. "How the Law School Fails: A Polemic." *Yale Review of Law and Social Action* 1 (Spring):71–90.

Ladinsky, J. 1963. "The Impact of Social Backgrounds of Lawyers on Law Practices and the Law." *Journal of Legal Education* 16 (2):127–44.

_____. 1976. "The Traffic in Legal Services: Lawyer-Seeking Behavior and the Channeling of Clients." *Law & Society Review* 11 (Special):207–31.

*Larson, M.S. 1977. *The Rise of Professionalism: A Sociological Analysis.* Berkeley: University of California Press.

  This is the most important book on the professions in recent years. It is a Marxist historical and structural account of how the major professions (law, medicine, engineering, and the newer "organizational" professions) in England and the United States simultaneously sought control over the market for their services and pursued a project of collective mobility.

Laumann, E.O. and J.P. Heinz. 1977. "Specialization and Prestige in the Legal Profession: The Structure of Deference." *American Bar Foundation Research Journal* 1977 (Winter):155–216.

Llewellyn, K.N. 1938. "The Bar's Troubles, and Poultices—and Cures?" *Law & Contemporary Problems* 5 (Winter):104–34.

Lochner, P.R., Jr. 1975. "The No Fee and Low Fee Legal Practice of Private Attorneys." *Law & Society Review* 9 (Spring):431–73.

Lortie, D.C. 1959. "Laymen to Lawmen: Law School, Careers, and Professional Socialization." *Harvard Education Review* 29 (Fall):352–69.

Maddi, D.L. and F.R. Merrill. 1971. *The Private Practicing Bar and Legal Services for Low-Income People.* Chicago: American Bar Foundation.

Marks, F.R. 1976. "Some Research Perspectives for Looking at Legal Need and Legal Services Delivery Systems: Old Forms or New?" *Law & Society Review* 11 (Special):191–205.

Marks, F.R. and D. Cathcart. 1974. "Discipline Within the Legal Profession: Is It Self-regulation?" *University of Illinois Law Forum* 1974 (2):193–236.

Marks, F.R., R.P. Hallauer, and R.R. Clifton. 1974. *The Shreveport Plan: An Experiment in the Delivery of Legal Services.* Chicago: American Bar Foundation.

Marks, F.R., K. Leswing, and B. Fortinsky. 1972. *The Lawyer, the Public and Professional Responsibility.* Chicago: American Bar Foundation.

Mayer, M. 1967. *The Lawyers.* New York: Harper & Row.

Mayhew, L.H. 1975. "Institutions of Representation: Civil Justice and the Public." *Law & Society Review* 9 (Spring):401–29.

Mayhew, L.H. and A.J. Reiss, Jr. 1969. "The Social Organization of Legal Contacts." *American Sociological Review* 34 (June):309–18.

Muris, T.J. and F.S. McChesney. 1979. "Advertising and the Price and Quality of Legal Services: The Case of Legal Clinics." *American Bar Foundation Research Journal* (1979):179–207.

Nader, R. 1970. "Law Schools and Law Firms." *Minnesota Law Review* 54 (Jan): 493–501.

O'Gorman, H. 1963. *Lawyers and Matrimonial Cases: A Study of Informal Pressures in Private Professional Practice.* New York: The Free Press.

Ohralik v. *Ohio State Bar Association.* 1978. 436 U.S. 447.

Pashigian, B.P. 1977. "The Market for Lawyers: The Determinants of the Demand For and Supply of Lawyers." *Journal of Law & Economics* 20 (Apr):53–85.

———. 1978. "The Number and Earnings of Lawyers: Some Recent Findings." *American Bar Foundation Research Journal* 1978(Winter):51–82.

Pfennigstorf, W. and S.L. Kimball, eds. 1977. *Legal Service Plans: Approaches to Regulation.* Chicago: American Bar Foundation.

Ramey, F.H. 1978. "Minority Lawyers in California: A Survey." *Los Angeles Daily Journal Report* 78-2(November 17).

Rathjen, G.J. 1976. "The Impact of Legal Education on the Beliefs, Attitudes and Values of Law Students." *Tennessee Law Review* 44 (Fall):85–118.

Reichstein, K.J. 1965. "Ambulance Chasing: A Case Study of Deviance and Control Within the Legal Profession." *Social Problems* 13:3–17.

Rosenthal, D.E. 1974. *Lawyer and Client: Who's in Charge?* New York: Russell Sage Foundation.

_____. 1976. "Evaluating the Competence of Lawyers." *Law & Society Review* 11 (Special):257–85.

Rosenthal, D.E., R.A. Kagan, and D. Quatrone. 1971. *Volunteer Attorneys and Legal Services: New York's Community Law Offices Program.* New York: Russell Sage Foundation.

Ross, H.L. 1970. *Settled Out of Court: The Social Process of Insurance Claims Adjustments.* Chicago: Aldine.

Rothstein, L.E. 1974. "The Myth of Sisyphus: Legal Services and Efforts on Behalf of the Poor." *Journal of Law Reform* 7 (Spring):493–515.

Rudd, M.H. and J.P. White. 1974. "Legal Education and Profession Statistics, 1973–74." *Journal of Legal Education* 26 (3):342–48.

Seligman, J. 1978. *The High Citadel: The Influence of Harvard Law School.* Boston: Houghton Mifflin.

Sikes, B., C.N. Carson, and P. Goral, eds. 1972. *The 1971 Lawyer Statistical Report.* Chicago: American Bar Foundation.

Silver, C.R. 1969. "The Imminent Failure of Legal Services for the Poor: Why and How to Limit Caseload." *Journal of Urban Law* 46 (2):217–48.

Smigel, E.O. 1969. *The Wall Street Lawyer: Professional Organization Man?* Bloomington: Indiana University Press.

Smith, R.H. 1919. *Justice and the Poor.* New York: Carnegie Foundation.

Stevens, R.B. 1973. "Law Schools and Law Students." *Virginia Law Review* 59 (April):551–707.

Stumpf, H.P. 1975. *Community Politics and Legal Services: The Other Side of the Law.* Beverly Hills, Calif.: Sage.

Taylor, J.B. 1975. "Law School Stress and the 'Deformation Professionelle.'" *Journal of Legal Education* 27 (3):251–67.

Tisher, S., L. Bernabei, and M. Green. 1977. *Bringing the Bar to Justice: A Comparative Analysis of Six Bar Associations.* Washington, D.C.: Public Citizen.

University of California Regents v. *Bakke.* 1978. 438 U.S. 265.

Virginia Law Review. 1975. "Legal Specialization and Certification." *Virginia Law Review* 61 (Mar):434–64.

Warkov, S. 1965. *Lawyers in the Making.* Chicago: Aldine.

Weisbrod, B.A., J.F. Handler, and N.K. Komesar. 1978. *Public Interest Law: An Economic Analysis.* Berkeley: University of California Press.

Weinfield, W. 1949. "Income of Lawyers, 1929–48." *Survey of Current Business* 29 (Aug):18–23.

_____. 1952. "Income of Physicians, Dentists and Lawyers, 1949–51." *Survey of Current Business* 32 (July):5–7.

Wexler, S. 1970. "Practicing Law for Poor People." *Yale Law Journal* 79 (May): 1049–67.

White, J.P. 1975. "Is That Burgeoning Law School Enrollment Ending?" *American Bar Association Journal* 61 (Feb):202–4.

Yale Law Journal. 1976. "Unauthorized Practice of Law and Pro Se Divorces: An Empirical Analysis." *Yale Law Journal* 86 (Nov):104–84.

York, J.C. and R.D. Hale. 1973. "Too Many Lawyers? The Legal Services Industry: Its Structure and Outlook." *Journal of Legal Education* 26:1–33.

Zehnle, R.F. 1975. *Specialization in the Legal Profession: An Analysis of Current Proposals.* Chicago: American Bar Foundation.

Ziegler, D.H. and M.G. Hermann. 1972. "The Invisible Litigant: An Inside View of Pro Se Actions in the Federal Courts." *New York University Law Review* 47 (May):157–257.

20 LEISURE SERVICES

Rabel J. Burdge

In the late 1800s, National Parks and National Forests were established more with an eye to protection from the woodsman's axe than to meet the leisure needs of an urbanizing population. New York and the New England states also established their own state park and forest preserve system as a response to increased destruction of natural and scenic areas. In that period of rapid industrialization and urbanization, natural areas, parks, and leisure services were not seen as important to a people that were at work on the land and in the factory.

In the depression that followed almost one quarter of the working population were without jobs. Yet, that free time was seen only as idleness until work could be found. World War II brought work in the form of military duty or in war related industries.

After World War II, (and in concert with the widespread availability of the private automobile) governments at all levels became more active in providing leisure opportunity. Based on a 1960 comprehensive survey of outdoor recreation activity among U.S. adults (Outdoor Recreation Resources Review Commission, 1962a) the Land and Water Conservation Fund of 1964 was designed to provide matching grants to federal, state, and municipal agencies for the provision of outdoor recreation facilities. Since that time, recreation facilities have been built at an accelerated pace in both the United States and Canada. This has not been true with urban recreation services, however. No federal or state funding sources have been established to identify and fund programs in the urban parts of North America. Urban leisure services rely upon locally allocated tax monies and are supervised by locally appointed park boards or city park commissions.

*I want to thank James H. Gramann and John R. Kelly for their critical review of the manuscript.

Sociologists have shown little interest in contributing either conceptually or substantively to applied leisure programs. Much of the study of leisure services has been done by persons carrying the label of social scientists, with degrees from forestry departments or departments of park and recreation, and using sociological concepts and techniques. Many are employed directly by the Park Service, the Forest Service, or the Corps of Engineers. Sociologists have made some promising attempts at developing conceptual guidelines for the study of leisure (Kaplan, 1960; Burch, 1965; Cheek, 1971; Hendee and Burdge, 1974; Cheek and Burch, 1976), but few of these have been tested in the empirical world. When compared to such areas as the delivery of health and educational services, the niche that sociologists have carved in research on leisure services is quite small. This chapter deals with that limited contribution.

WHAT ARE THE PROBLEMS?

Definition of Leisure Services

Leisure services delivered outside the home are generally provided free or at token cost and are paid for by tax monies and occasionally by private donations. Examples of leisure services include municipal parks and recreation programs, access to public lands and waters for outdoor recreation, historic sites and monuments, and programs designed for special categories of the population (i.e., the handicapped, youth organizations, adult enrichment, and education and leisure programs for the aged). Therefore, leisure services are defined as: any program, facility, or event funded from extramural public and private sources and designed to meet the leisure needs of the general public. Commercial recreation and entertainment designed to make a profit (movies, TV, and radio) are not included in this discussion, although they constitute an important use of leisure time. Finally, this discussion assumes that leisure services are a legitimate expenditure of public money, although it has not been empirically established that people "need" leisure (Driver, 1977).

Some sociologists who work in applied leisure research define leisure as time left over from work when individual and collective maintenance functions have been completed (Burdge, 1961; Cheek, 1971). Other sociologists believe that leisure must have meaning and is not just nonwork time (Kaplan, 1960). To them, free time and leisure have important individual and philosophical meanings. Neulinger (1974) maintains that leisure is an activity freely chosen for intrinsic reasons; work, therefore, could be leisure. This disagreement over the concepts of leisure and free time has made the delivery of services difficult. Some of the questions most often raised include: "If leisure is an individual activity, why should the government be involved in providing that service?" "If leisure is individual, should not people make their own decisions about what pleases them in their free time?" The persons who provide leisure services respond that most leisure needs are collective and, therefore, must be met by public service, because it is necessary to maintain the health and general welfare of the population.

Leisure and Recreation Professionals

Within the United States and Canada, municipal leisure and recreation services are staffed largely by graduates of college programs coming under the general label of "Recreation and Parks." The training emphasizes programming skills such as camping, softball, and crafts, as well as administration and facility maintenance. Persons working in municipal and county recreation departments must have a combination of sports talent, organizational and process skills, and at least some knowledge of ground and facility maintenance.

Most municipal park and recreation professionals have a physical education background or are trained under people who have such an orientation. The dominant teaching mode, which is commonly called "learning by previous experience," consists of sharing past experiences that have worked in particular park settings. Consequently, it is very difficult to apply sociological research to municipal park programs, since what works in one setting may not be applicable to another area. Success for the recreation professional depends to a large extent upon how many people visit the facilities and participate in the planned programs. Evaluation comes in the form of head counts and public comments about the programs.

Park and recreation managers continually talk about the "movement." This social movement is aimed at getting people to realize that more park and recreation programs and facilities are necessary to solve the "leisure problem"—and here it is assumed that people "need" leisure. Because so much emphasis is placed on the movement, recreation professionals approach their job with the zeal of crusaders. As such, many day-to-day decisions are based on emotional considerations. Research, particularly when done by outsiders, is viewed as naive and not practitioner oriented. Because many leisure professionals do not appreciate, accept, or understand research, they are not likely to heed present and future trends. For example, the decision to develop outdoor recreation facilities away from population centers was made despite repeated warnings that the population was becoming more urban and that transportation to these sites depended upon cheap energy. A counter proposal to develop more recreation facilities in urban and suburban locations received little political support (Dunn, 1980).

Equity in the Distribution and Location of Leisure Services

Except for city parks and school playgrounds, most leisure facilities are located away from major population concentrations. Outdoor recreation opportunities, both those provided by the state and by federal agencies, tend to be located in scenic areas or within the federal forest and park system. Wilderness areas, good hunting and fishing sites, and settings for such activities as white-water canoeing and backpacking are located at considerable distances from urban centers. As travel becomes more restrictive and seasonal, these facilities will be used less.

The explosion of outdoor facility development came in the 1960s and 1970s when energy was cheap and seemingly abundant and population projections were for continued and even accelerated growth. Expansion of remote recreational facilities continued despite warnings that important demographic indicators were changing. The populations of the United States and Canada are either moving to the city or to warmer climates. Unfortunately, none of these recreation facilities, developed at enormous public expense, are able to pick up roots and follow.

The users of most outdoor recreation facilities are middle-class and upper-middle class persons and/or their college-age children. Because of inaccessability due to location and cost, neither working-class nor lower-class persons—and in particular blacks—are able to visit many of the outdoor facilities (Conner and Bultena, 1980). Some income is, of course, necessary to use almost any recreation facility, but the location and availability of quality recreation facilities tend to be the biggest obstacles to their use (Beaman, et al., 1979).

Municipal recreation programs tend to be of higher quality in suburban, middle-class areas. Organized recreation programs are either not available or very unsatisfactory in rural areas and in lower-income and working-class portions of the cities. Recreation services for young people in these areas is a particularly critical problem (Burdge, et al., 1979).

In summary, the delivery of recreation services and the location of leisure facilities is plagued both by equity and distributional patterns. The quality outdoor recreation opportunities are located away from population centers and require money to visit. The best municipal recreation programs are located in the affluent suburbs and medium-sized cities and towns.

Leisure as a Residual Social Problem

A social problem, as defined by sociologists, is a condition that is disruptive and dysfunctional to the social system and to the general day-to-day welfare of the population. In the case of leisure, the social problem is either too much free time, which raises the question of how to cope with idle hours, or not enough leisure time, in which case the issue is balancing work or obligatory time with the available free time.

The United States has gone through cycles of not having enough free time to having too much. The early part of the century saw little leisure, because of the rush to industrialize. During the great depression of the 1930s, widespread unemployment produced leisure consisting of forced idle time. Leisure has been viewed as a social problem only during such periods of high unemployment and forced idleness among segments of the populations. In periods of high employment or during wartime, federal and state programs do not emphasize leisure services. In a sense, leisure becomes a problem when free time turns into idleness.

During the last two decades of the twentieth century, the population of North America will grow very slowly as the birth rate declines and stabilizes below the replacement level. Because the actual number of new babies will be less, the population will slowly age, resulting in more people in their retirement years and fewer people entering the ranks of the employed. Therefore, to maintain the society at its present levels of service and production, the demand for labor will be high and people will be working longer hours and more years. Leisure as a social problem will lose its political appeal because unemployment as a practical concern will not exist. How can leisure programs be justified when everybody is working? In the old U.S. tradition, the leisure problem will be solved by more work. In the short run, persons in service and administrative occupations will work more, but others, such as certain categories of blue-collar workers may work less. Long-run adjustments in the occupational composition of the labor force should reduce idleness.

WHAT DO WE KNOW?

Most of the systematic accumulation of research within the leisure and recreation services area deals with the following topics:

1. The characteristics of populations participating in leisure activities.
2. Substantive explanation of leisure behavior and motivations.
3. On-site studies of natural resource facility users.
4. Ethnographic studies of leisure interaction, places, and organizations.
5. Research on conflict and carrying capacity, mainly in natural resource settings.
6. Influence of the life cycle on leisure behavior.

Each of these topics will be discussed in some detail from the standpoint of what leisure sociologists presently know.

Characteristics of Users

Surveys were conducted by the Outdoor Recreation Resources Review Commission (1962a) in 1960 to determine nationwide outdoor recreation use patterns of U.S. adults. A similar study in Canada was labeled the Canadian Outdoor Recreation Demand Survey. These surveys found that users of outdoor recreation facilities—in terms of both frequency and variety of activities—tended to be relatively young, well-educated persons with white-collar or professional occupations and relatively high income (up to a point). They also tended to be urban residents. Two notable exceptions were fishing and hunting, which were more popular among working-class and rural people. Very few females go hunting, and they only go fishing with their families (Burdge, et al., 1975). Few blacks were found among the ranks of the outdoor recreation users, except for fishing in private pay lakes near urban centers (Burdge, 1967b). Winter sports such as downhill skiing and ice skating were the exclusive domain of the white, upper-middle class.

In short, the surveys of the early 1960s found that social class, age, race, and residency all affected participation in outdoor recreational activities.

Subsequent nationwide studies of persons using outdoor recreation facilities have reaffirmed those earlier findings (Bureau of Outdoor Recreation, 1977). An important recent trend, however, has been broader participation in outdoor recreation as a result of more disposable income and the expansion of the middle class. The basic relationship between demographic characteristics and recreational participation remain the same, but the numbers in the categories have increased. For example, the percentage of the total adult population that skied increased from 1 to 3 percent between 1960 and 1977, but the relationships remained the same. However, such trends have only been confirmed through the summer of 1977. In addition, as the post-World War II babies have reached adulthood, more people have been available to use these facilities. In addition, the recreation supply industry has greatly improved the quality of the equipment used in these activities. Finally, the opportunity to participate in outdoor recreation was aided by federal subsidies that made more facilities available.

Substantive Explanations of Leisure Behavior

At about the same time the Outdoor Recreational Resources Review Commission was gathering survey data, a few sociologists began to synthesize available research findings on leisure behavior into a framework. Max Kaplan (1960) was the first sociologist to publish a book in this field, and he and the French sociologist Dumazedier (1974) have been the leaders in conceptualizing what is meant by leisure.

Sebastian DeGrazia (1962) and Stanley Parker (1971) posed the idea that leisure could be either compensating or complementing. In a compensatory situation, one engages in leisure or seeks leisure satisfaction that cannot be obtained at work. In a complementary situation, one's free time leisure is similar to what one does at work—as exemplified by the bus driver who rides the bus on a free pass when off duty. Burdge (1965) found in a study of occupations and leisure activity in Pittsburgh in the early 1960s that favorite leisure time pursuits were indeed related to people's work. Mechanics worked on cars in their free time and accountants played the stock market. Unfortunately, the compensatory and complementary theories have not been translated into applied leisure research even though they have intuitive appeal. This explanation has been attacked as over simplistic and does beg the question as to whether work and leisure are related (Burch, 1969).

Burch (1965) and Yoesting and Burkhead (1973) propose that peer or parental leisure activity influences the individual. In a study of how persons got started camping, Burch found that most people were socialized into the activity by their parents. In contrast, Burdge and others (1975) found that women went fishing only with their spouse or families and never alone or with other females. The major socializing agent in this case was the family and not parents. Yoesting and Christensen (1978) in comparing adult and childhood leisure found partial support for the notion that what one did as a child carried over to the adult years. Kelly (1974) suggests that what one does for leisure is based on one's stage in the life cycle. Obviously, the presence of small children, a heavy work schedule, and old age all limit one's opportunities for certain forms of leisure. These findings suggest, however, that it may be possible to develop new programs to meet the needs of people at all stages of the life cycle.

Cheek (1971) proposes that what distinguishes leisure activity from other forms of behavior is that it is almost always done in the presence of others. With the exception of certain hobbies and skill sports, most recreation is done as a member of a social group. While this observation places leisure within the domain of sociology, translating it into program development is quite difficult, as discussed later in this chapter.

On-Site Studies of Natural Resource Facility Users

No other category of leisure participants has received as much sociological attention as those users of natural resource recreation facilities, especially those located near water. The major reason for this is that the U.S. National Park Service, the U.S. Forest Service, plus the Army Corps of Engineers—who own most outdoor recreation facilities in the United States—and their Canadian counterparts have money to conduct research on the people who visit the areas they administer. A basic feature of this on-site research is a daily count of visitors, either by mechanical or observational procedures. Many parks and campgrounds require registration, which provides demographic and travel data on a continuous basis. Periodic studies of user satisfaction, perceptions of crowding, and general comments on management strategies are also obtained. Such on-site studies are readily justified because they provide immediate feedback to managers, who then, supposedly, improve the quality of the recreation experience. Many managers also use variations of these on-site studies to evaluate the performance of their employees. Finally, studies on the differences between managers and users of recreation show that managers want the parks to remain in a more natural state, while users want them developed (Peterson, 1974a).

State departments of natural resources (or conservation) conduct studies of hunters, fishermen, and boaters within their administrative areas. In addition, each state develops and updates a comprehensive State Outdoor Recreation Plan that attempts to utilize sociological characteristics to predict future demands and provide a basis for acquisition and development of new areas when demand is forecast to outstrip supply.

In sum, much is known about users of recreation sites and their preferences and satisfactions regarding these leisure services. On-site studies do much to evaluate the delivery and quality of leisure services, but they do not place the findings in any larger perspective.

Ethnographic Studies of Leisure Activities and Organizations

The large-scale surveys of leisure behavior do a very adequate job of outlining trends in leisure use on national and regional scales. If these findings were heeded, development of recreation facilities could be shifted to more favorable locations. However, surveys must be repeated on similar populations at selected intervals to locate changes and trends in leisure behavior. An alternative to both site-specific and cross-sectional surveys is intensive studies of a leisure group or a leisure setting. Several sociologists, notably Lee (1972, 1977) and Devall (1973) studied the same leisure setting (such as a beach, zoo, or park) over a long period of· time. These investigations allow analysis of the changing social norms and cultural settings that govern all social behavior, including leisure. This type of leisure research enables managers to better understand the social processes that occur at their recreation sites.

A few sociologists (Cheek, et al., 1976; Bryan, 1977) have intensively investigated specific leisure and recreation activities, including mountain climbing, scuba diving, sport fishing, and chess playing. The typical conceptual framework for this research on individual leisure and sport activities is either their unique normative structure or the socialization patterns that dominate entrance into the activity.

Research on Conflict and Carrying Capacity

As an example of the expansion of outdoor recreation facilities, campsites used to be primitive and restricted to a few national parks. By 1980, thousands of well-maintained public and private campsites had been developed to accommodate both tents and luxury camping vehicles. However, transplanting large numbers of people from the nation's cities and suburbs to pristine outdoor settings has not been accomplished without alteration to that natural environment.

What were once predominant urban problems, such as crowding, conflict, noise pollution, littering, and vandalism, have now become problems for recreation areas. Examples include vandalism and destruction of campsites by both campers and locals (Clark, et al., 1971a); riding motorcycles on trails and through campsites, partying in campsites after "quiet hours," and harassment of fishermen by reckless boaters, among others. Problems in relationships among recreation users carry the potential for conflict when users with different recreation experience preferences occupy the same space (Buchanan, 1979).

Some of the classic conflicts reported in the leisure literature include those between the snowmobiler and the cross-country skiier and between the trailbiker and the hiker. It seems as if each recreation opportunity has a counter activity that detracts from the opportunity for leisure enjoyment. Carrying capacity and crowding research focuses on ways to alleviate conflict in leisure settings and to provide a recreation experience for all (Knopp and Tyger, 1973; Gramann and Burdge, 1981). Such research can provide the basis for the introduction of management practices like zoning and use limitations.

Influence of the Life Cycle on Leisure Behavior

With many forms of active leisure, what people do in their free time depends to a large degree on how old they are and what stage they are at in the family life cycle. Results from survey research consistently demonstrate that younger persons are physically more able to participate in outdoor recreation, particularly the more vigorous activities like hiking, mountain climbing, backpacking, and swimming (Outdoor Recreation Resources Review Commission, 1962a).

While participation in some activities such as fishing, picnicking, and hobbies often persist well into the retirement years, age does change the nature of leisure activity. So, too, does the family cycle. Small children require more individual attention than do older children, and they have difficulty participating in vigorous outdoor recreation, which may be more available to families with older children. Consequently, families with small children make less use of leisure services. At the same time, peer pressures of adolescents restrict leisure. Rapoport and Rapoport (1975) cite evidence that the underlying leisure interests of people change with advancement through the life cycle. Kelly (1974) also offers empirical support that with the birth of children leisure behavior tends to be more home centered.

WHAT ARE WE DOING?

This section discusses the major areas of leisure service to which sociologists are making contributions: 1) demand for outdoor recreation, 2) user groups in leisure settings, 3) crowd control and management procedures, 4) planning special recreation areas, 5) evaluating municipal recreation programs, and 6) recreation services as societal needs. It is important to recognize that the study of leisure has never been a legitimate area for sociologists. Sociologists still laugh when leisure is mentioned as a topic of research (Burdge, 1974). A person doing research on leisure problems is often seen as really playing and, therefore, not doing legitimate sociological "work." The American Sociological Association classifies leisure research with the arts, music, literature, and sport. It is not surprising that few sociologists list leisure among their specialty interests. Within the Forest Service, the National Park Service, and the Corps of Engineers, only five sociologists are working on recreation and leisure service issues. Finally, not one sociology department in the United States offers sociology of leisure as a graduate specialty.

Against this backdrop of minimal involvement and even less professional support, the contribution of sociologists to leisure service programs is restricted and at times esoteric.

Demand for Outdoor Recreation

Sociologists presently use standard demographic and social organization variables to explain why people participate in various leisure activities. They seek to determine what facilities will be needed in the future and how new facilities should be designed. Their goal is to match participation figures with demographic trends. The accuracy of these predictions has never been checked because follow-up verification data has not been collected. The studies assume that sociodemographic variables associated with participation in particular activities will remain constant through time and that demographic trend analysis is accurate.

Early studies by the Outdoor Recreational Resources Review Commission (1962a) and subsequent studies by the Bureau of Outdoor Recreation and each of the states in their SCORP reports (State Comprehensive Outdoor Recreation Plans) have shown that the number of days spent in outdoor leisure has increased over the last two decades. Therefore, sociologists have advised managers, planners, and decision makers to purchase more park land, to place desirable scenic areas under public ownership, and to expand the recreation management aspects of their operations. At the same time, these recommendations are tempered by the fact that certain forms of recreation, such as hunting, are on the decline (Cichetti, 1972).

User Groups in Leisure Settings

Groups and organizations have always been an important component in the use of leisure services, but only recently has sociological research been able to document that trend (Cheek and Burch, 1976; Cheek, et al., 1976), and then the research has been limited to families and tourists. The major findings have been that families comprise a major portion of all leisure service users and that leisure activities are almost always done with other persons. If social groups are an important unit of observation in the leisure setting, then many sociological findings from other settings can be applied here. Unfortunately, sociologists have done little to establish those linkages.

Another important organized category of leisure organization is tourists. Traditionally, Canada and Mexico have supplied most of the tourists coming to the United States. Currently, however, the Japanese, Europeans, and people from the Middle East are coming here in larger numbers. The declining exchange rate of the U.S. dollar and the increased wealth of other countries are two of the reasons given for this trend. Within the limits of available energy, travel to the United States may become more common than travel from the United States to countries outside North America. As more tourists come to the United States, sociological research should focus on problems of cultural conflict and native U.S. ethnocentrism. Furthermore, competition for recreation facilities could develop between foreigners and the U.S. natives who must stay home due to high costs of foreign travel.

Crowd Control and Management Procedures

Most park managers and rangers are taught that their job is to protect the fauna and the flora of the park they manage from the people who visit it. The notion that parks are for people represents a new concept that is alien to the training of the rangers. They are used to thinking of parks as places to conserve, not to enjoy. If large numbers of visitors are new to managers of remote parks, the problems they create are not new in urban recreation areas. Most large city parks are vacant at night for fear of crime and violence (Burdge, et al., 1979). Public and private recreation property is often a target of vandalism (Clark, et al., 1971b).

In former times, campgrounds were seen as safe places where people could leave food and gear unattended while enjoying a day's activity. Not so today. Equipment must be locked up or it most certainly will be stolen. Littering and destruction of natural outdoor areas is even more severe. Littering of parks and playgrounds is also a major problem (Burdge, et al., 1979).

Sociologists have developed management programs to provide incentives for keeping campgrounds and natural areas clean. The work of Clark and others (1971a) in this area is one of the best examples of social research meeting the needs of managers and thus being applied. These procedures provide positive rewards for maintaining clean areas and not destroying the fauna and the flora. In addition, sociologists now are integrating law enforcement procedures into management training. In urban areas and increasingly in rural areas, park police are becoming a permanent fixture of the outdoor environment.

Planning Special Recreation Areas

Sociologists have demonstrated that not all recreational needs are the same and that users of different leisure facilities represent quite different needs (Driver, 1977; Peterson, 1974b). While the development of massive recreation areas, such as reservoirs carved out of unscenic areas, may satisfy some important recreation and leisure needs, this is not true for all persons. Other people enjoy leisure that requires large capital outlays, such as for golf courses and resorts. Still others would be satisfied with a place to play chess and meet friends. These diverse leisure needs represent the gamut of recreation experiences, but some cost much more than others.

Growing out of the diversity of leisure needs is the policy issue of whether all recreational facilities should be publicly financed. Specifically, should tax money be used to develop "quality" recreation opportunities at locations far from population centers? Since only persons with money could reach these facilities, and since the upper class has its own private leisure outlets, public funding of such facilities may be unwarranted (Hendee and Burdge, 1974). Another tax related issue is whether public monies should continue to finance and subsidize outdoor facilities, such as campgrounds, that directly compete with private facilities.

Evaluating Municipal Recreation Programs

A few sociologists have studied the success or failure of local recreation programs (Christensen, 1979). This type of evaluation research begins with a summary of the demographic characteristics of the people within the study area. A questionnaire is then developed for administration to users as a way of determining what their recreation needs are and whether or not they are being met by the program under study. Studies of municipal recreation programs do not include all possibilities of potential leisure services. Finally, the program operators are evaluated to see if their employment goals are the same as those of the program. Some sociologists in this field have also conducted workshops on leisure management techniques using skills borrowed from business management, accounting, and administration (Crompton, 1977).

Recreation Services as Societal Needs

During the 1970s, rural sociologists pioneered large-scale studies to assess public needs. Included in the topics investigated were recreation and leisure services. Because they were defined as societal problems, they could be ranked with other problem areas like housing, job opportunities, health, and education (Burdge, et al., 1979; Warner and Burdge, 1975). From a needs assessment perspective, leisure services is a legitimate contender with other problem areas for state and municipal tax monies. Once these findings are translated into priority rankings, policy makers and politicians can decide how much of the tax pie to allocate to recreation services. In the case of the 1978 Illinois study recreation services ranked seventh out of 13 problem areas in order of importance. They were ranked ahead of areas such as health services, education, community services, and planning an zoning, and behind such problem areas as housing, job opportunities, and environmental issues. In the 1975 Kentucky study leisure services as a problem area ranked seventh overall and ahead of such areas as education.

WHAT HAVE WE ACCOMPLISHED?

This section reports some outcomes of the studies outlined in the previous section. These observations rest on the basic understanding that applied sociology has made precious little contribution to public policy in this area. For the few attempts by sociologists to provide input to leisure services and programs, it is extremely difficult to document any success.

Demand for Outdoor Recreation

The sociological studies of demand for outdoor recreation and other forms of leisure activity have shown that age and to some extent income are the most important predictors of outdoor recreation activity, but they are not very good predictors. With a young affluent population, the recommendation was to build more recreation facilities (Outdoor Recreation Resources Review Commission, 1962b). Migration to the suburbs also signalled a need for more park facilities and programs in those areas. Sociologists were often correct in predicting these trends, which led to the construction of many new facilities. However, sociologists did not alert the recreation services industry and organizations to slow downs in population growth. The failure to point out what an aging population means for leisure facilities was a damaging omission. The inability to predict visitation to national parks, national recreation areas and forest service areas has soured many leisure services managers on sociological predictions.

User Groups in Leisure Settings

Although leisure sociologists have demonstrated that the social group is the most crucial unit of analysis for leisure activities, that awareness has not been adopted by recreation and park managers. The group concept has not been articulated into a format that can be used in planning and management. For example, recreational facilities are designed as places for carrying out activities, rather than as settings to be used by groups engaging in leisure. While managers of leisure services have been alerted to the notion that people come to their areas in groups, the concept has not proved useful in differentiating among groups in crowds on peak use days. Filtering out a recreation group made up of family members from a group made up of family and friends is quite unrealistic in a management setting.

The importance of the social group for leisure management may be easier to see in the areas of tourism and travel, however. A group of 50 Japanese tourists arriving at the Yellowstone Lodge complete with tour guide and driver is readily identifiable. All persons involved in the delivery of services to these people will quickly grasp that they are a group, represent a separate culture, have specific leisure goals, and, therefore, must be managed in a particular manner.

Crowding and Management Procedures

The National Park Service, at the Grand Canyon Training Center, includes sociological concepts and problems in their training programs for all new rangers. The extent to which the new rangers apply this knowledge once they reach the field is not fully known. Nevertheless, exposure to these ideas and recognition by the Park Service that "people problems" exist in parks is a step in the right direction. In addition, the Park Service recognizes the utility of sociological research in the parks.

The Forest Service, through its experiment station in Seattle, conducts a series of studies and management options dealing with depreciative behavior in forest lands. Campground attendants and managers are instructed to offer awards to children to stop littering, to pick up litter, and to encourage others not to litter. Vandalism is controlled by reinforcing group surveillance and rewarding persons for leaving areas as they found them. These techniques combine behavior modification and peer support (Clark, et al., 1971a).

Evaluations of litter and vandalism levels following initiation of the programs show dramatic improvement. Moreover, these programs will undoubtedly increase forest rangers' awareness of "people problems."

Planning Special Recreation Areas

While studies of user groups have identified the need for special recreation services and programs, little has been resolved in the way of relevant policy decisions. However, lobby groups representing the National Recreation and Park Association have been successful in obtaining leisure services for special categories of the population at public expense. As Hendee and Burdge (1974) point out, wilderness areas within the National Parks and the U.S. Forest Service can only be used by persons with enough money to get to remote areas of the West. These persons, of course, are largely upper-middle class.

Other sociologists (Conner and Bultena, 1980) argue that distance from urban areas creates a barrier to leisure opportunities, so that monies should be funneled into recreational development in urban areas. The Forest Service has established an urban forestry program to improve forest recreation opportunities in urban areas. The program is to expand existing forests and the recreational use of them in urban areas. Money was allocated for the program based on the hope the Forest Service (an organization presently operating in rural areas) could do something about the leisure opportunities of urban people. However, these programs are underfunded and understaffed. It is very difficult to cite any instances in which sociologists have made important inputs into decisions on special use of public recreation services.

Evaluating Municipal Recreation Programs

Evaluation of leisure services lies on the border between research and consulting. The research consists of applying sociological and management concepts to recreation programs and the persons who use these facilities and programs. The outcomes of these evaluations have not been as useful as one would hope, mainly due to differences between what recreation practitioners want and what sociologists are able to provide.

Recreation practitioners are skeptical of social science research because their background does not make them aware of the generalizable nature of social science research. Their training stresses specific situations rather than general principles that could be applied in a variety of leisure situations. Practitioners want solutions to the problems they are dealing with at the moment and need justifications for their programs and budgets. For example, these managers want a rationale that parks and/or other leisure facilities are needed and, if possible, that so many should be built per 1,000 population.

University sociologists commonly do consulting or evaluation research either for extra income or to provide data for research and graduate students. The two objectives are not compatible and produce different expectations and findings. This problem is further complicated by the recreation manager talking at a practical level while the sociologist is talking at a conceptual level, the result being they talk past one another. The relationship could be left alone, except for the very real situation that the managers need the type of user and organizational analysis that sociologists can provide and the sociologists need the contact with practical problems.

Recreation Services as Societal Needs

A study cited earlier (Burdge, et al., 1979) found that recreation services ranked seventh in a list of 13 problem areas of concern to a sample of 10,000 Illinois adults. Ranking above recreation were such areas as government-citizen relations, housing, job opportunities, and pollution and littering. Several problem areas that are of critical concern to applied sociologists were ranked lower than recreation, however, including education, health services, community services, public safety, and planning and zoning. This kind of study has also been conducted in several other states with very similar results.

Of particular importance in defining recreation services as a problem area is the availability and adequacy of these programs and facilities (Burdge, et al., 1979). Generally speaking, leisure services as a problem is more important in suburban and rural areas than in the cities. In addition, the definition of critical recreation services varies with the locale. Recreation services for young people are often seen as most important in rural areas, while the availability of recreation and playground facilities is seen as more of a problem in urban areas.

In the Burdge, et al. study (1979) age was strongly related to perceptions of recreation services as a problem area. Recreation services for older people were considered a serious problem by the youngest age category in the sample (18 to 24 year olds) and least serious by the persons to which they were directed (those 65 and older). Providing recreation services for young people was seen as the most serious problem by the 18 to 24 age category and the least serious concern by persons over 65.

Information on public perceptions of recreation services as a problem area is helpful both for the policy makers and recreation managers. Such information can enable policy makers to determine which public services are being adequately provided, while managers can improve or add services to fulfill unmet needs.

WHERE ARE WE GOING?

Leisure as a Problem Area

Organizations are formed, programs are put together, and people are hired to conduct them after a social problem has been identified by the political structure. The onset of the great depression in the 1930s triggered the first public recognition that "idleness" might be a major problem. With upwards of 25 percent of the working population idle, public and private social agencies were instructed to find something for people to do. The response to this public outcry was the policy decision that federal agencies should get people back to work. One such agency, the Work Projects Administration (WPA), went to work rebuilding roads and constructing hospitals, public buildings, and schools. Hundreds of conservation projects were undertaken by the Park Service and the Forest Service. The theme during that era was that time away from gainful employment was temporary. The federal government was keeping people off welfare by "making" work.

In the post-World War II era, leisure was something that came in small additional doses each year. As working hours steadily declined during the 1950s and 1960s, some observers predicted that play days would soon outnumber work days, so that leisure would become the dominate theme in North America. However, those predictions have not materialized, for the following main reasons (Burdge, 1978). 1) Technology has not relieved people of most work obligations and provided unlimited opportunities for new life styles, as was often assumed. While some blue-collar jobs have been displaced by technology, more white-collar jobs have been created. 2) As population growth slows down, the size of the available labor force declines, which requires that more people work longer. Instead of a problem of too much leisure, the problem becomes not enough free time in which to enjoy leisure.

Who Will Pay for Leisure Programs

Health, education, and other service organizations have well-established funding niches and sources. Private money and federal and state funds often flow readily to support their activities and to develop new programs. Leisure services frequently have a very difficult time obtaining adequate funding, however, especially at the local level. Public support for new and expanded leisure programs is usually small and selective.

Some private funds could be used, but most recreation and leisure businesses are dependent on a market that is fickle, seasonal, and fadish. Private businesses are not likely to invest in facilities for leisure activities unless they can foresee a consistent and long-term public demand. As demonstrated by sociologists, many leisure activities are subject to unpredictable fashion and fad cycles (Meyersohn and Katz, 1957).

Local and municipal recreation services will continue to have the most difficulty justifying their funding, however, They are commonly supported by property taxes and special levies, which are quick to come under the scrutiny of tax cutters and politicians.

Special Leisure Populations

While a decline might take place in support for recreation and leisure services, such programs for special categories of the population will increase, because of federal mandates. These include programs for the handicapped, particularly sports and games. Within departments of parks and recreation this field is known as therapeutic recreation. These programs attempt to provide handicapped people with meaningful leisure opportunities, and they are also seen as an aid in rehabilitation. As public legislation continues to favor handicapped and other special populations, therapeutic recreation will likely receive more money, despite the fact that these programs require expensive equipment and high salaried personnel.

SUMMARY

Because very few applied sociologists specialize in the study of leisure, sociological involvement in leisure services has been very minimal. Our only significant contribution thus far has been to provide concepts and research techniques that can be applied to leisure problems. Unless applied sociologists begin to give serious attention to leisure services, the need for social research in this area will be met by people trained in other fields such as forestry, parks and recreation, and planning. Research by sociologists may then lose legitimacy in the eyes of leisure service managers and, ultimately, in the eyes of the policy makers who fund their programs.

REFERENCES AND SUGGESTED READINGS

Beaman, Jay, Stephen Smith, and Yoon Kim. 1976. "Measurement of Supply Using National Interview Data on Participation in Outdoor Recreation Activities." Ottawa: Parks Canada. Technical Note 29. *Canadian Outdoor Recreation Demand Study, Vol. 2.*

Beaman, Jay, Yoon Kim, and Stephen Smith. 1979. "The Effect of Recreation Supply on Participation." *Leisure Sciences* 2:71–89.

Bryan, Hobson. 1977. "Leisure Value Systems and Recreational Specialization: The Case of Trout Fishermen." *Journal of Leisure Research* 9:174–88.

Buchanan, T., J.E. Christensen, and R.J. Burdge. 1979. "Social Groups and Outdoor Recreation Experience Preferences." Paper presented at the annual meeting of the Midwest Sociological Society. Minneapolis (April 26).

Buchanan, Thomas. 1979. "Recreation Experience Preferences of Subgroups of Participants in Selected Water-Based Activities." Unpublished Ph.D. dissertation, University of Illinois, Urbana.

Burch, William R., Jr. 1965. "The Play World of Camping: Research into the Social Meaning of Outdoor Recreation." *American Journal of Sociology* 70:604–12.

_____. 1969. "The Social Circles of Leisure: Competing Explanations." *Journal of Leisure Research* 1:125–47.

Burdge, Rabel J. 1961. "The Protestant Ethic and Leisure Orientation." Paper presented at the annual meeting of the Ohio Valley Sociological Society. Cleveland (April).

_____. 1965. "Occupational Influences on the Use of Outdoor Recreation." Unpublished Ph.D. dissertation. The Pennsylvania State University, University Park.

_____. 1967a. *Outdoor Recreation Studies in Vacations and Weekend Trips.*

Agricultural Economics and Rural Sociology, Bulletin No. 65. Agricultural Experiment Station, The Pennsylvania State University, University Park.

_____. 1967b. *Outdoor Recreation Research: An Annotated Bibliography.* Agricultural Economics and Rural Sociology, Bulletin No. 66. Agricultural Experiment Station, The Pennsylvania State University, University Park.

_____. 1974. "The State of Leisure Research." *Journal of Leisure Research* 6:312–17.

Burdge, Rabel J., John S. Burch, and Donald R. Field. 1975. "Traditional Sex Roles and Group Influences on Sport Fishing Behavior." Paper presented at the annual meeting of the Rural Sociological Society. San Francisco (August).

_____. 1978. "Social Change and Leisure Activity." *Indiana Academy of the Social Sciences* 13:1–13.

Burdge, Rabel J., James E. Christensen, and Jacquelin P. Buchanan. 1979. "Blockages to Urban Park Use." Paper presented at the National Recreation and Park Association Research Symposium. New Orleans (October).

Burdge, Rabel J. and Jon Hendricks. 1972. "The Nature of Leisure Research—A Reflection and Comment." *Journal of Leisure Research* 4:215–18.

Burdge, Rabel J. and others. 1979. *Recreation Services in Illinois: The Citizen Perspective.* Special Series 6: Illinois: Today and Tomorrow. Illinois Agricultural Experiment Station, University of Illinois, Urbana.

Bureau of Outdoor Recreation. 1977. *Results of the 1975 Nationwide Survey.* Washington, D.C.: U.S. Government Printing Office.

Cheek, Neil H. Jr. 1971. "Toward a Sociology of Not-Work." *Pacific Sociological Review* 14:245–58.

*Cheek, Neil H., Jr. and William R. Burch, Jr. 1976. *The Social Organization of Leisure in Human Society.* New York: Harper & Row.

An advanced text in the sociology of leisure, this book combines cultural and social organization elements into an explanation of leisure behavior. Drawing heavily from Furkeheim and Sorokin, leisure is treated as a social institution, on a par with education, religion, government, and the family. The authors maintain that the primary function of leisure in industrialized society is to foster both interpersonal and community bonds. Leisure as a social institution is seen as threatened by public recreation programs, which are criticized as being too highly institutionalized and excessively programmed.

Cheek, Neil H., Jr., Donald R. Field, and Rabel J. Burdge. 1976. *Leisure and Recreation Places.* Ann Arbor, Mich.: Ann Arbor Science Press.

Christensen, James E. 1979. "Attitude and Interest Survey—Elk Grove Village." Champaign, Ill.: Management Learning Laboratory–Final Report.

Chicchetti, C. 1972. "A Review of the Empirical Analyses That Have Been Based Upon the National Recreation Surveys." *Journal of Leisure Research* 4:90–107.

*Clark, R., J. Hendee, and R. Burgess. 1972. "The Experimental Control of Littering. *Journal of Environmental Education,* 4(3):22–28.

This article reports the results of different experimental settings created to learn about control of littering and depreciative behavior in forest service campgrounds. It found that signs, warnings, litter bags, and other traditional forms of communication did not reduce the level of litter. However, the use of rewards—such as patches, badges, and recognition of antilittering activity—drastically reduced the level of littering and depreciative behavior.

Clark, R., J. Hendee, and F. Campbell. 1971a. "Values, Behavior and Conflict in Modern Camping Culture." *Journal of Leisure Research,* 2:143–59.

Clark, R., J. Hendee, and F. Campbell. 1971b. "Depreciative Behavior in Forest Campgrounds: An Exploratory Study." U.S. Forestry Service Research Note PNW-161. Portland, Ore.: Forest Experiment Station.

Conner, Karen A. and Gordon L. Bultena. 1980. "Social Class Differences in Reservoir Visits." Journal Paper No. J-9766, (unpublished). Iowa Agricultural Experiment Station. Iowa State University, Ames.

Crompton, John L. 1977. "A Recreation System Model." *Leisure Sciences* 1:53–67.

*DeGrazia, Sebastian. 1962. *Of Time, Work and Leisure.* Garden City, New York: Doubleday.

DeGrazia sees leisure as activity that is done for its own sake or as its own end. Leisure is freedom from the necessity of being occupied with labor or any other "necessary" activity. Except for the "idle rich," few people in modern society ever achieve leisure. DeGrazia also shows that time is now becoming an important factor for study (which had previously been ignored).

Devall, Bill. 1973. "The Development of Leisure Social Worlds." *Humboldt Journal of Social Relations* 1:53.

Driver, Beverly L. 1977. "Item Pool for Scales Designed to Quantify the Psychological Outcomes Desired and Expected from Recreation Participation." Mimeo. Fort Collins, Colorado: U.S. Department of Agriculture, Forest Service.

Dumazedier, J. 1974. *Sociology of Leisure.* New York: Elsevier.

Dunn, Diana R. 1980. "Urban Recreation Research: An Overview." *Leisure Sciences* 3:25–59.

Gramann, J.H. and R.J. Burdge. 1981. "The Effect of Recreational Goals on Conflict Perception: The Case of Water Skiers and Fishermen." *Journal of Leisure Research* 13:15–27.

Hendee, J.C. and R.J. Burdge. 1974. "The Substitutability Concept: Implications for Recreation Research and Management." *Journal of Leisure Research* 6:155–162.

Hendee, J.C. and others. 1968. "Wilderness Users in the Pacific Northwest—Their Characteristics, Values and Management Preferences." Portland, Ore.: Pacific Northwest Forest and Range Experiment Station PNW-61.

Kaplan, M. 1960. *Leisure in America: A Social Inquiry.* New York: John Wiley & Sons.

Kelly, J. 1974. "Socialization Toward Leisure: A Developmental Approach." *Journal of Leisure Research* 6:181–93.

Knopp, T.B. and J.D. Tyger. 1973. "A Study of Conflict in Recreational Land Use: Snowmobiling vs. Ski-Touring." *Journal of Leisure Research* 5:6–18.

*Larabee, Eric and Rolf Meyersohn. 1958. *Mass Leisure.* Glencoe, Illinois: Free Press.

This volume introduced the systematic study of leisure to sociologists. The book brings together significant research and theoretical perspectives on leisure from sociology, anthropology, history, and philosophy. The thesis pursued in the book is that what is done in one's free time is certainly as important as job-related behavior.

Lee, Robert G. 1972. "The Social Definition of Outdoor Recreation Places." In *Social Behavior, Natural Resources and the Environment,* edited by William R. Burch, Jr., Neil H. Cheek, Jr., and Lee Taylor, pp. 68–84. New York: Harper & Row.

_____. 1977. "Alone with Others: The Paradox of Privacy in Wilderness." *Leisure Sciences* 1:3–19.

Meyersohn, Rolf and E. Katz. 1957. "Notes on a Natural History of Fads." *American Journal of Sociology* 62(May):594–602.

Moore, Wilbet E. 1963. *Man, Time and Society.* New York: John Wiley & Sons.

Neulinger, John. 1974. *The Psychology of Leisure.* Springfield, Ill.: Charles C. Thomas.

Outdoor Recreation Resources Review Commission. 1962a. *National Recreation Survey.* Study Report No. 19. Washington, D.C.: U.S. Government Printing Office.

Outdoor Recreation Resources Review Commission. 1962b. *Outdoor Recreation in America.* Washington, D.C.: U.S. Government Printing Office.

*Parker, Stanley. 1971. *The Future of Work and Leisure.* New York: Praeger.

Parker has popularized two approaches to leisure. The first is the extension (spillover, familiarity) hypothesis, which maintains that leisure and work activities are similar and that one's leisure or work carries over into the other. The second approach is the opposition or compensatory approach. Here leisure is unlike work and one presumably compensates in leisure for the lack of satisfaction obtained during work. For Parker leisure involves freely chosen activities during nonwork time.

Peterson, George L. 1974a. "A Comparison of the Sentiments and Perceptions of Wilderness Managers and Canoeists in the Boundary Waters Canoe Area." *Journal of Leisure Research* 6:194–207.

_____. 1974b. "Evaluating the Quality of the Wilderness Environment: Congruence Between Perception and Aspiration." *Environment and Behavior* 6:169–93.

Rapoport, Rhona and Robert N. Rapoport. 1975. *Leisure and the Family Life Cycle.* London: Routledge and Kegan Paul.

Sofranko, A. and M. Nolan. 1972. "Early Life Experiences and Adult Sports Participation." *Journal of Leisure Research* 4:6–18.

Warner, Paul W. and Rabel J. Burdge. 1975. *Issues Facing Kentucky.* Tabloid (Dec). Department of Sociology, Cooperative Extension Service, University of Kentucky, Lexington.

Yoesting, D. and D. Burkhead. 1973. "Significance of Childhood Recreation Experience and Adult Leisure Behavior: An Exploratory Analysis." *Journal of Leisure Research* 5:25–36.

Yoesting, D. and J. Christensen. 1978. "Reexamining the Significance of Child-hood Recreation Patterns on Adult Leisure Behavior." *Leisure Sciences* 1:219–29.

Part
E

ENSURING
HUMAN
SURVIVAL

The processes through which society is preserved and social order is maintained are fundamental concerns of sociology. Over three decades ago Pitirim Sorokin argued that "As long as a group exists, it must maintain a certain degree of adjustment to its environment. Ceaselessly changing itself in an incessantly changing environment, it must preserve its internal equilibria.... Groups solve this twofold problem through constant adjustments to their environment and through the adjustment of their environment to themselves. To some extent all groups use both modes of adaptation."*

Although the principal modes of adaptation vary among societies, the dominant trend over the past century has been expansion. Societal expansion can be seen in population growth, exploitation of the natural environment for resources, rising levels of energy use, swelling economic production and consumption, and attempts to extend political influence over an ever-widening territory. With few exceptions, societies have not considered the consequences of such growth for the natural environment or for other societies.

Only during the past few decades have we begun to question the desirability of continued expansion and to recognize that human survival will be threatened if growth is not slowed or halted. Because of excessive population growth, severe stresses are being placed on the earth's carrying capacity. Critical shortages of food, energy, and raw materials are imminent in the near future. The natural environment is being polluted by the wastes of industry and human consumption. Conflicts over the territorial boundaries of nation-states threaten world peace. Societal growth cannot continue at its present pace without dire repercussions for humanity's future.

Applied sociologists have recently become involved in numerous efforts to combat excessive growth and to preserve the natural and social environments. Programs to reduce fertility have been initiated in almost every country of the world, and some governments are searching for ways to achieve a more balanced distribution of population. Recognizing that energy consumption is shaped by cultural values and social institutions, sociologists have sought ways of altering social behavior and organization to reduce energy consumption and to use energy resources more efficiently. Protection of the natural environment has become a major concern in all Western societies, and many people today argue that natural resources must be used for the common good rather than for private economic interests. Finally, applied sociologists have begun to demonstrate that they can contribute to the resolution of international conflicts.

---

*Pitirim A. Sorokin. *Society, Culture, and Personality: Their Structure and Dynamics* (New York: Harper and Brothers, 1947), p. 445.

Each of the topics addressed in the following chapters—population control, energy conservation, environmental protection, and peace promotion—demonstrates these efforts to apply sociological principles to a condition that threatens the survival of human society. Running throughout these chapters is the basic thesis that societal expansion must be controlled. A fundamental challenge for applied sociologists is to find ways of curbing expansion while improving the quality of life.

21 POPULATION CONTROL

Michael Micklin

During the last several decades the issues of how to control and change the size, growth, distribution, and composition of populations has become a major concern for policy makers and social planners, as well as many concerned citizens. We now recognize that current population trends are creating conditions that soon may threaten the very survival of the human species. Since population processes and characteristics are closely related to many other aspects of societal organization, governments and concerned private groups have turned to social scientists for basic population data, for studies of the causes and consequences of population trends, and for help in designing and evaluating programs for population control.

This chapter reviews the contributions of sociologists and other social scientists to efforts to implement population control. Discussion will be focused on the uses of sociological knowledge for understanding population growth and lowering fertility. Emphasis will be concentrated on the less-developed countries of the world.

WHAT ARE THE PROBLEMS?

At the global level, the two most significant population problems are the absolute number of people and the rate of population growth. It is estimated that the human population reached one billion in the first half of the nineteenth century. The second billion was reached around 1925, the third billion in 1960, the fourth billion in 1975, and by 1980 world population stood at 4.5 billion (Micklin, 1980:265-66). The average annual rate of population growth was around 0.5 percent from 1750 through 1900, but it increased to 0.8 percent between 1900 and 1950 and to 2.0 percent between 1950 and 1978. Projections

457

of future population growth indicate that the world is likely to have approximately 6 billion inhabitants by the year 2000 (van der Tak, et al., 1979:36-39). The ultimate size of the world's population when it eventually stabilizes, and the conditions under which growth is halted, will depend largely on how population control is managed during the next few decades.

Population problems vary from one country to the next, as well as among the world's geographic and cultural regions. The nature and extent of these problems depend on historical trends, relationships among demographic variables, and the nondemographic socioeconomic context. Nevertheless, it is possible to simplify the discussion of population problems by contrasting the situations of the less-developed and the more-developed nations. While there are some important variations within each of these categories, the differences between them underlie most critical generalizations about population problems.

The Less-Developed Countries

Approximately three-quarters of the world's population presently live in the poorer nations; in 1950 this figure was 66 percent (Demeny, 1974:149). The rising concentration of people in the less-developed countries during this period has resulted from their 2.3 percent average annual growth rate from 1950-77 in comparison to the 1.1 percent rate in the more-developed countries (calculated from U.S. Bureau of the Census, 1978:15, Table 2). The changes that have occurred in these rates over this period also demonstrate the more serious growth problems of the poorer countries. Their average rate of increase between 1950 and 1955 was 2.1 percent, but in 1975-77 it was 2.3 percent. In contrast, comparable figures for the more-developed countries were 1.3 percent and 0.7 percent, respectively.

What accounts for the high growth rates in developing nations during the past three decades? The principal demographic explanation is found in the changing balance between fertility and mortality and its effect on age composition. Although immigration and emigration can also affect population size, these factors are important in only a few countries. Hence, this discussion will concentrate on mortality and fertility.

Death rates in the less-developed countries have fallen dramatically since about 1920 as a result of improvements in medical technology, sanitation, popular education, and overall socioeconomic conditions (Davis, 1976:270-72). In many developing countries crude death rates were in the range of 20-25 per thousand inhabitants as recently as the 1940s, whereas today the average for all developing countries is around 15, and in many nations the rate is much lower. Death rates in the more-developed countries began to decline in the latter part of the nineteenth century and currently average around 9 per thousand persons (United Nations, 1973:108-15).

The picture is much different when birth rates are examined. From 1950 through 1970 there was only a slight decline in crude birth rates in the less-developed nations. United Nations (1977) estimates show the average figure to be 42 per thousand for the period 1950–55 and 38 for 1970–75. A more recent estimate for 1976 indicates the average crude birth rate to be somewhere between 34 and 39 per thousand (U.S. Bureau of the Census, 1978).

In the past few years a heated debate has emerged over fertility trends in the less-developed countries during the 1970s (Tsui and Bogue, 1978; Bogue and Tsui, 1979a, 1979b; Demeny, 1979a, 1979b; Kirk, 1979). While it is generally agreed that fertility has declined during the past decade, the debate hinges on several key issues, including 1) the extent of the decline and 2) fertility projections for the years to come. Tsui and Bogue examined fertility trends in 113 less-developed nations between 1968 and 1975 and concluded that the total fertility rate declined by 20 percent or more in 18 cases and by 10–19 percent in 19 cases. Overall, 95 (84 percent) of the less-developed countries showed a reduction in fertility. Demeny points out that the fertility declines estimated by Tsui and Bogue are greater than those calculated by other analysts. Moreover, he questions the accuracy and representitiveness of the data used by Tsui and Bogue for their calculations. Kirk (1979:397) reviews estimates of fertility for 1975 provided in nine separate studies and concludes that "the picture is clear: there has been a real decline in the birth rate in developing areas . . . in Asia and Latin America, but not in Africa." Bogue and Tsui (1979b; also see Tsui and Bogue, 1978) foresee even more rapid fertility reductions for the less-developed countries during the next century, and they predict zero world population growth by the year 2025. Whether fertility will decline this much and this rapidly, is, however, a matter of speculation and depends on changes in a variety of factors that influence fertility, which are discussed in detail below.

A critical demographic variable in the determination of potential fertility is the age composition of a population. The greater the number of women in the childbearing years, usually considered to be those 15–44, the greater the potential fertility, especially if most of these women are in sexual unions and are not contracepting. High fertility populations with relatively low or declining mortality show a pyramid-shaped age structure, with 40–50 percent of the population under 15 years of age (Demeny, 1974). As the younger cohorts of women age, the number of women who will be of childbearing age in the future is increased. The less-developed countries are currently feeling the effects of a sustained period of high fertility and declining mortality, as reflected by a growing proportion of women in the reproductive ages. Whether fertility increases, remains stable, or declines in future years will depend on the reproductive behavior of the currently young women as they pass through the child-bearing period (see Frejka, 1974: 176).

The demographic problems of the less-developed countries revolve around population growth and fertility. Mortality rates have leveled off and, with the exception of African nations, are generally comparable to those of the developed countries. While modest declines in fertility appear to have occurred in the past decade, birth rates are still high in most of these nations. The trends are promising, but the outlook for the future is not optimistic.

Global Problems

While the less-developed countries are responsible for the largest share of world population growth and exhibit much higher fertility than the more-developed nations, the consequences of continuing population expansion are felt by everyone. In recent years it has become widely recognized that we live in a finite, interdependent world (Ward and Dubos, 1976; Brown, 1978; Ridker and Cecelski, 1979). Population growth is threatening the carrying capacity of the planet (Catton, 1980) by increasing demand on natural resources and polluting the physical environment.

The detrimental effects of population growth are seen in growing scarcities of food, resources needed for economic production, and sources of energy. The world economy is characterized by increasing inflation and rising unemployment. All nations are experiencing housing shortages, and expanding settlements are reducing the supply of agricultural land. As world population increases, the amount of wastes dumped into the air and waters and on the land threatens to upset the ecological balance of nature and, ultimately, to make the earth unfit for human habitation.

In short, problems of population growth are felt even by those nations that have curtailed their own rate of increase. There is a growing recognition that it is in the interest of all countries to determine how best to slow, and ultimately halt, the rising number of people on the planet. Clearly, the immediate problem is to lower fertility. How to accomplish this feat is still an open question.

WHAT DO WE KNOW?

Empirical studies of the biological, cultural, economic, and social determinants of fertility now number in the thousands, although there is still little agreement on any comprehensive explanation of fertility trends and differentials. Nevertheless, implementation of any program that will result in fertility regulation requires that causal relationships be identified and that the underlying determinants be subject to manipulation. Stated otherwise, knowledge of the causes of fertility is a precondition of fertility control.

Despite its limitations, the "theory of the demographic transition" (Davis, 1945; Beaver, 1975; Teitelbaum, 1975; Coale, 1975) still provides a useful analytic framework for examining the causes of fertility. Briefly, transition theory argues that the social, economic, cultural, and demographic changes associated with the process of societal modernization bring about reductions first in mortality, then later in fertility, and, ultimately, in population growth. A problem with demographic transiton theory is that it includes a variety of explanatory variables that are related to one another and to fertility in complex ways. These variables include urbanization, individualism, rising levels of aspiration, occupational differentiation, education, the declining influence of traditional norms governing family organization and the status of women, the rise of mass communication, and increasing geographic and social mobility. While transition theory gives us a menu from which to select potential causes of variations in fertility, it does not help us to choose among alternative explanations that may involve direct, indirect, and interactive relationships.

Another problem with the transition theory is that it fails to specify how broad societal changes result in lower fertility. Logically, the answer must reside in the effects these social organizational variables have on the likelihood of intercourse, pregnancy, and gestation. In what has come to be a very influential argument, Kingsley Davis and Judith Blake (1956) identified three categories of "intermediate variables" that determine fertility. The first of these is exposure to intercourse, which is affected by such factors as 1) those governing the formation and dissolution of unions in the reproductive period (e.g., age at entry into sexual unions, proportion of women not entering sexual unions) and 2) those governing exposure to intercourse within unions (e.g., voluntary abstinence, coital frequency). The second category consists of factors affecting exposure to conception, including 1) infecundity, which may be voluntary or involuntary, and 2) use of contraception. The third category includes factors affecting gestation and successful parturition, such as voluntary and involuntary causes of foetal mortality (e.g., abortion). Subsequent attempts to modify this framework of intermediate variables (Bongaarts, 1976, 1978) have clarified the argument somewhat but do not challenge the validity of this perspective.

A final conceptual issue pertains to the level of analysis to be employed in explaining fertility. Fertility can be viewed as both an aggregate and an individual variable (Ryder, 1978). Populations are characterized by fertility rates and ratios, but it is individuals who act with regard to intercourse, marriage, contraception, abortion, and other fertility-related behaviors. Accordingly, studies of the determinants of fertility can be categorized in terms of their focus on aggregate or individual variables. The choice of level of analysis is not merely a matter of disciplinary or personal preference, or of the availability of data. The utility of research findings for affecting fertility control may depend on whether they reflect aggregate or individual variables. For example, suppose we find that education is inversely related to fertility. One strategy for using this information to lower fertility would be to alter the educational process in a society, perhaps by improving the quality of instruction or by establishing a mandatory minimum level of attainment. Alternatively, emphasis might be placed on increasing the motivation of young women to attend college through mass media campaigns or counseling. The difficulties of implementing these two strategies are likely to vary among populations, which emphasizes the significance not only of what we know, but also the likelihood of putting that information to use.

Determinants of Fertility

In recent years a number of studies have sought to inventory and synthesize knowledge about the various causes of fertility (Hawthorne, 1970; United Nations, 1973; McGreevey and Birdsall, 1974). The typical result is a list of variables, or perhaps a conceptual model, showing the direction and/or strength of relationships among social organizational or individual characteristics and fertility. Sometimes the findings are consistent with one another, but there is wide variation among the specific factors considered. The following discussion reviews the current state of knowledge regarding four broad categories of fertility determinants: socioeconomic characteristics, health and nutrition, psychological factors, and contraceptive practices.

Socioeconomic characteristics. Given the orientations provided by demographic transition theory and the intermediate variables approach, it is not surprising that efforts by social scientists to explain variations and trends in fertility have concentrated on identifying the effects of socioeconomic characteristics. The relationships most frequently considered are the following.

Marriage and family patterns. Age at marriage shows a strong inverse relationship to fertility. "Throughout the world, women who marry late—in their mid- or upper 20s—tend to have fewer children than women who marry early" (Henry and Piotrow, 1979:1). Delayed marriage results in lower fertility because it shortens the period during which a woman is likely to become pregnant and lengthens the interval between generations. Declining rates of marital fertility appear to be associated with societal movement through the demographic transition (Eberstadt, 1980:46). Nevertheless, intercourse is not confined to marital unions. The rising rates of premarital pregnancy throughout the world demonstrate that while marital fertility accounts for the large majority of births, average age at entry into sexual unions is a key consideration.

In societies where some type of corporate kin group is the basic social unit, fertility tends to be high. Children are valued because of their contribution to the economic and social functions of the group, and because they ensure its perpetuation (United Nations, 1973:92). Modernization, which results in a trend toward nuclear families, has the effect of lowering family size (Goode, 1963).

The status and roles of women. Numerous studies have shown that fertility is higher in societies where women's status is low and the variety of social roles they can assume is limited (Dixon, 1975, 1976; Oppong and Haavio-Mannila, 1979). In male-dominated societies females tend to be restricted to the household, their "proper" role being limited to domestic chores and childrearing. As these constraints are lessened and sexual equality is increased, communication between spouses becomes more egalitarian and women assume greater control over their lives. One consequence is that women have greater choice among alternative roles such as marriage, childbearing (including the number and spacing of births), education, and having a career.

Considerable attention has been given to the effects of female education and labor force participation on fertility. Generally, the higher the educational attainment and the greater the participation in the work force, the lower the fertility (Kasarda, 1971). These relationships have been supported with both aggregate and individual data, but the causal mechanisms in operation are not yet fully understood. Higher education and labor force participation influence a number of variables—age at marriage, aspirations, individualism, knowledge of contraception, occupational skills—that are related to fertility.

Education. Perhaps the most widely accepted finding in this area is the inverse relationship of fertility with literacy and/or educational attainment (Bogue, 1969:676-77). The logic underlying the education-fertility relationship has been elaborated by Holsinger and Kasarda (1976). They argue that schooling can influence fertility in three fundamental ways: 1) directly, through its effects on individuals' attitudes, values, and beliefs about small family size, 2) indirectly, through influences on other variables related to fertility (e.g., age at marriage, female labor force participation, social mobility, husband-wife communication, contraceptive knowledge), and 3) jointly, in interaction with other independent variables.

Careful consideration of the research literature suggests several flaws in our understanding of the education-fertility relationship, however (Cochrane, 1979; Graff, 1979). First, findings are inconsistent concerning the direction of the relationship. Cochrane's assessment of 50 studies shows that the expected inverse relationship occurs in only 29 cases and is more likely for women than men and in urban rather than rural communities. Second, the magnitude of the coefficient is not large, especially when other relevant variables are included in the analysis. Third, both the size and direction of the relationship depend upon the measures used and whether the analysis is based on individual or aggregate data. Fourth, the bulk of the evidence indicates that education has little direct effect on fertility but is more likely to exert an indirect influence through other variables such as age at marriage, women's labor force participation, and contraceptive knowledge. Finally, much more attention needs to be given to the differential effects of *quality* and *quantity* of education. Most studies have been concerned with how much education has been received rather than the types of information conveyed or the context of the schooling experience (Holsinger and Kasarda, 1976).

Income. Most people are familiar with the adage that "the rich get richer and the poor get children," but the empirical relationship between income and fertility is much more complex than this.

Cross-sectional studies generally show a fairly strong inverse relationship between income and fertility. This is true whether the analysis is intranational using family income, or international using such measures as per capita income or gross national product (King, et al., 1974:Appendix A). However, as with the relationship between education and fertility, the addition of other variables to the equation reduces considerably the relationship of income level to fertility and may result in a reversal of its direction.

Some of the resulting confusion over the income-fertility relationship can be cleared up by distinguishing between short-run and long-run effects of income change (Simon, 1976). For low-income countries, the immediate effect of a rise in income is to increase fertility. However, over a period longer than a few years, the result of an increase in national income is to reduce fertility, largely through indirect effects on education, employment, migration, child health, and the overall standard of living.

In recent years attention has shifted from the level of income to its distribution as a determinant of fertility (Rich, 1973; King, et al., 1974; Repetto, 1979; Simon, 1976:56-64). Although findings regarding income distribution are available for only a few countries and are subject to methodological criticisms (Eberstadt, 1980:48-49), the weight of the evidence suggests that fertility tends to decline when families or nations in the lower half of the income scale receive a greater share of the economic pie (Repetto, 1979).

Caldwell (1976) has revised the demographic transition theory to suggest another way in which income may affect fertility. Using data from Nigeria and Australia, he argues that the key factor is the direction of the flow of wealth in a society. When the flow runs from children to parents—as when children provide old age economic security for their parents—it is rational to have a large number of births. However, when the flow is reversed—as in the practice of parents making large investments in their childrens' educations—the economically rational thing to do is to have few children. Caldwell contends that a central component of the transition from high to low fertility is this reversal in the flow of wealth.

Urbanization. Another relationship that has received considerable attention is between urbanization and fertility (Micklin, 1969; United Nations, 1973; Goldberg, 1976). Many features of urban life—including the nuclear family, geographic and social mobility, formal education, and the mass media—create conditions that make it advantageous for parents to have small families. Although the argument is intuitively compelling, the supporting evidence is mixed.

In Latin America, urban fertility is consistently higher than in rural areas. In India and parts of Africa, the differential is nonexistent or even reversed (United Nations, 1973:98-99). The problem is that the process of urbanization encompasses numerous social, demographic, cultural, and economic changes, not all of which always occur simultaneously or with the same order of magnitude.

Health factors. Early versions of the demographic transition theory incorporated the notion that a high level of infant mortality gives rise to norms and practices supporting high fertility. On the other hand, it has been argued that the low levels of nutrition that occur in many less-developed nations may reduce the fecundity of women. In recent years increasing attention has been given to the effects of health, nutrition, and related factors on fertility.

Infant mortality. The expected direct relationship between infant mortality and fertility is commonly referred to as the "child survival hypothesis." A comprehensive summary of the available evidence has been offered by Schultz (1976:283). His conclusion is that "The evidence...uniformly suggests that in low-income countries the [reproductive] response [of parents to the declining incidence of child mortality] is likely to exceed one-half of the amount required to achieve a constant [i.e., in line with desired numbers] surviving family-size target."

Interpretations of the effect of infant mortality on fertility vary considerably, however (Heer and Smith, 1968; Preston, 1975). Part of the difficulty is due to the use of noncomparable data and less-than-adequate measures by different investigators. Moreover, the theoretical assumptions and propositions underlying this relationship have yet to be fully explicated (Schultz, 1976; Preston, 1978).

Health and nutrition. There is a paucity of good research concerning the effects of health and nutrition on fertility (Butz and Habicht, 1976). Our understanding of these relationships is complicated by the fact that such influences can operate through both biological and behavioral channels. Health and nutritional status can effect ages at menarche, menopause, and death; pregnancy outcome; postpartum sterility; and fecundity. However, the magnitude of these effects at the population level does not appear to be large (Bongaarts, 1980). Much more likely is the possibility that improvements in health and nutrition are correlated with socioeconomic and behavioral changes that operate directly on fertility.

Lactation. Lactation delays the renewed onset of ovulation and, thus, provides contraceptive protection (Preston, 1975; Butz and Habicht, 1976). However, socioeconomic modernization appears to be associated with a decline in the prevalence of breast-feeding, thus reducing its impact on fertility. Although the biological effect of lactation on fertility is well understood, the socioeconomic and behavioral determinants of breast-feeding practices have not been examined in any detail.

Psychological factors. Included in this category of fertility determinants are such variables as attitudes, values, norms, motivations, expectations, tastes, and preferences. The common element in these approaches is that subjective factors are believed to influence fertility decisions and reproductive performance (Davis, 1977).

Sex preferences. Societies around the world show wide variation in preferences for the sex of children, although the less-developed countries are more likely to show strong son preferences (Williamson, 1976; Repetto, 1972). A variety of societal factors—the level of urbanization and economic development, sex role norms, religious doctrine, the kinship system—are related to the patterning of sex preferences.

Although the existence of sex preferences has been reasonably well-established, their direct effects on fertility have not yet been documented satisfactorily. Williamson (1978:15) argues that the influence of sex preference on fertility depends on four conditions: 1) strong preference for one sex or the other; 2) a large deviation from the natural sex ratio at birth (105 males to 100 females), 3) a small to moderate number of children desired (i.e., one to four), and 4) the availability of effective birth control. Very few studies have been conducted in countries that meet all these conditions. The results of the existing research (all of which has been conducted in Asia), are mixed and subject to methodological shortcomings (Williamson, 1978:15-18; Ben-Porath and Welch, 1976). Son preference does appear to influence fertility in Korea, Taiwan, and China, but not in Japan, Singapore, and Hong Kong.

The Value and Cost of Children. In recent years a growing body of research has examined the influence of perceived values and costs of children on fertility behavior. Values and costs are usually conceptualized as either economic or noneconomic in nature. Economic values refer to ways in which children are viewed as economic assets—as a source of financial security in old age or as contributors to household production (Espenshade, 1977:5). Noneconomic values are the psychic benefits people associate with having children: adult status, companionship, vicarious achievement and so on (Hoffman and Hoffman, 1973). Economic costs include direct maintenance expenses and the economic opportunities parents give up when rearing children (Mueller, 1972a; Espenshade, 1977: 5-6). Noneconomic costs "include the emotional and psychological burdens children impose on parents" (Espenshade, 1977:6).

Studies conducted in Taiwan (Mueller, 1972b, 1976) and several Latin American countries (Simmons, 1974; Micklin and Marnane, 1975) suggest that although people have ambivalent images of large and small families, they are more likely to recognize the advantages of small families and the disadvantages of large ones. Bulatao (1979), using data from 14 countries, argues that fertility declines are accompanied by a transition in the value of children. Changes in economic structure associated with societal modernization result in a reduction of the productive capacity of children. As the economic value of children is reduced, noneconomic values are increasingly emphasized and children are seen as sources of psychic gratification for parents. However, "these primary-group values do not sufficiently offset the burdens on parents. . . . Increasingly also parents seek to escape from children, to enjoy personally more of the satisfactions that an expanding economy makes possible" (Bulatao, 1979:52; Caldwell, 1976).

Although evidence for the association between a shift in the value and cost of children and declining fertility is accumulating, it is premature to conclude that the relationship is causal. All of the research thus far has been cross-sectional rather than longitudinal in design, and it has not controlled adequately other fertility-related factors.

Fertility Norms. A common assumption in fertility research is that individual and collective values regarding family size have a bearing on birth timing and spacing and on completed fertility (Freedman, 1963; Yaukey, 1969). These fertility norms can be measured in a variety of ways, in terms of one's ideal, desired, intended, or expected number of children. The majority of these studies are descriptive in nature (Micklin and Marnane, 1975; Poffenberger and Sebaly, 1976). A recent innovation has been the attempt to disentangle the effects of preferences regarding sex and number of children and to determine the cross-cultural validity of such measures (Freedman and Coombs, 1974; Coombs, 1978). The results of these studies show that fertility norms are higher in developing than in developed countries but also suggest that statements of preferences should not be taken at face value (Ware, 1974).

Studies of relationships between fertility norms and actual fertility in developing countries are few in number. However, one such study conducted in Taiwan indicates that statements about wanting more children are highly predictive of subsequent births (Freedman, et al., 1975). On the whole, though, there is little evidence that fertility norms measured at the beginning of the reproductive period are good predictors of completed family size.

Other Factors. Psychological variables have been incorporated in studies of fertility trends and differentials for at least four decades. The underlying premise is that in the modern world fertility is increasingly a matter of volitional control, particularly when effective contraceptive technology is available (Back, 1967). A vast array of psychological variables have been related, directly and indirectly, to family size, fertility norms, and contraceptive use. For example, during the 1960s and 1970s hundreds of KAP (knowledge, attitudes, practice) studies were conducted around the world in an effort to identify cognitive and affective determinants of reproductive behavior (Mauldin, 1965; Berelson, 1966; Caldwell, et al., 1970). Other studies have examined the influence of psychological modernity on fertility, focusing on variables such as mobility aspirations, openness to innovation and change, fatalism, and orientation toward time (Hill, et al., 1959; Kahl, 1968; Fawcett and Bornstein, 1973; Miller and Inkeles, 1974). While such studies have resulted in a better understanding of psychological differences between people with large and small families, and of the psychological correlates of modernization, they have achieved relatively little in the way of identifying causal linkages with fertility behavior.

Contraceptive Practices. There is little doubt that if all sexually active couples used effective contraceptives regularly, excessive and unwanted fertility could be controlled. It is also clear that without birth control technology the world's fertility would be much higher than it is. Dorothy Nortman (1977:8) estimates that, *ceterus paribus,* the absence of birth control would result in a world birth rate of 45-50 per thousand rather than the 1977 level of 31 per thousand.

A wide variety of contraceptives are available that provide reasonably sure protection against pregnancy. Methods resulting in less than one pregnancy per 100 users include tubal ligation, vasectomy, pills, and condoms used in conjunction with a spermacidal agent. Other popular methods—intrauterine devices (IUDs), condoms, diaphragms, and spermacidal foam—show failure rates only slightly higher (1–3 pregnancies per 100 users) (Hatcher, et al., 1976).

Why, then, do we face such a severe problem of controlling fertility and population growth? Part of the answer is evident from an examination of patterns of contraceptive use. First, the proportion of couples in less-developed countries using any contraceptive method is relatively low. Considering married women of reproductive age in 29 developing nations, Nortman (1977) found that in only nine countries do more than one-third of these women practice contraception. In contrast, approximately two-thirds of such women in the United States are contraceptive users. Second, there is no guarantee that couples who report using contraceptives are doing so effectively and consistently. Finally, it is in the countries with the highest fertility, and presumably the greatest need for contraception, that we find the lowest rates of contraceptive use (Nortman and Hofstatter, 1980). While the type of contraceptive used has some effect on variations in fertility, the important issues revolve around use prevalence and continuation, strategies for making contraceptives readily available to persons who need them, and increasing motivation to control fertility through effective contraception.

Assessment

From the preceding discussion it should be clear that there are many gaps in our knowledge of the determinants of fertility. A variety of determinants have been suggested in one study or another, but few meet the test of showing a direct, strong, and statistically significant connection to reproductive behavior once other potentially relevant variables have been controlled. Nonetheless, implementation of effective programs and policies for fertility control requires that we know which variables to manipulate.

WHAT ARE WE DOING?

We know that societal modernization and economic development are associated with lower fertility and reduced population growth. Thus, changes in social and economic organization that are occurring independently of any concern with population problems are likely to produce some desirable demographic effects. Nevertheless, we also recognize that development alone will not reduce fertility to the replacement level, and in some nations it appears to have no effect at all. Moreover, rapid population growth is itself an impediment to social and economic development (Revelle, 1971:16–69). Effective population control, therefore, requires direct intervention to influence the immediate causes of high fertility.

Organized efforts to lower fertility in the developing countries have grown significantly during the past three decades and are evident at both national and international levels. Relevant activities include basic research, family planning programs, population education, and development of population policies. Social scientists have played key roles in many of these efforts.

Basic Research

Intervention to affect changes in fertility and population growth presumes knowledge of the problems, their causes, and their consequences. Since our understanding of these issues is far from complete, basic research continues to be of critical importance for population control.

Population Counts, Estimates, and Projections. To determine the effects of population size and growth on the standard of living and social institutions, we need to know how many people there are or will be in the future. An important activity of population researchers is to provide these basic data. While most industrialized countries take a population census every decade, only since the middle of this century have the less-developed countries done so with any regularity, and even now there are many areas of the world for which these data are either nonexistant or incomplete. Since the early 1950s the United Nations, through its Population Division, has provided technical assistance to less-developed countries wishing to develop an accurate population census. In addition, UN scientists generate estimates of population data—e.g., size, rate of growth, fertility, mortality—for areas lacking accurate information, and they also produce projections of future population trends (see Partan, 1973:86-96). U.S. groups active in the production of world population data include the International Division of the Bureau of the Census, the Agency for International Development, the Population Reference Bureau, and the Environmental Fund.

Determinants of Fertility. We observed earlier that in spite of the volume of research that has been conducted, we know relatively little about the determinants of fertility. Research on this topic continues, with particular emphasis on the less-developed countries and on discovering how fertility can be affected through social policies (Burch, 1975; Berelson, 1976.) Another concern is to identify complementarities among approaches to fertility analysis taken by investigators from different disciplines (Namboodiri, 1978).

The most significant step toward improving our knowledge of fertility trends and differentials is the World Fertility Survey (WFS). Begun in 1974, and conducted by the International Statistical Institute in collaboration with the United Nations and the International Union for the Scientific Study of Population, the WFS involves nationwide sample surveys of women in 50 to 60 developing countries and a smaller number of developed countries (Caldwell, 1973; Kendall, 1979). Using a standardized interview schedule (at least in the developing countries), the WFS provides data on household structure, socioeconomic background, maternity history, fertility preferences and expectations, contraceptive knowledge and use, marital history, fertility regulation, work history, and husband's background. The WFS should provide the basis for a quantum leap in our understanding of the determinants of fertility (Tsui, et al., 1978; Freedman, 1979a).

Family Planning Programs

Family planning programs have three principal goals: 1) provision of contraceptive technology (services), 2) provision of information about the advantages of family planning and about contraceptive methods, their safety, and their availability, and 3) generation of social support for small family size (Freymann, 1966). Although family programs have existed in developing nations for less than three decades, a recent survey (Huber, 1974) showed that 95 percent of the world's population lived in countries having some form of organized family planning services.

Of the three goals, primary emphasis has been placed on making contraceptives available to potential users. Four organizational strategies have been used for this purpose. The traditional approach has been to establish clinics in which medical personnel prescribe oral contraceptives, insert IUDs, and perform surgical sterilizations and abortions. The assumptions underlying this strategy are that 1) there is a "demand" for contraceptive methods, and 2) if they are made available they will be used (Ravenholt and Chao, 1974). A second and related approach is to integrate family planning services into already established facilities providing maternal and child health services (Taylor and Rosenfield, 1974; Omran and Omran, 1977). With this approach, family planning is promoted in the interest of improving the well-being of mothers and children, and fertility control is frequently down played.

In recent years two rather different approaches to contraceptive distribution have received increasing attention. One is to market contraceptives through a variety of nonmedical commercial outlets or through traveling vendors. This mechanism is typically referred to as "social marketing" or commercial retail sales (CRS) (Altman and Piotrow, 1980). The other is to take contraceptives directly to households, particularly in communities located far from the clinics (Huber, et al., 1975). These community-based distribution (CBD) programs are now being tried in more than a dozen developing countries (Gardner, et al., 1976, 1977).

Less extensive, but nevertheless important, efforts are being made to implement the other two goals of family planning programs. These activities include providing information about contraception and family planning and education designed to produce attitudes and values favoring small families. All such efforts depend on communication strategies (Rogers, 1973; Worrall, 1977), and a wide variety of communication channels have been used to convey family planning messages in less-developed countries. For example, radio, television, and newspaper advertisements carry messages such as "two children are better than three" and "the small family is a happy family." In Thailand the tradition of travelling entertainers and story tellers has been adapted for family planning purposes. And in Pakistan paramedical field workers call on eligible couples to urge them to use contraception and to provide supplies.

The role of social scientists in family planning varies among the different types of programs. It has been least important in clinical settings that are dominated by physicians, nurses, and paramedical workers. In integrated health and family planning programs, as well as CBD and CRS programs, social scientists have played a larger role. Because these services are provided within the contexts of families and communities, social scientists are needed to determine how social structure and interaction processes influence program effectiveness. Sociologists, psychologists, and economists have also identified ways in which people can be motivated to adopt family planning and have designed strategies for family planning communication. Indirectly, social scientists have contributed to family planning programs through their criticisms of simplistic "availability" strategies, arguing that in order to get people to use contraceptive technology, we must first understand the values, norms, and attitudes underlying their approaches to family formation and conjugal relations. In the past few years the trend away from clinic-based family planning to programs rooted in the community has increased the role of social scientists.

Population Education

In recent years there has been a concentrated effort to develop specialized programs of population education in both school and nonschool settings. (Burleson, 1974; UNESCO, 1978). Although the goals of population education vary widely among countries, they are generally designed "to enable learners to acquire the knowledge, skills, attitudes and values necessary (a) to *understand* and (b) to *evaluate* the prevailing population situation, the dynamic forces which have shaped it, and the effect it will have on the present and future welfare of themselves, their families, communities, societies, nations and the world; (c) *to make conscious* and *informed decisions* (based on their understanding and evaluation); and (d) to *respond* (either by an intention to act or by an action itself) to population situations and problems in a conscious and informed manner" (UNESCO, 1978:36).

While more than 50 countries now have population education programs in one form or another, less than half of these countries have initiated comprehensive national programs. In Asia and Latin America a common strategy has been to develop regional workshops for educators with the aim of improving and disseminating curricular materials. Some countries have sponsored national seminars. In other countries population education has been incorporated into various levels of school curricula. In addition to these school-based programs, efforts are evident in some countries to stimulate population education through community, religious, and public welfare organizations (see UNESCO, 1978:28–32).

The principle role of social scientists in these efforts is to provide information and conceptual frameworks for understanding population issues and their bearing on individuals and groups. Only at the university level of the educational system, and in a few nonschool programs, are social scientists typically involved directly in the educational process.

Population Policy

For some years, it has been recognized that population control is unlikely to be achieved without the support of national governments. It is clear that high birth rates in the developing nations cannot be reduced appreciably through social and economic development alone. At the very least, governments in high-fertility countries must permit organized family planning programs to operate. To the extent that governments actively support fertility reduction and control of population growth through the commitment of resources and the formulation of operational strategies, these objectives are increasingly likely to be realized.

In its broadest sense population policy refers to measures and programs that, whether by design or not, are likely to influence population variables (Weiner, et al., 1974:86-87). This discussion is limited to policies related to fertility and, less directly, to population growth.

Social scientists have proposed a wide variety of policy interventions to influence fertility (Davis, 1967; Berelson, 1969, 1977; Ridker, 1976b; Berelson and Haveman, 1979). These suggestions can be grouped into the following general categories: 1) family planning programs, 2) social and economic development strategies, 3) procedural, administrative, and organizational rearrangements at the community level, and 4) official incentives, pressures, or sanctions against undesired fertility behavior or for desired behavior (Berelson, 1978:596). The specific policies that have actually been implemented, however, have concentrated on family planning and development.

National Policies. As of 1978 population policy data were available for 132 developing nations (Nortman and Hofstatter, 1980). Only 35 (27 percent) of those countries had any official policy to reduce the rate of population growth, although they contain 77 percent of the population of the less-developed world. Another 31 countries advocated family planning for nondemographic (primarily health) reasons.

The details of these policies, as well as the extent to which they are enforced, vary widely from one country to the next, as suggested by the following summaries (taken from Nortman and Hofstatter, 1980:Table 6).

Egypt: A presidential decree of 1965 established a national policy to reduce the population growth rate. The target adopted in 1978 was to achieve by 1982 a crude birth rate of 23.6 and a population not to exceed 41 million. The family planning program is emphasizing child spacing for younger women, and in the interests of health, birth limitation for women over age 35. In addition to a revitalized family planning program, plans are to encourage female employment, raise the legal status of women, and redistribute the population toward new urban centers.

Turkey: The official policy, expressed in the 1965 family planning law, advocates voluntary planning for the desired number of children. The program has been publicized through the mass media, but organized national efforts have been modest. Family planning and maternal and child health services are being expanded.

China: The government's goal (1979) is to achieve zero population growth as soon as possible, as early as 1985 and no later than 2000. The state advocates and encourages family planning and equal rights for men and women. Medical and health services are being developed to facilitate planned population growth. The government advocates "later" marriage, "longer" birth intervals, and a one-child norm. Several economic and social incentives and disincentives have been instituted to promote these policies.

The World Population Plan of Action. In 1974 a World Population Plan of Action (WPPA) was adopted at the World Population Conference in Bucharest (United Nations, 1975, Vol. I:155–67). The significance of this document lies in the fact that "the Conference was the first occasion on which the topic of population was considered in an international arena by high ranking government officials" (Miro, 1977:422). The essence of the WPPA consists of a statement of principles and objectives, a set of recommendations for action, and a set of recommendations for implementation. The WPPA addressed a wide range of population and related issues.

Several aspects of the WPPA are of particular relevance for policies on fertility and population growth. First, population and development are assumed to be interrelated, so that population policies are constituent elements of socioeconomic development policies, never substitutes for them. Second, all couples and individuals have the basic right to decide freely and responsibly the number and spacing of their children and to have the information, education, and means to do so. Third, the Plan of Action recognizes the responsibility of each government to set its own policies and devise its own programs of action for dealing with the problems of population and economic and social progress.

The WPPA is, thus, based on the assumption that social and economic development strategies are the key means of resolving population problems (Robinson, 1975; Stamper, 1977; Todaro, 1977). It leaves the details of population policy up to individual governments and upholds the freedom of individual couples to decide how many children they will have. In short, the WPPA does not recommend much in the way of normative goals for national population growth or family size.

Social Science and Population Policy. Few social scientists ever assume policy-making roles in government, although this is more likely in developing countries. Nevertheless, social scientists are frequently employed as consultants to policy makers or are contracted to conduct research on policy issues. For example, most of the research needed by the U.S. Agency for International Development's Office of Population is conducted by contractors such as the Population Council and the Battelle Memorial Institute's Population and Development Policy Program.

Assessment

There is considerable activity by social scientists in the areas of fertility and population growth. The bulk of their work consists of research aimed at discovering factors underlying population trends, the determinants of fertility, the conditions under which family planning programs are or are not successful, and the information needed to develop effective population policies. In a limited way social scientists have also been involved directly in programmatic efforts to deal with population problems.

WHAT HAVE WE ACCOMPLISHED?

Organized efforts to control fertility and population growth in the less-developed nations have been pursued for less than three decades, and in many countries these activities were begun much more recently. Consequently, a major limitation on any assessment of accomplishments is that not enough time has passed for effects on fertility or growth rates to be obvious. Another problem with such an evaluation is that our programmatic efforts to reduce fertility are based on an incomplete understanding of its causes. Fertility control programs have been focused on selected determinants, but, since the effects of other potential causes have not been measured, the results obtained are equivocal. Finally, in addition to birth and growth rates, a number of other outcomes of population control efforts may be equally significant. For example, in the long run, a rise in the age at marriage or an increase in the rate of female labor force participation may be good indicators of the success of current efforts to control future fertility. In short, "accomplishments" should not be viewed too narrowly, nor should we expect to find sizeable effects given the restricted period during which social science knowledge has been applied.

Fertility Rates

The debate over recent fertility trends in the less-developed nations was mentioned earlier in this chapter. The overall conclusion—that fertility has declined in a number of less-developed countries during the past 15 years—is not at issue. Rather, disagreements among investigators center on which countries have shown how much of a drop in the birth rate. (Some of the difference in results is due to the use of different sources of data for the same country, while other variations result from the use of different measures of fertility). In an absolute sense, somewhere between 77 and 84 percent of the world's developing countries showed *some* decrease in fertility between 1965 and 1975 (calculated from data presented by Mauldin and Berelson, 1978 and Tsui and Bogue, 1978). However, the majority of countries (nearly 70 percent) had a relatively small decrease (less than 10 percent over the decade) and most of them (80 percent) still had crude birth rates of at least 35 per thousand of population in 1975 (Mauldin and Berelson, 1978:Table 3). These figures should temper our optimism about accomplishments in lowering fertility in the developing countries, although WFS data suggest substantial declines among younger women in Costa Rica, Colombia, Thailand, The Dominican Republic, and Peru (Kendall, 1979).

Even if we cannot claim much success in reducing birth rates, other results of population control efforts that will eventually influence fertility are more encouraging.

Family Planning Programs

Accomplishments in the area of family planning can be measured in several ways. "Use-prevalence rates" indicate the number or proportion of women in the reproductive ages using particular types of contraceptives. Also important is the number of such women who begin using contraceptives in a given year (typically referred to as "acceptors"). Another indicator of success is the "continuation rate," i.e., the number or proportion of users or acceptors who are still using a given method (or sometimes any method) at a later date. Finally, the impact of a family planning program is frequently measured in terms of changes in ideal family size or the level of knowledge regarding birth control.

Contraceptive prevalence data are available for a relatively small number of developing countries (Nortman, 1977; Nortman and Hofstatter, 1980), although recently there has been an effort to increase coverage through brief surveys designed specifically for this purpose. In addition, results from the WFS will add to both the scope and accuracy of this knowledge. Generally, a relatively low proportion of women in developing nations, especially those under 30 years of age, are using contraception. While the exact figure varies considerably among countries, it rarely exceeds 50 percent (Nortman and Hofstatter, 1980:Table 22). It is also important to note that contraceptive use is more prevalent among women who have already had three or four children.

Data on acceptors are limited, but a few countries show increases during the mid 1970s (Nortman and Hofstatter, 1978:Table 16). A major deficiency in efforts to evaluate progress in family planning programs is the typical lack of information on continuation rates. A recorded increase in the prevalence of users or acceptors may be deceiving unless we know what proportion of these women continue to practice contraception.

KAP surveys, discussed earlier, have been conducted in most countries, often to provide baseline data for eventual evaluation of the effects of family planning programs. Preliminary results from the WFS suggest increased knowledge of contraceptive methods and more favorable attitudes toward lower fertility (Kendall, 1979), although it is uncertain how much of this change can be attributed directly to organized family planning programs.

Often neglected in social scientists' evaluations of the success of family planning programs are institutional barriers that override program efforts. For example, governments may impede the availability of modern contraceptives through customs restrictions, continued high prices, tying accessibility to inadequate medical facilities, rigid application of religious rules regarding women's right to control their own bodily functions, and medical restrictions on abortion, sterilization, and contraceptive prescriptions (Denman, 1980). Clearly, the accomplishments of family planning would be increased if these barriers were removed.

Family Planning versus Development

In recent years numerous studies have been conducted to determine the relative effects on fertility of family planning programs, as opposed to improvements in socioeconomic conditions (e.g., Freedman and Berelson, 1976; Birdsall, 1977; Srikantan, 1977; Cassen, 1978; Mauldin and Berelson, 1978; Ross and Forrest, 1978). Results from such studies provide guidelines for where to invest available resources (primarily money and personnel), so as to achieve the maximum payoff in terms of reducing fertility and population growth (see Berelson and Haveman, 1979).

The most comprehensive analysis conducted to date examines factors associated with fertility change in 94 developing nations for the period 1965-1975 (Mauldin and Berelson, 1978). Using a large number of measures of socioeconomic development and family planning programs and a variety of analytic procedures, these investigators find that social setting variables account for close to two-thirds of the variance in fertility, while program effort adds another 15-20 percent to the explained variance. Although they caution the reader that these results should not be "taken too seriously" (because of limitations of the data and the analytic procedures), Mauldin and Berelson (1978:123) conclude that "(1) the joint effect is more effective than either alone; (2) program effort makes a substantial difference, not merely a trivial one; (3) for policy purposes, given the wide disparity in developmental and family planning funding, great precision is not needed for economic judgments as to policy; and (4) from the scientific standpoint, it is in any case not attainable at this time." In other words, both socioeconomic development and family planning program effort can be effective strategies for reducing fertility, especially when they are implemented together.

Population Policy

During the 1970s an increasing number of governments in the developing world adopted official population policies (Nortman, 1977:4-6). These policies range from pronatalist stands in a few countries to coercive efforts to control fertility (as exemplified by Indira Ghandi's unsuccessful attempt to institute mandatory sterilization in India.) Although only with time can we determine the effectiveness of these policies, it is safe to say that in most cases existing policies do not deal directly with the causes of high fertility (Davis, 1967) or cannot be implemented on a large scale because governments lack the necessary resources.

The 1974 Bucharest conference was the first attempt to formulate a general policy on population growth among developing countries, and it has been hailed as "a turning point in the consideration of population problems" (Urquidi, 1967: 91). The resulting World Population Plan of Action, with its emphasis on reducing fertility and population growth through socioeconomic development, has been praised by some (Wahren, 1979), while others contend that "the Bucharest judgment that family planning effort is of little consequence is itself of little consequence" (Mauldin and Berelson, 1978:124).

Whether or not one agrees with the WPPA recommendations, the Bucharest conference appears to have had a significant political impact (Miro, 1977). A number of national, regional, and world conferences have been devoted to development of strategies for implementing the WPPA. International donors are reconsidering funding priorities, although the largest share of resources is still assigned to family planning programs. A number of governments are attempting to broaden their approaches to population policy. Nevertheless, Miro (1977:437) concludes that "disparity continues to exist between the declared aims of the Plan and the treatment of Population matters in other spheres of activity within intergovernmental bodies, particularly those of the United Nations." In short, the WPPA is still a long way from effective and widespread implementation.

Assessment

While worldwide population control is far from being accomplished, there is evidence of progress toward this end. Fertility rates do appear to be declining in the large majority of developing nations, although major reductions are evident for only a few of them. Organized family planning programs are increasing in number and level of effort, and governments are becoming more cognizant of the need for explicit and effective population policies. Both family planning and development strategies appear to have an effect on fertility, though the debate continues as to which of the two should receive highest priority. However, in spite of these accomplishments, the spector of Malthusian tragedy remains with us.

WHERE ARE WE GOING?

There are many ways in which sociologists and other social scientists can contribute to more effective strategies to lower fertility and population growth rates. Basic research on the determinants of fertility will continue to be a high priority, but the emphasis must be shifted. We cannot continue to "reinvent the wheel" through repeated studies that accomplish nothing more than verifying what we already know. Rather, we must focus our attention on synthesizing available knowledge and discovering causal connections among individual and organizational characteristics, social processes, and reproductive behavior. Such efforts will point to topics that truly require additional research. Recent pleas for increased attention to motivational factors (Ryder, 1976; Davis, 1977; Freedman, 1979b), the social dynamics of local communities (McNicoll, 1978), and relationships between parents and children in different types of economies (Caldwell, 1976, 1978) exemplify these innovative directions for research.

Additional work is needed to determine how family planning programs can be made more effective. Many institutional barriers inhibit dissemination of contraceptives and the flow of information about family planning (Mamdani, 1972; Micklin, 1976), and those influences must be counteracted. Efforts to take family planning programs directly to communities and households cannot succeed without greater knowledge of the social and cultural contexts within which these services are offered.

Population policies currently lack specificity and realistic means for implementation. Until recently they were composed largely of family planning supports with little attention to the principal objective of improving societal welfare (Demerath, 1976). We are now beginning to recognize that population and development policies must be integrated through institutional linkages (Etzioni, 1979). Moreover, increased attention must be given to formulating population policies in terms of manipulable variables that have an effect on fertility (Ridker, 1976a).

Social scientists frequently feel that their work is ignored by policy makers. If this is the case, perhaps it is because we have not paid enough attention to translating our results from conceptual jargon and methodological caveats into concise statements that can be acted upon. Sociologists have a wealth of useful knowledge to contribute to efforts to resolve the critical problem of world population growth, but our voices will not be heard as long as we choose to speak only among ourselves.

REFERENCES AND SUGGESTED READINGS

Altman, D.L. and P.T. Piotrow. 1980. "Social marketing: Does it work?" *Population Reports,* Series J, No. 21. Washington, D.C.: U.S. Government Printing Office.

Back, K.W. 1967. "New frontiers in demography and social psychology." *Demography* 4:90–97.

Beaver, S.E. 1975. *Demographic Transition Theory Reinterpreted.* Lexington, Mass.: D.C. Heath.

Ben-Porath, Y. and F. Welch. 1976. "Do sex preferences really matter?" *Quarterly Journal of Economics* 9(May):285–307.

Berelson, B. 1966. "KAP studies on fertility." In *Family Planning and Population Programs,* edited by B. Berelson, et al., pp. 655–68. Chicago: University of Chicago Press.

_____. 1969. "Beyond family planning." *Studies in Family Planning* 38(Feb): 1–16.

* _____. 1976. "Social science research on population: A review." *Population and Development Review* 2(June):219–66.

Berelson gives an overview of social science knowledge on population and its bearing on population policy. He summarizes "what we know" and points to a number of topics for future research. He argues that selection of new studies should be based on criteria of substantive importance: doability, specificity, number of years before results can be expected, cumulativeness, and policy responsiveness.

_____. 1977. "Paths to fertility reduction: The policy cube." *Family Planning Perspectives* 9(Sept/Oct):214–19.

_____. 1978. "Prospects and programs for fertility reduction: What? Where?" *Population and Development Review* 4(Dec):579–616.

Berelson, B. and R.H. Haveman. 1979. "On the efficient allocation of resources for fertility reduction." *International Family Planning Perspectives* 5(Dec): 133–42.

Birdsall, N. 1977. "Analytical approaches to the relationships of population growth and development." *Population and Development Review* 3(Mar/June):63–102.

Bogue, D.J. 1969. *Principles of Demography.* New York: John Wiley & Sons.

Bogue, D.J. and A.O. Tsui. 1979a. "A reply to Paul Demeny's 'On the End of the Population Explosion'." *Population and Development Review* 5(Sept): 479–94.

_____. 1979b. "Zero world population growth?" *The Public Interest* (Spring): 99–113.

Bongaarts, J. 1976. "Intermediate fertility variables and marital fertility." *Population Studies* 30(July):227–41.

_____. 1978. "A framework for analyzing the proximate determinants of 'Fertility'." *Population and Development Review* 4(Mar):105–32.

_____. 1980. "Does malnutrition affect fecundity? A summary of evidence." *Science* 208(May 9):564–69.

Brown, L.R. 1978. *The Twenty-Ninth Day: Accommodating Human Needs and Numbers to the Earth's Resources.* New York: W.W. Norton.

Bulatao, R.A. 1979. "Further evidence on the transition in the value of children." Papers of the East-West Population Institute, No. 60-B. Honolulu: East-West Center Press.

Burch, T.K. 1975. "Theories of fertility as guides to population policy." *Social Forces* 54(Sept):126–38.

Burleson, N. 1974. "Population education: Problems and perspectives." *Educational Documentation and Information: Bulletin of the International Bureau of Education* 193:entire issue.

Butz, W.P. and J.P. Habicht. 1976. "The effects of nutrition and health on fertility: Hypotheses, evidence, and interventions." In *Population and Development: The Search for Selective Interventions,* edited by R.G. Ridker, pp. 210–38. Baltimore: The Johns Hopkins University Press.

Caldwell, J.C. 1973. "The world fertility survey: Problems and possibilities." Occasional Papers, No. 2, World Fertility Survey. Voorburg, Netherlands: International Statistical Institute.

_____. 1976. "Toward a restatement of demographic transition theory." *Population and Development Review* 2(Sept/Dec):321–66.

_____. 1978. "A theory of fertility: From high plateau to destabilization." *Population and Development Review* 4(Dec):553–77.

Caldwell, J.C., H.M. Choldin, L.F. Noe, D.L. Sills, and F.F. Stephan. 1970. *A Manual for Surveys of Fertility and Family Planning: Knowledge, Attitudes, and Practices.* New York: The Population Council.

Cassen, R.H. 1978. "Current trends in population change and their causes." *Population and Development Review* 4(June):331–53.

Catton, W.R., Jr. 1980. *Overshoot: The Ecological Basis of Revolutionary Change.* Urbana, Ill.: University of Illinois Press.

Coale, A.J. 1975. "The demographic transition." In *The Population Debate: Dimensions and Perspectives.* Papers of the World Population Conference, Bucharest, 1974. Vol. I. Population Studies No. 57. New York: Department of Economic and Social Affairs.

Cochrane, S.H. 1979. *Fertility and Education: What do we really know?* Baltimore: The Johns Hopkins University Press.

Coombs, L.C. 1978. "How many children do couples really want?" *Family Planning Perspectives* 10(Sept/Oct):303–8.

Davis, K. 1945. "The world demographic transition." *Annals of the American Academy of Political and Social Science* 273(Jan):1–11.

_____. 1967. "Population policy: Will current programs succeed?" *Science* 158 (Nov 10):730–39.

_____. 1976. "The world's population crisis." In *Contemporary Social Problems,* 4th ed., edited by R.K. Merton and R. Nisbet, pp. 265–303. New York: Harcourt Brace Jovanovich.

_____. 1977. "Population policy and the theory of reproductive motivation." *Economic Development and Cultural Change* 25(Supplement):159–79.

Davis, K. and J. Blake. 1956. "Social structure and fertility: An analytic framework." *Economic Development and Cultural Change* 4(Apr):211–35.

Demeny, P. 1974. "The populations of the underdeveloped countries." *Scientific American* 231(Sept):148–59.

_____. 1979a. "On the end of the population explosion." *Population and Development Review* 5(Mar):141–62.

_____. 1979b. "On the end of the population explosion: A rejoinder." *Population and Development Review* 5(Sept):495–504.

Demerath, N.J. 1976. *Birth Control and Foreign Policy: The Alternatives to Family Planning.* New York: Harper & Row.

Denman, D. 1980. Personal communication.

Dixon, R.B. 1975. "Women's rights and fertility." *Reports on Population and Family Planning* 17(Jan):1–20.

_____. 1976. "The role of rural women: Female seclusion, economic production, and reproductive choice." In *Population and Development: The Search for Selective Interventions,* edited by R.G. Ridker, pp. 290–321. Baltimore: The Johns Hopkins University Press.

Eberstadt, N. 1980. "Recent declines in fertility in less developed countries and what 'Population Planners' may learn from them." *World Development* 8 (Jan):37–60.

Espenshade, T.J. 1977. "The value and cost of children." *Population Bulletin* 32 (Apr):3–47.

Etzioni, A. 1979. "Beyond integration, toward guidability." In *World Population and Development: Challenges and Prospects,* edited by P.M. Hauser, pp. 538–65. Syracuse, N.Y.: Syracuse University Press.

Fawcett, J.T. and M.H. Bornstein. 1973. "Modernization, individual modernity, and fertility." In *Psychological Perspectives on Population,* edited by J.T. Fawcett, pp. 106–31. New York: Basic Books.

Freedman, R. 1963. "Norms for family size in underdeveloped areas." *Proceedings of the Royal Society, Series B* 159:220–34.

_____. 1975. *The Sociology of Human Fertility*. New York: John Wiley & Sons.

_____. 1979a. "Issues in the comparative analysis of world fertility data." Papers of the East-West Population Institute, No. 62. Honolulu: East-West Center Press.

_____. 1979b. "Theories of fertility decline: A reappraisal." *Social Forces* 58 (Sept):1–17.

Freedman, R. and B. Berelson. 1976. "The record of family planning programs." *Studies in Family Planning* 7(Jan):1–40.

Freedman, R. and L.C. Coombs. 1974. *Cross-Cultural Comparisons: Data on Two Factors in Fertility Behavior*. New York: The Population Council.

Freedman, R., A.I. Hermalin, and M. Chang. 1975. "Do statements about desired family size predict fertility? The case of Taiwan, 1967–1970." *Demography* 12(Aug):407–16.

Frejka, T. 1974. *The Future of Population Growth*. New York: John Wiley & Sons.

Freymann, M.W. 1966. "Organizational structure in family planning programs." In *Family Planning and Population Programs: A Review of World Developments*, edited by B. Berelson, et al., pp. 321–34. Chicago: University of Chicago Press.

Gardner, J.S., M.T. Mertaugh, M. Micklin, and G.W. Duncan, eds. 1977. *Village and Household Availability of Contraceptives: Africa/West Asia*. Seattle: Battelle Human Affairs Research Centers.

Gardner, J.S., R.J. Wolff, D. Gillespie, and G.W. Duncan, eds. 1976. *Village and Household Availability of Contraceptives: Southeast Asia*. Seattle: Battelle Human Affairs Research Centers.

Goldberg, D. 1976. "Residential location and fertility." In *Population and Development: The Search for Selective Interventions*, edited by R.K. Ridker, pp. 387–407. Baltimore: The Johns Hopkins University Press.

Goode, W.J. 1963. *World Revolution and Family Patterns*. New York: The Free Press.

Graff, H.J. 1979. "Literacy, education, and fertility, past and present: A critical review." *Population and Development Review* 5(Mar):105–40.

Hatcher, R.A., G.K. Stewart, F. Guest, R. Finkelstein, and C. Godwin. 1976. *Contraceptive Technology 1976–1977*, 8th rev. ed. New York: Irvington.

*Hauser, P.M., ed. 1979. *World Population and Development: Challenges and Prospects*. Syracuse, N.Y.: Syracuse University Press.
     This is a collection of papers covering a variety of aspects of population and of social and economic development. Topics discussed include recent demographic trends, societal and environmental consequences of population change, programs for population control, and population policies.

Hawthorn, G. 1970. *The Sociology of Ferility*. London: Collier-Macmillan.

Heer, D.M. and D.O. Smith. 1968. "Mortality level, desired family size, and population increase." *Demography* 5:104–21.

Henry, A. and P.T. Piotrow. 1979. "Age at marriage and fertility." Population Reports, Series M., No. 4. Washington, D.C.: U.S. Government Printing Office.

Hill, R., J.M. Stycos, and K.W. Back. 1959. *The Family and Population Control*.

Chapel Hill: The University of North Carolina Press.

Hoffman, L.W. and M.L. Hoffman. 1973. "The value of children to parents." In *Psychological Perspective on Population,* edited by J.T. Fawcett, pp. 19–76. New York: Basic Books.

Holsinger, D.B. and J.D. Kasarda. 1976. "Education and human fertility: Sociological perspectives." In *Population and Development: The Search for Selective Interventions,* edited by R.G. Ridker, pp. 154–81. Baltimore: The Johns Hopkins University Press.

Huber, S.C. 1974. "World survey of family planning services and practice." In *Survey of World Needs in Family Planning,* pp. 57–72. London: International Planned Parenthood Federation.

Huber, S.C., P.T. Piotrow, M. Potts, B. Chir, S.L. Isaacs, and R.T. Ravenholt. 1975. "Contraceptive distribution: Taking supplies to villages and households." *Population Reports,* Series J., No. 5. Washington, D.C.: U.S. Government Printing Office.

Kahl, J.A. 1968. *The Measurement of Modernism: A Study of Values in Brazil and Mexico.* Austin: University of Texas Press.

Kasarda, J.D. 1971. "Economic structure and fertility: A comparative analysis." *Demography* 8(Aug):307–18.

Kendall, Sir M. 1979. "The world fertility survey: Current status and findings." *Population Reports,* Series M., No. 3:73–103. Washington, D.C.: U.S. Government Printing Office.

King, T., et al. 1974. *Population Policies and Economic Development.* A World Bank Staff Report. Baltimore: The Johns Hopkins University Press.

Kirk, D. 1979. "World population and birth rates: Agreements and disagreements." *Population and Development Review* 5(Sept):387–404.

Mamdani, M. 1972. *The Myth of Population Control: Family, Caste, and Class in an Indian Village.* New York: Monthly Review Press.

Mauldin, W.P. 1965. "Fertility studies: Knowledge, attitude and practice." *Studies in Family Planning* 7(June):1–10.

_____. 1978. "Patterns of fertility decline in developing countries." *Studies in Family Planning* 9(Apr):54–61.

*Mauldin, W.P. and B. Berelson. 1978. "Conditions of fertility decline in developing countries, 1965–1975." *Studies in Family Planning* 9:90–147.

The authors provide a comprehensive review of the relative effects of family planning and development strategies for reducing population growth in 94 less-developed countries. A number of measures of family planning effort and socioeconomic development are analyzed using a variety of statistical procedures. Results indicate that both strategies have a substantial affect on fertility decline and that the most effective policy approach is to combine strong family program effort with socioeconomic progress.

McGreevey, W.P. and N. Birdsall. 1974. *The Policy Relevance of Recent Social Research on Fertility.* Occasional Monograph Series, No. 2. Washington, D.C.: Interdisciplinary Communications Program, Smithsonian Institution.

McNicoll, G. 1978. "On fertility policy research." *Population and Development Review* 4(Dec):681–93.

Micklin, M. 1969. "Urban life and differential fertility: Specification of an aspect of the theory of the demographic transition." *The Sociological Quarterly* 10(Fall):480-500.

_____. 1976. "Contraceptive distribution and family planning at community and household levels: Institutional barriers and evaluation strategies." In *Village and Household Availability of Contraceptives: Southeast Asia,* edited by J.S. Gardner, R.J. Wolff, D. Gillespie, and G.W. Duncan, pp. 19–29. Seattle: Battelle Human Affairs Research Centers.

_____. 1980. "Population and demography." In *Sociology: An Introduction,* 2nd ed., edited by R. McGee, pp. 256–88. New York: Holt, Rinehart and Winston.

Micklin, M. and P.J.H. Marnane. 1975. "The differential evaluation of 'large' and 'small' families in rural Colombia: Implications for family planning." *Social Biology* 22(Spring):44–59.

Miller, K.A. and A. Inkeles. 1974. "Modernity and acceptance of family limitation in four developing countries." *Journal of Social Issues* 30:167–88.

Miro, C. 1977. "The world population plan of action: A political instrument whose potential has not been realized." *Population and Development Review* 3(Dec):421–42.

Mueller, E. 1972a. "Economic cost and value of children: Conceptualization and measurement." In *The Satisfactions and Costs of Children: Theories, Concepts, Methods,* edited by J.T. Fawcett, pp. 174–205. Honolulu: East-West Population Institute, East-West Center Press.

_____. 1972b. "Economic motives for family limitation: A study conducted in Taiwan." *Population Studies* 26(Nov):383–403.

_____. 1976. "The economic value of children in peasant agriculture." In *Population and Development: The Search for Selective Interventions,* edited by R.G. Ridker, pp. 98-153. Baltimore: The Johns Hopkins University Press.

Namboodiri, N.K. 1978. "On fertility analysis: Where sociologists, economists and biologists meet." In *Major Social Issues: A Multidisciplinary View,* edited by J.M. Yinger and S.J. Cutler, pp. 295–309. New York: The Free Press.

Nortman, D. 1977. "Changing contraceptive patterns: A global perspective." *Population Bulletin* 32(Aug):3–37.

Nortman, D. and E. Hofstatter. 1980. *Population and Family Planning Programs,* 10th ed. New York: The Population Council.

Omran, A.R. and K.R. Omran. 1977. "Family planning and health: The vital connection." In *Village and Household Availability of Contraceptives: Africa/West Asia,* edited by J.S. Gardner, M.T. Mertaugh, M. Micklin, and G.W. Duncan, pp. 35–58. Seattle: Battelle Human Affairs Research Centers.

Oppong, C. and E. Haavio-Mannila. 1979. "Women, population, and development." In *World Population and Development: Challenges and Prospects,* edited by P.M. Hauser, pp. 440–85. Syracuse, N.Y.: Syracuse University Press.

Partan, D.G. 1973. *Population in the United Nations System: Developing the Legal Capacity and Programs of UN Agencies.* Durham, N.C.: Rule of Law Press.

Poffenberger, T. and K. Sebaly. 1976. "The Socialization of Family Size Values: Youth and Family Planning in an Indian Village." Paper No. 12. University of Michigan, Ann Arbor, Center for South and Southeast Asian Studies.

*Population Council. 1975–76. *Population and Development Review.* New York: The Population Council.

This journal contains articles by sociologists, economists, demographers, political scientists, anthropologists, and policy analysts reflecting the latest thought on problems of population and development. It also publishes useful notes and commentaries, descriptions of data sources, official documents, and abstracts of current literature.

Population Reference Bureau. 1976. *World Population Growth and Response, 1965–1975: A Decade of Global Action.* Washington, D.C.: Population Reference Bureau.

Preston, S.H. 1975. "Health programs and population growth." *Population and Development Review* 1(2):189–200.

_____. 1978. "The next fifteen years in demographic analysis." In *Social Demography,* edited by K.E. Taueber, L.L. Bumpass, and J.A. Sweet, pp. 299–313. New York: Academic Press.

Ravenholt, R.T. and J. Chao. 1974. "Availability of family planning services: The key to rapid fertility reduction." *Family Planning Perspectives* 6(Fall): 217–23.

Repetto, R.G. 1972. "Son preference and fertility behavior in developing countries." *Studies in Family Planning* 3(4):70–76.

_____. 1979. *Economic Equality and Fertility in Developing Countries.* Baltimore, Md.: The Johns Hopkins University Press.

Revelle, R., ed. 1971. *Rapid Population Growth: Consequences and Policy Implications.* Baltimore, Md.: The Johns Hopkins University Press.

Rich, W. 1973. *Smaller Families Through Social and Economic Progress.* Washington, D.C.: Overseas Development Council.

Ridker, R.G. 1976a. "Perspectives on population policy and research." In *Population and Development: The Search for Selective Interventions,* edited by R.G. Ridker, pp. 1–35. Baltimore, Md.: The Johns Hopkins University Press.

*_____. ed. 1976b. *Population and Development: The Search for Selective Interventions.* Baltimore, Md.: The Johns Hopkins University Press.

This multidisciplinary collection of papers assesses the effects of socioeconomic factors on fertility and population growth. Factors examined include income levels and distribution; costs and value of children; education; nutrition, health, and mortality; the roles of women; mass media and consumer goods; and residential location. Each chapter assesses available evidence and suggests research and/or policy interventions that will improve our ability to control fertility and population growth.

Ridker, R.G. and E.W. Cecelski. 1979. "Resources, environment, and population: The nature of future limits." *Population Bulletin* 34(Aug):3–41. Washington, D.C.: U.S. Government Printing Office.

Robinson, W.C. 1975. *Population and Development Planning.* New York: The Population Council.

Rogers, E.M. 1973. *Communication Strategies for Family Planning.* New York:

The Free Press.

Ross, J.A. and J.D. Forrest. 1978. "The demographic assessment of family planning programs: A bibliographic essay." *Population Index* 44(Jan):8–27.

Ryder, N.B. 1976. "Some sociological suggestions concerning the reduction of fertility in developing countries." Papers of the East-West Population Institute No. 37. Honolulu: East-West Center Press.

_____. 1978. "Some problems of fertility research." In *Social Demography*, edited by K.E. Taueber, L.L. Bumpass, and J.A. Sweet, pp. 3–13. New York: Academic Press.

Schlutz, T.P. 1976. "Interrelationships between mortality and fertility." In *Population and Development: The Search for Selective Interventions*, edited by R.G. Ridker, pp. 239–89. Baltimore: The Johns Hopkins University Press.

Simmons, A.B. 1974. "Ambivalence toward small families in rural Latin America." *Social Biology* 21(Summer):127–43.

Simon, J.L. 1976. "Income, wealth and their distribution as policy tasks in fertility control." In *Population and Development: The Search for Selective Interventions*, edited by R.G. Ridker, pp. 36–76. Baltimore: The Johns Hopkins University Press.

Srikantan, K.S. 1977. *The Family Planning Program in the Socioeconomic Context*. New York: The Population Council.

Stamper, B.M. 1977. *Population and Planning in Developing Nations: A Review of Sixty Development Plans for the 1970s*. New York: The Population Council.

Taylor, H.C., Jr. and A.G. Rosenfield. 1974. "A family planning program based on maternal and child health services." *American Journal of Obstetrics and Gynecology* 120:733–45.

Teitelbaum, M.S. 1975. "Relevance of demographic transition theory for developing countries." *Science* 188(May 2):420–25.

Todaro, M.P. 1977. "Development policy and population growth: A framework for planners." *Population and Development Review* 3(Mar/June):23–43.

Tsui, A.O. and D.J. Bogue. 1978. "Declining world fertility: Trends, causes, and implications." *Population Bulletin* 33(Oct):3–55.

Tsui, A.O., D.J. Bogue, and D.P. Hogan. 1978. *A Work Plan for a Family Planning Analysis of World Fertility Survey Data*. Chicago: Community and Family Study Center, University of Chicago.

UNESCO. 1978. *Population Education: A Contemporary Concern*. Educational Studies and Documents, New Series, No. 28. Paris: United Nations Educational, Scientific, and Cultural Organization.

United Nations. 1973. *The Determinants and Consequences of Population Trends: New Summary of Findings on Interaction of Demographic, Economic, and Social Factors. Volume I*. Population Studies, No. 50. New York: Department of Economic and Social Affairs.

_____. 1975. *The Population Debate: Dimensions and Perspectives*. Papers of the World Population Conference, Bucharest, 1974. Vols. I. and II. Population Studies, No. 57. New York: Department of Economic and Social Affairs.

_____. 1977. *Levels and Trends of Fertility throughout the World, 1950–1970*.

Population Studies, No. 59. New York: Department of Economic and Social Affairs.

U.S. Bureau of the Census. 1978. *World Population: 1977. Recent Demographic Estimates for the Countries and Regions of the World.* Washington, D.C.: U.S. Government Printing Office.

Urquidi, V. 1976. "On implementing the world population plan of action." *Population and Development Review* 2(Mar):91–99.

van der Tak, J., C. Haub, and E. Murphy. 1979. "Our population predicament: A new look." *Population Bulletin* 34(Dec):3–41, 46–48.

Viederman, S. 1974. "Towards a broader definition of population education." *International Social Science Journal* 26:315–27.

Wahren, C. 1979. "Population: The forgotten factor." *People* 6(2):8–10.

Ward, B. and R. Dubos. 1976. *Only One Earth.* New York: W.W. Norton.

Ware, H. 1974. "Ideal family size." Occasional Papers, No. 13, World Fertility Survey. Voorberg, Netherlands: International Statistical Institute.

Weiner, M., et al. 1974. *In Search of Population Policy: Views from the Developing World.* Washington, D.C.: National Academy of Sciences.

Williamson, N.E. 1976. *Sons or Daughters: A Cross-Cultural Survey of Parental Preferences.* Beverly Hills, Calif.: Sage.

_____. 1978. "Boys or girls? Parents' preferences and sex control." *Population Bulletin* 33(Jan):3–35.

Worrall, R.P. 1977. "Communicating population and family planning." *Population Bulletin* 31(Feb):3–39.

Yaukey, D. 1969. "On theorizing about fertility." *The American Sociologist* 4 (May):100–4.

22 ENERGY CONSERVATION

Frederick H. Buttel and Michael R. Hattery

Energy conservation is one of the major challenges for applied sociology and applied social science generally. The whole history of U.S. socioeconomic development has occurred in a milieu of energy extravagance. Because energy has always been inexpensive and abundant, U.S. economic institutions have become dependent on prolifigate energy use. An applied sociology of energy conservation, then, must involve some fundamental changes in production, consumption, and political institutions.

WHAT ARE THE PROBLEMS?

The Meaning of Energy Conservation

In many ways, energy consumption is a deceptively simple goal—using less. Applied social scientists have a remarkably diverse set of images of what energy conservation entails. On one hand, we can distinguish between *input-altering* and *output-altering* energy conservation. Input-altering energy conservation entails delivering the same mix of goods and services in the society with less energy by changing the kinds of inputs used in production and consumption activities. A good example of input-altering conservation is to use home insulation, which allows the same level of ambient heat with less fuel input. Another example is the use of more efficient central-station generators in electrical power production. Output-altering energy conservation involves shifts in the mix of goods and services produced, from those that embody high energy intensity to those that have less heavy energy requirements. Such conservation would mean changes in life styles and production patterns. For example, the extensive use of passenger cars could be supplanted by more use of public transportation, or the waste heat from electrical energy production could be used to heat water through a process called "cogeneration" (Craig, et al., 1976).

Another approach to distinguishing between forms of energy conservation is to ask whether these actions are intended only to increase economic efficiency or attempt to go beyond that criterion. A large variety of energy-conserving measures could be implemented in households and firms to reduce costs or expenditures. In this case energy conservation is "an act of enlightened self-interest" (Demand and Conservation Panel, CONAES, 1978). Because the economic benefits of these energy conservation activities—reduced energy bills—exceed their costs, they are economically efficient. If conservation actions were all so beneficial, encouraging energy conservation would be a rather straightforward problem. However, many observers argue that energy conservation must go beyond the criterion of economic efficiency. It is frequently suggested that a major goal of energy conservation should be to establish U.S. self-sufficiency in energy (especially petroleum), so that the country will not be vulnerable to cutoffs or price fluctuations wrought by the OPEC cartel and could reduce its balance-of-payments deficits for imported oil (Lindberg, 1977). Watt, et al. (1977) and Illich (1974) both point out that the high level of energy and materials used in "overdeveloped" societies such as the United States leads to "suffocation" and actual *deterioration* of the quality of life. They argue for vastly reduced energy use patterns that go far beyond the criterion of economic efficiency. Finally, many social scientists have come to believe that the efforts of individual families or firms to maximize their economic welfare do not lead to economic efficiency in the use of energy and other natural resources. This is because, among other factors, the price system cannot adequately take account of the value of nonrenewable resources to future generations. The price system tends to undervalue scarce nonrenewable resources, so that there is a powerful incentive to rapidly exhaust these resources in the short term. Therefore, it is argued that conservation should go far beyond the level that can be achieved by firms and households seeking to optimize their profits or welfare.

These rival images of energy conservation belie the apparent simplicity of the concept and must be considered when we examine the available research literature on applied conservation efforts. Before we examine that literature, however, we will first review the economic and resource problems that make conservation a desirable option. We will then discuss some of the constraints or tradeoffs involved in implementing conservation strategies.

The Case for Energy Conservation

The call for massive energy conservation is a rather recent phenomenon, having begun barely ten years ago. Why is conservation becoming such a dominant national concern—if only in lip service—when such a plea was almost never uttered in the 1950s and early 1960s? The emergence of energy conservation reflects an evolving trend toward high dependence on nonrenewable energy resources. The culmination of this trend was the rapidly deteriorating energy situation of the 1970s.

Less than 100 years ago over 90 percent of the energy used in the United States came from renewable energy resources, principally wood. Presently, about 94 percent of total energy consumption is derived from three major nonrenewable sources: petroleum, natural gas, and coal (Hayes, 1976). Although there is vigorous debate as to how much of these three nonrenewable energy resources can eventually be recovered, they are all ultimately finite. The rationale for energy conservation is that it can extend considerably the time over which nonrenewable energy resources can be stretched to meet production and consumption needs, giving us more time to develop renewable sources such as solar power.

The rapidly changing energy situation during the past seven or eight years has dramatically hastened the call for conservation. U.S. production of petroleum and natural gas peaked in 1970 and 1974, respectively (Foley, 1976) and is now declining in absolute terms. As a result, energy imports (especially oil from the Middle East) have rapidly expanded. The Arab oil embargo, along with diminished domestic production of petroleum and natural gas, has produced both escalating prices and insecurity of supply.

The supplies of the two principal fossil fuels used in the United States—petroleum and natural gas—appear to be shaky beyond 1990 (Kent, 1976). Coal and nuclear power are often cited as substitute energy sources, but both have decided disadvantages that make the case for conservation even more compelling. Coal is the largest domestic energy resource, and various projections suggest that U.S. coal reserves might be sufficient for 400 years (Holdren, 1976). However, the environmental consequences of accelerated coal production would be staggering (Steinhart and Steinhart, 1974). Coal mining techniques such as strip mining are extremely destructive to forest and arid ecosystems, and the combustion of coal involves massive air pollution. Further, it is doubtful whether coal production can be increased at a rate sufficient to compensate for declining domestic production of petroleum and natural gas (Hayes, 1976).

Nuclear power is frequently presumed to be a cornerstone of any strategy to compensate for declining petroleum and natural gas production. But nuclear power also has a number of shortcomings. The uranium supplies that make nuclear fission possible are finite. Perhaps the most intractable problems of the nuclear option are safety and expense, however. Nuclear power production involves potentially serious risks to human health and safety as a consequence of reactor accidents and waste disposal (Berger, 1976). The capital investment requirements for nuclear power are massive. Lovins (1976, 1977) and Kent (1976) suggest that extensive reliance on nuclear power would divert gigantic amounts of investment capital from already tight capital markets. Many observers are also suggesting that nuclear power is more expensive than coal-generated electricity or electricity from solar or other renewable sources (Lovins, 1977). Finally, like coal, it is quite unlikely that nuclear power production can be increased rapidly enough to make up for anticipated shortfalls of petroleum and natural gas toward the end of the next decade. Thus, both coal and nuclear power are decidedly limited in their ability to compensate for decreased availability of conventional fossil fuels.

The ultimate case for energy conservation is the fact that without conservation, our national energy consumption will continue to increase rapidly each year (Ophuls, 1977; Ford Foundation Energy Policy Project, 1974). Although annual percentage changes have fluctuated greatly, U.S. energy consumption has grown at an exponential rate since World War II. The average annual percentage increase since that time has been 3.5 percent, and the average growth rate from 1964–1973 (the ten years prior to the OPEC oil embargo) was 4.5 percent. Two independent energy forecasting studies (Edison Electric Institute, 1975; Ford Foundation Energy Policy Project, 1974) have concluded that without extensive conservation or rapid deployment of renewable energy sources such as solar power, the average annual percentage increase in U.S. energy consumption from the present to 2000 will be roughly 3.5 percent. This continued high rate of energy growth would necessarily increase our environmental problems and intensify the risks of nuclear power deployment. In contrast, energy conservation can "stretch" existing reserves of petroleum and natural gas as well as diminish the threats of coal and nuclear power to human health.

Energy and Economic Growth

The United States is not the only advanced industrial society that is highly dependent on inanimate fossil fuels. It has long been recognized that the production and consumption activities of industrialized societies require high levels of energy inputs (Cottrell, 1955). Figure 22.1 provides dramatic evidence of the intimate association between energy use and economic growth or development. It shows a substantial linear relationship between per capita energy consumption and per capita Gross National Product (GNP).

This well-known relationship between economic growth and energy consumption implies that an aggressive energy conservation program might involve some diminution of economic well-being. If continued growth in energy consumption is required to support further economic growth, conservation is likely to be opposed by groups whose economic fortunes are tied to growth. As we shall see below, however, there is growing social scientific awareness of the fact that growth in energy consumption can be "decoupled" from growth in economic activity. Energy conservation need not result in deterioration of living standards or quality of life. Nevertheless, it is important to recognize that energy conservation may conflict with economic goal of growth, particularly if there is little change in the basic economic structure of the nation.

Economic and Spatial Structure

Compared to most other developed Western societies, the spatial structure of U.S. cities and the basic structure of the U.S. economy are highly energy intensive (Darmstadter, et al., 1977). U.S. cities are where the bulk of the U.S. population resides and the vast majority of energy consumption occurs. Our urban systems have been increasingly characterized by "the enormous growth of sprawling suburbs, the concentration of financial and managerial offices in the city center, the separation of work and homes with its consequent need to commute long distances, and the almost complete dependence on the automobile for movement" (Walker and Large, 1975:969). In addition, the principal symbol of urban growth—the large, single-family detached house, typically in the suburbs—tends to be a voracious energy consumer. In the short term, these energy-consuming spatial relationships and urban forms are largely fixed. Sunk investments in housing, highways, and places of employment cannot be rapidly discarded in the interest of energy conservation. These features will definitely constrain any programs for energy conservation.

Figure 22.1 Energy Consumption and GNP Per Capita

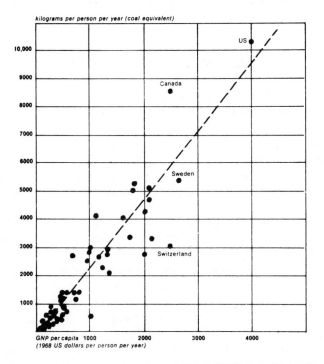

Source: Reprinted by permission from *THE LIMITS TO GROWTH: A Report for The Club of Rome's Project on the Predicament of Mankind*, by Donella H. Meadows, Dennis L. Meadows, Jorgen Randers, William W. Behrens III. A Potomac Associates book published by Universe Books, N.Y., 1972. Graphics by Potomac Associates.

The historical trajectory of growth in the U.S. economy has been closely tied to the success of a handful of energy-intensive industries. Walker and Large (1975) noted that three mutually-reinforcing sectors of increased energy use and corporate expansion have been at the heart of U.S. growth and prosperity: the automobile, urban development, and energy-intensive manufacturing. The automobile has largely supplanted less profitable and less energy-intensive public transport systems. It has also facilitated the dispersal of urban populations to the suburbs. Suburbanization has, in turn, stimulated the other two energy-intensive sectors of the economy: the housing and highway construction industry, and the manufacture of consumer goods for use in single-family detached homes (such as refrigerators, air conditioners, etc.). One might also add the energy industry to Walker and Large's triumverate to form a mutually-reinforcing cluster of economic sectors that are gigantic energy consumers. These sectors include the most profitable U.S. industries and account for a significant proportion of the total GNP. The power and economic prominence of these industries will likely be a significant barrier to energy conservation because their profitability depends greatly on the stimulation of energy-intensive consumption.

Low Energy Prices

It is a cardinal economic rule that it is irrational to use a cheap resource sparingly. Historically, U.S. energy prices have been extremely low relative to other Western societies (Darmstadter, et al., 1977). This inexpensive energy has been made possible primarily by the once-abundant supplies of petroleum and natural gas in the North American continent, plus the policy of the U.S. government to subsidize energy production and consumption. For example, favored tax treatment of the oil industry has lowered the industry's costs and thus decreased the price of oil. Public subsidization of highways has encouraged energy-wasteful truck transportation and undermined the more energy-efficient railroad industry.

If energy prices are too low to encourage conservation, the obvious strategy would be to increase those prices. Several actions (in addition to eliminating government subsidization of cheap energy) have been suggested. First, a variety of economic studies has demonstrated that moderate to substantial amounts of energy can be saved if prices of energy resources are increased (Darmstadter, 1975). Second, economic inducements to conserve may take the form of taxes that make the purchase of an energy-inefficient commodity or other extravagant uses of energy economically formidable. A frequently advanced example is a horsepower or weight tax on automobiles. Third, conservation can be encouraged through "positive" inducements such as a tax credit for homeowners who install insulation.

One of the major weaknesses of this pricing strategy, which we will expand upon later, is that higher energy prices disproportionately disadvantage the poor and are likely to be resisted by low-income persons. Higher energy prices also benefit only a very small fraction of U.S. industry, principally the energy companies and utilities. Most other corporations—including the automobile industry, which is currently being pinched by pressure to build smaller and less profitable automobiles—are likely to resist price increases. It thus appears that a pricing approach to energy conservation is both politically untenable and threatening to economic growth.

Energy and Equity

The energy crisis of 1973–74 dramatically demonstrated a major social and political problem of conservation policy. This is the tendency for the poor to be hurt most by energy price increases. The OPEC embargo had a substantial impact on energy prices (U.S. Bureau of the Census, 1975). While the overall consumer price index rose by 17.9 percent from 1972 to 1974, the price of fuel and utilities expanded by 25.1 percent. Morrison, in a comprehensive review of the socioeconomic consequences of the energy crisis, pointed out that:

> It is self-evident that higher energy prices are harder on those who have less money. But there is much that is not so obvious about the impact of energy price increases on different socioeconomic layers. Chief among such impacts is the fact that, like regressive taxes which make the poor pay at a higher *rate* than the affluent, higher energy prices, in effect, take away a larger share of the income of the poor than of others. (Morrison, 1978:165)

Morrison notes that although low-income households use substantially less energy than high-income households, lower-income persons spend a greater proportion of their incomes on energy. He cites a number of studies indicating that the energy price increases of 1973–74 were a much greater burden on the poor than the affluent and had the effect of redistributing income from the poor to the rich. Morrison notes with irony that while the poor are the nation's best energy conservers (albeit involuntarily), the dislocations caused by the energy waste of the upper social classes are largely borne by the poor.

Unlike the affluent, the poor have very limited opportunities to reduce their energy consumption. Low-income families tend to live in poorly insulated dwellings and to use less-efficient appliances and automobiles. At the same time, they lack the money to invest in more energy-efficient housing and other items. Morrison argues that if the United States is to reduce energy waste while not placing undue burdens on the poor, the affluent must shoulder a greater share of the cost. An equitable transition to greater energy efficiency would require the upper socioeconomic strata to provide funds for income transfers through governmental channels to the poor. These income transfers would soften or eliminate the regressive impacts of energy price increases and enable the poor to make investments in more efficient housing, appliances, and transportation. However, Morrison suggests that this course is unlikely to be taken in the short term because it will threaten the consumption expectations of the affluent. The experience of the past few years bears out Morrison's anticipations.

Schnaiberg (1975) has noted that the effects of energy price increases in the wake of the 1973–74 energy crisis were not confined to differential consumption impacts on households of varying incomes. The poor suffered more than the middle and upper classes because the energy crisis caused some layoffs of blue-collar workers, while white-collar workers did not tend to lose their jobs. Schnaiberg also presents evidence that the overall life styles of the poor were affected more than those of the affluent. In addition, the Nixon administration used the energy crisis and the austerity it fostered to justify eliminating or curtailing many "nonessential" federal programs that were primarily aimed at assisting the poor and indigent.

The moderate energy price increases that appeared after the 1973–74 oil embargo proved to be devastating to many of the nation's poor families, but it is evident that energy prices are still too low to stimulate significant conservation efforts. The tendency for energy price increases to further penalize the poor implies that this cannot be the sole approach to promoting energy conservation.

The Supply Expansion Bias of U.S. Energy Policy

U.S. energy policy—to the extent that a clear-cut policy exists—has largely emphasized supply expansion over energy conservation (Walker and Large, 1975; Lindberg, 1977). In contrast to conservation, supply expansion policies accept the quantities of energy being consumed and the ways in which energy is being used and seek to ensure that sufficient energy is produced to meet those needs. There are two major types of governmental supply expansion policies. The first involves government subsidization of energy firms through massive tax breaks such as investment tax credits or accelerated depreciation. This decreases the costs and increases the profits of these firms, which in turn keep energy prices low and encourage expanded investments in fossil fuel energy production. The second type of supply expansion policy is federal underwriting of the research costs of new technologies to obtain greater production from existing reserves or to develop new fossil fuel energy sources. Supply expansion policies, thus, undercut conservation by eliminating—but only in the short run—conditions such as higher energy prices and public concern over energy shortages that encourage conservation (Walker and Large, 1975).

Applying Sociology to Energy Conservation:
A Matter of Theory and Method

Energy conservation is a complex problem with no obvious solutions. When we examine the approaches that social scientists have taken toward this problem, we can see major differences in their assumptions about the way society functions and how energy use is related to the social structure. This section describes some of the differences in approaches and assumptions that underlie these styles of research and action.

Perhaps the most common type of applied sociological research on energy conservation employs what might be termed a "cognitive" (Olsen and Goodnight, 1977) or "social-psychological" approach. The underlying assumption of this approach is that inducing energy conservation is ultimately a problem of social values and cognition. The most useful approach to conservation is, therefore, to foster attitude and value changes among consumers that will lead to greater voluntary conservation (usually in the household unit, although the technique may be extended to business, industry, and government).

A second type of research utilizes a "behavioral-incentive" (Olsen and Goodnight, 1977) or "economic-inducement" approach. Its principal assumption about the conservation problem is that there are insufficient economic incentives for consumers to conserve. Hence, the greatest leverage on the conservation problem can be gained by implementing economic incentives that encourage consumer conservation. A third approach might be described as "critical" sociology. The major underlying assumption of the critical approach (Walker and Large, 1975; Lindberg, 1977; Hammarlund and Lindberg, 1976) is that the principal barriers to conservation are the political power and economic privilege of those who benefit most from energy extravagance (especially energy companies, industrial firms, construction interests, and so forth). Therefore, little progress can be made toward energy conservation unless steps are taken to dismantle this structure of power and privilege and to restructure the political economy.

These three alternative approaches to energy conservation lead to quite different styles of applied social science research. The major method employed by the cognitive approach is the laboratory or field experiment, in which the researcher measures the extent to which variations in cognitive variables (such as energy conservation information) affect energy use. The behavioral-incentive approach has employed both experimentation and "energy modeling," in which the research attempts to simulate the effects of various economic incentives on the energy decisions of households and business firms.

The critical approach is not characterized by any particular research methods. It frequently employs both quantitative (e.g., energy modeling) and qualitative (e.g., exploration of the power structure of the energy industry) methods. Ultimately what is most characteristic of this approach is its use of research findings to critique prevailing policies and to provide groups with the information they need to challenge existing energy-related policies (Henderson, 1978).

WHAT DO WE KNOW?

Conservation Experiments: Cognitive and Behavioral Research

Considerable research has examined the possibilities for conservation in the household sector. These studies typically compare a "treatment group" that receives conservation information or a behavioral inducement with a "control group" that does not. For the most part, these "conservation experiments" examine only conservation of direct energy use and ignore the 45 percent of household energy use that is "indirect" (embodied in the manufacture of goods and the provision of services).

A variety of cognitive and behavioral techniques have been used in attempts to alter the energy consumption of family units (Olsen, 1978). Cognitive approaches use communication to achieve commitment by individuals to desired attitudes, values, and goals. This approach assumes that as individuals' attitudes and thoughts change, their behavior will change in correspondence. Behavioral approaches use influence to achieve compliance by individuals to desired forms of action. In contrast to the cognitive approach, the behavioral approach assumes that altered behavior patterns of individuals will lead to changes in values and attitudes.

Most cognitive experiments have involved transmitting energy-related information to households. This information has dealt with the benefits of conservation, ways of saving energy, and feedback on current household energy consumption. Heberlein (1975) and Becker (1978) examined the effects that these kinds of information have on cognitive attitudes and found that they bear little relation to changes in conservation activity. By incorporating household conservation goal setting with feedback information, Becker (1978) achieved a relatively high level of conservation behavior, but this procedure is beyond the capability of most large-scale public information programs.

The inability of purely informational approaches to change energy-consuming behavior is no surprise. Sociological research on the relationship between attitudes and behavior has discovered little evidence that attitudes can be changed by cognitive appeals or that attitude changes can significantly alter established behavior patterns. These generalizations have been substantiated by survey research studies that have explored the link between belief in the reality of the energy problem to the perceived importance of energy conservation and actual conservation behavior. In general, belief in the need for conservation or belief in the reality of energy shortages does not lead to significant conservation behavior. Thus, although approximately half of the U.S. population (Olsen and Goodnight, 1977) believes in the reality of the energy crisis, very few people have taken major conservation actions.

Leik and Kolman (1978) point out a set of behavioral components that pose major barriers to personal or household acts of conservation, and, hence, are important for the success of the cognitive approach to energy conservation. These include the perception of the reality of a shortage, felt personal responsibility to take conservation action, the ability to monitor one's own consumption, belief that conservation efforts will be equitably rewarded (so that the conserver will reap the benefit of his or her conservation), and belief that it is necessary to act now to conserve. All except the first of these conditions presumes the importance of conservation, and the absence of any one of them would inhibit taking a conserving action when the importance of conservation was an accepted belief. These "barriers" dramatize the gap between attitude and behavior in the case of energy conservation.

The principal behavioral approach to energy conservation is the use of pricing mechanisms such as increasing energy prices to discourage consumption. This mechanism overcomes the various cognitive barriers between attitude and action noted above. However, we saw earlier that there are major economic and distributional problems with the pricing approach to conservation. Since energy use represents a large share of the total household budget for low-income families, increased energy prices will have much greater impacts on their budgets than in more affluent households. Thus, increased prices may lead to conservation, but they will also create distributional problems that must be dealt with in any overall policy solution (Morrison, 1978).

Herendeen (1974), on the basis of 1960–63 data, has noted that direct energy use in the household increases with income and then levels off as income rises above about $22,000 in 1979 dollars. However, total energy—including indirect use embodied in goods—continues to grow as income increases. The direct-to-total energy ratio decreases with income from about two-thirds for the lowest-income class, to one-third for the highest-income class. Therefore, attempts to conserve energy by increasing the price for direct household use will have less proportional impact on the consumption of the affluent than on the poor.

Another limitation to the pricing strategy is the high level of price increases that is necessary to stimulate a substantial reduction in home energy use. Lopreato and Meriwether (1976), using a set of hypothetical questions, discovered that an increase of 10 percent or less in gas and electricity bills would induce little or no effort to reduce consumption. They found that to induce substantial reductions in gas and electric consumption across a majority of the population, prices would have to rise by 40 percent or more.

Household consumers of energy may also be unresponsive in the short run to energy price increases because of the energy-consuming economic system in which they live and because a relatively small portion of their household budget is typically spent on direct use of energy. Existing housing patterns and transportation structures, as noted earlier, tend to mitigate against household energy conservation and limit its magnitude in the short run. If those who use the most energy are relatively unaffected by small price changes, then the social desirability of energy consumption will overwhelm the conservation incentives of small price changes. But if we institute large energy price changes in order to encourage conservation in the household sector, the effects upon the poorer households could be devastating.

Evidence from Economic Analyses: The Emergence
of a Critical Perspective on Energy Conservation

Applied sociologists interested in energy conservation cannot ignore the economic rooting of energy problems. The work of economists has important implications for developing effective conservation policies. Economic data can provide the applied sociologist or policy maker with working parameters within which conservation can occur without inducing economic dislocation or significant deterioration in the quality of life.

Unfortunately, the economic studies relevant to energy conservation do not always provide consistent and unambiguous findings. The traditional interpretation of national economic phenomena has related energy availability to the level of unemployment through the use of the Phillips curve. This curve can be roughly interpreted as the ratio of the price level, and consequently of inflation, to employment. The outcome of that approach generally was the prediction that reduced energy supplies or higher energy prices would lead to a higher rate of unemployment, holding constant the price of other factors of production. The policy implication of such analysis was that energy supplies must be expanded to maintain employment and income levels and to sustain growth in the GNP. Within such a framework, energy conservation is thought to slow down production, employment, and real income.

The implicit assumption in analyses based on the Phillips curve is that energy, capital, and labor are complementary inputs in aggregate production. "Complementarity" means that an increase (or decrease) in the use of a particular factor of production such as energy must necessarily be accompanied by an increase (or decrease) in labor and capital inputs. Chapman (1977) and Berndt and Wood (1977), in reviews of recent empirical microeconomic studies of the complementarity of the basic factors of production, provide evidence that the complementarity assumption may be invalid. The evidence suggests that labor and energy are substitutes in production, with one replacing the other. Capital and energy, meanwhile, may be either complements or substitutes, depending upon the context. The implication of these findings is that, all things being equal, reduced energy input into the production process due to changes in energy prices will increase employment (rather than decrease employment, as implied by analyses based on the Phillips curve). In other words, energy consumption may be reduced without necessarily diminishing economic growth, while simultaneously increasing employment. And these results probably underestimate the substitution that might occur under conditions of high and rapidly increasing energy prices over periods of time long enough to permit the turnover of energy-intensive capital stock.

Altering the mix of inputs in the production process is one way of conserving energy within the economy. Another major source of conservation is an alteration in the composition of outputs, decreasing energy-intensive outputs and increasing outputs that require less energy. For example, an aggregate shift from private automobile use to some form of mass transit would represent a change in the output of transportation services that would likely produce considerable energy savings. Using input-output analysis of data on U.S. industrial, commercial, and household activity, the Energy Research Group of the Center for Advanced Computation at the University of Illinois has begun to document the capacity for conservation through sectoral shifts in the economy. Many of these energy-conserving shifts would also result in greater employment (Hannon, 1977).

A central concern in many discussions of shifts in the economy is the rate of return on investment. Existing figures indicate that investments in energy conservation will yield a higher rate of return than investments in greater energy production, even if current energy prices are discounted and inevitable higher future prices of energy are ignored. In other words, it takes less money to conserve a barrel of oil than it does to produce one. Schipper states the case explicitly:

> New energy production facilities demand large and ever increasing amounts of capital per BTU produced or per unit of capacity. The energy sources most often cited as vital to our energy future—nuclear energy, oil shale, enhanced recovery of oil and natural gas—would, if historical trends continued, require capital investments over the next 25 years totaling trillions of dollars, making the energy industries' share of all investment grow faster than the economy as a whole. This means that consumers, industry, and government would have to forego both consumption and investment, through higher interest rates, higher prices, or higher taxes in order to finance the expansion of the energy industry.... It can be shown that proper conservation techniques save more energy than new energy sources can produce, per dollar invested. (Schipper, 1976:493–94)

These recent economic studies of the potential for energy conservation make a solid case for shifting away from energy production and toward energy conservation activities. If there is significant room for energy conservation within the economy, and significant disincentives to investment in costly energy/production facilities, why is conservation not being vigorously pursued? As will be discussed below, there are a number of institutional barriers to conservation in the realm of governmental policy and private control of energy resources.

Galbraith (1973) has developed a theoretical model of the role of large corporate enterprises in the economic system. He argues that large corporations are not bound by the traditional constraining forces of consumer choice, investor control, or government regulation of monopolies. These enterprises act to maximize growth and stability rather than merely maximize profits. Both of the large institutions that dominate the energy supply and distribution system in the United States—the petroleum companies and the investor-owned utilities—bear a close relation to Galbraith's model of growth monopoly. This correspondence leads to several consequences: extensive government subsidization through various tax and explicit transfer programs, average rather than marginal cost pricing (in other words, underpricing) of energy, and marketing and corporate objectives that seek to maximize sales volume and market control rather than profits.

The functioning of the investor-owned utilities as private corporations encourages expansion of generating capacity, rather than more public-service-oriented goals of minimizing investment and discouraging extravagant use of electricity.

Government policy has aided these expansion-oriented goals of investor-owned utilities by subsidizing expansion of generating capacity through tax provisions and by establishing policies that justify charging the heaviest energy consumers the lowest rates. Publicly-owned utilities, on the other hand, have tended to exhibit markedly different goals and performance. In particular, the public utilities tend to be more oriented toward conservation than the investor-owned utilities. However, it should be kept in mind that not all publicly-owned utilities perform with the same level of attention to conservation. It appears, in fact, that when publicly-owned utilities are insulated from public participation and control, they tend to perform like investor-owned utilities (Morgan, et al., 1976).

WHAT ARE WE DOING?

Early applied sociological research on energy conservation was heavily oriented toward the cognitive and behavioral approaches. Within a year following the Arab oil embargo numerous experimental studies of cognitive and behavioral inducement of energy conservation were launched. While these studies did produce some useful results, it is clear that this research approach has not achieved significant breakthroughs that would make promoting energy conservation a simple or routine matter. It has also become apparent that focusing so much attention on direct use of fuels in the residential sector is not consistent with that sector's status as a consumer of energy. Direct household use of fuels accounts for roughly 34 percent of total national energy consumption (Leik and Kolman, 1978), so that even if massive conservation successes were registered in this sector, its aggregate impact on national energy consumption would be limited. For these reasons, applied conservation researchers have increasingly turned to more structural issues in conservation and to identifying structural strategies for implementing conservation policies at the national or local level.

Gross National Product, Social Welfare, and Energy
Consumption: Exploring the "Decoupling" Issue

We noted earlier that there is a relatively close cross-national relationship between per capita energy consumption and per capita GNP. Roughly the same finding prevails when we examine energy use historically in a society such as the United States. As per capita GNP rises, per capita energy consumption also tends to rise (Craig, et al., 1976). This evidence has led many social scientists to argue that a reduction in energy use per capita would have undesirable impacts on GNP and social welfare (Federal Energy Administration, 1974).

This notion has not gone unchallenged, however. Many social scientists have begun to generate theory and evidence suggesting that it is possible, at least in part, to "decouple" growth in GNP or social welfare and growth in energy consumption. Daly (1977) has pointed out that increases in per capita GNP do not always signal improvements in social welfare for the majority of a nation's population, especially when per capita GNP is already at a high level. This argument is largely supported by available empirical evidence for the developed market economies. From 1955 to 1970 there was relatively little correlation between change in per capita GNP and change in a wide variety of indicators of quality of life or social welfare (Buttel, 1979). Consequently, even if rising energy consumption does lead to increased GNP, improvements in social welfare or quality of life will not be automatically forthcoming.

A second line of argument supporting the decoupling perspective is that societies with similar levels of per capita GNP (or similar levels of quality of life) have markedly different levels of per capita energy consumption (Buttel, 1978). The most frequently cited example is that of the United States and Sweden, which have broad similarities in their levels of economic activity. Sweden, however, consumes only about one-half as much energy as the United States does on a per capita basis (Schipper and Lichtenberg, 1977). This observed difference in energy consumption has stimulated a number of comparative studies seeking to discover if the United States could achieve the energy efficiencies apparent in Sweden and other developed societies (Darmstadter, et al., 1977). This research has suggested a number of technical routes toward greater energy conservation in the United States, such as improved automobile designs, cogeneration of industrial waste heat, and the like. Applied energy research has also indicated that the energy efficiency of countries such as Sweden is partially accounted for by their comparatively higher energy prices.

One of the key issues in the decoupling debate has been the likely impacts of conservation on employment. A dramatic consequence of the 1973–74 energy crisis was a substantial increase in the unemployment rate. Therefore, it has been widely assumed that the effects of an aggressive conservation program might depress employment even further. Recent research, however, casts doubt on whether these fears of escalating unemployment are warranted. Many conservation measures, such as retrofitting existing buildings, would require a large labor force. Conversely, the most important outlets for projected increases in energy consumption would be for electrical power generation and electrical plant construction—two of the sectors of the economy that employ the fewest persons per dollar of investment (Hayes, 1976:60; Hannon, 1975). Also, insofar as energy is used to mechanize economic processes (that is, displace human power with power from inanimate energy), increases in energy consumption would aggravate unemployment.

An interesting example of the logic behind the decoupling notion is the experience of the State of Oregon with its recently invoked "bottle bill." This bill, which requires the use of returnable bottles, is estimated to be saving 1.4 trillion BTUs of energy in Oregon annually—enough energy to heat the homes of 50,000 Oregon residents for an average winter. While this bottle bill did eliminate jobs in the industries that formerly manufactured nonreturnable bottles and cans, it is estimated that there has been a net increase in employment in the beverage industry in Oregon of 55 to 365 full-time jobs (Waggoner, 1974). The Oregon bottle bill experience, thus, suggests that energy conservation may enhance the ability of the economy to provide its citizens with jobs.

Proponents of the notion that the United States can begin to decouple growth in energy, GNP, and social welfare do not assume that the decoupling process can be implemented rapidly. The main reason why the 1973–74 energy crisis proved so disruptive to the U.S. economy was that it involved an abrupt decrease in energy consumption without sufficient time for the economy to accommodate to a lower level of energy use. It also should be recognized that not all forms of energy conservation will simultaneously increase employment and enhance social welfare. We noted earlier that the Energy Research Group at the University of Illinois has been greatly concerned with generating estimates of the conservation and employment impacts of sectoral shifts in the economy. Only some of these shifts both conserve energy and increase employment. Nevertheless, their work has been extremely influential in establishing the plausibility of, and the most desirable routes for, the decoupling of energy from GNP and social welfare. Finally, there are undoubtedly limits beyond which energy consumption cannot be lowered without affecting the quality of life. Quite clearly, this issue of decoupling energy consumption from economic well-being will be one of the most important foci for ongoing conservation research.

WHAT HAVE WE ACCOMPLISHED?

The intimate connections between energy use and the socioeconomic fabric of life make it impossible to separate energy policy from public policy in general. Therefore, even though the United States has yet to formulate a coherent national energy policy, the government has clearly been shaping the nature of energy use through various economic and natural resource policies. As we view the future of energy use, it is apparent that whether we pursue the path of energy supply expansion or a more energy conservation-oriented path, both will require substantial initiative and support from the public sector.

The principal effect of public policy to this point has been to depress energy prices and make energy relatively more attractive as a factor of production. Through the now discontinued oil depletion allowance and the various tax provisions alluded to earlier, petroleum and gas price ceilings have been maintained below market or marginal cost prices. Present tax policy operates to distort factor prices—decreasing the cost of capital relative to labor—and therefore provides incentives for capital-intensive energy production.

It should be obvious by now that energy conservation differs from most other areas of applied social science because many influential government decision makers do not readily accept the importance of establishing an effective energy conservation policy. The conservation researcher must often grapple with forces in public policy making that continue to favor energy supply expansion over conservation. A significant area of ongoing work by applied sociologists is, therefore, attempting to understand and possibly counteract those powerful forces that are encouraging the energy supply expansion "bias" of the federal government. In particular, applied conservation researchers who hold a critical perspective have argued that the hesitancy of the federal government to encourage energy conservation is no accident. They suggest that government preoccupation with supply expansion closely reflects the overall structure of U.S. society and the interests of those groups that are most influential in public policy making. Walker and Large (1975) have suggested that the dominant corporations in the U.S. economy (especially the automobile, petroleum, metals, and chemical industries) have clear-cut interests in stimulating energy consumption. Furthermore, with the exception of energy corporations, the profitability of these dominant corporations depends on the availability of cheap and abundant energy. General Motors, for example, would find it much more difficult to sell automobiles if gasoline were priced at $5.00 per gallon.

Researchers holding a critical perspective have also documented the sensitivity of the economy to the fortunes of these dominant energy-intensive industries. The "automobile complex" (including all firms that sell and repair motor vehicles, parts, and gasoline) alone accounts for 10 percent of the total U.S. GNP (Hardesty, et al., 1971:88-89). An aggressive national energy conservation policy might well reduce the profitability of this handful of large, energy-intensive industries, hence at least temporarily aggravating recessionary tendencies in the U.S. economy. Because of the importance of these energy-intensive corporations in the national economy, government officials encounter severe limitations in their efforts to implement energy conservation.

While applied researchers have not totally ignored the federal arena in their energy conservation efforts, they have recently focused much more attention on state and local governments. Although the national government has thus far not been able to go beyond its supply expansion orientation to energy policy and generate a national energy conservation policy, there are many hopeful indications of emerging local energy conservation policy initiatives.

The existence of publicly-owned utility systems seems to be a key facilitating factor. One bright spot in this regard has been Seattle, Washington. Seattle City Light was well on its way to investing in nuclear generating plants to provide for projected future electricity demands when a number of community groups and local government leaders began to question the advisability of that policy. This concern resulted in an extensive study of energy alternatives for the community and eventual adoption by the City Council of a policy of meeting future electricity needs through conservation rather than new generation facilities. Seattle City Light created an Office of Conservation, which is vigorously promoting energy conservation throughout the city. Its programs include conducting energy management seminars to train local commercial and industrial businesses in developing effective energy conservation programs, establishing heat loss standards for new houses and new residential electric heat installations, operating insulation programs for low income households with electrically-heated homes, providing free home energy checks, community conservation education meetings, and establishing a research and development program that includes demonstration projects for wind and solar technologies (Olsen and Cluett, 1979).

Seattle is not alone in these efforts. Amory Lovins (1977) has noted that several hundred communities in the United States are now pursuing policies that emphasize a "soft energy path." Morgan, et al. (1976) have found that localities from California to Massachusetts are focusing their public policies on renewable energy sources and conservation, especially where public utilities exist. However, the Tennessee Valley Authority (TVA) experience demonstrates that the mere existence of "public" control over energy resources does not necessarily lead to creative energy policies. The TVA has had a history of environmental abuse and conflict with local public authorities. Its structure of authority, which is built around a board of federal appointees, effectively insulates TVA actions from local public initiatives. Nevertheless, a growing body of evidence supports the notion that when publicly-owned energy authorities operate under the scrutiny and participatory control of their constituencies, more responsive and energy conserving policies are likely to emerge.

The city of Davis, California, has become widely known for its adoption and implementation of a coherent community plan for energy conservation by its residents, businesses, and government. The city has made many changes in building code standards to encourage energy conservation, including regulations governing window area and orientation, insulation, etc. A new solar building code also encourages replacing electricity and fossil fuels with renewable energy sources (Hammond, et al., 1974). It is interesting to note that local successes in cities such as Seattle and Davis have led to a widespread reorientation among applied energy researchers. Barriers to effective national policies have heightened the attention given to state and local programs. A number of national organizations, such as the Conference on Alternative State and Local Public Policies (CASLPP), have also adopted the position that meaningful alteration of national policy is essentially hopeless because of the powerlessness of citizens in the face of corporate domination of public policy. The energy project of CASLPP has become an especially effective vehicle for disseminating information about the possibilities for energy conservation at state and local levels.

It is useful to distinguish between knowledge obtained and the actual level of conservation achieved when discussing the accomplishments of applied energy research. In the brief time that sociologists have concerned themselves with energy conservation, the accumulation of relevant knowledge has been impressive. We know in a much more precise manner the nature of the problems to be solved, the kinds of techniques that will or will not be effective, the benefits and costs of prospective shifts in production inputs and outputs, and the barriers to meaningful conservation programs. Applied conservation sociologists have a relatively firm grasp of the kinds of policies that would induce significant energy conservation, in an equitable manner, without increasing unemployment or reducing the quality of life. However, the difficulties inherent in implementing such policies have not been surmounted, especially at the national level. The major accomplishments in energy conservation are being made at local and state levels, particularly in the Pacific Northwest and California. The actual level of conservation obtained from these efforts is extremely difficult to quantify precisely in terms of BTUs of energy saved. Nevertheless, the accomplishments in certain states and localities have been sufficiently impressive to warrant more attention to future possibilities for energy conservation.

WHERE ARE WE GOING?

Applied social scientific research on energy conservation is presently in a state of flux. The ambiguity of the future directions that this research will take is due to several interrelated factors. The limits of voluntary conservation induced by information and modest incentives have become apparent. It is generally accepted that the public sector—particularly at the national but also at state and local levels—must play an important role in implementing more effective conservation programs. However, the reluctance of the federal government and many state and local governments to go forward with aggressive conservation policies tends to undermine the traditional role models (i.e., the "technocratic"and "enlightenment" models of Street and Weinstein, 1975) for applied sociologists. Applied sociologists have tended to assume that their proper role was to supply enlightened public decision makers with the information necessary to formulate prudent policies. In large part, this approach to social change has failed to bear fruit in the conservation area. Another related source of ambiguity for many applied energy sociologists is that the need for energy conservation is overshadowed in the minds of major public policy makers by issues such as inflation and general economic stagnation. The dominance of these issues at the present time implies that conservation is not likely to attract progressively-more-limited federal funds and that the short-term "health" of the economy is unlikely to be sacrificed for long-term goals such as energy conservation.

Because of this situation, applied conservation sociology may likely exhibit several changes in the form (although probably less so in the content) of its research. The major change in form will perhaps be an alteration in the perceived constituency of the applied conservation sociologist. Whereas public policy makers were once generally assumed to be the major constituents of applied sociology, citizen groups, community organizations, and political action organizations may increasingly become the sociologist's major constituents. In this new milieu, the goal of applied research becomes using available information to challenge public policy and policy makers, usually through public interest or other voluntary organizations. It is significant that many of the accomplishments of local communities such as Davis have not come about through a consensual process of local public officials unilaterally implementing conservation-oriented policies. Rather, local public officials have typically had to be prompted into action by political activities of citizens and applied social scientists. This marks a considerable departure from the customary relationship of the sociologist to the public policy maker and raises fundamental questions about the appropriate role of the social scientist in public affairs.

One of the more significant ongoing changes occurring among sociologists concerned with this problem is to consider energy conservation and the use of renewable energy sources (solar energy, energy from wood and other biological materials, wind energy, and the like) as being complementary and mutually reinforcing practices. Both conservation and the use of renewable sources of energy have the ultimate impact of reducing the consumption of scarce fossil fuels. The implementation of alternative, renewable energy sources is particularly important in demonstrating that fossil fuel use can be dramatically reduced without reducing living standards or threatening a return to preindustrial life styles. In practice, the most successful local initiatives in energy conservation (such as in Davis) have been closely tied to strong encouragement of alternative energy sources. The intimate connection between these two approaches will likely become much more influential in conservation-oriented sociological research.

The role of the sociologist concerned with energy conservation undoubtedly will bear a close relationship to the future course of the changing U.S. energy situation. Conservation will become a much more important policy priority during periods in which the society is faced with severe energy supply shortfalls and other "energy crises." Applied sociologists must become accustomed to the notion that the major role of energy conservation research will not be to prevent energy crises, but rather to cope with existing crises. In this situation the role of sociological energy researchers will not be to provide guidelines for rational planning, but to assist in energy "crisis management."

It is tempting to end this discussion on a note of impending doom, viewing energy conservation researchers and proponents as lone wolves crying at the moon. Nevertheless, conservation researchers *can* demonstrate to citizens and private organizations that energy conservation is necessary, can be equitable, can be compatible with the employment interests of the vast majority of families, and can improve the nation's quality of life and social welfare in many quantitative and qualitative ways. Furthermore, we are increasingly recognizing that our inability or unwillingness to implement conservation is a significant cause of many of the problems (such as inflation and unemployment) that seem to be more immediately pressing than extravagant energy consumption.

REFERENCES AND SUGGESTED READINGS

Becker, Lawrence J. 1978. "Joint Effect of Feedback and Goal Setting on Performance: A Field Study of Residential Energy Conservation." *Journal of Applied Psychology* 63:428–34.

Berger, John J. 1976. *Nuclear Power: The Unviable Option.* San Francisco: Ramparts Press.

Berndt, Ernst R. and David O. Wood. 1977. "Consistent Projections of Energy Demand and Aggregate Economic Growth: A Review of Issues and Empirical Studies." M.I.T. Energy Laboratory Working Paper No. MIT-EL-77-024WP.

Buttel, Frederick H. 1978. "Social Structure and Energy Efficiency: A Preliminary Cross-National Analysis." *Human Ecology* 6:145–64.

_____. 1979. "Social Welfare Correlates of Energy Intensity: A Comparative Analysis of the Developed Market Economies." In *Sociopolitical Impacts of Energy Use and Policy,* edited by C.T. Unseld, et al., pp. 295–327. Washington, D.C.: National Academy of Sciences.

Chapman, Duane. 1977. "Energy Conservation, Employment, and Income." Cornell Agricultural Economics Staff Paper No. 77-6. Cornell University, Ithaca, N.Y.

Cottrell, Fred. 1955. *Energy and Society.* New York: McGraw-Hill.

Craig, Paul P., Joel Darmstadter, and Stephen Rattien. 1976. "Social and Institutional Factors in Energy Conservation." *Annual Review of Energy* 1: 535–51.

Daly, Herman E. 1977. *Steady-State Economics.* San Francisco: W.H. Freeman.

Darmstadter, Joel. 1975. *Conserving Energy.* Baltimore: The Johns Hopkins University Press.

Darmstadter, Joel, Joy Dunkerley, and Jack Alterman. 1977. *How Industrial Societies Use Energy: A Comparative Analysis.* Baltimore: The Johns Hopkins University Press.

Demand and Conservation Panel, Committee on Nuclear and Alternative Energy Systems (CONAES). 1978. "U.S. Energy Demand: Some Low Energy Futures." *Science* 200:142–52.

Edison Electric Institute. 1975. *Economic Growth in the Future.* New York: McGraw-Hill.

Federal Energy Administration. 1974. *Project Independence Report.* Washington, D.C.: U.S. Government Printing Office.

*Foley, Gerald. 1976. *The Energy Question.* Baltimore: Penguin.
    The book provides basic background on energy problems of advanced industrial societies in a highly readable fashion. Part III, "Futures," is specifically devoted to the problems and prospects of energy conservation as a means for solving these energy problems.

Ford Foundation Energy Policy Project. 1974. *A Time to Choose.* Cambridge, Mass.: Ballinger.

Galbraith, John Kenneth. 1973. *Economics and the Public Purpose.* Boston: Houghton Mifflin.

Hammarlund, Jeffrey R. and Leon N. Lindberg, eds. 1976. *The Political Economy of Energy Policy.* University of Wisconsin-Madison, Institute for Environmental Studies.

Hammond, Jonathan, et al. 1974. *A Strategy for Energy Conservation.* Winters, Calif.: Living Systems.

Hannon, Bruce. 1975. "Energy Conservation and the Consumer." *Science* 189: 95–102.

_____. 1977. "Energy, Labor and the Conserver Society." *Technology Review* (Mar/Apr):47–53.

Hardesty, John, Norris C. Clement, and Clinton E. Jenks. 1971. "The Political Economy of Environmental Destruction." In *Economic Growth vs. the Environment,* edited by W.A. Johnson and J. Hardesty, pp. 85–106. Belmont, Calif.: Wadsworth.

*Hayes, Denis. 1976. *Energy: The Case for Conservation.* Worldwatch Paper #4. Washington, D.C.: Worldwatch Institute.

This short piece lays out the rationale for emphasizing conservation rather than expanded production of conventional energy sources as a strategy for adapting to reduced fossil fuel supplies. Hayes points out possibilities for significant energy conservation in the areas of transportation, buildings, food production and distribution, and industry. The final section is a "personal conservation guide" that suggests how individuals and families can greatly reduce their energy consumption.

Heberlein, Thomas A. 1975. "Conservation Information: The Energy Crisis and Electricity Consumption in an Apartment Complex." *Energy Systems and Policy* 1:105–18.

Henderson, Hazel. 1978. *Creating Alternative Futures.* New York: Berkeley Windhover.

Herendeen, Robert E. 1974. "Affluence and Energy Demand." *Mechanical Engineering* 9:18–22.

Holdren, John. 1976. "Energy Resources." In *Environment: Resources, Pollution, and Society,* edited by W.W. Murdoch, pp. 121–45. Sunderland, Mass.: Sinauer Associates.

Illich, Ivan. 1974. *Energy and Equity.* New York: Perrenial Library.

Kent, Paul G. 1976. "Energy Supply." In *The Political Economy of Energy Policy,* edited by J.R. Hammarlund and L.N. Lindberg, pp. 57–59. Madison, Wis.: Institute for Environmental Studies, University of Wisconsin-Madison.

Leik, Robert K. and Anita Sue Kolman. 1978. "Isn't it More Rational to Be Wasteful?" In *Energy Policy in the United States: Social and Behavioral Dimensions,* edited by S. Warkov, pp. 148–63. New York: Praeger.

*Lindberg, Leon N., ed. 1977. *The Energy Syndrome.* Lexington, Mass.: D.C. Heath.

This edited book compares several societies (primarily advanced industrial ones) according to how their energy policies have been formulated during recent decades. By the "energy syndrome" Lindberg means the rather consistent tendency for these policies to emphasize energy production rather than energy conservation; to disproportionately benefit energy producers; and to present massive political, institutional, and structural obstacles to the development of renewable energy resources. The final two chapters offer some useful ideas on how obstacles to energy conservation and alternative energy sources can be removed.

Lopreato, Sally Cook and Mirian Wossum Meriwether. 1976. "Energy Attitudinal Surveys: Summary, Annotations, Research Recommendations." University of Texas, Austin, Center for Energy Studies.

Lovins, Amory. 1976. "Energy Strategy: The Road Not Taken." *Foreign Affairs* (Fall):65–96.

* _____. 1977. *Soft Energy Paths.* Cambridge, Mass.: Ballinger.

Lovins has written a confident–almost messianic–book on the need and mechanisms for achieving energy conservation and greater utilization of renewable energy sources. By "soft energy paths" he means strategies that attempt to meet energy needs through conservation and renewable energy resources, rather than continuing down the "hard path" of expanded production of fossil fuels. The most interesting parts of this book are the sections pointing out the hidden economic, social, and ecological costs of continuing along the hard path, together with the long-term social and political advantages of shifting to a soft energy path.

Morgan, Richard, Tom Riesenberg, and Michael Troutman. 1976. *Taking Charge: A New Look at Public Power.* Washington, D.C.: Environmental Action Foundation.

Morrison, Denton E. 1978. "Equity Impacts of Some Major Energy Alternatives." In *Energy Policy in the United States: Social and Behavioral Dimensions,* edited by S. Warkov, pp. 164–93. New York, Praeger.

Olsen, Marvin E. 1978. "Public Acceptance of Energy Conservation." In *Energy Policy in the United States: Social and Behavioral Dimensions,* edited by S. Warkov, pp. 91–109. New York, Praeger.

Olsen, Marvin E. and Christopher Cluett. 1979. "Evaluation of the Seattle City Light Neighborhood Energy Conservation Program." Seattle: Battelle Human Affairs Research Centers.

Olsen, Marvin E. and Jill A. Goodnight. 1977. "Social Aspects of Energy Conservation." Portland, Oreg.: Northeast Energy Policy Project of the Pacific Northwest Commission.

Ophuls, William. 1977. *Ecology and the Politics of Scarcity.* San Francisco: W.H. Freeman.

Schipper, Lee. 1976. "Raising the Productivity of Energy Utilization." *Annual Review of Energy* 1:455–518.

Schipper, Lee and A.J. Lichtenberg. 1977. "Efficient Energy Use and Well-Being." *Science,* 194:1001–13.

Schnaiberg, Allan. 1975. "Social Syntheses of the Societal-Environmental Dialectic: The Role of Distributional Impacts." *Social Science Quarterly* 56: 5–20.

Steinhart, John S. and Carol E. Steinhart. 1974. *Energy.* North Scituate, Mass.: Duxbury.

Street, David P. and Eugene A. Weinstein. 1975. "Problems and Prospects of Applied Sociology." *The American Sociologist* 10(May):65–72.

U.S. Bureau of the Census. 1975. *Statistical Abstract of the United States, 1975.*

Washington, D.C.: U.S. Government Printing Office.

Waggoner, D. 1974. "Oregon's Bottle Bill—Two Years Later." Portland: Portland, Oregon Environmental Council.

Walker, Richard A. and David B. Large. 1975. "The Economics of Energy Extravagance." *Ecology Law Quarterly* 4:963–85.

Watt, Kenneth E.F., Leslie F. Molloy, C.K. Barshney, Dudley Weeks, and Soetjipto Wirosandjono. 1977. *The Unsteady State.* Honolulu: The University Press of Hawaii.

*Warkov, Seymour, ed. 1978. *Energy Policy in the United States: and Behavioral Dimensions.* New York: Praeger.

This collection of articles by leading scholars in the sociology of energy problems contains several pieces dealing with social aspects of energy conservation, most of which are either written from an applied perspective or have major implications for the application of sociological knowledge to energy problems. The papers by Klausner, Gladhart and his co-workers, Olsen, and Morrison are especially useful.

23 ENVIRONMENTAL PROTECTION

William R. Catton, Jr.

Evolving culture has made *Homo sapiens* a phenomenally successful species—but culture operates in a material biosphere, not in a void. Facts known to ecologists are incompatible with sanguine or optimistic views of the human prospect derived from doctrinaire cultural determinism. Immense as the world may seem, "man has reduced its biomass and is beginning, with pollution, to affect [adversely] its productivity. The relation of an exponentially increasing human population and industry to the biosphere is thus unstable" (Whittaker and Likens, 1973:357). Doubt has been expressed as to whether environmental limits will ever permit the majority of the world's people to overtake the high living standards attained by the industrialized minority (Keyfitz, 1976). It is becoming apparent that human well-being is in jeopardy unless the environment that sustains human life can be protected from some of the consequences of its human use. The task of finding ways to adapt human customs, values, and decision making to ecosystem constraints should afford many opportunities for applying sociological principles and research procedures. This chapter explores some of the efforts in that direction and examines influences that have seriously limited those efforts.

WHAT ARE THE PROBLEMS?

More than three decades ago, when people commonly supposed that improving our political and economic systems was equivalent to solving the basic problems confronting society, one writer urgently pointed out that to raise standards of living, or even to survive, "mankind must reach a sound, healthy relationship with its *total* environment.... The need is especially pressing to

511

reach a favorable biophysical relationship with the earth" (Vogt, 1948:x). As a result of not usually recognizing that need, human societies "have an inherent tendency to overshoot the limits that should be set by their resources" and to discount the cumulative but delayed consequences of environmental damage (Whittaker and Likens, 1973:367). From the beginning of civilization in Mesopotamia until the present, human societies have time and again altered ecosystems by technological and organizational means, at first thereby making available increased human sustenance, but eventually bending the system beyond its tolerance limits and reducing its human carrying capacity (Eckholm, 1976).

Accordingly, by the time the United Nations convened its Stockholm Conference on the Human Environment in 1972, three important conclusions about mankind's relationship to the biosphere had become apparent to a group of researchers at M.I.T. commissioned by the Club of Rome to study limits to growth: 1) Within the next century, present trends in industrialization, pollution, resource depletion, food production and population growth would reach the limits of our planetary environment, and these limits would turn the trends around, resulting in sudden and uncontrollable declines in human numbers and industrialization. 2) It was still possible to opt for a state of sustainable equilibrium instead of continuing these environment-damaging trends. 3) The sooner the world began to pursue this alternative the greater the chance of success (Meadows, et al., 1972).

Today, investigations in various disciplines indicate that many global environmental changes (some of them substantially anthropogenic) are potentially detrimental to mankind. These include a measurable increase in the earth's surface albedo (reflectance), especially in the Northern Hemisphere (Otterman, 1977), an accelerating increase in the carbon dioxide content of the atmosphere (Woodwell, 1978), and a sharp rise in the acidity of rain and snow falling over wide areas (Likens, et al., 1979). Climatologists now believe human societies are dangerously vulnerable even to natural climatic variability (Schneider, 1977). Inadvertent human contributions to that variability, though not altogether predictable, are certain to be unevenly distributed over the face of the earth and are more likely to aggravate the disruptive impact on food production and other human activities than to reduce that impact. "Man has apparently become a major geological and geophysical agent in his own right, able to influence the physical and biological conditions of his future, deliberately or inadvertently, in a way not open to our ancestors" (Cooper, 1978:519).

By the end of the 1960s environmental impairment had become defined in almost every industrial nation as a "social problem"—a condition requiring political decisions and social action. In the 1970s, however, doubts began to be expressed whether existing institutions could provide remedies that would have more than marginal effectiveness (Lundqvist, 1973; Anderson, 1976).

WHAT DO WE KNOW?

Clearly, here is a realm of problems crying out for applied sociological attention. But sociologists have been conceptually incapacitated, so that applied environmental sociology has until very recently remained confined to microscopic issues—worthy enough topics by traditional standards but not commensurate with the enormity of our predicament. Conventional sociological concepts virtually precluded asking how far world industrialization could go before running afoul of ecosystem constraints that might transform it from blessing to curse.

This section begins by briefly summarizing sociological views of the nature of human personality, culture, and society—for these views are basic premises for whatever sociology purports to know about environmental impairment or protection. Two examples of specific lines of environmental inquiry by sociologists are then examined: 1) sociological contributions to forest fire control, and 2) sociological studies of procedures for curbing "depreciative behavior" in outdoor environments such as campgrounds. After looking briefly at the developing need for a "camping ethic," we will turn to a more extensive consideration of research pertaining to the possible emergence of an "environmental ethic."

Basic Sociological Premises

If adaptation to conditions set by the environment is prerequisite to the life of all organisms, a major part of the human adaptive process is cultural. For any human group, behavior (whether adaptive or not) is patterned by norms that are conveyed from the collectivity's more senior members to its recruits. The distinctively human means of transmission is through symbols or language, as contrasted with the biochemical (genetic) means of transferring information from ancestors to descendants that is common to all species. *Homo sapiens* has an unparalleled capacity for communication through language, but language is a shaper as well as a conveyer of perception and thought.

A major premise of modern sociology is that individuals become human through experiences in groups. A further premise is that humans can do things collectively they could not do without organization and a social heritage.

In on-going group activities norms develop and groups impose sanctions to minimize deviation from their norms. One reason for the occurrence of deviant behavior is the occurrence of inconsistencies among norms that evolve in different contexts. Within a given culture, however, there tends to be a strain toward normative consistency.

Apart from enforcement of norms by sanctions, members also comply with group expectations as a result of absorbing them in the socialization process. Socialization is a means of heritage bestowing that is far more highly developed among humans than among other species. It imparts not only shared attitudes and social standards of judgment, but also habits, skills, and appetites. It is a lifelong process, and each person is not only a product of its cumulative influences, but also an agent engaged in socializing all others with whom he or she interacts.

Not all norms arise out of ecological adaptation, but some sociologists argue that norms that require behavior consistent with environmental opportunities can be more readily enforced than those that require ecologically improbable behavior. Despite whatever influence ecological constraints may have on human behavior, virtually all sociologists maintain that differences in the actions and expectations of people in different nations or regions can arise from cultural differences attributable to the particularities of their histories, and not just from direct influences of their physical and biological environments.

Social organization also extends human capabilities. The basis for elaborating organization among humans is provided by social differentiation. If all humans were alike, there could hardly be any division of labor, and the complex organizations by which industrial societies undertake complex tasks would be impossible. People are not all alike. Many human differences are socially produced; other differences are socially endowed with meanings not inherent in their biological origins. Human diversity is especially important for large-scale pursuit of elaborate technical goals. This pursuit tends to foster bureaucratic formal organizations.

Social organization is resistive to change. In some ways this is especially true of the bureaucratic form of organization, but some aspects of bureaucracy may sometimes facilitate innovation and change. Innovative behavior results from imperfect socialization, which bestows skills but fails to prevent them from being used in unconventional ways or toward unconventional ends. Rates of innovation vary in different times and different social contexts. Rates of acceptance of innovations depend partly on their perceived utility, but how useful an innovation will appear to be can depend on numerous additional factors.

For most sociologists, the propositions in the preceding seven paragraphs have become virtually axiomatic (Catton, 1979:94-97). These propositions state the kinds of things we *know* about people and societies, but as Claude Bernard pointed out, what we think we know can prevent us from learning (Coser and Larsen, 1976:xv). Sociological studies undertaken for various environment-managing agencies naturally tend to incorporate these premises. Useful increments of knowledge obtained from such studies are, therefore, not likely to contain many surprises.

Desensitizing Concepts

If sociological inquiry in what Eckholm (1976:18) has called "the world war to save a habitable environment" is largely devoted to topics that must increasingly be viewed as "skirmishes compared to the uncontested routs being suffered" as human societies violate the limits of natural systems and destroy the basis of their own livelihood, let us consider the conceptual incapacity behind this stance. Part of it has resulted from a tendency among sociologists to use the word "environment" in a way that desensitizes them to society's involvement with ecosystems. In sociological writing, "environment" has not meant the biosphere or a local portion of it (Gould and Kolb, 1964:241). Instead, it has meant the surrounding cultural and social factors that influence people's behavior. Basically, for sociologists "environment" has been the antonym of "heredity" (Dunlap and Catton, 1979b:244-45).

Today, people who are not social scientists take "environmentalism" to mean something like "concern for environmental quality or for protection of the (physical) environment," but when sociology was emerging as a new discipline, "environmentalism" was a word that meant commitment to the view that "environmental" influences were more appropriate explanations for behavior than "hereditary" factors. Ambiguity remained, however, as to what kinds of nongenetic influences were most important (Zadrozny, 1959:109). In some contexts, "environmentalism" came to represent the view that social and cultural patterns were primarily caused by the geographic environment. But "geographic determinism" was as offensive as genetic explanations to the deep-seated sociological taboo against "reductionism." Disavowing all efforts to explain social facts by relating them to nonsocial facts (Durkheim, 1950:xxxix,xlvii-liii,97-112), most sociologists chose not to be "environmentalists" in this sense.

More recently, "environment" has ostensibly meant in sociology "all phenomena, including other social systems, that are external to and have influence upon" the people under study (Berry and Kasarda, 1977:14). However, sociologists have tended to remain preoccupied with the environment's social and cultural components (Dunlap and Catton, 1979a:65,77). Due to this preoccupation, as well as an aversion toward anything that seems reductionist, sociologists have largely disregarded the dependence of human societies on ecosystems, have exaggerated the supposed exemption of humans from ecological principles, were startled in the 1970s by the crescendo of public concern with the biophysical environment, and were slow to acknowledge the reality and social importance of environmental degradation.

Sociological neglect of the biosphere has been so nearly complete that the term "environment" has not appeared with that meaning in any article title in the *American Sociological Review* during its 45 years of publication. Except for rare papers about an extractive occupation (Hayner, 1945), social implications of soil erosion (Hypes, 1945), the rural hinterland (Jones, 1955), and the influence of natural resource distribution upon urbanization (Gibbs and Martin, 1958), sociologists have seemed almost unaware of the existence or sociological relevance of natural environments.

Despite Duncan's (1961:142) effort to demonstrate the importance of the "ecosystem" concept and to show that its utility derives from the way it transcends boundaries between social, organic, and inorganic "levels" of phenomena, traditional sociological preconceptions quickly led to a substitution of "location" for the "environment" component of Duncan's "ecological complex" (Lundberg, et al., 1968:119-22). Further, sociologists have assumed that technology was capable of creating an almost completely artificial environment for human life (Berry and Kasarda, 1977:15). Consequently, the phrase "environmental protection" has at best merely meant "channeling future [urban] growth away from areas suffering from environmental overload or possessing qualities worthy of special protection, toward areas where disruption of the environment can be minimized" (Berry and Kasarda, 1977:405). A summary review of the sociological treatment of "human ecology" (Hoselitz, 1970:31-32) reflects the wide gulf between sociologists' preoccupation with urban environments and the meaning of environment in genuine ecology.

A Neglected Precedent

Sociologists should have been able to grasp the importance of environment in the biosphere sense, however, for there was an important precedent in respected sociological literature that had given genuinely ecological consideration to environmental protection. In developing the concept of "cultural lag," Ogburn (1922:202-10) devoted eight pages to an ecological example of the phenomenon. With a narrowed meaning, the cultural lag concept took hold among sociologists, but that example and its ecological implications were forgotten.

According to Ogburn, a large part of our environment consists of life's material conditions. He used the term "adaptive culture" to refer to that portion of a society's nonmaterial culture that is adapted to these material conditions. As material conditions change, for whatever reasons, adaptive culture may get out of adjustment and will also need to change. The required changes may take time. For a while, therefore, there may be maladjustment or stress in the cultural system due to a lag between changes in material conditions and our adaptation to them. To illustrate this idea, Ogburn cited changes in forestry in the United States.

At one time, U.S. woodlands were superabundant for the timber needs of a small population, and standing forests controlled soil erosion and preserved water quality in the nation's streams. Wood for fuel, building, or manufacture was plentiful and accessible. In fact, forests were so extensive that vast tracts were burned to make way for agriculture. Under material conditions like these, outright "exploitation" was adaptive. Subsequent population growth, industrialization, and forest depletion made this prodigal policy obsolete. It nevertheless continued. New methods of sustained yield forestry were needed, such as restricted and selective harvesting combined with reforestation. A policy of "conservation" was required both to protect timber resources and to prevent soil erosion and loss of water quality. But the necessary new policy was slow in developing; the old mores of exploitation persisted long after they began having notable adverse effects. Not until the time of Theodore Roosevelt's administration was forest conservation institutionalized. In Ogburn's view, this was at least a quarter century after the need became evident.

Applied Studies

Now that the nation can no longer afford wanton destruction of its forests, many problems require immediate attention. Among these are questions of the relation between human behavior and forest fires (Brown and Davis, 1973: 272ff.). Man-caused fires can result from negligence or from arson. In either case, a critical combination of circumstances is involved that must be understood if forest fires are to be prevented. For example, unintentional smoker-caused fires might be prevented by excluding from combustible forests any of the following elements: smokers, smoking materials, matches (or lighters), or careless smoking habits. Prevention of incendiary fires, on the other hand, would require exclusion of any of the following: people, motives for burning, or incendiary devices. Studies have been numerous (Folkman, 1972) and have suggested assorted measures such as education and regulation to deal with these factors.

Sociological perspectives have been valuable in approaching each of the above topics, and sociologists have been involved in many of the studies. Here are some representative examples. Bernardi (1970) tested the effectiveness of fire prevention TV films. Siegelman and Folkman (1971) studied children who had set forest fires and found that multiple-fire setters were characterized by multiple personal problems such as aggression, hyperactivity, psychosomatic conditions, and school or family difficulties. Folkman (1979) studied urban users of wildland areas, finding them markedly different in socioeconomic characteristics from nonusers, generally aware of the fire problem, in favor of fire prevention efforts, and familiar with fire prevention messages, but nevertheless displaying gaps in their knowledge of behavior appropriate in vulnerable areas. In the South, where incendiarism has been particularly prevalent, Bertrand and Baird (1975) found that neither local people nor local law enforcement authorities deemed the setting of forest fires a serious offense. In California, Sarapata and Folkman (1970) found that among employees of the state's Division of Forestry, the Division's fire prevention program was felt to be accorded less prestige and priority by management than its program of fire detection and suppression.

Another area in which environment protection research has become important is wildland recreation (Catton, 1971). To predict the volume and types of use to be expected on recreation sites, researchers have studied demographic characteristics of wildland recreation visitors (Hendee, 1969; White, 1975), social ties among visitors (Hendee and Campbell, 1969), and the attitudes and values of visitors (Clark, et al., 1971; Hendee, et al., 1971). Problems of overuse, sometimes necessitating restricted access to popular recreation sites, have led to research on "recreational carrying capacity" (Dunlap and Catton, 1979b:248).

Visitor activities sometimes harm the recreation environment. Studies of "depreciative" behavior in places like campgrounds were therefore undertaken. Such behavior sometimes damages biological or physical features of the seminatural environment; more often it detracts from the value of recreational visits.

Littering, a pervasive form of depreciative behavior in modern society, occurs in forest campgrounds and National Parks, and applied sociologists have participated in investigating techniques for controlling it. Several studies have found widespread apathy and indifference among bystanders who witnessed campground littering, as well as minimal readership of antilittering leaflets handed out to campers (Clark, et al., 1972). However, experiments have demonstrated the potential of an incentive procedure for reducing campground litter levels, when nominal rewards are offered to children for picking up litter.

Theft, vandalism, destructive play, illegal camping, campground rule violations, as well as littering—and camper recognition of these problems—were studied by Campbell, et al. (1968). An urban "norm of noninvolvement" seemed to prevent campers from acting to deter each other (or to sanction each other's children) from engaging in such acts. According to these investigators, campers' pleasure-seeking activities also sometimes became destructive because of reduced campground contact with rangers during periods of heavy use, and because of a tendency to think of pleasure-impeding rules as intended to control others but inapplicable to oneself. As a partial solution to the problem, the researchers proposed strengthening park authorities' police powers, but more especially they proposed devising ways to persuade campers to be more vocal in their disapproval of wrongdoing so as to eliminate the erosive effects of the norm of noninvolvement.

In short, what appeared to be needed were ways of strengthening the socialization of campers to a camping ethic. Similarly, it has been suggested that larger problems of environmental protection call for development of an environmental ethic (Leopold, 1933). Ethical development can be one result of the tendency for interdependent individuals or societies to evolve modes of cooperation—what biologists call "symbioses." An ethic is a normative code restricting the kinds of actions that may occur in the struggle for existence. An ethic differentiates social from antisocial behavior. Over many centuries there have occurred notable extensions of prevailing ethics. Instead of property norms governing the treatment of slaves, for example, standards of right and wrong conduct toward fellow human beings have become applicable.

According to Leopold (1933), ethics at first prescribed allowable relations between one individual and another; later, ethics became concerned with relations between an individual and society. But man's relationships to land and to nonhuman animals and plants growing on the land are not yet governed by an ethic. Land and the biotic communities upon it are still treated according to property norms, as slaves once were. The extension of ethical norms to man-ecosystem relations is, however, an ecologically possible adaptation. The extension has become necessary: "Civilization is not...the enslavement of a stable and constant earth. It is a state of mutual and interdependent cooperation between human animals, other animals, plants, and soils, which may be disrupted at any moment by the failure of any of them. Land despoliation has evicted nations, and can on occasion do it again" (Leopold, 1933).

The author of these remarkable insights into the development and adaptive importance of human normative systems was no sociologist. Leopold was a forester (turned game manager, turned ecologist). But some sociologists have recently undertaken to investigate whether or not people have begun to embrace a "land ethic" such as Leopold advocated. Heberlein (1972), extending a previous analysis by Schwartz (1968), inferred that environmental decisions were coming to be made on moral grounds rather than by standards of economic expediency. Thus, Leopold's "land ethic" was, Heberlein supposed, becoming reality. Similarly, Burch (1975:78) noted how "life scientists are beginning to have some voice in land decisions" because of growing recognition that such things as "airsheds, watersheds, the oceans, natural beauty, and agricultural lands have reasons that real estate markets cannot understand." On the other hand, Dunlap and Van Liere (1977) argued that such changes did not truly constitute realization of an ethic that regarded humans not as dominant overlords of biotic communities but as coordinate members along with other species. The norms encouraging restraint in environmental use, they said, were still based on consideration of the consequences for humans, not consequences for other biotic entities.

When new norms are needed, one way their development can sometimes be stimulated is through the organized efforts of a social movement. Perhaps because of growing awareness of such environmental threats to human welfare as carcinogenic pollution and burgeoning dependence on rapid depletion of fossil fuel deposits, a broadly-based social movement dedicated to environmental protection has become an enduring feature of the social scene. Early studies of public attitudes toward environmental problems documented levels of concern, but we learned little of the social bases for this concern, since much of the research was rather atheoretical (Dunlap and Catton, 1979b:249). Public support for environmental protection now appears to have passed a peak and begun declining (Dunlap, et al., 1979), in spite of continued warning from knowledgeable observers that ecological problems are serious and persistent. However, membership in environmental organizations has continued to increase (Mitchell and Davies, 1978).

The environmental movement has been the subject of a number of sociological studies (Buttel and Morrison, 1977). Some sociologists have examined its origins (Albrecht and Mauss, 1975:587-90; Gale, 1972:283-86; Harry, 1974; Schnaiberg, 1973:606-9). Others have focused on environmental organization members—their socioeconomic status (Mitchell and Davies, 1978; Sills, 1975: 26-29), their reasons for joining and participating (Faich and Gale, 1971), and their attitudes toward environmental problems and possible solutions (Stallings, 1973). The evolving ideology, goals, and tactics of the movement have been studied (Morrison, et al., 1972; Gale, 1972). Typologies for classifying environmentalists have been constructed (Dunlap, 1976; Schnaiberg, 1973). Bases of opposition to the movement—both economic and ideological—have also been examined (Albrecht, 1972; Dunlap, 1976; Morrison, 1978). Some critics have deemed the movement "alarmist," and some have persisted in the cornucopian view of limitless resources perpetually available from an environment not seen as vulnerable to human overuse (Sills, 1975).

According to McEvoy (1972:234), various surveys have indicated public readiness to bear a higher tax load for environmental protection and to have additional tracts of public land reserved as national parks, wildlife refuges, etc. Environmental protection appears to be mainly a middle-class innovation; the young, the better educated, and the more affluent tend to be the most concerned about environmental problems. (These are the kinds of people one might expect to have the intellectual skills necessary to comprehend ecosystem processes, without absorbing inhibitions against departing from "conventional wisdom" about the inevitability of "progress.")

In sum, there appears to exist a growing body of knowledge, substantially sociological, with which one might assess the probable *social* feasibility of implementing various environmental protection measures as the need for them becomes imperative. Assessing their *ecological* effectiveness, of course, remains another matter.

WHAT ARE WE DOING?

The mass media were slow to acquire a suitable vocabulary that would enable them to observe and report holistic environmental concerns (Schoenfeld, et al., 1979). Media treatment of environmental matters, thus, exemplified the cultural lag concept. At the federal government level, however, there was apparent progress. In the 1970s two new federal agencies—the Council on Environmental Quality (CEQ) and the Environmental Protection Agency (EPA)—began to wield noteworthy influence both on other segments of government and on powerful industrial interests (Albrecht, 1976). New topics for sociological investigation arose. Responses of industry to pollution were examined (Rickson, 1974), and factors associated with the adoption of water pollution control practices were traced in a sample of 102 industrial organizations in Minnesota. Attitudes of industrial executives toward pollution control regulations and their enforcement were also measured (Rickson, 1977).

The two new government agencies were a major departure from the previously endemic (and sociologically expectable) fragmentation of government concern for protection of environments. "Circumscribed role expectations" had certainly characterized the federal bureaucracy. Responsibility for bits and pieces of environmental protection had been allocated to various agencies in a structure that had evolved crescively rather than by design—leaving no bureau charged with preserving the environment. This piecemeal development antedated environment sociology, but there is no evidence that environmentally interested sociologists contributed to the establishment of the more holistically oriented CEQ or EPA.

To clarify the disjunction between policy and sociology, consider a little history. The United States "started life more richly endowed than perhaps any other new country" and later there were enormous additions to its domain. The Constitution gave Congress power to manage or dispose of environmental resources. Congress soon made "some decisions that proved more durable than prudent," the most fundamental of which was a decision that "resources should not be developed by the government, but should be desocialized by sale for nominal considerations and without a covenant restrictive of the use to be made by private owners" (LeDuc, 1965:23-24).

In the second half of the nineteenth century, rapid advances in science and technology, industrial expansion and diversification, and the resulting urban growth escalated the national appetite for fuels and raw materials. By the early years of the twentieth century a vigorous conservation movement had arisen, partly in reaction against the actions of private corporations. Leaders of the movement assumed that unless corporations were controlled the nation's basic resources would become concentrated in the hands of a few wasteful and profligate users pursuing a quick profit without concern for the long-range benefit of the people (Maass, 1968:275-76). Note that what worried the movement in the beginning was more nearly the human inequities being perpetrated by industrial empire builders rather than the ecological damage their actions would inflict. The movement did not arise from sociological studies, but its ideology certainly was congruent at that stage with the sociologist's anthropocentric neglect of societal involvement in the larger web of life.

Two federal bureaus evolved, whose respective definitions and practices of conservation differ as a result of their histories. The sociological research fostered by the policies and programs of each of these bureaus tended to remain equally at the "skirmish" level in the war for environmental protection.

The Department of Interior was created in 1849. Its original activities dealt mainly with administering and disposing of the public domain, but in the twentieth century it became the largest unit of the federal government concerned with managing and developing diverse resources (Highsmith, et al., 1969:16-17). In 1916 the National Park Service was established within this department. It gave radically new institutional expression to a version of conservation derived from environmental values extoled in the writings of George Catlin, Henry David Thoreau, and John Muir. It focused on protection of esthetic, spiritual, and recreational qualities of natural environments (Nash, 1974:4-6). National Parks in the United States were established, it has been argued, not to protect portions of the biosphere as such, but to preserve natural spectacles. "Monumentalism, not environmentalism, was the driving impetus" (Runte, 1977:65,71)–at first. Over the years, however, the mission of the National Park Service has broadened. It became concerned with imparting a perceptive understanding of humanity's place in the universe and of "the incredible complexity of the plant and animal communities that made up wilderness America" (Everhart, 1972:v–vi,241).

The Department of Agriculture, on the other hand, was created for very practical purposes in 1862, and in it, in 1881, Congress established a Division of Forestry. As this division evolved, the focus of its version of conservation remained utilitarian. Gifford Pinchot, who became its chief in 1898, was the first American actually trained in Forestry (in France). The Division under his leadership became the Bureau of Forestry, acquired from the Department of Interior jurisdiction over the nation's forest reserves, and became in 1905 the U.S. Forest Service (Highsmith, et al., 1969:17–20). Pinchot brought from Europe an understanding of the scientific principle of sustained-yield forestry, which eventually became a formal policy of the U.S. Forest Service. Some convergence with the National Park Service version of conservation evolved as Forest Service "wilderness areas" were created after 1924 and as millions of acres under Forest Service jurisdiction went into a National Wilderness Preservation System authorized by Congress in 1964 (Nash, 1974:11–13).

As this convergence occurred, it sometimes entailed huge transfers of land management jurisdiction between Forest Service and Park Service. Insights from sociology were expressly sought by the editors of the *Journal of Forestry* when they invited a sociologist to prepare a paper for inclusion in their symposium concerning the pending establishment of a North Cascades National Park (Catton, 1968: cf. Hendee, 1966). We do not know, however, how many members of Congress read the symposium or similar materials in the course of deciding whether or not to create the proposed park.

Both the Park Service and the Forest Service have sponsored research on environmental topics by university sociologists, and each service has also found it worthwhile to employ sociologists to conduct research. Whether such employment by an environment-managing agency is conducive to thinking and writing from a holistic perspective on macroscopic environmental issues seems doubtful, although some sociologists working in these settings have managed to write about global topics while also studying smaller applied problems (Burch, 1965, 1966, 1967, 1970, 1971, 1975).

Conservation literature is permeated with an idea that agencies like the Forest Service are needed to protect the public interest against the selfish interests of private operators with financial power. Studies have shown, however, that public versus private ownership of resources may do less than the size of the holdings to determine whether conservation is practiced. The quality of forest practices is poorest on small private holdings, whereas the quality of these practices in both large private industrial forests and on federal lands is comparably sound. Likewise, prevention of overgrazing can be more readily achieved when livestock are run on federal rangeland in large numbers by few permittees (who can afford a substantial percentage cut in allowable numbers grazing) than when many permittees are running small numbers and cannot tolerate a marginal reduction (Maass, 1968:276–77).

In addition to such research bearing on specific components of environmentalist ideology, organizational problems faced by government resource management agencies have become applied research topics for some sociologists. For example, Reeves and Bertrand (1970) studied high turnover among rangers in Yellowstone National Park. Devall (1973) analyzed the dilemma of the U.S. Forest Service arising from its dual commitment to providing "sustained yields" of both recreational opportunities and marketable timber. Multiple uses can conflict. It is well to bear this in mind in view of the way "multiple use" serves as a Forest Service shibboleth in rivalries with other agencies such as the Park Service.

Problems of other agencies, such as those involved in water resource development, have also drawn sociological attention (Field, et al., 1974). Today the Army Corps of Engineers, for example, has come to believe that "the social aspects of water resource development and management equal or exceed the physical problems," and it deems both physical and social scientists "essential to the successful development of the nation's water and related resources" (Harrison, 1977:1). Topics that have been studied have included variations in public tolerance for both environmental and social change (e.g., community relocation) arising from water development projects (Andrews and Geertsen, 1970; Love, 1977; Napier and Moody, 1977).

Summing Up

Environmental protection policies have a history of piecemeal development in and by assorted agencies that have evolved crescively rather than by design. Coordination and synthesis have just begun. Sociological inputs to agency and policy development have been few and peripheral, but considerable sociological activity is involved at the tactical, administrative, and public relations level, where it has been useful. Insofar as bits and pieces of the environment are being given protection, the aims and procedures tend to be substantially compatible with currently accepted sociological knowledge, especially its least ecologically sophisticated tenets. There is much to be done.

WHAT HAVE WE ACCOMPLISHED?

What can sociologists now say about the results of efforts to develop national and international policies for environmental protection? Have these efforts assured the biosphere's capacity to sustain human life permanently?

Dangerous Treadmill

Industrialism has placed mankind in an ecological situation that environmental sociologists have begun to recognize as fatefully precarious. In an important book, Schnaiberg (1980:230–49) has described the structure of advanced industrial societies as a "treadmill" of expansion of production and consumption in mutual positive feedback. This treadmill is ecologically dangerous because increasing its speed involves increased "environmental withdrawals and additions." Theoretically, government could regulate the treadmill's "externalities— from unemployment to resource depletion." In reality, however, policies of governmental regulatory agencies that are meant to correct abuses have been turned toward suppression of competition and further entrenchment of the treadmill in our lives. Schnaiberg believes government restructuring of the treadmill is unlikely in the United States, and internationally it is blocked by the power of multinational corporations. The longer the treadmill operates, the more people become dependent upon it, the fewer the alternative options available, and the less the economic influence of opposing forces. Consciousness of the treadmill's failure to achieve sustained social welfare and increasing recognition of environmental and energy problems, have heightened the sense of vulnerability. Alternatives to the treadmill have become conceivable, but their serious implementation cannot begin while the labor and social equity movements remain uncoordinated with the environmental and appropriate technology movements.

Yet, there have been some organizational developments that possibly do constitute real and significant steps toward biosphere protection. Management of world fisheries for maximum sustained yield, while still far from actual achievement, would require eventual cooperation of all nations, and numerous treaties already adopted do reflect considerable international recognition of this need (Highsmith, et al., 1969:389). United States involvement in global conservation activities is likewise indicated by U.S. funding for and participation in such United Nations agencies as the Food and Agricultural Organization (FAO), the United Nations Education, Scientific, and Cultural Organization (UNESCO), and the World Meteorological Organization (WMO), whose objectives include encouraging development of wind and solar energy resources, as well as improvement of agriculturally useful weather forecasting (Highsmith, et al., 1969:391–92).

Sociologists are, nevertheless, still peripheral to the work of these organizations, partly because we tend to define them as peripheral to the interests of our discipline.

Eye-Opening NEPA

Sociological recognition of the human relevance of natural environments (and organizations concerned with their protection) broadened after passage in 1969 of the National Environmental Policy Act (NEPA) and as a result of the celebration of Earth Day in the following year. An event that "radicalized" many citizens and helped stimulate enactment of NEPA, the 1969 offshore oil spill at Santa Barbara led to a study of the impacts of an environmental disaster on people's attitudes (Molotch, 1970). Sociological interest in the impact of attitudes on environments may yet catch up.

NEPA required that environmental impact statements (EISs) be included in every federal project proposal significantly affecting environmental quality, and a new role for applied sociologists began to be envisioned. In response to a resolution put forward by a group attending a business meeting of the American Sociological Association, the ASA Council authorized the formation of a committee "to develop guidelines for sociological contributions to environmental impact statements" (Dunlap and Catton, 1979b:246). It is problematic whether the subsequent proliferation of social impact assessments really foreshadows a more holistic understanding among sociologists of the global environmental effects of industrialism. For now, however, a major activity absorbing the efforts of applied sociologists in the area of environmental protection is the preparation of social impact assessments.

Assessing Impact Assessment

The original ASA committee was unable to complete the task of formulating guidelines for sociological involvement, perhaps because its members disagreed on whether doing social impact analyses was the only way, or even the major way, in which sociologists might involve themselves in environmental impact assessment. A subsequent committee did develop a list of suggested social impact variables and data sources. Members of that committee felt that the EIS requirement of NEPA had "allowed the country to think in a very systematic way about the impacts of administrative and development decisions" (Burdge, et al., 1978).

It is not clear, however, that becoming preoccupied with project-centered social impact assessment suffices to sensitize sociologists to the seriousness of macroscopic environmental problems. Consider, for example, the quest for fuels. As sociologically interesting as indexes of social disorganization in energy boom towns may be (Cortese and Jones, 1979), this impact of society's energy appetite is probably not the one most threatening to the future of our species. Nor is it reason enough to regard industrialism as a precarious mode of living. Moreover, even though new in name, the idea of assessing social impacts is not without precedent in sociology. Cottrell (1951) long ago analyzed the effects of technological change upon a specific railroad-dependent community, and Chase (1929) as well as Ogburn (1938) examined the effects of modern technology on society in general. None of these studies addressed the now salient question: Is industrialism a permanently viable way of life for a human species on a planet the size of ours?

Social impact assessment asks what difference a proposed development is likely to make in the lives of residents of the targeted area (Gold, 1978). This is not the same as asking what difference the proposed change will make in the durability of the ecosystem upon which the human community depends; in the long run that may be the most important question. If sociologists are inclined to leave the latter question alone because it seems "nonsociological," we can, nevertheless, quite legitimately study the correlates of asking or not asking it. They may have social ramifications more profound than the impacts of a specific development project. Certainly it is within the purview of sociology to wonder what kind of society does, and what kind does not, ask whether its basic sustenance-producing activities entail environmental effects that preclude their permanent practice.

Social impact assessment may, as Gold says, consider the perspectives not only of the local residents but also of industrialists, construction workers, and others significantly concerned with the development project. However, insofar as social impact assessment is site-specific in its focus, it probably does little to engage sociologists in consideration of global biospheric changes affecting mankind. As Gold points out, social impact research can give attention to "important hyphenations" such as the sociopsychological, socioeconomic, and even the sociobiological effects of a project. But if project-specific impact assessments are considered *the* way for sociologists to contribute to environmental protection, then the currently abundant opportunities for sociologists to engage in that kind of research may function as opportunities for avoiding genuinely ecological consideration of larger ways in which our normal activities threaten the environmental basis for continuation of our present way of life.

United Nations Efforts

Somewhat more holistic attempts at devising environmental protection policies can be found if attention is turned to international agencies. The proposal to convene a United Nations Conference on the Human Environment was first submitted to the UN Economic and Social Council in 1968 by the leader of Sweden's mission at the UN. He was apprehensive that it might go nowhere because the institutionalized sovereignty of nations might fatally obstruct recognition of humanity's global interdependence and impede international cooperation for coping with environmental problems (Rowland, 1973:33-34). Among the steps taken to prepare for the 1972 conference and for ongoing cooperative environmental protection efforts was the 1971 launching by UNESCO of an intergovernmental and interdisciplinary research program on Man and the Biosphere, in which sociology was included. In Stockholm in 1972, in spite of their political, economic, ideological and religious differences "delegates of 114 nations...were able to agree on an Action Plan and a Declaration of Principles based on the common realization that the Earth is a closed, ecological system and man continues to modify it at his peril" (Lewis, 1973:6). Perceptive reading of these documents reveals, however, that at a number of points they remain attuned to the anthropocentric perspective that has characterized a cultural determinist sociology, even though elsewhere they invoke principles of ecology. For instance: "In the developing countries most of the environmental problems are caused by underdevelopment...[and] ...to safeguard and improve the environment...industrialized countries should make efforts to reduce the gap between themselves and the developing countries." Further, it was asserted that "the capability of man to improve the environment increases with each passing day" (Rowland, 1973:141).

Thus, there is no magic in going international; the UN, too, has treadmill commitments.

Becoming a Nation of Adversaries

If international cooperation, difficult to achieve, is essential for protecting the biosphere, nations can hardly afford erosion of their internal cooperative relations. It appears, however, that just such erosion may be a significant effect of NEPA, despite its environmentalist intentions.

Schnaiberg (1980:326) doubts the protective efficacy not only of social but also of environmental impact statements. Each EIS theoretically addresses the question, "What would the world be like with, versus without, this project?" But reliable assessments of the effects of past projects are rare enough to make impact forecasting dubious. It is also necessary to ask, "How would policy making differ with, versus without, the writing of EISs?"

A sample of about 200 environmental impact statements from the 2,400 actions subject to environmental analysis in the first two years of NEPA was studied to see if any of them resulted in a proposed action being avoided or reversed. In no case was the proposed project abandoned as a result of adverse comments in the environmental impact statement. In many instances the project had already reached a technological stage that made any change of plans extremely difficult (Kreith, 1973).

Eight years after passage of NEPA, a political scientist who had been instrumental in having the EIS requirement included in NEPA, acknowledged that in practice the intent of environmental impact analysis had been subverted. A new growth industry—EIS writing—had arisen. Agencies employed "instant ecologist" consultants to write the required statements. The test of their effectiveness was not the protection of the environment, but the survival of the agency's project or program upon challenge in the courts (Caldwell, 1978). Remedy for the abuse, he felt, depended on existing powers of the executive branch of government and required no legislative changes.

Adversary proceedings in courts and administrative forums have become a major means of delaying projects that opponents regard as environmentally harmful. NEPA has generated a new field of litigation (Smith, 1973:35). "Frequently, environmentalists are able to obtain injunctions which halt the environmentally damaging practice while the issue is being adjudicated....The total impact of existing environmental legislation is that, at the present time, it is more effective to go into court than into the streets" (Gale, 1972:293). A crucial question remains unanswered, however. As a way of defending ecosystems, isn't it self-defeating to become a nation of litigious factions? If the environment is threatened because industrialized humanity has overloaded it, and if overload is a condition we want to avoid because it intensifies the competitiveness of human relations, what is the use of attempting to protect the environment by a means that turns competitors into adversaries? Perhaps there is much to be undone.

WHERE ARE WE GOING?

Applied environmental sociology must ask questions more daring and of larger scope. Humans can do more damage to the environment than other species because machines supplement human bodies as processors of environmental substances. Not only human lungs, but also steel mills, engines, and furnaces inhale oxygen and exhale carbon dioxide. The environment's capacity to absorb, transform, and recycle noxious and toxic substances produced by human-machine metabolism is limited. There is an urgent and persistent need for studies of the social ramifications of this condition. If the per capita industrial productivity of the rest of the world were raised to the U.S. level, so that the world's total human population would be imposing six times the present burden upon ecosystems, what then? It is doubtful whether the world's ecosystems could bear such a load. If not, then some or all of the world's human population must be destined not to reach (or retain) the high standard of living a few have attained and more aspire toward. If ecologically there has to be an end to economic growth, serious problems of equity lie ahead. Already a lively sociological interest in this issue is evident (Morrison, 1976, 1978; Schnaiberg, 1975), and the topic will need to be studied quite extensively and carefully in years to come.

Equity issues aside, "No organism has yet been discovered that can perpetuate itself in an environment saturated with its own waste products, and there is little reason to suspect that man is an exception" (Everhart, 1972:242). This means that many more sociologists must become familiar with the ecological concept of *carrying capacity*.

Something like this concept has been known to those few sociologists who have sought ways of protecting wild areas from overuse by recreational visitors. The National Park Service sponsored a study of river running in the Grand Canyon, for example, in which sociologists sought to develop methods of measuring "recreational carrying capacity." That term was used to mean the maximum number of visitors who could be in an area without impairing each other's recreational experience—rather than without impairing the physical environment (Heberlein and Shelby, 1977). Perhaps for this reason, it turned out to be extremely difficult to determine at precisely what volume the recreational use of such an environment became excessive (Nielsen and Endo, 1977; Nielsen, et al., 1977).

Still, it ought to be clear that if people can overuse a national park, they can also overuse a planet. Carrying capacity is an indispensable concept; it ought to become focal to applied research in environmental sociology. It can be simply defined as the maximum load a species population (human or nonhuman) may impose upon an ecosystem *without reducing the environment's ability to bear that load* (Catton, 1980:4,34).

For other animals, where there is not (within a species) so much interindividual variation in resource appetites or environmental impact, "maximum permanently supportable population" has sufficed as a definition of an environment's carrying capacity. For the human species, which displays tremendous variation in per capita appetite for resources and per capita impact on habitat, carrying capacity cannot be adequately defined in mere head-count terms. This appears to have tempted sociologists to disregard the concept as if it were inapplicable to humanity, instead of refining it by combining population counts with measures of per capita demand and impact. It has distracted us with debates over the clumsier concept of "optimum population" (Catton, 1978:231–32).

Sociological neglect of the ecosystem dependence of human societies (and the limits of environmental resilience) has also caused us to miss another point about carrying capacity that is well known in the science of range management. Carrying capacity refers to the load a given area of land can support indefinitely. Omission of this time element from sociological versions of the concept has precluded recognition by sociologists that environments can be overloaded and, thus, damaged (Wisniewski, 1980). It has kept sociology inattentive to the often delayed but inexorable human consequences of environmental degradation.

The main question requiring answers in the years ahead, therefore, is this: What things that people and societies are going to be capable of doing must they refrain from doing in order to protect their future? It is heartening, in view of the need for answers to that question, to see the range of topics being explored by those applied environmental sociologists who are studying rainfall stimulation, fog dissipation, hail suppression, hurricane modification, etc. They have not only looked into the distribution of costs and benefits of weather modification and the processes of decision making about it, but have also studied public doubt as to whether so monumental a manifestation of the human urge to engineer the environment should be tolerated (Farhar, 1977; Haas, 1973). More of the latter type of investigation (on other ominous forms of society-environment interaction) will be needed in years to come.

As we move deeper into the future, the scope of such inquiries has to become more global. We must discover, for instance, how much the public may comprehend, why and how much it resists, and how educable it might be toward propositions like the following:

The principal defect of the industrial way of life with its ethos of expansion is that it is not sustainable. Its termination within the lifetime of someone born today is inevitable—unless it continues to be sustained for a while longer by an entrenched minority at the cost of imposing great suffering on the rest of mankind. We can be certain, however, that sooner or later it will end…in one of two ways: either against our will, in a succession of famines, epidemics, social crises, and wars or in a way we want it to—because we wish to create a society that will not impose hardship and cruelty upon our children—in a succession of thoughtful, humane, and measured changes. (Goldsmith, et al., 1974:3)

Sociologists must recognize the applied potential in cross-cultural and historical studies designed to isolate the most fundamental causes of environmental degradation. A first step in that direction might be comparing the environmental repercussions of capitalism versus socialism (Anderson, 1976; Buttel, 1978), but it may ultimately be more crucial to contrast industrial with nonindustrial societies. The earth has less carrying capacity, Goldsmith, et al. are telling us, for industrial than for nonindustrial societies.

As the United States moved from agrarianism into industrialism, public attitudes toward the environment became divided into what environmental historians have called the "transformational orientation" (desire to conquer and control nature for utilitarian ends) versus the "preservationist orientation" of the wilderness movement (McEvoy, 1972:215-16). Unless industrialism is inherently fatal, it may be vital to discover the prospects for diminishing popular commitment to transformationalist values. Environmental protection studies would, thus, need to include some monitoring of media indicators of the persistence of that orientation (Sporn, 1969). Of even greater and increasing importance, especially if survival turns out to depend on outgrowing industrialism, will be imaginative research on changes in the values that shape our ways of interacting with our planetary environment (Cotgrove, 1975, 1976, 1979).

In the final analysis the problem of environmental protection is this: how to induce members of human societies to opt for a state of sustainable equilibrium instead of continuing environment-damaging trends in ecosystem exploitation.

REFERENCES AND SUGGESTED READINGS

Albrecht, S.L. 1972. "Environmental Social Movements and Counter-Movements: An Overview and an Illustration." *Journal of Voluntary Action Research* 1(Oct):2-11.

_____. 1976. "Legacy of the Environmental Movement." *Environment and Behavior* 8(June):147-68.

Albrecht, S.L. and A.L. Mauss. 1975. "The Environment as a Social Problem." In *Social Problems as Social Movements*, edited by A.L. Mauss, pp. 536-

605. Philadelphia: Lippincott.

Anderson, C.H. 1976. *The Sociology of Survival: Social Problems of Growth* Homewood, Ill.: Dorsey.

Andrews, W.H. and D.C. Geersten. 1970. "The Function of Social Behavior in Water Resource Development." Utah State University, Logan, Institute for Social Research on Natural Resources and Center for Water Resources Research.

Bernardi, G.C. 1970. "Three Fire Prevention Television Films Varying in 'Threat' Content." USDA Forest Service Research Paper PSW-63. Berkeley, Calif.: Pacific Southwest Forest and Range Experiment Station.

Berry, B.J.L. and J.D. Kasarda. 1977. *Contemporary Urban Ecology.* New York: Macmillan.

Bertrand, A.L. and A.W. Baird. 1975. "Incendiarism in Southern Forests: A Decade of Sociological Research." Starkville: Social Science Research Center, Mississippi State University.

Brown, A.A. and K.P. Davis. 1973. *Forest Fire Control and Use,* 2nd ed. New York: McGraw-Hill.

Burch, W.R., Jr. 1965. "The Play World of Camping: Research into the Social Meaning of Outdoor Recreation." *American Journal of Sociology* 70(Mar): 604-12.

_____. 1966. "Wilderness—the Life Cycle and Forest Recreational Choice." *Journal of Forestry* 64(Sept):606-10.

_____. 1967. "The Social Characteristics of Participants in Three Styles of Family Camping." Portland, Ore.: Pacific Northwest Forest and Range Experiment Station, USDA Forest Service Research Paper PNW-48.

_____. 1970. "Resources and Social Structure: Some Conditions of Stability and Change." *Annals of the American Academy of Political and Social Science* 389(May):27-34.

*_____. 1971. *Daydreams and Nightmares: A Sociological Essay on the American Environment.* New York: Harper & Row.
    This book is a pioneering effort by a sociologist who had done micro-level environmental protection research for the government to turn toward a macro-level orientation. It explores the myths about man and nature that enabled Western civilization to create an environmental crisis.

_____. 1975. "Land Use, Ethics, and Property Rights—a Western View from the East." *Journal of Range Management* 28(Jan):77-79.

Burdge, R.J., W.R. Burch, Jr., R.L. Gold, G. Krebs, Sue Johnson, and T.L. Napier. 1978. "Social Components of Environmental Impact Statements." In *Environmental Impact Analysis: Emerging Issues in Planning,* edited by R.K. Jain and B.L. Hutchings, pp. 117-32. Urbana: University of Illinois Press.

Buttel, F.H. 1978. "Environmental Sociology: A new Paradigm?" *The American Sociologist* 13(Nov):252-56.

Buttel, F.H. and D.E. Morrison. 1977. "The Environmental Movement: A Research Bibliography with Some State-of-the-Art Comments." Exchange Bibliography No. 1308. Monticello, Ill.: Council of Planning Librarians.

Caldwell, L.K. 1978. "The Environmental Impact Statement: A Misused Tool." In *Environmental Impact Analysis: Emerging Issues in Planning,* edited by R.K. Jain and B.L. Hutchings, pp. 11–25. Urbana: University of Illinois Press.

Campbell, F.L., J.C. Hendee, and R.N. Clark. 1968. "Law and Order in Public Parks." *Parks and Recreation* 3(Dec):28–31, 51–55.

Catton, W.R., Jr. 1968. "Decision in the North Cascades." *Journal of Forestry* 66(July):540–46.

_____. 1971. "The Wildland Recreation Boom and Sociology." *Pacific Sociological Review* 14(July):339–59.

_____. 1978. "Carrying Capacity, Overshoot, and the Qualify of Life." In *Major Social Issues: A Multidisciplinary View,* edited by J.M. Yinger and S.J. Cutler, pp. 231–49. New York: The Free Press.

_____. 1979. "The Recreation Visitor: Motivation, Behavior, Impact." In *Recreational Use of Wild Lands,* 3rd ed., edited by C.F. Brockman and L.C. Merriam, Jr., pp. 91–117. New York: McGraw-Hill.

* _____. 1980. *Overshoot: The Ecological Basis of Revolutionary Change.* Urbana: University of Illinois Press.

This is an ecological interpretation of human history that shows how mankind mistook means of evading the world's limits for means of raising them. It develops an ecological paradigm to replace obsolete thoughtways that prolong dangerous reliance on phantom carrying capacity and provides conceptual tools for realistically facing a difficult future and for perceiving ways to minimize the environmental degradation by which we continue to aggravate the future's burdens.

Chase, S. 1929. *Men and Machines.* New York: Macmillan.

Clark, R.N., R.L. Burgess, and J.C. Hendee. 1972. "The Development of Anti-Litter Behavior in a Forest Campground." *Journal of Applied Behavior Analysis* 5(Spring):1–5.

Clark, R.N., J.C. Hendee, and F.L. Campbell. 1971. "Values, Behavior, and Conflict in Modern Camping Culture." *Journal of Leisure Research* 3:143–59.

Cooper, C.F. 1978. "What Might Man-Induced Climate Change Mean?" *Foreign Affairs* 56(Apr):500–20.

Cortese, C.F. and B. Jones. 1979. "Energy Boomtowns: A Social Impact Model and Annotated Bibliography." In *Sociopolitical Impacts of Energy Use and Policy,* edited by C.T. Unseld, D.E. Morrison, D.L. Sills, and C.P. Wolf, pp. 101–63. Washington, D.C.: National Academy of Sciences.

Coser, L.A. and O.N. Larsen, eds. 1976. *The Uses of Controversy in Sociology.* New York: The Free Press.

Cotgrove, S. 1975. "Technology, Rationality, and Domination." *Social Studies of Science* 5:55–78.

_____. 1976. "Environmentalism and Utopia." *The Sociological Review* 24 (Feb):23–42.

_____. 1979. "Catastrophe or Cornucopia?" *New Society* 47(Mar 22):683–84.

Cottrell, W.F. 1951. "Death by Dieselization: A Case Study in the Reaction to Technological Change." *American Sociological Review* 16(June):358–65.

Devall, W.B. 1973. "The Forest Service and Its Clients: Input to Forest Service

Decision Making." *Environmental Affairs* 2:732–57.

Duncan, O.D. 1961. "From Social System to Ecosystem." *Sociological Inquiry* 31(Spring):140–49.

Dunlap, R.E. 1976. "Understanding Opposition to the Environmental Movement: The Importance of Dominant American Values." Paper presented at the annual meeting of the Society for the Study of Social Problems. New York.

Dunlap, R.E. and W.R. Catton, Jr. 1979a. "Environmental Sociology: A Framework for Analysis." In *Progress in Resource Management and Environmental Planning*, Vol. I., edited by T. O'Riordan and R.C. d'Arge, pp. 57–85. Chichester, England: John Wiley & Sons.

* _____. 1979b. "Environmental Sociology." *Annual Review of Sociology* 5: 243–73.

Drawing upon more than 200 sources, this review article traces the development of a sociology of environmental issues and the emergence of an environmental sociology. Areas of research in environmental sociology are briefly surveyed.

Dunlap, R.E. and K.D. Van Liere. 1977. "Land Ethic or Golden Rule: Comment on 'The Land Ethic Realized' by Thomas A. Heberlein." *Journal of Social Issues* 33(Summer):200–7.

Dunlap, R.E., K.D. Van Liere, and D.A. Dillman. 1979. "Evidence of Decline in Public Concern with Environmental Quality: A Reply." *Rural Sociology* 44:204–12.

Durkheim, E. 1950. *The Rules of the Sociological Method*. Glencoe, Ill.: Free Press.

Eckholm, E.P. 1976. *Losing Ground: Environmental Stress and World Food Prospects*. New York: W.W. Norton.

Everhart, W.C. 1972. *The National Park Service*. New York: Praeger.

Faich, R.G. and R.P. Gale. 1971. "The Environmental Movement: From Recreation to Politics." *Pacific Sociological Review*, 14(July):270–87.

Farhar, Barbara C., ed. 1977. "Hail Suppression: Society and Environment." University of Colorado, Boulder, Institute for Behavioral Science.

Field, D.R., J.C. Barron, and B.F. Long, eds. 1974. *Water and Community Development: Social and Economic Perspectives*. Ann Arbor, Mich.: Ann Arbor Science Publishers.

Folkman, W.S. 1972. "Studying the People Who Cause Forest Fires." In *Social Behavior, Natural Resources, and the Environment*, edited by W.R. Burch, Jr., N.H. Cheek, Jr., and L. Taylor, pp. 44–64. New York: Harper & Row.

_____. 1979. "Urban Users of Wildland Areas as Forest Fire Risks." USDA Forest Service Research Paper PSW-137. Berkeley, Calif.: Pacific Southwest Forest and Range Experiment Station.

Gale, R.P. 1972. "From Sit-in to Hike-in: A Comparison of the Civil Rights and Environmental Movements." In *Social Behavior, Natural Resources, and the Environment*, edited by W.R. Burch, Jr., N.H. Cheek, Jr., and L. Taylor, pp. 280–305. New York: Harper & Row.

Gibbs, J.P. and W.T. Martin. 1958. "Urbanization and Natural Resources: A Study in Organizational Ecology." *American Sociological Review* 23 (June):266–77.

Gold, R.L. 1978. "Linking Social with Other Impact Assessments." In *Environmental Impact Analysis: Emerging Issues in Planning,* edited by R.K. Jain and B.L. Hutchings, pp. 105–16. Urbana: University of Illinois Press.

*Goldsmith, E., R. Allen, M. Allaby, J. Davoll, and S. Lawrence. 1974. *Blueprint for Survival.* New York: New American Library/Signet.

A milestone in the environmental literature, this book offers persuasive evidence that routines of modern industrial societies disrupt ecosystems upon which their life depends and calls for major social change to achieve a stable society affording new satisfactions more than compensating accustomed ones man must learn to forego.

Gould, J. and W.L. Kolb, eds. 1964. *A Dictionary of the Social Sciences.* New York: The Free Press.

Haas, J.E. 1973. "Social Aspects of Weather Modification." *Bulletin of the American Meteorological Society* 54:647–57.

Harrison, R.W. 1977. "Introduction." In U.S. Army Corps of Engineers, Institute for Water Resources, Social Scientists Conference Proceedings, Memphis, September 20–24, 1976, Vol. 1.

Harry, J. 1974. "Causes of Contemporary Environmentalism." *Humboldt Journal of Social Relations* 2(Fall/Winter):3–7.

Hayner, N.S. 1945. "Taming the Lumberjack." *American Sociological Review* 10(Apr):217–25.

Heberlein, T.A. 1972. "The Land Ethic Realized: Some Social Psychological Explanations for Changing Environmental Attitudes." *Journal of Social Issues* 28(Fall):79–87.

Heberlein, T.A. and B. Shelby. 1977. "Carrying Capacity, Values, and the Satisfaction Model." *Journal of Leisure Research* 9:142–48.

Hendee, J.C. 1966. "An Evaluation of the North Cascades Study Report." Institute of Forest Products, Contemporary Forestry Papers, Contribution No. 2, University of Washington, Seattle.

———. 1969. "Rural-Urban Differences Reflected in Outdoor Recreation Participation." *Journal of Leisure Research* 1:333–41.

Hendee, J.C. and F.L. Campbell. 1969. "Social Aspects of Outdoor Recreation—The Developed Campground." *Trends in Parks and Recreation* 6:13–18.

Hendee, J.C., R.P. Gale, and W.R. Catton, Jr. 1971. "A Typology of Outdoor Recreation Activity Preferences." *Journal of Environmental Education* 3(Fall):28–34.

Highsmith, R.M., Jr., J.G. Jensen, and R.D. Rudd. 1969. *Conservation in the United States,* 2nd. ed. Chicago: Rand McNally.

Hoselitz, B.F., ed. 1970. *A Reader's Guide to the Social Sciences,* Rev. ed. New York: The Free Press.

Hubbert, M.K. 1967, "Mineral Resources and Rates of Consumption." *Proceedings of the World Population Conference,* Belgrade, August 30–September 10, 1965. Vol. 3:318–24. New York: United Nations.

Hypes, J.L. 1945. "The Social Implications of Soil Erosion: A Case Study." *American Sociological Review* 10(June):373–82.

Jones, L.W. 1955. "The Hinterland Reconsidered." *American Sociological Review* 20(Feb):40–44.

Keyfitz, N. 1976. "World Resources and the World Middle Class." *Scientific American* 235(July):28–35.

Kreith, F. 1973. "Lack of Impact." *Environment* 15(Jan/Feb):26–33.

LeDuc, T. 1965. "The Historiography of Conservation." *Forest History* 9(Oct): 23–28.

*Leopold, A. 1933. "The Conservation Ethic." *Journal of Forestry* 31(Oct): 634–43.

This is the original version of an article later incorporated in revised form as a chapter in Leopold's *A Sand Country Almanac,* widely read in recent years. Sociologically insightful, poetic in style, fervent in aim, it argues the need for humans to outgrow the urge to enslave nature. It advocates learning to act with ethical restraint toward all our fellow citizens (other animals, plants, the soil) in biotic communities to which we owe our lives.

Lewis, R.S., ed. 1973. *The Environmental Revolution.* Chicago: Educational Foundation for Nuclear Science.

Likens, G.E., R.F. Wright, J.N. Galloway, and T.J. Butler. 1979. "Acid Rain." *Scientific American* 241(Oct):43–51.

Love, Ruth L. 1977. "Responses to Innovation: A Perspective for Social Profiling or How to Avoid the Laundry List Syndrome." In U.S. Army Corps of Engineers, Institute for Water Resources, Social Scientists Conference Proceedings, Memphis, September 20–24, 1976, Vol. 1.

Lundberg, G.A., C.C. Schrag, O.N. Larsen, and W.R. Catton, Jr. 1968. *Sociology,* 4th ed. New York: Harper & Row.

Lundqvist, L.J. 1973. "Environmental Quality and Politics: Some Notes on Political Development in 'Developed' Countries." *Social Science Information* 12(Apr):43–85.

Maass, A. 1968. "Conservation: Political and Social Aspects." In *International Encyclopedia of the Social Sciences, Vol. 3,* edited by D.L. Sills, pp. 271–79. New York: Macmillan and The Free Press.

Malin, K.M. 1967. "Food Resources of the Earth." *Proceedings of the World Population Conference,* Belgrade, August 30–September 10, 1965, Vol. 3:385–90. New York: United Nations.

McEvoy, J. III. 1972. "The American Concern with Environment." In *Social Behavior, Natural Resources, and the Environment,* edited by W.R. Burch, Jr., N.H. Cheek, Jr., and L. Taylor, pp. 214–36. New York: Harper & Row.

Meadows, D.H., D.L. Meadows, J. Randers, and W.L. Behrens, III. 1972. *The Limits to Growth.* New York: Universe Books.

Mitchell, R.C. and J.C. Davies, III. 1978. "The United States Environmental Movement and Its Political Context: An Overview." Discussion Paper D-32. Washington, D.C.: Resources for the Future.

Molotch, H. 1970. "Oil in Santa Barbara and Power in America." *Sociological Inquiry* 40(Winter):131–44.

Morrison, D.E. 1976. "Growth, Environment, Equity and Scarcity." *Social Science Quarterly* 57(Sept):292–306.

_____. 1978. "Equity Impacts of Some Major Energy Alternatives." In *Energy Policy in the United States: Social and Behavioral Dimensions,* edited by S. Warkov, pp. 164–93. New York: Praeger.

Morrison, D.E., K.E. Hornback, and W.K. Warner. 1972. "The Environmental Movement: Some Preliminary Observations and Predictions." In *Social Behavior, Natural Resources, and the Environment,* edited by W.R. Burch, Jr., N.H. Cheek, Jr., and L. Taylor, pp. 259–79. New York: Harper & Row.

Napier, T.L. and Cathy W. Moody. 1977. "The Social Impact of Forced Relocation on Rural Populations due to Planned Environmental Modification." *Western Sociological Review* 8(July):91–104.

Nash, R. 1974. "The American Conservation Movement." Forums in History, FA 049. St. Charles, Mo.: Forum Press.

Nielsen, Joyce M. and R. Endo. 1977. "Where Have All the Purists Gone? An Empirical Examination of the Displacement Hypothesis in Wilderness Recreation." *Western Sociological Review* 8(July):61–75.

Nielsen, Joyce M., B. Shelby, and J.E. Haas. 1977. "Sociological Carrying Capacity and the Last Settler Syndrome." *Pacific Sociological Review* 20(Oct): 568–81.

Ogburn, W.F. 1922. *Social Change.* New York: Viking.

_____. 1938. *Machines and Tomorrow's World.* New York: Public Affairs Committee.

Otterman, J. 1977. "Anthropogenic Impact on the Albedo of the Earth." *Climatic Change* 1:137–55.

Reeves, J.B. and A.L. Bertrand. 1970. "Employee Mobility and Community Cohesion in a National Park." *Journal of Leisure Research* 1:342–47.

Rickson, R.E. 1974. "Social and Economic Factors in the Adoption by Industry of Water Pollution Measures in Minnesota." University of Minnesota, Minneapolis, Water Resources Research Center, Bulletin 67.

_____. 1977. "Dimensions of Environmental Management: Legitimation of Government Regulation by Industrial Managers." *Environment and Behavior* 9(Mar):15–40.

Rowland, W. 1973. *The Plot to Save the World: The Life and Times of the Stockholm Conference on the Human Environment.* Toronto: Clarke, Irwin.

Runte, A. 1977. "The National Park Idea: Origins and Paradox of the American Experience." *Journal of Forest History* 21(Apr):64–75.

Sarapata, A. and W.S. Folkman. 1970. "Fire Prevention in the California Division of Forestry: Personnel and Practices." USDA Forest Service Research Paper PSW-65. Berkeley, Calif.: Pacific Southwest Forest and Range Experiment Station.

Schnaiberg, A. 1973. "Politics, Participation, and Pollution: The Environmental Movement." In *Cities in Change: A Reader on Urban Sociology,* edited by J. Walton and D. Carns, pp. 605–27. Boston: Allyn & Bacon.

_____. 1975. "Social Syntheses of the Societal-Environmental Dialectic: The Role of Distributional Impacts." *Social Science Quarterly* 56(June):5–10.

_____. 1980. *The Environment: From Surplus to Scarcity.* New York: Oxford University Press.

Schneider, S.H. 1977. "Climate Change and the World Predicament: A Case Study for Interdisciplinary Research." *Climatic Change* 1(Mar):21–43.

Schoenfeld, A.C., R.F. Meier, and R.J. Griffin. 1979. "Constructing a Social Problem: The Press and the Environment." *Social Problems* 27(Oct):38–61.

Schwartz, S.H. 1968. "Awareness of Consequences and the Influence of Moral Norms in Interpersonal Behavior." *Sociometry* 31:355–69.

Siegelman, Ellen Y. and W.S. Folkman. 1971. "Youthful Fire-Setters: An Explanatory Study in Personality and Background." Berkeley, Calif.: Pacific Southwest Forest and Range Experiment Station. USDA Forest Service Research Note PSW-230.

Sills, D.L. 1975. "The Environmental Movement and Its Critics." *Human Ecology* 3:1–41.

Smith, W.J.J. 1973. *Environmental Policy and Impact Analysis: Origins, Evolution, and Implications for Government, Business, and the Courts.* New York: The Conference Board.

Sporn, P. 1969. "Energy for Man and Environmental Protection." *Science* 166 (Oct 31):555.

Stallings, R.A. 1973. "Patterns of Belief in Social Movements: Clarifications from an Analysis of Environmental Group." *Sociological Quarterly* 14:465–80.

Vogt, W. 1948. *Road to Survival.* New York: William Sloane.

White, T.H. 1975. "The Relative Importance of Education and Income as Predictors in Outdoor Recreation Participation." *Journal of Leisure Research* 7:191–99.

Whittaker, R.H. and G.E. Likens. 1973. "Primary Production: The Biosphere and Man." *Human Ecology* 1(Sept):357–69.

Wisniewski, R.L. 1980. "Carrying Capacity: Understanding Our Biological Limitations." *Humboldt Journal of Social Relations* 8(Summer):55–70.

Woodwell, G.M. 1978. "The Carbon Dioxide Question." *Scientific American* 238(Jan):34–43.

Zadrozny, J.T. 1959. *Dictionary of Social Science.* Washington, D.C.: Public Affairs Press.

24   PEACE PROMOTION

Louis Kriesberg

Of all the problems to which sociology might be applied, preventing war would seem to be paramount. Yet, the magnitude and complexity of this problem—as well as traditional disciplinary boundaries—have constrained efforts by sociologists to study peace promotion. Before examining what we know, what we are doing, and what we have accomplished in this area, we will identify the major issues in applying sociology to the specific problems of promoting peace.

WHAT ARE THE PROBLEMS?

Major Issues

Severe value and conceptual issues confront sociologists working in this field. A fundamental value issue concerns the relative importance of avoiding violence and war versus ending injustice. Some people give highest priority to advancing freedom, justice, or equality—even if that means waging wars. Others, however, give highest priority to preventing the destruction of people's lives and property—even at the price of accepting a social order that is not optimal. Sociologists practicing in this area are, therefore, sometimes forced to make value choices between advancing peace versus justice. In many ways, however, peace and justice are mutually dependent rather than contradictory, and we can seek ways to maximize both.

This value issue is related to several difficult conceptual issues. Should peace be defined simply as the absence of war, or as a positive condition in which justice prevails? Should violence be defined as actions intended to cause physical harm to humans or their goods, or as structural conditions that interfere with people realizing full and wholesome lives (Galtung, 1969; Dedring, 1976)? In this chapter we adhere to the prevailing conception of peace as the absence of

538

war among organized military units. Warfare is a form of organized violence, and violence—directly physically damaging people or their artifacts—is in turn one type of coercion. Coercion itself is one of the several ways in which conflicts are pursued. Since conflict is endemic in social life and is conducted in a variety of ways, peace does not mean the absence of conflict or even the threat of violence. Conflict refers to any relationship between parties who believe they have incompatible objectives (Kriesberg, 1973).

To say that a conflict exists when parties believe they have incompatible objectives raises the issue of whether or not such beliefs are based on reality. The extent to which a conflict is realistic or not has grave implications for the way in which the dispute can or should be managed, as well as its eventual resolution. For our purposes it is best to assume that all international conflicts blend realistic and unrealistic components. *Realistic* conflict refers to adversaries correctly perceiving the incompatibility of their objectives. Several qualities of conflicts may be regarded as unrealistic. The methods used by adversaries in seeking their goals can be inappropriate or too costly. Redress from a grievance can be sought from the wrong adversary. Or the adversaries can ignore interests they have in common. *Unrealistic* components generally derive from internal factors within one of the actors and not from the relationship between the adversaries. The distinction between realistic and unrealistic conflict elements is not inherent in the conflict, but depends on the observer's assessment of the situation. Our assumptions about the realistic or unrealistic character of an international conflict largely determine the importance we attach to misunderstandings in generating and resolving that conflict.

Applied Problems

On the basis of the above discussion, we can distinguish three kinds of applied problems: how to minimize violence, how to minimize conflicts, and how to reduce injustice that might lead to conflict and war. This review will not discuss how to wage war effectively, even if such efforts might be viewed as a means of liberating people, resisting or detering aggression, or establishing a lasting peace (Bowers, 1967).

The problem that most concerns sociologists working on peace promotion is how to prevent warfare. This concern focuses particularly on the prevention of nuclear war between the United States and the Soviet Union. At the same time, widespread persistence of nonnuclear limited wars has revived social scientists' interest in so-called conventional warfare.

In addition to working to prevent wars, applied sociologists can contribute to the control of conflicts generally. Three phases of conflicts are relevant here. First is the latent phase. There are numerous objective conditions that generate grievances that people feel can be remedied if others will yield something. One task in promoting peace, then, is to reduce the conditions that underlie the emergence of disputes. This is where the reduction of injustice is relevant to promoting peace. The second phase is emergence of conflicts into awareness. Although there are innumerable latent conflicts, only a few emerge as recognized disputes. Sociological knowledge may be used to inhibit the emergence of disputes, for example, by establishing cooperative bonds that counterbalance the conflicting issues. The third phase is conflict escalation and deescalation. Once a conflict has emerged, the means that adversaries use in their struggle may be more or less violent. One factor greatly affecting the escalation of conflict is its degree of regulation. Since highly regulated conflicts tend not to be violent, applied sociologists can help to promote peace by furthering conflict regulation.

Early U.S. sociologists recognized war as an important part of social life, but they were more interested in the consequences of wars than in dealing with its emergence, conduct, or control. World War II marked a change in these regards. Sociologists became involved in research and consultation about the origins and conduct of the war. During the Cold War period, many social scientists continued to participate in programs related to war and peace. They helped interpret Soviet conduct, studied human relations within the armed forces, and developed ideas for counterinsurgency.

Currently, a wide variety of sociologists work in the area of peace promotion. They differ in the specific questions they seek to answer, in the institutional base for their work, and in their values and theoretical orientations. This review draws on work by social scientists who vary in all these regards. It includes references to political scientists, psychologists, economists, and others whose work draws on or contributes to applied sociology.

WHAT DO WE KNOW?

A short and honest answer to the question of "what do we know?" is "not enough." The issues in this area are so complex and the data and analyses are so limited that we presently possess little definite knowledge. Moreover, there are fundamental contradictions between what we seek to know as social scientists and as practitioners (Crawford and Biderman, 1969). Social scientists typically seek to discover generalizations, and their findings are commonly stated in probablistic terms such as: if "X" happens, then "Y" also tends to follow, other conditions being equal. Practitioners in contrast, are clinicians concerned with particular cases. They want to know what will happen in each unique case, taking everything into account. The knowledge needed by a practitioner is, therefore, different from that provided by a social scientist. Furthermore, social scientists often seek the basic causes of a wide range of phenomena. This means paying attention to fundamental forces and processes, which are often not susceptible to manipulation. A practitioner, however, would likely study those factors that could be intentionally modified in order to promote peace. This review covers both perspectives, examining probablistic findings concerning major social forces, as well as findings with immediate applicability.

Basic Research

Much of the scholarly research about war and peace is focused on the major factors that underlie outbreaks of warfare. It is important to understand what those factors are, even if they are not currently modifiable, because they may set limits to policies that would counter them. Furthermore, knowing what social conditions are conducive to peaceful international relations may suggest new social structures that should be created. As a result, when alternative policies with varying sets of outcomes are being considered, policy makers are more likely to select those that have long-run desired consequences as well as immediate benefits. For example, sociologists and other social scientists generally agree that institutionalized structures for managing conflict tend to reduce coerciveness in conflict resolution. We also know that the development of such conflict management structures must rest upon a recognized community of shared interests and values. Efforts to establish a strong supranational structure without an underlying community of interests and values are therefore doomed to failure (Etzioni, 1965). Consequently, procedures for handling conflicts that tend to enhance a sense of community among the adversaries would normally be preferred over means of conflict management that lack such a consequence.

Explanations for war can be found in three sets of factors: the world system, specific interstate relations, and domestic conditions. The following paragraphs explore these factors.

The World System. As it pertains to international conflict, the world system is generally viewed as consisting of sovereign countries with independent governments. But there are many other units in the system: international governmental organizations such as the United Nations; multinational corporations; social movements and organizations based on ethnicity, religion, and political ideology; and nongovernmental international organizations related to professions, trade unions, and other special interests. Sociologists are particularly attentive to the nongovernmental components of the world system, on the grounds that these transnational organizations could form a network of relations that would crosscut and, hence, mitigate conflicts among national governments (Angell, 1969; Evan, 1974; Kriesberg, 1972).

The units comprising the world system are related to each other in a variety of ways. Political scientists and most policy makers generally see power relationships as primary. They are concerned with the effects of different structures of power relationships, such as a bipolar system (dominated by two major rivals) or a balance of power system (with several major actors, some of whom shift sides to prevent any one power from becoming too dominant). Sociologists tend to give greater attention to other aspects of the world system. They are concerned with the degree to which peoples and leaders in different areas of the world share common values and understandings. They also tend to be interested in the way in which the world as a whole constitutes a stratified system, in which some countries dominate others economically, politically, and culturally (Horowitz, 1972). Thus, the Third World nations may be regarded not as developing countries seeking to catch up with the developed ones, but rather as dependent and peripheral countries that are prevented from developing by the economically advanced core countries within the world system (Chase-Dunn, 1975; Chirot, 1977). This world stratification system pits the peripheral countries against the core and core countries against each other in continual rivalry. Moreover, the multiple ways in which countries are ranked results in numerous inconsistent rankings. Some countries are dominant in certain ways but not in others, and these rank inconsistencies may be conducive to aggressive action (Galtung, 1964).

Interstate Relations. The world system provides a necessary context if disputes between governments are to be understood. But the particular issues in contention between adversaries and the relationships among them also must be considered. Adversaries may struggle to control resources, peoples, or other objectives that they both value. In these cases, they agree about the desirability of the objective but want to acquire it for themselves and deny it to others. Such conflicts are called *consensual*. Conflicts may also be based on value differences. In those cases, one side tries to impose a particular religious or political creed on the other. These are *dissensual* conflicts. Of course, every international struggle involves some elements of both consensual and dissensual conflict, as when a government seeks to extend its military power in order to advance its political ideology.

There has been relatively little analysis of the issues over which governments and other world actors struggle. Such research would have to confront, in one way or another, the difference between realistic and unrealistic conflicts. An international conflict is a kind of social interaction between the leaders of the contending countries. Not only are the goals of each party important for their interaction, but also the perceptions that each party holds about the goals of the other party to the conflict. In addition, each side forms images of how its goals are perceived by the other side and uses those images to interpret the meaning of the other side's reactions to its own moves. There is certainly room for misunderstanding in that sequence. Gamson and Modigliani (1971) studied the conduct of the U.S. and Soviet governments toward each other between 1946 and 1963. They concluded that each government acted as if it saw its own goal as purely consolidation, assumed that this was recognized by the other government, and thought that the goal of the other government was expansion. The subjective belief systems of the officials in each government, however, were different. For example, U.S. Secretary of State Dulles believed that the Soviet goal was expansion, that the Soviet leaders knew it was so perceived by the West, and thought the Western goal was only consolidation. Furthermore, Dulles believed that the Western goal was indeed consolidation, that this goal was correctly perceived by the Soviets, and that the Soviet goal was correctly perceived by the West to be expansion. The Soviet official belief system was a mirror image of this: that the West's goal was expansion and that the West knew that the Soviets correctly perceived this goal.

International conflicts emerge when parties with grievances believe they can gain redress. Thus, as subjugated or relatively deprived groups or governments gain strength, they are likely to make claims that bring latent conflicts into the open. Furthermore, the dominant group or government is likely to perceive this action as a threat and may try to increase its domination to forestall that threat, thus intensifying the conflict. As conditions become more symmetrical between contending parties, therefore, conflicts may increase. As conditions actually approximate symmetry, however, stabilization and conflict regulation become more likely. The previously dominant group may even become more hesitant in pressing aggrandizing goals and, thus, reduce the incidence of international disputes.

Sociologists have also studied cooperative and complementary interactions across national borders, such as student exchanges, postal trade and other communications, investments, travel, and immigration (Pool, 1965). A major concern of these studies is the extent to which such interactions mute international conflicts. A common assumption—for which there is supporting empirical evidence—is that high rates of these interactions promote the growth of an international community, and that conflicts are not likely to escalate into armed violence when they are embedded within a dense network of cooperative and complementary relations (Deutsch et al., 1957). Hopkins (1973), examining contiguous countries, found that high levels of transactions were positively related to institutionalization and that high levels of transactions limited violence. In general, countries that are relatively extensively involved in international organizations and international trade tend to use global level intermediaries in handling international conflicts (Wolf, 1978). Furthermore, high levels of social and economic integration can provide the basis for transnational structures that promote economic or political unification. Once some steps are taken along that route, people within the developing international community began to act in terms of the new structures, which facilitates further steps in this direction (Etzioni, 1965; Kriesberg, 1960). But this movement is not inevitable (Lerner and Aron, 1957).

Domestic Conditions. Many characteristics of a society affect its foreign policy and, thus, help explain the outbreak of war. The most frequently examined societal characteristics include: public opinion about other countries and about foreign policy issues, national character, political leadership, internal dissent and conflict, and the military-industrial complex (Gamson and Modigliani, 1966; Pilisuk, 1972; Mills, 1956; Lieberson, 1971).

Along with other observers, sociologists have drawn attention to the relative autonomy of leading U.S. political, military, and industrial officeholders in determining foreign policy and in making decisions about military weapons systems. Insofar as such decisions are based on calculations of advantages to be gained by domestic elite groups, rather than on considerations of how national objectives can be obtained in relationship to external adversaries, unrealistic and perhaps threatening elements may be added to international conflicts (Kurth, 1971; Mills, 1956). These observations are relevant to all countries, not just the United States.

Applied Research

Four areas of applied research in peace promotion are discussed in the following paragraphs: alternative means of conducting conflicts, accuracy of perception and communication, conflict dynamics, and conflict regulation.

Conducting Conflicts. World conflicts, like all others, can be pursued through the use of coercion (violent and nonviolent), persuasion, or contingent rewards. Whatever we can learn about the effectiveness of alternative ways of conducting conflict will certainly be relevant for policy makers in choosing strategies to promote peace.

Coercion undoubtedly is a major inducement in all international conflicts. Recognizing this, some peace researchers attempt to document the social consequences of warfare, pointing out the anticipated as well as the unanticipated high costs of war (Dentler and Cutright, 1963). Others stress the limited effectiveness of war as a means of altering national standing in comparison with more fundamental social changes (Barbera, 1973). Such research indicates the limits and inefficiencies of warfare (Finsterbusch and Greisman, 1975).

Much contemporary thinking assumes that the threat of violence acts as a deterrent to its outbreak, but the evidence on this issue is unclear. Several scientists have analyzed cases of successful and unsuccessful deterrence since World War II in an effort to learn how to make deterrence credible and effective. For instance, George and Smoke (1974:531) concluded that "Deterrence success will be favored, but not insured, by the defender's offering compensation elsewhere as a *quid pro quo* in return for a tacit or explicit agreement by the potential initiator not to challenge deterrence."

A few sociologists have examined the role of nonviolent coercive action in international conflicts, including analyses of revolutions and resistance to foreign occupation (Sharp, 1973; Wehr, 1979). These studies indicate that with popular support, resistance can be effective in limiting the power of a government that is regarded as illegitimate. And nonviolent civilian defense methods are being examined by some defense departments, as in Sweden (Boserup and Mack, 1975).

Persuasion and rewards, generally mixed with coercion, are also important inducements in international conflicts, but they are relatively unstudied. Most analyses of persuasive efforts pertain to psychological warfare aimed at the armed forces or civilian population of an enemy country in order to weaken that government's ability to exercise coercion (Janowitz, 1961). In addition, governments sometimes direct appeals to people in other countries in order to gain support for their national policies. In general, such efforts are most effective when they reinforce existing values and beliefs. Persuasion of government leaders by other government leaders, although constantly attempted, has not been examined outside the context of negotiations (to be discussed later). Similarly, rewards are usually viewed solely as concessions offered in the process of negotiation. But rewards can also involve a promise of increased benefits to an adversary or to particular components within an adversary coalition.

Perception and Communication. The second major area of applied research pertains to the accuracy of perception and communication. In varying degrees, international conflicts emerge and escalate through misunderstandings and faculty information (Jervis, 1976). Sociologists can help to reduce such intelligence mistakes in several ways. Trained in studying and understanding cultural variations and subjective definitions of situations, they are able to develop sound information about an adversary's mode of thinking and intentions. In addition, sociologists have examined the way in which intelligence is ignored by governments and have made suggestions for improving its quality and utilization, such as maintaining diverse sources of information (Wilensky, 1967). When persons in decision-making positions try to establish policies, they are subject to a variety of circumstances that reduce clear thinking. For example, there is evidence that a sense of crisis increases rigidity and that group meetings can fail to elicit the wide variety of perspectives they are supposed to provide (Janis, 1972). Suggestions for structural changes to avoid or lessen the undesirable consequences of these processes have been made by social scientists and sometimes implemented. For example, Janis (1972) suggests holding "second thought" meetings in which participants have a chance to say anything they want about the decisions they reached in previous meetings. Another method was used by President Kennedy in handling the 1962 Cuban missile crisis. He did not attend many sessions of his advisory group in order to encourage the members to freely consider a full range of alternatives.

Conflict Dynamics. The third area of applied research pertains to the dynamics of conflict, particularly escalation and de-escalation. Perhaps the most fundamental aspect of escalation and de-escalation is the interaction between the adversaries. If one party threatens another, will a conciliatory reaction invite further threat and aggression and, hence, escalate the conflict, or will this reaction lead the initiator to reduce its threats to match the response? On the other hand, if the reaction is very strong, will it precipitate a rapid escalation, or will it intimidate the initiator to terminate further threats? Experimental studies and historical analyses suggest that responses that are at about the same level or only slightly less threatening than the initial action tend to promote de-escalation (Kriesberg, 1973; Snyder and Diesing, 1977). In other words, a "tit for tat" strategy seems to mitigate against either side in a conflict escalating either its demands or the intensity of the struggle.

Conflicts often tend to escalate sharply, but they also de-escalate. Sociological research can provide insights into the factors that produce these shifts and, hence, suggest guidelines for policies that will prevent escalation or bring about de-escalation. One way to reduce the chances of runaway escalation is to plan a series of discrete steps, starting at a low level, with pauses at each step, that provide time to gauge the opponent's response and to think about the likely consequences of taking the next step on the escalatory ladder (Wehr, 1979).

Public support for, or disaffection with, hostile governmental policies toward an external adversary is a major area of sociological research pertaining to escalation and de-escalation. Sociologists have long been concerned with the effects of external conflict upon internal solidarity or dissension. Clearly, popular support for war efforts is essential to the waging of contemporary international conflicts. Generally, struggles for objectives that are perceived as limited and nonvital will not sustain support when the sacrifices they require are great and unequally distributed. Thus, the limited U.S. objectives in Vietnam and the inequality of gains and losses in waging that war undoubtedly contributed to the growth in popular disaffection with the war (Kriesberg, 1973; Smith, 1970).

Other social science research has considered how adversaries can communicate with each other in order to reduce tension. Osgood (1962) suggested that unilateral concessions, clearly made with the expectation of reciprocal concession but without specifying the expected concession, are a way of accomplishing this. In bitter and enduring conflicts, techniques for breaking through barriers of mistrust are particularly important and often require dramatic acts. President Sadat's visit to Jerusalem was such an action for it enabled the Israeli government to make concessions it otherwise could not have offered.

A fundamental condition affecting conflict escalation and de-escalation is the interlocking character of international conflicts. Any particular struggle is embedded in many crosscutting, superimposed, nested, converging, and linked conflicts. For example, each government is made up of many groups and must, therefore, be responsive to several constituencies. It also has allies and potential allies. One consequence of the interlocking character of conflicts is that each party relates to many audiences at the same time and shares some common interests with at least certain groups on its adversary's side. It must, therefore, try to appear as reasonable as possible. This provides a basis for appeals and promises that tend to de-escalate the struggle. On the other hand, the interlocking character of conflicts also makes it difficult for the parties to offer unambiguous concessions and promises.

At the same time a concession is offered or a promise is made, allies or constituencies must be reassured that little is being yielded, even though this undercuts the value of the offer to the adversary. Although we lack systematic research on ways of dealing with these circumstances, practitioners have made some pertinent suggestions (Fisher, 1969). It is sometimes useful to isolate a specific dispute from the welter of interlocking conflicts in which it is embedded. It is also useful to break up a complex dispute into several smaller issues and deal with them one at a time. These techniques are more easily applied in consensual than in dissensual conflicts.

Conflict Regulation. A fourth area of applied research is conflict regulation, which is discussed here in four subtopics: third party intercession, negotiations, institutionalization, and peace-keeping forces. A growing amount of research is focused on the ways in which individuals or representatives of nonaligned parties intercede in a conflict to assist the contending parties in reaching an agreement. Much of the sociological work in this area has dealt with this intermediary role in community, environmental, and ethnic conflicts rather than international disputes (Wehr, 1979). Nevertheless, this research—as well as studies of intercession in world conflicts—reveals the many roles that intermediaries can and do play in conflict regulation.

One activity that such intermediaries often perform is transmitting information. Official diplomats sometimes serve as indirect communication links between adversaries whose animosities and mistrust make it difficult or impossible to send or hear messages. In addition, persons acting in various private capacities serve as informal diplomats (Berman and Johnson, 1977). Davison (1974) examined the many ways in which journalists affect international negotiations and suggested ways in which their activities can facilitate reaching agreements. The media, for example, are a readily available vehicle for sending signals to an adversary and, hence, testing whether or not the time is appropriate for serious negotiations.

Intermediaries can also assist adversaries in hearing what each has to say by providing "good offices," a neutral place to meet, and a safe audience toward which each side can vent its feelings without provoking a reaction. They can also help structure the communication between adversaries. This may occur, for instance, in special workshops for official and nonofficial representatives from adversary countries held under the auspices of academics (Burton, 1969; Doob, 1970). In these settings a variety of techniques are employed to assist participants from adversary countries to hear each other and think innovatively about possible proposals for resolving the issues in contention. The intermediaries act as facilitators of this process and usually refrain from making direct suggestions.

In other situations, however, third party intervenors play an active role in offering suggestions. Proposals offered by a third party often appear salient and can become the focus of mutual concessions with less loss of face than would be true for a proposal made by one of the adversaries (Schelling, 1960). Third parties can also introduce additional resources into the negotiations and thus eliminate the zero-sum character of the conflict.

Although we are familiar with the variety of activities that intervenors perform, we have little certain knowledge about the circumstances that make one set of activities effective and another set ineffective. An intermediary cannot perform all roles, since some are mutually contradictory. It seems reasonable that the most effective combination of activities will depend on the nature of the dispute, the disputants, and the intermediary, but we have only the beginnings of such assessments (Young, 1967; Kelman, 1977; Kochan and Jick, 1978).

There is general consensus, however, that even when intermediaries offer suggestions, it is best if they assist the adversaries in taking a problem-solving approach to their conflict.

The second area of applied research in conflict regulation relates to negotiations. Numerous analyses, particularly social experiments, have focused on different bargaining conditions, strategies, negotiators, and outcomes of the negotiation process (Deutsch, 1973; Druckman, 1977; Zartman, 1976).

One set of findings, as summarized by Bartos (1974:302), indicates that a negotiator's toughness (maintaining a high level of demands) when matched by the opponent's softness improves the negotiator's payoff, but it also tends to decrease the chances of an agreement. Furthermore, when both parties maintain the same level of toughness, their joint payoff tends to be low. This helps explain why a strategy of matching concessions and demands (tit for tat) tends to render an opponent cooperative.

Pruitt and others (Pruitt and Lewis, 1977) have examined "integrative" bargaining that yields an agreement with high joint utility. In this case, the outcome is valuable to both bargainers, rather than being a compromise in which one side gains from the concessions of the other. Since most negotiations involve many dimensions and values, if both sides are rigid about the ends they seek but flexible about the means, they can often discover solutions that provide much of what they both want. Experimental work has been done on the conditions that are conducive to such integrative bargaining. For example, negotiators who are less accountable to other people on their side and less subject to surveillance are more likely to reach integrative solutions.

Analyses of actual negotiations have tested some of the ideas developed in these experimental studies. This research has also given attention to the effectiveness of threats of coercion, persuasive efforts, and promises of reward as inducements to reach an agreement. Snyder and Diesing (1977), for example, studied bargaining in 16 international crises during this century. They concluded that crises are more likely to be resolved expeditiously and peacefully if both parties are initially firm, since this helps clarify the balance of bargaining power and the structure of the crisis. They also concluded that bargaining theories are well complemented by theories about how information is processed. For example, since they believe that "the outcome of a crisis is determined by relative power, which is function of comparative resolve as perceived by the parties" (Snyder and Diesing, 1977; 494–95), then perceiving such resolve is critical in shaping the negotiation process and its outcome.

A third area of applied research on conflict regulation deals with the process of institutionalizing disputes within international organizations as a means of promoting world peace. An analysis of international conflicts between 1920 and 1965 (Kriesberg, 1973:223) indicates that third party intervention in the form of mediation, adjudication, involvement of international organizations, or multilateral conferences tends to result in outcomes that are relatively likely to be compromises or third party awards; while forced submission, withdrawal, deterrence, conquest, or annexation are relatively infrequent. Furthermore, the outcome is less likely to be determined by military force than by nonviolent means when third party intervention procedures are used (Wolf, 1978).

Finally, some research has been on the effectiveness of peace-keeping forces. Moskos (1976), for example, studied the soldiers of the United Nations force in Cyprus. He found that those soldiers adapted and adhered to general constabulary standards, regardless of the country from which they came, their prior training, or their attitudes. This behavioral adherence was learned informally in the field situation. He also found that these experiences did not foster internationalist values among the soldiers.

WHAT ARE WE DOING?

Most sociologists in the area of peace promotion teach and do research in academic institutions, but some of them are based in numerous other settings and conduct a wide variety of other activities.

Bases of Operations

Many sociologists working on peace promotion are employed in sociology departments and in university-related peace studies centers. Those centers are usually interdisciplinary—with members from sociology, psychology, history, political science, and other disciplines. Although in the United States such centers are university associated and primarily emphasize teaching, in several other countries peace centers are more autonomous, engage in research programs, and in some cases are partially supported by government grants in addition to funds received for contract research. This is true, for example, of the International Peace Research Institute, Olso and the Stockholm International Peace Research Institute.

Other bases for applied sociologists in this field are the many semiofficial organizations, foundations, independent research centers, and private voluntary associations that conduct peace related activities. The following list of such organizations gives some idea of their variety: the American Friends Service Committee, SANE, Federation of American Scientists, Institute for World Order, Carnegie Endowment for International Peace, International Peace Academy, RAND, Institute for Policy Studies, United States Strategic Institute, and the Pugwash Conferences. Sociologists are not active in all of these organizations, but they have been involved in many of them at one time or another and may participate more in the future.

Finally, many national and international governmental organizations employ sociologists in various peace-promoting activities. Among United States agencies, the most important have been the Agency for International Development (AID) and the International Communications Agency. In addition, sociologists have served in the Department of Defense, the various military branches and their associated research centers, the U.S. State Department, and the Peace Corps.

Several specialized agencies of the United Nations, as well as the United Nations Organization itself, conduct many activities related to peace promotion. Many of these focus on providing assistance for social and economic development, while others engage in direct conflict management. The United Nations Institute for Training and Research (UNITAR) carried out many research projects as well as training programs for diplomats from countries around the world.

Activities

Sociologists working on peace promotion engage in educating, advising, and participating in conflicts.

Educating. Perhaps the most fundamental way in which sociologists attempt to promote peace is by conveying their orientation and knowledge to others through teaching and writing. The interpretations that sociologists develop about the genesis, development, and management of international conflicts help shape the alternatives considered by participants in international conflicts. Publics in the United States and elsewhere support or oppose policies on the bases of their interpretations of their own interests, the interests of adversaries, and the probabilities of specific outcomes resulting from alternative policies. These interpretations are often implicit, but they are, nevertheless, significant. To a considerable extent, images of other governmental leaders and of what works in foreign affairs are shaped by interpretations of the past and present that are formulated by sociologists, historians, political scientists, psychologists, as well as by journalists and involved participants.

In addition, sociologists educate students. Sociological interpretations of international conflicts are conveyed through college courses on war and peace and social conflict (Boulding, et. al., 1974). Graduate training in this area, however, is very limited, consisting primarily of interdisciplinary programs in international relations and related areas.

The education process also includes training programs for practitioners such as diplomats and military officers. Such training is conducted at universities or by special academies such as the International Peace Academy and UNITAR. This training includes lectures and workshops in which insights and skills are developed through role playing and simulation (Bloomfield and Gearin, 1973). In conjunction with such training, guides for practitioners have been prepared (Fisher, 1978).

Advising. The second major activity performed by sociologists in peace promotion is advising and consulting. The following paragraphs focus on advising and consulting on request; lobbying and offering unsolicited advice will be discussed later.

A common device for advising and consulting is contract research. A government agency, for example, may want specialized assistance in carrying out its activities. It will, therefore, contract with sociologists and other social scientists with the necessary edge and skills to conduct the desired research. The scope of contract research in this area is indicated by the fact that in fiscal year 1975 the U.S. government spent almost one million dollars for research on foreign affairs by outside consultants, and this did not include any funds spent by the Central Intelligence Agency and the National Security Council (Rochester and Segalla, 1978). Social scientists also receive funding for research on peace from private foundations, or they may work without external financial support. Three kinds of advising and consulting activities are described next: providing information, evaluating programs, and making suggestions.

One of the most fundamental activities of sociologists and other social scientists in peace promotion is providing information to policy makers. Much of this information is based on studies of adversary countries, leaders, and policies. Other information concerns groups and countries who are allied to one or another side of a conflict, or whose friendship or at least neutrality is being sought. Such information may also concern the processes by which foreign policy objectives might be gained. Even knowledge about one's own country's agents is important. Thus, studies of the military profession or the State Department can provide useful understanding about the career and organizational problems of persons in these occupations and how those problems affect the formulation and implementation of policies (Janowitz, 1967). For example, studies of the careers of military officers after retirement from active service can indicate how political-military decisions might be influenced by retired officers who occupy high positions in defense industries or elective political offices (Biderman, 1964). Sociologists are working now on issues related to the volunteer character of the armed forces and the integration of minorities and women into the military services.

Another major area of study is evaluation research, which assess how effectively and efficiently government programs are achieving their objectives. For instance, numerous evaluation studies have been made of International Communications Agency efforts and cultural exchange programs (Bogart, 1976). The Agency for International Development has developed methods for assessing the consequences of its projects, and these are incorporated into the projects.

The third type of activity, offering suggestions, is least likely to be solicited by policy makers. But such solicitation does occur, since policy makers find it useful to hear the opinions of persons who can speak freely and independently of bureaucratic career concerns. Advisory committees provide one vehicle through which such opinions can be elicited and communicated. Another way in which sociologists can express their views is by acting as advisors to political leaders who are out of office or are seeking higher elective office. Special task forces or regular committees may also meet to formulate foreign policy alternatives. Finally, nongovernmental organizations working in peace-related areas often carry out activities that draw on the skills of applied sociologists. Such organizations include trade unions, business and professional associations, and churches.

Participating. The third major activity of sociologists in peace promotion is taking direct action, pursued in three kinds of roles: as intermediaries, as insider partisans, and as outsider activists.

Social scientists can and do play a variety of intermediary roles in international conflicts. They may act as messengers, transmitting information between adversaries. Information garnered through research abroad or at international conferences may be passed back to the home government as negotiating ideas. They may instigate informal discussions or other mutual efforts among adversaries to reach agreements prior to official meetings (Berman and Johnson, 1977). They may also work with representatives of adversary groups, assisting them to develop mutual understanding or to devise new solutions to old problems (Burton, 1969; Doob, 1970; Kelman, 1977).

Some applied sociologists work in or through nongovernmental organizations committed to nonviolence, functioning as partisans or as third party intermediaries in world conflicts (Hare and Blumberg, 1977). Such actions have included intervening in Culebra when it was being used for target practice by the U.S. Navy, in Bangladesh when it was being repressed by Pakistan, and in Cyprus prior to the invasion by Turkish military forces. These actions were not merely symbolic demonstrations. Relief supplies were brought directly to people in Bangladesh without recognizing Pakistan's governmental claims. And Greek and Turkish Cypriot youths were brought together in a work camp to construct houses for resettling Turkish refugees.

Applied sociologists also work as staff persons within agencies engaged in peace-related activities. One activity they frequently perform is evaluation research. For example, sociologists in the International Communications Agency study the state of world opinion and responses to U.S. information programs all over the world. This research draws upon public opinion surveys and content analyses of news media. The results of these analyses affect policy formation as well as its presentation abroad. Within AID, research in demography, community organization, and information diffusion is particularly relevant for program planning and assessment.

Finally, many sociologists engage in activities outside any formal governmental position, urging particular proposals or general changes in national policy. They argue their case as publicists and lobbyists, sometimes helping to mobilize public opinion and sometimes merely-offering personal statements about particular policies. Such activity has been especially notable in the arms race between the United States and the Soviet Union, as well as the Cold War generally (Etzioni, 1964; Mills, 1958). Sociologists have also been active in promoting policies concerning economic development in the Third World and regarding the Middle

East conflicts. In some of these cases the participants are acting merely as concerned citizens and do not draw on their professional knowledge, but much of the time their efforts do reflect a sociological orientation and utilized specialized information that has been acquired through sociological research.

The products of research and theoretical reasoning pertinent to peace promotion appear in books, articles, pamphlets, and special reports of the sponsoring organizations. Among the several journals that publish articles in this field are the following: *Journal of Peace Research, Journal of Conflict Resolution, Insurgent Sociologist, Armed Forces and Society, Social Problems, International Studies Quarterly,* and *Bulletin of Peace Proposals.*

WHAT HAVE WE ACCOMPLISHED?

Applied social scientists have contributed to the effectiveness of organizations promoting peace in several ways. They have helped in training persons to deal with crises and in developing organizational structures for crisis management. They have helped develop policies to diversify recruitment into the foreign service to help broaden class, ethnic, and gender representation within it. Sociologists have helped to increase awareness of the organizational and career dilemmas of persons in governmental organizations. An example of this is the dilemmas encountered by foreign service officers when their activities change as a result of new means of communication or multilateral meetings and negotiations (Niezing, 1973:31-64). Within the Peace Corps, a sociologist helped to construct methods for placing volunteers in effective training groups (Hare, 1966).

Sociologists have also contributed to shaping the patterns of interaction among countries comprising the world system. One way of doing this is to alter people's images of the way the global system works and how it is changing. For instance, sociologists tend to stress the role of nongovernmental factors in the world system. They also frequently emphasize functional relations and major social forces underlying government actions. When policy makers give greater attention to mutual interdependencies among nations and broad social trends, their objectives tend to become more realistic and more modest. This in turn inhibits the use of forceful intervention to impose particular policies on other governments.

Sociological attention to nongovernmental actors also has led to involvement in and research about international trade unions, professional and scientific organizations, and multinational corporations. Such work can contribute to the effectiveness of multilateral conferences and programs, as well as minimizing the socially disruptive consequences of those efforts.

One major shift in governmental activities has been particularly affected by sociological research and writing about economic development in the Third World. For many years after World War II, the policies of the World Bank regarding assistance for economic development stressed industrialization as a primary goal. Governments of developing countries also sought industrialization and emphasized growth of the urban centers. Sociological and anthropological studies of peoples in those countries, as well as evidence about investments and income distribution, showed that most people in developing countries were not benefiting from these policies. Although there were some increases in personal wealth and some expansion of capital investment, most people living in rural subsistence economies were not being helped. Inequalities were often aggravated, and in some ways rural conditions actually deteriorated. Furthermore, capital investment was often devoted to industries producing products for export. The economies of these countries were not producing products needed in the local economy, and they were becoming increasingly dependent on the advanced industrialized countries. Sociologists and other social scientists analyzed this situation as a system of relationships between developed "core" countries and "peripheral" countries that were kept in a state of perpetual dependence (Kahl, 1976; Cockcroft, Frank, and Johnson, 1972).

In recent years AID and World Bank policies have changed to emphasize rural development and programs that will improve the living standards of the poor sectors within developing countries. Many governments in Third World countries have also shifted to an emphasis on agricultural development, in response to new intellectual understandings as well as popular pressures.

A third area of accomplishments concerns specific international conflicts. The primary international conflict since World War II has been the Cold War between the United States and the Soviet Union. Sociologists have contributed in various ways to preventing open warfare between these countries and promotin détente. In the early years of nuclear weapons and missiles, procedures designed to prevent accidental firings neglected human factors. Sociologists helped draw attention to this oversight and correct it (Etzioni, 1967a). More broadly, applied sociologists have contributed to a reinterpretation of the emergence and basis of the Cold War, emphasizing views of U.S. and Soviet interests that were supportive of détente (Gamson and Modigliani, 1971).

Sociological emphasis on the importance of underlying social forces also supports efforts at building ties between various groups in the United States and the Soviet Union. It helps provide an intellectual and popular understanding of the basis for détente. Understanding is also facilitated by analyses of the convergences among all industrialized societies.

Techniques for de-escalating conflicts have been applied at the direct or indirect suggestion of sociologists. For example, ideas about how graduated unilateral initiatives can be effectively conducted may have played a role in the remarkable 1963 series of agreements between the United States and the Soviet Union. Etzioni (1967b) has analyzed the interactions, led by Kennedy and Khrushchev, that resulted in the partial nuclear test ban treaty, the sale of U.S.

wheat to the Soviet Union, the agreement to refrain from placing any objects carrying nuclear weapons in orbit around the earth, and other agreements between these countries. In particular, Kennedy's speech at American University in June 1963 seems to have provided a context within which unilateral de-escalatory actions were effectively made and to have led to this series of treaties.

Sociologists have also contributed to intermediary efforts in a number of specific international conflicts. The results of such efforts have often been limited, but at the least some bridging ties at the interpersonal level have resulted. Such effects have occurred in conflicts in the Middle East, the Horn of Africa (relating to Somali), the U.S. intervention in the Dominican Republic, and the India-Pakistan dispute (Kelman, 1977; Wedge, 1971; Yarrow, 1977).

Many of the methods developed by practitioners and students of mediation were used by President Carter and U.S. State Department officials in their interventions in the 1978–1979 Egyptian-Israeli negotiations. For instance, when the negotiations became deadlocked at one point, leading Egyptian and Israeli officials were sequestered in a castle in Leeds, England, not to negotiate, but to explore areas of agreement in an informal atmosphere. Another example was the extraordinary meetings at Camp David among President Sadat, Prime Minister Begin, and President Carter. Carter and his aides played an active intermediary role in these sessions. Since neither the Egyptian nor Israeli treaty drafts provided an acceptable basis for bargaining, a comprehensive draft prepared by U.S. officials became the basis for comments and suggestions by the Egyptians and Israelis. Twenty-two revisions were drafted until the Egyptians and Israelis were asked to say yes or no to the whole agreement (Caltani, 1979).

WHERE ARE WE GOING?

We need to learn a great deal more about international conflicts, but in recent years there has been a significant growth in research on this topic. We need, and are gaining, basic research on the emergence and course of conflicts. Recently we have begun to devote more attention to alternative ways in which struggles are and can be pursued, including nonviolent and even noncoercive means such as persuasion and promises of benefits. We need, and are beginning to get, assessments of the effectiveness and consequences of different conflict modes. With the expansion of intermediary activities, we need careful evaluations of the appropriateness of different combinations of such activities for promoting peace in different kinds of conflicts. These are important areas that, one hopes, will be studied vigorously during the next several years.

Not many sociologists presently work in the applied field of peace promotion. There are signs, however, of increased activity. In general, sociologists are becoming more involved in applied activities, partially as a result of developments within the discipline and partially as a consequence of expanding career opportunities in nonacademic settings. And more particularly, there is a renewed interest in the subject of international conflict within the discipline.

More institutional roles that will support professional careers in peace promotion are also needed. The expansion of international organizations, both governmental and nongovernmental, will facilitate this trend. Within the United States, centers for peace studies are maintaining themselves, despite the financial strains being experienced by many colleges and universities. The U.S. Congress and several departments within the executive branch are showing signs of renewing support for research on conflict and foreign area studies, which have been relatively neglected in recent years. In 1978 Congress passed a bill to establish a commission to examine the possibilities of forming a U.S. Peace Academy (Laue, 1978).

In this review, we have indicated some of the many ways in which sociologists serve to promote peace. The task is immense and never ending. But sociologists have many colleagues in and outside of other academic disciplines who are also engaged in these efforts. Our knowledge and skills are growing, and the opportunities to utilize them are all around us.

REFERENCES AND SUGGESTED READINGS

Angell, Robert C. 1969. *Peace on the March: Transnational Participation.* New York: Van Nostrand Reinhold.

Barbera, Henry. 1973. *Rich Nations and Poor in Peace and War.* Lexington, Mass.: Lexington Books.

Bartos, Otomar J. 1974. *Process and Outcome of Negotiations.* New York: Columbia University Press.

*Beitz, Charles R. and Theodore Herman, eds. 1973. *Peace and War.* San Francisco: W.H. Freeman.

This book has a wide range of selections by partisans and observers of international conflicts. The readings are about the war system (the morality of war, war as an instrument of policy) and about ways of building a peace system (world government, reforming the state system, domestic change, civilian resistance).

*Berman, Maureen R. and Joseph E. Johnson, eds. 1977. *Unofficial Diplomats.* New York: Columbia University Press.

The editors review the growing role of unofficial diplomats and include 13 reports of such activities. Participants report about unofficial meetings, intermediary roles in international dealings, and various conflict resolution workshops.

Biderman, Albert D. 1964. "Sequels to a Military Career: The Retired Military Professional." In *The New Military,* edited by Morris Janowitz, pp. 287–366. New York: John Wiley & Sons.

Bloomfield, Lincoln P. and Cornelius J. Gearin. 1973. "Games Foreign Policy

Experts Play: The Political Exercise Comes of Age." *Orbis* 16(Winter: 1008–31.

Bogart, Leo. 1976. *Premises for Propaganda.* New York: The Free Press.

Boserup, Anders, and Andrew Mack. 1975. *War Without Weapons: Non-Violence in National Defense.* New York: Schocken Books.

Boulding, Elise M., et al. 1974. "Teaching the Sociology of World Conflicts: A Review of the State of the Field." *The American Sociologist* 9(Nov):187–93.

Bowers, Raymond T. 1967. "The Military Establishment." In *The Uses of Sociology,* edited by Paul F. Lazarsfeld, William R. Sewell, and Harold L. Wilensky, pp. 234–74. New York: Basic Books.

Burton, John W. 1969. *Conflict and Communication: The Use of Controlled Communication in International Relations.* London: MacMillan.

Caltani, Richard J. 1979. "New Methods for Solving Disputes." *Christian Science Monitor* (Jan 16):12.

Chase-Dunn, Christopher. 1975. "The Effects of International Economic Dependence on Development and Inequality: A Cross-National Study." *American Sociological Review* 49(Dec):720–38.

Chirot, Daniel. 1977. *Social Change in the Twentieth Century.* New York: Harcourt Brace Jovanovich.

Cockcroft, James D., Andre Gunder Frank, and Dale L. Johnson. 1972. *Dependence and Underdevelopment.* Garden City, N.Y.: Anchor Books.

Crawford, Elisabeth T. and Albert D. Biderman, eds. 1969. *Social Scientists and International Affairs.* New York: John Wiley & Sons.

Davison, W. Phillips. 1974. "News Media and International Negotiation." *The Public Opinion Quarterly* 38(Summer):174–91.

*Dedring, Juergen. 1976. *Recent Advances in Peace and Conflict Research: A Critical Survey.* Beverly Hills, Calif.: Sage.

This work provides a comprehensive bibliographic survey of current peace-related research, drawing on work from throughout the world. The author critically reviews work about peace and conflict systems, conflict theory, perceptual factors in conflict, the dynamics of conflict interactions, and games and simulations.

Dentler, Robert A. and Phillips Cutright. 1963. *Hostage American.* Boston: Beacon Press.

Deutsch, Karl. W., S.A. Burrell, R.A. Kann, M. Lee, Jr., M. Lichterman, R.E. Lindgren, F.L. Loewenheim, and R.W. Banwagenen. 1957. *Political Community and the North Atlantic Area.* Princeton, N.J.: Princeton University Press.

Deutsch, Morton. 1973. *The Resolution of Conflict: Constructive and Destructive Processes.* New Haven, Conn.: Yale University Press.

Doob, Leonard W., ed. 1970. *Resolving Conflict in Africa: The Fermeda Workshop.* New Haven, Conn.: Yale University Press.

Druckman, Daniel, ed. 1977. *Negotiations: Social Psychological Perspectives.* Beverly Hills, Calif.: Sage Publications.

Etzioni, Amitai. 1964. *Winning Without War.* Garden City, N.Y.: Doubleday.

———. 1965. *Political Unification.* New York: Holt, Rinehart and Winston.

_____. 1967a. "Nonconventional Uses of Sociology as Illustrated by Peace Research." In *The Uses of Sociology,* edited by P.F. Lazarsfeld, W.H. Sewell, and H.L. Wilensky, pp. 806–38. New York: Basic Books.

_____. 1967b. "The Kennedy Experiment." *Western Political Quarterly* 20 (June):361–80.

Evan, William M. 1974. "Multinational Corporations and International Professional Associations." *Human Relations* 27:587–625.

Finsterbusch, Kurt and H.C. Greisman. 1975. "The Unprofitability of Warfare in the Twentieth Century." *Social Problems* 22(Feb):450–63.

Fisher, Roger. 1969. *International Conflict for Beginners.* New York: Harper & Row.

*Fisher, Roger with the help of William Ury. 1978. *International Mediation: A Working Guide.* New York: International Peace Academy.

The authors analyze international negotiation and mediation and provide detailed suggestions for mediators. They suggest how to diagnose and approach the basic problems, the inventing of possible solutions problem, and the procedural problems.

Galtung, Johan. 1964. "A Structural Theory of Aggression." *Journal of Peace Research* (2):95–119.

_____. 1969. "Violence, Peace, and Peace Research." *Journal of Peace Research* (3):167–91.

Gamson, William A. and Andre Modigliani. 1966. "Knowledge and Foreign Policy Opinions: Some Models for Consideration." *Public Opinion Quarterly,* XXX (Summer):187–99.

_____. 1971. *Untangling the Cold War: A Strategy for Testing Rival Theories.* Boston: Little, Brown.

George, Alexander L. and Richard Smoke. 1974. *Deterrence in American Foreign Policy.* New York: Columbia University Press.

Hare, A. Paul. 1966. "Planning for Utopia—A Sociologists in the Peace Corps." In *Sociology in Action,* edited by A.B. Shostak, pp. 249–53. Homewood, Ill.: Dorsey Press.

Hare, A. Paul and Herbert H. Blumberg, ed. 1977. *Liberation without Violence: A Third-Party Approach.* London: Rex Collings.

Hopkins, David Morse. 1973. "Conflict and Contiguity: An Empirical Analysis of Institutionalization and Conflict in Contiguous Dyads." Unpublished Ph.D. dissertation, International Relations, Syracuse University.

Horowitz, Irving Louis. 1972. *Three Worlds of Development,* 2nd. ed. New York: Oxford University Press.

Janis, Irving L. 1972. *Victims of Groupthink.* Boston: Houghton Mifflin.

Janowitz, Morris, ed. 1961. "Mass Persuasion and International Relations." *Public Opinion Quarterly* 25(Winter):560–70.

_____. 1967. *The New Military: Changing Patterns of Organization.* New York: John Wiley & Sons (originally published 1964).

Jervis, Robert. 1976. *Perceptions and Misperception in International Relations.* Princeton, N.J.: Princeton University Press.

Kahl, Joseph. 1976. *Modernization, Exploitation, and Dependency in Latin America.* New Brunswick, N.J.: Transaction Books.

Kelman, Herbert C. 1977. "The Problem-Solving Workshop in Conflict Resolution." In *Unofficial Diplomats,* edited by M.R. Berman and J.E. Johnson, pp. 168–200. New York: Columbia University Press.

Kochan, Thomas A. and Todd Jick. 1978. "The Public Sector Mediation Process." *Journal of Conflict Resolution* 22 (June):209–40.

Kriesberg, Louis. 1960. "German Leaders and the Schuman Plan." *Social Science* 35 (Apr):114–21.

_____. 1972. "International Nongovernmental Organization and Transnational Integration." *International Associations* 24(11):520–25.

*_____. 1973. *The Sociology of Social Conflicts.* Englewood Cliffs, N.J.: Prentice-Hall.

This book provides a comprehensive survey and synthesis of research on the full range of social conflicts, including international conflicts. The book is organized according to stages in the conflict cycle: their underlying bases, emergence into awareness, alternative conflict modes, escalation and de-escalation, terminations and outcomes, and long-run consequences.

Kurth, James R. 1971. "Widening Gyre." *Social Policy* 19 (Sept):373–404.

Laue, James H. 1978. "Community Peacemaking: Its Role in a United States Academy for Peace and Conflict Resolution." In Hearings before the Subcommittee on International Operations of the Committee on International Relations House of Representatives, 95th Congress, 2nd Session, pp. 33–53. Washington, D.C.: U.S. Government Printing Office.

Lerner, Daniel and Raymond Aron, eds. 1957. *France Defeats EDC.* New York: Praeger.

Lieberson, Stanley, 1971. "An Empirical Study of Military-Industrial Linkages." *The American Journal of Sociology.* 76(Jan):562–84.

Mills, C. Wright. 1956. *The Power Elite.* New York: Oxford University Press.

_____. 1958. *The Causes of World War Three.* New York: Simon & Schuster.

Moskos, Charles C., Jr. 1976. *Peace Soldiers: The Sociology of United Nations Military Force.* Chicago: University of Chicago Press.

Niezing, Johan. 1973. *Sociology, War and Disarmament: Studies in Peace Research.* Rotterdam, Netherlands: Rotterdam University Press.

Osgood, Charles E. 1962. *An Alternative to War on Surrender.* Urbana: University of Illinois Press.

Pilisuk, Marc. 1972. *International Conflict and Social Policy.* Englewood Cliffs, N.J.: Prentice-Hall.

Pool, Ithiel de Sola. 1965. "Effects of Cross-National Contact on National and International Images." In *International Behavior,* edited by Herbert C. Kelman, pp. 104–29. New York: Holt, Rinehart and Winston.

Pruitt, Dean G. and Steven A. Lewis. 1977. "The Psychology of Integrative Bargaining." In *Negotiations,* edited by Daniel Druckman, pp. 161–92. Beverly Hills, Calif.: Sage.

Rochester, J. Martin and Michael Segalla. 1978. "What Foreign Policy Makers Want from Foreign Policy Researchers: A Data-Based Assessment of FAR Research." *International Studies Quarterly* 22 (Dec):435–61.

Schelling, Thomas C. 1960. *The Strategy of Conflict.* Cambridge, Mass.: Harvard University Press.

Sharp, Gene. 1973. *The Politics of Nonviolent Action*. Boston: Porter Sargent.

Smith, Robert B. 1970. "Rebellion and Repression and the Vietnam War." *The Annals of the American Academy of Political and Social Science*. 391 (Sept):156–67.

Snyder, Glenn H. and Paul Diesing. 1977. *Conflict Among Nations: Bargaining, Decision Making, and System Structure in International Crises*. Princeton, N.J.: Princeton University Press.

Wedge, Bryant. 1971. "A Psychiatric Model for Intercession in Intergroup Conflict." *The Journal of Applied Behavioral Science* 7:733–61.

Wehr, Paul. 1979. *Conflict Regulation*. Boulder, Colo.: Westview Press.

Wilensky, Harold L. 1967. *Organizational Intelligence: Knowledge and Policy in Government and Industry*. New York: Basic Books.

Wolf, Peter. 1978. "International Social Structure and the Resolution of International Conflicts, 1920 to 1965," In *Research in Social Movements, Conflicts, and Change*, Vol. 1, edited by Louis Kriesberg, pp. 35–53. Greenwich, Conn.: JAI Press.

Yarrow, C.H. "Mike." 1977. "Quaker Efforts Toward Conciliation in the India-Pakistan War of 1965." In *Unofficial Diplomats*, edited by M.R. Berman and J.E. Johnson, pp. 89–110. New York: Columbia University Press.

Young, Oran R. 1967. *The Intermediaries: Third Parties in International Crises*. Princeton, N.J.: Princeton University Press.

Zartman, I.W., ed. 1976. *The Fifty-Percent Solution*. Garden City, N.Y.: Doubleday.

EPILOGUE: THE FUTURE OF APPLIED SOCIOLOGY

Marvin E. Olsen

> Unless sociology undergoes a radical change, the field will be deprived
> of the resources it now commands. Those resources now exceed our
> collective accomplishments, and sooner or later there will be an ac-
> counting. Directors of governmental agencies and officers of founda-
> tions will commence giving sociologists a medium hello, and the begin-
> ning of the end will be signaled when a tough dean puts this question to
> the head of a sociology department: What have you people accomplished
> in over a century? Even a glib head will have a difficult moment.
>
> This vision of doom is tempered by the promise of contingent salva-
> tion, in the form of another prophecy: Sociologists will avoid collective
> extinction only by pursuing theories and research that have policy im-
> plications. A theory has policy implications if it makes assertions about
> *realizable* means to goals sought by a group whose interests transcend
> scientific and scholarly activities. Correlatively, research has policy
> implications if it bears on the empirical validity of an assertion about
> such means....
>
> My plea for theory and research with policy implications reduces
> to this: do something or say something that someone might find both
> interesting and useful. (Gibbs, 1979:79–85)

These contrasting prophecies about the future of sociology, as envisioned by
Jack Gibbs, pose a sharp challenge that applied sociologists cannot ignore. Confronting and responding to that challenge during the 1980s could be highly invigorating. To launch that quest, we must face a demand, surmount a dilemma,
resolve a paradox, respond to an imperative, and answer an ultimate question.
To carry out that quest we must also clarify our analytic perspective, select the
kinds of roles we seek to enact as applied sociologists, and learn to communicate
clearly with policy makers.

561

THE DEMAND: BE RELEVANT OR BE IGNORED!

Even if an academic dean did ask a sociology chairperson to recite the accomplishments of his discipline, the dean would be very unlikely to say: "Produce or get out." The scientific rhetoric of "contributing to the accumulation of basic knowledge about ourselves and our world" can always be invoked to justify one's niche in the academic community. The outside world is much less tolerant of useless theorizing and data collecting, however, especially when it is paying the bill for those activities. It wants to know: "What can you as a sociologist tell me that will help solve this problem."

The most insistent demands that sociology be relevant to real problems are being made by government agencies at all levels. Public officials—from heads of federal departments to local office managers—are charged with the responsibility of using public resources wisely to accomplish their missions. They have a job to do and many of them sincerely believe that sociology could assist them in that effort. But they also have limited time and financial resources, and they must demonstrate some identifiable accomplishments from their efforts. Hence, they are insisting that sociologists contribute directly to the attainment of agency goals if they are to receive either a hearing or funding.

Although sociologists have made far fewer inroads into private business and industry than into government, sophisticated corporate managers are becoming aware that many of their problems—both inside and outside the firm—have social as well as technical and economic aspects. Going beyond traditional concerns with employee satisfaction and public image, corporations are now hiring sociologists to examine organizational structures, communication patterns, and changing life styles. In business, however, the bottom line is always the final arbiter. Hence, sociologists must demonstrate that they can contribute to the positive side of that balance sheet or else go job hunting.

Another expanding employment opportunity for sociologists is private consulting and research firms, ranging from one-person operations to organizations employing hundreds of researchers in various disciplines. All such firms depend on the research contracts they can secure from public and private organizations. Those sponsors fund research to obtain answers to questions and problems with which they must deal. Hence, the research firm must be able to give the sponsor whatever information or advice it needs. The sponsor calls most of the shots in this process, and the target is research that is both relevant and useful.

Is there nowhere for the "pure scientist" to go to escape these incessant demands for relevance? Is not academia still a safe haven? Although deans are undoubtedly more tolerant of pure science than are government officials and business executives, they often feel the pains of tightening budgets. To justify its budget, a department must be able to demonstrate that it is carrying its share of the overall teaching load. Its courses must, therefore, attract students. A faculty member who insists on teaching his or her esoteric specialty to a handful of disciplines jeopardizes both the departmental budget and the status of the discipline in the academic community. So even here the demand for relevance cannot be ignored.

Finally, although the average citizen may remain relatively unaware of, and unconcerned about, the day-to-day work of sociologists, the educated public does form opinions about the contributions that various fields are making to society. The criteria they use in forming these judgments are not theoretical rigor or technical precision, but rather relevant and meaningful insights into the workings of our society and ways of solving the social problems that confront us. Michael Harrington's *The Other America* (1963), for instance, may not be viewed by many sociologists as a sophisticated piece of social research, but it sparked massive public concern and action to eliminate poverty in the United States. How many journal articles on status attainment could make such a claim? In this fundamental sense, therefore, sociologists must demonstrate to the educated public that their work is worthy of respect.

Many sociologists—especially those attempting to do applied sociology—are increasingly accepting the challenge to be relevant, for they do not want their discipline to be ignored. Having crossed the first hurdle, another one then looms ahead.

THE DILEMMA: TO VALUE OR NOT TO VALUE?

Somewhere in their professional training, virtually all aspiring sociologists are exposed to the ideal of "value-free sociology." From Max Weber (1949) and countless other writers on this topic, they learn that as scientists they should put aside all their own personal values and beliefs and maintain an ethically and morally neutral stance toward everything they study. Lengthy lists of guidelines have been developed to assist students in learning to desensitize themselves to all personal values in their research. The purpose of science, they are told, is to understand the world, not to save it. Leave that to religion, or philosophy, or psychiatry. Admittedly, we all hold many values and beliefs quite strongly, so that value-free sociology always remains something of an unobtainable ideal, but we should constantly strive to be as value-neutral as we possibly can. In addition, as a check on our human frailty, we should keep our work fully open to inspection and criticism by others, so that they can catch any biases that may unintentionally or intentionally slip into our work.

This prescription of value-free sociology places the researcher or the teacher squarely on the horns of a double dilemma. First, is this goal even partially attainable, or do values and beliefs so thoroughly pervade our work that it is sheer hypocrisy to pretend otherwise? Isn't the mantle of value-neutrality often evoked to cloak values and beliefs that we don't want to acknowledge openly?

Wouldn't it be much more honest to state clearly the value positions that underlie our research and teaching, so that others can take them into account when evaluating our work? That should eliminate "hidden agendas" and subtle "manipulative strategies," as well as exposing the full scope and depth of our thinking. If we follow this path of complete "value emersion," however, do we not become political polemists rather than scientists?

The second side of this dilemma is perhaps more vexing. Even if we could remain relatively neutral in our work as sociologists, is this compatible with being relevant to the real world? If applied sociologists are to come to grips with pressing social problems and contribute to their solution, how can they possibly remain value-neutral? If one is investigating the causes of poverty or racial discrimination and formulating policy proposals to eliminate such conditions, has one not taken a clear moral stand against those conditions? In reality, how many sociologists would state: "Here are the main factors contributing to poverty in contemporary society. You can vary them as you like, to either increase or decrease poverty—it makes no difference to me as a sociologist." In fact, were not the founders of the discipline, such as Marx and Durkheim, strongly committed to eliminating conditions like worker exploitation and suicide? If we pretend to be neutral social technicians or social engineers who are just "tinkering with society to find out how it works," will we have fooled anyone but ourselves? And if we should fool others, how can we expect them to view our work as relevant to the pressing concerns of real life?

We can transcend both of these apparent dilemmas by brushing them aside. We can proclaim boldly that value-free sociology is not an ideal, but rather a totally unrealistic, undesirable, and potentially deceitful myth. All sociology is value-involved, and it must be so if it is to be relevant and respected.

Will this stance destroy sociology as a science and reduce it to nothing but emotional polemics? Certainly there are people who call themselves sociologists but whose only interest is espousing a personal cause such as the "right to life" or the "workers revolution." Before we abandon the field to these crusaders, however, let us stop to distinguish between neutrality and objectivity. Rejecting the myth of value-free sociology does not require us to discard any of the cannons of objective science. There is no incompatability, for instance, in stating, "I am convinced that energy conservation is a vital goal for our society, and I will do everything I can to promote it," and then exploring the effectiveness of various implementation strategies in a totally professional and objective manner. Nonneutrality, or value-involvement, pertains to the goals we seek in our professional work, while objectivity refers to the methods of research and teaching that we employ in seeking those goals. Although no scientist is so perfect as to be totally objective in his or her work, the established practice of open publication and criticism—letting "the world bite back"—will sooner or later correct whatever lapses of objectivity unintentionally or intentionally slip into scientific endeavors. Polemics may even become highly interwoven with scientific analysis—Marx made no attempt to separate them—but eventually the polemical chaff is separated from the scientific wheat and discarded.

If we accept the idea of value-involved (but scientifically objective) sociology, we then confront a paradox.

THE PARADOX: GOOD SOCIOLOGY IS BOTH BASIC AND APPLIED

A paradox is an assertion that appears to be contradictory but actually may not be. The distinction between the science of "basic sociology" and the practice of "applied sociology" has a long and venerable history in the discipline, as in many other fields. The basic scientist views himself or herself as a scientist dedicated to the pursuit of knowledge for its own sake, while the applied sociologist identifies himself or herself as a practitioner who contributes to solving or eliminating social problems. Since these two forms of sociology are commonly presumed to be incompatible, role segregation is often advocated as a means of avoiding the conflict that might arise if one were to combine them. In any given setting, one must supposedly choose to be either a scientist or a practitioner but not both simultaneously.

During the political and intellectual upheavals of the 1960s, basic sociology was severely criticized by numerous members of the academy, including Mills (1959), Lazarsfeld, Sewell, and Wilensky (1967), Horowitz (1968), and Gouldner (1968). Among the many charges they levelled at traditional sociology were that 1) much of what passes for basic empirical research in this field is merely trivial date manipulation, 2) a great deal of our "theory construction" is really just meaningless categorization and other mental gymnastics, 3) pursuing pure science without any concern for its applied relevance is intellectually and morally indefensible, and 4) the public will not continue for much longer to tolerate or support a field that makes no appreciable contribution to the welfare of society.

On the other side of the fence, the limitations of straightforward applied sociology, undertaken without any pretense at scientific investigation, are also well known. As summarized by Denzin (1970), they are that: 1) the sociologist in this role exercises little or no control over the topics he or she studies, 2) most of this work is totally atheoretical and usually makes no lasting contribution to the discipline, 3) much applied research is simply data accumulation for "program evaluation," which often becomes "program justification," and 4) the applied sociologist tends unwittingly to become a supporter rather than a critic of existing social, economic, and political conditions.

The obvious resolution of this paradox is not further role segregation, but role integration. Integrated sociology tears down the fence separating basic and applied work, merging the scientist and practitioner roles into one. Both endeavors benefit enormously from this synthesis. Basic sociology becomes oriented toward answering questions and solving problems that are important to people outside the discipline and that affect the quality of life in society. Applied sociology, meanwhile, becomes intellectually challenging and rewarding and contributes to our fundamental knowledge of human social life.

What might be done to integrate sociology? Here are a few suggestions. 1) Always select topics for research and teaching that directly or indirectly pertain to a critical social problem. If you are interested in the family, for instance, don't study or lecture on "the role of the oldest child in traditional Chinese families" when more and more people in our society are struggling with the task of managing a single-parent family. 2) Begin your study or course with a survey of all the theoretical ideas that are relevant to the topic, regardless of how straightforward or routine that topic may be, and identify theoretical questions that can be addressed in your work. Even if you are doing market research for a soap company, you might ask how various theories of communication and attitude change apply to your task. 3) Organize your data collection and analysis or the content of your course so that it will both shed light on those unresolved theoretical issues and provide answers to practical questions. In a race relations course, for instance, you might examine the use of law as both a general agent of social change and as a strategic weapon in the continuing war against racism in this society. 4) Draw two sets of conclusions from your efforts, one dealing with broad theoretical concerns and the other with specific pragmatic concerns, and then demonstrate how they complement one another. In a study of supervisor-worker relationships, for example, you might first conclude that they are most stable when the supervisor's authority rests on demonstrated expert knowledge rather than on delegated authorization, then recommend that the supervisors in the office being studied make a greater effort to keep abreast of new developments in their fields, and then suggest ways in which that specific technique might be generalized to improve supervisor-worker relationships throughout the entire organization. 5) Distribute your results to reach both the scientific community and the interested public. In addition to writing the usual professional journal article or monograph, consider writing a newspaper article or magazine story, speaking to concerned groups and organizations about your work, and testifying at school board meetings or rate commission hearings.

In short, there need be no distinction between the science of basic sociology and the practice of applied sociology. Good sociology will contribute to both goals. But as we set out to do integrated involved sociology, we will likely find that our training, role expectations, and job requirements are seriously out of alignment. At this point we encounter an imperative.

THE IMPERATIVE: REORGANIZE THE PROFESSION

Sociologists are occupational elitists, no matter how much we decry inequality in society. The doors of the profession are closely guarded against outsiders who might accidently stray into our territory—such as journalists or social critics—or who might intentionally try to invade our fortress—such as pollsters, social workers, management consultants, or governmental "program analysts." To reach a door to the profession, one must run a four- or five-year obstacle course that is designed to eliminate everyone except those with single-minded dedication to the discipline (to the virtual exclusion of all other intellectual concerns), a total commitment to "pure science,"and a sincere conviction that only "professional sociologists" can do real sociology.

With degree at last in hand, we are allowed to pass through the door of the sociological mansion and are led to the bottom of a narrow, steep, and seemingly endless staircase labeled "professional achievement." We are informed that we have been provisionally admitted to the cellar of the mansion, but if we want to get out of the servants' quarters we must start climbing the staircase. Two good research papers in refereed journals will get us to the ground floor, we are told, where we will be let into the kitchen to eat. If we want to mount to the second floor and become a full-fledged member of the profession, however, we must publish several more articles (in the "big three" journals) or a sound book or two and then pass the initiation rites of "tenure evaluation." At that point we can stop climbing if we wish, although it does not take long to discover that the staircase continues on to an "upper chamber" where most of the crucial decisions affecting the profession are made. We are told that the doors of this upper chamber are always open to anyone who wants to become involved, but by this time we are certainly familiar with Robert Michels' "iron law of oligarchy."

All professions dwell in similar mansions, so that sociologists are not unique in this respect. We are all quite jealous of our professional status and exercise eternal vigilance to ensure that we are not overrun by the hoards of untutored and uncredentialed commoners whom (we believe) are constantly attempting to storm our fortress. (The possibility that they are dancing in the streets and enjoying life, while we stand lonely guard duty on the ramparts above, has apparently not occurred to most of us—except for those few who don a mask and go out to join the festivities under the guise of doing "participant observation.")

Sociology differs from most of the other professions in two major respects, however. First, most other professions dwell in mansions with more diverse accommodations. In economics, for instance, a person with an M.A. or even just a B.A. in the field is commonly permitted to identify with that field and to work for government or business in a semiprofessional role. Although these people may never attempt to climb very far up the professional staircase, there is room for them in the mansion: they perform many vital jobs for society, they demonstrate the importance of the field to the public, and they free the professional elites from having to perform many rather routine and noncreative duties. In return, these semiprofessionals receive several benefits, including relatively high social status (in the eyes of the general public), satisfying use of their occupational skills, good incomes, and fairly accessible opportunities for mobility into full professional careers if they choose.

In contrast, until quite recently sociology has been extremely reluctant to admit any semiprofessionals into its mansion—probably for fear of jeopardizing its recently acquired and still quite tenuous legitimacy as a professional field. Individuals who attempted to carve out such occupational roles for themselves in government, business, and other organizations were discouraged from calling themselves sociologists, were granted only second-class citizenship in professional associations, and were otherwise shunned by professional sociologists. This situation has loosened somewhat in recent years, but the number of people in such semiprofessional sociological roles is still quite small.

The second major way in which the house of sociology differs from many other professional mansions is that we have (also until quite recently) insisted that all sociologists must climb a single staircase of professional achievement. There has been nothing in sociology analogous to the separate career routes in experimental and clinical psychology. We could adopt a similar strategy of role segregation and establish a separate career staircase for applied sociology—and some members of the profession have been attempting to do this. Alternatively, we could—as advocated above—recognize the paradoxical nature of the basic/applied distinction and simply widen the existing staircase to accommodate integrated involved sociology.

Opening the doors of our castle and widening its staircase are intriguing ideas, but how might we accomplish these alterations without destroying the entire mansion? Let us first examine the doors. It is important, for several reasons, to maintain some control over entry into the profession. We could, however, take two steps to encourage the development of a semiprofessional role within sociology. The first step would be for sociology departments in universities to work more closely with schools of social work, to ensure that social work students in the areas of group work, community organization, and public policy formation received sound training in the principles and methods of sociology. As an alternative to the psychological orientation that pervades social case work, students whose interests were more social in nature could be offered enough sociology so that they could function with a sociological perspective and imagination. This collaboration between sociology and "macro social work" could also be expanded into professional associations, research, and program development.

A second possible step toward creating a semiprofessional role within sociology would be for sociology departments to offer a new type of program and degree. This would be a two-year master's program, similar to the M.S.W. with integrated classroom and field work. It would focus on social research rather than on social services, however, and might be called a Master of Social Analysis (M.S.A.) degree. These social analysts would receive considerable training in research methods and data analysis, courses in basic social theory, some exposure to other social sciences (especially economics), and a chance to develop a substantive speciality. With an M.S.A. degree they would be prepared to do a wide variety of social research tasks, especially of a more applied nature. The principal arguments for this step are that much social research does not require Ph.D. training, the Ph.D. requirements drive away many people who want to and are capable of doing good (if relatively routine) social research, and many employers who would like to have some sociologists on their staff do not want to hire Ph.Ds ("they cost too much and their ambitions are too high"). Conversely, Ph.Ds who end up doing routine research tasks—and much applied research is quite routine in nature—often feel frustrated and deprived because their own role expectations exceed the opportunities available. M.S.As would presumably have career ambitions that were more in line with realistic opportunities and, hence, would be more likely to derive personal satisfaction from their work. They could have their own career path with status and income advancements, their own associations, and even their own journals. More importantly, they would constitute an adequately trained work force who could carry social research out of academia into "real world" settings where it could contribute directly to pressing problems.

Let us now turn to widening the staircase of our mansion so that it can accommodate integrated involved sociology. The people climbing this staircase (with a few exceptions) would be professional sociologists with Ph.D.s. Their goals might be similar or identical to those of more traditional sociologists, but they would face expanded criteria for professional advancement. Research publications, minimal competence in the classroom, and a bow to public service would no longer by sufficient. To move up the staircase, they would also have to demonstrate that their work had policy or program relevance and that they were applying it in the classroom and/or the community and the society. If a person's specialty were social stratification, for example, he or she would have to express a clear value commitment (presumably toward decreasing at least some forms of inequality, although conceivably one might argue for maintaining or increasing inequality). If the person were teaching, his or her courses should cover current policy issues pertaining to inequality. The person's research would have to demonstrate direct or at least indirect relevance to practical issues and problems of social inequality. And the person would have to show that he or she was applying this professional knowledge to real-world situations through writing, speaking, consulting, testifying, serving on committees or boards, holding public office, or otherwise reaching outside academia. Ideally, there would also be room on this staircase for sociologists who opted to be either "pure scientists" or "straightforward practitioners," but presumably their upward progress would be considerably slower than that of persons doing competent, involved, integrated sociology.

If sociologists do eventually succeed in putting their house in order along the lines suggested here, one ultimate question remains to be answered.

THE QUESTION: WILL ANYONE LISTEN TO US?

Facing the demand for relevance, surmounting the dilemma of value involvement, resolving the paradox of basic versus applied work, and responding to the imperative to reorganize the profession are all intermediate steps toward the ultimate goal of bringing our sociological perspective and knowledge to bear on improving the human condition. We cannot meet that final challenge, however, unless the rest of the world—or at least some portion of it—is willing to listen to us seriously and adopt some of what we have to say. Without that, the entire effort will be fruitless.

If the world is to listen to us, we must first have something important and useful to say. This book has been an effort to demonstrate the numerous ways in which sociologists are today struggling to find something to say about a wide range of applied social concerns. In each of the areas surveyed it is obvious that we presently know very little and are extremely frustrated by our ignorance. Nevertheless, in every one of these areas we know more today than we did even five or ten years ago. And we certainly know more than nonsociologists about the social aspects of each of these areas. Ignorance is frustrating, but it can also be challenging—calling us to enlist as much help as we can gather from concerned semiprofessionals and from our scientist colleagues and then to continually expand our efforts to apply sociology to the real world.

ALTERNATIVE PERSPECTIVES

Most sociologists live and work in a highly encapsulated intellectual world. They talk mainly with other sociologists and sociology students, they read primarily sociologically oriented books and journals, and their research and writing assumes a sociological perspective that is rarely questioned or examined. Within these confinements, we frequently forget that we are a very small minority of the population. Even if we narrow our focus to the policy makers, public officials, organizational leaders, practicing professionals, and community activists whom we seek to influence through our applied work, few of these people share our sociological view of the world. They are more likely to hold one of four other basic perspectives on social life: technological, economic, legal, or psychological. All of these alternative perspectives are relevant for applied sociology, however, since each one captures a portion of social reality. Hence, applied sociologists must be familiar with all of them, aware of the contribution that each one can make to resolving social problems, and able to communicate and work with persons who hold these perspectives. The four perspectives are illustrated in the following paragraphs with examples from energy conservation studies, but they are likely to be encountered in virtually any type of applied sociological work.

Technological Perspective

This orientation is especially prevalent in areas based on physical or technical processes. In its most extreme form, the technological perspective asserts that there is a "technical fix" solution for every problem and that solution awaits only the development of more effective engineering techniques and/or equipment. If we have an energy shortage, build more nuclear reactors or other high technology toys like solar satellites or synfuel plants. If we want to conserve gasoline, build more fuel-efficient automobiles so that we can preserve our mobile life styles.

Less doctrinaire technologists recognize that people must accept and utilize new technologies if problems are to be solved and hence are willing to adapt their technical designs to the needs and desires of potential users. They are anxious to take the "human factor" into account and solicit sociological input that can contribute to the acceptance and use of new technologies. Nevertheless, the technological perspective still prevails, and the applied sociologist is expected to work within that framework to help people adapt to the technology that will presumably solve their problems. Since many managers in technically-oriented government agencies were originally trained as engineers, the technological perspective tends to be pervasive in those settings.

Economic Perspective

Most engineers are at least willing to admit that they don't understand human behavior and welcome sociologists as collaborators. In contrast, persons who hold an economic perspective often have little use for sociologists unless they act primarily as methodologists or social psychologists. This perspective is not confined to professional economists, but is widespread among managers and others trained in business administration, as well as budget-conscious public officials. An economic view of the world espouses a belief system whose major tenet is that economic principles and theories are sufficient to explain most or all important human activities. Hence public policy formation must not only take economic factors into consideration, but must be based solidly on them. If energy conservation is not being taken seriously by the public, it is because energy is still too cheap, and the way to encourage conservation is to keep raising the price until people start reducing their consumption. If we want people to install solar hot water heaters in their homes, offer a tax credit against the cost of installation.

People who are strongly committed to the economic perspective frequently contend that sociologists do not understand the "hard realities" of the world or that our models and research results are too vague and imprecise to be of any practical use to decision makers. This posture can perhaps be explained by the fact that the sociological perspective attempts to explain many of the same empirical phenomena as the economic perspective, but without making most of the assumptions necessary for economic modeling. Some economists are beginning to take sociological considerations seriously (as in Hirsch's 1976 analysis of the social limits to economic growth), while others are at least willing to admit that some areas of social life cannot be understood from an economic perspective. Nevertheless, the economic perspective still remains the most adamant challenge to the sociological perspective in many policy realms.

Legal Perspective

People who approach policy formation with this perspective are often trained in law, although they may also have studied political science or public administration. They rarely totally reject the sociological perspective and frequently welcome applied sociologists as valuable members of an interdisciplinary research team. Their particular stance is that all sociological (as well as technical and economic) factors must be viewed within a context of what is "institutionally" possible.

Terms like "institutional analysis" and "institutional barriers" have become quite popular among policy makers in recent years, as a result of the efforts of legally-oriented policy analysts. The uninitiated sociologist may at first be rather puzzled by these terms, since their meaning does not correspond to any of sociology's diverse definitions of "institution." In the world of policy analysis, "institution" includes not only legal statutes, court decisions, and case law, but also the prevailing operating patterns and practices of all involved agencies and organizations, all functional linkages between those units, relevant job descriptions and role expectations, and virtually all other aspects of social structure and culture. If a research team were planning a study of the social impacts of a proposed energy program, a person with this orientation might likely state; "I'll handle all the institutional aspects of this problem; you sociologists can measure people's attitudes toward the program." The legal perspective is probably more penetrable by sociologists than are the technological and economic perspectives, but when doing this we must guard against becoming engulfed in the vague mist of "institutional analysis."

Psychological Perspective

Applied sociologists are continually challenged to distinguish their sociological perspective from the psychological perspective of clinical psychologists, many social workers, and nonprofessionals who have read the latest books espousing pop-psychology. In addition, this perspective is very popular among "humanistically oriented" policy makers who are anxious to demonstrate that they have grown beyond simple technological and economic viewpoints. Sociologists do not deny the importance of psychological and emotional factors in most social situations. Our conflict with psychologically-oriented researchers and policy makers is over the importance of these factors for public policies and programs. For instance, it has taken several years to convince public policy makers that information and persuasion campaigns will not, by themselves, produce any significant increases in energy conserving practices. An even more difficult task is explaining to policy makers the critical difference between an individual attitude favoring energy conservation (which does not predict individual conservation behavior) and a cultural "conservation ethic" (which is related to conservation actions on the aggregate level).

Most sociologists and psychologists realize that their contributions to applied problem solving can be fully complementary and mutually reinforcing. Nevertheless, there are many subtle differences between these two perspectives, which often produce disagreements concerning how public policies should be designed and implemented. Sociologists are frequently at a disadvantage in these skirmishes, since our variables tend to be less tangible and more difficult to measure than many psychological variables. One effective tactic in such cases is to say to the psychologically-oriented policy maker: "OK, carry out your advertising campaign, and after you discover that it doesn't change people's actions, I'll be anxious to work with you again." This tactic requires patience, but it has been effective in the realm of energy conservation research.

Sociological Perspective

Most sociologists—basic and applied—share a common sociological perspective on the world, as emphasized by C. Wright Mills (1959) many years ago. But what is the essence of this perspective? Regrettably, there is no simple answer to that question. At the very minimum, the sociological perspective contains a strong emphasis on the reality of social structure and culture and the effects of these factors on individual behavior and social interaction. Many sociologists would also probably include some form of system model as a convenient way of describing and analyzing the complex patterns of relationships that exist among social actors. We would most likely agree that consensus and conflict are both vital processes within all social organization and that neither is inherently more desirable or important than the other. Many of us might also stress the crucial role of power, influence, and control throughout all aspects of social life, as well as the patterns of inequality that result from the exercise of social power. Finally, from an ethical standpoint we might agree that human beings must be the measure of all social policies. From there, however, we tend to take diverse paths according to our particular theoretical viewpoints and empirical concerns. Nevertheless, we seem to have no trouble identifying a sociological perspective whenever we encounter it and realizing that we are dealing with a kindred mind.

APPLIED SOCIOLOGICAL ROLES

A favorite topic in many discussions of applied sociology is the kinds of roles that sociologists can enact to influence public policy formation. A variety of applied sociological roles have been identified by several writers (Crawford and Biderman, 1969:233–43; Finsterbusch and Motz, 1980:7–10; Janowitz, 1972a and 1972b; Scott and Shore, 1979:36–48; Weiss, 1977:1–22; Weiss and Bucuvalas, 1977:226). A critical examination of these diverse typologies suggests that they can be combined into five major applied sociological roles, plus a sixth one that only a few sociologists have attempted. These roles are not mutually exclusive, and most applied sociologists probably enact several of them during their careers, either sequentially or simultaneously.

Observer

The work of applied sociologists who act as scientific observers is quite similar to that of basic sociologists, except that it focuses on conditions that are defined as social problems or policy issues. Hence, an alternative term for this role might be "problem explorer." Such work can involve gathering data on prevailing social conditions, trends, or rates of behavior; formulating concepts of particular activities or situations; developing theories to explain the causes or consequences of various social problems; or constructing social indicators with which to measure changing social trends and then collecting data with which to monitor those trends. Much of this applied social observation is done by sociologists in academic settings, although some of it is carried out by persons working in government agencies, research institutes, and even private industries.

Analyst

This role takes the applied sociologist more directly into the realm of policy formation and program development, but strictly as a social researcher. The social analyst carefully distinguishes his or her role from that of a decision maker or program director, defining the analyst role solely in terms of research and avoiding any involvement in valuative issues. Hence, an alternative term for this role might be "policy researcher." It can involve analyzing proposed or current policies in terms of their likely implications and effects, assessing the potential social impacts of proposed programs and projects, or evaluating the success of programs in attaining their objectives. Also included in this role is the analysis of how policies are formulated and programs are enacted, although in this case the researcher is concerned with generic processes and procedures rather than with substantive policies and programs. Policy analysis and evaluation research are commonly done on a contractual basis by nonacademic research firms and independent consultants, but some academically based sociologists also do this kind of research and consultation. For sociologists employed in government agencies and other operating organizations, policy analysis and evaluation is their principal work.

Enlightener

In the enlightenment role, applied sociologists seek to give policy makers (and ultimately the general public) a new and presumably more sophisticated understanding of social life, based on the sociological perspective. As this perspective becomes increasingly prevalent, applied sociologists can contribute to policy formation and social change by "challenging the ideas currently in vogue and providing alternative cognitive maps....In time, these alternative images of reality can yield new ways of addressing policy problems and new programs of procedures for coping with needs (Weiss and Bucuvalas, 1977:226). The importance of the enlightenment role has been emphasized by Crawford and Biderman (1969), Janowitz (1972a and 1972b), and Weiss (1977:17). Scott and Shore (1979:37), meanwhile, argue that applied sociology contributes to public policy formation primarily by "disabusing people of erroneous ideas that they may have about societal conditions; by disclosing complexity where others may see only simplicity...by uncovering latent functions and unanticipated consequences of established practices; and, in general, by helping policy-makers to comprehend better the inner workings of society and its main institutions." In short, this is a "sociology teacher" role.

Until fairly recently this role has not been taken very seriously by many applied sociologists, however. It has usually been viewed as a residual and relatively automatic by-product of other applied work. More specifically: 1) Because we have commonly assumed that our research has at least some enlightenment effects on policy makers, we have tended to see this role as a last-ditch justification for doing applied sociology. If all other attempts to affect the policy process fail, we can always console ourselves that "at least our work broadened the perspectives of the sponsors." As a result, the importance of this enlightenment activity as a means of influencing public policy has been severely minimized. 2) Because policy enlightenment has been seen as a residual outcome of applied work, little attention has been given to how this process occurs or how its effectiveness might be enhanced. We have naively assumed that it happened automatically, as if policy makers absorbed the sociological perspective whenever they were exposed to our work. As a result, applied sociologists rarely think of enlightenment as an objective to be self-consciously pursued in their research.

Planner

The social planner is concerned not just to analyze policies or to enlighten policy makers, but also to assist in implementing policies and programs. The emphasis of this role is on application rather than research, so that an alternative term for it might be "social engineer." Policy formation is still left to others, such as public officials or legislative bodies, but once a policy has been adopted the social planner begins exploring ways of implementing it. This can involve such activities as preparing community or organizational plans; designing action programs; developing and testing strategies for program enactment; communicating information about plans and programs to the public, or perhaps conducting citizen participation programs; and developing procedures for mitigating undesirable social impacts. Persons doing this kind of work will likely view themselves as practicing sociologists but often do not describe themselves as social scientists. Most of these people are employed by public or private agencies or other nonacademic organizations, some of them work as independent consultants, and a small minority of them hold academic appointments.

Activist

An applied sociologist who chooses this role has elected to concentrate on applied action rather than research. Two principal characteristics distinguish the social activist: 1) this person takes a clear stand on public issues and policies, making no pretense of value neutrality; and 2) he or she becomes directly involved in facilitating or conducting action programs to achieve valued goals. Many different terms might be applied to a sociologist enacting this type of role, depending on one's activities: "program director," "social change agent," "clinical sociologist," "conflict mediator," "policy advocate," "community organizer," or "lobbyist." These role variations differ in many crucial ways, but all of them entail direct involvement in efforts to solve social problems, promote social change, and achieve desired social goals. Some academically based sociologists undertake these kinds of activities in addition to their scholarly work, but most social activists find that other employment opportunities are more conducive to their concerns. These include social action agencies, voluntary associations, community organizations, and private consulting.

Effector

This final role has not been enacted by many sociologists, despite the urgings of Lester Ward (1883) long ago that sociologists should seek to become policy makers. A few sociologists have headed major government agencies, and Arnold Rose was a member of the Minnesota state legislature for many years, but most members of the sociological profession have shied away from positions in which they would have official responsibility for public decision making and policy formation. Although this role would provide an ideal setting for translating the sociological perspective into public policy, it presently remains a largely unexplored avenue for doing applied sociology.

APPLIED SOCIOLOGICAL COMMUNICATION

Applied sociologists may share a common sociological perspective in their work, but it is often difficult to convey this view of the world to policy makers and others as we enact our various applied sociological roles. The most effective way of communicating the sociological perspective is clearly not to lecture on its virtues, but rather to demonstrate its usefulness while doing applied sociology.

Techniques

The following paragraphs discuss several ways in which applied sociologists can intentionally convey the sociological perspective to policy makers and project sponsors while conducting applied research or action.

Writing a proposal. Government officials and others who issue "Requests for Proposals" (RFP) for applied research often have only a general notion of the kind of information they need. When writing a proposal based on an RFP, one must respond to its stated provisions, but it is always permissible to expand upon those provisions. A proposer can, therefore, frequently indicate to the sponsor what research is really required to meet its needs or what kinds of information would be of most benefit to it. In this manner, one may be able to introduce more sociological considerations into a study than intended by the sponsor.

Designing the study. Once a contract is signed and the study is actually being designed, an even more proactive stance can be taken with many sponsors. It is as if there were an unspoken understanding between sponsor and researcher that: "Now that we've played the legally required RFP/Proposal game, let's get down to business and decide what is really going to be done in this research project." Many features of the proposed research design can usually be modified during this negotiation process, so countless opportunities will arise to build more aspects of the sociological perspective into the project. Sponsors are generally quite willing to accept these modifications as long as they appear to strengthen the study and do not increase its costs.

Interacting with the sponsor. During the course of a study, the researcher will often interact informally with the sponsor on a regular basis, in addition to submitting whatever periodic progress reports are required. The researcher will, therefore, have numerous opportunities to discuss sociological ideas with the sponsor and explain why various sociological considerations are relevant to the problem at hand. It may also be possible to incorporate some of these concerns into the study as it progresses.

Writing the report. An applied research report can be written in a manner that clearly demonstrates the value of the sociological perspective. This is done by describing the sociological approach to the problem and discussing its value for understanding and dealing with the problem. The sociological perspective can then be contrasted with other orientations commonly applied to the problem, showing how these perspectives differ from a sociological viewpoint, discussing the strengths and weaknesses of the sociological approach in comparison with the other orientations, and demonstrating the ways in which a sociological perspective can shed new light on the problem.

Recommending program actions. Most applied research reports contain a set of recommended actions based on the results of the study. The applied researcher can explicitly show how these recommendations reflect the sociological perspective and how their outcomes would differ from the outcomes of actions based on alternative perspectives. The report can then conclude with an assessment of the benefits to be gained from applying a sociological perspective to the problem and adopting program strategies that are consistent with that perspective.

Attending policy conferences. In addition to conducting applied research projects that utilize the sociological perspective, there are several other ways in which sociologists can introduce their ways of thinking to policy makers. One of these is to attend conferences dealing with applied problems at which policy makers discuss research agendas and action strategies with people from various disciplines. The importance of this kind of activity was stressed some years ago by Amitai Etzioni (1967:824): "When attending various meetings of sociologists with policy makers, I have found again and again that the main virtue of specific sociological recommendations was the expression of a viewpoint, a way of looking at things that would otherwise have been neglected."

Serving on local committees. Even if one does not have many opportunities to attend national conferences, a similar educational function can be performed in one's local community. There are numerous opportunities in most communities for sociologists to serve on voluntary citizen groups, task forces, local project steering committees, and agency boards. Considerable time and effort may be required to participate actively in such groups, but they offer excellent forums for sociologists to acquaint local decision makers with the sociological perspective and inject that perspective into local programs.

Writing for the general public.. Most of the writing we do is aimed at our sociological colleagues who already share our perspective. If we seek to spread the sociological perspective outside our discipline, one highly effective procedure is to rewrite our technical reports into books, magazine articles, or newspaper stories for the general public. This requires developing a quite different writing style from the one we use in our professional writings. But if we can learn to communicate with the public in this manner, we can contribute to creating a climate of public opinion that will support or even demand sociological approaches to societal and local problems.

A Two-Way Bridge

Thus far we have been focusing on communicating the sociological perspective to policy makers. This communication process goes two ways, however, as implied by Nathan Caplan (1977:196) in the conclusion to his recent study of social science utilization by government officials: "What is needed to increase the level of utilization is to bridge the social science and policymaker perspectives." In addition to introducing policy makers to our view of the world, sociologists must be willing to learn how they think if we are to have any influence on their actions.

Applied sociologists must learn to understand and appreciate the total policy-making process, including the incremental approach to problem solving, the use of satisfying rather than maximizing action strategies, the importance of manipulable as opposed to explanatory variables, and the ways in which policy makers act as mediators among conflicting interest groups in society. We must also become familiar with the strengths and weaknesses of the technological, economic, legal, and psychological perspectives, so that we can effectively demonstrate how the sociological perspective is either complementary or superior to them in any given situation. All of these factors often limit the ability of applied sociologists to influence public policy formation, but they are crucial elements of the policy process that we cannot afford to ignore if we want policy makers to listen to us.

Clarity and Humility

Even if applied sociologists do have something important and useful to say to the world, neither policy makers nor the general public are likely to listen seriously unless we speak to them with clarity and humility. Both qualities are crucial. Who among us really enjoys reading the typical sociological journal article or even fully understands it if it is outside our narrow sphere of current expertise? How, then, can we possibly hope that nonsociologists (no matter how literate) will pay attention to our work? Profound thoughts can always be expressed in clear language: "Treat others in the way you would like to be treated." Incomprehensible writing is often merely a way of disguising confused ideas. In this regard, most sociologists have a great deal to learn about writing clear English.

A stance of sincere humility as we address the world may also be difficult for many sociologists to assume. The isolation of the cloistered, value-free, "pure-science" mansion in which most sociologists dwell tends to breed a sense of superiority or even arrogance among many of us. From Comte on, we have secretly dreamed of forming a priesthood of sociologists to run society in a rational (?) and benevolent (?) but autocratic manner. We often lose sight of the fact that the sociological perspective is only one of many different ways of understanding and conducting human life. We can face the world with confidence, knowing that, as applied sociologists, we have something important and useful to say, but we must speak with genuine humility in light of both our vast ignorance and our narrow perspective.

A FINAL THOUGHT

When sociologists initially begin doing applied work, they frequently expect policy makers to immediately adopt and act on the results of their sociological research. When this does not happen—which is usually the case—applied sociologists frequently react with puzzlement and frustration. In addition to being ignorant of the complex political context within which policies are formulated and enacted, we often fail to understand that most policy makers are operating with perspectives different from our own. Adopting the approach suggested here of emphasizing the policy enlightenment role and self-consciously incorporating it into all our applied research and other professional activities will not result in our exerting direct influence on any particular policy decision. In the long run, however, this approach could reshape the overall intellectual context of public policy formation and enactment to reflect the sociological perspective on the world. To the extent that occurs, applied sociology will have been eminently successful.

Applied sociology certainly does have a bright future. The world will indeed listen to us if we ensure that our work is truly relevant, is value-involved but scientifically objective, combines the best features of both basic science and applied practice in a creative synthesis, encourages many others to join us in this effort, speaks to the world with clarity and humility—and then says something that is important and useful.

The current frontiers of applied sociology that are sketched in this book all await further expansion.

REFERENCES

Caplan, Nathan. 1977. "A Minimal Set of Conditions Necessary for the Utilization of Social Science Knowledge in Policy Formation at the National Level." In *Using Social Research in Public Policy Making,* edited by Carol H. Weiss, pp. 183–97. Lexington, Mass.: Lexington Books.

Crawford, Elizabeth T. and Albert D. Biderman, eds. 1969. *Social Scientists and International Affairs.* New York: John Wiley & Sons.

Denzin, N.K. 1970. "Who Leads: Sociology or Society?" *The American Sociologist* 5(May):125–27.

Etzioni, Amatai. 1967. "Nonconventional Uses of Sociology as Illustrated by Peace Research." In *The Uses of Sociology,* edited by Paul Lazarsfeld, et al., pp. 806–38. New York: Basic Books.

Finsterbusch, Kurt and Annabelle Bender Motz. 1980. *Social Research for Policy Decisions.* Belmont, Calif.: Wadsworth.

Gibbs, Jack P. 1979. "The Elites Can Do Without Us." *The American Sociologist* 14(May):79–85.

Gouldner, Alvin W. 1968. "The Sociologist as Partisan: Sociology and the Welfare State." *The American Sociologist* 3(May):103–16.

Harrington, Michael. 1963. *The Other America.* Baltimore, Md.: Penguin Books.

Hirsch, Fred. 1976. *Social Limits to Growth.* Cambridge, Mass.: Harvard University Press.

Horowitz, Irving L. 1968. *Professing Sociology.* Chicago: Aldine.

Janowitz, Morris. 1972a. "Professionalization of Sociology." *American Journal of Sociology* 10:105–35.

———. 1972b. *Sociological Models and Social Policy.* Morristown, N.J.: The General Learning Press.

Lazarsfeld, Paul F., William H. Sewell, and Harold L. Wilensky, eds. 1967. *The Uses of Sociology.* New York: Basic Books.

Mills, C. Wright. 1959. *The Sociological Imagination.* New York: Oxford University Press.

Scott, Robert A. and Arnold R. Shore. 1979. *Why Sociology Does Not Apply: A Study of the Use of Sociology in Public Policy.* New York: Elsevier.

Ward, Lester. 1883. *Dynamic Sociology or Applied Social Science, as Based upon Statistical Sociology and the Less Complex Sciences.* New York: Appleton.

Weber, Max. 1949. *Max Weber on the Methodology of the Social Sciences.* E. Shills and H.A. Finch, ed. Glencoe, Ill.: Free Press.

Weiss, Carol H. 1977. "Introduction." In *Using Social Research in Public Policy Making,* edited by Carol H. Weiss, pp. 1–22. Lexington, Mass.: Lexington Books.

Weiss, Carol H. and Michael J. Bucuvalas. 1977. "The Challenge of Social Research to Decision Making." In *Using Social Research in Public Policy Making,* edited by Carol H. Weiss, pp. 213–34. Lexington, Mass.: Lexington Books.

NAME INDEX

SUBJECT INDEX

Abortion, 115; and adolescents, 118, 121, 125, 127, 129; government aid for, 121, 125; and attitudes, 63, 291

Access-to-Justice Project, 79

Achievement: and aspiration, 348; and autonomy, 126, 128; and conformity, 126; and education, 14; and the elderly, 323–24, 329–30; and equality, 200–201, 206; and illegitimacy, 120–21; and initiative, 126; and motivation, 343; and obedience, 126; and passivity, 126; and self-direction, 126, 128; and self-esteem, 348; and work, 14

ACORD (Action Program of Organizational Development), 187–88

ACTION (Chicago), 145

Action for Children's Television, (ACT), 166

Adolescents: and abortion, 118, 121, 125, 127, 129; and contraception, 118, 121, 125, 127, 129, 381; death of, 371; disability of, 371; formal support for, 145, 147; and illegitimacy, 117–18, 120–22, 124–25, 126–27, 129; marriage education for, 129–30; mental illness in, 395; reproduction of, 117–18, 120–22, 124–25, 126–27, 129, 276; sexuality of, 117–18, 120–22, 124–25, 126–27, 129; and single parents, 145, 147

Advertising: and lawyers, 411, 414, 422, 423; as propaganda, 161; and recreation choices, 177

Advocacy: in conflict intervention, 68, 69; in family crisis, 76

Affirmative action: in corporations, 235, 259–60; and employment, 299, 304, 307,

309, 312, 313–14; evaluation of, 264; impact of, 3; and income, 299–300, 304, 309, 312, 313–14; programs for, 264–65; requirements of, 98; and social indicators, 17 (*see also* minority groups; Office of Economic Opportunity; women)

Age: and blacks, 324; and conservatism, 326; constraints of, 320–34; and divorce, 122; and equality, 223; and fertility, 459, 462; and gender role, 296; and health care, 373–74; and media, 329–30; and mental illness, 395; and physician visits, 373–74; and recreation, 435, 439, 442–43; and single parenthood, 119; and unemployment, 324–28 (*see also* age discrimination; elderly)

Age discrimination, 320ff; in corporations, 324–28; 330–34; defined, 320; and demographic trends, 333; and education, 327; and employment, 324–28, 330–34; legislation on, 330–34; and Medicaid, 327; origins of, 321–24; prevalence of, 324–28; and race discrimination, 324; and retirement, 326, 330–34; types of, 324–28

Age Discrimination Act (ADA) of 1975, 330–34

Age Discrimination in Employment Act (ADEA), 324–25, 327, 330–34

Ageism, 320ff; and culture, 322–24; defined, 320 (*see also* age discrimination, elderly)

Agency for International Development (AID), 33, 469, 473, 549, 551, 552, 554

Aggregation: of indexes, 9, 10; in social indicators, 10

Aggression: and violence, 168–69

Agriculture: and the media, 167, 169–70;

ABOUT THE EDITORS AND CONTRIBUTORS

RICHARD L. ABEL holds a Ph.D. from the School of Oriental and African Studies at the University of London and a J.D. from Columbia University. He is Professor of Law at the University of California at Los Angeles and is concerned with such areas as the sociology of the legal profession, the provision of legal services, and legal aspects of health and safety. Dr. Abel has been the editor of *Law and Society Review* and of *African Law Studies* and has edited two volumes of essays on *The Politics of Informal Justice*. Most recently he has written a critique of the proposed American Bar Association Model Rules of Professional Conduct.

GARY L. ALBRECHT, who received a Ph.D. in sociology from Emory University, is an Associate Professor of Health Resources Management in the School of Public Health at the University of Illinois. His specialty is social aspects of physical disability and rehabilitation. His works in this area include *Disability and Rehabilitation: The Consequences of Social Choice, The Sociology of Physical Disability and Rehabilitation,* and *Cross-National Rehabilitation Policies.* Dr. Albrecht is presently studying the social control of rehabilitation services.

ROBERT C. ATCHLEY, whose specialty is the sociology of aging, received a Ph.D. in sociology from American University. He is Director of the Scripps Foundation Gerontology Center at Miami University, which offers undergraduate and graduate programs in gerontology. Dr. Atchley is Editor-in-Chief of the Gerontology Monographs of the Gerontological Society of America and has written *The Sociology of Retirement* and *Families in Later Life*. His applied research has included evaluations of various types of retirement planning programs and of CETA programs for older people.

RABEL J. BURDGE has a Ph.D. in rural sociology from Pennsylvania State University and is Professor of Rural Sociology, Environmental Sociology, and Leisure Studies in the Institute for Environmental Studies at the University of Illinois at Urbana-Champaign. He is a former editor of *The Journal of Leisure Research*, founder and coeditor of *Leisure Sciences: An Interdisciplinary Journal*, and author of *Social Change in Rural Societies: A Rural Sociology Textbook*. Dr. Burdge is presently studying the impacts of navigation and associated operations on recreation, potential wilderness, and cultural resources of the Upper Mississippi River Basin.

FREDERICK H. BUTTEL holds a Ph.D. in sociology from the University of Wisconsin-Madison and is an Assistant Professor of Rural Sociology at Cornell University. His research interests deal primarily with energy and environmental issues, especially as they relate to the agricultural and rural sectors of the United States. Dr. Buttel is coeditor of *The Rural Sociology of the Advanced Societies* and coauthor of *Environment, Energy, and Society*. He has contributed to the Sociopolitical Effects Resource Group of the Committee on Nuclear and Alternative Energy Systems of the National Academy of Sciences.

WILLIAM R. CATTON, JR., who earned his Ph.D. in sociology from the University of Washington, is Professor of Sociology at Washington State University. His research concerns include wilderness, recreation use, adaptations to energy and other resource scarcities, and the ecological basis of human society. He is the author of *From Animistic to Naturalistic Sociology* and *Overshoot: The Ecological Basis of Revolutionary Change* and was the first chairperson of the Environmental Sociology Section of the American Sociological Association. Dr. Catton recently spent a year studying adaptations of New Zealanders to reduced access to oil imports and export markets.

JOHN A. CLAUSEN, who received his Ph.D. in sociology from the University of Chicago, is Professor of Sociology at the University of California, Berkeley and also holds a research appointment in the Institute of Human Development at that university. He does applied work in mental health and illness and in social and psychological aspects of smoking. His most recent project deals with planning services to meet the needs of families in which a parent becomes a mental patient. Among Dr. Clausen's many writings on mental illness are papers on "Socio-cultural and Social Psychological Factors in Social Response to Mental Disorder," "The Impact of Mental Illness: A Twenty-Year Follow-up," "Madness and Work: Short and Long Term Effects of Mental Illness on Occupational Careers" (coauthor), and "The Impact of Parental Mental Illness on Children" (coauthor).

JUDY CORDER-BOLZ has a Ph.D. in sociology from Indiana University and is presently a Project Director at Southwest Educational Development Laboratory in Austin, Texas. Her major area of work is sex roles, including strategies for use with adolescents in vocational planning, and litigation in support of sex and race employment discimination law suits. Her writings in these areas include "Sex Roles and Occupational Aspirations" and (with others) "The Status and Sex-Typed Dimensions of Occupational Aspirations in Young Adolescents." Dr. Colder-Bolz is presently concerned with the problems of translating research findings into intervention strategies to affect the occupational plans of adolescents from a variety of racial, ethnic, and socioeconomic backgrounds.

KURT FINSTERBUSCH, an Associate Professor of Sociology at the University of Maryland, received his Ph.D. in sociology from Columbia University. His applied work spans such topics as the process of social impact assessment, community social indicators, and community and neighborhood functioning. He is a coauthor of *Social Research for Policy Decisions*, the author of *Understanding Social Impacts: Assessing the Effects of Public Projects*, and the co-editor of *Methodology of Social Impact Assessment*. Typical of Dr. Finsterbusch's research on social impact assessment was a recent study of the impacts of transportation developments on urban neighborhoods.

HOWARD H. GARRISON holds a Ph.D. in sociology from the University of Wisconsin—Madison. He is a Social Science Analyst in the Office of Program and Policy Analysis of the U.S. Commission on Civil Rights. Dr. Garrison's principle interests are in race and ethnic relations and sex roles, and he is currently doing research on unemployment and underemployment among minorities and women for the Civil Rights Commission, as well as a review of recent studies on sex roles.

EDWARD GROSS, a University of Chicago Ph.D. in sociology, is Professor of Sociology at the University of Washington. His research has dealt primarily with the sociology of work and complex organizations, and his writings include *Work and Society, Industry and Social Life*, and *University Goals and Academic Power*. Dr. Gross is a past president of the Pacific Sociological Association. At the present time, he is engaged in a study of organized crime, using organizational theory.

RICHARD H. HALL received his Ph.D. in sociology from Ohio State University. He is a Professor of Sociology at the State University of New York—Albany, where he previously served as Acting Vice President for Research and Dean of Graduate Studies. Within the field of complex organizations, Dr. Hall is particularly interested in organizational theory as applied in administrative work. Among his writings are *Organizations: Structure and Process, The Formal Organization*, and, most recently, "A Mismatch: Organizational Theory as Applied in Higher Education."

DONALD A. HANSEN holds a Ph.D. in sociology from the University of Minnesota and a Ph.D. in education from Northwestern University. At the University of California, Berkeley, he is Associate Professor and Chairman of Sociology of Education in the Graduate School of Education, as well as an Affiliate Professor in Mass Communications. In addition to the areas of sociology of education and mass communications, he is also interested in the family and socialization. Dr. Hansen's writings include *On Education: Sociological Perspectives, Explorations in Sociology and Counseling,* and *An Invitation to Critical Sociology*. His applied projects have dealt with such topics as the social contexts of learning in bilingual classrooms, family-school articulations and classroom learning, and the new media and families as educators.

MICHAEL R. HATTERY is a doctoral candidate in developmental sociology at Cornell University. His principle research interest is with the relationship between energy and local economic development in nonmetropolitan areas. He is currently working on a Ph.D. dissertation dealing with the impacts of unconventional production organizations, such as community development corporations and cooperatives, on energy utilization and community development in the Northeast.

VICKY A. JOHNSON holds a Ph.D. in educational psychology from the University of California, Berkeley, where she is now a research psychologist in the Graduate School of Education. Her research has dealt with such topics as the social contexts of learning in bilingual classrooms, experience-based moral education at home and school, and family life and adolescent moral reasoning. She is also interested in teacher training and school and neighborhood violence. In collaboration with Donald A. Hansen, she has written papers on "Sociology, Developmental Theory, and the High School Curriculum," and "Rethinking Family Stress Theory: Definitional Aspects."

JAMES R. KLUEGEL obtained his Ph.D. in sociology from the University of Wisconsin—Madison and is Associate Professor of Sociology at the University of Illinois at Urbana-Champaign. His specialty areas include public attitudes toward social welfare programs, racial discimination, and criminal sentencing and victimization. Dr. Kluegel's writings include "Social Inequality and Predatory Criminal Victimization: An Exposition and Test of a Formal Theory" (coauthor) and "The Causes and Cost of Racial Exclusion from Job Authority."

LOUIS KRIESBERG, who is Professor of Sociology at Syracuse University, received his Ph.D. in sociology from the University of Chicago. Most of his work has dealt with such topics as international conflicts, international government and nongovernmental organizations, and social inequality. He has edited *Social Processes in International Relations* and edits an annual series on *Research in Social Movements, Conflicts and Change*. His writings include *The Sociology of Social Conflicts, Social Inequality,* and *Mothers in Poverty*. Dr. Kriesberg has chaired the Sociology of World Conflicts section of the American Sociological Association and the division on International Tensions of the Society for the Study of Social Problems. His applied work has included conducting conflict management training programs for persons engaged in negotiating and mediating international and community conflicts.

JAMES H. LAUE holds a Ph.D. in sociology from Harvard University. He is Director of the Center for Metropolitan Studies and Associate Professor of Sociology at the University of Missouri—St. Louis. He works in the areas of community conflict resolution and change, race relations, urban problems, and social policy. Dr. Laue recently served as Vice-Chair of the U.S. Commission on Proposals for the National Academy of Peace and Conflict Resolution and as a mediator for the negotiated investment strategy in Gary, Indiana. He is co-author of *The Role of Community and School Groups in School Desegregation: Strategies for Crisis and Change* and has written papers on "The Ethics of Intervention in Community Disputes" and "Intervening in School Desegregation Conflicts: The Role of the Monitor."

EDWARD H. LEHMAN, who received his Ph.D. in sociology from Columbia University, is Professor and Chairman of the Department of Sociology at New York University. Within his specialty of political sociology he is particularly interested in relationships between government and other parts of society, such as higher education. He is the author of *Political Society: A Macrosociology of Politics* and *Coordinating Health Care: Explorations in Interorganizational Relations*. Dr. Lehman has done applied research on the structure of policy research centers and how their structure affects their influence on policy making, and research on minority utilization of a community mental health center.

MICHAEL MICKLIN holds a Ph.D. in sociology from the University of Texas at Austin. He is Director of the Population and Development Policy Program at the Battelle Human Affairs Research Centers in Washington, D.C., which sponsors and provides technical assistance to research projects on population and development problems in Latin America, Asia, Africa, and the Middle East. In addition to this work with population and socioeconomic development, Dr. Micklin also does research on population policy and youth and employment. He is the editor of *Population, Environment, and Social Organization* and the coeditor of *Sociological Human Ecology: Contemporary Issues and Applications*.

JUDITH INNES de NEUFVILLE received her Ph.D. from the Department of Urban Studies and Planning at Massachusetts Institute of Technology, with a focus on quantitative methods and social policy. She is an Assistant Professor in the Department of City and Regional Planning at the University of California, Berkeley. Her major research interest is in the role of information in policy and implementation processes, and her recent work has dealt with developing a set of social indicators of basic human needs for use by the U.S. State Department's Bureau of Human Rights in its reports on human rights conditions around the world. Dr. de Neufville has authored *Social Indicators in Public Policy: Interactive Processes of Design and Application* and edited *The Land Use Policy Debate in the U.S.*

MARVIN E. OLSEN holds a Ph.D. in sociology from the University of Michigan. He is Professor of Sociology at Washington State University and a Visiting Research Scientist at the Battelle Human Affairs Research Center in Seattle. His applied interests include energy conservation and renewable resource strategies and policies, social impact assessment, program evaluation, and citizen participation. Dr. Olsen's applied research has dealt with such topics as evaluating Washington state energy conservation programs, examining the social impacts of conservation technologies, analyzing the conservation policies of Western European countries, designing citizen involvement programs dealing with nuclear waste repositories, and evaluating CETA training programs. His publications include *The Process of Social Organization: Power in Social Systems, Power in Societies*, and *Social Aspects of Energy Conservation*.

SONIA R. ROSENBAUM obtained her Ph.D. in sociology from Purdue University and is presently Research Director for Cibola Investment Consultants, Inc., in Northhampton, Massachusetts. Much of her work has dealt with applied methodologies such as evaluation research, applied statistics, and time series analysis, and that focus is evident in her books on *Quantitative Methods and Statistics* and *Evaluation: A Systematic Approach* (with P. H. Rossi and H. E. Freeman). Dr. Rosenbaum also has substantive interests in income maintenance, having worked on the New Jersey Income Maintenance Experiment and in natural disaster recovery processes.

PETER H. ROSSI took his Ph.D. in sociology at Columbia University. He is Professor of Sociology and Director of the Social and Demographic Research Institute at the University of Massachusetts at Amherst. His work has been concerned largely with the application of social research methodologies to social issues, and he is presently doing research on the long-term effects of natural disasters on communities and on the treatment of released prisoners. His recent writings include *Evaluation: A Systematic Approach* (with H. E. Freeman and S. R. Wright), *Money, Work, and Crime*, and *After the Clean-Up: Long-Range Effects of Natural Disasters*. Dr. Rossi is a past president of the American Sociological Association.

JACK ROTHMAN holds an M.S.W. degree from Ohio State University and a Ph.D. in social psychology from Columbia University. He is a Professor in the School of Social Work at the University of Michigan. A continuing theme in his work has been the systematic application of social science knowledge to contemporary issues of policy and practice, as exemplified by research on developing strategies for community intervention and on the utilization of social research by the British government. Among Dr. Rothman's many books are *Changing Organizations and Communities* (coauthor), *Social R&D: Research and Development in the Human Services,* and *Using Research in Organizations: A Guide to Successful Application.*

JOHN SCANZONI, a Professor of Sociology and Family Relations at the University of North Carolina—Greensboro, obtained his Ph.D. in sociology from the University of Oregon. His work has focused on family policy, with particular emphasis on synthesizing insights from sociological theory with applied issues. This theme is reflected in his most recent books: *Sex Roles, Women's Work, and Marital Conflict: A Study of Family Change, The Black Family in Modern Society: Patterns of Stability and Security,* and *Men, Women, and Change: A Sociology of Marriage and Family* (coauthor). Dr. Scanzoni is presently working on a book that examines public policy relating to the family, together with micro-level programs and clinical approaches, in an effort to present an agenda for family research and practice in the twenty-first century.

ARTHUR B. SHOSTAK received a Ph.D. in sociology from Princeton University and is Professor of Sociology at Drexel University. He has taught courses in applied sociology for 20 years, has been a consultant on organizational development for colleges across the country, and has worked with a wide range of public agencies and business concerns. Recently he has been involved in evaluating CETA youth employment programs and designing new programs in applied sociology for several colleges and universities. Among Dr. Shostak's numerous books are *Modern Social Reforms, Putting Sociology to Work,* and *Sociology in Actions.*

JOHNATHAN H. TURNER received a Ph.D. in sociology from Cornell University and is Professor of Sociology at the University of California, Riverside. His principle area of interest and work is inequality and stratification, as indicated by his book *Inequality: Privilege and Poverty in America* (coauthor). Dr. Turner is also concerned about a wide range of problems in contemporary societies, as presented in his basic texts *Social Problems in America* and *American Society: Problems of Structure.*

DONALD I. WARREN is an urban sociologist who holds a Ph.D. from the University of Michigan. He is currently Professor of Sociology at Oakland University in Rochester, Michigan. He is particularly interested in neighborhood social structure and community support systems and has conducted research on helping networks in urban communities and on strategies of home placement of the developmentally disabled. Dr. Warren is coauthor of *Neighborhood Organizers Handbook*, "Local Neighborhood Social Structure and Response to the Energy Crisis of 1973-74," and *Black Neighborhoods: The Dynamics of Community Power*.

ALAN WELLS obtained a Ph.D. in sociology from Washington University in St. Louis and is Associate Professor of Sociology at the University of Rhode Island. In addition to his work in mass communication, he also is interested in the field of military sociology and is beginning an investigation of Army enlistment problems. Dr. Wells is the author of *Picture Tube Imperialism* and editor of *Mass Media and Society* and *Contemporary Sociological Theories*.